HUNTS' GUIDE TO
SOUTHEAST MICHIGAN

By DON and MARY HUNT

MIDWESTERN GUIDES
Waterloo, Michigan

CONTENTS

Map of Southeast Michigan 3
Map of Detroit Metro Area 4

DETROIT

Detroit profile   5
Downtown   15
   Profile 15 Points of Interest 17
   Restaurants 37
   Map of Downtown Detroit 14
Rivertown   43
   Profile 43 Points of Interest 44
   Restaurants 50
Belle Isle   52
   Points of Interest 55
   Map of Belle Isle 54
East Side   59
   Profile 59 Points of Interest 60
   Restaurants 73
Historic Auto Factories   76
Southwest Detroit   79
   Profile 79 Points of Interest 80
   Restaurants 86
Cultural Center   88
   Profile 88 Points of Interest 90
   Restaurants 101
Albert Kahn   103
New Center   106
   Profile 106 Points of Interest 108
   Restaurants 112
Detroit Lodgings   113

THE INNER SUBURBS

Hamtramck   114
   Profile 114 Points of Interest 117
   Restaurants 120
Grosse Pointe   121
   Profile 121 Points of Interest 125
   Restaurants 132
Dearborn   134
   Profile 135 Points of Interest 138
   Restaurants 151 Lodgings 153
   Map of Dearborn 134
Royal Oak   155
   Profile 155 Points of Interest 156
   Restaurants 161
Southfield   163
   Profile 163 Points of Interest 164
   Restaurants 165 Lodgings 166

THE OUTER SUBURBS

Grosse Ile   167
   Profile 167 Points of Interest 169
   Restaurants 171

Plymouth   172
   Profile 172 Points of Interest 174
   Restaurants 177 Lodgings 178
Northville   179
   Profile 179 Points of Interest 180
   Restaurants 183 Lodgings 184
Birmingham   185
   Profile 185 Points of Interest 190
   Restaurants 198 Lodgings 200
   Map of Birmingham 187
Bloomfield Hills   201
   Profile 201 Points of Interest 203
   Lodgings 208
Troy   209
   Profile 209 Restaurants 210
   Lodgings 210
Pontiac   211
   Profile 211 Points of Interest 213
   Restaurants 215 Lodgings 216
Rochester/Auburn Hills   217
   Profile 217 Points of Interest 217
Milford   219
   Profile 219 Points of Interest 220
   Restaurants 226

BEYOND DETROIT

Monroe   227
   Profile 219 Points of Interest 231
   Restaurants 237 Lodgings 238
Ypsilanti   239
   Profile 239 Points of Interest 243
   Restaurants 248 Lodgings 248
Ann Arbor   249
   Profile 249 Points of Interest 254
   University of Michigan 272
   Restaurants 284 Lodgings 287
   Map of Ann Arbor 250
Fenton   289
   Profile 289 Points of Interest 292
   Restaurants 292 Lodgings 292
Holly   293
   Profile 293 Points of Interest 294
   Restaurants 296
Flint   297
   Profile 297 Points of Interest 304
   Restaurants 315 Lodgings 317
Port Huron   318
   Profile 318 Points of Interest 320
   Restaurants 323 Lodgings 324

OTHER

Nightspots 325
Sports Ticket Info 327
Shopping Malls 328
Recommended Reading 331
Index 333

Copywrite 1990 by Mary and Don Hunt

All rights reserved. No part of this book may be reproduced or utilized in any form or by any means, electronic or mechanical, including photocopying, recording or by any information storage and retrieval system, without permission in writing from the Publisher. Inquiries should be addressed to Midwestern Guides, 8330 Waterloo Road, Grass Lake, Michigan 49240.

ISBN 0-9623499-0-9

A Midwestern Guides Book

Printed in the United States of America

Cover Designer & Design Consultant:
Chris Golus
Map Designer: Sharon Carney Solomon

Illustrations

Ahern, Rich, p. 275
Albert Kahn Associates, 76, 77, 78, 103, 105, 108
Archives of Labor and Urban Affairs, Wayne State University, p. 5, 96, 302
Barcus, Frank, p. 69, 146
Farmer, Silas, *History of Detroit*, pp. 8, 9, 46, 49, 67, 93, 99
Flint Area Convention & Visitors Bureau (Aran Kessler), 297
General Motors, p. 225
Harper's Magazine, 1886, p. 31
Hirneisen Photography, p. 207
Historic Fort Wayne, 83, 84
Jaronski, Paul, p. 253, 268
Kemnitz, Milt, p. 251
Korab, Balthazar, p. 28.
Klein, V., p. 36
Kruz, Debbie Axelrod, p. 228
Mancinelli, Mark, p. 100
Marketing Communications, University of Michigan, p. 275.
Michigan Travel Commission, p. 12, 15, 18, 45, 55, 57, 82, 218, 241, 295, 318, 320
Motown Museum Historical Foundation, p. 111
Polk Michigan State Gazetteer (1889), p. 239.
Schervish Vogel Merz, p. 47, 60
Scott, Nelson Gerald, p. 292
Smith Hinchman & Grylls, p. 19
State Archives of Michigan, p. 6, 135, 299, 300
Wineberg, Susan, p. 118, 179
Woodward, William T., Grosse Ile Historical Society, p. 167, 169
Yamada, Takeshi, p. 261

Rich Ahern's prints of campus views are available at the Caravan Shop in Ann Arbor.

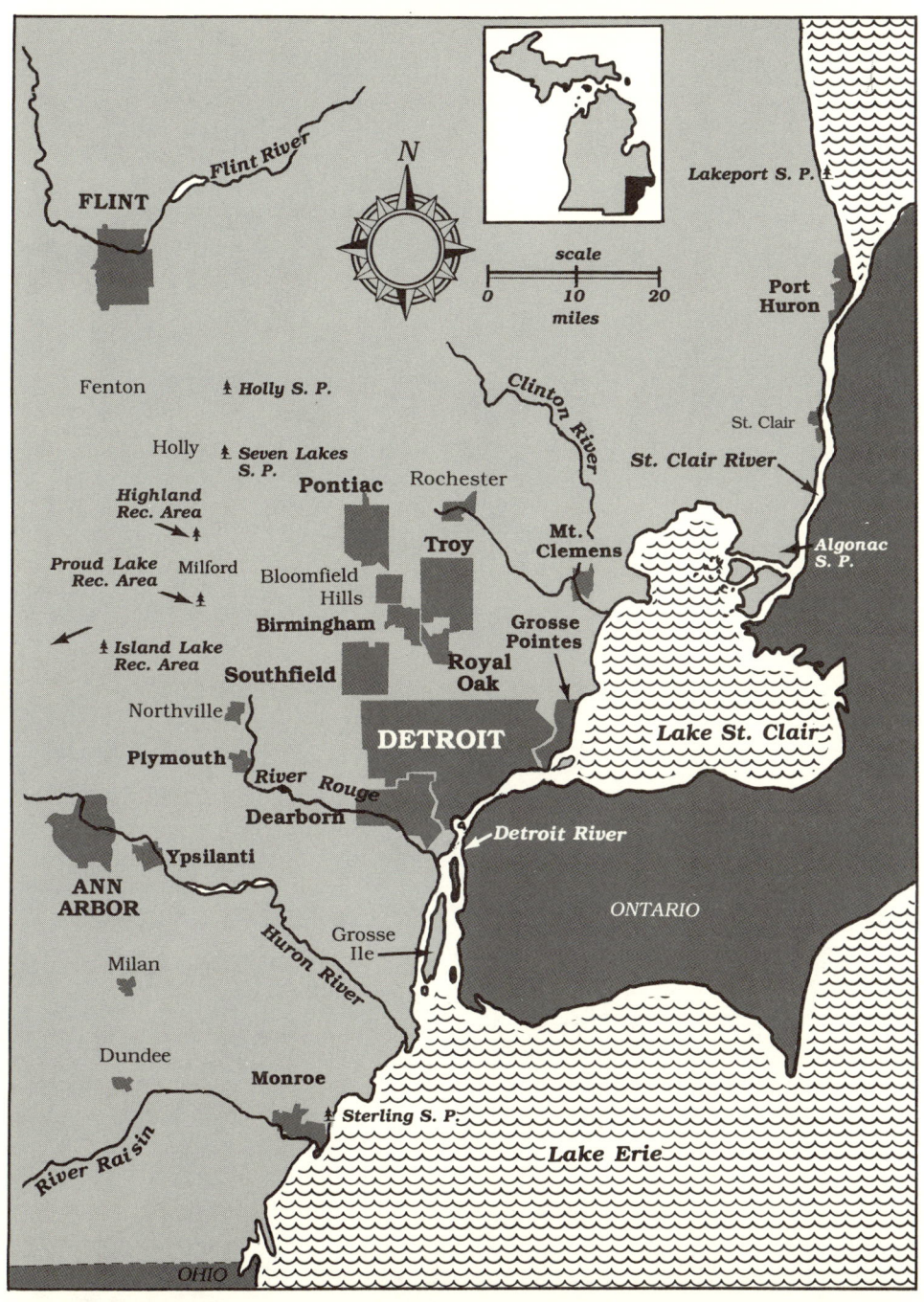

· SOUTHEASTERN MICHIGAN ·

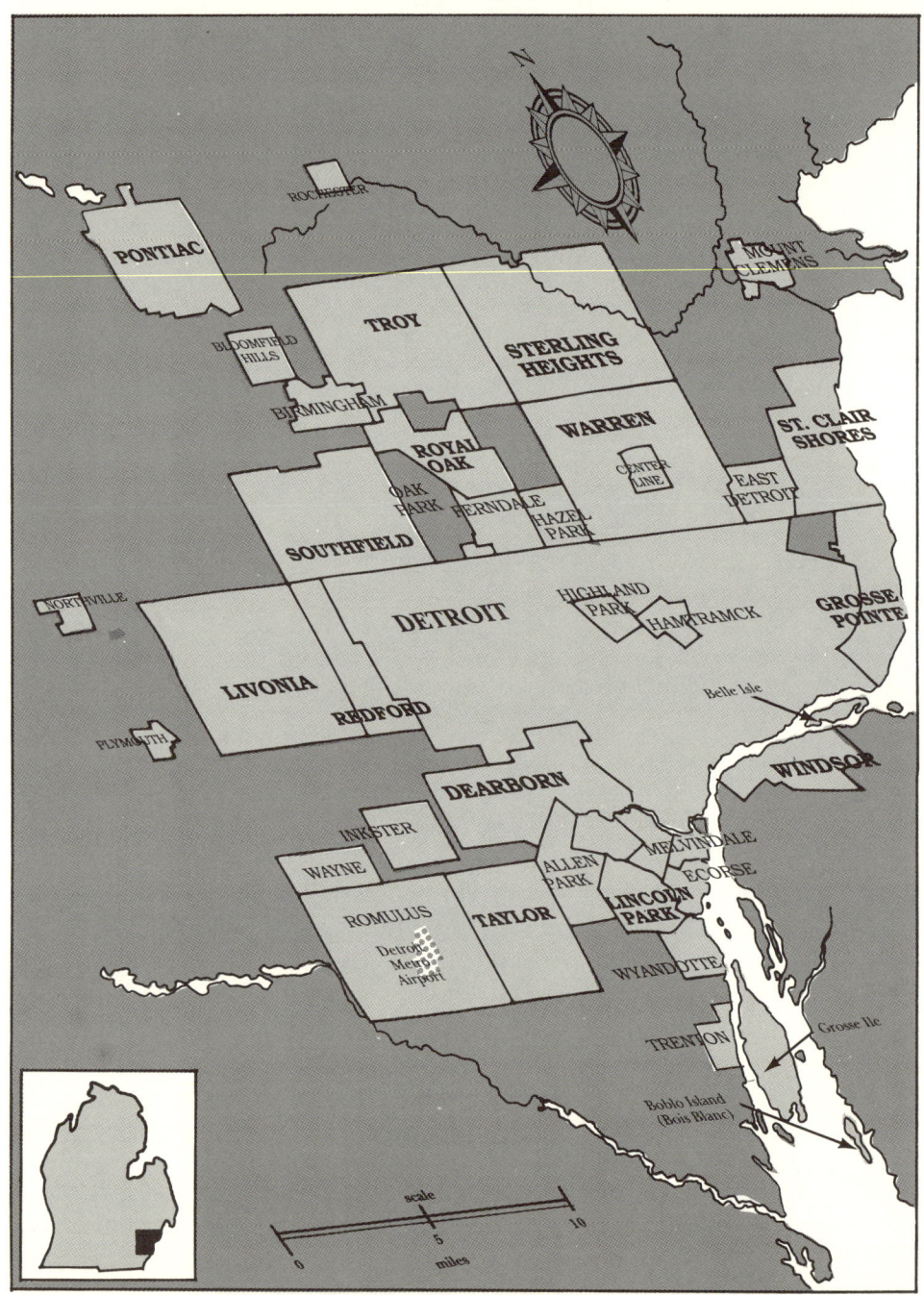

· METROPOLITAN DETROIT ·

Detroit

Modern Detroit, the birthplace of the assembly line, isn't like other old American metropolises. Though the city is nearly 300 years old, what you see today is the aftermath of a giant 20-century boom town. The boom began with the great surge in auto manufacturing soon after 1900, swelling this medium-sized turn-of-the-century industrial center into one of the country's biggest cities. Many of the most extraordinary sights Detroit has to offer visitors come from this boom of the 1910s and 1920s: lavish Art Deco skyscrapers, opulent auto baron mansions, a major symphony, a world-renowned art museum, the spectacular Fox Theater.

By 1930 the city's population had grown to over 1.5 million. Well over half the cars in the world were made here. The billions of dollars flowing into Detroit positioned it to rival Chicago as the financial center of the Midwest.

The boom ended abruptly with the Depression, then revived again during World War II, when the auto plants were converted to war production. It continued into the 1950s, as automakers worked overtime to fill demand pent up during the war years. But by the 1950s the auto companies were building their new factories outside the Motor City. The prosperous Detroit of the 1950s was a city living on borrowed time. The 1910-vintage auto plants, life blood of Detroit's working-class neighborhoods, were becoming obsolete.

Detroit's population reflects its history
1850: 21,019
1860: 45,619
1870: 79,577
1880: 116,340
1890: 205,876
1900: 285,704
1910: 465,766
1920: 993,698
1930: 1,568,662
1940: 1,623,452
1950: 1,849,568
1960: 1,670,144
1970: 1,514,063
1980: 1,203,339

Although founded in 1701, Detroit didn't become much more than a village until the Erie Canal was completed in 1824, encouraging the Michigan land rush. It remained only a medium-sized city until this century, when it exploded in population to become fourth largest in the land. The population peaked in the 1950s at about 2 million and is now declining at a rate of 20,000 a year.

People flocked to Detroit to earn good wages in its auto plants. They came from Michigan farms and mining towns, from Eastern Europe, and the Near East, and — after World War I cut off immigration — from the American South. This photo shows Ford line workers in the 1950s.

A dramatic decline

Today Detroit's public image has become synonymous with decline. It will be the first American city of over one million people to fall back below a million.

Detroit's civic leaders of the 1920s would no doubt be astounded were they to view their city today. Its population is decreasing by twenty thousand a year. Of the remaining households, 45 per cent were below the poverty level in 1985 — double the figure only five years earlier. The murder rate is among the country's highest. Two thousand buildings a year are torn down, while almost no new homes are being built, except for riverfront luxury apartment complexes. Most of the fine old downtown shops and department stores are gone. Detroit is the only major older U.S. city without a downtown department store. Many of the once-grand office buildings and hotels lie empty. Though some Detroit neighborhoods remain desirable, and inspiring tales of tough, spunky people working to improve their blocks abound, the fact remains that vast neighborhoods are crumbling, and many Detroit homes sell for $10,000 and less.

This aerial view of Detroit in 1930 shows the streets of Judge Woodward's plan radiating from Grand Circus Park and the cluster of 1920s skyscrapers between Larned and Fort, the fruit of Detroit's auto boom. Notice how the riverfront was completely blocked from downtown by docks and warehouses — a problem recently remedied by demolition and the building of a series of parks.

Capitol of the French fur-trading empire

Although Detroit didn't become one of the country's biggest cities until the 20th century, few American cities are older. Founded in 1701, its strategic location at a narrow point on the Detroit River made the fort town a keenly fought-over prize and gave it an unusually rich history. Five times it changed sovereignty. Twice it was under Indian siege. Twice it surrendered to invading armies. In 1805 Detroit burned to the ground after the wind took hold of a spark from a baker's pipe.

Detroit was founded by the ambitious, arrogant youngest son of a French noble. In the waning years of the 17th century, Antoine de la Mothe Cadillac served King Louis XIV and successfully used Detroit as a feudal-style administrative center controlling the rich fur trade over an immense territory.

Strategic military location

Cadillac chose the site for Detroit not for its specific transportation advantages, as was typical for early American cities, but for its strategic military importance. The French were concerned lest the English to the east move in on their lucrative fur-trading territories in the upper Great Lakes. By erecting a fort on the stretch of the Detroit River that the French called "the straits" or *d' etroit,* the French controlled access to this territory. Cadillac built his fort on the highest bank on the narrowest part of the river, a point where it was only half a mile wide. In 1701 Fort Pontchartrain arose between what is now Jefferson and Griswold, Larned and Shelby streets in downtown Detroit.

Despite its important role in ruling a giant portion of America's interior, Detroit remained for many decades a tiny outpost, first French and later British.

Crime and Detroit — two insiders' views

"I feel very safe in Detroit," says Detroit News jazz critic Jim Dulzo, a native who has visited nightspots in every part of the city several nights a week for the past 10 years. "The landscape makes people apprehensive. It looks so bleak and harsh, it really does something to your perception of people and everything else. You adjust to it when you get to know the city. The main thing you've got to watch out for here is your car."

"A lot of suburbanites act like they're allergic to Detroit," says John King, owner of John King Books downtown, who goes all over the city and country buying collections. "I can think of lots of places more dangerous than anyplace in Detroit — parts of Chicago, or San Francisco, or New York, or LA. Hollywood and Vine, for instance, is so creepy you want to look around you three times before getting out of your car."

The overwhelming majority of Detroit crime occurs between people who know each other. Most of it is drug-related. By far the greatest threat to personal safety is not peculiar to Detroit at all: drunk drivers.

Detroit in 1796, the year it came into U.S. possession. Although almost a century old, the village consisted of fewer than 200 houses inside the log stockade, around St. Anne's Church.

Even after the city was ceded to the U.S. in 1796, there was little growth. As late as 1810 Detroit had fewer than 800 residents.

The original French-Canadian vassal farmers, called *habitants*, did little better than subsist on their narrow ribbon farms. These fronted along the river east and west of the fort, stretching far inland. Many downtown and eastside streets (including Beaubien, St. Aubin, Chene, Joseph Campau) were named after the French families whose property lines they follow.

Eccentric Judge Woodward and his plan

Shortly after a fire devastated the little town in 1805, Judge Augustus Woodward arrived. His friend Thomas Jefferson had appointed him to supervise rebuilding the leveled village. A highly learned and eccentric character, Woodward was known for his bizarre judicial decisions, his grubby apparel, and his fondness for brandy. Judge Woodward devised an elaborate new street system, based on Charles L'Enfant's street plan for Washington. Woodward's 1805 plan was based on repeated circular parks connected by spoke-like arteries. Although it has been largely replaced by a conventional grid system, Woodward's plan configured a good part of present-day downtown, creating office buildings with unusual shapes and an interesting web of streets, plazas, and parks.

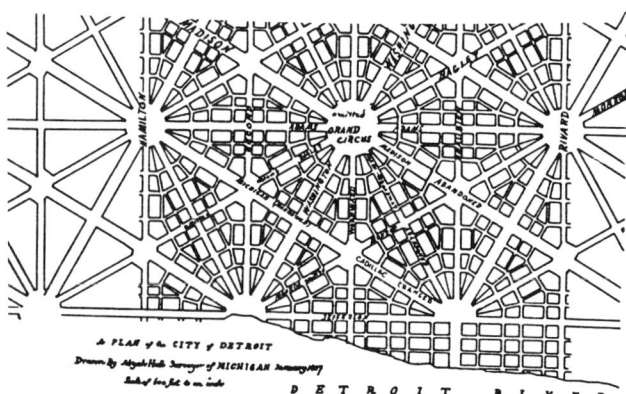

Only downtown are there remnants of Judge Woodward's 1807 circle-and-spoke street plan of Detroit. L'Enfant's plan for Washington D.C. inspired Woodward's boulevards radiating from circular parks.

Lumber, fishing, agriculture, and cast iron created old Detroit money

For a city destined to become an industrial giant, Detroit didn't show much manufacturing prowess until well into the 19th century. Not until 1830 did the city begin to grow. At that time the new Erie Canal led to a deluge of American immigrants coming to Michigan from upstate New York and New England. On some days in 1836, two thousand pioneers arrived in Detroit by boat across Lake Erie. By 1840 there were more Irish Catholics than French Catholics in Detroit, and the French influence on public affairs had become quite small.

Until the final quarter of the 19th century, the region's major wealth was generated by agriculture, lumbering, and fishing. Detroit's chroniclers of that era would boast of how Detroit whitefish could be found as far away as Natchez, Cincinnati, and New York. Coupled with Great Lakes shipping, new railroad lines in the 1850s made Detroit a regional transportation center. That same decade, the city started to become the major Great Lakes boatbuilding center and a national leader in the manufacture of railroad cars. The one area in which Detroit clearly led the nation before the turn of the century was in the manufacture of stoves.

The surprising emergence of the Motor City

Historians have sought in vain for a simple explanation of Detroit's extraordinary, unexpected rise between 1900 and 1915 to dominate the world of auto manufacturing. One factor was the presence of wealthy citizens with fortunes from ebbing industries such as lumbering who could supply capital. Also, the city had by then considerable experience in the metal-working and manufacturing engines. Henry Ford, for instance,

In 1900, on the eve of the auto boom, Detroit was a city of just 285,000, about the same size as metropolitan Kalamazoo today. Its biggest industry was the manufacture of stoves. The Detroit Stove Works, here depicted in Silas Farmer's 1884 history, occupied the later Uniroyal Tire site just west of the Belle Isle bridge.

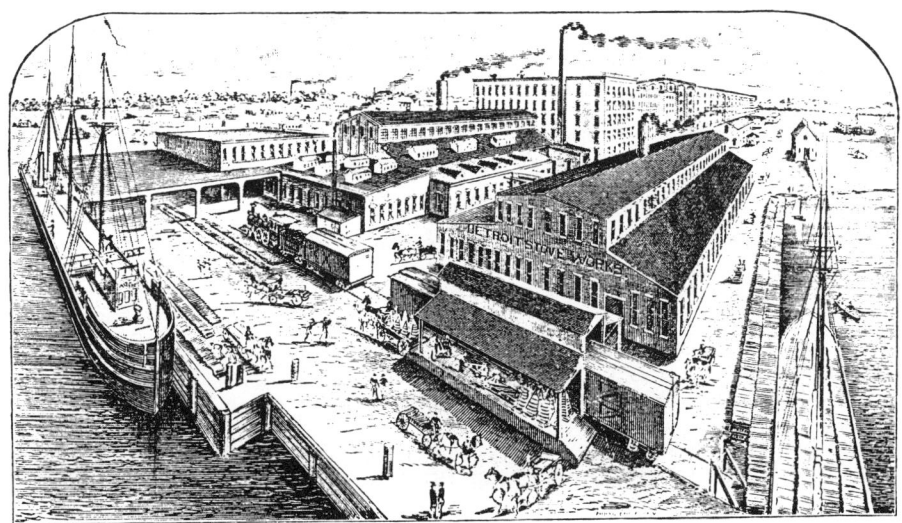

first became acquainted with the manufacture of engines through his job at Detroit Dry Dock, the city's largest boat builder.

Michigan had other advantages. It already led the country in producing buggies and wheels. Detroit is midway between the coal fields of West Virginia and Pennsylvania and the iron ore deposits along Lake Superior. Rogers City and Alpena furnished limestone for Detroit's blast furnaces.

But other cities had more sophisticated industrial bases. What set Detroit apart was the presence of a few remarkably capable and aggressive entrepreneurs — Henry Joy, Henry Leland, the Dodge Brothers, Henry Ford, among others — who pushed ahead to create the high-volume production necessary to lower the cost of manufacturing and to undercut competitors.

In 1905, autos were made in 175 American cities, none of them dominant. By 1910 Detroit had become the industry's center. It had grown from a medium-size city on the order of Toledo into the nation's fifth-ranking city. Dozens of Detroit automobile factories sprang up, making Cadillacs, Packards, Fords, Studebakers, Huppmobiles, Hudsons, Dodges, Lincolns — to name a few. A feverishly inventive auto-manufacturing culture developed here akin to Silicon Valley's recent high-tech culture on the West Coast. Automobile talk was the talk of the town.

The city's boom times got a powerful boost with the Ford workers' famous five-dollar day in 1914. Soon storefronts stretched along streetcar lines for miles, not only out Woodward but Gratiot, Michigan, Grand River, Warren, Livernois, and Mack. Detroit had far more commercial strips than older cities developed in earlier eras, where small corner clusters of stores were the rule. With suburbanization and the coming of the giant shopping centers (pioneered by Detroit's J. L. Hudson Company), these miles of car-line storefronts have mostly become desolate streetscapes, boarded-up structures brightened periodically by the bold colors of party stores. For many visitors this bleak view is the dominant image of Detroit. Actually, many of the neighborhoods behind the old strips are in much better shape than the commercial arteries would suggest.

Homeownership: the workers' reward

Boomtown Detroit of 1910-1930 was erecting row upon row of small single-family homes for the newly prosperous autoworkers — tens of thousands of them. Apartments were less common here than in other cities. Detroit long enjoyed the highest rate of homeownership of any major city, between 70 and 80 per cent. As late as the 1980 census, only 42 per cent of its households were renters.

Ironically, Detroit's extraordinary rate of homeownership — testimony to its ability to fulfill the American

Detroit's ethnic diversity
Because Detroit boomed after 1910, it attracted a far larger variety of peoples from Eastern Europe and the Middle East than older industrial cities. Metro Detroit has unusual numbers of African-Americans, Albanians, Belgians, Chaldeans, Lebanese, Maltese, Palestinians, Poles, and Yemeni, along with substantial numbers of Germans, Hungarians, Irish, Italians, Jews, and Mexican-Americans.

Dream — contributes to its problems today. Tough Michigan anti-condemnation laws, designed to protect homeowning industrial workers during the Depression, make it unusually difficult and slow to tear down abandoned homes. Detroit today has a glut of modest mostly frame worker homes that are not as attractive to urban rehabbers as the 19th-century brick row houses of, say, St. Louis or Baltimore. Housing values in Detroit have dropped so low and tax rates risen so high that many property owners just walk away from houses that it doesn't pay to fix up.

Just as Detroit in the 1950s was peaking with over two million residents, the adjacent suburbs began to boom. The little village of Warren, home of the GM Technical Center and a tank plant, skyrocketed from a 1950 population of 727 to over 89,000 in 1960. Today it is Michigan's third biggest city. Livonia, Roseville, East Detroit, Madison Heights, Birmingham, Royal Oak, Garden City, Southfield — all experienced their biggest growth in the 1950s.

Roots of racial segregation

Almost all the Detroiters moving to these nearby new suburbs were white. Restrictive real estate practices kept blacks in the city. Metro Detroit's suburbia was not only one of the biggest and newest in the U.S., it was also one of the most segregated—and remains so today.

African-Americans in Detroit numbered only 5,700 back in 1910. But beginning with labor shortages during World War I, when European immigration was curtailed, the auto companies started recruiting Southerners, black and white. Some 30,000 Southern blacks arrived in Detroit in 1916-17. World War II again produced a labor shortage, and the African-American population rose to a quarter of a million. These blacks had the bad luck of arriving in Detroit after the city's auto boom had peaked.

Early suburbanization

It is widely but incorrectly thought that the mass exodus of Detroit whites to the suburbs was precipitated by "white flight" from the increasing black population. Actually, the bulk of the whites' departure was a simple matter of prosperity and upward mobility. The new housing developments of the postwar years beckoned as better places to live than the tight-packed neighborhoods built during the first auto boom. When demand for older neighborhoods softened, banks and real estate firms opened them to black people. Blockbuster scare tactics were sometimes used to hasten the transition of neighborhoods from black to white.

The effect of the middle-class exodus — first of whites, and in recent years also of blacks — eventually devastated the city. Most of its more affluent residents

Detroit's freeways, among this country's very first, spurred suburbanization. Not surprisingly, the Motor City and the state of Michigan had the money and desire to build one of the nation's earliest and most sophisticated freeway systems. Freeways reinforced Detroit's tendency to sprawl, caused by the fact that its major growth occurred during the automobile age. Even in the 1930s, visitors noted, it was a remarkably spread-out city of single-family homes built without regard to public transportation lines. Here, the Fisher Freeway (top to bottom) intersects with the Lodge near Tiger Stadium on Michigan Avenue (diagonal).

are now gone. The tax base declined with property values, putting more stress on remaining residents to pay for expensive big-city services.

By the 1960s the steady loss of hundreds of thousands of auto-related jobs in the city of Detroit had begun, even though the auto industry still prospered. The Motown Sound, based on the widespread talent in Detroit's black community, gave a successful new pop cultural identity to the city even as its economy was souring. Those with the least job security were most affected, especially African-Americans. At the same time, the war on poverty was raising the expectations of young black Americans. They compared themselves not with blacks in other cities who were less well off than they, but with area whites, who had more. The city was becoming less white, but the police department (like the school system and other longstanding institutions) remained staffed largely by whites, who had trouble understanding the perspective of many Detroit blacks.

The climax to these building tensions came with the stunning riots of 1967, characterized as the worst civil disorder experienced by an American city in the 20th century. Ironically, the riots occurred in a city that had won national acclaim as a model of progressive enlightenment in fighting poverty and discrimination. But a raid on a black-owned blind pig escalated into 10 days of rioting. In all, 43 people died, 7,231 were arrested, 682 fires were started, and 1,700 stores looted. It took federal troops to restore order.

For both blacks and whites, the alarming riots were a turning point, dramatic evidence of radical change. Many more whites hastened to leave the city, and many

A sprawling city
As Detroit prospered, almost every autoworker had a car. Car ownership per capita led the nation. As a result, public transportation was never well developed in the Motor City and bus service today is poor.

suburbanites turned their backs on it. For blacks and sympathetic whites, the riot and the attention focused on police-community relations set the stage for the 1974 mayoral victory of state representative and labor hero Coleman Young as Detroit's first African-American mayor. His deal-making skills have shaped today's "Renaissance city," a thin riverfront strip of glitzy hotels, office buildings, apartments, and parks.

The cost of living in Detroit

Affluent residents in the more desirable Detroit areas like Indian Village and Palmer Woods, where property values have held up, pay a stiff premium for living in the city. Property taxes are high – fifth highest among major U.S. cities. With Detroit's 3 per cent personal income tax, it's no wonder that relatively few high-income people choose to live in the city. The financially strapped Detroit public school system is generally viewed as inadequate, except for a few elite high schools (Cass Tech and Renaissance) and special elementary schools.

The strategy for the city's regeneration consistently implemented by Mayor Coleman Young's administration has been to concentrate limited resources on making the downtown and riverfront alluring for new development, while attracting with huge subsidies new plants and their jobs to the city. Young's strategy is bearing some fruit. Two big new auto plants will have gone up during his term of office. New condos and marina-residential developments along the river are drawing suburbanites — almost exclusively young singles, divorced men, and couples with grown children or no children at all.

But Detroit has a long way to go in regaining its onetime status as a great place to raise a family. The Young administration has a disappointing track record in neighborhood improvement compared to many large industrial cities. While the city's riverfront blossoms and stable neighborhoods are dotted throughout the city, most neighborhoods have continued to decline, largely because of drug-related problems sweeping the U.S.

Some of the many people who love this city maintain it can't get any worse, that things have bottomed out, and that soon the low cost of land and the city's considerable cultural and geographic advantages will result in a turnaround. Others see no concrete grounds for optimism yet.

The cost of an imperial mayor
Now in his fifth four-year term as mayor, Coleman Young has grown more isolated and arrogant with time. "The most devastating thing Coleman Young has done was to keep down a secondary level of black leadership," says one liberal Detroit lawyer. "Most on the council are an absolute joke."

Signs of the Motor City
Driving along Detroit's many freeways, a visitor will quickly see that this remains very much an automobile town. There is a huge three-story Uniroyal tire along I-94 in Dearborn. Three big digital signs update motorists on the number of U.S. cars built so far in the year. The largest is at the Chrysler Freeway-Ford Freeway interchange, where a 96-foot-long sign sponsored by Goodyear Tire keeps counting upward, its rate based on weekly forecasts of Automotive News. Another is located on the Lodge Freeway at Clairmount, and a third on the Ford Freeway near Metro Airport.

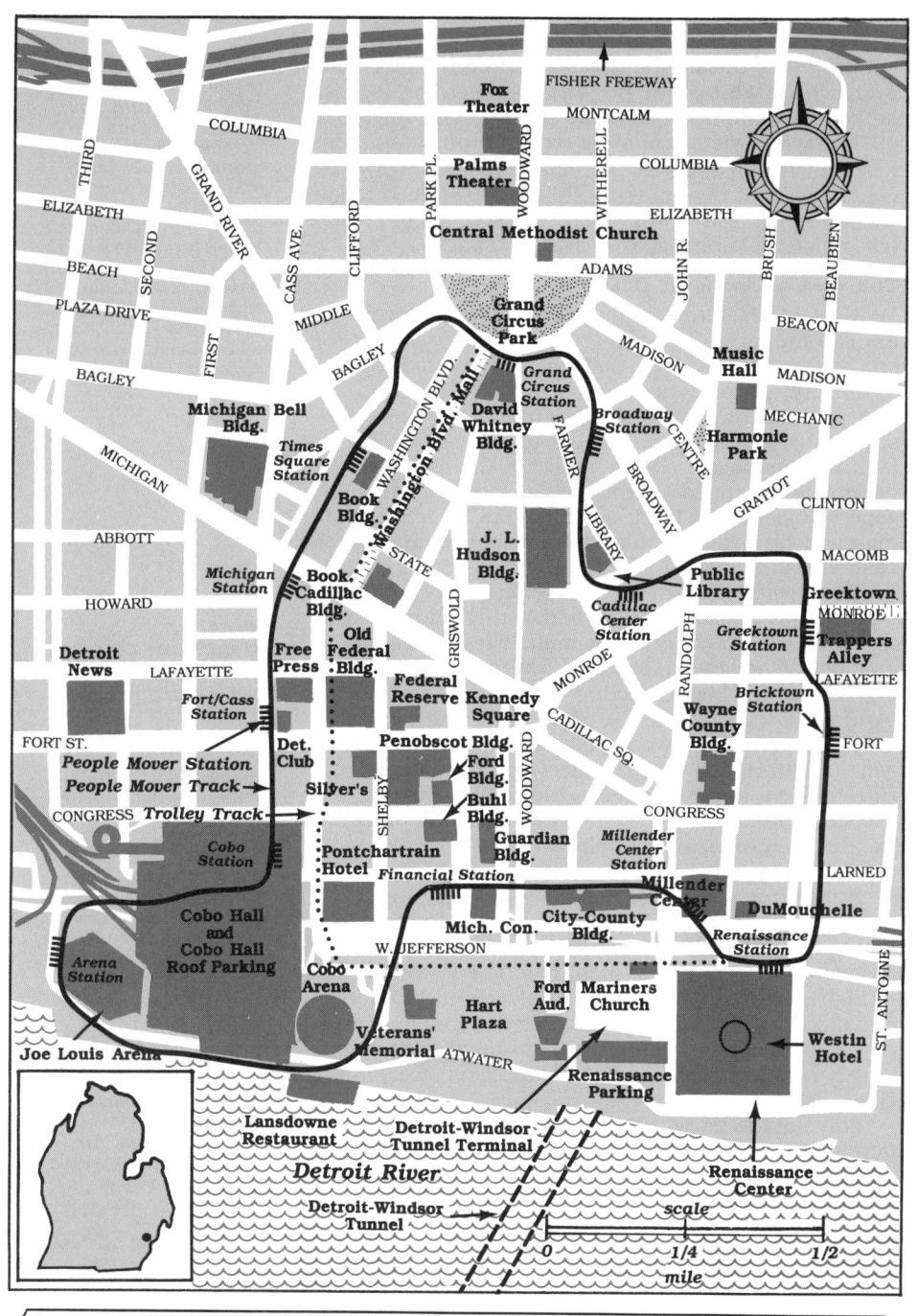

· DOWNTOWN DETROIT ·

Downtown Detroit

Today downtown Detroit is an infrequent destination for many suburbanites, who have been put off by the erroneous impression that downtown is dangerous and has little to offer. They miss out on a lot. In fact, downtown Detroit is as safe as most other major U.S. downtowns, and it's considered safer than many, including Los Angeles and New York. Exceptional restaurants at all price ranges are plentiful (see **Downtown Restaurants**), and Detroit's culinary stars like the Money Tree and the Rattlesnake Club are bargains compared with their peers on the Coasts. Downtown has some impressive architecture, from the Beaux-Arts County Building to some of the most impressive Art Deco office towers found anywhere. High-quality public sculpture abounds, from an ornate allegorical Civil War monument to an important Calder stabile.

The unique elevated **Detroit People Mover** offers an exciting, comfortable bird's-eye view of the center city, and a trip to the RenCen's 72nd-story restaurant offers a map-like view of the Detroit River connecting lakes Erie and St. Clair. **Greektown**, a perennial tourist draw, retains its colorful, bustling atmosphere. **Trappers Alley** festival marketplace has greatly enhanced the nearby **Bricktown** area as a visitor draw, with an eclectic range of bars and nightclubs. The riverfront is blossoming with parks and picnic areas, with more restaurants, clubs, and taverns nearby. Each weekend in summer there is entertainment and

Detroit's most dazzling sight is the downtown skyline reflected in the Detroit River from Windsor at night. Other good vantage points are from the west tip of Belle Isle and from Chene and St. Aubin parks. At the left of this photo is the landmark ball on the 47-story Penobscot Building. The RenCen is at the right.

activites (mostly free, and sometimes of very high quality) at the riverfront parks: **Hart Plaza** downtown, **St. Aubin Park** just to the east, and **Chene Park**. The spectacular **Fox Theater** renovation on downtown's northwestern edge promises to be a catalyst for further arts and entertainment development in the **1920s theater district** at Woodward and Grand Circus Park.

The riverfront blossoms; downtown waits

The lion's share of new development in Detroit is occurring along the beautiful Detroit River from downtown to Belle Isle. Here the removal of old factories and warehouses is creating space for riverside parks. Tall office buildings and apartment complexes are going up. The centerpiece of the colossal, controversial **Renaissance Center** office complex is the world's tallest hotel. Many of the liveliest nightspots can now be found in converted old brick buildings on the riverfront east of the RenCen. Building up an attractive core of riverfront development is a key part of tough, irascible Mayor Coleman Young's game plan for creating a healthy new Detroit by the 21st century.

The hundreds of millions of dollars invested in Detroit riverfront development dwarfs new activity in the older downtown and threatens the grand old skyscrapers. They must compete for tenants with the gleaming new buildings. Many ornate old hotels and office buildings lie empty, their futures uncertain. Outside of specially created enclaves such as Trappers Alley, the Renaissance Center, and Millender Center, the downtown retail climate looks dismal. The loss of the huge Hudson's on Woodward at Grand River still hurts. For generations of Detroiters, it was the heart of the city. Actually, there are clusters of noteworthy shops — on Congress near Griswold, around Beaubien in Bricktown, around Grand Circus Park, and, on Broadway, a mix of tough old survivors like Henry the Hatter and trend-setters like City Slickers, where famous entertainers buy $800 snakeskin shoes. But you have to know where to find them.

For a city the size of Detroit, the downtown is quite compact, easy to walk through without getting tired. And if you do get tired, the magnificent People Mover is there to whisk you form one side to another, or just give you a spectacular view of downtown. Parking downtown is a snap compared to Birmingham, East Lansing, or Ann Arbor, and if you go to the right lots, it need cost no more than $2 a day.

To round out a downtown excursion, just minutes away are the fabulous **Detroit Institute of Arts**, the **Eastern Market** (a food-lover's paradise of high-quality bargains), and beautiful **Belle Isle** with its aquarium, zoo, and ship museum.

"The Spirit of Detroit" **by Marshall Fredericks.**

Detroit: Downtown 17

POINTS OF INTEREST

Detroit People Mover ★★★

Downtown Detroit (See map for route.) 1-800-541-7245 ; from Detroit, 962-RAIL. Mon-Thurs 7 a.m.-11p.m., Fri 7 a.m.-midnight, Sat 9 a.m.-midnight, Sun noon-8 p.m. Fare: 50¢. (Two quarters or a token necessary to operate turnstile.)

If you only have half an hour to spend in Detroit, take a ride on the People Mover. This spectacular elevated rail system runs in a 2.9-mile loop around the downtown, offering extraordinary views of the central city, the river, and Windsor. Big, colorful works of art by top area artists make it an adventure to pass the entryways and platforms in each of the 12 stations. Call the People Mover for a splendid brochure on "Art in the Stations." Even in winter, the People Mover is fun.

This must be the most expensive public transport in history: the 2.9 miles cost federal and state taxpayers a whopping $200 million, vastly more than initial projections. What's more, the system, a pet project of Mayor Young, has attracted one-third fewer riders than projected (about 11,500 a day), requiring the city to subsidize it to the tune of over $9 million a year.

Still, the People Mover is a visitor's delight: beautifully designed, clean, safe, and frequently patrolled. It's a smooth-working system which gives the rider an unparalleled view of the glories and desolations of downtown Detroit. It takes only 15 minutes to make the entire loop. You may want to take several trips to take it all in: the beauty of the aqua Detroit River on a sunny day, the ornate 1920s skyscrapers, the VIPs' cars double-parked for lunch at the elite Detroit Club, Grand Circus Park, the once proud and now sadly abandoned hotels and office buildings on the north part of the loop, the towering Renaissance Center, lively Bricktown and Greektown. Special highlights: the swing out over the Detroit River by the Joe Louis Arena and the close glimpse of City-County Building employees at their desks.

1920s office towers in the Financial District ★★★

Between Washington and Woodward, from Lafayette to Larned.

During the 1920s, the go-go national economy and Detroit's auto boom combined to make Detroit third (after New York and Chicago) in the volume of new construction. Soaring, individualistic skyscrapers vied for attention, creating the jagged, energetic, proud skyline so esteemed by American city dwellers. These giants turned Griswold Street into a veritable canyon in only four years. The firm of Smith, Hinchman and Grylls won most of the office-building design work, and entrusted it to designer Wirt Rowland, a gifted student of architectural theory and admirer of Gothic architecture.

It was Cranbrook's Eliel Saarinen who had earlier set the standard for the new way of treating tall buildings as boldly aspiring towers with streamlined setbacks, rather than building tall boxes and covering them with bits and pieces of facades borrowed from the past. Although Saarinen took up residence at nearby Cranbrook in 1926, he never designed a skyscraper built in Detroit.

The following tour from Fort to Congress combines dazzling architectural ornament with chances to eat and shop. It shows how quickly Rowland shifted from an archaeological, cathedral-like conservatism to designing the exuberant Guardian Building.

Guardian Building ★★★
*500 Griswold at Congress.
(313) 965-2430. Mon-Fri 9-5.*

This ornate 1929 skyscraper is a flamboyant banking tribute to the go-go years of the 1920s. It also symbolizes the financial excesses of that time, for its occupant and owner, Guardian National Bank, was the very first in a nationwide domino-like chain of banks to close in 1933, greatly intensifying the national Depression.

The notched Aztec front facade is unusual in itself. Specially made bricks clad the 535-foot-high building, enlivened with bands of colored tiles. The bricks, less costly than the more typical granite or limestone exterior of a major building, allowed architect Rowland to use the savings on a variety of spectacular visual effects.

The most stunning are in the main lobby and the adjacent banking room half a story up. Over the main entrance is a Pewabic-tiled half dome. Covered over in the 1950s, it

From the Detroit River, the cubistic mass of the 47-story Penobscot Building dominates the Financial District skyline. Its radio tower and illuminated ball are landmarks. The cross-shaped Buhl Building is in front of it to the right. The Guardian Building with its top band of geometric decorations is to the far right.

has since been restored by its present occupant, Michigan Consolidated Gas. The walls of the main lobby are blood-red Numibian marble. Rowland had to re-open an African mine to quarry it. The lobby's mosaic mural was designed by noted artist Ezra Winter. Thomas DiLorenzo designed the ceiling of the main banking room to the south. It is painted on canvas, behind which is a 3/4-inch mat of horsehair to mute the sound in the vast room.

Ernest Kanzler, the brother-in-law and close friend of Edsel Ford, built the Guardian Building. His Guardian Group became the major banking power in Detroit with the financial help of Edsel Ford, who put millions of his and Ford Motor Company's money into Kanzler's banking syndicate. So successful was this group that there was even talk that Detroit would overtake Chicago as the financial center of the Midwest. Then the 1929 stock market crash put increasing strain on the overextended bank. Despite a personal plea from President Hoover, Henry Ford refused at a critical juncture to bail the bank out, even though his son lost up to $20 million with its failure.

When Guardian National closed its doors in 1933, it was the first of a chain reaction that led to the closing of every bank in the country.

Buhl Building ★★
Southwest corner, Griswold at Congress. (313) 962-8300.

The 1925 Buhl Building feels like a church, a true temple of commerce, with the dark, enclosed, rich effect of heavy medieval masonry and Romanesque decorative embellishments. Architect Wirt Rowland was designing two churches at the same time, and it shows. The marble lobby with its Italian bronzes is a splendid setting for the dark, richly decorated **Buhl Cafe and Bar** and the elegantly simple little corner cafeteria, **Quattro Punti** (see p. 39).

In the Guardian Building's banking hall, a map of Michigan is the centerpiece of a long barrel vault. It is surrounded by the geometric steps and zig-zag motif repeated throughout the building.

Penobscot Building ★★
Corner of Griswold and Fort. (313) 961-8800. 6:30 a.m.-6 p.m.

In this 47-story skyscraper, finished in 1928, architect Wirt Rowland designed a simple, H-shaped shaft. Setbacks above the 30th floor form an interesting cubistic pattern topped by an observation deck and a big blinking aircraft beacon, once a hallmark of the city. Inside, the warm-colored marble floors feature geometric designs, with Indian eagles on the elevator doors and mailboxes. The interior shops include a Doubleday bookstore, the **Epicurean Cafe** (see p. 38) and **John T. Woodhouse Sons** tobacconist, whose wood-inlaid interior is a period delight.

Silver's/People's State Bank ★
151 W. Fort at Shelby. 963-0000. Mon-Fri 8:30-5:30.

This stylish, sophisticated office and gift store occupies the marble-faced bank space that is Detroit's only building designed by the famous Beaux Arts architects McKim, Mead and White. It dates from 1900. Hawkins Ferry says Stanford White himself was much involved, and that "the exquisite refinement of its details and proportions [indicate] the handiwork of the most gifted and fastidious of the partners." Balustrades, allegorical sculpture, and two Ionic columns make it appropriately bank-like, but huge arched windows let in lots of light. This pedigreed neoclassicism sets the standard against which to measure the nearby skyscrapers' innovations.

Today the dignified banking floor showcases gifts and accessories, plus room arrangements of office furniture. It feels a little like a museum of serious good design. The gifty, impulse-oriented lower level (opening onto Congress) is jazzy, with trendier items and good sales on glassware and dishes, cards, candies (including the highly regarded, locally produced Gayle's Chocolates), and the excellent and very popular cafeteria-style **Britt's Cafe**. (See p. 37.)

**Money Museum/
National Bank of Detroit** ★★
611 Woodward at Congress. (313) 225-1000. Mon-Fri 9-4.

Even if you have little interest in coins and currency, this large lobby display is surprisingly appealing. Nate Shapiro, owner of the old Cunningham drugstores, collected all kinds of money — from New Guinea dog-tooth currency to Lydian silver pellets from the 7th century B.C. There are conventional coins of all ages, local and national currencies, private U.S. gold pieces, and emergency money, which is in some ways the most fascinating of all. In Germany's hyperinflation of the early 1920s, for instance, when it could cost a million marks to mail a letter, money was sometimes made of materials that had intrinsic worth — coins of Meissen porcelain, fabric bills in striking Expressionist designs (if they lost all value, you could make a quilt out of them) and coins of pressed coal issued by the town of Rothenbach, bearing the motto, "In spite of everything, we will survive."

Beautifully engraved bills from all over the world are so subtly colorful and graphically interesting, they put dull American currency to shame. Bills picturing African landscapes, hair designs, and textiles are especially appealing. Local history is well represented, with exhibits about Michigan's 1837 banking crisis and commemorative medals for cities and auto manufacturers.

Hart Plaza ★★
At the foot of Woodward between Jefferson and the Detroit River.
Visitors Information Center *in front of Ford Auditorium is open 9-5 Mon-Fri. (Pull in to 15-minute free parking spots, and some short-term parking, off Jefferson.) Call (313) 567-1170 for specific events programming and suggestions on what to do.* **Park** *at Cobo Arena or Ford Auditorium garages.* **People Mover:** *exit at Millender Center and walk across Jefferson or the RenCen skywalk. The* **Downtown Trolley** *(see p. 36) stops and turns around on Jefferson Ave. side of Mariners' Church.*
Summer Riverfront Festivals *(see below) from late April through Labor*

The changing spray patterns of Noguchi's Dodge Fountain in Hart Plaza are fun to watch.

Day weekend. Hotline: (313) 224-1184. For season schedule, write Detroit Rec. Dept., 1707 Water Board Bldg., Detroit 48226.

A lot of memorable things come together at this popular gathering place. Eight acres of interestingly designed, multi-level pavement lead down from Jefferson to the Detroit River and the very spot on which Cadillac built Fort Pontchartrain in 1701. Hart Plaza is a splendid place to be in nice weather, as attested by crowds of downtown workers at lunch and weekend visitors to the summer-long Riverfront Festivals. Regulars play chess at concrete tables near the **Dodge Fountain,** by famed sculptor Isamu Noguchi. It's easy to be mesmerized by the fountain's changing water patterns, which shoot up from the center and down from the futuristic stainless steel "doughnut" propped up by round angled supports. Noguchi also designed the plaza and its 120-foot twisted **Pylon Sculpture**, meant to suggest the DNA molecules that, he explained, "we all are made of."

On the one side of the Plaza there's a view of Detroit's impressive **skyline.** The other looks out on the river, with views of the **Ambassador Bridge** and **Windsor,** Detroit's Canadian neighbor to the south. The **Star of Detroit** cruise boat and the **Lansdowne** floating restaurant are docked here. The plaza's many levels make it interesting to explore. Down at the lawn by the river, a few tables encourage picnics.

All sorts of things around Hart Plaza convey the coming-together of past and present. Here in the same view you see:
♦ the **Renaissance Center**, a nearly omnipresent backdrop downtown.
♦ the historic 1849 **Mariners' Church.**
♦ the center of local government, the 19-story **City-County Building** on Woodward at Jefferson. In front of it is the **Spirit of Detroit** statue by Detroit sculptor Marshall Fredericks.

Also known as the "Jolly Green Giant," it's the city's logo, seen on every garbage truck and police car. The huge seated figure is the spirit of humanity, holding in one hand a gilt sphere emanating rays (representing God) and in the other a tiny family, representing "the noblest human relationship."
♦ the giant sculptural **Joe Louis fist** at Woodward and Jefferson. It memorializes Detroit's famous Brown Bomber, who vanquished Max Schmelling (and by implication Hitler's theory of white racial supremacy) to become world heavyweight boxing champion in 1938.
♦ the bright-painted **Downtown Trolley** cars. The antique trolley cars wait by Mariners' Church between regular runs to Grand Circus Park. (See p. 36.)

On summer weekends food, live music and dance in the Hart Plaza outdoor amphitheater are part of popular, low-key weekly **ethnic festivals**, plus several big festivals: the mid-May **Downtown Hoedown** (world's largest free country music fest), the mid-June **Grand Prix** (with a free day Friday), the big Detroit-Windsor **International Freedom Festival** with fireworks on the July 4 weekend, and the **Montreux-Detroit Jazz Festival**, on Labor Day Weekend. Except for a few big events, these are free. Call 313-224-1184 weekdays for a schedule.

Mariners' Church

170 E. Jefferson east of Woodward. (313) 259-2206. Open for casual visitors Tues, Thurs, Fri 10-3. Services Thurs noon, Sun 8:30 & 11.

This historic church served the crews of the Great Lakes ships, many of whom were laid up in Detroit for the winter. It was donated by Julia Anderson, who came to Detroit with her husband in 1819 on the Lakes' first steamboat, Walk-in-the-Water. The first services were held Christmas Eve in 1849. Though Great Lakes shipping is a fraction of what

Mariners' Church, finished in 1849.

it used to be, a good many sailors still attend services here. The church is Episcopal, but the services are non-denominational. At the Blessing of the Fleet on the second Sunday of every March, dozens of captains bring the flags of their ships to be blessed. The closest Sunday to November 10 is a memorial service for the crew of the sunken Edmund Fitzgerald.

The building, all six million pounds of it, received national attention in 1955 when it was moved 800 feet due east to fit into the new Civic Center complex. After the move, some fine stained glass windows were installed. The rose window, in the shape of a ship's compass, was donated by the family which owned the Boblo ships and Boblo Island. In the window's center is a ship with the faces of the 12 apostles. The compass design shows symbols for the Four Evangelists at north, south, east, and west.

Civic Center

From Ford Auditorium to Joe Louis Arena, between Jefferson and the river.

A 1940 travel guide to Michigan stated that Detroit, like many river cities, had turned its back on the river. "The stream now flows, almost unobserved from the city, past a rampart of warehouses, elevators, and other buildings." In 1977 Hart Plaza culminated the first phase of winning back the river as a sort of village common, a great ribbon of public space along which the city is reorienting itself. First came the **Ford Auditorium** performing space (1955), the home of the Detroit Symphony Orchestra until 1989, but widely despised by musicians for its acoustics. It was followed by **Cobo Hall** (1960) at the foot of Washington Boulevard. Cobo's round convention hall, at 12,000 seats, is big enough to host a national political convention. Cobo's huge exhibit space was doubled and remodeled for $200 million in 1989, to become the largest one-floor convention center in the U.S. It hosts events like the Detroit Auto Show in January.

In 1979, the 20,000-seat **Joe Louis Arena** was finished just to the south of Cobo Hall. The Republican National Convention nominated Ronald Reagan here the next year. Both Cobo and Joe Louis unfortunately cut off downtown from the river, but Cobo's cafeteria and ballroom offer sweeping river views, as does the People Mover here.

Renaissance Center ★★

E. Jefferson at Brush on the Detroit River. Open 7 a.m.-11 p.m. **Shops** *open 10-6, closed Sun. Second-story* **bridges across Jefferson** *connect with the Millender Center and People Mover Station.* **Information kiosk** *in Jefferson Ave. lobby.* **Park** *in "A" transient lot off Beaubien east of Jefferson. Rates encourage short-term and off-hours parking: $1 for 3 hours weekdays 10-6, $2 week nights after 6, 12 hours for $2 weekends. Rates for over 3 hours start at $6.60. To get a helpful* **directory and map**, *call (313) 568-5600 weekdays, write Renaissance Center Venture, 100 RenCen #1400, Detroit 48243, or stop at the information kiosk in the Jefferson Ave. lobby.*

Huge and controversial, the RenCen includes the world's tallest hotel (73 stories high), over 2 million square feet of office space, and dozens of shops and restaurants. The architect was John Portman, who had revolutionized hotel design with the Hyatt Regency's spectacular multi-story interior atriums in Atlanta and Los Angeles.

The RenCen is built on the site of an old warehouse right next to the tunnel to Canada. Completed in 1977, it instantly became the symbol of Detroit. Since then it has also come to exemplify for many a wrong-headed urban revitalization project cut off from the city it is supposed to revive.

From Jefferson in front, the RenCen, sitting behind a massive concrete wall, looks like a fortress intended to protect its occupants from neighboring vandals. And, in fact, this "circle the wagons" psychology seems central to the design. The idea for the RenCen grew out of the aftermath of the 1967 Detroit riot. Though the riot occurred in a poor neighborhood miles from downtown Detroit, it accelerated the exodus of whites and money from the city's center. And it increased suburbanites' fear of downtown as dangerous.

It was Henry Ford II who pushed through this formidable project. He cajoled Ford suppliers and other major Detroit businesses to cough up the hundreds of millions to help build the riverside complex. Ford, like his grandfather, had a deep if erratic idealistic streak. He felt the RenCen was essential to reverse the Motor City's disastrous decline.

When it opened in 1977, the gleaming RenCen was impressively stocked with glamorous shops: Mark Cross, Gucci, and Cartier, among others. The RenCen quickly became notorious as a bewildering circular maze for casual visitors. Without memorable landmarks, the space connecting four similar round towers surrounding the Westin Hotel proved disorienting. Moneyed suburbanites were not drawn to the forbidding, confusing place. Many retailers pulled out, while the big hotel suffered from a low occupancy rate. By 1983, the original investors had defaulted on their loans, and the RenCen was taken over by the insurance company which held the mortgage. Beginning in 1985, $27 million was spent to make the complex more user friendly.

The revamped RenCen is better but still confusing, and it still doesn't draw many suburban visitors downtown. Nonetheless, the massive complex is credited with helping to launch the succeeding wave of riverfront office and residential projects. The RenCen's 50-odd shops and service businesses and 25 or so eateries have achieved a stable presence, due mainly to the 12,000 people who work for the 140 companies with offices here. The restaurants range from numerous fast-food outlets (some open for breakfast) to the spectacular, 72nd-story **Summit Steak House & Lounge**, with Tex-Mex, Japanese, Greek, and seafood

The RenCen's towers (hotel in the center, flanked by office and elevator towers) soar behind the Civic Center. In the foreground are Hart Plaza's amphitheater, Pylon (left) and Dodge Fountain (right). Behind it to the right is the white wall of the Ford Auditorium.

sit-down restaurants in-between. The **River Bistro**, tucked away on the Promenade Level, is expensive and underappreciated at dinner, "one of the untapped culinary jewels of Detroit," says *Detroit Monthly*.

The shops, which close at 6 and on Sundays, include Anton's menswear, Gantos, Alvin's, Winkelman's, and five other women's wear stores, and a small assortment of typical mall outlets for cookies, books, cards and gifts, plus a complete range of office and visitor services.

One RenCen visitor attraction is without doubt remarkable: the **view** from the revolving **Summit Steak House** on the hotel's 72nd floor. You're up so high it's like looking at a living map of the Detroit River and its islands, up to Lake St. Clair and down almost to Lake Erie. Just a trip on the elevator to the lounge, without a meal or drink, isn't cheap ($3/adult, $1 for kids 5-12, free for seniors and preschoolers). But lunches begin at just $6 and let you take in the view at your leisure. Sunday brunch (10:30-2:30) is $7 to $17. For a quick, free view, take one of the glass-sided elevators attached to each office tower. From the 400 Tower you can see Hart Plaza, downtown, and downriver.

Detroit-Windsor Tunnel

Foot of Randolph St., just west of the Renaissance Center. Fare: $1.50 per car (one way)

It's a bit eerie taking this dark, damp route to Canada under the Detroit River — certainly not as scenic as the Ambassador Bridge downstream. The 5,135-foot-long tunnel was finished in 1930. The center section of 2,200 feet was created by sinking nine steel tubes, each 31 feet wide, in a trench 45 feet under the riverbed.

If you want to make the trip, be aware that at times there are considerable delays waiting to get through customs on either side. Weekday mornings are least busy.

Millender Center

Jefferson between Brush and Randolph, across from the RenCen.

This 20-story, mixed-use complex includes the **Omni Hotel**, apartments, offices, and shops. The prefabricated construction, a trademark of Cleveland-area developer Forest City Dillon, features lots of block-like cube details, done up in mauve and beige. The **"Atrium Retail Stores"** are not unusual specialty stores, but ordinary businesses (fast-food eateries, a card shop, a magazine stand, a pleasant little book store) geared to serve residents and workers. **Blossoms,** the informal, creative flower shop on the street level, stands out. The shops are clustered between the hotel lobby and the second-level pedestrian skybridge across Jefferson to the RenCen, not far from the People Mover station.

Michigan Society of Architects/Beaubien House

555 E. Jefferson. (313) 965-4100. Mon-Fri 9-5.

Beautifully renovated, this 1870s Italianate townhouse on Jefferson near Beaubien would be a good first stop for people interested in making their own tour of downtown and "Rivertown" historic architecture. Several free pamphlets and maps are available. In the elegant front parlor are worthwhile changing exhibits related to architecture or people involved in architecture in Michigan.

DuMouchelle Auction Galleries ★

409 E. Jefferson across from the Ren Cen. (313) 963-6255. Mon-Sat 9:30-5:30. Free valet parking on auction dates. Pick up a free illustrated brochure for the upcoming auction here or at the Hart Plaza visitor information booth.

The region's premier auction spot, this is where the furniture, art, jewelry, and bibelots of the very rich are put on the block. Its home, once Detroit's first Cadillac dealership, is one of the few remaining older buildings on East Jefferson downtown. The big display windows now are full of things like chandeliers (over 60 are typically on hand), porcelain, paintings, cut crystal, silver, rugs, and furniture. These are priced items for sale right from the floor.

Auctions take place once a month, usually the second or third week. This event not uncommonly attracts people from all over the world. Items are available for inspection the week before the auction from 9:30 to 5:30. The auction lasts three days, beginning Friday at 7 p.m., Saturday at 11 a.m., and Sunday at noon. Items go for anywhere from $10 to $200,000. A Tiffany lamp recently sold for $49,000. A silk Oriental rug from the Shah of Iran's palace was picked up for $60,000. And the high bid for an Andy Warhol "slipper collage" was $10,000.

Bricktown ★

Between Greektown (Monroe St.) and Larned, Brush to St. Antoine. **Park** *at Greektown structure, between Monroe and Macomb just east of St. Antoine.* **People Mover Bricktown station:** *Beaubien at Fort.*

In recent years energy from bustling Greektown (p. 26) has spilled south into the area now being called Bricktown, strategically located between Greektown and the RenCen. Here scattered warehouses, storefronts, and townhouses of 19th-century Detroit have been restaurants, nightclubs, galleries, and shops — some elegantly renovated.

Opus One, downtown's most opulent restaurant, is at 565 East Larned, just across from the unpretentious **Bea's Comedy Kitchen.** Tucked across the street from the slick modern office building that also houses **Lynn Portnoy's** stylish women's wear shop is **St. Andrew's Hall,** a sober, dark turn-of-the-century Gothic building at 431 East Con–gress. By day it houses a Scottish men's club and, in the basement by night, the loudest and most innovative rock music in Detroit.

Other Bricktown sights of note:

Detroit Focus Gallery
743 Beaubien (take elevator or stairs to third floor). (313) 962-9025. Wed-Sat noon-6.

This respected nonprofit gallery is run by artists. It shows the work of established and new artists in juried and curated shows. As part of its public outreach programs, it publishes *Detroit Focus Quarterly* (available free at the gallery), a collection of articles, interviews, and reviews, mostly about artists in Michigan.

Muccioli Studio Gallery/ Little Things
(313) 962-4700/ 965-1510. 511 Beaubien. Tues-Sat 11-6.

It's fun to peek into this elegantly renovated, hundred-year-old townhouse. Downstairs, Nate Muccioli creates and redesigns jewelry; his mother, Anna, displays her paintings, drawings, and sculpture.

Upstairs, Little Things offers distinctively dramatic handmade jewelry and fashion accessories.

Lynn Portnoy
440 E. Congress at Beaubien. (313) 964-0339. Mon-Fri 10-6, Sat 10-2.

This shop features bright, stylish, practical, and well-made clothes for career women, coupled with wardrobe consulting and alterations. Lynn Portnoy is a downtown fashion pioneer who has made it. Good sales and a friendly staff.

Flood's Bar & Grill/ Detroit Cornice and Slate
733 St. Antoine between Lafayette and Fort.

The entire street facade of this handsomely restored 1897 building was made of galvanized steel, manufactured by its original occupant— a late and unusual example of metal fronts imitating stone. Much of the delicate ornament was hammered by hand. The downstairs bar still has its original pressed-metal ceiling. The offices of the distinguished Detroit architectural firm of William Kessler and Associates are upstairs.

Greektown ★

Monroe St. between St. Antoine & Beaubien. Most restaurants open 11 a.m.- 2 a.m. or later, 7 days a week. **Park** *at large, 24-hour city structure just east of Greektown, entered off Monroe or Macomb.* **People Mover Stations:** *Greektown (Monroe and Beaubien), Bricktown (Beaubien and Fort).*

With its six Greek restaurants and numerous other Greek shops, this bustling, busy block of Monroe Street between Beaubien and St. Antoine has long been one of Detroit's most popular tourist attractions. It's one of the few areas in Detroit where the 19th-century city holds its own. With the addition of Trappers Alley festival marketplace, there's even more to see and do.

This really is the core of a Greek neighborhood going back to 1915 or so, with its old bakeries, grocery stores, and coffee houses where old-timers drink coffee and play cards. (The coffee houses are now tucked behind more profitable video arcades.)

The handsome, red brick St. Mary's Catholic Church, built in 1885 for the Germans who preceded the Greeks, forms a strong backdrop. The Detroit Police Department, the jail, and Detroit Recorder's Court are all a block or so north of here, so Greektown also functions as a neighborhood meeting place for lawyers, cops, and city workers.

Greektown, writes Martin Fischhoff in his fine *Detroit Guide*, "is a success story right out of some urban planner's dream (though planning had nothing to do with it). It's about the only place in Detroit that's alive around the clock."

Overpopulation caused hard times that drove over a fourth of the Greek labor force off their native rocky farmlands between 1890 and 1920. Greek men found their way to then-booming industrial towns throughout Michigan, from Detroit and Flint to Dowagiac and Calumet. They parlayed earnings from factory and construction work into small business opportunities opening up in rapidly urbanizing America: shoe repair, groceries, rooming houses and downtown commercial property, and above all, confectioneries and restaurants. And they did it so quickly and successfully that it's hard to believe that they were mostly farmers thrust into a totally unfamiliar environment, hailing from remote rural villages that first got electricity well after World War II.

Most Greektown families have long since moved onward and upward, scattered throughout the metro area. But many Greek-Americans still patronize Greektown establishments. Restaurant menus feature gyros, shish kebob, spinach pie, Greek salads, egg-lemon soup, rice pudding, baklava, and the like. Locals joke that it's really all prepared in one giant kitchen. See p. 39 for Greektown restaurants.

Notable Greektown points of interest are:

Stemma Bakery
514 Monroe. (313) 962-1898. Mon-Thurs 9 a.m.-10 p.m., Fri 9 a.m.-1 a.m. Sat 9:30-2 a.m. Sun 10 a.m.-11 p.m.

> **Groceries in Greektown**
>
> Hours at Greektown's two old-world grocery stores are so long ('til 9 p.m. at the earliest) that you can both dine and shop for groceries. Greek bread, cheese, and wine can be the center of simple, delicious meals. Greek feta cheese, made from sheep's milk, is richer and quite unlike the domestic variety. Creamy white Kasseri cheese is like a mild cheddar. It can be cut into cubes, dredged in seasoned flour, and pan-fried 'til it's soft. Greeks serve it with lemon, crusty Greek bread, and a red wine like the dry red from the highly recommended Nemea (pronounced "nuh-MAY-uh) region. An excellent, very light white wine is made by Boutari. Both are about $7 a bottle. Retsina wine, flavored with rosin, is admittedly an acquired taste even when served correctly (very, very cold). Greeks like to drink it with fish, or with olives, bread, and fresh tomatoes.

The window of Michigan's oldest Greek bakery presents old-fashioned arrangements on lace doilies of baklava and related honey-nut sweets, plus rum cakes, cannoli, and big loaves of Greek bread. It's beautiful, but some people who shop around think it's also a little overpriced.

Athens Grocery and Bakery ★
527 Monroe. (313) 961-1149. Mon-Thurs 9-9, Fri & Sat 9-10:30, Sun 9-8:30.

Both Greektown groceries enjoy good reputations among Greek-Americans, and they smell wonderfully of fresh bread (in the morning) and spices. The crusty loaves, soft in the middle, sell for under a dollar apiece. The Athens' old-fashioned front window, filled with neatly arranged produce, nicely balances Greektown's neon glitz.

Monroe Grocery and Bakery ★
573 Monroe. (313) 964-9642. Sun-Thurs 9-9, Fri & Sat until 10 or 11.

Open the beat-up wood screen door, and you feel you're in a time warp. Ornate, shiny tins of olive oil and imports have a turn-of-the-century look, while pistachios, Greek cheeses, olives, pastas, and filo dough are sold in bulk at the counter.

Athens Bookstore
520 Monroe (also entered from Trappers Alley). (313) 963-4490.

The place to find Greek-language publications, cassettes of Greek music, ornate coffee urns, gaudy religious icons, along with a wide selection of tacky Detroit souvenirs.

Susan Hoffmann Pastries ★★
1219 St. Antoine. (313) 965-1692. 7:30 a.m.-6 p.m., Fri til midnight.

Delicious muffins, cakes and tortes (13 kinds, from Sacher tortes to whiskey cake and carrot cake, mostly at $2.25 a slice), cookies, 95¢ muffins, quiche (vegetable $2.25/slice, seafood $2.75), and pasta salads. There are a few tables, or you can eat on benches by the parking structure outside.

Old Shillelagh
349 Monroe. (2 blocks west of Greektown). 964-0007. Mon-Fri 11 a.m.- 2 a.m., Sat noon-2 a.m., Sun 2 p.m.-2 a.m.

The downstairs of this Irish pub is open all week, with darts, live folk music (Irish and not), competently performed. Upstairs on weekends, big audiences sing along with Irish folk bands, starting at 9. No food except for lunch, when inexpensive burgers, steak pies, and Cornish pasties are available.

Trappers Alley ★
Beaubien between Lafayette and Monroe. (313) 963-5445. **Parking:** *see Greektown. Mon-Thurs 10-9, Fri & Sat 10-11, Sun noon-7.*

Right in Greektown is Detroit's

Trappers Alley, an old tannery, is an interestingly designed environment to explore.

festival marketplace. While it doesn't compare with Boston's Fanueil Hall or Baltimore's Harborplace, this spectacular, four-level space is a pleasant place to wander around. The rich brick facades of old buildings are juxtaposed with crisp, colorful tiles and lush foliage. These buildings once were part of the huge tannery operations of Traugott Schmidt and Sons.

Schmidt immigrated from Germany in 1852, already a knowledgeable furrier. This complex was built between 1872 and 1901, while he was becoming one of the leading U. S. processors of leather, fur, and wool. Operations ceased in 1924.

In the early 1980s the city of Detroit approached a leading developer of festival marketplaces, Cordish Embry & Associates of Baltimore, to develop the then-vacant buildings. Trappers Alley opened in 1985; it was recently sold to the owners of the Pegasus Taverna, who have become prominent developers.

The main handicap of Trappers Alley is that except for one very fine restaurant (the Blue Nile, the only Ethiopian restaurant in the area), the 70 establishments here are not all that remarkable. The shops tilt too strongly in the direction of formula formats and frivolous gift shops: stuffed animals, T-shirts, candles, greeting cards. One shop even specializes in items of just one color: purple. Predictably, there's the ubiquitous Benetton sportswear shop, part of that international sportswear chain that seems snugly at home in the festival marketplace setting.

Detroit Recorder's Court

Frank Murphy Hall of Justice, 1441 St. Antoine south of Gratiot.

Criminal mystique has been one of Detroit's hottest cultural exports lately, thanks to area detective writers Elmore Leonard and Loren Estleman, who set many of their stories here. The Recorder's Court is where Leonard and Estleman get much of their material, and where Harrison Ford hung out to pick up atmosphere for a recent movie. A model of efficiency under difficult conditions, the court recently won a prestigious national award for its operation.

"Watching criminal investigations in Recorder's Court is better than going to the movies, and it's free," says a Leonard character. Judge Michael Talbot gets rave reviews from the *Detroit News*. "Talbot is so articulate, he's been accused of sitting up nights with a thesaurus before he hands down sentences. He must know a thousand synonyms for 'scumbag.'"

Cadillac Square ★

From Woodward at Monroe to Randolph. (It is the eastern terminus of Michigan Avenue.)

The **Bagley Memorial Fountain** (1887) is the only work left in Michigan by that extraordinary architect, H. H. Richardson. It is a simple work, but eye-catching, a water fountain with leafy Romanesque decoration, modeled after a medieval canopy in St. Mark's in Venice. Former governor (1873-1877) and tobacco magnate John Bagley donated it. Richardson accommodated the governor's request for the water fountain to provide water "cold and pure as the coldest mountain stream" by leaving space underneath for thousands of pounds of ice.

Across Monroe Street from the fountain is one of the country's first Civil War memorials, the 1867 **Michigan Soldiers and Sailors Monument** by Randolph Rogers. An Ann Arbor baker's son, he spent most of his adult life in Italy as one of the 19th century's best-known American sculptors. Giorgio Gikas of River Rouge recently restored this splendidly complex sculpture in his campaign to clean acid-rain corrosion from the city's grand public statues.

The octagon-shaped monument belongs to the multi-level, wedding-cake genre so popular in the late 19th century. On top of a base layer of eagles, bronze military figures alternate with relief portraits of Lincoln, Grant, Sherman, and Farragut, topped with seated allegorical female figures (Victory, Union, History, and Emancipation, who is a Negro). An aggressive-looking female figure representing Michigan waves her shield over the whole affair.

The two long blocks of Cadillac Square between Woodward and Randolph served as the city market from 1835 and 1893. Later they connected two grand, domed public buildings of the Age of Elegance: City Hall and the massive, high-towered Wayne County Building. City Hall was demolished after a bitter fight in 1961; Kennedy Square now occupies the site. The market area is now used for bus stops.

Wayne County Building ★

Randolph at Congress and Cadillac Square.

Cost was apparently no concern in constructing the Wayne County Building in a florid, pull-out-all-the-stops Roman Baroque style between 1896 and 1903. "At the time it was unquestionably the most sumptuous building in Michigan. . . . The interior is aglow with every variety of imported and domestic marble," wrote architectural historian Hawkins Ferry. Above the entrance, unfortunately so high they're hard to take in, are two chariots driven by dramatically gesticulating female figures, Victory and Progress, their robes blowing heroically in the wind. The County Building was recently restored to its original glory, inside and out, through an ingenious arrangement (no longer possible after the 1988 Tax Reform Act), in which the county leases back the building from new private owners.

J. L. Hudson Building

Woodward between Gratiot and Grand River.

Hudson's huge flagship store, erected between 1924 and 1929, was once the largest department store in the country. Today it sits empty, the single most dramatic symbol of downtown's decline.

This was downtown's anchor, the place which for decades brought together Detroiters from all walks of life. Now Hudson's is part of Dayton-Hudson, headquartered in Minneapolis. And Detroit is the only older U.S. city without a downtown department store.

Not coincidentally, metro Detroit is where in the 1950s Hudson's pioneered the suburban mall (see p. 331) which accelerated the decline of downtown retail shopping. The many fine old retailers have now all but fled downtown Woodward. At Woodward and Grand River, where retailers boasted the state's highest dollar volume in sales per square foot in 1952, three corners stand empty today. The fourth has a wig shop. The big storefront at 1201 Woodward built for **S. S. Kresge #1** (the progenitor of K Mart) remains occupied by a variety store, McCrory's. The street has a kind of wild, Third World vitality, with big, loud, colorful signs screaming out bargains — the kind of thing you see in Mexico or India.

Harmonie Park

Bounded by Randolph, Centre, and East Grand River, a block north of Gratiot. Northwest of Greektown, southeast of Grand Circus Park.

The stately, neoclassical Harmonie Club, built as the home of one of the German singing societies so common in late-19th-century Detroit, presides over this delightful, hidden-away triangular park. The park is formed by the odd angles of Judge Woodward's 1805 plan. In the 1970s the park was transformed into a leafy little downtown oasis, with stone benches and walls, a plashing fountain, and a sculpture. The **Detroit Artists Market** and the **Preston Burke Galleries** (specializing in "corporate art") face the park, which is currently frequented almost exclusively by street people.

Next to the Harmonie Club in the Madison-Lenox Hotel is the tiny (45-seat) **Harmonie Park Playhouse**, Michigan's only black professional theater company. To find out about its four or five productions a year, call 965-2480. Two top jazz spots, **Bo-Mac's Lounge** and the **New World Stage** loft, are also near the park (see p. 327). On East Grand River just down from Preston Burke, a string of sometimes-interesting little shops culminates in the **Gypsy Dome Rainbow Tea Room** (313-963-5069; open Mon-Sat 11-3:45) on the 7th floor of the old Merchants Apparel Building. You buy tea and sandwiches for $20, and your fortune is told free. (It's illegal to tell it for money.)

The architecture, planning, and development firm behind many riverfront projects, Schervish Vogel Merz, plans to revitalize and develop the Harmonie Park area, which they consider a "hidden jewel." They intend to renovate the now-empty Harmonie Club and to rehab for themselves an old office building around the corner on Broadway and Gratiot and move in there.

Detroit Artists Market

1452 Randolph at Centre (313) 962-0337. Tues-Sat 11-5. Park on Harmonie Park next door ($2 all day) or on the street.

Changing exhibits are held in this large, two-story exhibit space. Shows feature new and established artists in the area. Some are juried, others are selected by a single curator.

The Detroit Artists Market was established by collectors and art-lovers to provide a place where new art could be seen and sold. Board members typically include leaders of the Detroit Institute of Arts and other notables. In contrast, the nearby Focus Gallery is run by artists themselves. The gallery shop carries two-dimensional art, sculpture, jewelry, and other crafts.

David Whitney Building ★

1553 Woodward at Washington Blvd. and Grand Circus Park. (313) 965-0190. A People Mover station is attached to the building.

The remodeled white porcelain street facade of this 18-story office building, erected in 1915 by lumber tycoon David Whitney, doesn't suggest the restored elegance inside. The building was designed by the famous Chicago architectural firm of Daniel Burnham & Co. The lower floors were for doctors and dentists. Every office opens onto a beautiful four-story interior courtyard, recently restored to show off its Renaissance motifs in fresh white and gold. The owners who restored the building lobbied successfully for a People Mover station that connects to the courtyard. Note over in the station platform's eastern corner the wonderfully realistic sculpture of the man reading a newspaper.

Today the building's storefronts and atrium offices are occupied by a colorful variety of shops and galleries, almost all oriented to African and African-American cultures. Some are highly sophisticated, some verge on the amateurish, but all are energetic and interesting. It's worth checking out every floor, especially for anyone interested in art based in African cultures dispersed around the world.

At ground level, the **Diva Boutique** carries dramatic sweaters, sportswear, and dresses, while the Pakistani-owned **Hilal Books** has Middle Eastern clothing, jewelry, and essential oils for mixing your own perfumes, in addition to Islamic books. Free piano concerts are given in the grand court at noon weekdays.

Also in the David Whitney Building:

G. R. N'Namdi Gallery
David Whitney Building #315. (313) 963-4838. Tues-Sat 11-5.

Vibrant, colorful art by contemporary artists with national and international reputations, including Al Loving, Howardene Pindall, and Richard Hunt. Many but by no means all are of African descent. Different exhibits from the same stable of artists are shown at N'Namdi's Birmingham gallery.

National Conference of Artists
David Whitney Building #214. (313) 964-5775. Wed-Sat 11-5.

The Michigan chapter of this organization of African-American and transplanted African artists has space for changing exhibits and an attractive small shop with books on African, Caribbean, and African-American art; ceramics, paintings, jewelry, and note cards.

Grand Circus Park and vicinity ★
Woodward at Adams

This semi-circular park, bisected by Woodward Avenue, was once downtown's jewel. Today, Grand Circus Park has a bigger array of old and new sculptural features, a resident population of street people, and a backdrop of stately, often vacant buildings from 1915-1925.

The park's distinctive shape arises from Detroit's 1807 circle-and-spoke street pattern. This has been a park since 1844. In 1886, when the Grand Circus was still mainly residential, *Harper's Magazine* gives this account of downtown Detroit: "The first and most agreeable things that strike the eye are not the work of man but of nature. These are the numerous small parks that everywhere dot the landscape — the

Grand Circus Park, 1886.

oases of green in a wide waste of brick and stone. One of the these, and the most beautiful, the Grand Circus, is adorned with two fine fountains. Here the tired citizen comes of sultry nights, and in the spray-laden air finds refreshing coolness."

Today the park is an interesting place to walk through, if somewhat depressing in contrast to its onetime grandeur. The street people are loud but harmless, and the underground parking garage is inexpensive, never full, considered safe, and convenient to the People Mover station in the David Whitney Building.

In the western half, the big bronze figure of **Hazen Pingree,** seated on a simple chair, looks past the traffic on Woodward as if he's about to get up and talk to someone. The former Detroit mayor was a true folk hero. Owner of a large shoe manufacturing company, he was put into office by other capitalists in the Republican machine intent on preserving their unjust privileges. Pingree, however, turned out to be quite a champion of the people, a Republican populist in the manner of Theodore Roosevelt. The inscription on the 1903 monument reads, "A gallant soldier, an enterprising and successful citizen, four times elected mayor of Detroit, twice governor of Michigan. He was the first to warn the people of the great danger threatened by powerful private corporations, and the first to awake to the great inequalities in taxation and to initiate steps for reform. THE IDOL OF THE PEOPLE."

When Pingree was elected governor in 1896, he was replaced as mayor by a political enemy and early financial backer of Henry Ford, **William Maybury.** Maybury's statue is to the back of Pingree's. The one modern sculpture in the park is **The Entrance,** John Piet's 1975 vertical abstraction in orange-red steel.

Across Woodward in the eastern half of Grand Circus is the **Alger Memorial Fountain,** created in 1920 by the designer of the Lincoln Memorial, Daniel French. The female figure, a personification of the State of Michigan, holds a shield with the state's coat of arms on it. General Russell Alger (1836-1907), a U.S. Senator, governor, and Secretary of War under McKinley, was part of the local Republican establishment Pingree dared to buck.

Surrounding Grand Circus Park is some of Detroit's more important architecture. On the east side of Woodward at Adams, the handsome Gothic **Central United Methodist Church** (1867) with its tall corner spire and steeple has for decades been a center of social activism in Detroit. It was designed by the Englishman Gordon Lloyd, termed by Hawkins Ferry one of Detroit's two architectural giants of the 19th century. Lloyd was a Gothic Revivalist in the simple, rather spare manner of the style's master, Richard Upjohn. The steeple and front wall were moved back some 28 feet when Woodward was widened in 1936. Ask at the office to see the interior, and to visit the **Small World Shop,** where Third World handcrafts and souvenirs can be purchased.

A short stroll down Adams passes several interesting spots. **India Brass** (33 E. Adams; Mon-Fri 10-5, Sat 10-4) offers two floors of Indian imports, from jewelry and brass trays, boxes, and other accessories to women's clothing and carved tables. **The Value Shop** (41 E. Adams, open Tues-Sat 11-3) is a resale shop operated by Central Methodist. **Swords into Plowshares** (45 E. Adams; 313-965-5422; open Tues, Thurs, and Sat 11-3) terms itself a peace art center, with a gift shop of handcrafts and exhibits such as narrative applique pieces made by relatives of people who have disappeared in Chile. **The Detroit Council of the Arts** (47 E. Adams; 313-224-3482; open Mon-Fri 9-5) is a city arts coordinating agency whose Front Room Gallery showcases local visual artists. It's a good place to pick up information on the local arts scene.

On the west side of Woodward at Adams is a striking example of Gothic commercial architecture, the 11-story **Fyfe's Shoe Store Building** (1919), designed by the distinguished Detroit firm of Smith, Hinchman, & Grylls. At Park and Washington, on the circle side of the park, is the once-luxurious, now-empty **Statler Hotel,** designed by George Post, the architect of Cornelius Vanderbilt's Fifth Avenue chateau in New York. When the 800-room hotel opened in 1914, it set a new standard for Detroit hotels. Each room had a bath. Subtle Italian details set a refined, sophisticated tone.

Theater District

On and nearby Grand Circus Park.

Today the outlook for Detroit's theater district, those grand, gilded old picture palaces around Grand Circus Park, is bright, thanks to the foresight of real estate investor Charles Forbes and the resounding success of the renovated Fox as a major entertainment venue. In the late 1970s, Forbes, a former Ford real estate and marketing executive, envisioned a revived theater district planned as a whole, with coordinated parking and restaurants. He purchased the State, the 500-seat Gem, and the giant Fox, where he'd had his first date. ("You couldn't get any bigger than to go to the Fox," he recalls.) And he assembled 40 properties on and just off Woodward between Grand Circus Park and the Fisher Freeway for parking and restaurants.

Detroit's auto boom had coincided with the era of palatial movie theaters put up across America by Hollywood studio owners. The Grand Circus Park area developed an unusual concentration of opulent theaters, each designed to outdo the last. On West Adams across from the park, the **Madison and Adams Theaters** opened in 1916 and 1917. It was the Madison that established the nationwide reputation of Detroit architect C. Howard Crane as a designer of movie theaters; he eventually designed 250 picture palaces across the continent, including 52 in the Detroit area. A block away on Bagley, another famous theater architecture firm, Rapp and Rapp, designed the **Michigan** (1925, the state's most splendid movie theater until upstaged by the Fox and the Fisher), and **United Artists** (1928). Three other large theaters were nearby: the **Capitol** on Broadway (1922), and on Woodward the 3,000-seat **State** (1925) and the fabulous, 5,000-seat **Fox** (1928). Of these, all but the Michigan remain.

In 1987 Mike Ilitch and Little Caesar's Pizza bought the Fox and adjacent properties in a three-way deal that required the city of Detroit to invest $5 million in lights and other area public improvements. Forbes still owns the Gem and the State. In fall, 1989, the State was transformed into **ClubLand,** one of entrepreneur Steve Jarvis's razzle-dazzle nightclubs installed in spectacular historic movie theaters. (See Nightspots, p. 326.) By night, its sophisticated sound and video system and ClubLand Dancers attract a fashion-conscious young crowd; by day, its video system is used for banquets and corporate training sessions. Forbes plans to restore the Gem as a live performing and film theater for alternative, off-Broadway-style productions. The Century Club will move its restaurant there.

The **Michigan Opera Theater,** anxious to control its own performing space, has purchased the **Grand Circus Theater** and, for rehearsal space, the **Capitol Theater.** It is mounting an ambitious $17-million fundraising campaign to restore the theaters and acquire adjoining property.

With these developments, plus billionaire shopping center developer Al Taubman's support for the long-range possibility of a big performing-arts center near the Detroit Institute of Arts, it looks as if the momentum for arts and entertainment may well return downtown.

Marian and Mike Ilitch and daughter Denise Ilitch Lites stand on the Fox's grand staircase. Mike Ilitch, who owns the family-run Little Caesar's Pizza chain and the Detroit Red Wings hockey team, is self-effacing in contrast to the area's other pizza baron, Domino's Tom Monaghan. For Ilitch, restoring the Fox and moving his headquarters from the suburbs into the adjoining office building, is a way to give something back to the city where he got his start.

Fox Theatre ★★★

2211 Woodward between Montcalm and Columbia. (313) 567-6000 for events information and assistance. Parking across Woodward. $2 all day, $5 for evening events.

During Detroit's extraordinary boom decade of the 1920s, a number of flamboyant structures went up. But none was more utterly and unabashedly gaudy than the 5,000-seat Fox Theatre on Woodward, opened in 1928 and restored in 1988. Part of the nationwide 250-theater Fox chain, this $6 million picture palace was the flagship of the empire, the pinnacle of Detroit architect C. Howard Crane's successful career as a movie theater designer.

The eclectic Asian interior was designed by owner William Fox's wife, Eve Leo, who humorously called it "Siamese Byzantine." The six-story lobby was designed to look like an ancient temple in India. In the main auditorium you can see a two-ton stained-glass chandelier. Walls feature peacocks, serpents, Buddhas, Chinese tomb guardians, Greek masks, Egyptian lions, and other motifs from Hindu, Persian, Indian, Chinese, and southeast Asian art. Gushed the *Free Press* at the opening, "One feels that he is in the midst of nobility, treading among treasures of the mind and of the subtler senses, as ancient and immortal as the exquisite Hindu art that has been modernized in the new drama-temple." This era of unbridled opulence was not to last long. Fox lost control of his theaters during the Depression, which left him $91 million in debt.

The Fox was designed for both movies and live performances. By the 1950s, it began suffering from neglect. But thanks to hometown booster Mike Ilitch, owner of Little Caesar's Pizza and the Detroit Red Wings hockey team, a careful $15 million restoration has been completed, and the Fox is packing in crowds with over 250 widely varied acts a year. For the first half of 1989 it was the top-grossing venue anywhere in the U.S. Bill Cosby, Chuck Berry and Jerry Lee Lewis, Bonnie Raitt, The Red Army Chorus, Donald O'Connor and Mickey Rooney, Barbara Mandrell, and the Eurythmics were among the acts in a recent two-month period. If you go, don't miss **"Peacock Alley,"** a hallway above the main alley, which displays some of the theater's paintings, furniture, and artifacts assembled by Eve Leo from around the world.

Ilitch is renovating the 10-story office building attached to the Fox as the new world headquarters of Little Caesar's, now in Farmington Hills. It will be the first major firm to move to the city in over 30 years.

Washington Boulevard

Between Grand Circus Park and Michigan Avenue. Accessible via the Times Square or Cass Ave. People Mover stations or via the Downtown Trolley from Hart Plaza.

This boulevard of once-elegant buildings was designed to be Detroit's Fifth Avenue or Champs Elysees, lined with fine shops and well-dressed patrons. For several decades in this city of rapid economic cycles, it was. But downtown retaling deteriorated in the 1970s, and the likes of Himmelhoch's and Winkelman's are long gone. Nevertheless, on a fine day, the boulevard, softened by greenery, is still one of the prettiest public spaces in the city if you focus on the architecture and not the lack of healthy shops.

The puzzling metal truss-like "monkey bars" that run along the length of the boulevard were part of an attempt to revitalize it as a retail and restaurant street by enhancing its pedestrian ambiance. The intrusive, fluorescent-lit truss itself was ill-conceived as a way to unify the streetscape. But the accompanying seating and other pedestrian improvements have been more successful, greatly appreciated by office workers at lunch. An unusual, **sound-activated fountain and light sculpture** at the Grand River intersection creates an interesting light show. Its varying intensity is based on the randomly occurring ambient sounds nearby.

All this jazzy streetscaping hasn't yet changed the reality that the riverfront is hot property, while elegant old office buildings are a glut in this market. **Trolley Plaza**, a large prefabricated apartment building from Cleveland's Forest City Residential Development, is the only new construction attracted here so far.

At the turn of the century, youthful real estate heir J. B. Book, Jr. dreamed of developing the then-declining Washington Boulevard, where his family owned property, into Detroit's equivalent of Chicago's Michigan Avenue. He studied the grand boulevards of Europe. When his father died in 1916, he had his chance. With his brothers' help, Book came to control 60 per cent of Washington Boulevard's frontage.

Detroit architect Louis Kamper, a Bavarian inclined to operatic splendor, shared the Books' devotion to the grand manner. Their first creation, the relatively simple 13-story **Book Building** on Washington at Grand River (1917), still attracts attention because of the 12 nude female figures that, like columns, support the cornice. The 21-story Washington Boulevard Building was followed in 1924 by the huge, 23-story **Book-Cadillac Hotel** on Washington at Michigan Avenue. The interiors received lavish touches, with monumental Corinthian columns, rich woods and murals, lots of gold and bronze, colored crystals and red brocades. Detroit's grandest hotel is now empty. The luxurious interiors have long since been replaced with plainer, more modern decor. A plaque points out that President Kennedy's last speech on his ill-fated western tour ending in Dallas was given here.

The boulevard's need for an impressive tower was filled in 1926 with the 36-story **Book Tower** at Grand River (1926). It was an ungainly carryover from the old school of design that used horizontal cornices to organize tall buildings into parts rather than emphasizing their verticality with stepped-back skyscraper styling. If the Depression hadn't put an end to Detroit's building explosion, downtown would have been dwarfed by a second Book tower, fashionably streamlined and as high as the RenCen.

In the boulevard median at the busy Michigan Avenue intersection, a statue of Polish Revolutionary War hero **Casimir Pulaski** faces a hero of the War of 1812, **General Alexander Macomb**, leaning into an imaginary wind. His father, a partner of the fur trading magnate John Jacob Astor, owned most of what is today Macomb County as well as Belle Isle and Grosse Ile. Across the street, a state historical plaque commemorates the old **Chicago Road,** now Michigan Avenue. The first major Michigan highway, it was built between 1829 and 1836 to connect Detroit with Chicago.

Just to the north at 1234 Washington Boulevard is **St. Aloysius Church** (1930), a striking, richly detailed Romanesque Catholic church adorned with 12 bronze Apostles. Because of the confined space, the main floor is below street level. Instead of stained glass, this church is dominated by mosaics, tiles, and marble. You can step inside weekdays anytime between 6 a.m. until 6 p.m. and from 9 until 5:30 Saturdays.

A block away at Michigan and Cass, outside the headquarters of the Michigan Bell Telephone Company is Alexander Calder's 1970 stabile, **Jeune Fille et sa Suite.** In this 20-ton abstract steel sculpture, the whimsically curvaceous "girl" is followed by a "suite" of spiky, geometric attendants.

Downtown Trolley ★

Route goes along Washington Blvd. and Jefferson between Grand Circus Park and Hart Plaza/Mariners Church. Mon-Fri 7 a.m.-6 p.m., weekends 10 a.m.-6 p.m. Cars depart from either end on the quarter-hour at 15-minute intervals. **Fare:** *45¢.*

There never was a streetcar line on Washington Boulevard until

Mayor Coleman Young dedicated this trolley track in 1976 to cap the Washington Boulevard revitalization effort. Federal, state, and private grants paid for it. The seven antique trolleys (four made in St. Louis in 1899) are fun to ride and to look at; ask for the descriptive brochure. Some are housed in the trolley barn at the Grand Circus terminus and easily viewed through the windows.

If it's a nice day between Memorial Day and the end of September, by all means try to take the car with the open upper deck — America's only operating open-top doubledecker. If you happen to take the green trolley, sponsored by Nestle Chocolate, you'll get a free sample.

John King Books ★★

901 W. Lafayette at the Lodge Expressway (U.S. 10) and Sixth St. Park on expressway side of building. (313) 961-0622. Mon-Sat 9:30-5:30.

Housed in a big old former work-glove factory just west of downtown, John King Books has quickly become a national leader in used and rare books. Its workaholic owner, John King, flies all around the country in search of big lots of used and remaindered books to fill his store's over 30,000 square feet. (A separate warehouse has another 20,000 square feet.) At 750,000 volumes, his may be the biggest book store in the country. The stock is well organized, and browsing is comfortable. The store will search for hard-to-find titles for $1. There's always a box of free books out front.

A fascinating variety of framed pictures, printed ephemera, postcards, and collectibles are artfully displayed in several rooms of this pleasant catacomb.

King's philosophy for acquiring books is to stay general, partly because he finds it "too boring" to specialize. He keeps the prices reasonable, and he and his staff do a good job weeding out the drivel.

John King has transformed an old work glove factory on downtown's west edge into what's probably the biggest U.S. bookstore, with 750,000 volumes of well-organized used and rare books, plus interesting graphics and printed ephemera.

RESTAURANTS

FINANCIAL DISTRICT AND VICINITY

American Coney Island

115 W. Michigan between Griswold and Shelby. (313) 964-6542. Open 24 hours, 7 days. Beer. No credit cards.

A beloved 75-year-old Detroit institution, this efficiently run eatery serves an extraordinary cross-section of humanity at all hours of day and night. Along with its neighbor, the Lafayette (owned by cousins), it offers breakfasts in addition to the mainstay coney dog. In a very short time you'll get your $1.30 hot dog with chili (cheese 25¢ extra). You can choose from 15 beers on hand. Other offerings: a loose hamburger ($1.50), chili fries with cheese ($2).

Britt's Cafe at Silver's ★

151 W. Fort in the basement of Silver's, Congress at Shelby. (313) 963-4866. Mon-Fri 11:30-3. Continental breakfast 9:30-11. Entrees $4.50-$4.75; sandwiches $4. No alcohol or credit cards.

Lodged in the basement of a jewel-like historic bank building designed by the legendary American architectural firm of McKim, Mead, & White, Britt's is a fine place to rest during a walk around downtown. The cafeteria ambience inside Silver's office supply store is austere, but the food makes up for it. Most famous is the Caesar salad, followed by the warm pasta salad. Among sandwiches, the No-Mayo Chicken Salad is a favorite, along with the Vegetarian Delight: 3 cheeses, pesto, red peppers, and olives. Scones ($1) are available Wednesday and Fridays; muffins (75¢) on Monday, Tuesday, and Thursday.

Epicurean Cafe

Basement of the Penobscot Building, Griswold at Fort. (313) 965-4998. Mon-Fri 6:30 a.m.-4. p.m. Cafeteria entrees $4.25-$4.95. No alcohol.

This is a great place to eat lunch if you like big, bustling cafeterias. As a bonus, it is located in one of downtown Detroit's finest 1920s skyscrapers, giving the visitor a colorful glimpse of office workers in the heart of the Motor City. The Epicurean serves a whopping 2,000 customers at lunch daily (a third or so are take-out orders) and seats 400. But service is brisk, and no more than a 10-minute wait is standard. Alcohol is not served, but the manager takes pride in the variety of drinks for sale here (30 in all), from Australian fruit juices to V-8. A best seller is Greek moussaka — eggplant with ground beef and cheese sauce. Beer-battered fish is popular on Fridays. A big selection of desserts includes fruit and Boston cream pies.

Lafayette Coney Island

117 W. Michigan between Griswold and Shelby. (313) 964-8198. Open 24 hours a day, all year around. Beer, no credit cards.

Next door to American Coney Island, Lafayette has the same egalitaian mystique and pretty much the same food , too, including breakfast. Each has its devotees. At night people who've come after concerts in their Porsches and BMWs rub elbows with bums. The coneys are $1.40 here and chili is $2.

Lindell AC

1310 Cass at Michigan. (313) 964-1122. 8 a.m.-2 a.m. (Closed only on Christmas Day). Full bar.

This is Detroit's original sport bar, the place visited by legendary local sports figure (many of them often), including Gordy Howe, Alex Karras (a one-time partner), Mark Fidrich, and Al Kaline. Memorabilia of prominent visitors encrust the walls. The menu is short: hamburgers, cheeseburgers, and small $3 steaks (each served with French fries).

London Chop House ★★★

155 W. Congress between Shelby and Griswold. (313) 962-0277. Mon-Sat 11:30 a.m.-12:45 p.m. Cocktails; excellent wine list. Major credit cards.

"The Chop," which looks more like a men's club than a private restaurant, has long been the place for Detroit's wealthy power elite to see and be seen (especially at VIP booth #1), and pampered as well. Beset by increased competition as the area's premier status restaurant, and hurt by downtown's still-limited dinner market, it has been bailed out, amid a publicity barrage, by a group of loyal customers. They were determined not to see Detroit's version of 21 go down the tube.

The old aura, service, and understated top-of-the-line quality have been retained. To its traditional American dishes like prime rib, frog legs, and grilled breast of chicken have been added updated versions of steaks and fresh seafood, including clams, oysters, and lobster served in many ways. A la carte dinner entrees ($18-$30) include inventive garnishes but no starch or salad. Recommended appetizers include polenta ($4.25) and oysters champagne. The Caesar salad ($6.50) is perfect.

Lunch favorites include the Poncho burger ($8.95) with its trademark

---

Riverfront Dining

Options are still limited. Consider a boat, the **Star of Detroit**, p. 42, or the **Lansdowne** (259-6801), moored near the RenCen at 201 E. Atwater. Average meals are $6.25-$12.95. Open Mon-Thurs 11-11, Fri & Sat 10-midnight, Sun noon-10. The RenCen's **Summit Steak House** offers an eagle'eye, almost geographical view, while the **Riverfront Cafe** in Al Taubman's Riverfront apartments has the best ship's-level river view. Call (313) 393-5100 for reservations (to clear security).

special sauce and the lobster club sandwich ($12.95) with tomato, avocado, and mango chutney. Both come with shoestring potatoes.

If you can't afford dinner, you're most welcome to stop in for coffee ($2.25) and famously lavish desserts ($6.50) such as chocolate raviolis or the Stairway to Paradise, with white and dark chocolate mousse laced with raspberry sauce.

Money Tree ★★★

333 W. Fort at Washington Blvd.. (313) 961-2445. Lunch Mon-Fri 11:15-2:30. Dinner Tues-Wed 6-9, Thurs-Sat 5:30-10. A la carte entrees: $6.75-$8.50 (lunch); $15-$22 (dinner). Average dinner for 2 without wine: $55-60. Cocktails, excellent wine list. Major credit cards.

One of Detroit's consistently outstanding restaurants, the Money Tree features "hearty French cooking with high standards but without pretensions," according to critic Molly Abraham. Its food and desserts are excellent. The menu changes daily, but is more daring at dinner, when Tom Foydel, one of Detroit's best chefs, showcases his eclectic style. But it is much less expensive at lunch. Grilled salmon and tuna are favorites. Some sort of excellent wild game and free-range chicken is usually offered. The setting is pleasant but not fancy, with a view of busy Fort Street and a theme (money) borrowed from its location in a bank parking structure.

Pontchartrain Wine Cellars ★★

234 W. Larned (east of Washington Blvd.) 963-1785. Lunch Mon-Fri 11:30-2:30. Dinner Mon-Fri 5-9:30, Sat 5:30-11. Closed first 2 weeks in July. Entrees $6.75-$14 (lunch); $16-$21(dinner) include potato and vegetable. Wine and beer; extensive wine list.

Opened in 1935, this is one of Detroit's most respected restaurants. Bistro classics like sauteed lake perch (a specialty), escargots, braised sweetbreads, noisettes of lamb, pork chops, fried clams, and salmon are simply presented. It offers excellent service, a good wine list, and consistently tasty, nonflashy French-American cuisine in a French country atmosphere. Cold duck, incidentally, was invented here.

Quattro Punti ★

First floor of Buhl Building, 535 Griswold at Congress. (313) 961-0400. Mon-Fri 7 a.m.-2:30 p.m. No alcohol or credit cards.

The Buhl Building is one of Detroit's wonderful, ornate, well-preserved skyscrapers — almost church-like in atmosphere. Its big, two-tiered lobby best conveys the feel of what the downtown big-business district was like decades ago when elegant shops thrived downtown. The Quattro Punti is a classy new addition to the scene. Also a cafeteria, it's smaller than the Epicurean nearby, with more interesting (and expensive) dishes. Thursdays and Fridays feature delicious Louisiana crab cakes ($6.10). Fresh lemon pepper scrod filet is $5.75. Pasta, made fresh here daily, is used in many $4-$5 dishes, including Cajun seafood pasta and fettucine primavera. The name "Quattro Punti" means "four points" in Italian, for the four points of the globe, reflecting the eclectic Italian range of dishes.

BRICKTOWN/GREEKTOWN

The Blue Nile ★★★

508 Monroe (Trappers Alley, second floor). (313) 964-6699. Daily 5-10. Lunch a future possibility. Full bar. Major credit cards.

This superb Ethiopian restaurant, begun by an Ethiopian couple in a storefront on Woodward, now provides Trappers Alley with a much needed destination restaurant that's original and first-rate. Diners sit on quite low chairs with goatskin cushions, and eat off low basket-like tables from a communal platter. It is covered with bread, on which meat dishes (lamb, chicken, and beef) and vegetable stews are placed. These range from bland to moderately spicy. Instead of silverware, you eat with your hands (steaming cloths are provided for washing before and after the meal) and tear off pieces of the fresh bread to scoop up food and sop up the fragrant juices. This complete, all-you-can-eat "Ethiopian feast" is $13.90 with four meat and six vegetable dishes, $10.90 vegetarian.

Greektown

Monroe St. between St. Antoine and Beaubien. Most restaurants open 11 a.m.-2 a.m. or later, 7 days/week. All have full bars, accept most major credit cards. Park in city structure to the east, entered off Monroe or Macomb.

The food at these popular restaurants is reasonably priced ($6 or $7 will buy a typical entree with salad and bread) and pretty much the same. They attract a wide mix, from downtown workers to visitors here for sagnaki (flaming kasseri cheese) presented with "Opa!" and a festive flourish. Reputations and kitchens of Greektown restaurants shift frequently, but some restaurants are definitely better than others, and each has its followers.

The Laikon (569 Monroe, 313-963-7058) is rated "most authentic" by a native Greek who's knowledgeable about food. He loves their homestyle bean soup and the pan-fried cod with garlic sauce. The kitchen is run by the owners themselves, and vegetables like okra and beans are likely to be fresh.

The **Grecian Gardens** (562 Monroe, 313-961-3044), here since 1942, has improved greatly and updated the decor. Recent specials included barbeque lamb with rice, $7.45, and broiled sweetbreads with peas and potatoes, $6.25.

Pegasus Taverna (558 Monroe, next to Trappers Alley, 313-964-6800) has adequate food in a big, busy, theatrical setting that some people really like. Plastic grapes hang from the ceiling for a vineyard effect, and people can sit at a big bar while waiting for tables. Owners Ted Gatzaros and Jim Papas now own a great deal of prime Greektown property, including Trappers Alley, the International Marketplace office building, and the International Hotel under construction.

New Hellas (583 Monroe at St. Antoine, 313-961-5544), a Greektown pioneer, does the biggest volume.

Lindos Taverna (511 Monroe, 313-961-2070) offers some less common homestyle dishes in a setting of whitewashed walls, fool-the-eye windows, and murals of the Greek countryside.

Jacoby's Since 1904 ★

624 Brush between Congress and Fort (behind the historic Wayne Co. Bldg.). (313) 962-7067. Mon-Thurs 11-10, Fri & Sat 11-11. Full bar, big beer selection. Major credit cards.

This favorite lawyers' hangout has the atmosphere of an authentic German saloon (which it is), despite losing some of its well-worn patina in a fire. It's solid and down-to-earth, convivial and loud. Downstairs is now spiffy tile and oak, while the upstairs still has the plain look of a bierstube. The reliable fare consists of good salads, a corned beef sandwich and a highly regarded burger with fries ($4.50) plus staples of *gute buergerliche kuche*: sauerbraten ($8.25) and wienerschnitzel ($9.75), served with potatoes and vegetable; German potato salad ($1.75); and meat salad with vinaigrette.

Niki's Taverna

735 Beaubien just south of Monroe. (313) 961-2500. Sun-Thurs 10 a.m.-3 a.m., Fri & Sat 10 a.m.-4 p.m. Full bar. Visa, AmExpress, Diners, MC.

One of Detroit's very best pizzas — with a blend of kasseri and brick cheeses — is served here, along with an expanded menu that includes all the Greek standards, plus chops, ribs, and steaks. The downstairs pizza parlor, which stays open very late, is cheaper than the mauve-and-burgundy dining room and bar upstairs. Sample upstairs prices: moussaka with rice $5.45, barbeque ribs with vegetable $7.95 1/2 slab, $12.95 full.

This is the very space where the Dodge brothers, having failed to make a go of it in their Windsor bicycle parts factory, got their start in auto manufacturing and made transmissions for the famous 1903 curved-dash Olds. It may well have right here that Henry Ford called on the Dodge brothers to get them to make the engine and running gear for the Model A. Ford had no cash to capitalize his own auto, but the Dodges trusted him to assemble and sell it, and they all became legends as a result.

Opus One

565 E. Larned between Beaubien and St. Antoine, 2 blocks east of I-375. Mon-Fri 11:30-2, 5:30-10, Sat 5:30-11. Full bar. Major credit cards. Lunch $20-$30, dinner $50.

Chef Peter Loren calls his highly acclaimed food "progressive cosmopolitan cuisine," a blend of traditional French and stylized regional American fare. Opus One has one of the city's most opulent dining atmospheres, with loads of marble and etched glass. Notable dishes include grilled gulf swordfish with pesto butter and sauce chron ($27 a la carte at dinner) and sauteed medallions of pork tenderloin with toasted almond and apple Roquefort sauce ($22.50).

See also: *Old Shillelagh (weekday lunches only), p. 27.*

THEATER DISTRICT

Elizabeth Street Cafe

2100 John R at Elizabeth 2 blocks east of Woodward. Mon-Fri 7:30-2:30. Everything is under $5. No alcohol or credit cards.

This intimate cafe on the north edge of downtown serves cheap, excellent breakfasts (eggs, pancakes, oatmeal, etc.) and lunches. For breakfast the blueberry muffins (75¢) are popular. For lunch, the crustless quiche ($3.95 with side salad) is a standby, as are the grilled chicken breast sandwich ($3.95) and chicken salad ($4.50). A specialty is the South of the Border BLT ($4.25) which includes turkey, guacamole, red onion, bacon, lettuce, and tomato on a sourdough bread.

Elwood Bar & Grill

2100 Woodward at Elizabeth, across from the Fox. (313) 961-7485. Mon-Wed 11-midnight, Thurs-Fri 11-2 a.m., Sat noon-2 a.m. Meals average $8-$10 including potato and salad. Full bar. MasterCard, Visa.

This handsome diner right across from the Fox Theater, in operation since 1936, had gone steadily downhill until 1987, when new owners gutted it and created a smashingly smart Art Deco watering hole, a big hit with Yuppies after work.

The Elwood's menu, periodically changed, emphasizes veal, including an excellent veal meat loaf ($9.50 at dinner, $4.75 in a sandwich at lunch) and Texas chili with veal, beef, and pork ($10.50 including walnut cornbread at dinner). Also recommended are the homey chicken and dumplings ($8.95 at dinner), the tomato soup and the whipped potatoes flavored with vegetables or herbs. All dinner entrees come with soup, potato, and vegetable. Homemade potato chips ($1.50) are great, and burgers ($3.95 at lunch) are good, too. This place is packed at lunch and on theater nights; voices bounce off its hard surfaces for a high-energy effect.

For theater dining see also: *The Gnome and Traffic Jam in Cultural Center, p. 101.*

ELSEWHERE DOWNTOWN

Star of Detroit ★

20 E. Atwater (docked at Hart Plaza Waterfront) (313) 259-9160. Season: mid-April through late October, possibly longer. Dinner cruise packages: Sun-Thurs 7-10 p.m., $43.45; Fri & Sat $45.45. Lunch Mon-Fri 11-1:30, $22.45. Sunday brunch 11-1:30, $25.45. Early Sunday dinner 3-5:30, $30.45. Cash bar. AmExpress, MasterCard, Visa, Discover.

The 500-passenger boat "Star of Detroit" offers reasonably good food and quite pleasant cruises from downtown Detroit to the mouth of Lake St. Clair, past Belle Isle. The buffet-style meals include all you want to eat of New York strip, filet of sole, stuffed chicken breast, along with pasta and green salads. For dessert, there's blueberry sour cream coffee cake and triple chocolate Chambord layer cake. Reservations are needed, and it's best to board half an hour before departure.

Carl's Chop House

3020 Grand River. From southbound Lodge take Grand River exit and make a right. (313) 833-0700. Mon-Sat 11:30-midnight, Sun 2-10. Full bar. Major credit cards. Luncheon specials $7.75, dinners $10-$30.

Carl's is perhaps Detroit's most popular steakhouse, a boisterous place which has been around for decades. Prime rib ($16.95) is especially popular. Dinner prices include soup and a salad or potato, and a big relish tray from days of yore, with cottage cheese, celery, olives, and marinated herring.

See also: *Rivertown restaurants, p. 50, Maxie's Leftfield Deli, p. 86.*

Rivertown

Ten years ago, this four-block strip consisted mainly of old warehouses and factories, along with remnants of docks and shipbuilding industries. Now that industry has departed, Rivertown has become a thriving entertainment district with some of the most expensive land in the city. Scattered nightspots range from the wild dance club **Taboo** (1940 Woodbridge; 567-6140) to the elegant but only slightly more subdued **Rhinoceros** (265 Riopelle; 259-2208), the earthily casual and eclectic **Soup Kitchen Saloon** blues and jazz club (1585 Franklin at Orleans; 259-1374), and the **Woodbridge Tavern** (289 St. Aubin at Woodbridge; 289-0578), an unpretentious and genuine local landmark (see p. 51). For more on selected nightspots, see p. 326.

As part of Mayor Coleman Young's grand plan to encourage tourism and attract business and residents to Detroit, the city has successfully attracted two large mixed-use luxury developments, **Harbortown** and **Stroh River Place**, formerly the Parke-Davis pharmaceutical headquarters and manufacturing facility. Stroh Brewery, now being sold, has its headquarters there. (Parke-Davis is now part of Warner-Lambert, headquartered in Morris Plains, New Jersey.) The city owns and is marketing for development a third big riverfront site, the 39 acres by the Belle Isle bridge. Six thousand workers made Uniroyal tires here from 1906 up through 1980. Before that, the giant Detroit Stove Works was here.

A number of downtown businesses projecting a creative image have relocated here in Rivertown, notably Crain Communications (publishers of *Detroit Monthly* and *Crain's Detroit Business Week*) and in Stroh River Place, Ross Roy advertising. But enough of the old buildings and businesses like the Globe Trading Company and Medusa Cement remain to give the place a kind of gritty, real-world visual atmosphere, without being dangerous. (One early attraction for development, in fact, was that the area was isolated from the rest of the city and devoid of residents.) Some warehouses have been converted to apartments. There's still a lot of vacant land here, which is good for parking at nightspots but doesn't yet make for the dense and lively pedestrian area Rivertown could become some day.

The city's three Linked Riverfront Parks at the feet of St. Aubin, Chene, and Mt. Elliott streets were planned early in the Coleman Young administration as

Boat tours on the Detroit River aboard the 41-passenger Renaissance Queen currently leave St. Aubin Park on Fridays (5:30 and 7 p.m.) and Saturdays (1:30, 3, and 4:30 p.m). $5/adult, $2/under 12 for a one-hour tour. Call to confirm: (313) 341-7881.

Rivertown's location is between Jefferson and the river, from the Renaissance Center to Belle Isle. Streets paralleling the river are (from Jefferson) Woodbridge, Franklin, Wight, Guoin, and Atwater.

catalysts for more riverfront development. Now they are coming on line. (Chene Park, opened in 1984, was so popular it had to be expanded. The cost, which vastly exceeded original projections, has been a source of considerable controversy. But it is not out of line with construction of this elaborateness elsewhere.) Eventually the parks are to be linked by bicycle paths and walkways to form a riverfront trail between downtown and Belle Isle.

All the linked parks were designed by the architecture, landscape, and development firm of Schervish Vogel Merz, with offices in an attractively renovated carriage house on Woodbridge near St. Aubin.

The Rivertown Rambler Trolley Bus leaves the Renaissance Center every 30 minutes on the hour to go out Lafayette and Jefferson to Harbortown and Rivertown. Currently it runs from June through early September, Fridays 3-11, Saturdays 11-11, Sundays 11-10. Call (313) 941-3252 for route and schedule information.

POINTS OF INTEREST

Detroit River

This wide, deep river connects the upper Great Lakes (Huron, Superior, and Michigan) with the lower Great Lakes of Erie and Ontario. Its 2,200-foot width made it difficult in wartime to stop ship traffic, which is why in 1701 the French set up a fort at this relatively narrow point, perching cannon on the high northern ground to repel enemy English ships.

For Detroit's first two hundred years, shipping from the downtown wharfs was central to its economy, connecting the city with New York to the east and Chicago to the west. Although the river still carries the world's largest tonnage of cargo, Detroit is no longer a significant port. After years of neglect, the city's waterfront is reemerging as the one hot spot of new building, with new hotels, office buildings, and parks going up every year.

Tip: An especially splendid over-night place to watch the freighters go by as well as get a dramatic view of downtown Detroit is the **Holiday Inn** of Windsor. Be sure to ask for a room on the Detroit River side, and you'll get your own personal outdoor porch overhanging the water from which to view the spectacle. One usually needs to call ahead for reservations at (519) 963-7590. Rooms are about $60 a night and up.

On a warm, not-too-windy day, the banks of this attractive aqua river are a wonderful place to watch the big boats go by. Belle Isle is your best bet for a close-up glimpse of the river traffic. But you won't see nearly as many ships on the river today as a quarter century ago. In the late 1960s, freighters passed an average of once every 12 minutes. Today only about 25 to 35 a day pass by Detroit. Waits of over an hour to see one are not uncommon.

There are several reasons for this decline in Great Lakes shipping:

◆ Less iron ore is needed for automobiles manufactured in the Midwest because they are smaller, less numerous, and use more plastic in place of steel.

◆ The Great Lakes steel industry, faced with much greater foreign competition, no longer produces as much.

◆ In the past decade or so, giant thousand-foot-long Great Lakes freighters have replaced many of the smaller freighters. One superfreighter can do the job of six conventional freighters.

It's a thrill to see these massive boats pass by, some with up to 60,000 tons of cargo. Adding to the mystique is the fact that a freighter may be coming from or going to literally any port in the entire world. The superfreighters, however, can't get through the Welland Canal in Canada to reach the Atlantic. The

Detroit: Rivertown 45

The Detroit River and Ambassador Bridge, with Belle Isle and Lake St. Clair in the distance and Windsor to the right. Cadillac built Fort Ponchartrain in 1701 at the narrowest point (just west of the RenCen) so his cannons could reach passing enemy ships.

saltwater boats, in order to get through the St. Lawrence Seaway, can't be over 730 feet long. The generally larger Great Lakes boats go up in size to the mammoth 1,013-foot William Delancey.

Many of the saltwater boats, which might be Japanese or Soviet or Greek, are picking up grain in Thunder Bay, Canada or Duluth, Minnesota. But there are also stranger cargoes, such as sugar beet pulp from Michigan's Thumb area which is shipped to Europe and Africa for fertilizer.

Regardless of their size, the big boats typically have 35-man crews. The food on board is said to be excellent. In off hours, crew members can watch TV or play ping-pong in the boat's rec room.

St. Aubin Park

On Atwater between Orleans and St. Aubin. Open for fishing during daylight hours. (313) 259-4677 or 1-800-338-6424. Call for info on special weekend Boat Festival events or on marina. Moorage fees: $10 (day rate 9 a.m.-4 p.m. or for a dinner stay) or $15-$40 overnight. Advance reservations available for $25 extra.

Half of this 12-acre, $8 million park is devoted to a 67-slip transient marina, the only one between Lake Erie and Metropolitan Beach on Lake St. Clair. For non-boaters there's a covered shelter, picnic tables and restrooms, two **fishing shelters**, a grassy **picnic area**, and two **river overlooks**. The canopies are colorful and offer some shade, but it will take a while for the new trees to make this a settled, shady place.

Phase Two, to be finished in 1990, includes improved dockage for visiting boats, a play sculpture with concrete sailboats, and **interpretive walkways** on riverfront history and

Detroit's Great Lakes connection. The park itself is on the site of the former Detroit Dry Docks, a major historic shipyard. Near the entrance to the east promenade, which takes you out on the landscaped breakwater, is an illustrated commemorative wall, **"The Black Presence in Detroit,"** mounted on a 15-foot semicircle of concrete. Paths and walkways will link the park with nearby Chene Park.

Tall ships and Great Lakes vessels are planned to visit the park weekends as part of an ongoing, summer-long St. Aubin Park Boat Festival.

Old Riverfront Industries

Northern Engineering
210 Chene at Atwater.
Lauhoff Manufacturing
241 Chene between Franklin and Atwater.
Medusa Cement
On Atwater at the foot of Dubois.

These operating businesses represent the river's recent industrial past. The last industrial shipping in Rivertown unloads cement at Medusa's silos for distribution to area construction sites. Every 10 days or so, the Challenger, a boat as long as two football fields, unloads cement from northern Michigan. Unloading can be observed from Chene Park.

Since 1899 Northern Engineering

The Eagle Iron Works on Woodbridge, pictured in 1884, made engines and boilers. One of many iron works near the river, it resembled buildings like Northern Engineering that still stand.

has made cranes in this four-story brick factory, formerly the Frontier Iron Works. Lauhoff Manufacturing, said to be the oldest manufacturer in Detroit, makes and exports a variety of specialty machines, including flakers and pressure cookers for making cornflakes.

Chene Park

On Atwater at the foot of Chene and Dubois, between St. Aubin Park and Stroh River Place. For specific program information on the **Chene Park Summer Arts Festival** *and other riverfront concerts, call (313) 224-1184 from 8:30 to 5:30, or the 24-hour Leisure Line (313) 224-2732. For general brochures for the season's events, write Detroit Recreation Dept., 1707 Water Board Bldg., Detroit 48226.*

The first of the linked riverfront parks, nine-acre Chene Park combines low-key fishing and riverfront access with an expanded, 6,500-seat amphitheater that promises to become a riverfront concert venue on the order of Meadowbrook. Chene Park's catchy contemporary design won a number of awards for Schervish Vogel Merz and launched the firm on a notably successful path of urban design projects.

When Chene Park opened in 1984, its arts festival programming attracted such crowds that the amphitheater, concession and restroom facilities are being expanded and redesigned, to open in 1990. Expect the same mix of free and ticketed **concerts** and diverse programming, with a classical series and occasionally the Detroit Symphony Orchestra. Chene Park's jazz series has featured top local talent and names like Wynton Marsalis, Ornette Coleman, Tito Fuente, and Weather Report. Pop acts have ranged from Suzanne Vega and Jeffrey Osborne to Second City comedy. Concertgoers can walk along the river and small pond rather than being confined to the amphitheater.

Fishing is encouraged here, and good-size trees provide a pleasant, shady canopy on hot summer days. A warming shelter will be open in winter for **ice skating** on the artificial riverside pond.

Stroh River Place

At the foot of Joseph Campau, corner of Atwater. Valet parking, or park on a nearby street and walk. (313) 446-5000.

What once was the campus-like headquarters and manufacturing facility for Parke-Davis pharmaceuticals occupies this beautiful, 30-acre riverfront site. The giant drug firm began here in 1873. These plain, handsome brick buildings were built between 1900 and 1930. Many were designed by Albert Kahn. The Stroh Brewery purchased the property in 1981, renovated and developed it in first-class style, and relocated its headquarters in the renovated Parke-Davis offices. 300 River Place, the old factory, now contains offices and famed chef Jimmy Schmidt's Rattlesnake Club, one of Detroit's best restaurants. (See p. 51.) The project also includes shops and 300 apartments and townhouses, and River Place Inn luxury hotel. The civic-minded, family-run Stroh's, a Detroit fixture since the 1850s, is in the process of being sold. In the fiercely competitive, advertising-driven, be-big-or-die beer business, Stroh's both lost market share and increased its debt after it acquired Schlitz in 1980.

Mt. Elliott Park

On Atwater at the feet of Mt. Elliott, Iron, and Meldrum. Shoreline improvements scheduled for completion by summer, 1990, with interpretive phases to follow in 1991 or 1992. Call (313) 224-1184 for information.

This park is being designed to interpret the history of the late 19th-century riverfront metal-working industries that helped get Detroit's auto industry off to a fast start. The superstructure of a former steel factory here will become a picnic shelter and activity area where machinery and exhibits can be displayed. The park may become the home of the giant Michigan Stove, a wood replica first

The Coast Guard operations building (center) and Harbortown apartments (right) form the backdrop for the new Mt. Elliott Park.

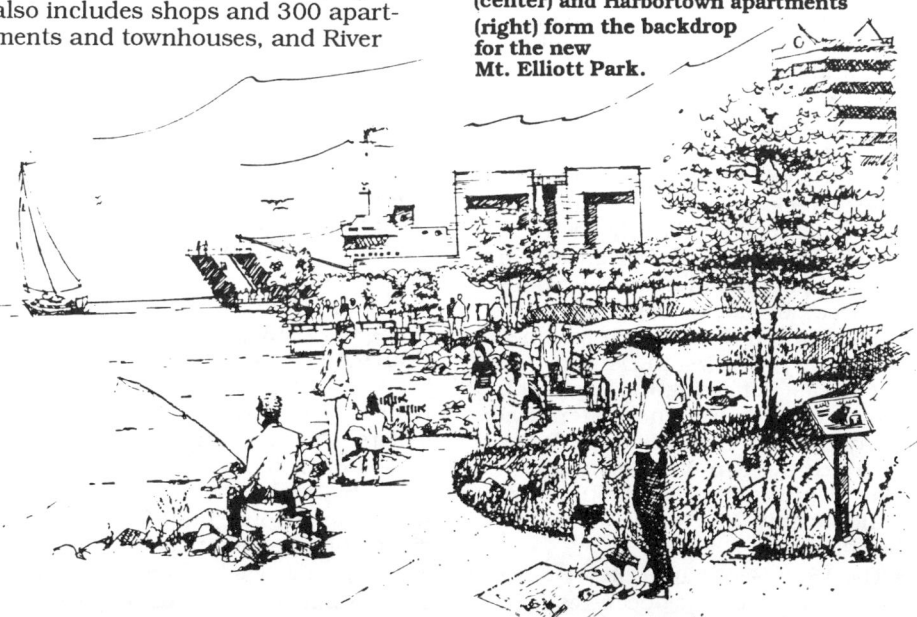

made for the Chicago World's Fair of 1893 and familiar to generations of Detroiters in outdoor locations by Belle Isle and later the Fairgrounds.

Mt. Elliott Park will incorporate as an interpretive center the former **Coast Guard Lighthouse Depot**, a four-story building from the late 19th century used for storing oil, coal, soap, and other supplies for maintaining buoys and other navigational aids. The **Coast Guard** ice-breaking, rescue, buoy-tending, and policing operations are in expanded quarters at the foot of Mt. Elliott. They can be readily observed from the park.

Fishing, considered outstanding here, will be easier to get to with the park's new landscaped shoreline treatment.

History on Jefferson Avenue

Between I-75 and Riopelle, just east of downtown.

In the 1850s, "before the days of multi-storied buildings, the skyline of Detroit was dominated by soaring church spires," commented architectural historian Hawkins Ferry. "As a whole the city must have been a pleasing sight. . . . The scars of industrialism were still relatively unobtrusive, and life assumed an easy balance between the stimulus of the city and the rustic joys of the nearby countryside."

Pre-Civil War Detroit, with its gentle Greek Revival and Gothic Revival buildings, has largely been erased. But pieces of old Detroit can still be seen on Jefferson, especially on these two blocks, beginning with Christ Church Detroit with its limestone belfry, the first in Detroit.

On East Jefferson, the parade of 19th-century homes (now often used as stylish offices) is occasionally interrupted by turn-of-the-century apartment buildings and clubhouses of the wealthy. Starting just east of the church:

♦ The 1848 Georgian **Sibley House** (976 E. Jefferson) has been restored as the headquarters of the Detroit Junior League, an active group in programming and promoting riverfront events.

♦ The six-story limestone **Palms Apartments** (1001 E. Jefferson at Rivard), with a marble lobby and tearoom, was an early luxury apartment in this city of homes.

♦ **The Trowbridge House** (1380 E. Jefferson) is very old for Detroit (1826), but much remodeled.

♦ The English Tudor **University Club** (1411 E. Jefferson) was a late addition (1931).

♦ For the Greek Revival **Moross House** at 1460, see p. 49.

♦ At 2170 E. Jefferson at Dubois is the 12-story **Pasadena Apartments** (1898-1902), the street's earliest apartment building. It offered a wide variety of apartment sizes and plans to wealthy people who did not care to maintain a single-family residence.

Other noteworthy buildings farther out on Jefferson include, in sequence:

♦ The 1850s Federal-style Chene House, now **Little Harry's Restaurant** (2681 E. Jefferson past Chene).

♦ The 1925 **Phelps Advertising Company** office at 2767 East Jefferson, brimming with Northern Italian Renaissance arches and columns. It has a playful statue of a town crier on its east side.

♦ Across the street, the medieval-inspired 1896 **Franklin Walker House** (2730 E. Jefferson), built for one of the family of distillery-owners who left Detroit for Windsor during Prohibition.

♦ Just up from it at Joseph Campau, the 9-story, 32-unit 1915 **Garden Court Apartments**, built for another Walker distillery family member. It typifies the apartments built along Jefferson early in the 20th century.

♦ Next door, the very old (circa 1830) **Joseph Campau House**, a modest white frame house built for a leading citizen of an old French family.

♦ On the north side of the street, the 1888 Romanesque **John Bagley House** (2921 E. Jefferson) and its many-turreted neighbor at 2931, the **William Wells House**.

◆ Finally, **The Players** (3321 E. Jefferson), a Florentine Renaissance playhouse with gargoyles and arched windows with picturesque balconies on front. It is still used by a men's theatrical group.

Christ Episcopal Church

906 E. Jefferson. (313) 259-6688. Ask at office (open weekdays 9-5) to see church interior.

This prominent and beautiful 1863 Gothic Revival church was the first in the city designed by Gordon Lloyd, the talented Canadian architect who designed so many Gothic Revival buildings in Detroit and outstate Michigan. Ask at the office to see the interior with its original butternut woodwork. "Suffer Little Children to Come Unto Me" is the theme of the 1905 Lyster Window, which honors the family of the church's first rector, William Lyster. He went on to found several missions in the Irish Hills between Adrian and Jackson. Indeed, Lyster is the one who coined the name "Irish Hills" because its glacial hills and lakes reminded him of his native Ireland. Photographs of the Lyster family were sent to the Munich window-makers, who reproduced them faithfully. In the south transept, a Tiffany window depicts the legend of St. Elizabeth of Hungary in a beautiful garden.

Moross House/ Detroit Garden Center

1460 E. Jefferson (south side) west of Riopelle. (313) 259-6363. Tues-Thurs 9:30-3:30. Free, docent-guided tour of the house and garden, with a slide show, are on the 2nd and 4th Tuesdays of the month from 1-3, or by appointment. The Detroit Garden Center offers classes and lectures to members ($10/year and up).

This 1840 brick Greek Revival townhouse is the headquarters of the Detroit Garden Center. Its brick-walled rear garden, a vine-clad oasis on this busy street, can be visited whenever the house is open. After the Center took over the city-owned house less than 20 years ago, the rear garden was landscaped with brick walkways and a gazebo and planted with mid-19th-century plant materials: lilacs, peonies, perennials, spring-flowering bulbs, a wisteria-covered pergola, and some espaliered trees. It has now become so lush and settled-looking, it seems much older.

Complete with garden bench, this makes a fine rest stop on a walking tour of historic Detroit. A garden center staffer will tell you about the choice small herb garden. Another vestige of a remote era peeks over the wall: the copper roof and brick walls of the Yondotega Club (also known as the "Yawn"), an old Detroit men's club concealed from the street by a high brick wall.

The Moross House, built sometime between 1843 and 1846, is Detroit's oldest existing brick dwelling. Though not a pretentious house, it was chosen to be photographed and drawn by the prestigious Historic American Buildings Survey in the 1930s. Brickmaker Christian Moross, from an old French family in Detroit, built it from money earned supplying brick during Detroit's post-statehood growth surge in the 1840s. He rented it out for income and lived in a smaller house behind it.

The parlor, front stair hall, and an upstairs area have been furnished with mid-19th-century antiques from old Detroit families, including a rosewood horsehair sofa, oriental rugs, Hitchcock chairs, and whale oil lamps. Compared with later Victorian excess, it's a spare, airy look, complemented by beautiful Belgian lace curtains. Visitors are welcome to peek in, or schedule a tour.

Visitors can also use the extremely pleasant second-floor **gardening library** and consult (by phone or in person) with the center's staff of experienced gardeners about plant problems. A small **gift shop** is on the premises.

Stearns Building/ The Lofts at Rivertown

6665 E. Jefferson between Beaufait and Bellevue, west of the Belle Isle Bridge.

The 1899 headquarters of this old Detroit pharmaceuticals company and the adjoining eight-story reinforced concrete factory are being renovated into one hundred luxury condominium units, in the first Detroit loft rehab project on the scale of similar East Coast developments. Stearns' success was based on being the first to package and market cough syrup in consumer-sized portions. The original office building, designed by Stratton and Baldwin, is full of medieval and Arts & Crafts touches. Two timbered great rooms are under the upper gables.

Harbortown

Between Jefferson and the river, bounded by Adair and Mt. Elliott. (313) 259-2200.

This new apartment, condo, and shopping project, designed by Skidmore, Owings and Merrill, has created a lot of excitement, not just with its thousand units of luxury tower apartments and super-popular condo townhouses but because the small shopping plaza has finally brought a top-quality grocery store, the **Harbortown Market**, to the underserved east side. It's a good place to buy takeout food for picnics at nearby riverfront parks.

Though eastside crime is actually declining as its population decreases, excellent security is a prerequisite for selling upper-income projects like Harbortown. So Harbortown's oversize postmodern gates between the Jefferson Avenue shopping center and the residential areas are an apt design statement. They instantly communicate the image of a friendly fortress. Applied sailboat motifs emphasize the oversize toy castle effect. Amenities include a swimming pool, tennis courts, bridges and walkways around three lagoons, and a marina.

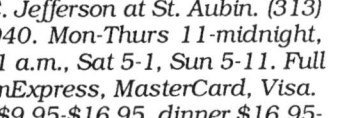

1940 Chop House ★

1940 E. Jefferson at St. Aubin. (313) 567-1940. Mon-Thurs 11-midnight, Fri 11-1 a.m., Sat 5-1, Sun 5-11. Full bar. AmExpress, MasterCard, Visa. Lunch $9.95-$16.95, dinner $16.95-$38.95.

Detroit's fanciest steakhouse — in a formal, moderne 1940s vein that's true to its name — features excellent Angus prime rib of beef (12 oz. for $20.95). Another popular entree is broiled rack of lamb ($32.95). Meals come with baked potato and lettuce wedge — another 1940s touch. Good house wine costs just $15 a bottle.

Rattlesnake Club ★★★
Stroh River Place at the foot of Joseph Campau. Take E. Jefferson 1.5 miles from downtown, turn south onto Jos. Campau just past Doctors' Hospital. (313) 567-4400. Mon-Thurs 11:30 a.m.-11 p.m., Fri & Sat 'til 1 a.m. Full bar, noteworthy wine list. Major credit cards. Valet parking.

The atmosphere in celebrity chef Jimmy Schmidt's $3 million riverfront restaurant is bright, contemporary, sophisticated, and lively — the place was designed for people-watching — and the outstanding food is surprisingly affordable and wide-ranging, to suit the most conservative and sophisticated palates alike.

Lunch prices range from $4.50 sandwiches to $14.95 filet of beef; most dinner entrees are under $20, with one at $10.95. All entrees come with starch and vegetable. Some dishes repeat on the seasonally changing menu: pickerel with herb tartar sauce ($12.95 lunch, $15.95 dinner), porterhouse steak ($24.95 at dinner), Schmidt's specialty shrimp, crab and salmon cakes. For dinner, rack of lamb with artichoke and celery root is an award-winner, as is the persillade swordfish with citrus sauce and ginger. Many diners order an appetizer like angel hair pasta with rock shrimp ($6.95/$8.95) or poached oysters in champagne sauce ($9.50) and salad. Schmidt's chocolate desserts are famous. An outdoor patio is pleasant in summer.

Woodbridge Tavern ★
289 St. Aubin at Woodbridge. (313) 259-0578. Mon-Sat 11 a.m.-2 a.m., Sun noon-10. Full bar. Major credit cards. Live music (usually rock oldies, sometimes Dixieland) begins at 8:30 Thurs, 9:15 Fri & Sat, 4 p.m. Sun.

In the 1920s, places like this lined the waterfront, part grocery, part ship supplier, and part speakeasy. (It was an easy matter to bring illegal booze across the river here.) When the Belgian founders' granddaughter took over in 1975, she reopened the restaurant and built a roof deck, but had the good judgment not to change its beat-up, utterly plain character. It is popular with yuppies and preppies of all ages. The menu, extensive for a bar, features soup and chili; six meal-size salads with and without meat ($4-$6); over a dozen sandwiches ($4-6) from fried cod and perch and 1/3-pound burgers with loads of options ($3.25 and up) to chargrilled chicken and a chicken pita sandwich with tomatoes, onions, and hummus. Deep-dish pizza ($6, $8, and $13) is a favorite. So is baked brie ($5.95) and Key Lime Pie ($2.50). Fish, steak, and chicken dinners come with salad, potatoes, and rolls ($6.50-$12).

Takeout is available to nearby parks. The young wait staff is cheerfully individualistic. From the large deck you can see the moon, the Ren-Cen and the towers of nearby Medusa Cement. The luxuriant back grape arbor, where founder Euphrasie Brunelle hung out her wash, is another delightful spot.

See also: *Soup Kitchen Saloon (p. 325).*

Belle Isle

Belle Isle is one of the most interesting and beautiful urban parks in the world. Here you can get a dramatic **view of downtown Detroit**, a panoramic **view of the grand Detroit River** with its international freighter traffic, and an equally sweeping **view of Canada** and the big distillery right across the river. On the 981-acre island itself, you can find waterfront **picnic areas** throughout, two long **fishing piers**, and, on Central Avenue near Inselruhe, an elaborate **playground** for kids along with a **giant slide**. There's a delightful **zoo**, an extraordinarily beautiful **aquarium**, a fascinating **Great Lakes museum**, a sizable plant **conservatory** and formal gardens, and a **nature center** with nature trails through forests filled with deer. A quaint **floral clock** still graces the entrance in summer. And to top it all off, you'll find one of the most striking fountains in the Midwest. No wonder some ten million visitors see the island each year. Even if you don't get out of your car, it's pleasant to drive around the park with its old cast-iron street lights, fanciful old picnic pavillions, and frequent monuments.

Still an attractive and safe Detroit showplace

Generations of Detroiters, including Mayor Coleman Young, have fond childhood memories of picnics and outings at Belle Isle. Maintaining that tradition has been a high priority for Young's 16-year administration, and he has succeeded in many ways. Substantial investments have been made in the Belle Isle Zoo, restoring the Scott Fountain, installing the Kresge Promenade by the Casino, and improving maintenance and police patrols. In other details, however, there's a lot of room for improvement. The canoe rental facility is poorly maintained. The Casino needs to be repaired. Friends of Belle Isle, a group of supporters and watchdogs intent on preserving the park for low-key recreational uses, has effectively helped squash developers' ideas like building a posh gambling casino here.

The crush of visitors creates problems on the island. At times maintenance personnel cannot keep up with the accumulation of trash. Some areas are scarred and need upgrading. On warm evenings teenagers cruising with loud portable stereos can create so much congestion that this is one of the last places you would want to visit, despite the efforts of the Belle Isle

A brochure with map, "Detroit's Beautiful Belle Isle Park," describes the full range of activities and sights. It is available weekdays 8-3:30 at the park office, which is in the White House on Inselruhe at the canal, or by writing Detroit Recreation Dept., 735 Randolph #2006, Detroit, MI 48226.

Sports and activities include handball, basketball, 10 lighted tennis courts, a cinder track, bicycle trail, canoe and paddleboat rentals, model boat basin, 20-station fitness trail, half-mile swimming beach with lifeguard, and 9-hole golf course in addition to ball fields.

More about freighters and river traffic is on page 44.

police to control it. Evenings and weekends in early and midsummer are best avoided.

There is a **police station on** the island, at Inselruhe and Central Avenue, with enough patrols to make it safe for visitors day or night, (The island is never closed.) By big-city standards, Belle Isle is quite safe.

From a pasture to a grand park

The city bought Belle Isle in 1879 for $200,000. A century earlier, it had been a common grazing ground for the French farmers whose narrow strip farms fronted on the river. They called it "Isle au Cochons" or "Hog Island." But by 1845 it had become a popular picnic ground, especially for Detroit's gentry, who renamed it Belle Isle. The picturesque names of the island's streets reflect its 19th-century romantic heritage: The Strand, Loiterway, and Inselruhe. In the 1880s the great landscape architect Frederick Law Olmstead, designer of New York's Central Park, created a plan for Belle Isle which included a grand central drive. The idea was eventually rejected in favor of a local newspaperman's proposal for a series of canals and lakes.

Today the major thoroughfare is around the island's perimeter. Originally swampy throughout, most of the park has been elevated with fill. Only the eastern wooded area looks the way it did a century ago. Canals allow canoeists to traverse the length of the island.

The first bridge to the island wasn't built until 1889. Today's splendid MacArthur Bridge, designed by Emil Lorch, was built in 1923. East of the bridge on the mainland, the Luna Amusement Park used to be where Gabriel Richard Park now is. West of the bridge, the famous curved-dash Oldsmobile, the world's first mass-production car, was first made in a factory on the site of the now-vacant Uniroyal property. The city holds this plum parcel to award to an especially desireable development project.

Monumental sculpture in the park

Several sculptures on Belle Isle, nicely described in the book *Art in Detroit Public Places*, are worth a visitor's attention:

◆ **Father Gabriel Richard** *(1940; at the E. Jefferson entrance to the Belle Isle bridge).* This simplified, severe granite sculpture by Leonard Jungwirth (who also designed M.S.U.'s famous Sparty) depicts one of Detroit's key figures during its early American years. Father Richard, among many other things, helped found the initial University of Michigan, served in Congress, and started the city's first newspaper.

◆ **James J. Brady Memorial** *(1928; on Central Ave. between Picnic Way and Inselruhe).* This bronze figure stands on Central Avenue between Picnic Way and

Fishing on Belle Isle
Belle Isle has four special fishing spots. The two long piers are especially interesting. They're at either end of Inselruhe. Fishing bulkheads are at the island's east end, one on the south side (just west of the Coast Guard Station) and one on the north, across a channel from the Detroit Yacht Club.

Sizable catches are common. Among the fish caught are silver bass, bluegill, perch, sheephead, catfish, salmon, pickerel and pike.

*A bait shop is four blocks west of the MacArthur Bridge: **Jefferson & Meldrum Service** (6220 E. Jefferson, 259-1176). It can fix you up with a cane pole, hook, line, and sinker for under $10. Don't forget a fishing license. Minnow and worms are $1.50 a dozen. Worms are mainly used in summer, while minnows are used in the winter for pike and pickerel.*

Belle Isle Casino
Designed by Albert Kahn in the Mediterranean style and opened in 1908, it has seen better days. Its back porch still offers an excellent view of the river. The snack bar is open daily from 10 to 6.

Inselruhe. Sculptor Samuel Cashwan's bronze sculpture of the man who founded the Old Newsboys philanthropic organization in 1914 shows him with a newspaper for sale, shielding a small, barefoot girl.

◆ **Dante Alighieri** *(1927, at Central and Vista avenues).* To commemorate the great Italian poet's 600th anniversary, Italian sculptor Raffaello Romanelli created this bust.

◆ **Major General Alpheus Starkey Williams** *(1921; Central at Inselruhe).* Sculptor Henry Shrady's intriguing bronze shows a once well-known Civil War and Mexican War officer perusing a map during a battle in stormy weather.

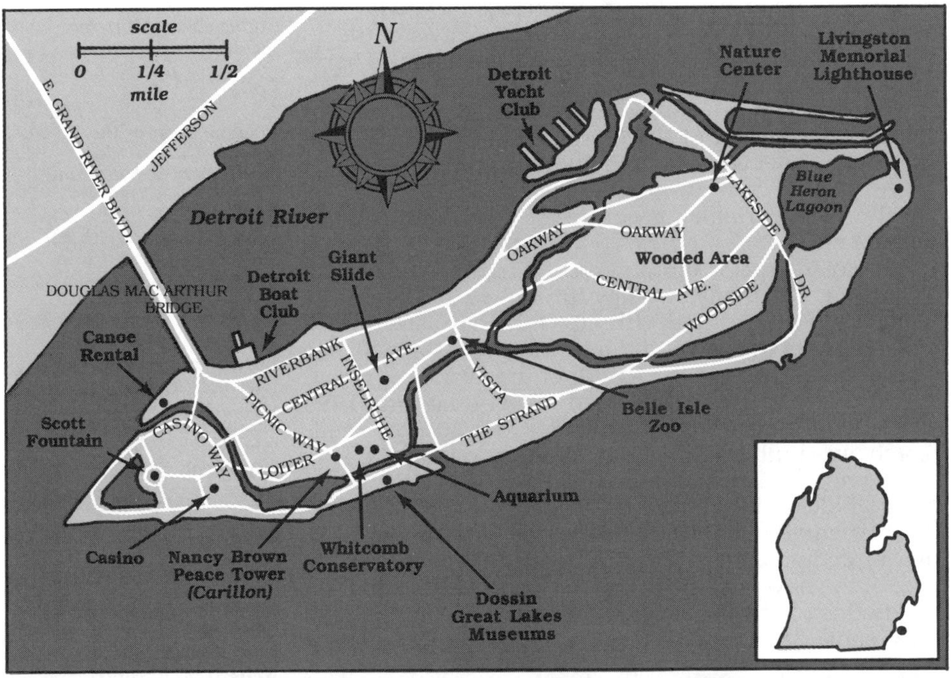

· BELLE ISLE ·

POINTS OF INTEREST

Scott Fountain ★★

West tip of Belle Isle, overlooking downtown.

To make room for this huge and ornate fountain, Belle Isle was actually extended one thousand yards on its western end. From that western tip you can see not only the fountain but its reflection in the specially constructed lagoon. Italian white marble — some 20,000 square feet of it — was used to create the monument, which the city was at first reluctant to build. The half million dollars were supplied in the bequest of James Scott when he died in 1910. But Scott was viewed as such a local scoundrel that the city at first refused to honor his request to spend the donation on an imposing monument in his honor. As Tom Holleman suggests in his delightful *Bicycle Tours of Detroit*, a prominent Methodist minister proposed a statue "about 2 1/2 inches high."

Eventually the city held an international competition, won by the eminent Beaux-Arts architect Cass Gilbert. (The following year he also was hired to design Detroit's Public Library.) For the fountain, Gilbert came up with a complex series of bowls, basins, and fountains, complete with spewing turtles, dolphins, lionesses, Neptunes, and animal horns. Sculptor Herbert Adams created the required bronze statue of Scott. It graces the fountain's west side. Some say the spot was chosen so that prevailing winds keep him wet much of the time.

Now for the first time in decades, all four pumps work, and the central spray reaches a height of over 75 feet.

Dossin Great Lakes Museum

The Strand (the Canada-side perimeter drive) at Picnic Way, west of Inselruhe. (313) 267-6440. Wed-Sun, 10-5:30. Closed holidays. $1 donation requested.

Overlooking the Detroit River, this is one of the niftiest museums in Michigan. Outside you'll find two big cannons from Commodore Perry's key naval victory in the Battle of Lake Erie, the turning point of the War of

1812, which preserved American independence.

Entering the museum, you are confronted with a splendid carved oak and stained glass interior from the 1912 steamer, the *City of Detroit*. This was the Gothic Room, where the male passengers came to smoke and talk. The reconstruction from the boat's original materials vividly conveys a vanished era when passengers could cruise the Great Lakes inexpensively yet in luxurious comfort.

In the next room leading toward the river, a giant three-dimensional relief map of the Great Lakes clearly reveals the relative depths of the five lakes, from shallow Lake Erie (only 210 feet at its deepest) to Lake Superior (1,333 feet).

Carefully crafted models of Great Lakes ships are displayed throughout the museum. So are large photos of boat christenings and spectacular wrecks. One display promotes Great Lakes shipping, which today takes a back seat to rail and truck. It points out that to deliver by boat 15 million tons of ore to Chicago from the East Coast takes just 24 million gallons of fuel, compared with 35 million gallons by rail and 123 million gallons by truck.

At the end of the room, an authentic-looking reconstruction of a steamer's pilot house allows the visitor to look right out over the river through the pilot house's windows. Above it is an observation deck, a splendid place to look at passing steamers. Their radio messages can be heard from a nearby speaker. On the river's near bank are signs showing the distance and direction to frequent freighter destinations:

```
        < Marquette  481 miles
        < Green Bay  507 miles
        < Alpena     219 miles
        < Duluth     728 miles
          Montreal   618 miles >
          Toronto    299 miles >
```

Next to the pilot house and observation deck is the most popular museum item of all: a working

Steamers like this once plied the Great Lakes.

submarine periscope. Looking through it, past the crosshairs designed to guide torpedos at enemy ships, you get a great preview of what's coming up and down the river as well as a full 360° view of the island.

Aquarium

On Loiterway just west of Inselruhe. (313) 267-7159. 10-5 daily, including holidays. Free.

This is not only the oldest public aquarium in the U.S. but one of the most visually striking. It was built in 1904, designed by the legendary Albert Kahn. Carved dolphins, now mostly covered by vines, grace the entrance. The interior, with muted, indirect lighting, has a delightful aura created by the serene green-tiled ceiling contrasted with the black-tiled lower level. The effect, augmented by the many strange fish in crystal-clear aquaria, is that of entering a fantastic new world.

Over 100 species of fish are kept here. The rarest is the tiny and endangered Desert Pupfish from the southwestern U.S., where rampant development is dangerously lowering the water table. Most popular is probably the huge and ugly electric eel, which delivers a hefty 650 volts to stun prey. Visitors can hear a dramatic indication of the big eel's electric output when it is fed at 10:30, 12:30, 2:30 daily (and at 4:30 Sunday). Often big crowds gather to experience the noisy performance.

Informational signs in this striking aquarium are also excellent. Neither frustratingly brief nor overly long, they provide interesting nuggets of information. The sign next to the piranha exhibit reads: "Outside of the movies, piranhas have never been known to kill a person. In fact, people swim and bathe in rivers where piranhas live. Piranhas use their razor-sharp teeth and strong jaws to feed on fish. An injured animal that falls into piranha-infested waters may be reduced to bones in minutes."

Because of corrosive vapors from salt water, the aquarium no longer keeps saltwater fish. But you can see most major groups of freshwater fish, including a big 2,800-gallon tank of Great Lakes fish: Largemouth Bass, Lake Sturgeon, Spotted Gar, and Long-nose Gar. Some 10,000 gallons of refrigerated water is used to keep muskies, trout, and salmon.

Whitcomb Conservatory ★

On Loiterway just west of Inselruhe. (313) 267-7134. Open 9-6, every day of the year. Free.

Capped by an imposing 85-foot glass dome, this Albert Kahn building, opened in 1904, was made of parts of an exhibit at the St. Louis World's Fair of the same year. The giant palms in this central space are spectacular. Adjoining rooms

Winter and summer, the Whitcomb Conservatory is an oasis filled with exotic plants. The floral displays in the formal garden in front of it are also worth a look.

feature cactus, ferns, tropical plants, an unusually large collection of orchids, and seasonal displays. Labels are erratic. This is more a place for looking at plants and enjoying them than learning much about them.

In front are formal gardens and a delightful fountain capped by a bronze gazelle, created by Marshall Fredericks in 1936. At the base are four animals native to the island: a hawk, rabbit, otter, and grouse.

Belle Isle Zoo

Between Central Ave. and Loiterway toward the east end of the island. (313) 398-0900. Open May 1-Oct 31, 10-5 daily. Admission: $2 for 13 years up, 50¢ for kids 5-12, under 5 free.

Set amid splendid, shady trees, this small, 13-acre zoo is an exceptionally pleasant place to spend a warm summer day. Much of its charm is created by the 3/4-mile-long elevated walkway from which most of the animals are viewed. Looking down into the animals' settings, you get a more three-dimensional, interesting view of their habitats. The naturalistic settings are ample enough to allow most of the 160 species to roam freely. Especially for brief visits or people with small children, a visit the Belle Isle Zoo may well be more satisfying than the much larger and more

expensive Detroit Zoo in Royal Oak.

Among the rarer animals on display are the endangered maned wolves from South America. They are known as "foxes on stilts" because their long legs enable them to see over tall vegetation. Another endangered species here is the spectacled bear, the only bear native to South America. These bears have light-colored markings around their eyes. They love to climb and eat fruits, leaves, roots, and young shoots.

New to the zoo are a pair of siamangs, primates of the gibbon family which have extraordinary leaping and acrobatic skills. They live in mountainous forests of Indo-China. Siamangs make terrific zoo exhibits because they are such active and noisy creatures.

Nature Center

At the east end of the island, on Oakway Rd. at Lakeside Dr. (313) 267-7157. 10-5, closed Mondays. Free. Special weekend family programs.

Belle Isle's nature center is, appropriately enough, situated on the eastern side of the island where the forest and marsh remain in their natural state. This low area is subject to flooding. Also, two feet under is a layer of clay hardpan which neither water nor tree roots are usually able to penetrate. As a consequence, many trees blow over in big storms. A particularly bad flood in the early 1980s killed many trees and resulted in increased populations of woodpeckers, cattails, and wrens, which love tall grass.

The two self-guided nature trails, one 3/4 of a mile long, the other 1/4, give a good view of the native wildlife in the 200-acre natural area. For wheelchair users there's a short paved trail as well.

On a recent January 1, some 49 bird species were counted here — a creditable number for a large city. Here you can also see, in the drier parts of the wood, the now tame and abundant European Fallow Deer, brought to the island in 1937. You are best off not coming in April, when the trails are likely to be underwater.

The snakes, birds, turtles, and mammals inside are mostly temporarily held injured animals or illegal confiscated pets such as ferrets and foxes. An outside animal shelter also houses such animals. Once rehabilitated, those which can survive in the wild are released. One animal which won't be released because someone cut off its rattle is a Massasauga rattlesnake, Michigan's only poisonous snake species.

Livingstone Memorial Lighthouse ★

Visible from Lakeside Dr. at the island's east end. Not open to visitors.

This beauty, made of Georgian marble, is topped by a bronze lantern cap. Detroit's famous architect Albert Kahn designed it to commemorate the president of the Lake Carriers' Association. The lighthouse is almost 70 feet tall, and its light can be seen 15 miles away in the middle of Lake St. Clair. At the base is a heavy bronze door and bronze portrait of Livingstone.

European Fallow Deer, smaller than the whitetail, roam the island and are especially noticeable in winter. When the population builds up over a hundred, the parks department rounds some up to trade two-for-one with deer breeders, thus reducing their numbers and diversifying the gene pool.

East Side

Detroit's east side is easily the most varied part of the city. It has beautiful **Belle Isle** and the **Detroit River**. Along the river are remnants of some of the city's oldest industries: shipbuilding, iron works, and pharmaceutical companies. Many are now converted into nightclubs and offices in the district today called Rivertown. Some of the behemoths of Detroit's early 20th-century industrial boom are on the east side, including Chrysler's Mack and Jefferson avenue plants. **City Airport** has been recently expanded as a handy, popular airport for commercial flights, after much neighborhood controversy.

For many outsiders, the east side is best known for the **Eastern Market,** a concentration of wholesale-retailers around a big public market. It's a fabulous, earthy place for people who love good food. Metro Detroit's huge size and big mix of distinct ethnic groups make the market much more complex and interesting than those in most cities.

The east side has both historic and up-to-the-minute luxury apartments between Jefferson and the river. Long streets of well-maintained, early 20th-century mansions make up **Indian Village,** not far from stretches of some of the city's oldest, most decrepit housing.

Some of the most stable middle-class neighborhoods in Detroit are here, too. Streets of charming, medium-sized Tudor houses are just west of the Grosse Pointes in "Copper Canyon," so called because many police live there. **Lafayette Park**, whose apartment towers and townhouses were designed by master modernist Mies van der Rohe, has been a model middle-class neighborhood for all its 30 years. Streets of modest, primly maintained bungalows lead from Jefferson toward the quaint fishermen's cul-de-sac and marina on Harbor Island and a cottagey riverside trailer park just west of Grosse Pointe Park.

To be from the east side has always suggested coming from a place where most people work with their hands: skilled tradesmen, tool and die workers, factory workers, owners of shops that make small parts. That stands in contrast with the Woodward corridor and west, always more stylish, which was largely developed for people "in business" — often Jews, also many Irish.

The big eastside ethnic groups in the early 20th century were Germans, who originally lived near Gra-

Grayhaven Marina Village on Lenox near the Fisher Mansion is on the site of the mansion built by Detroit boat manufacturer Gar Wood, who invented the hydroplane. Grayhaven represents the new type of eastside residential development: self-contained, with a security gate, on-site athletic facilities, and often with river access and boat slips. Rents run from $690 to $1,100. The typical tenant: a divorced suburban executive with a boat.

tiot; Poles; Italians; Flemish and French Belgians; and some Christian Lebanese. Macomb County just north of here is today dominated by eastside Germans, Italians, and Poles who have moved out of Detroit.

The oldest and most decrepit part of the east side away from the river (ironically named "Paradise Valley") was deemed suitable for blacks who had come up from the South. Diplomat Ralph Bunche, who won the Nobel Peace Prize in 1950 for helping negotiate a cease-fire between Israel and Egypt, grew up over a barbershop on Hastings Street. By the 1920s, Hastings Street had become a nationally-known center of blues, jazz, and night life. The Brewster Project, built when blacks finally gained access to public housing in overcrowded, booming Detroit, was the home of a number of Motown musicians, including Diana Ross of the Supremes.

Thanks to the boating boom, the riverfront here is seeing big new development projects: apartment and townhouse enclaves with marinas, swimming, tennis, and jogging facilities, and sometimes their own shopping. Gates and security checkpoints are a necessary marketing feature. It's too soon to say whether these self-contained projects will eventually lead to the revival of nearby neighborhoods of houses and flats.

POINTS OF INTEREST

Eastern Market ★★★

From Gratiot 1 mile east of downtown, take Russell north over the Chrysler Freeway. Signs clearly direct visitors from Gratiot to the market. Eastern Market Central Administration: (313) 833-1560. **Market hours:** *Mon-Fri 5 a.m.-noon (but most farmers are gone by midmorning), Sat 5 a.m.-6 p.m.* **Retail store hours:** *typically 8 a.m. (earlier on Saturday) until 4 p.m. or 2 p.m. Sat.* **Parking** *is free in and along the market square and on adjoining streets (both jammed on Saturdays) and in the little-used public parking structure off Riopelle, parallel to Russell but two blocks east.*

Since the 1890s, this colorful, bustling market has been where Detroiters come to buy produce from local farmers and to buy meats, fish, coffee, nuts, produce, fruit, spices, wine, and cheese from the stores around the market. Surrounding the large open-air stall area called "the sheds," where up to 800 farmers can sell their produce, are wholesale-retail specialty shops. The entire area has an appealing, earthy atmosphere. Wholesalers have been leaving the old marketplace storefronts for less congested, more functional, single-story quarters in the blocks just north of here. Visitor-oriented retailers are replacing them. But for now the blocks of Russell and Market in front of the sheds still have a satisfyingly workaday feel. There's lots of commotion as forklifts load and unload trucks, jockeying among shoppers' cars.

The Market is a genuine vestige of old Detroit: a great medley of smells and sounds and colorful sights, and a vast variety of food appealing to the city's diverse populations and cultures. It's quite a sight to see the wonderful array of nationalities who congregate here Saturday mornings.

Next to the **Gratiot Central Market** across from the Eastern Market sheds, the aroma of nuts pervades the air at **Germack's**, the oldest pistachio importer in the U.S. Pungent spices greet you in several Middle Eastern shops; an Islamic slaughterhouse is a few blocks away. Nearby at **Capital Poultry**, live ducks (a favorite with Detroit's many Poles) and chickens cackle away. Feathers are mixed in the dirt in the gutter outside. In front of **Ciaramitaro's**, the third-generation Italian produce business on Market and Winder, you'll see dozens of crates of onions being unloaded, followed by piles of burlap bags of potatoes, as customers buy grapefruit and celery from the stand that's in front of the store, winter and summer.

In a city that's known great ups and downs, people love the Eastern Market because it's still the same. It's a touchstone to former Detroiters, who can come back and see this vital remnant of the city they loved when they were kids. Even the freeways haven't carved up the market and isolated it. You hardly notice that the Fisher Freeway, recessed in a giant ditch, separates the sheds and square from the Gratiot Central Market.

Old-timers will tell you that it was really something to see the market in the 1920s, when some two thousand produce peddlers converged here to load their wagons with the day's goods to sell in the neighborhoods. (This crowded scene is shown in historic photographs by the cashier at the Roma Cafe at the end of Riopelle.) The oldest market hall and the wholesale houses alongside it date from the 1890s, when the farmers' market moved from the long block of Cadillac Square downtown between Woodward and what's now the historic Wayne County Building. The city's house of corrections used to be here, along with an old Indian burial ground. Wholesalers at the market today are likely to be descended from Belgian, German, and Polish farmers who sold at the market generations ago, or from Italian and Syrian street peddlers who first catered to Detroit's booming population of industrial workers beginning about 1910. Many older merchants are boyhood chums from Our Lady of Help and St. Joseph High nearby. Its pupils in the 1920s and 1930s were Germans, Italians, and Lebanese — a common ethnic mix in eastside Detroit.

There's much more to the market area than just the old brick buildings facing the main market hall. Actually, there are three market buildings: the familiar **main sheds**, with planner Alex Pollack's funny chicken murals on its ends; the taller, somewhat newer, heated **Shed #5** just north of it on Adelaide (some farmers sell

here on Saturdays only), and, still farther north between Riopelle and Russell, the big, modern **truck terminals** where semis with produce come in from California and the South.

It's true that today the Eastern Market, like smaller suburban markets, has fewer area farmers coming to sell their produce — a result of the declining farm population. But this place is still fascinating in all its guises, which change with the time and day of the week.

♦ **Saturday mornings.** The market's madhouse persona is now, especially from 7 to 10. It's most familiar to the general public. Food-lovers from far and wide converge here for weekend shopping. Eastern Market ranks with the Detroit Institute of Arts and Tiger Stadium as favorite destinations of suburbanites otherwise ignorant of Detroit.

♦ **Early weekday mornings.** The wholesalers' weekday work is mostly done before sun-up. Around 1 a.m. trucks from the South and Southwest arrive to be unloaded. Some produce is already destined for distributors like I.G.A., Spartan, and Abner Wolf, and some is sold at the market, either direct to retailers or to old-line Eastern Market wholesale houses like Del Bane, Vitale, and Ciaramitaro. They in turn sell and even deliver it to retail customers. Farmers in market stalls compete with these out-of-state producers for retail buyers, and a lot of bargaining takes place.

Throughout the early-morning hours, trucks of all sizes are coming and going, unloading and loading. In the old days, musicians used to stop by after hours and check out the market scene, just as Les Halles was a gathering spot in Paris. But there aren't any all-night restaurants here any more. By the time restaurants open around 6 or 7 a.m., the main

Sal Ciarmitaro of Ciarmitaro Brothers Produce is one of many third-generation Eastern Market wholesalers. Part of the market's charm is its continuity with the past and its emphasis on food as a basic bulk commodity.

> Farmers at the market are prepared to sell wholesale to distributors, retailers, and restaurants, and retail to the general public, but consumers can try their hand at bargaining down to wholesale prices, especially if they buy in quantity.

part of the work day is over, and it's time for a break.

◆ **Weekdays in the mid-morning and afternoon.** Now the atmosphere is positively leisurely — a good time to get the undivided attention of the knowledgeable clerks at R. Hirt and Cost Plus Wine. The farmers are gone by late morning, but wholesale-retail produce places remain well stocked.

The retail areas around the market actually extend well beyond the main market hall itself into the surrounding streets. The thickest concentration is on Russell just north of the market. There, low new buildings house a variety of retail stores, including the venerable and highly recommended **Al's Fish and Seafood** (2929 Russell, 313- 393-1722) and **B & S Produce** (3111 Russell, 313-833-6133), where you can get big bags of onions and potatoes, 5 pounds of raw peanuts for $4.59, fresh-roasted peanuts for $1.25 a pound, or choose from five kinds of watermelon in season.

North of the market between Gratiot and Mack are several more blocks of wholesalers and meat packers, who cut up and package carcasses for retailers. Every odd turn reveals something else: **Rudy's New and Used Restaurant Equipment**, **Berry & Sons Islamic Slaughterhouse** (one of the few slaughterhouses left here), **Amrine's** Middle Eastern grocery near the Gratiot Central Market, the **Jenuwine Candy & Tobacco** wholesale/retailers on Russell (pun intended), **Fuchs Religious Goods** across Gratiot from the Gratiot Central Market, the **Farmers' Restaurant** on Market and Division, and the **Meat Cutters Inn** at 2638 Orleans ("Fine Food, open 7 a.m.-7 p.m., Hires Root Beer"). That's not to mention the many, more visible retail stores. You could come here every week for months and each time have different places to explore.

Here are some of the Eastern Market's most notable shops:

Cost Plus Wine Warehouse ★
2448 Market. (313) 259-3845. Mon-Fri 8:30-6, Sat 7-4:30.

It's a real pleasure to deal with Irishman Tim McCarthy. Knowledgeable without being condescending or snobbish, he is a great guide to good wines. He puts his own label (Tara Hills) on a very good Michigan Riesling produced by Chateau Grand Traverse and sells it for only $5 a bottle.

R. Hirt Jr. Company ★★
2468 Market at Windsor. (313) 567-1173. Mon-Fri 8-5, Sat 7-2.

This century-old Detroit institution has a great range of merchandise: cheese, sausage and ham products, crackers, bottled waters, beans and rice, coffee, mustards and condiments, and all sorts of imported pastas, jams, sparkling waters, olives, and fancy foods. What's more, you can sometimes get premium-quality food at less than supermarket prices.

Hirt's is big-hearted and resolutely old-fashioned, even when old-fashioned means somewhat inefficient. You take a basket, load up on shelved merchandise, then go to the counterperson, who gets your cheese from the ancient, walk-in wood refrigerator, cuts it straight from the wheel, wraps your purchases, and

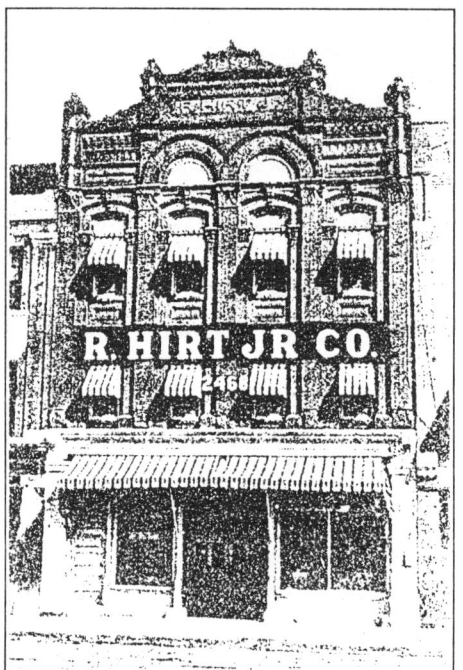

Shopping at the Eastern Market's R. Hirt, the friendly, old-fashioned cheese shop and fancy foods grocery, is a weekly tradition for quality- and value-conscious customers. Swiss immigrants started Hirt's in 1887 as wholesalers in cheese, butter, and eggs. Their handsome building was erected just after Eastern Market started in 1893. (The first one burned shortly after completion.)

writes up a bill. This you pay at the separate cashier's, then return to pick up your purchases. Saturdays are crazy, what with the big, convivial crowds who seem to enjoy the opportunity to socialize in line and pick up food ideas. (There's no number system to streamline the wait.) On weekdays, it's quiet, and the service is attentive, prompt, and knowledgeable.

As at many Eastern Market wholesale-retailers, Hirt's prices are somewhere between wholesale and normal retail prices. Its wholesale operation, over three-fourths of its total volume, has moved to single-story quarters a few blocks away.

For years Hirt's was a general grocery store, the first in Detroit to sell Swiss cheese and fresh mushrooms. Today Hirt's has evolved to occupy the specialty foods niche without being geared to the super-trendy, Oakland County market. That's what gives the place its special allure. The owner-buyers are pros who really know their cheese (and beans and rice and other merchandise they wholesale). A few stores may have more varieties of cheese, but the DeVries family who owns and runs Hirt's looks for "the best quality at a fair price," as Tom DeVries matter-of-factly says.

Excellent values, chosen by the *Detroit News*'s outstanding food and restaurant writer Sandra Silfven, include:

◆ Leerdamer Swiss cheese from Holland: low in fat (like all Swiss) but sweeter and more deeply flavored. Cheaper than domestic Swiss at the supermarket.
◆ Parmesan and provolone made in Wisconsin by a noted Italian producer, thus cheaper than imports but better than other domestics.
◆ Canadian Red Leaf cheddar, aged longer than other cheddars, creamy and sharp but not bitter.
◆ Shannon, a Gouda-style cheese smoked in oak and considered the best smoked cheese available.

Writes Silfven, "Bet you didn't know Hirt's has Medjool dates from California, air-dried Swiss beef, macadamia nut brittle, porcini mushrooms from Italy, extra-virgin olive oil in 5-liter containers, and some of the world's best vinegars from France." We came upon other outstanding values ourselves: 5 pounds of honey for $4.60; Swiss-style sharp mustard sold under Hirt's own Market Street brand, 8 ounces for 69¢; from Dearborn Sausage, honeybaked ham for $3.10/lb. (compared with over $4 for the popular Honey Baked brand), cappicola ham $3.65/lb., and ring bologna $2.20/lb.

Hirt's non-food treasure trove is the third-floor wicker and basket department, where you can find classics ($5 laundry baskets, $2 door mats, tomato, bushel, and berry baskets, covered picnic baskets), decorator items (including decorative tins, hampers, $55 Adirondack chairs and 4-piece wicker furniture groups for $500), and a huge variety of shapes and sizes of all kinds of baskets. Cheap cheese boxes can double as toy boxes or end tables.

Ciaramitaro Brothers produce
2506 Market at Winder. (313) 567-9064. Mon-Sat 5:30 a.m.-2 p.m.

Ciaramitaro's (pronounced "SHERM-uh-ta-ro's) and many other market old-timers started as "commission houses" that took farm produce and resold it at a percentage. Today Ciarmitaro's is mainly a wholesale food purveyor. The colorful, year-round sidewalk retail operation is more of a sideline run by retirees. Its prices on a wide range of fruits and vegetables are attractive. The ancient-looking frame building is said to have been a tavern and inn going back to the 1840s.

Eastern Market restaurants

There are a variety of popular eating places in the Market to pick up a cheap breakfast or lunch. **Zef's Coney Island** (2469 Russell, 313-259-4705, Mon-Sat 5:30-4) is where John DeLorean breakfasted during his trial for fraud. There pancakes and two eggs sell for just $1.55, and an ample corned beef sandwich with pickle is $1.99. The new **Russell Street Deli** (2465 Russell, 313-567-2900; current hours Mon-Fri 11-2:30, Sat 8:30-2) stands out above the rest with its excellent homemade soups, changing daily, and fresh-roasted turkey sandwiches. Classic deli sandwiches mostly run $3 to $4. Also in the vicinity: **Joe Muer's** outstanding fish restaurant on Gratiot at Vernor (see p. 74), the venerable **Roma Cafe** (p. 73), and, on the inexpensive, takeout end, the highly regarded **Louisiana Creole Jambalaya** on the opposite side of Gratiot just north of Joe Muer's.

Joe's Wine and Liquor ★
2933 Russell. (313) 393-3125. Mon-Sat 7-6, Fri until 7.

"Dave Anderson has the best collection of beers in the state, including the most exotic Belgian entries, which many connoisseurs consider the most interesting in the world," says *Detroit Monthly*. For homesick Berliners longing for "eine Weisse mit einem Himbeer Schuss" (light beer with a shot of raspberry syrup), this is the place to come.

Rafal Spice Company ★
2521 Russell. (313) 259-6373. Mon-Fri 7-4, Sat 7-2.

Even if you don't need any spices, be sure to stop in here just to smell the 400 herbs and spices on hand. It's a visual treat, too, to see row upon row crammed with everything from asafoetida powder to burdock root. Rafal also carries 85 kinds of coffee beans (at attractive prices), 60 kinds of bulk teas, and a large assortment of hot sauces, plus potpourri, oils, and books with recipes for concocting your own scents. The founder's grandson runs the place.

Gratiot Central Market
1429 Gratiot. It faces Gratiot on one side and the Fisher Freeway Service Drive on the other. Mon-Fri 8-5, Fri until 6, Sat 7-7. **Park** *on the service drive or Gratiot, or take the pedestrian walkway over the Fisher Freeway.*

This colorful amalgam of butchers and other shops is in the white building with the terra cotta cow heads over the entrances. **Ronnie's Meats** (313-567-3226) offers a wide range of meats. *Detroit Monthly* calls its babyback ribs the best in town. Goat is butchered to Islamic halal standards. **Joe Wigley Meats** (313-567-2857) is famous for its lamb and kosher-style corned beef.

Capital Poultry
1466 E. Fisher Freeway next to the Gratiot Central Market. Tues-Sat 7:30-5.

Here you can actually pick out a live chicken to be dressed and picked up later. Free-range chickens grown by northern Indiana Amish are sold for very reasonable prices. An exotic assortment of other poultry is also available, including guineas, pigeons, and wild game in season.

Germack Pistachio Company
1416 E. Fisher Freeway, near the Gratiot Market. (313) 393-0219. Mon-Fri 8:30-4:30, Sat until 2.

America's oldest pistachio processor (since 1924) offers natural and red pistachios; cashews and mixed nuts; squash, sunflower, and pepita seeds; peanuts (roasted, salted and blanched, honey toasted, or butter toffee) and raw shelled nuts, also many kinds of dried fruit. Roasting is done on the premises, so you know they're fresh. Holiday gift packages or plain plastic bags are available.

Paradise Valley/ Lafayette Park ★

Between Lafayette and Gratiot, Chrysler Freeway (I-75) to Orleans.

Lafayette Park's high-rise apartments and popular townhouses designed by Mies van der Rohe show how attractive an environment this great architect could create. A drive or walk through the townhouse section, where the lush landscaping sets off the elegantly simple buildings, is a special treat.

Lafayette Park stands on the site of a neighborhood of small frame homes, built in a hurry for German immigrants in the 1850s. It became famous as the Negro ghetto of Paradise Valley and "Black Bottom." The near east side was the oldest and poorest area of Detroit, and Paradise Valley was the poorest of all. During the auto boom, black people poured in here from the agricultural South to make $5 a day in the auto plants. Boxer Joe Louis grew up here; so did Mayor Coleman Young.

By the 1920s the adjoining bar district along Hastings Street had become fabled for its music — big-band jazz and urban blues. The 17 nightclubs on Hastings Street were popular spots not only for blacks but for whites. The area's black-and-tan cabarets featured black entertainers geared to white audiences. The Detroit-based McKinney's Cotton Pickers played here often; so did Mississippi Delta bluesman John Lee Hooker (he came north in 1943 to work in Detroit's "Arsenal of Democracy") and Jackie Wilson, whose 1956 "Reet Petite" was an early crossover pop hit.

In the 1940s these 129 acres of crowded, decrepit housing were targeted for slum clearance in the nation's first urban renewal project. Hastings Street would later succumb to the Chrysler Freeway. By 1954 Paradise Valley was levelled to build middle-class housing that was part of Mayor Albert Cobo's grand plan to stem the hemorrhage of Detroit's middle class to the suburbs. Residents were supposed to be relocated to public housing projects, but demand for low-cost housing so far outstripped supply that most simply crowded into other old houses nearby. Today, of all Paradise Valley's many black-owned businesses, only the **Horse Shoe Lounge** at 1907 St. Antoine remains.

Chicago builder Herbert Greenwald brought in none other than the guru of modernism, Mies van der Rohe ("Form follows function") to plan the area as a single huge superblock arranged around a central park. As built, his part of Lafayette Park is a splendidly realized example of the low-density modern urban village. Such decentralized superblocks and lawns aimed to bring rural qualities of fresh air and open spaces into the city — an ideal that architects and planners have now discredited and replaced by the romantic notion of a high-density, pedestrian-oriented, medieval-style city. Nevertheless, Lafayette Park was a popular success. Only recently have the towers begun to be eclipsed by newer riverfront housing.

Mies designed three parts of the project. Each shows the technical elegance of detailing for which he is famous.

◆ **Lafayette Park Pavillion Apartments** (1 Lafayette Plaisance, 1959). A 22-story tower of concrete, aluminum, and gray glass.

◆ **Lafayette Towers** (1963). Twin 21-story towers, much like the Pavillion Apartments, separated by a parking garage with a swimming pool on the roof.

◆ **Lafayette Park Court Houses** (1959). 186 townhouses and apartments grouped around courts. They have blank brick end walls and window walls crisply framed by the black outlines of exposed structural steel.

Rigorous and doctrinaire, Mies influenced a lot of cold, impersonal architecture, but Lafayette Plaisance today is a beguiling in-town oasis of calm and neighborly congeniality.

"From the beginning, the neighborhood attracted an amazing mix: doctors, lawyers, congressmen, cops," according to a 1989 *Detroit News* article. "At one time the *Times* of London called Lafayette Park the smartest neighborhood in the whole world. The neighbors, black and white, hung out together like well-to-do pioneers. 'If somebody said "hello" to you on the sidewalk, there would be a cocktail party then and there.' . . . There wasn't much the new neighborhood didn't promise in 1959: cold martinis, limbo dancing, Jestons-style kitchens, blacks and whites living together in peace and harmony."

After builder Greenwald died in a plane crash, the rest of Lafayette Park was developed and designed by others. One building approaches Mies's in quality: **1300 Lafayette East** (Birkerts & Straub, 1964), an elegantly thin, finely detailed 30-story apartment building designed in part by the nationally respected Birmingham architect Gunnar Birkerts.

Between Lafayette Park and the historic Elmwood Cemetery, 500 acres were later cleared and developed as **Elmwood Park**. Its less distinguished apartment tower and townhouse projects are for families with average incomes and below.

Elmwood Cemetery

Elmwood Ave. at E. Lafayette; entrance on Elmwood.

The city's oldest cemetery, started in 1846, incorporates the romantic landscaping principles of Boston's famous Mount Auburn Cemetery: winding lanes and a casually picturesque English style of landscaping. The rolling site, with surprising valleys, has many mature trees. The topography of much of Detroit was like this before the street grid and dense buildings flattened it out.

The pointed arches of the 1856 Gothic Revival entrance gate underscore the cemetery's otherworldly, romantic mood. This attractive place is a favorite spot for history-minded Detroiters because of its big variety of interesting old monuments and well-known people buried here, from eminent statesman Lewis Cass to travelog host George Pierrot.

Many prominent African-Americans are buried here, including

Elmwood Cemetery gatehouse

abolitionists George DeBaptiste and William Lambert, who helped some 30,000 fugitive slaves escape to Canada. A former valet to President William Henry Harrison, DeBaptiste was a clothier, caterer, and owner of an excursion steamer in Detroit.

Heidelberg St. Project ★★

On Heidelberg between Mt. Elliott and Ellery. From downtown, take Gratiot to Mount Elliott, turn right. Three blocks past Mack, turn right onto Heidelberg Street.

"Fun House" is the first abandoned Heidelberg Street house decorated by artist Tyree Guyton a few years ago. It is a weathered frame house splashed with color and decorated with old toys, dollhouses, pictures, plastic bottles, and the like.

Now this transformation has extended to a whole environment on Heidelberg Street, and to several abandoned houses on nearby Benson and Charlevoix. Heidelberg Street itself sports a tangle of colored lines. Bright shoes march up a tree trunk. Stately pedestal drinking fountains are in the vacant lot across the street. Black and white splotches decorate the dead tree behind them.

Photos can't convey the magical, powerful feeling of this place. Coming here is a very special experience, especially if you have a talk with Guyton's philosopher grandfather, Sam Mackey. He is often out on the park bench installed for the steady stream of visitors. Mackey has lived in the neat, green house next door for 40 years. He has seen the neighborhood become spotted with abandoned homes that invite arson, drugs, and other crimes.

For Guyton, the project has been both a way to stabilize the neighborhood, which has now turned into a popular tourist attraction, and to work out his own personal demons. As a child he lived in poverty on this street. His mother was overwhelmed by family responsibilities. He was abused by a family friend and teased for his interest in art. Only his grandfather encouraged his art.

As an adult, Guyton studied at Detroit's Center for Creative Studies and has pursued art as a career. "Fun House" got him started using color, imagination, and cast-off toys to transform a depressing environment into a wild and appealing fantasy of the childhood he never enjoyed.

The project has been the subject of national publicity since it first hit the local papers in the summer of 1988. Since then, it has been featured in *People*, *ArtNews*, *Vogue*, and *Connoisseur*. "It's good we got it goin' this way," says Mackey. "Everybody cooperated — the police, neighbors, the Grey Lines bus drivers. [The project is on its city tour.] The city lets us do more houses." Nevertheless, one decorated house fell victim to the city's catch-up demolition blitz of abandoned homes in 1989. Donated discards for the project arrive regularly.

Incidentally, the well-known Capuchin monastery and soup kitchen is a few blocks south on Mt. Elliott.

Jefferson Avenue from Belle Isle to Grosse Pointe

Jefferson Avenue is one of Detroit's two important show streets along which prestigious institutions and residences were built. Like Woodward, Jefferson leads to elite suburbs. By paralleling the Detroit River, Jefferson has nearby marinas, riverfront parks, and baronial homes with boat houses. It also has a good share of old Detroit industries. On Jefferson between downtown and Belle Isle are some of Detroit's oldest buildings. (See p. 48-9.)

A drive out Jefferson to Grosse Pointe shows a somewhat newer but equally interesting slice of Detroit, in which fine old buildings, often beautifully maintained, and fast food restaurants aren't far from clusters of street people, boarded-up storefronts, and party stores brightly wrapped in protective armor.

Right at the Belle Isle bridge are two pretty good restaurants, the **New Detroiter** (soul food) and the **Acapulco** (Mexican food). (See p. 74.) At Van Dyke and Jefferson, you're at the intersection of the prestigious **Indian Village** historic district, a long, narrow strip of mansions along Seminole, Iroquois, and Burns, and its slightly less imposing neighbor, **West Village**. (See p. 70.) Some interesting shops and restaurants, including the sumptuous, superb Van Dyke Place, are clustered at Van Dyke and Jefferson.

Across from the foot of Seminole at 800 East Jefferson is **Solidarity House**, the tall glass headquarters of the United Auto Workers, one of the most progressive and socially enlightened American labor unions. The UAW's many bloody battles with auto management turned Detroit, once one of the most anti-union cities in the U.S., into a bastion of unionism.

Just east of the Glass House is Detroit's version of Chicago's Gold Coast, a string of stately apartments including the **Whittier Hotel** on Burns, now a retirement residence. It faces **Memorial Park**, a public park with good parking and access to the river. It's good for fishing or looking at the Detroit Yacht Club across the channel on Belle Isle. The other side of the park, along Marina Drive off Jefferson, has a playground and basketball court. On the north side of Jefferson here is **The Kean**, a remarkable Art Deco apartment tower.

Just past Memorial Park, three small side streets between Jefferson and the river comprise the Berry subdivision. These fine homes are not so old or grand as those in Indian Village, except for "The Castle" on Parkview. Once a boys' school, it is now part of the **Blanche House Bed and Breakfast**. (See p. 113.) The mayor's official residence, the beautifully landscaped **Manoogian Mansion**, backs up to the river on Dwight. In a city not known for speedy police response time, neighbors love living near the reclusive mayor with his security squad. The mansion was donated to the city by Alex Manoogian, the founder of Detroit's extremely successful Masco Industries empire built on plumbing supplies. His son, Richard, is the celebrated art collector whose collection of 19th-century American paintings was a surprise hit at the Smithsonian in 1989.

Next on Jefferson comes **Waterworks Park** between Parkview and Marquette. Its 1893 **Hurlbut Memorial Gate** stands out in bombastic, statue-bedecked Beaux Arts grandeur. Chauncey Hurlbut, a Detroit Board of Water commissioner, left a bequest to beautify the park. Art historian Denis Nawrocki praises the gate's "fine balance between lavish areas of ornamentation and smooth, unadorned surfaces." **Waterworks Tower** (1876), 185 feet tall, stands in the background. The water intake and purification facility here is now one of five in the city.

Across from the park is the famed **Pewabic Pottery**, again producing architectural tiles and open to visitors. (See p. 70.) **The Roostertail**, a banquet hall known as the scene of

The Hurlbut Memorial Gate at Waterworks Park has been a Jefferson Avenue landmark since 1893. Detroit water consistently scores very high in taste tests.

many elite parties, is at the foot of Marquette just east of the park. A block east on the river at the foot of St. Clair, is **Sindbad's**, popular for its casual, boating atmosphere and excellent hamburgers. (See p. 74.)

About a mile east, the pedestrian overpass at 12200 East Jefferson announces the giant **Chrysler Jefferson Assembly Plant**, now closed. Here 1,200 workers most recently made Omni and Horizon autos. The facility, built by Albert Kahn between 1907 and 1916, eventually totaled almost 2 million square feet on 47 acres. The plant's history shows how volatile the early history of auto manufacturing was. First it was owned by the Thomas Motor Company. In 1911 it became the Chalmers Motor Car Company and was leased to the Maxwell Motor Car Company in 1917. Finally, in 1924 it became a keystone of the Chrysler Corporation. Saxons, Chryslers, and DeSotos have all been built here.

The eastside ring railroad line built by a consortium of expansion-minded industrialists around 1913 begins here. The lifeline of many big eastside plants, it heads northwest from the river alongside Conner and connects Chrysler's Mack Avenue Stamping Plant, the Harper Avenue headquarters of Fruehauf, and the industrial enclave in Highland Park.

Indian Village & West Village ★

Indian Village is on Burns, Seminole, and Iroquois between Jefferson and Mack. West Village extends from Seyburn to Parker between Jefferson and Mack, just west of Indian Village.

Some of Detroit's finest-quality and most interesting architecture is being restored and preserved here. Indian Village coincided with the blossoming of medieval and Arts and Crafts styles in the Detroit area, so those styles are well represented, along with a wide range of early 20th-century revival styles from Italian Renaissance to Georgian. The large mansions on Indian Village's three long streets were built between 1895 and the mid-1920s. West Village is more eclectic, a mix of stately apartments, occasional row houses, and large but not quite grand houses on smaller lots.

During the 1920s in older large cities across the U.S., the elite basically withdrew to the suburbs. Grosse Pointe, Birmingham, and Bloomfield Hills grew rapidly. Threatened with decline as the city became less desirable, Indian Village organized in 1938 to protect itself as a neighborhood of single-family homes, with rigorous zoning and design review.

Today pride of place is evident in Indian Village's often stunningly landscaped yards. More heterogeneous West Village spans the gamut from elegant to funky. To find out about the spring homes tour of some of these beautifully crafted homes, call Preservation Wayne, (313) 577-3559.

Pewabic Pottery ★★★

10125 E. Jefferson between Cadillac and Hurlbut, across from Waterworks Park. (313) 822-0954. Tues-Sat 10-5. Free admission.

"Hundreds of years from now, the names of your motor cars and drug factories may be forgotten, but people will know that Pewabic Pottery was made in Detroit because this beauty will live," said the great Detroit art collector Charles Lang Freer. He made his fortune manufacturing railroad cars, then devoted himself to becoming one of the world's foremost connoisseurs of Oriental art. Early in this century Freer inspired Pewabic founder Mary Chase Perry to develop her famous iridescent pottery. He brought her a shard of unusually beautiful Babylonian pottery to emulate. It took her years of experimentation, but by 1906 she succeeded.

Perry was part of the turn-of-the-century Arts and Crafts movement,

The architecture of the Pewabic Pottery studio and gallery on Jefferson across from Waterworks Park exemplifies the simple, English cottage look that dominated the Arts & Crafts movement in Detroit. Today Pewabic is again making the unique iridescent glaze tiles used to decorate buildings across the country.

which promoted a return to simple, pre-industrial art forms, She never attempted to exploit her exclusive glaze by mass-producing her art. Some of her most striking work was in architectural tiles, which can be found from the Nebraska State Capitol to the Shrine of the Immaculate Conception in Washington, D.C. You can see her work all over town, including the entrance of the Guardian Building in downtown Detroit and at Christ Church Cranbrook in Bloomfield Hills, where extraordinary Pewabic tiles decorate the choir floor.

Perry established Pewabic Pottery in 1903. "Pewabic" is an Indian word for copper. Her work was so well received that in 1906 she and her associate, Horace Caulkins, had this pleasant gallery and workshop built in the style of an old English country inn. She later married its architect, William Stratton. Perry refused to reveal the formula for her iridescent glaze. The center declined after her death in 1962.

But since 1982 there has been a revival under the auspices of the newly organized Pewabic Society. Production is once again underway.

After much experimentation, glazes quite similar to Perry's are now being created. There are classes for beginners, residencies for experienced craftspeople, and a **gallery** which shows both new works and some of Perry's original ceramics. With a staff of 25 professional artists, Pewabic is again a national center for the design and production of architectural tile. Contemporary designs in Pewabic tiles adorn four People Mover stations downtown.

The visitor is given free rein to wander through the two-story building, which looks much as it did decades ago. For sale in the **consignment gallery** at quite reasonable prices are some beautiful pieces including bowls, dinner plates, and tiles. For as little as $4 you can buy a small Buddha or pony. In the rear **studios** downstairs, artists can be

Mary Chase Perry Stratton combined strong artistic and entrepreneurial abilities to develop Pewabic Pottery as a famous manufacturer of architectural tile.

seen shaping their works and using the big kilns.

Fisher Mansion   ★★★

383 Lenox. Take Jefferson to Dickerson (east of the Chrysler plant), turn south. Dickerson becomes Lenox. (313) 331-6740. Tours Fri & Sat 12:30, 2, 3:30, & 6; Sun 12, 1:30, 3, & 6. $4 admission ($3 seniors and children)

This fascinating and fancifully lavish mansion is one of the truly extraordinary sights of Detroit. It was built in the 1920s by the playboy head of Cadillac Motors. Its style has been described as "glitz bordering on garish." Neglected after owner Lawrence Fisher's death, the mansion has been purchased, restored, and maintained by an improbable team of Hare Krishna converts — Alfred Brush Ford, great-grandson of Henry Ford, and Elisabeth Reuther Dickmeyer, daughter of legendary UAW head Walter Reuther. Today it serves a small community of Hare Krishna followers, who use the ballroom for their chanting hall. On the second floor is the excellent **Govinda's** vegetarian restaurant (see p. 75), also run by the Hare Krishnas.

Lawrence Fisher was one of the seven Fisher Brothers who helped revolutionize the auto industry in the early 20th century by building enclosed bodies for cars. Up until then the standard auto was an open vehicle. The Fishers signed up with GM to make their car bodies, and Fisher Body later became a GM division. Lawrence was a big, beefy bachelor who squired the likes of Jean Harlow and threw opulent parties. No elitist, he invited local tradespeople as well as celebrities to these events. Champagne flowed continuously during parties from the mouth of a solid silver head of Neptune in the entryway.

The home of publishing magnate William Randolph Hearst, Fisher's good friend, inspired this mansion on the Detroit River. Hearst's San Simeon then set the standard for California opulence, mixing a dazzling array of florid architectural styles. Fisher's 50-room mansion follows in this grandiose tradition. The entranceway of the cream-colored stucco spread gives a flavor of

William Randolph Hearst's San Simeon inspired the most opulent of all the mansions built by Detroit auto barons — that of his friend Lawrence Fisher, head of Cadillac Motors. It can be toured Friday through Sunday.

its no-holds-barred approach to architecture. The black Majorcan tiles on the floor have gold insets. Art Deco tiling surrounds the silver head of Neptune. Tile work alternates long Roman tiles with Detroit's famous Pewabic tile. The marble columns are Corinthian Greek. In all, 75 ounces of golf leaf and inlay were used on the mansion's ceilings and moldings, and 140 ounces of silver.

Always impeccably dressed, Fisher remained a bachelor until, at 62, he married his childhood sweetheart, then 67. One of his great loves was his dogs. He frequently dined alone with his cocker spaniel, who ate out of a silver bowl. When the dog suddenly disappeared one day, the disconsolate auto baron personally went door to door in the neighborhood, offering a $10,000 reward for its return, to no avail. When another dog drowned in the adjacent swimming pool, he had the pool filled in. He buried two of his beloved pooches in signed, silver Tiffany caskets on the mansion's grounds. It is said that one of the first things a subsequent owner did upon taking possession was to dig up the caskets, dump the bones in the trash, and sell the silver.

Sailing was another of Lawrence Fisher's passions. Hence, the mansion is strategically situated at the mouth of the Detroit River. Fisher had a wide canal built up to the house, with large enclosed boat houses on each side. The larger held his 106-foot yacht. The smaller housed the vessel which later became President Kennedy's presidential yacht.

The ornate details throughout this extraordinary home are too many to mention. The beautifully tiled bathrooms have fixtures of 24 carat gold. The ballroom is in the style of a Spanish courtyard, complete with Venetian parapet and delicate white clouds painted on the blue ceiling. During Fisher's festive parties, a machine projected stars on this ceiling, and lighting was adjusted to simulate dusk or dawn, whichever time it might be. In the music room, with organ and piano, an ornate Japanese ceiling accompanies walls of African zebrawood and a black parquet floor. Liberace once played for guests here. Some of the world's top wood-carvers were brought to work on the detailing. In some cases a carver would spend over a year on a single door. Not much of a reader, Fisher ordered the hand-tooled leather books in the library by color rather than title.

Amazingly, this splendid mansion was sold by a bank in the early 1960s for just $80,000. The Hare Krishnas have for the most part respected the historical integrity of the place. Their own colorful religious paintings hang on some walls, but they don't obscure the feel of the place when Fisher lived there. One startling exception is an upstairs room in which sits a full-sized, bluish seated statue of their deceased guru. Our tour was given by a highly knowledgeable and entertaining member of the local 80-member Hare Krishna community.

RESTAURANTS

Roma Cafe

3401 Riopelle at Erskine a few blocks north of the Eastern Market. From Gratiot, turn north onto Russell, right onto Erskine. From I-75, take the Mack exit east to Russell, south 2 blocks to Erskine, left to Riopelle. Mon-Fri 11-10:30, Sat 11-1 a.m. Full bar. Major credit cards. A la carte lunch entrees $8-$12, dinner entrees $11.25-$18.

This friendly place, with its 100-year-old carved back bar, may be Detroit's most popular Italian eating spot. Not a trend in sight — the waiters wear tuxedos, and the sauce is an honest tomato red. Veal is a specialty here, with veal Parmesan and veal tosca (both $16.25 at dinner) the two most popular. Baked lasagna ($11.75), shrimp scampi, fettucine Alfredo, homemade cannelloni ($2.50 for dessert) — all the old favorites are well prepared, as are the vegetables. Prices are a la carte; soup is $1.75 extra, salad $1. People rave over the $14.50 Monday-night pasta buffet.

Joe Muer's Seafood ★★

2000 Gratiot at St. Aubin, 1 1/2 miles northeast of downtown Detroit. Take I-75 to Gratiot exit, turn left, 1/4 mile on right. (313) 567-1088. Mon-Thur 11:15-10, Fri 11:15-10:30, Sat 5-11. Lunches $8.50-$15, dinners $14.75-$28. Full bar, extensive wine list. Major credit cards. Reservations for large groups only.

Now 60 years old, Muer's is Detroit's premiere fish restaurant, known for superb service and consistently excellent fish, 25 selections in all. A specialty is flounder stuffed with crabmeat ($22.75 at dinner). Also popular is the broiled Lake Superior white fish ($16.75). The delicious shrimp scampi a la Muer ($21.50) has a crushed almond coating. Lunch entrees come with choice of boiled potato, stewed tomatoes, spinach, or cole slaw. Dinner price includes soup, salad, and choice of vegetable.

New Detroiter

7339 E. Jefferson at Sheridan, 2 blocks east of Belle Isle bridge. Park in front or rear. (313) 822-2642. Sun-Thurs 7 a.m.-1 a.m., Fri & Sat 7 a.m.-4 a.m. No alcohol. Visa, MasterCard, Discovery.

Soul food — home cooking familiar to any Southerner, black or white — is prepared simply and deliciously here, and the view of the Belle Isle bridge is great. Catfish chunks fried in a cornmeal batter were a fabulously light and tasty dinner ($8.95). Pit barbeque is the biggest seller. Most dinners are $8.95 — half a dozen ribs, or baked fish, or barbeque chicken. Weekly specials are $2 or $3 less. Dinners include cornbread and choice of three sides, all of which are pretty good: macaroni and cheese, greens, green beans, pintos, lima beans, blackeyed peas, salad. carrots, candied yams, carrots, soups, or mashed potatoes. Some people make a meal of the sides, $1 and when ordered separately. For dessert, there is sweet potato pie and several cakes.

Hearty breakfasts include starch (hash browns, rice, or grits) and two sides. Bacon and eggs are $3.50, steak and salmon patties $4.95.

Sindbad's

At the foot of Marquette on the Detroit River. Go east on Jefferson 4 1/2 miles from downtown, turn south onto Marquette just past Waterworks Park. (313) 822-7817. Winter hours: Sun-Thurs 11 a.m.-midnight, Fri & Sat 11 a.m.-2 a.m. Summer hours: 11 a.m.-2 a.m. 7 days.

This boaters' hangout, also popular with landloving locals, has 40 available slips if you care to arrive by the river. There's a marina next door; in summer, 70 per cent of the clientele is boaters and therefore very casual. Once you're inside, there is virtually no river view. Service can be brusque and lines long, but the atmosphere is convivial, even clubby, and the portions huge. Burgers are $3.25 plain, $3.75 with cottage cheese; sides of fries are just 50¢. Specialties include a 12-ounce steak sandwich ($11.95) and fried or broiled pickerel ($12.95). Dinner entrees come with salad, roll, and potato.

Van Dyke Place ★★★

649 Van Dyke, 3 buildings north of Jefferson. Mon-Fri 6 p.m.-9:30. Sat 5:30 p.m.-10. Full bar. AmExpress, MasterCard, Visa. Entrees $26-$35. Reservations strongly advised.

The setting alone is very special — a beautifully restored turn-of-the-century mansion just west of Indian Village, the kind with lots of carving and elaborate plaster ornament. The table is set with cut crystal and orchids, elegance matched by the distinguished French haute cuisine served up here. Representative a la carte entrees include chicken and shrimp with scallops and leeks and shellfish cognac ($27.50) and lamb chops with a potato-filled artichoke and roasted garlic ($28.50). Soups are $5, vegetables $4.50.

In the informal basement **Cuisine de Pays**, thrifty, top-quality French farmhouse cooking reigns. Simple dishes like steamed mussels, interesting sausages, and risottos cost from $7 to $12. Currently this room is used Thursdays through Saturdays as a cabaret ($35 for the show and dinner).

Cadieux Cafe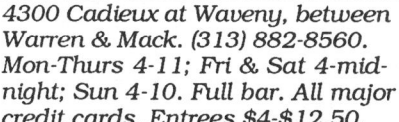

4300 Cadieux at Waveny, between Warren & Mack. (313) 882-8560. Mon-Thurs 4-11; Fri & Sat 4-midnight; Sun 4-10. Full bar. All major credit cards. Entrees $4-$12.50.

This warm, tidy corner tavern, a period holdover from the early 1950s, serves the sizable community of Belgians here on Detroit's far east side and in nearby Grosse Pointe. (See p. 72.) Now many have moved on to the suburbs of Sterling Heights and St. Clair, but they still come back to the Cadieux for their traditional mussel dinners, feather bowling, and dart-throwing contests. Mussels are $10 a bucket, $6 a half-bucket. You can request the mussels Belgian style (steamed in onions, celery, and carrots). Other dinners ($9-$15) include pickerel, perch, steaks, and shrimp, with choice of two: salad or slaw, potato, or soup, all competently prepared. Mashed potatoes with spinach and nutmeg are a Belgian specialty. Sundays the Cadieux serves an $8.50 rabbit dinner: roast rabbit with vegetables, mashed potatoes, and rabbit gravy. There's a big selection of Belgian beers, often considered the world's best.

Feather bowling takes place in an adjacent hall on dirt alleys. Contests usually get under way by 7 or 8 p.m. on Thursday, Friday, and Saturday it's always busy. You can sit at a table, watch, and play if no one has reserved the alley. Or call to reserve it yourself. Dart-throwing leagues are Thursday nights. The Cadieux is also headquarters for other Belgian sports: bicycling and pigeon racing.

Govinda's

383 Lennox, off E. Jefferson between the Chrysler plant and Golightly Vocational Center, 3/4 mile west of Grosse Pointe Park. From Jefferson turn south onto Dickerson. It turns into Lennox. (313) 331-6740. Fri & Sat noon-9, Sun noon-7. Complete Indian dinner $7.50 lunch, $8.50 dinner. Reservations recommended. No alcohol. Visa, AmExpress, MasterCard.

The Hare Krishna owners of the extraordinarily ornate Fisher Mansion, most lavish of the all auto barons' 1920s palaces, run an excellent vegetarian Indian restaurant in the Cadillac president's opulent dining room. (See p. 72 for more on the mansion.) Nothing here is plain. The columns undulate sinuously. The floor is of onyx-like Italian marble. Walls are of burled walnut, African zebrawood, and teak. Pewabic tile decorates a fountain.

The affable Hare Krishna offer a delicious Indian feast without proselytizing. Dinner includes two vegetables in yogurt and tomato sauces; a fried rice patty in yogurt; basmati rice with spices, nuts, and vegetables; lentil soup; a wonderful puffy Indian bread; and two fresh vegetables dipped in chick pea flour batter and deep-fried in butter. Applesauce is for dessert. More mundane appetites may be appeased with sandwiches (grilled cheese is $3.50), pizza, and nachos.

See also: *Eastern Market restaurants, p. 63, 65.*

Detroit's Historic Auto Factories

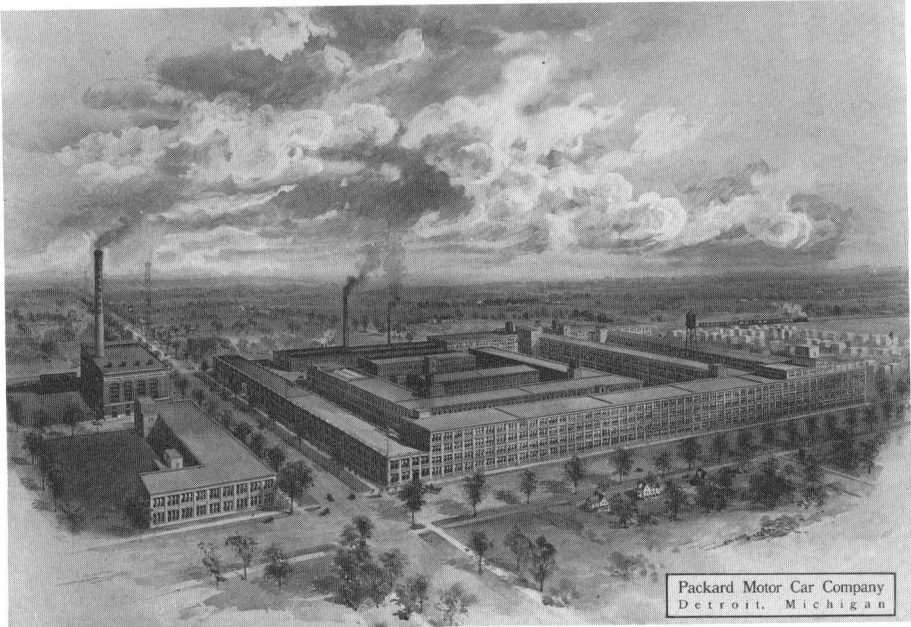
Packard Motor Car Company
Detroit, Michigan

By 1900, automobile manufacturers were beginning to spring up all over the U.S. Detroit, far from dominating the infant automobile industry, was not even yet the most significant auto-manufacturing city. But then, due mostly to the audacious drive of several key people living here, Detroit auto companies quickly wiped out most of the competition with their cheap, mass production of reliable automobiles. By 1910, Detroit was becoming the Motor City.

Today the city of Detroit manufactures just a tiny fraction of the country's autos. Only one assembly plant is presently in operation. But there was a time when Detroit auto factories were making well over half of all the cars in the world. In the first three decades of the century, dozens of these often mammoth factories were built here. Long idle, many have yet to be torn down.

Detroit's oldest auto factories were in established industrial areas, mostly

(Above). **The Packard Motor Car Company moved to Detroit in 1903, when auto enthusiast Henry Joy, son of Michigan Central Railroad magnate James Joy, encouraged other wealthy Detroit heirs to invest in expanding the infant auto manufacturer. Joy was alarmed by recent Detroit fire disasters, and he searched out the architect of the luxury Palms Apartments on Jefferson, constructed of fireproof concrete, specially reinforced. The designer turned out to be young Albert Kahn. The 1903 Packard plant, his first industrial commission, became the prototype for 20th-century factories. It can still be seen at 1580 East Grand at Concord.**

on the east side, along main railroad lines.

Crowding and obsolescence

Auto factories require not only railroad tracks but large amounts of space. That's why the first large ones were located beyond built-up 19th-century Detroit — out past Grand Boulevard and on the farmland of present-day Hamtramck and Highland Park, but still close enough for workers living in the city to get there easily. Soon those factories were surrounded by dense rows of workers' housing and by tool-and-die shops and parts shops. This crowding forced newer plants outside of Detroit. Only in the 1970s, when Detroit's depopulation made large tracts of central-city land available, could new auto plants locate in the city.

Many historic factories still stand

If you drive around the city, you can still see the ghost-like remains of the factories which launched many of America's legendary cars (Plymouth, Ford, Cadillac, and Packard, to name a few) and made Detroit the Motor City. Here are the most important:

◆ **Ford Motor Company** (Piquette at Beaubien between I-94 and Grand). This historic plant, built in 1904, was where Henry Ford first produced the Model T. After making over 10,000 cars here in 1909, Ford moved the following year to the famous Highland Park plant. In 1911 he sold this complex to Studebaker.

◆ **Ford Highland Park Plant** (15050 Woodward at Manchester). Begun in 1910, this once-massive complex designed by Albert Kahn is where Henry Ford

At the Ford Highland Park plant, designed by Albert Kahn, the continuously moving assembly line was perfected between 1912 and 1915. The original 1910 building shown here has been demolished, but several six-story concrete buildings at Manchester just east of Woodward remain.

perfected the assembly line, the key to the mass production which cemented Detroit's supremacy in car production. Four stories high, 875 feet long by 75 feet wide, upon completion it was the largest factory under one roof anywhere, and the largest building in Michigan. Here in 1914 workers began receiving the unheard-of sum of $5 a day. It was during the Highland Park era that Ford began to outsell all the other car manufacturers combined. Most buildings of this "Crystal Palace" (so-called because of the large expanses of glass) have been torn down, but you can still get a sense of its scale from what remains. Ford began moving operations to the Rouge Plant in Dearborn in 1917.

◆ **Cadillac Motors** (450 Amsterdam at Cass). Henry Leland founded Cadillac in 1902 and built this 1905 plant with then-new reinforced concrete. Subsequently Cadillac plants sprouted up all over the city. In 1921, all Cadillac operations were consolidated at the big facility at 2860 Clark at Michigan Avenue, which only recently stopped making GM's flagship model.

◆ **Packard Motors** (1580 E. Grand Blvd. at Concord). Managed by Henry Joy, Packard moved to Detroit from Warren, Ohio, in 1903, when the first building in this complex was built. Here you can see the first of many Albert Kahn auto factories. The tenth building was the first reinforced concrete building in Detroit. It created for the first time large sections (32 by 60 feet) of clear work space between columns. Packards were made here until 1956, when Studebaker bought the company and closed the facility.

◆ **Lincoln Motors** (6200 Warren at Livernois). After a dispute with GM founder Billy Durant, Henry Leland and his son left Cadillac in 1917, founded Lincoln, and began building this complex. Here were made the Lincoln Zephyr, the Mercury, and the Lincoln Continental. In 1952 operations were moved to Wayne, Michigan, and the complex was sold to Detroit Edison.

◆ **Plymouth Motors** (6334 Lynch at Mt. Elliott). Until GM built its Detroit Hamtramck assembly plant in 1985, this 1928 facility was the newest major auto plant built in Detroit. It was built by Walter Chrysler, who timed the introduction of his cheap Plymouth to coincide with Ford's long changeover from the Model T to the Model A. At the time 1,000 cars a day were produced here.

Innovations in reinforced concrete technology by structural engineer Julius Kahn, Albert's brother, were a cornerstone of Kahn's industrial success. Big spaces with few columns, shown here in the 1910 Highland Park plant, made for flexible layouts of large machines, plus huge windows with good ventilation and lighting.

Southwest Detroit

Southwest Detroit has four main visitor draws. On Michigan Avenue just west of downtown, there's endangered **Tiger Stadium,** one of the few remaining grand old ball parks with real mystique. Nearby, **Mexican Town** has a concentration of popular, good Mexican restaurants. Not far away, at the foot of Clark Street near the Ambassador Bridge, there's the dock for the excursion boats to the **Boblo Island** amusement park, next to two docks where some big freighters still unload their cargo, and **Riverside Park,** a good place for watching shipping activity. A little farther west on the river off Jefferson, there's **Historic Fort Wayne**, one of the last generation of star-shaped fortresses, with interesting museums on Detroit military history, Great Lakes Indians, and the Tuskegee Airmen, the Air Force's famous all-black flying unit during World War II.

Surrounding these sights are neighborhoods of modest older housing long occupied by workers at the area's big employers — huge plants that are often, significantly, just outside the Detroit city limits: the Ford Rouge steel foundry and auto plant in Dearborn and Great Lakes Steel in Ecorse. Historically, Detroit's chemical industry has also been located on the river here — an additional source of pollution.

In general these neighborhoods have not aged well. The lively Hispanic neighborhood around Vernor and Junction and residence hotels along Michigan Avenue are ports of entry for immigrants without much money. Nearby Clark Park, a drug dealers' hangout, is the scene of "Take Back the Park" marches.

Today Spanish-speaking populations (historically Mexican-American, with recent arrivals from Cuba, Puerto Rico, and other Caribbean islands) dominate most of the area south of I-94 and north and east of I-75. Few traces remain of the vibrant Hungarian community in **Delray**, south of Fort and west of Livernois. In the 1910s and 1920s, Hungarians moved here to work at the nearby Solvay Process Company, Peninsular Stove Foundry, and Detroit Graphite Company. Their yards had big vegetable gardens, poultry houses, smokehouses for each year's pig, and root cellars. Sausages, bacons, and hams hung in their attics, along with hot peppers and spices. Today Hungarians live in newer downriver suburbs, especially Taylor and Southgate.

The Maltese migration to Southwest Detroit
Overpopulation forced residents of the tiny Mediterranean islands of Malta, midway between Italy and Africa, to emigrate between 1910 and 1930. Booming Detroit with its plentiful auto factory jobs was their preferred destination. Many worked in the building trades. These Catholic descendants of the ancient Phoenicians were fluent both in English and Maltese (a blend of newer Italian words on an Arabic base), and they assimilated quickly. Today southeast Michigan's estimated 44,000+ Maltese are dispersed, but Corktown around Michigan Ave. and Fifth St. remains their old neighborhood, the home of the Maltese-American Benevolent Association. Maltese old-timers, who own a good deal of Corktown rental property, have played an important stabilizing role in this originally Irish area.

One neighborhood to improve in recent years is **Corktown**, the historic Irish neighborhood a few blocks south of Tiger Stadium. The Irish have long been dispersed, though a few old Irish taverns remain on Michigan Avenue. Today Corktown is a safe, friendly neighborhood, home to a stable combination of longtime residents and newcomers. The old-timers are Maltese, Eastern European, and perhaps 50 to 70 old Irish families. The newcomers include Hispanics and blacks and a substantial number of multiethnic artists, filmmakers, architects, teachers, lawyers, and more — some with family roots in the area, all drawn by its closeness to downtown.

A big economic shot in the arm for the Corktown area is due to occur when the empty colossus of the old **Michigan Central Station**, just south of Michigan at 14th Street, is renovated as a world trade center by one of the developers of the World Trade Center in New York. A monumental piece of Beaux Arts architecture with a 14-story office building on top, the impressive train station is now an eerie, peeling ghost of its former self. Detroit is well positioned to profit as an exporting center when U.S.-Canadian tariffs are dropped in 1992. Detroit Amtrak passengers must today scurry ignominiously to a bleak trailer-like prefab station in a dreary, unpaved parking lot to the west.

Mexican-American roots in Detroit
Between 1910 and 1920, many Mexican-Americans came to Detroit, settling close to Tiger Stadium. Some came because the railroads they worked for transferred them here. Ford's $5 work day attracted others. Pickle producers brought yet more to Detroit.

POINTS OF INTEREST

Boblo Island ★★★

By boat only, from docks at Detroit, Amherstburg (Canada), or Gibralter. Detroit dock is at the foot of Clark St., just south of Fort and the I-75 Clark St. exit. Gibralter dock is just north of the foot of Gibralter Rd. east of Jefferson and about a mile east of I-75 exit 29A (Gibralter Rd.). Amherstburg dock is at Front Rd. and Simcoe St., 16.5 miles south of Windsor.
Park open *mid May-Labor Day. 11 a.m. until 5:30 (week–days through mid-June); until 8:30 weekends through mid-June, weekdays thereafter; until 10:30 summer weekends.*
For departure times, *call (313) 843-0700.* **Cost**, *including boat trip from Detroit or Gibralter and all rides and shows: $15.95 ($9.95 after 3 p.m.) for ages 7-50, $13.95 for 51 and over, and $9.95 (ages 3-6).* **Moonlight** **cruises** *from Detroit dock: 11-1 Fri & Sat, plus Sun on Mem. & Labor Day weekends, $10.95.*

A trip to Boblo Island makes for a splendid outing. The boat ride between Detroit and the island is an exceptional treat by itself. And the amusement park, dating back to 1898, has enough amusing spectacles to entertain adults as well as children.

By far the best boat ride is on the big, old original Boblo steamers from the Detroit dock. The oldest is the SS *Columbia*, built in 1902. It carries 2,500 passengers and weighs 969 tons. Both the *Columbia* and the *Ste. Claire* offer game rooms for kids, concession stands, and superb river views from the top deck. The scenery is also a lot more interesting when you leave from Detroit. You get a great view of the Ambassador Bridge and downtown Detroit. As you sail downriver, the one-hour ten-minute trip takes you by the once bustling and now mostly quiet Detroit freighter dock area. You pass river traffic, big

The scenic 70-minute boat ride to Boblo Island from the Detroit dock is a memorable experience in itself.

old steel mills, chemical factories, Zug Island, Grosse Ile, impressive riverfront estates, Amherstburg, and the open expanse of Lake Erie. As long as you're not being lashed by a chilly wind, it's an exhilarating outing.

Boblo Island is in the Canadian half of the Detroit River. Its name is a confused English pronunciation of the original French "Bois Blanc," which refers to the white poplar trees on the 272-acre island. The island was militarily strategic because it faced out toward the opening of Lake Erie. You can still see a blockhouse built by the British in 1837, and the first lighthouse built on the Great Lakes. The great Indian chief Tecumseh held a war council on Boblo during the War of 1812.

Though Boblo rides don't compare with Cedar Point in Sandusky, Ohio, there are enough here to amuse all but the most demanding thrill-seekers. Over 75 rides include all the stock classics: the **octopus, tilt-a-whirl, corkscrew roller coaster, falling star, dodge 'em** car rides, and **log flume.** The **Ferris wheel** and **sky tower** offer fine views of the surroundings. The colorfully restored turn-of-the-century **carousel** is complete with twirling mirrors and a band organ. The two-mile **train ride** around the island was marred on our visit by a loud but inaudible PA system used by a bored guide. Smaller kids seem to greatly enjoy **Fort Fun,** complete with ball crawl, rope climb, punching bag forest, and other exhausting activities.

The new Nightmare **enclosed roller coaster** is a 90-second ride in the dark, punctuated by special sound effects and lighting. It's the centerpiece of the **International Pavilion** (built as the dance pavilion in 1913, recently renovated for $1.9 million), with food booths, shops, and an arcade. Admission to Boblo also covers several shows, including animated singing characters and waterskiing.

The grounds here are very well maintained. Over $15 million in improvements were made to the landmark amusement park during AAA Michigan's 5-year tenure, including expansion of the marina to 131 slips. Boblo is now owned by International Broadcasting Corporation. Ride attendants are for the most part sullen teenagers. Food ranges from the very bad to the uninspired; you might want to take along a picnic lunch.

Ambassador Bridge/ Riverside Park

Bridge entrance at 21st and Porter Streets. Fare: $1.25 per car (one way). Park is on Jefferson at the foot of West Grand, 1 block south of Fort.

At the time it was completed in 1929, this 1.8-mile-long bridge between Detroit and Windsor was the world's longest suspension bridge. The two steel towers holding the central 1,850-foot span are 363 feet high.

Boblo tips: don't visit windy Boblo on a cool day. Try to arrange your visit for a weekday: weekends and holidays you'll wait too long for the rides.

You used to be able to walk across the bridge, and a magnificent walk it was. Because of prolonged construction, the pedestrian walkway is now closed, and it is unclear when (if ever) it will reopen.

Detroit is an eagerly-awaited port for most Great Lakes sailors, for it is the only place in the world where ships in motion regularly receive deliveries of mail, passengers, machine parts, laundry, cigarettes, snacks, and such. The service is provided by the S.W. Westcott Company. Its little 45-foot boat pulls up beside each passing freighter, looking alarmingly fragile next to the giant it is servicing. The freighter's crew drops down a line with a bucket at its end to receive shipments. Mail going to these passing freighters even has a special zip code, 48222. The best place to see this interesting spectacle is at **Riverside Park.** To find out if a freighter is com-

If you're lucky, you can see a freighter being unloaded from one of the marine terminals near Riverside Park. The overseas traffic they handle has diminished since the busy 1960s. Today they chiefly export steel from nearby McLouth, Great Lakes, and Rouge Steel. They import blast furnace coke for them, plus steel and heavy equipment.

ing anytime soon, you can call the Westcott Company at (313) 496-0555.

Historic Fort Wayne ★★

*6325 W. Jefferson at Livernois. (313) 297-9360. Adults $1; children and seniors 50¢. Season: first week in May through Labor Day. Wed-Sun 9:30-5. Tours of the **National Museum of the Tuskegee Airmen** and the **Great Lakes Indian Museum** can be arranged throughout the year by calling (313) 297-9360.*

This old U.S. Army fort, now a Detroit museum, has been connected with a good deal of important U.S. military history. Though it was built in the 1840s and 1850s, its design was based on principles of warfare developed in the 17th century, and the fort is closer to a medieval fortress than a 20th-century military base. It's a reminder of how rapidly warfare has changed in the past century compared with the previous six centuries.

Like a castle, Fort Wayne depends on an encircling moat, thick walls,

> **Special events at Historic Fort Wayne** include informal weekend concerts and events. Major events are **Civil War Day** (first weekend in May), in which hundreds of people depict life at the fort during the Civil War and demonstrate tactical weapons; **Fort Night** (same night as the big Detroit River fireworks display at the pre-July 4 International Freedom Festival), with patriotic band music and viewing of the downtown fireworks spectacle; **Highland Games** (first weekend in August), bagpipe bands and athletics sponsored by Detroit's St. Andrew's Society in the oldest big continuous Highland games in North America; and a large **antique car show** (May).

and heavy studded doors to repel attacks. Its odd quasi-star shape allows cannon firing grapeshot out of embrasures to repel attackers who approach the 22-foot-high outer wall.

Fort Wayne also hearkens back to the time when the U.S. was still in conflict with Great Britain. Situated on a narrow bend in the Detroit River three miles south of downtown, its purpose was to stop enemy vessels from heading up the river to attack Detroit. Cannons firing 64-pound balls were to be placed on a V-shaped promontory overlooking the river to sink enemy ships that dared to pass. The fort was one of a network of 14 northern defense posts planned in 1840, stretching from Lake Superior to Maine.

In fact, Fort Wayne never was involved in a conflict, or even armed. By the time it was finished, a British attack from Canada was no longer a threat. The fort garrisoned infantry regiments over the decades, was a training ground for Michigan Civil War soldiers, and served as a parts depot during World War II. All its varied uses led to additions and modifications. But since the Army declared the fort surplus property and gave it to the city of Detroit, it has been stripped down to look much as it did in the mid-19th century.

Visitors can explore the tunnels within the outer walls and walk through the handsome three-and-a half-story barracks near the fort's center. Where possible, living history is told by costumed "residents" of the historic fort, and cannons are fired twice a day. (Call for times.) The fort's first two floors house exhibits telling the story of Detroit's military history, from the coming of the French in 1701 through the Indian Wars of the 1890s, fought in part by Michigan's famous Seventh Cavalry. Uniforms, firearms,

Star-shaped Fort Wayne, built in the 1850s, is closer in design to a medieval fortress than a modern military facility. It was never attacked, but a realistic battle is staged on Civil War Day in May. A museum of Detroit military history is in its old stone barracks. Officers' Row is outside the fort to the right.

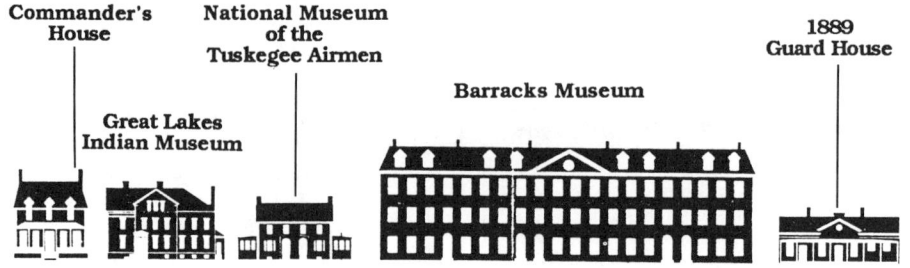

Historic Fort Wayne also includes interesting small museums and restored accessory buildings.

and swords from various eras can be seen. One room reconstructs a Civil War barracks.

Smaller museums are housed in the separate buildings of officers' row, outside the old star fort. The **commanding officer's house** has been restored to an authentically furnished 1880 Victorian residence. In the **guard house** and prison, furnished as it was during the Spanish-American War in 1898, a costumed soldier talks about his life as a guard.

National Museum of the Tuskegee Airmen ★★

Part of Historic Fort Wayne. Same hours and fees. Also open by special appointment, often guided by an Airman. Call (313) 297-9360.

Here is told the story of the struggle of African-Americans to achieve equality in their country's armed forces during World War II. In the navy, for instance, blacks were relegated to jobs as stewards and cooks. The 20,000 Airmen were an all-black Air Force unit, formed in 1940-41 at the instigation of civil rights leaders, and stationed in Tuskegee, Alabama. In the North African and Italian campaigns, the Airmen proved their skill as flyers, mechanics, and bombardiers to doubting Air Force brass.

Of the many nationwide Airmen veterans' groups, the Detroit chapter took the lead in raising $280,000 for this first-rate small museum. It helped that the city of Detroit owns Historic Fort Wayne and that Mayor Young was an Airman himself.

Great Lakes Indian Museum ★★

Part of Historic Fort Wayne. Same hours and fees. Also open by appointment for groups. (313) 297-9360.

This informative museum gives an especially sympathetic view of how white invaders repeatedly betrayed Indians. It has one of the finest collections of Woodland Indian artifacts in the U.S., including beautiful quillwork, beaded moccasins and ceremonial clothing, and early trade goods.

Tiger Stadium ★★★

Michigan Ave. at Trumbull, one mile west of downtown Detroit. Call (313) 962-4000 for schedule and ticket reservations.

This grand old ball park is a scruffy, glorious representative of that endangered species. It ranks right up with Wrigley Field and Fenway Park. On a Smithsonian-sponsored tour of the Midwest's four old parks, the *Wall Street Journal* reported, "tour members who were ready to sacrifice Comiskey [Park] as a crumbling relic [were] eager to fight for Tiger Stadium, offering moral and financial support" to the Tiger Stadium Fan Club. The exploits of Tigers past — Ty Cobb, Charlie Gehringer, Mickey Cochran, Al Kaline, and the ecstatic World Series victory in 1968, the year after the riots — not to mention Lou Gehrig's last game and Reggie Jackson's 1971 All-Star home run onto the upper-deck roof — all these resonate in the minds of knowledgeable visitors to the venerable park, where the cast-iron supports of the old seats were embellished with tiger heads.

Tiger Stadium has several hundred seats behind pillars, and more cheap seats than any other ball park. That jeopardizes it in the new economics of baseball. "With player payrolls soaring and cities bidding wildly for scarce professional sports franchises, team owners have both the need and the leverage to get new, publicly financed facilities stuffed with revenue-producing luxury skyboxes and premium-priced box seats," states the *Journal*. The city of Detroit owns Tiger Stadium, and its emperor mayor, Coleman Young, has long campaigned for a domed stadium to show Detroit really is a big-league city. Pizza baron Tom Monaghan, who owns the Tigers, wants an open-air design. But only 16 percent of the fans in a *Detroit News* poll wanted a new ball park at all — another instance of how Monaghan has ended up upsetting huge segments of the area's pizza-buying public. Alternative plans for a new stadium were unveiled shortly after Tiger Stadium was placed on the National Register of Historic Places. In response, the Tiger Stadium Fan Club organized a giant hug-in, in which they linked arms, surrounded the old ball park, and hugged it.

The Tigers were already playing at this site (then called Bennett Park, capacity 8,500) when a 23,000-fan steel and concrete stadium was built in 1912, the core of today's Tiger Stadium. In 1924 double decks were constructed from first to third base. They extend all the way out over the lower deck, providing some of baseball's best upper-level seats, right on top of the action. In 1936 more double decks in the right field pavilion and bleachers were added, and still more seats in 1938, bringing the capacity to 53,000. The stadium was then renamed Briggs Stadium, after Tiger owner (and auto body maker) Walter Briggs. Lights were installed in 1948, and the place renamed Tiger Stadium in 1961.

With this beloved anachronism in jeopardy, don't miss a chance to watch a game when you're in town.

Corktown

South of Michigan Avenue between 6th and 14th streets, extending south to Porter and the train tracks.

Corktown residents like to promote it as Detroit's oldest extant neighborhood. It dates to the 1830s, when Irish immigrants from County Cork were first able to move out of rented housing downtown and build their own homes here, on the subdivided back lots of three old French ribbon farms.

The frame cottages, townhouses, and Queen Anne houses were built by Corktown's founding Irish working-class residents between the 1830s and about 1900. Today they are in varying stages of repair and renovation. Exteriors are often the last to be finished. Historic houses alternate with new subsidized townhouses and vacant land created by urban renewal. Renovation jobs are showcased on a homes tour the weekend after Mother's Day; for particulars, call the Corktown Citizens' District Council at (313) 962-5660.

To get to Leverette, Corktown's show street, turn south off Michigan onto 11th Street. Corktown isn't architecturally impressive by the standards of sleepy, intact small towns in Michigan, but Corktown makes it up with diversity and spirit.

Holy Trinity Church on Porter at 6th Street, where the 10:30 Mass is in Spanish, still has a special status among the Irish, who return on St. Patrick's Day. Holy Trinity, founded by the Irish in 1834, was Detroit's first English-speaking parish. Today the interior of the later brick Gothic Revival church has been beautifully restored, with a plaza that's a neighborhood focus. Ask at the church office to see inside.

Mexican Town

On and off of Bagley, half a mile or so southwest of Tiger Stadium.

I-75 splits the Hispanic business district on Bagley; you have to cross over it on Vernor, a block north. West of the freeway you'll find most of the popular restaurants and an interesting Mexican import shop. A wide selection of Mexican groceries and beers is at **La Colmena** (the Honey Bee) grocery to the east, on 2443 Bagley at 17th. It stays open until 8,.

Though the restaurants attract people from all over, this is no Greektown geared mainly to visitors. Businesses here and on Vernor between Grand River and Livernois serve Detroit's sizable Hispanic population — at least 30,000 in 1980.

Michigan Gallery

2661 Michigan Ave. at 20th St, 1 mile west of Tiger Stadium. Park on the street; look for entrance door with bronze relief and white sign, and buzz. Tues-Sat 11-5, Fri until 8. Call first (313) 961-7867 for special events or to see if a show is up.

Detroit's biggest artist-run alternative arts space is in this 5,400-square-foot former garage. Each year it sponsors 24 exhibitions, 6 to 10 artist-run workshops, life drawing sessions, lectures, film festivals, concerts, and more. This programming is designed to foster "constructive and creative interaction" between and among professional and amateur artists and the public. Detroit art patrons may lack the confidence to get behind their own artists before they've made it somewhere else, but the city and its attendant struggles foster camaraderie among artists.

RESTAURANTS

Maxie's Leftfield Deli ★★

1266 Michigan (north side of street) at Brooklyn, 2 blocks east of Tiger Stadium. In a white diner whose sign reads "Corktown Deli & Chowder House" and not "Leftfield Deli." (313) 961-7968. Mon-Sat 7:30-3. No alcohol or credit cards.

Presided over by gregarious Maxie Silk since 1968, this unpretentious joint is a joy to visit. The loyal clientele, from all parts of society, is like an extended family, and Maxie himself, a former boxer and bar owner friend and admirer of the late Father Kern, has had his philanthropic career described in *U.S. News and World Report*. In addition to lending a sympathetic ear to all his customers, he funds a school for poor children.

Maxie's soups are famous — six kinds each day, from black bean to chicken noodle. One connoisseur considers his wild omelets (made with onions, peppers, pastrami, corned beef, and the like) the best in town. The corned beef sandwich ($3) is delicious. A Friday favorite here is seafood chowder, thick with shrimp, crab, and clams ($2.50). On Wednesdays the grated potato pancakes with sour cream and applesauce are also popular ($2.50).

Xochimilco ★★

3409 Bagley at 23rd St., just west of I-75. From I-75, take exit 47B.(313) 843-0179. From Tiger Stadium/ downtown, take Vernor across I-75, turn left onto 23rd. Daily 11 a.m.-4 a.m. Full bar. AmExpress, Visa, MasterCard. Entrees: $3.75-$8.75.

Of the half-dozen Mexican Town restaurants near Bagley and 23rd, this and the similar but somewhat slicker El Zocalo across the street are the most highly regarded. Evenings there are often lines, so it's a good idea to call for a reservation. The standard Mexican fare of enchiladas, tostadas, and burritos are better than what you'll find in the typical Mexican restaurant up North. The guacamole is excellent. One favorite is the botana: corn chips with refried beans, tomatoes, and chorizo (Mexican sausage).

Al's Lounge ★

7940 South at West End, 2 blocks south of Fort St. near the Detroit Union Produce Terminal and 5 blocks north of West Jefferson. 3/4 mile west of Historic Fort Wayne. West End is the southerly extension of Springwells. From nearby I-75, take Springwells exit. Lighted, guarded parking. (313) 841-5677. Mon-Fri 11-9, Sat 3-9, Sun noon-9. Full bar. No credit cards.

"We're quite quaint," says a staffer at this Hungarian restaurant that's one of the only vital remnants of the once-bustling immigrant community of Delray. "All our cooking, including our homemade [noodle-like] dumplings and our cabbage rolls, is done by little ladies back in the kitchen." The juke box plays some Hungarian music. Outsiders are often charmed by this unpretentious spot, run by the family of Al Kazensky for the past five decades. It exists in a strange time warp here among the pheasants and chemical pollution from infamous Zug Island a scant quarter mile away. Pheasants, along with tumbleweed, flourish in overgrown vacant lots near the century-old brick and aluminum-sided building. They have come to symbolize ultimate urban decay. These pheasants are helped along by the friendly folks at nearby Historic Fort Wayne, who feed them.

Chicken paprikash with dumplings in sour cream gravy ($6 at lunch and dinner) is the star of Al's menu, which also features cabbage rolls ($5.50), roast beef and pork, beef stew, shrimp, frog legs, and blackboard specials of the day like Monday's hot chicken sandwich. Meals include starch, vegetable, and salad.

After dinner, outsiders are often dazzled by the dramatic riverfront sights: the twinkling lights on the downriver chemical factories, and the backlit smoke billowing from big stacks of Allied Chemical, Detroit Coke, and Great Lakes Steel on Zug Island. It's easy to see why this is the most polluted part of metro Detroit.

Giovanni's

330 S. Oakwood just west of Fort, in extreme southwest Detroit just south of the Ford Rouge in Dearborn. Take Springwells exit from I-75 heading south, Oakwood exit from I-94 heading east. Mon 11-3, Tues-Thurs 11-10, Fri 11-11, Sat 4-11. Full bar, good Italian wine list. Major credit cards. Sandwiches $3.95-$4.95, lunches $5.95-$7.95, dinner $8.95-$13.95.

This exceptional home-style Italian restaurant makes its own pasta. Its Cappelletti Verde Pesto (spinach raviolis filled with beef or veal and cheese, $10.50) are famous. Thin pizza with white cheese ($1.50 a person) is also popular. For vegetarians, the sauteed strips of zucchini and sweet onions over spinach fettucine ($10.95) is a hit.

Cultural Center

Detroit's cultural center is anchored by those grand marble palaces of culture that face each other across Woodward: the renowned Detroit Institute of Arts (DIA) and the great Detroit Public Library. A block west on Cass begins the campus of Wayne State University, one of the nation's leading big-city public research universities. Surrounding this core, in addition to numerous educational and cultural institutions, is an odd assortment of testimonials to different stages of the city's history: splendid mansions and churches from the 1880s and 1890s, stylish early 20th-century apartment buildings, and more recently, cleared land and crumbling neighborhoods, gas stations and fast food franchises — a most undignified development for stately Woodward.

As a whole, the Cultural Center area is full of the jarring juxtapositions of present-day American cities: beauty and ugliness, order and disorder. It's stimulating if you know your way around, but not conventionally pretty at all. So suburbanites tend to zip in and out of the DIA's handy garage and ignore the rest. It's easy to miss the surprising beauty of Wayne State's sculpture-studded interior malls, or the charming, cobblestone-paved block of Canfield between Second and Third, with its restored houses from the 1870s.

Briefly an elite neighborhood

In the 1880s, Detroit's captains of industry first moved out here from downtown to build their very showy homes where the air was cleaner. The area was then so rural that the Ferry Seed Company's seed farms and test gardens covered vast tracts on East Ferry Street. The farm superintendent's 1885 Eastlake-style house at 612 East Ferry still stands, recently renovated.

The impressive churches of Detroit's elite still bear testimony to Woodward's past as a show street of imposing residences and churches. Every few blocks all the way to downtown they punctuate a bleak landscape of mostly decaying commercial buildings and cleared land.

By 1910, barely 10 years after some of Detroit's business leaders had built their homes here, most of them were moving on to new mansions even farther out — out Jefferson Avenue to Indian Village and even Grosse Pointe, and in greater numbers to new subdivisions out Woodward past Grand Boulevard.

Parking hints
The DIA's underground garage on Farnsworth (60¢/hour, $2 max.) or the Science Center lot on John R at Farnsworth ($1.25 all day) are probably your best bets for long-term parking in the area.
Parking is tight because of Wayne State. If you find on-street parking but let the meter expire, you're almost sure to get a ticket. Away from the campus/DIA area, on-street parking is plentiful, and you can drive from one place to another.

The monumental scale and compelling attractions of the fabulous Detroit Institute of Arts (right) can discourage people from exploring on foot the rest of the Cultural Center. For a refreshing walk, there's the bustling, attractive Wayne State campus off Cass, the magnificent mansions on Ferry Street, or the Center for Creative Studies' Sarkis Gallery in the Park-Shelton Apartments (left).

The auto boom was already making Detroit a goldmine for retailers as well, and Jewish businessmen built the next wave of fine homes here. In 1903 Temple Beth El had built what is now Wayne State's domed **Bonstelle Theater.** That 20th-century Roman Pantheon with Louis XVI embellishments is a mile southeast on Woodward south of Mack.

The City Beautiful movement in Detroit

Detroit in 1910 was caught up by the City Beautiful movement, inspired by Daniel Burnham's Great White City at the 1893 Chicago World's Fair. Detroit seemed destined to become a great city, and its leaders agreed the emerging Motor City deserved a more impressive look.

Edward Bennett, a Burnham associate, finished a Detroit city plan in 1915 which included a center of arts and letters out Woodward two miles from downtown. That year an important public competition to design a new library was won by Cass Gilbert, one of America's leading architects. The library, grand and massive, opened in 1921, followed by the even more impressive Detroit Institute of Arts in 1927. Built later than their counterparts in other American metropolises, they were also more splendid.

A region of myriad institutions

Agencies, fraternities, women's clubs, and private schools began occupying the big mansions in the 1920s, a use that still continues. At 217 Farnsworth, the **Scarab Club,** a group of artists, designed and built an unusual Arts and Crafts-style space for classes and exhibits. Then in 1927 the 14-story **Maccabees Building** (now the **Detroit Public Schools Administration Building**), designed by Albert Kahn, was completed at Woodward and Putnam, near the library.

Knights guard its entrance; stenciled beams and a vaulted mosaic ceiling decorate the lobby. The Depression soon curtailed further office towers here.

During the 1930s, The Lone Ranger and the Green Hornet radio programs were born in the WXYZ studio on the Maccabees Building's top floor. And in a basement laboratory at 67 East Kirby, now the **Children's Museum**, R. P. Scherer invented the machine for making the now ubiquitous soft gelatine capsules used by drug companies.

By the 1940s African-American professionals and entrepreneurs were occupying many old mansions in the neighborhood. East Ferry between Woodward and Brush was home to the Lewis Business School, the Omega Psi Phi Fraternity (still there), and several black-owned hospitals. Motown founder Berry Gordy grew up on Farnsworth, when it was one of Detroit's best addresses for middle-class black families. Restrictive real estate practices kept blacks east of Woodward until open housing in the 1960s.

Preservation Wayne, the city-wide historic preservation umbrella organization, has offices in the home of Wayne State's first president at Cass and Canfield. Stop by weekdays or call 577-3559 for a free brochure with an excellent architectural walking tour of the Cultural Center area and for information on other Detroit historic districts, homes tours, and activities.

POINTS OF INTEREST

Detroit Institute of Arts ★★★★

5200 Woodward between Kirby and Farnsworth. (313) 833-7900. Tues-Sun 9:30-5:30. Free; donations welcome. Occasional charge (typically $3) for special exhibitions. **Parking** *in a secure, lighted parking garage on Farnsworth: $2 maximum. Lighted surface Science Center lot at John R and Farnsworth, $1.25.* **Guided tours:** *Tues-Sat 12:15; Sun 1 & 2:30.*

Detroit is blessed with one of the world's great art museums, surpassed in this country only by four or five others. It is encyclopedic, giving the visitor a view of great art from Meso–potamian through modern eras. It may be the only major art museum that charges no admission.

Credit for the DIA's emergence as a great art museum goes to donations from auto magnates and to

Diego Rivera's famed Detroit industry murals (above), Van Gogh's self-portrait, and Breughel's Wedding Dance are among the DIA's many masterpieces.

the museum's outstanding former director, William Valentiner. A persuasive, knowledgeable German, Valentiner advised the Rockefellers and J. P. Morgan on the creation of the Museum of Modern Art. He came here to help plan the museum, which opened in 1917. With the often anonymous financial assistance of Edsel and Eleanor Ford, Valentiner was able to purchase many modern paintings at bargain prices. He acquired a van Gogh self-portrait, for example, for just $4,200. He established the first North American Indian art collection and acquired the first Matisse bought by an American museum.

The museum's very size presents the visitor with the problem of excess. You need to be careful not to become numbed by the thousands of pieces on display. This tendency is reinforced by the disorienting labyrinth of halls and corridors linking the original museum with additions. Refiguring the existing space is part of the planned massive $75 million renovation and expansion project, to be designed by Postmodern superstar architect Michael Graves.

One helpful antidote is a one-hour guided tour. (See above for times.) It gives a quick view of the highlights. Also helpful are the knowledgeable staff at the information desks. They will be happy to suggest a route based on your tastes and time.

The museum's greatest strengths are in American, Italian Renaissance, Dutch-Flemish, and German Expressionist art. While there are dozens of masterpieces throughout, the following are generally considered the museum's most important:

The Wedding Dance (Pieter Bruegel the Elder), ca. 1566. A colorful, realistic view of a peasant wedding.
Detroit Industry (Diego Rivera), 1932-33. An enormous series of frescoes focusing on the auto industry.
Cotopaxi (Frederic Church), 1862. A grand, mystical oil painting of an active volcano in the Andes.
Self Portrait (Vincent van Gogh), 1887. One of the great artist's sunnier self-portraits.
Reclining Figure (Henry Moore), 1939. A large sculpture in elm wood of a female.
Nail Figure (from the Western Kongo), ca. 1875-1900. A 46-inch wooden icon which served an African community's mystical needs.
Early Autumn (Qian Xuan), 13th or 14th century. A delicate handscroll in ink and color of insects in autumn.
Seated Bather (Pierre-Auguste Renoir), 1903-6. A sensuous, languid nude painted when the artist was in his sixties.
Saint Jerome in His Study (Jan van Eyck), ca. 1390-1441. A small, richly symbolic oil painting by the great Flemish painter.
The Visitation (Rembrandt), 1640. A dramatic presentation of the Biblical scene in which Mary and Elizabeth encounter God.
Gudea of Lagash (Mesopotamian), ca. 2141-2122 B.C. A superb stone sculpture of the ruler of a city-state.

Of course, many other important works are worth mentioning— major

---

Film, poetry, children's theater at the DIA

The Detroit Film Theater. Popular film series showing high-caliber films (seldom-seen ones Fri, classics Sat, special series Sun) under technically excellent conditions in a plush auditorium. $3/ticket. Reservations advised. Usually 7 and 9:30. Info line (313) 832-7676. Call 832-2730 to get a schedule. Shown in the auditorium off John R. Lighted, guarded parking across the street.
Afternoon Film Theater. Odd and interesting films shown at 1 p.m. Tues-Sun. $1.25. (313) 832-2730.
Lines: New Writing. George Tysh's poetry series brings in "all kinds of on-the-edge contemporary poets of international status," says a savvy fan. (313) 832-2731.
Detroit Youtheatre. Interesting range of high-caliber dramatic and musical performances for children of different ages. $4 admission is a deal. Oct.-May. Call for (313) 832-2731 for schedule.

pieces by Whistler, Picasso, Miro, Kokoschka, Gauguin, Seurat, Degas, Cezanne, and Matisse, among others.

Don't miss the striking **Kresge Court** (Tues-Sat 11-4, Sun 1-4). It's a vast, open dining area inspired in part by the courtyard of the Bargello Palace in Florence. Here you can eat cafeteria- style, sip coffee, or drink beer and wine. There is also a popular sit-down restaurant with full bar and nouvelle cuisine, **La Palette** (11:30-2, reservations recommended).

The **museum shop** by the Farnsworth entrance (10:30-5) carries a sophisticated selection of art books, cards, reproductions, jewelry, and gift items, but is weak on inexpensive things that appeal to kids.

Museum of African-American History

301 Frederick Douglass between John R and Brush. From Woodward, take Kirby to John R, turn right, then left. (313) 833-9800. Wed-Sat 9:30-5; Sun 1-5. Free.

The self-proclaimed mission of this handsome museum is "the documentation and education of the general population on the life, history and culture of Africans and African-Americans and their struggle for freedom and dignity." The museum itself, however, is more of a plodding and superficial march through African-American history than the insightful and moving illumination one would hope for.

To be sure, there's a lot of history here, from pre-slavery life in African villages through the Underground Railroad. But little is presented in a way that would rival in impact a really good book or article on the topic. Even the museum's most dramatic display, a full-scale mock-up of part of a slave ship below deck, complete with sound effects, is curiously unable to convey how atrocious conditions were on these horrific journeys. This is an expensively furnished museum, but it lacks so far the guiding intelligence to make it a really fine one.

Detroit Science Center

5020 John R. (313) 577-8400. Mon & Tues 9-6; Wed-Sat 9-9; Sun 10-7. Adults $5. age 6-18 $4; 5 & under $2.

Housed in a impressive-looking brick building, this hands-on museum fails to deliver inside what its exterior promises. On display in one big space are the items now familiar in hands-on museums: computer games, a giant soap bubble device, anatonomical displays, geological formations, fossils, etc.

On our visit, many of the most interesting-looking displays, such as a fiber optics demonstration and a natural gas exploration game, didn't work. What's here now is definitely minor-league.

The big draw is the **Omni-Max Theater**, a huge tilted screen which conveys a sense of motion in specially filmed movies. Science-related films are shown every hour on the half hour from 10:30 until 3:30.

International Institute

111 E. Kirby at John R. 871-8600.

This United Foundation agency, founded in 1919 by workers at the YWCA, still welcomes new immigrants to metro Detroit, providing English-language and citizenship classes and counseling. The volunteer shops are a good place to find gifts that help support its worthy cause. The basement **Melting Pot Cafe** (Mon-Fri 11-2), a lunch counter appealingly decorated in international folk art motifs, is a handy alternative to the DIA's often overcrowded eating facilities.

The ground-floor **gift shop** (Mon-Fri 11-3) offers good values on imported gifts and cards from around the world: Indonesian masks, Central American worry people, jewelry, and lots of appealing trinkets for kids. The **UNICEF Shop** in the basement

(Mon-Fri 10-4) carries a full line of the popular cards, calendars, and gift items, including puzzles, popup books, *Games of the World: How to Make Them and Play Them*, and *The Little Cooks* ($11), a wonderful wipe-off children's cookbook with mainstream international recipes.

Center for Creative Studies/ Sarkis Gallery

Park Shelton Apartments, Woodward and Kirby. (313) 872-3118. Mon-Fri 9-4, Sat 11-3.

With almost one thousand degree-seeking students, the Center for Creative Studies' College of Art and Design is one of the seven largest undergraduate professional schools of art and design in the U.S. It was founded in 1906 by the Detroit Society of Arts and Crafts, devoted to promoting good design and handcraftsmanship. Ironically, the Center owes much of its growth to the needs of the local auto industry for auto and advertising design. Detroit has the nation's third-largest concentration of advertising agencies, which employ over 3,000.

The CCS gallery, which shows faculty and alumni work, has recently been moved to a much larger space in the Park Shelton Apartments at Woodward and Kirby.

Detroit Historical Museum ★★

5401 Woodward at Kirby (across from Detroit Institute of Arts). Park behind museum off Kirby. (313) 833-1805. Wed-Sun 9:30-5. Admission free, donation requested

Detroit has had an especially rich, eventful history. It was founded in 1701 and ruled by France and then England before joining the U.S. in 1796. This museum captures some of that history quite well.

In the Round Hall near the entry is

Great old churches
anchor many of Detroit's major boulevards, especially Woodward and Jefferson. Today they are often flanked by gas stations and fast-food outlets, but when they were built, the city's finest homes were their neighbors.

Above left, the **Cathedral Church of St. Paul** (1911), 4800 Woodward at Warren, the mother church for the Episcopal Diocese of Michigan, was designed by the famous Gothic Revivalist Ralph Adams Cram. Above right, the **First Congregational Church** (1891) at Woodward and Forest, a rich blend of Romanesque Revival and Byzantine details in red sandstone. Below, the **Fort Street Presbyterian Church** (1855), right downtown at Fort and Third. It is widely admired for its lacy stone Gothic details and graceful silhouette.

a 15-foot-high carved mahogany clock, built between 1892 and 1904. At noon a procession of figures from around the world marches in native costume around a globe while a music box plays.

On the main floor behind the gift shop is a vast display, **From Outpost to Industry. Detroit: The Early Years: 1701-1900.** Under a long chronological band beginning with 1701 are historical artifacts to match the dates. The items aren't terribly interesting, and the explanatory placards aren't especially illuminating. One important point the chronology ignores is just how small Detroit was for over two centuries.

> **The Detroit Historical Society**, headquartered here, sponsors **tours of historic churches** (first Monday of each month) and **Sunday strolls** through historic areas (every other week). Send a stamped, self-addressed envelope for a schedule.

However, this exhibit is being upgraded and will eventually become part of a new permanent exhibit, "Motor City," to open in 1992-3.

A real highlight is **The Streets of Detroit** in the basement. It's a three-quarters-scale, realistic nighttime recreation of Detroit commercial streetfronts in the 1840s, 1870s, and at the turn of the century. Along cobblestone and then brick streets you walk by banks, a printing shop, a drug store, a bicycle shop, and a grocery store, among others. The darkened ambience makes the settings seem lifelike. It's a rich step back into the past, no doubt magical for many children. The idea came from the York Castle Museum in England. Though most of the shops, especially those from the 1840s, are imaginative recreations, the dime store and pharmacy are fairly accurate portrayals of actual Detroit businesses. Particularly wonderful is the old Kresge & Wilson Big 5 and 10¢ Store, which once occupied the spot where the National Bank of Detroit now stands across from Kennedy Square. "Nothing over 10¢ in this store" was its motto. S.S. Kresge went on to establish dime stores across the nation, building the giant company which evolved into today's K Mart Corporation, now headquartered in nearby Troy.

Behind the Streets of Detroit is the new **National Toy Gallery**, with changing exhibits from one of the world's largest collections of toys, including the notable Glancy Trains.

On the museum's second floor is a gallery with changing fasion exhibits and a fashion library for historical research.

The attractive first-floor gift shop features a wide assortment of antique reproductions, posters of Detroit scenes, books, toys, and souvenirs.

Detroit Public Library ★

5201 Woodward between Kirby and Putnam. (313) 833-1000. Mon-Sat 9:30-5:30, Wed 9-9.

A few years ago, this fabulous library (1,637,000 volumes) was making headlines with budget cutbacks and curtailment of new book purchases. Now it receives part of the state's support for the Cultural Center, and any Michigan resident can use its remarkable reference collections and services. You can also stop and listen to records in the Music and Performing Arts Department.

The Burton Historical Collection (Detroit history; open regularly) and **National Auto History Collection** (Tues, Thurs-Sat 1-5, Wed 5-9) are tops of their kind.

The 1921 building itself is one of those grand cultural monuments based on the Italian Renaissance and designed to impress with the seriousness of its mission. The noted architect Cass Gilbert based it on the Boston Public Library, designed by his famous ex-employers McKim Mead & White. But he gussied up the interior with more ornate 16th-century decorations in the style of Brunelleschi. There are coffered ceilings, murals in the grand staircase resembling Raphael's arabesques in the Vatican, and the obligatory portraits of great artists, musicians, and writers on the walls. Most interesting to Detroiters are the romantic historical scenes of early Detroit in the vaulted, second-floor **Adam Strohm Hall**, painted by Gari Melchers, the city's most renowned artist of the day. Changing exhibits of old photographs and topics from baseball to travel are mounted here.

Wayne State University ★★
Along Cass north of Warren; exit I-94 at John R.

The sprawling, 185-acre central campus of this important urban research university lies behind the Detroit Public Library on Woodward and stretches all the way from Cass on the east to the Lodge Freeway on the west, from the Ford Freeway on the north to Forest to the south. As the neighborhoods and business districts around it deteriorated during the past quarter century, there was talk of walling off the university. Instead, Wayne State has admirably positioned itself to be an integral part of the city. The pedestrian-oriented part of the campus, separated from the street, is a surprisingly stimulating, pleasant place to visit.

Wayne State started as a collection of five existing colleges — education, medicine, law, pharmacy, and liberal arts. In 1933 they joined to form Wayne University. It remained governed by the city's Board of Education until the state assumed control in 1959 with the new name of Wayne State University. (**Old Main,** the 1896 Romanesque Revival pile on Cass and Warren, is Detroit's old Central High.) Thanks to its meteoric rise after World War II, Wayne is now the third most prominent Michigan university, behind Michigan and Michigan State, but with a distinctively urban mission. Faculty research is frequently geared to Detroit industries and social problems. Programs endowed by local ethnics teach some unusual subjects — Armenian studies, for instance, and modern Greek.

"Wayne started out as a community ed project. It still is, and that's what's good about it," says one faculty member. He likes teaching students who work and who are usually the first generation in their families to go to college. "This is a place where you can't be a professor, because nobody knows the role. Students aren't sequestered in dorms. A lot of reality-

> **Events and exhibits at Wayne State**
> For information on today's events, call (313) 577-5345. For upcoming events, contact sponsoring departments:
> Theater (577-2972), Art (577-2980), and Music (577-1795).
> **Theater:** At the **Hilberry Theater** (in the former Christian Science Church at Cass and Hancock), graduate student actors, including some returning Equity actors, perform in a revolving 2- or 3-play repertory. It's much more polished than most college theater. Undergraduate productions are at the **Bonstelle Theater,** Woodward and Mack. Ask about nearby lighted, guarded parking; also about the highly regarded **Black Theater Program, Movin' Theater** (dance history), and varying summer programs. Season: Oct.-May, Thurs Fri, & Sat. Phone (313) 577-1795.

testing goes on here." Alum Lily Tomlin, who first won attention in Wayne theater productions when she studied pre-med here, is a generous supporter.

Almost 90 per cent of the 30,000 students here come from the metropolitan area. Wayne State encourages those in the Detroit area who might not ordinarily be able to go to college, providing them an extraordinary opportunity to attend a major university. About 94 per cent of the students commute, and only a tiny proportion live in dorms. Three out of four work full- or part-time. Twenty-four per cent of its students are African-Americans, the highest proportion of any major university in the country. Arab-Americans and Asians also attend in considerable numbers.

Under President David Adamany, Wayne State's financial situation has improved, new buildings have sprung up, and research funding has skyrocketed. But his tough leadership has had a cost: a large percentage of the faculty dislike his dictatorial style. A chief criticism is that he budgets too much for the physical plant and too little for students and instruction. On the other hand, one faculty member points out, "Today

In 1946, Walter Reuther and his supporters were jubilant when he beat out the communist candidate and was first elected president of the United Auto Workers. This photo is part of the world's biggest collection of labor history materials in Wayne State's Walter Reuther Library.

the campus looks good. When Adamany came here, it looked like a toilet, a dump — very depressing. He inherited a bankrupt university and balanced the books, built a good relationship with the governor, took a piece of the pie from Michigan State and the U. of M."

Notable facts about Wayne State:
◆ Its Hilberry Theatre program has the country's only graduate repertory company.
◆ It has one of the country's best nursing colleges.
◆ Its men's glee club, featured in a Wall Street Journal article, is one of the very finest in the country.
◆ Its engineering college is particularly strong in combustion engines research.
◆ Two-thirds of Wayne State students are undergraduates, with the largest number taking degrees in business and management (15%) and the health professions (13%).
◆ The big medical campus, southeast of the main campus across Woodward at Canfield and Brush, is the largest single-campus medical school in the U.S.

Campus highlights include:

Gullen Mall
Enter from any open space along Cass. The mall, formerly Second Avenue, parallels Cass. The walk from the Walter Reuther Library to the Art Building and Student Center

Detroit: Cultural Center

is especially nice.

The pedestrian-oriented interior of Wayne's campus is a lushly planted oasis, liberally accented with sculptures. It's a tribute to the success of an intelligently planned and planted "superblock" with buildings grouped around interconnected courts. The campus consists mainly of well-designed, contemporary buildings no higher than four stories, and quite plain except for the highly regarded **McGregor Conference Center** by noted architect Minoru Yamasaki, with its signature zigzag roof of prestressed concrete and reflecting pool. (It's behind the Arts Building, facing what was Ferry Street.) Occasional leftover mansions are incorporated into the scheme with good results. "In the superblock there will be no autos, no city traffic and confusion," proclaimed Yamasaki, who planned much of the campus. "A walk from one building to another will be a series of delightful surprises. Each court will be different,— one paved, one grassy, one with a fountain and statues, another with trees." Today the superblock concept has been somewhat discredited, like its spiritual cousin, the downtown mall. But this well-executed campus shows how well it can work. Don't miss the striking view of the Fisher Building from Gullen Mall.

Community Arts Gallery
In the Art Building, facing Kirby Mall. (313) 577-2980. Mon-Fri 10-5.

Shows relating to Wayne State programs, mostly art, are mounted in this large, attractive exhibit space.

Student Center Building
Gullen Mall (Second Ave.) at what was Kirby. Limited weekend hours; closed weekends in summer.

The attractive eating area across from the fast-food outlets here is a great place to have a quick meal or snack and take in the diversity of Wayne's student body. You'll hear a lot of Arabic and Chinese as well as English. There's reasonably priced lasagna and pizza at **Little Caesar's,** pita sandwiches, soups, and salads at **Friar Tuck's,** burgers at **Burger King,** and ice cream at **Baskin Robbins.** Information about campus events is posted at the Student Resource and Info Center nearby.

Walter Reuther Library of Urban Affairs
Cass at Kirby. (313) 577-4024. Mon-Fri 9-5.

Changing exhibits about labor and labor history are mounted in the big first-floor **gallery** of this archive, the world's largest repository of labor records and publications. It was funded largely by the United Auto Workers to honor their late leader. Researchers come from all over the world to use the papers of the UAW, the United Farm Workers, AFSCME, CIO, IWW, Airline Pilots and Flight Attendants, Detroit Mayor Jerry Cavanaugh, and the United Fund.

Shopping and browsing

Campus Treasure Shop ★
5704 Cass at Palmer. (313) 646-9288 Open Wed only, 2:30-11 p.m. Ask about the warehouse and its hours.

Marguerite Hague started this eccentric shop of used paraphernalia to benefit Wayne State University's beautification fund. "GOOD THINGS ARE HAPPENING IN DETROIT" is Hague's motto. Much of the stuff for sale here comes from soon-to-be-demolished buildings which Hague has personally cleaned out. The university lets Hague use the shop rent-free, but last year utility and other costs put her over $6,000 in the hole, which she had to make up out of her own pocket. She has found her philanthropic enterprise rewarding, but many of her Birmingham friends think she's nuts to run such an arduous project.

The array of stuff in this cluttered storefront is hard to catalog, but it's all cheap. What's more, if you don't like the price, the clerk will quickly point out it's negotiable. Along with stacks of old magazines, there's quite a collection of salvaged hardware. Old glass doorknobs, for example, sell for $3 a set. Boxes in the basement are full of ancient nuts and bolts. Light fixtures, used clothes, books, flowerpots, old chopping boards, and picture frames are here in abundance, along with unexpected discoveries: a motorcycle helmet, old office equipment, a scribbled sign beneath a neat row of little bottles saying, "Bottles found in crawl area of centennial farm home."

Cass Corridor Food Co-op
4201 Cass at Willis. (313) 831-7452. Mon-Sat 11-6, Fri until 7, Sun 12-5.

Here's a good selection of unprocessed, chemical-free bulk foods and spices, dairy products, and the like — plus sandwiches and salads to take out — in an attractively folksy setting. The bulletin board is a good way to find out about local alternative culture events.

Willis Gallery
422 Willis just south of Cass. Ample on-street parking. (313) 567-0860. Wed-Sat noon-6. Call first to be sure a show is up.

This alternative, artist-run art space is funded by exhibitors and highlights work in the vein of the Cass Corridor artists who founded it in 1971: "raw, energetic, and concerned with the urban/ industrial environment," in the words of its directors. Today "it features works of emerging artists and is an appropriate setting for works that are experimental in nature."

Favor Ruhl
4863 Woodward at Warren. (313) 833-9616. Mon-Fri 8:30-6, Sat 9-5.

Detroit's biggest store for art and drafting supplies and furniture. Cash-and-carry discounts.

A sampling of historic mansions

For a free, illustrated guide to many more historic buildings in the Cultural Center, stop in at Preservation Wayne weekdays in the David Mackenzie House, 4735 Cass at Forest.

Smiley Bros. Music Co./ Col. Frank Hecker House. ★★
5510 Woodward at Ferry. (Louis Kamper, arch., with John and Arthur Scott; 1889).

An adaptation of an early French Renaissance chateau built by Frank Hecker. He made a fortune manufacturing freight cars — one of pre-automobile Detroit's big industries, along with stoves. Today its salons and ballroom, with embossed and gilded leather-covered walls, carved paneling, and stained glass windows, are piano and organ showrooms, open to the public.

Merrill-Palmer Institute/Charles Freer House ★★
71 E. Ferry. (Wilson Eyre, 1890).

In contrast to Hecker's unsophisticated love of display, his partner, Charles Freer, became one of America's most discriminating collectors. He helped plan this simple, rough-textured Shingle Style house, designed by a master of the style. It had a bare-walled viewing room rather than a cluttered gallery, so Freer could admire his carefully pruned collection of American and Oriental prints, paintings, and porcelains one at a time. In 1904 Freer purchased the celebrated Peacock Room, decorated by his friend James McNeill Whistler, and installed it in his remodeled stable here. Today it is the showpiece of the Smithsonian's Freer Gallery, which Freer established and endowed. Incidentally, Hecker and Freer were notorious for the low wages they paid their employees.

Your Heritage House/ William Jackson House
110 E. Ferry (1887). Mon-Fri 9:30-5, Sat 10-3. (313) 871-1667.

This part of East Ferry has one of Michigan's most outstanding remaining groups of opulent late Victorian homes. This Romanesque mansion was built for the president of the Michigan State Telephone Company. It's the home of a children's art and drama school whose international focus is based on an African perspective. There's a small gallery and doll exhibit. The mood here is wonderfully serene.

Charles Warren House/ Dunbar Hospital
580 Frederick (1892).

This Romanesque Revival home of the jewelry-store founder became, in 1916, the first home of Dunbar Hospital, Detroit's first nonprofit hospital. It was organized by black physicians who couldn't practice or get their patients in existing Detroit hospitals. It evolved into Southwest Detroit Hospital. The Detroit Medical Society is restoring the richly embellished house and installing the Dunbar Museum to show the history of medicine in Detroit's black community.

W.S.U. Development Offices/George Beecher House.
5575 Woodward at Ferry (H.J.M. Grylls, 1893).

Inside, the grand staircase is highlighted by a window from the Tiffany studios.

First Unitarian-Universalist Church Parish House/ Perry McAdow House
4605 Cass at Forest (John Scott; 1893).

McAdow struck it rich gold-mining in Montana, then built this eclectic, sandstone-trimmed brick mansion to establish himself and his wife in society. Today it houses church offices and the busy child care center next door. Both contribute much to the area, aesthetically and socially.

Preservation Wayne/ David Mackenzie House
4735 Cass near Canfield. (Malcomson & Higgenbotham, 1895).

When this Queen Anne home of Wayne State's founder and first dean was slated to be demolished in 1977, it sparked the formation of Preservation Wayne, Detroit's active preservation umbrella organization. Its offices are among those here today. Stop in weekdays for publications on upcoming neighborhood tours and

Canfield between Second and Third is paved with cobblestones and lined with restored brick houses like these, built in 1875 (left) and 1883 (right). West Canfield, in the core of the upper Cass Corridor's urban revival, became Detroit's first historic district in 1970.

activities. (313) 577-3559.

The Whitney/ David Whitney, Jr. House. ★★
221 Woodward at Canfield (Gordon Lloyd, 1894).

It took four years to finish this pink jasper mansion for lumber baron and developer David Whitney, Jr. Jasper is so hard it that it takes a great deal of time and patience to cut. When finished, the *Free Press* proclaimed this the "most pretentious modern home in the state." Architecture critic Hawkins Ferry says architect Lloyd misunderstood Romanesque Revival and made it too animated. Today The Whitney is a four-star restaurant, and "the carved woodwork, mosaic tile, marble and onyx fireplaces, stained glass windows, and original light fixtures, all in a remarkable state of preservation keep patron's necks craning," writes Molly Abraham in *Restaurants of Detroit*. It's expensive, but nobody minds if you just order an appetizer ($10) or dessert. See p. 102.

Orchestra Hall/ Detroit Symphony Orchestra ★★
3711 Woodward at Parsons. **Program and ticket information:** *(313) 567-1400. Main series ($16-$45) Thurs, Fri, & Sat evenings. Other series include occasional 10 a.m. Fri coffee concerts ($11-16); chamber concerts; Saturday Young People's Concerts ($9); Orchestra Hall Presentation series (classical recitals, dance, and jazz); Classical Roots series drawing on the African heritage of much American music.*

World-class artistically and seriously troubled financially: these same up-and-down themes are shared by the intertwined stories of the Detroit Symphony Orchestra and the acoustically extraordinary Orchestra Hall. After the auto boom was well underway, carmaker Horace

Orchestra Hall's outstanding acoustics, considered among the very best in the U.S., were a lucky fluke. Two Detroit Symphony Orchestra musicians led the successful drive to restore the hall and again make it the Symphony's home.

Dodge and lumberman William Murphy felt it was time Detroit had a great orchestra. As the DSO's first conductor they hired the then-renowned pianist Ossip Gabrilowitsch. Knowing how badly they wanted him, he pushed for a permanent home for the orchestra. To satisfy his demands, in the summer of 1919 the 2,500-seat hall was built in just four months and 23 days.

In designing the hall, Gabrilowitsch worked closely with architect C. Howard Crane. It was Crane's first big project, and it launched his career as a prolific designer of movie theaters — over 250 in all, including the Fox. The hall's brilliant acoustics are regarded as a lucky accident. Musicians put it in the top three or four U.S. performing spaces.

In 1939, the symphony left Orchestra Hall for larger quarters downtown. As the Paradise Theater from 1941 to 1951, the hall was a famous venue for the likes of Duke Ellington, Count Basie, and Charlie Parker.

The symphony itself eventually disbanded, to be brought back by Matilda Dodge Wilson. Eventually it settled in the Ford Auditorium on the riverfront, where the acoustics are only adequate at best. DSO musicians initiated the successful two-decade campaign to "Save Orchestra Hall." On bumper stickers the slogan appeared all over southeast Michigan.

Now the hall has been magnificently restored by a civic fundraising group separate from the DSO. Next to it, Orchestra Place is a handsomely landscaped plaza developed with city funds. Orchestra Hall is now on solid financial footing, while the financially shaky DSO itself is trying to increase its endowment and develop a bigger audience among people under 45 and Detroit's big population of middle-class blacks.

RESTAURANTS

The Gnome ★

4124 Woodward between Alexandrine and Willis. 1 block north of Orchestra Hall, 4 blocks south of DIA. (313) 833-0120. Sun-Thurs 11-10:30, Fri & Sat 11-2:30. Major credit cards. Full bar. Lunches $3.95-$7.95, dinners $7-$16.

Housed in the lobby of the old Majestic Theater on an otherwise grim block, the Gnome offers American favorites and does a good job of Middle Eastern dishes, including marinated chicken breast shish tawook ($11.95), baked eggplant ($7.95), stuffed grape leaves, and tabouli. Dinner prices include salad, rice, and stir-fry vegetables. The popular fatoush salad (parsley, cucumber, tomatoes, toasted pita bread) is $4.25. Creamy rice pudding ($2.25) is outstanding.

Customers come from nearby Wayne State and the medical center for the popular $6.95 lunch buffet; dinner attracts theater- and concert-goers. Sunday brunch ($12) with live classical music is September-May.

Homemaker's Pantry ★

4648 Woodward at Forest, next to Church's Fried Chicken. (313) 833-8430. Call ahead for carryout. Mon-Fri 7-4. Sometimes sells out earlier. No alcohol or credit cards.

In this tiny, onetime White Tower are prepared copious quantities of home cooking, soul food-style, plus decorated cakes and party trays. Most business is carryout; eat-in customers expect to wait. Lunches ($4.60-$6) consist of entrees like perch or whiting filets, baked or BBQ chicken, beef short ribs, meat loaf, or baked ham; two side dishes (pinto beans, macaroni and cheese, slaw, cabbage, yams, potato salad), mostly made from scratch, and corn bread. Desserts include cake every day and specials like banana pudding and sweet potato pie. Breakfast features fish and grits with biscuits, or, for $2.85, more standard eggs, meat, grits or hash browns with toast.

Thelma Grisson feels she's been sent here to run this inner-city beacon for a reason, to make contact with people. Letting go of her old life as a government employee, she found herself guided by the previous owner and by customers. All her children help out. The walls are decorated with inspirational sayings ("When you come to the end of your rope, hang on" and "Don't take life too seriously; it's only temporary") and photos of cakes produced in this tiny kitchen.

Traffic Jam & Snug ★★

511 W. Canfield at Second, two blocks south of the Wayne State campus. Lighted, patrolled parking. (313) 831-9470. Mon 11-3 p.m., Tues-Thurs 11-10:30, Fri 11-midnight, Sat 5-midnight. Full bar. MasterCard, Visa. Entrees $6.95-$8.95; sandwiches $5.50-$6.95; salads $2.25-$6.75.

A diverse crowd patronizes this extraordinarily eclectic restaurant. Many customers are on their way to someplace else, so service is fast. By day it's heavy on business people, employees at the medical center and Wayne State, and ladies who lunch. At night you can see concertgoers in furs and suits alongside students from the neighborhood in jeans.

It's the only restaurant in Michigan with its own dairy. Traffic Jam cheeses have won 11 ribbons at the Michigan State Fair. All breads and desserts are made on the premises. A different and distinctive bread each day shows up in the complimentary bread basket; specialty breads, cookies, and such are for sale at the bakery counter. Wines here are a great value, marked up only 50% over wholesale, compared with 100% to 200% at other places. Customers select them in the foyer display area; there's no wine list as such. A micro-brewery, to produce stronger European-style beers, is expected to be operating by 1990.

Some come here specifically for the huge desserts, the most famous of which is the Carlotta Chocolate Ice Cream Cheese Cake (topped with ground espresso) — at $5.95 the restaurant's most expensive. Others come here for no other reason than the Tex-Mex Lentilburger sandwich ($6.50). The menu (the same for lunch and dinner) changes weekly, with some perennial standards and daily extras — surprises are part of the owners' game plan.

The Whitney ★★★

221 Woodward at Canfield, between Orchestra Hall and the Cultural Center. (313) 832-5700. Lunch 11-2 weekdays, dinner Mon-Thurs 6-10, Fri & Sat 5-midnight, Sun brunch 11-3, dinner 5-8. Light menu on 2nd floor at dinner. Full bar, extensive wine list. AmExpress, Visa, MasterCard, Carte Blanche, Diners.

The food lives up to the expectations established by The Whitney's setting: a super-spectacular mansion built in 1894 by lumber baron David Whitney, who lavished it with stained glass, carved woodwork, and turrets. Today it's remarkably preserved and restored, and furnished with silver butter pots, heavy linens, monogrammed china, and other accoutrements of the Gilded Age. (See p.100 for the house's history.) The upstairs rooms are only slightly less elaborate than the downstairs music room, library, drawing room, etc.

The menu, changed monthly, features American classics (oysters Rockefeller, grilled filet mignon, broiled swordfish and Dover sole, veal Oscar, and the like). They are "refreshed with sometimes surprising accompaniments," says the *Free Press's* Molly Abraham, such as a garlic-mustard crust and potato noisettes with the rack of lamb ($29). Broiled salmon ($22.50) comes with sauteed cucumbers and tiny shrimp with lemon mint sauce. The oven-roasted double pork chop ($16.50 lunch, $22.50 dinner) is stuffed with hazelnuts, apples, and onions and served with cranberry relish and herbed mashed potatoes. A la carte dinner entrees with garnish run from $18.50 to $38, soups are $5.75, and salads $5.75-$10.75. Or you could come for dessert and coffee, or put together a simpler, cheaper meal with soup or salad and an hors-d'oeuvre like the "warm scallop sandwich" ($8.75) between potato pancakes with lemon butter.

Lunch entrees, also a la carte, run from $9 (for a much-praised chicken pot pie) to $24.50, with soups and salads mostly $4.75. Lighter dishes include shredded duck salad with avocado ($7.95) and fried calamari in garlic with tomatoes ($6.75).

The third-floor Winter Garden bar has a pianist and singer from 9 to 1 Tuesdays through Saturdays.

See also: *DIA Kresge Court and La Palette (p. 92), Melting Pot Cafe (weekday lunches, p. 93), Wayne State Student Center food court (p. 98), Alvin's Finer Delicatessen (p. 326).*

Albert Kahn:
The Motor City's Quintessential Architect

It's not surprising that the career of the twentieth century's most influential industrial architect should have been based in the Motor City, where Henry Ford perfected the assembly line. Albert Kahn (1869-1942) pioneered the modern, light-filled factory in which reinforced concrete opened up large, flexible spaces. In no other major American city have the important buildings of an era been more fully the product of one architect than have the hundreds of Detroit-area buildings designed by Kahn's office. Albert Kahn Associates designed mansions and auto factories, skyscrapers and college buildings.

Son of a poor rabbi in Germany, Kahn had moved with his family to Detroit in 1884. Discovered by the prominent Detroit artist Julius Melchers, he soon progressed from Melchers' drawing class to apprenticeship in the architectural office of Mason and Rice, adept in the reigning historical styles of the day.

Though Albert Kahn designed everything from neoclassical Italian villas to Gothic-inspired office towers, his revolutionary factories brought him international fame. Their airy spaciousness allowed unprecedented flexibility for manufacturers, and art critics praised their spare, elegant functionalism. The 1938 Dodge Half-Ton Truck Plant in Warren (above) won acclaim for its roof, supported by cantilevered bent steel beams. The 1939 press shop at the Ford Rouge Plant in Dearborn (left) required more steel than had ever been used in a single building.

Kahn's pragmatism, combined with his natural respect for good taste and tradition, fit in with the eclectic firm and its wealthy clients.

The Kahn brothers' concrete-based architecture

When this small, modest man opened his own office, he and his brother Julius, a structural engineer with his own firm, were passionately focused on how to formulate a new architecture based on concrete. A large-scaled industry like automobile manufacturing required big spaces unimpeded by columns. Reinforced concrete was cheaper than structural steel, fireproof, stronger than existing mill construction and more resistant to vibration. Also, wide spans between columns allowed for more window area with better lighting and ventilation. Julius's "Kahn system" of concrete beams reinforced with horizontal tension bars strengthened with stirrups provided the breakthrough. Kahn's Building No. 10 at the new Packard plant on East Grand Boulevard at Concord, designed for Henry Joy in 1905, became the first reinforced concrete factory in Detroit and possibly the U.S.

Work designing factories for the booming auto industry soon flooded the office. Collaborating with the demanding, efficiency-obsessed Henry Ford on the revolutionary Highland Park plant (1910-1914) and Rouge complex (1917-1936) certainly helped Kahn to come up with even more brilliant solutions. Among a host of Detroit-area factories, Kahn designed the Chalmers Motor Car plant (1907), now Chrysler, the Hudson plant (1910), and the Continental Motor plant (1912) — all on East Jefferson — and the Dodge brothers' big Hamtramck plant (1910).

Kahn's non-industrial designs were quite competent but unexciting when measured by standards of originality and new approaches to design. Philosophically, he preferred to stress continuity with the great architecture of the past in his nonindustrial buildings. This suited his clients. With the noteworthy exceptions of Charles Freer and George Booth, Detroit's newly wealthy industrialists lacked the self-confidence or desire to push accepted architectural conventions and take risks with new directions. Most of Kahn's houses — Tudor, Georgian — were traditional and designed to impress. In his own homes, Kahn indulged his love of simplicity and good taste, ideals which made him a founding member of Detroit's Society of Arts and Crafts. His own Tudor Arts & Crafts-style house at 208 Mack at John R, built in 1906 and today the home of the Detroit Urban League, was unencumbered by what Hawkins Ferry calls "oppressive souvenirs of the Middle Ages." It provided a "point of departure" for Kahn's house for George Booth at Cranbrook.

In Grosse Pointe, a great many of the mansions on Lake Shore Road are his, as is the exclusive **County Club of Detroit** there and the handsome **Grosse Pointe Shores Village Hall** (1915). On Belle Isle, the **Casino**, the **Conservatory**, and the beautiful **Aquarium** are all Kahn designs.

A good deal of everything built during Detroit's boom years was designed by Kahn's office. (Smith Hinchman & Grylls also became very large during this period, and designed the biggest downtown skyscrapers.) Downtown, Kahn built big office buildings for the competing dailies, the ***Free Press*** and the ***News***, both on West Lafayette. The **National Bank Building** at Woodward and Cadillac Square and the **Detroit Trust Building** at Fort and Shelby are his. His **Woodward Building** at Woodward and Clifford was built in 1915, the same year as Kahn's **Detroit Athletic Club** at 251 Madison. In the New Center (Grand Boulevard at Second) Kahn designed two of his most monumental commercial buildings: the ornate **Fisher Building** (1928) and the **headquarters for General Motors** (1922).

Most of the big buildings on the central University of Michigan campus came out of Kahn's office: **Angell Hall, Hill Auditorium,** the **Natural Sciences Building, Clements Library,** the **General Library,** and **West Engineering** (1903), his first big commission, with the landmark Engin Arch.

An international career spawned in Detroit

By the 1920s Kahn was famous around the world. His office worked on every continent. In 1928 he and Ford Motor took on the vast program of Soviet industrial expansion, building 531 Soviet factories, including the famous Stalingrad tractor factory, and training 4,000 Soviet engineers to carry out the program. In 1938 Kahn's 400-person office accounted for 19 per cent of the architect-designed industrial building in the U.S.

Kahn's architectural office was organized to be super-efficient and fast in designing industrial facilities, a great advantage in building factories for war production as Detroit became "the Arsenal of Democracy" during World War II. The great architect died in 1942 before the completion of his **Willow Run Bomber Plant,** the biggest plant in the world.

Kahn, pictured here in 1940, was a poised and genial man. Extraordinarily energetic but never proud, he liked to say, "When I began, the real architects would design only museums, cathedrals, capitols, monuments. The office boy was considered good enough for factories. I'm still that office boy."

New Center

This 60-block area three miles north of downtown is built around two majestic office buildings of the 1920s: the **GM Building** and the **Fisher Building**. The Fisher, one of the most lavishly ornate buildings in an already flamboyant architectural era, is alone worth a visit to the New Center. But there is also theater and jazz here, plus a remarkable contemporary crafts gallery and some upscale shops. And you can wander around the vast, bustling lobby of GM's headquarters.

The New Center got off the ground in 1922 when General Motors, wishing to avoid downtown's increasing congestion, built its giant headquarters here. A few years later, the seven Fisher brothers, who had become enormously rich by developing the enclosed auto body and selling Fisher Body to GM, decided to use some of their vast fortune to create the world's most beautiful office building. Behind the Fisher Building on Lothrop they also built a much more austere office building, now called the **Albert Kahn Building**.

In 1983, a third major office/retail building was added, **New Center One**, as well as the fancy 117-room **Hotel St. Regis**, whose rooms go for $145 a night and up. Skybridges connect the New Center buildings north of Grand with the GM Building to the south; 10,000 people work in these six buildings alone.

A Fisher Building historical brochure filled with interesting historic photos and information about the building's fabulous decoration can be picked up at Trizec Properties' office, 450 Fisher Building. The Fisher's 60,000 square feet of polished granite is said to be the largest amount of polished granite ever ordered.

For New Center entertainment information:
Attic Theater — (313) 875-8284
Fisher Theater — (313) 872-1000
Club Pentha — (313) 972-3760.

Skywalks interconnect the main New Center buildings, making for a pleasant environment to explore in winter. From left, the GM Building, the St. Regis Hotel, the trapezoidal-shaped New Center One, the Fisher Building with its famous Golden Tower, and the Albert Kahn Building.

Two important theaters are here: the superbly equipped Fisher Theater, which stages popular Broadway plays and musicals, and nearby the **Attic Theater**, which produces and imports off-Broadway plays. The Fisher has weekend matinees. A new entertainment hit is **Club Pentha** jazz club in the Fisher Building basement, patronized by the likes of Aretha Franklin. Three black professionals started it as a step up from their celebrated parties.

On the New Center's western border is the prestigious **Henry Ford Hospital**, and just west of that, the **Motown Museum** in that entertainment conglomerate's modest birthplace. South of the GM Building at York and Second Streets is the former Burroughs Corporation headquarters. Now it is one of two **Unisys** headquarters, with 1,850 employees. In all, 27,000 people work in the New Center area.

GM's $400 million neighborhood improvement

The New Center was so called because, when built, it was virtually at the center of the region's population and handy to the burgeoning suburbs. Today it remains conveniently accessible from any direction (barring rush-hour traffic), as it's just blocks from the Ford, Chrysler, and the Lodge freeways.

In recent years GM has funded the renovation of 18 blocks of once rundown homes just north of the center. Today these handsome houses, on redesigned courts with beautiful landscaping and a private security patrol, cost between $90,000 and $120,000. Another 400 housing units have been built with GM sponsorship. **New Center Commons**, as the area is known, is now one of Detroit's most convenient and desirable neighborhoods, with shopping and entertainment right at hand, and an easy drive to downtown, the Cultural Center, or Wayne State.

In all, GM has invested $400 million here in an effort to rescue its headquarters, which had come to sit in the middle of a seriously rundown neighborhood. It has been joined by Trizec Properties, headquartered in Calgary, Ontario, and the largest real estate development firm in North America. New Center retailing was in decline (the Saks and several other exclusive stores had closed) until Trizec purchased the Fisher and Albert Kahn buildings in the 1980s and developed New Center One as the city's only shopping center with a department-store anchor.

Woodward Avenue still doesn't look too good here. But the New Center's massive upgrading has been so successful that GM now uses the location in its promotional literature. What makes this an especially congenial complex to explore in the winter are fabulous interior spaces in the Fisher and GM buildings and the six skywalks that connect the main buildings and adjacent parking.

Free summer concerts featuring a big variety of area popular music acts are held at the stage in the park on the south side of Grand at Second, across from the GM Building. Times: Wednesday lunchtime from 11:30 to 1 and Thursday evenings from 5:50-8:30, from June 1 to Labor Day.

The Arcade of Flags is a popular Fisher Building tradition during July and August. A brochure enables visitors to identify 84 banners made for the Fisher Building's opening in 1928, including some for countries that no longer exist, like the Orange Free State, East Prussia, Serbia, and Sarawak.

The GM Building as it appeared upon its completion in 1922. Albert Kahn designed it and the Fisher building across Grand Boulevard. Note the boulevard's parkway planting of trees, since removed for street widening.

POINTS OF INTEREST

General Motors Building ★
W. Grand Blvd. between Second Ave. & Cass. Mon-Fri 8:30-5:30.

Although it is just 15 stories high, the sprawling GM headquarters was the world's second-largest building in square footage when finished in 1922. It was originally named the Durant Building after Billy Durant, GM's deal-making founder and two-time CEO. Durant, audacious as an empire-builder but not personally ostentatious, opposed the construction of such a huge and expensive headquarters. After he was replaced in 1920 with more conservative leadership, the building was renamed, but the ornate "D" over the entrance remains.

The building's site was at the time the geographical center of Detroit. With plenty of room on which to build, architect Albert Kahn opted for four huge cross wings instead of a skyscraper. This decision to build outside of the Detroit downtown area was part of a trend toward removing automobile operations from central Detroit.

There is a sense of drama as one walks around the GM Building's big, bustling lobby, amid the brisk-paced, conservatively dressed executives of one of the world's biggest corporations. Will these blue-suited managers pull their company out of the tailspin which caused its American market share to plummet from over 50 per cent to well below 40 per cent? One is reminded of ex-GM vice president John DeLorean's critical and foreboding memoir which portrays the building's fabled 14th floor as a hushed sanctum where the corporation's insulated top executives met in meeting after numbing meeting.

The grand marble lobby with its richly colored and embellished Renaissance ceiling is worth a look. Current model cars are displayed on the eastern side, along with occasional special shows of race cars, perhaps, and historical displays. Of the 14 businesses here, most are service-related. Exceptions are LeClair Men's Wear, Washington Clothiers, Truan's Candies, Connolly-Brown Jewelers, and the New Center Cafe, with a wine store and card and camera shop in the basement.

Fisher Building ★★★
W. Grand Blvd. at Second Ave. Open Mon-Fri 8 a.m.-9 p.m., Sat 9-6.

Built across the street from the GM Building, this Albert Kahn creation ranks with the Guardian Building downtown as the most elaborate of Detroit's remarkable collection of 1920s office buildings. The interior is what's most spectacular, for the Fisher brothers wanted the building to be not only the world's most stunning office center but a shopping and entertainment mecca as well. The Fisher Building's exterior is a simplified Gothic, capped by the famous Golden Tower — which architects consider a detraction from the dramatic vertical massing. Inside, the building is full of "pagan splendors," to use architectural historian Hawkins Ferry's evocative words, executed in a combination of geometric and stylized naturalistic motifs. The lobby's three-story grand arcade is fully 600 feet long. Its vaulted ceiling is decorated with 60 stylized nude cherubs, muses, and other figures, along with oranges, hemlocks, eagles, vines, and folk art motifs. Rich greens and oranges make for a rather Persian effect, lavishly gilded with gold leaf. From the ceiling hang Art Deco crystal chandeliers weighing one to three tons each.

By all means go up to the second and third floor mezzanines running along the length of the arcade. They offer close-up views of the ceiling as well as fascinating glimpses of the busy corridor below you. "Upon the walls gleam 40 different varieties of marble that would dazzle even the most jaded Roman emperor," remarked Ferry. On the top floor is the Great Lakes' number-one radio station, **WJR**, which has made "from the golden tower of the Fisher Building" its audio logo. Tours are available for groups of 10 to 15; call 875-4440.

As in most status office towers of the 1920s, elevator doors and mailboxes were treated as works of art, which makes it interesting just to look around. Unusual amenities here included free babysitting in a richly decorated nursery, white-dressed parking attendants, and, in the theater lobby, banana trees, a pond of goldfish and turtles, and wandering macaws fed by moviegoers.

The lavish, brilliantly colored interior of the **Fisher Theater**, inspired by pre-historic Central American art, was removed in 1961, at the end of its moving picture days. The Fisher brothers transformed it into Detroit's preeminent legitimate theater. Its acoustics, stage, and orchestra pit make it superb for even the biggest and most elaborate musicals. Hits including *Hello, Dolly* and

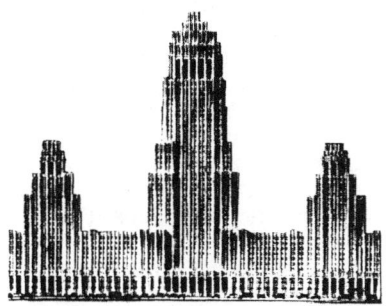

The Depression curtailed the Fisher brothers' grand plan to build a duplicate of the existing Fisher Building on Grand at Third and connect them with a 60-story tower.

Fiddler on the Roof originated here before moving to Broadway.

A number of interiors that go back to 1928 can still be seen in the Fisher Building. A bank's sumptuous Aztec plaster decoration and ornate vault are now part of the affordably priced **Pegasus in the Fisher** restaurant (see p. 113). The elaborate fixtures remain at Forster & Laidlaw florists at the Lothrop entrance. Next door, the romantic plaster ribbons of Julie's Frocks are now part of the Research Federal Credit Union. Next to it are a spiral staircase, vaulted ceiling, and a Pewabic tile floor that was recently uncovered when the Detroit Gallery of Contemporary Crafts moved down here.

For coffee, pastries, sandwiches, and salads, there's **Jacques Patisserie** in the north-south wing off the main arcade. **The Willow Tree** and **Fashion Place** women's wear stores and **Poster Gallery** are also on this corridor.

Detroit Gallery of Contemporary Crafts ★★

Fisher Building main lobby, near Lothrop St. entrance. (313) 873-7888. Mon-Sat 10-6, until 8 on theater nights.

This unusually interesting gallery, opened in 1976, offers a select array of American crafts, handmade by hundreds of top craftspeople from across the country. Attractive displays combine media: furniture, rugs, toys, pottery, glass, jewelry, clothing, quilts, and dolls. Prices range from $25 to $500. Special shows change, but each year includes a glass show, "Clothes for the Collector" in fall, and "Objects of Wonder and Delight" before the holidays.

Beautiful floors of Pewabic tile, some with animal imprints, others forming a sunburst design, were uncovered when the gallery recently moved downstairs.

New Center One

On Second between Grand and Lothrop. Shop hours: Mon-Fri 9-6, Sat 10-5. (313) 874-4444.

The lower two stories of this new office building are retail. A large **Crowley's** department store is at street level, with a Waldenbooks and General Nutrition Center. On two are Gantos and Winkelman's women's fashions, a Burger King and Gertie's Garden Restaurant (featuring salads), a one-hour photo, and two stores of unusual interest. **Little Women** was founded by two unusually small career women who wanted to dress like professional women and not little girls; it now carries sizes 0-13. **Boulevard Luggage** offers an outstanding selection of better handbags and luggage to a large and enthusiastic base of upscale customers. (**London Luggage**, four blocks away at 5955 Woodward just north of I-94, is also well known; it offers a wider range of prices and also deals in award incentive gifts.)

Motown Museum ★★

2648 W. Grand Blvd., west of the Lodge Freeway and 1 1/2 blocks west of Henry Ford Hospitals. (313) 875-2264. Mon-Sat 10-5, Sun 2-5. Admission $3/adult, $2 12 and under.

Pop music legends — scores of them — were made in these modest two-story houses due to the musical intuition, persistence, and organizing skills of Berry Gordy, Jr., a former boxer and autoworker. His father, a Mississippi farm worker who came to Detroit in 1922, was a part of the great migration to the North. They had achieved middle-class status in the Motor City's flush decades.

Under Gordy, Motown Records broke down rock and roll color lines and launched an amazing number of stars whose music remains current today: Michael Jackson, Stevie Wonder, Diana Ross and the Supremes, Marvin Gaye, Martha Reeves and the

Starting in 1959, Motown songwriters and producers working and even living in this house produced an unparalleled string of pop hits that broke Top 40 music's color barrier. The long list of Motown stars, largely from Detroit, indicates the tremendous amount of grassroots talent that, when developed and managed well, can rise to the top.

In the Motown Museum, founder Berry Gordy's portrait is surrounded by awards and honors. Despite his great wealth, the museum, run by his sister, is curiously underfunded.

Vandellas, Smokey Robinson and the Miracles, the Temptations, Lionel Richie, Gladys Knight and the Pips, the Isley Brothers, Junior Walker, and more.

Records produced in the small, crudely fashioned rear studio here were among the first 45s by black artists to break out of the R&B charts. They became the signature music of the entire generation of Americans growing up in the 1960s. Within a few years of its founding in 1959, Motown had become the biggest black-owned company in America, with an impressive office on Woodward just north of the Fisher Freeway.

In 1971 Gordy left Detroit for Los Angeles to pursue movie and television projects, which have recently included "Lonesome Dove." These at first centered on Diana Ross's career as an actress and singer. She was showcased in Motown's first movie, "Lady Sings the Blues." Motown movies, like Motown music, were aimed at bringing black subjects into the American mainstream. Music industry analysts date the decline of Motown Records to its departure from Detroit and its inability to develop new talent in Los Angeles to replace its increasingly independent stars and songwriters. In 1988 Motown sold its recording arm to MCA-linked investors for $61 million.

The Motown Museum takes you back to a much simpler, earlier era. By the early 1960s, so many local kids flocked here to Hitsville, USA, as Motown's headquarters was known, that traffic on West Grand was jammed for blocks. Some wanted to glimpse the stars who recorded there. Others hoped to audition informally on the front porch, a approach that had succeeded for more than one Motown star.

Gordy's dramatic rise is an inspirational tale of black entrepreneurial success. He grew up on nearby Farnsworth Street in the then-middle-class black neighborhood behind the Detroit Institute of Arts. Each member of his upwardly mobile, hard-working family contributed $10 a month to build an enterprise fund from which any family member could draw. After his jazz-oriented record shop went bankrupt, Gordy began focusing on writing and producing rhythm and blues songs for local groups. At a critical juncture, Gordy borrowed $800 from the family fund to start his own record production company. "Shop Around," written by Smokey Robinson, was the first big hit he produced.

A talented manager and an autocratic disciplinarian, Gordy perfected the assembly-line style of hit production. He hired teams of writers who, as one critic describes it, put out "a wholly mechanical style and sound that roared and purred like a well-tuned Porsche." The Supremes recorded 12 #1 pop hits in five years, written by the great songwriting team of Lamont Dozier and Eddie and Brian Holland. Gordy so carefully orchestrated Motown affairs that charm coaches were hired to polish the manners and dress of Motown recruits.

In the museum, rooms are crowded with Motown memorabilia collected by director Esther Gordy Edwards, Berry's sister: publicity photos and scrapbook shots, letters, album jackets, newspaper clippings, plaques and gold records. Highlights of a visit include the recording studio, with original sheet music on the music stands just as it was, and the modest 4-track board from which most of Motown's greatest hits were engineered.

The Motown Museum is curiously underfunded, considering Gordy's great wealth and the respect paid him in museum displays. Michael Jackson donated $125,000 from a Detroit concert to the museum; so far no major changes have been made.

RESTAURANTS

Lelli's ★
7618 Woodward 4 blocks north of Grand Blvd. Enter at rear only. Lighted, guarded parking. (313) 871-1590. Mon 11 a.m.- 2 p.m., Tues-Fri 11-10, Sat 11-11. Full bar. Major credit cards. Entrees $6.80-$18.30 (lunch); $15.75-$23.95 (dinner).

This big Italian restaurant has been around since 1939. It's a favorite of theatergoers and Chrysler and GM executives, whose headquarters are both nearby. Lelli's seats a whopping 650 people in 10 dining rooms. For lunch, the spaghetti with meat sauce ($6.80), accompanied by bread sticks and a simple salad, is quite good. Steaks, veal, chicken cacciatore ($8.95), and breaded haddock ($7.95) are also served. For dinner, there's broiled filet mignon ($22.95), a favorite of many, and chicken Kiev with wild rice ($17.75).

Mr. Fofo's Deli ★
8902 Second Ave. at Hazelwood, 2 blocks west of Woodward, 3/4 mile north of Grand. Only closed Sun 8 a.m.-1 p.m. Carryout; Solarium restaurant to open soon. Sandwiches $2.50-$6.45. Dinners $5-$14.

This big, bustling takeout does a mammoth business in both deli sandwiches and barbeque. Customers include many of Detroit's famous black celebrities. The delicious corned beef sandwiches use top-quality meat and rye bread. The regular one is $4.90; the famed triple-deck New Yorker ($6.55) could feed two or three. A single chunk of Mr. Fofo's famous five-layer cakes ($2.85 in double chocolate, German chocolate, yellow batter and coconut) weighs in at over 1 1/2 pounds. Deep-dish peach cobbler ($2.45 small, $2.95 large) is especially popular.

To entertain crowds waiting at the deli, there are huge aquariums with unusual fish.

Pegasus at the Fisher
In the Fisher Building lobby, West Grand at Second. (313) 875-7400. Mon-Fri 11 a.m-11p.m., Sat 4-midnight. Full bar. Major credit cards.

Updated, moderately priced American food (no more Greektown fare) is served in an opulent, sensitively restored Art Deco space in the fabulous Fisher Building (see p. 109).

LODGINGS

DOWNTOWN

Westin Hotel
(313) 568-8300. In the Renaissance Center on E. Jefferson at Brush on the Detroit River downtown.
1,200 rooms on 73 floors.
$116-$174 single; $136-$194 double (the higher the room, the higher the rates). $99 weekend special for 2 includes $30 free food or beverages in hotel's restaurants. Indoor swimming pool. Health club, Nautilus equipment, jogging track, aerobic workout space, masseuse. 3 restaurants and 3 lounges. Wet & dry sauna. Pay movies ($6.35). This center tower of the giant Renaissance Center complex is the world's tallest hotel. Upper rooms have spectacular views of the Detroit River, Belle Isle, or Hart Plaza.

Hotel Pontchartrain
(313) 965-0200.
2 Washington Blvd. at Jefferson Ave. I-94 to U.S. 10 to Jefferson St. exit.
419 rooms, 5 floors. $125-$150 single; $135-$160 double. Outdoor pool, health club. HBO. 3 restaurants. Upper stories offer good views of river. Bankruptcy sale pending.

Omni Hotel
(313) 222-7700.
333 E. Jefferson at Randolph.
354 rooms, 21 floors. Mon-Thurs $145-$165, Fri-Sun $69 room only, $99 with breakfast, valet parking, health club. View of river from some rooms, downtown Detroit from others. HBO, Spectravision, full-service restaurant and bar. Olympic-size indoor pool. Fitness center with weight room and sauna $5 extra.

Day's Inn
(313) 965-4646 (800) 325-2525.
Michigan Ave. at Washington Blvd.
287 units, 16 floors. 65 single; $75 double; weekends: $55 single; $65 double. Exercise room. Free shuttle to area restaurants, free breakfasts. Pay TV movies ($6.35). Many rooms with good views of the Detroit River and downtown Detroit.

RIVERTOWN/EAST SIDE

Shorecrest Motor Inn
(313) 568-3000 (800) 992-9616 (out of state). 1316 E. Jefferson, 2 blocks east of RenCen.
2 floors, 54 rooms. $44-$54 single; $50-$62 double. Showtime, ESPN. Restaurant. Refrigerator in all rooms. Convenient Rivertown location.

River Place Inn
(313) 259-2500.
Stroh River Place at Jos. Campau, 3 blocks south of Jefferson.
108 rooms on 5 floors. $135-$155 single, doubles up to $500. Fri & Sat packages $120 (with continenetal breakfast), $175 (with buffet breakfast, champagne, and dinner). Half the rooms in this luxuriously renovated former headquarters of Parke-Davis have views of the Detroit River. Others have view of landscaped gardens. Health and fitness center, indoor pool. Excellent restaurants.

Blanche House Bed & Breakfast
(313) 822-7090.
506 Parkview Dr. south off Jefferson, 1.25 miles east of Belle Isle Bridge and just west of Waterworks Park.
7 rooms. $60-80. Large, turn-of-the-century house just down the street from the mayor's residence. Large rooms attractively restored by innkeeper, a friendly, knowledgeable Detroit native, and her family, who are working on converting the remarkable next-door castle, once a prestigious boys's school, into additional space. River access via canal.

NEW CENTER

Hotel St. Regis
(313) 873-3000. W. Grand at 2nd Ave.
223 rooms on 6 floors. $125 single. $140 double. Weekends $69 single; $84 double. HBO. Excellent restaurant. Skywalks connect with the General Motors Headquarters and Fisher Building, with shopping and restaurants.

Hamtramck

This city of just two square miles, totally surrounded by Detroit, is Michigan's most ethnically distinctive community. As a Polish stronghold, it goes back to 1914. A continuing influx of Polish immigrants over the years constantly reinforces the Polish culture. Drive along its bustling main street of Joseph Campau and you'll see Polish bakeries, Polish meat shops, Polish bookstores, Polish clubs. At the corner of Belmont and Joseph Campau is a tribute to the Polish Pope, a large statue of Pope John Paul.

For years now, Detroiters have been discovering the gritty charm of a trip to Hamtramck: eating heartily in its good, cheap restaurants; browsing in the small, budget-oriented shops, bakeries, and meat markets; and, more recently, dancing to some of the area's most innovative rock at Lilli's Bar. Joseph Campau's long retail blocks have the vintage appeal of a living, thriving blue-collar relic from the 1930s or 1940s before chains came to depersonalize retailing and before malls had sucked the vitality out of most American downtowns. It's an amazing contrast with the boarded-up bleakness of similar 1920s shopping strips in nearby Detroit.

Hamtramck's Polish population is actually declining today. Once nearly 60 per cent, Poles now make up only 40 per cent of the residents. For years, Polish families have moved from Hamtramck to the northeast into Warren, Sterling Heights, and Utica. Hamtramck's Ukrainian population, centered in the brick houses around Mitchell and Gallagher, is 20 per cent and also dwindling. Taking up the slack are Albanians from Yugoslavia, who occupy much of the rental neighborhood south of Holbrook. They are now 20 per cent of the population and growing.

Dense neighborhoods of auto workers

Driving along its residential streets, you see why Hamtramck has the highest population density of any Michigan city. The neat, small two-story houses are packed within a few feet of each other on 30-foot lots. Most were originally two-family flats, with the owner-occupant living downstairs. They were built for auto workers' families in one amazing gush between 1914 and 1920, when the village's population skyrocketed from 3,589 to 45,615, the largest such increase in that decade anywhere in the U.S.

Poles in metro Detroit number over 350,000; only Chicago has more. Most emigrated between 1880 and 1920 as poor peasants from semi-feudal estates. A small earlier wave of aristocrats and intellectuals emigrated for political reasons. In the late 19th-century, Detroit's big railroad car manufacturers hired representatives in Poland to recruit workers.

Big Great Lakes onion eaters Because of their huge populations of Germans, Poles, and other Central and East Europeans, Great Lakes metro areas like Detroit, Cleveland, and Chicago have populations which consume 26 pounds of onions per person a year, twice the national average.

The sudden growth occurred in part because the Dodge Brothers started building a big plant in the southern part of Hamtramck in 1910, where they made auto parts for Ford. When Dodge expanded to make its own cars in 1914, the original Polish neighborhood centered along Chene just to the south in Detroit spread upward into Hamtramck.

Poles came from other heavily Polish areas such as Chicago, Cleveland, Buffalo, and the Pennsylvania coal fields, drawn to Hamtramck's high-paying automotive jobs at Dodge Main. Ford's nearby Highland Park plant was another major employer for these Poles.

Before Dodge Main was built, this unincorporated area had been a sleepy German farming township. It was named after Colonel John Francis Hamtramck, the Canadian son of a Luxembourg immigrant. He was an American army strategist during the post-Revolutionary Indian wars and the first American military commander of Detroit. Initially Hamtramck Township had been a French farming area; the Germans became dominant soon after they arrived in the 1850s.

Surrounded by Detroit

Unlike many neighboring Wayne County villages, Hamtramck refused to be annexed to Detroit. The most important reason was the desire of Hamtramck Poles to retain their identity. The close-knit Polish community is still a place where church and fraternal organizations abound. Important also were the considerable tax revenues from the town's huge factories, which would have gone into the common Detroit pot had Hamtramck been annexed.

By 1920, Hamtramck had become known as "the world's largest village," with a population of 48,615. Under the Germans, the village government had already won a reputation as a rural backwater soft on

St. Florian Church's Strawberry Festival, the weekend with the first Sunday in May, is a major event in Hamtramck. There are booths with games, lots of homemade food, and polka bands with folk dancing.

Home and church: St. Florian, Hamtramck's great cathedral-like Gothic church, is surrounded by streets of quite modest, tightly-packed houses, most all neatly maintained. The Polish familes who lived here in the 1920s donated considerable portions of their incomes to build this magnificent church.

vice, principally bootlegging and gambling. As a Polish city after 1922, Hamtramck became even more widely known as a wide-open town through sensational exposes. One of the Midwest's most notorious brothels was located in the Hamtramck Hotel. Gambling dens abounded and could even be found in city hall offices. "Every soft-drink place sells hard liquor," complained a judge. Two mayors went to prison.

Those wild days are long past. By the 1950s, Hamtramck was far less crowded and calmer, a great family town known for its famous sports teams. Locals love to list Hamtramck's state championships and homegrown stars: Rudy Tomjanovich in basketball, Tom Paciorek in baseball, and Jimmy Pietrzak in football. In 1959 Hamtramck boys won the National Little League Championship, the only Midwestern team so far to do so. This blue-collar enclave called itself "Tennis Capital of the World" when an elementary physical education teacher, Jean Hoxie, coached the high school tennis team to 19 state Class A championships and, with her husband, established a world-famous summer tennis school. Lack of tennis courts didn't bother her; she had kids hitting the ball against brick walls. Local teen tennis phenomenon Peaches Bartkowicz became a national star in the 1950s.

Surprising stability

As Detroit's surrounding commercial districts have severely eroded, Hamtramck has survived in surprisingly good shape. Its housing stock, modest to begin with, is now 70 years old, occupied increasingly by widows. In many neighborhoods it remains meticulously maintained. Joseph Campau has continued to be a bustling commercial avenue, also serving many Detroiters and Highland Park residents.

The "land-lust" of the Polish peasant settlers helps explain the stability of core Hamtramck neighborhoods. "One of the greatest joys for a Pole is to be able to transform a certain plot of land into his home," explains Hamtramck native Frank Serafino.

Most ethnic groups clustered together after arrival. But the Poles clustered more tightly than most out of a greater need for support in an extremely unfamiliar and hostile environment. They were poor peasants who came to the U.S. between 1880 and 1920 — too late to get much good farm land. Their lives were organized around the Catholic Church, supplemented by social institutions like the neighborhood tavern, sports teams, and a host of fraternal and political organizations from the Polish Century Club and the Polish Falcons to the Polish National Alliance. Poles continued speaking their native language at home far longer than most ethnic groups. Polish is still heard frequently in Hamtramck shops.

Parades in Hamtramck are a big deal, and Labor Day is the biggest of all, growing every year. Marching bands, floats from clubs, the Budweiser Clydesdales, and firefighters from neighboring communities all participate. It starts around 1 p.m. and lasts 2 1/2 hours.

Hamtramck's special status among Polish-Americans has brought many presidential campaign visits and, in 1987, the visit of Pope John Paul II.

As population declines, city troubles mount

Today, even with the declining Polish presence in Hamtramck, its commercial district has a distinct Polish feel to it. But there is an increasingly shabby aura to parts of Hamtramck. Some say as the city's tax base plummets, the city's infrastructure — garbage pickup, road repair, police and fire service — is suffering badly. Hamtramck's population peaked around 1930 at about 56,000. By 1980 it was down to 21,000 and is expected to drop below 18,000 by 1990.

A major blow to the community was the 1979 closing of the giant Dodge Main plant. It had always been Hamtramck's life blood, even though it had more recently become known for poor working conditions, bad race relations, low plant morale, and unusually high absenteeism and substance abuse. The GM Poletown plant which has since been built on some of the same land is two-thirds in Detroit. Its 3,000 jobs, half of what GM anticipated, haven't come close to replacing the 11,000 Dodge workers. Dana Corporation's departure in 1986 cost the city hundreds more jobs.

Eventually the Polish presence in Hamtramck may diminish to the extent that it will no longer be the distinctive ethnic enclave it has been for over half a century. This makes Hamtramck's distinctive Old World atmosphere all the more precious. Enjoy it while you can.

*Neighborhood taverns, off the main drag, are great Hamtramck institutions best observed after work. Many have inexpensive food and/or entertainment. They include **Artie's Locker Room** (31421 Caniff at Charest), **G's Place** (2764 Florian), **Dr. Dave's Waiting Room Lounge** (3216 Carpenter), and **Paycheck's Lounge** (2932 Caniff).*

POINTS OF INTEREST

Polish Art Center

9539 Joseph Campau at Norwalk. (313) 874-2242. Mon-Sat 9-6, Mon & Fri 'til 7.

This delightful shop, owned and run by Raymond and Joan Bittner, has such an attractive array of Polish arts and crafts that people visit it from all over the U.S. Here you can find Polish folk art rugs from $35 to $300. Beautiful wooden plates inlaid with metal are $8 to $50. The Polish leaded glass ranges from $11.50 to $400. Costume dolls are $2.50 up. The brightly painted Russian nesting dolls start at just $6 a set. Sparkling and intricate tinfoil nativities, called *szopka*, are $15 to $55.

Colorful Easter eggs, including Ukrainian goose and ostrich eggs, are on hand, as are the supplies (dyes, wax, tools, unfinished eggs) with which to embellish them yourself. There are inexpensive paper cuttings (and books on this gay Polish folk art), amber jewelry, replicas of antique Polish swords, and Polish greeting cards.

New Palace Bakery

9833 Joseph Campau between Yemans and Evaline. (313) 875-1334. Mon-Sat 5 a.m.-7 p.m., Fri 'til 8.

Hamtramck is known for its Polish bakeries, and the New Palace is a favorite among the locals. One Polish specialty is angel wings, a very light dough fried with a powdering of sugar. Another favorite is *paczki*, jelly-filled doughnuts. On the

Independent shoe stores, meat markets, bakeries, even a ladies' hat shop give Joseph Campau, Hamtramck's main shopping street, a dense, old-time flavor. Signs are painted on walls (a no-no in gentrified suburbia); offices and artists' studios occupy second stories. Vibrant murals of folk life in Poland are from an early 1980s beautification campaign.

day before Lent, lines form by 7 a.m. to buy these traditional delicacies. Lemon tortes, cinnamon-raisin breakfast rolls, and pumpernickel and rye breads are other standbys.

Monument to Pope John Paul II

Corner of Belmont and Joseph Campau.

It's not surprising that this distinctively Polish city would want to do something special to commemorate the installation of the first Polish pope. The idea for an imposing statue was first conceived by the local Knights of Columbus, but it eventually became a project most local Poles participated in. Much of the funding has come from the proceeds of a festival held for four days around Labor Day, when over 700,000 visitors flock to the city. The austere little park is enlivened by the colorful and well-executed mural of costumed folk dancers in a historic Polish street scene. The original entrance gates to the late, lamented Dodge Main plant, Hamtramck's reason for being, form the fence.

Ciemniak Meat Market ★

9629 Joseph Campau between Norwalk and Edwin. (313) 871-0773. Mon-Fri 9-6, Sat 8-6.

Lots of people around Hamtramck think this is the best meat market in town. Ciemniak's own smokehouse is in back, where they make such things as hunter's sausage ($3.98/lb.) and smoked kielbasa (with veal and pork, $3.39/lb.). Their fresh pork kielbasa is $2.79 a pound. Kiszka ($1.59/lb.) is made with buckwheat, beef blood, liver, and pork.

Kowalski Sausage

2270 Holbrook.

Although this Polish sausage maker is small enough to refer you to the general manager if you call with

Kowalski Sausage on Holbrook, with its landmark sign, is now Hamtramck's second-largest employer. Its **17 area retail stores offer takeout golabki (cabbage rolls), pierogi (dumplings), nalesniki (blintzes or crepes) and soups in addition to kielbasa and cold cuts.**

questions, Kowalski is now Hamtramck's second-largest private employer (after GM) with a work force of 300. Its big neon hot dog in front of the plant is a local landmark. The plant, founded in 1920, produces about 10 million pounds of sausage a year. The most popular is kielbasa, that large uniquely Polish sausage made with coarse ground pork and beef. Kowalski flavors it with garlic and smokes it in its old-fashioned hardwood-fired ovens. The company has 17 retail outlets in the region, including two in Hamtramck: **9405** and **10212 Joseph Campau**.

St. Florian Church ★

Faces Florian St. one block west of Joseph Campau. (313) 871-2778. Church is open to visitors from 8:30 a.m.-6 p.m.; enter from back door on Poland St. next to the church offices.

This magnificent Gothic church, completed in 1926, is on the scale of a great European cathedral. Serving one of the region's largest parishes, it holds 1,800. The church was designed by Ralph Adams Cram, America's high priest of the 20th-century Gothic Revival. The interior is awesome, with an enormously high ceiling. Massive stained glass windows fill the high walls.

A set of nine windows were made by the famous Mayer Studios in Munich in 1936. As Nola Huse Tutag explains in *Discovering Stained Glass in Detroit,* "The St. Florian windows by Mayer demonstrate a rediscovery of the essential character of medieval glass, which prefers a simpler and more austere technique. The figures of The Crucifixion are simplified and stylized, pot-metal glass is used, and the pieces of glass are smaller and jewellike, with leading boldly outlining the design. The colors are deep blue, red, and green used by the medieval craftsman." The altar windows show five Polish saints: Casimir, Stanislaus, Hedwig, Hyacinth, and Florian.

Cadillac Detroit-Hamtramck Assembly Center ★★

Just north of I-94 between Mt. Elliot and I-75. (313) 972-6000. Tours by reservation only (booked up months in advance) Tues & Wed 9 a.m., Thurs noon.

The highly roboticized new Poletown plant makes Cadillac Sevilles, Buick Rivieras, and Oldsmobile Toronados. The 1 1/2-hour tour begins with a 12-minute slide show. Highlights include the Dimensional Verification Area where laser cameras check the exact dimensions of the body build, and the Robogate, where a series of robot welders simultaneously weld the side frames to the underbody.

Because this is the only Detroit-area auto plant tour, tours are booked months in advance.

An extended, wrenching controversy and much pain was created when the city of Detroit condemned and tore down a whole neighborhood and the Immaculate Conception church so GM could build its big new Poletown plant here in the city, incorporating the site of the old Dodge

Main plant. Actually only a small part of this 77-acre facility, the power house, is in Hamtramck. A good percentage of homeowners were happy to find a buyer for their modest frame homes. But others, including many elderly original owners and their defiant parish priest, were heartsick to see their neighborhood and parish destroyed with the cooperation of labor unions and the Catholic Archdiocese.

Contrary to the impression left by national media, the new plant did not destroy the entire Poletown neighborhood, the site of Detroit's original Polish community, but only its northern third. Half the displaced residents were Polish; many of the rest were black. But the demolition did effectively kill off customer traffic in the Chene Street commercial area and handsomely refurbished Chene-Ferry Market. The area had bustled on Saturdays in 1979; now a single farmer sells at the empty market.

RESTAURANTS

Polonia ★★

2934 Yemans, just east of Joseph Campau. (313) 873-8432. Tues-Thurs 11-7, Fri & Sat 11-8, Sun noon-7. Lunches and dinners: $3.95-$5.95. No bar. No credit cards.

Back in the 1930s, when this was the Detroit Workingman's Co-op Restaurant, Marxists and socialists gathered here. The portrait of FDR remains, now joined by the Pope. The bustling Polonia, established here in 1986, has transformed the plain decor with that fresh, informal Polish folk look that blossomed in Hamtramck in the 1980s. Here it's in sort of a country grape arbor guise, with a mural of a lush garden scene with people in folk dress, plus colorful plates and paper cuttings by the booths and counter. All the expected Polish favorites are here. A good idea for newcomers is the combination plate ($5.95), with stuffed cabbage, homemade sausage, dumplings, a crepe, mashed potatoes, and sauerkraut.

Under the Eagle ★

9000 Jos. Campau, 3 blocks south of Holbrook. (313) 875-5905. Mon & Tues 11-7; closed Wed. Thurs-Sun 11-9. Meals $5-7. No bar or credit cards.

Duck soup (actually duck's blood soup) and dill pickle soup are served here daily. There is good rye bread and all the other standbys of homey, satisfying Polish cooking — tastily prepared, and at the low prices typical of Hamtramck restaurants. The $6.05 combination plate is a meal and a half. Bright plates and other Polish artifacts, and waitresses in folk costume, make for a comfortable, cheerful atmosphere that stops short of being contrived. Roast duck is a Sunday specialty.

Buddy's Pizza ★★

17125 Conant at Six Mile— in Detroit, but just north of Hamtramck's northeastern border out Conant. (313) 892-9001. Mon-Thurs 11-11, Fri & Sat 11-midnight, Sun noon-10 p.m. Visa, MasterCard, AmExpress. Full bar.

Buddy's thick, square pizza has been rated tops in Detroit for decades. It's loaded with pepperoni, cheese, and onions, with a thick, chewy crust. Now Buddy's has six suburban locations, but this, the original Buddy's, remains a favorite spot for families from Hamtramck and vicinity. It's a plain, lively, unpretentious place with pitchers of Bud, Labatt's, Michelob, and Miller Lite from the tap. A large, 8-square pizza is $8.68 (cheese only), $11.18 (with pepperoni and onion). "So good you want to cry," says Sandra Silfven. "Solid, satisfying fare," says Molly Abraham. As good as ever, opines Bob Talbert.

Grosse Pointe

This famous string of five affluent suburbs is a splendid place to tour by car or bicycle, thanks to its combination of beautiful Lake St. Clair and handsomely landscaped estates. What is loosely referred to as "Grosse Pointe" is actually five separate municipalities just east of Detroit. All but one stretch along Lake St. Clair.

The western Grosse Pointes are much closer to downtown Detroit than most of that sprawling city itself. The prominent old families of three of these municipalities — Grosse Pointe, Grosse Pointe Shores, and Grosse Pointe Farms — are about as close as Detroit comes to having an aristocracy. Many scions of the founding auto barons still live in Grosse Pointe, while most of the current top auto executives favor more distant, newer Bloomfield Hills.

There's more inherited money and a less hard-driving ethos in Grosse Pointe than in Bloomfield Hills. Most of the women you see shopping on Kercheval have that low-key, preppy look — a practical style of dressing, without much makeup, that barely seems to change from one generation to another. It's a far cry from Birmingham's trendy Maple Road.

"It's true, Grosse Pointe is very conservative, but it's not right-wing," says a native in his mid-thirties. What he likes about Grosse Pointe is that "there are very few insufferable snobs on this side of town. People who are fabulously wealthy walk around in ripped T-shirts and Topsiders. They're not self-conscious, and they don't

Grosse Pointe map
Getting around Grosse Pointe can be surprisingly tricky. An easy-to-read map is available for $1.25 through the Grosse Pointe Board of Realtors, 710 Notre Dame, Grosse Pointe, MI 48230, or from any of the many real estate offices along Kercheval on "The Hill."

The Cotswold-style Edsel and Eleanor Ford House on Lake St. Clair sums up the charm of Grosse Pointe's dwindling number of lakeside estates. Its architecture is beautifully detailed, and the setting lush and leafy. Famed landscape architect Jens Jensen designed the plantings according to naturalistic principles, using only native plant materials.

have to prove themselves." This is definitely George and Barbara Bush territory, he says, with the tone set by down-home people at ease with their wealth.

What many people are surprised to discover is the diversity that lies behind the Grosse Pointe stereotype. The tweed-clad clubbie takes his place alongside many Belgians, robust Italian personalities, a surprising number of Poles, some Lebanese, and a few old French families, not to mention executive transferees to the Detroit area.

Million-dollar estates and tidy bungalows

Property on the lake is always expensive — often over a million dollars per home. Some of the choicest streets are Vendome, Provençal (overlooking the Country Club of Detroit), and Lake Shore Road. But away from the lake, Grosse Pointe Park has a lot of comfortable but modest 1920s houses in the six blocks just east of Alter Road that sell for $100,000 and under. A good number of three-bedroom ranches in Grosse Pointe Woods and Grosse Pointe Farms sell for around $120,000.

A lot of people say they chose to live in Grosse Pointe not for the image but because it offers excellent schools and good housing values, fabulous parks, lots of affordable activities for kids, and reasonably-priced dockage for boats—although there's a five-year-long waiting list for public slips. Downtown Detroit is a short 15- to 20-minute commute. Police response is excellent — a far cry from neighboring Detroit.

It's still true there aren't many Jews or Democrats in any of the Pointes, and in 1980 the black population was well under one per cent. For years into the 1950s, prospective Grosse Pointe home buyers were excluded by the Grosse Pointe Realtors' infamous point system. Prospective buyers were assigned points to qualify for the privilege of living here. A maximum score was 100, with 50 points the minimum for ethnically inoffensive applicants. But Poles had to score 55 points, Greeks 65, Italians 75, and Jews 85. The private detectives hired to fill out the reports didn't even bother to rate blacks or Asians. The questions included:

1. Is their way of living typically American?
2. Appearances—swarthy, slightly swarthy, or not at all?
3. Accents—pronounced, medium, slight, not at all?
4. Dress—neat, sloppy, flashy, or conservative?

Anatomy of the Pointes

The exclusive Grosse Pointe image best fits Grosse Pointe Shores (pop. 2,800). It's a three-mile strip of shoreline, only half a mile deep, just south of St. Clair Shores. Behind the Shores is Grosse Pointe Woods (pop. 17,000), the largest and newest of the Pointes, filled with moderately expensive, mostly colonial-style

The Belgian builders of Grosse Pointe
Detroit's east side is the home of the largest concentration of Belgians outside Europe. Around 1900, skilled Belgians in the building trades started emigrating from the Flemish part of rural Belgium to Michigan and Illinois. Belgians helped build many of Grosse Pointe's great mansions. Many lived in Grosse Pointe Park. Detroit's Cadieux Cafe nearby remains the Belgian community's cultural center to this day. See p. 75.

The older parts of Grosse Pointe and adjoining Detroit boast some wonderfully embellished Art Deco commercial buildings, like this service station on Mack.

homes. Post-World War II homes predominate in Grosse Pointe Farms (pop. 9,600), the middle community. It split off from Grosse Pointe, its southern neighbor, in 1893, when its residents objected to liquor sales.

"The City" (Grosse Pointe, pop. 5,500) and "the Park" (Grosse Pointe Park, pop. 13,800, planned as a buffer along the Detroit border) have a higher percentage of pre-1939 housing stock than just about anyplace else in Michigan — 66 per cent of the Park's housing units, third statewide after Hamtramck and Jackson.

Grosse Pointe and Grosse Pointe Park have a dense, urban feel, complemented with mature street trees, including some fabulous streets of still-healthy American elms. They are really pre-1925 streetcar suburbs, laid out on the presumption that homeowners would walk to the car lines along Jefferson and Mack to take the streetcar downtown to work—a convenient, 20-minute ride. One fun surprise in touring Grosse Pointe is discovering well-preserved commercial relics of the urban 1920s and 1930s along Jefferson, Kercheval, and Mack: Art Deco gas stations and corner drugstores, old-timey grocery stores, and the jazzy Art Deco Esquire Theater on Jefferson. It was recently closed and is in foreclosure after a series of fights and stabbings among teens from Detroit attracted by dollar movies.

A jarring contrast

It's a dramatic transition when you drive out Jefferson and go from Detroit into Grosse Pointe Park. From a decrepit, largely black ghetto, you suddenly enter a green, kempt domain of big trees and beautiful buildings. Even before Detroit's decline accentuated the contrast, this was for many people a magical transition, especially on hot summer days, when you could feel the temperature drop because of all that shade.

The Pointes' tactics for keeping Detroit at bay go back a long, long time and have always applied to both white and black nonresidents. You can't turn from Alter, the dividing line, onto Windmill Pointe Drive, for instance. Only card-carrying residents can use Grosse

Pointe's guarded lakeside parks. When this book was being prepared, the manager of the exclusive Grosse Pointe Yacht Club didn't even want it to be mentioned.

French ribbon farms on the lake

The five Grosse Pointes are sandwiched between Lake St. Clair and Mack Avenue. Mack was once an old elevated Indian trail which, thousands of years ago, was the gravelly beach of a much larger lake. The present shoreline was first settled by French who left Detroit after Britain took it over in 1760. These French families began establishing their distinctive ribbon farms along Lake St. Clair. The narrow farms, only three hundred to six hundred feet wide, extended a mile or more back into the hinterland, permitting each farmer access to the lake for transportation. Orchards were a French specialty, and it is said that a few ancient, gnarled French pear trees can still be found.

The first Englishman to live in the area nicely set the grandiose residential tone of later lakefront mansions. He was the commander of the English Navy on the Great Lakes, Captain Alexander Grant. On his 640 acres, he built a 280-foot-long, two-story log cabin called "Grant's Castle." Located where Grosse Pointe Academy (off Moran Road in Grosse Pointe Farms) is today, it became the social center for Detroit's upper crust in the 1760s.

A 19th-century summer retreat

Wealthy Detroiters began building summer homes in the Grosse Pointe area as early as the 1840s, but few who worked in Detroit dared live year-round so far out. The problem was the marshy area that extended from today's Waterworks Park in Detroit almost to the eastern end of Grosse Pointe Park. In 1851 a plank road was built to Detroit, but it still took two to five hours to get there, depending on how wet it was. Wealthy businessmen often commuted by yacht to Detroit from these summer residences. A dozen or so families even secured a launch which motored them to the city on a

Scenic ride
For a scenic 10-mile round-trip bike ride or drive through the Pointes, start at Windmill Pointe. Stay close to the lake heading west and make a series of jogs onto Bedford, St. Paul, and Fisher to Grosse Pointe Blvd., then to Moross and to Lake Shore Rd. Turn around at Lakeshore and 8 Mile.

An early Grosse Pointe summer cottage. Some businessmen who summered here commuted to downtown Detroit by boat. The bleak landscape is a legacy of the earlier French farms here. This 1882 house belonged to Hugh McMillan, vice president of the largest railroad car manufacturer in the U.S.

regular morning and evening schedule. Some of these fine old Victorian summer residences are still standing. (See Lake Shore Road, p. 128.)

In the mid-1870s the marsh was drained, yielding another 900 acres for development between Jefferson and the lake. By 1887 an interurban was built, creating Grosse Pointe Boulevard.

Home of the auto barons

Beginning around 1910, wealthy auto magnates began building the lakeshore estates which would make Grosse Pointe famous. In 1912 architect Albert Kahn designed Rosecroft for the president of Continental Motors. Another Kahn house at 8 Carmel Lane was built in that year for the director and largest stockholder of the Packard Motor Company, Philip McMillan. In the 1920s Henry's son Edsel Ford built his estate here (see p. 131). Two of the most famous of all have sadly been torn down: Mrs. Horace Dodge's Rose Terrace and the Dodge Castle, commissioned by the elder Dodge brother, John. This Tudor mansion at Harbor Hill, costing $3 million at the time, had 118 rooms and a tunnel under Lake Shore Road to a private wharf. Dodge died in 1920 before it was completed. For years the place remained empty, protected by a high wire fence, its shrubbery growing in wild, unkempt masses. In the late 1970s it was torn down to build a number of smaller houses on the choice site.

POINTS OF INTEREST

Jefferson Avenue/ Lake Shore Road ★★★

Some of the most spectacular mansions built along this remarkable drive have been razed to make way for more modest half-million-dollar homes. But this remains a very fine drive, especially when the sun is shining on the stunning turquoise blue of Lake St. Clair. Where Jefferson becomes Lake Shore Road, no houses obstruct motorists' views of the lake.

Entering the Grosse Pointes from Detroit, you pass a number of historically interesting homes. Just off East Jefferson at **938 Three Mile Drive** is the house built in 1927 by architect William Stratton and his wife, Mary Chase Stratton, the founder of Pewabic Pottery. (See page 70.) William Stratton had designed the Pewabic studio in Detroit. He and his wife collaborated on this beautiful, Spanish-inspired Arts and Crafts home.

Farther east, at **16939 East Jefferson**, is the Isadore Cadieux House, one of the oldest in the close-in metro area. A simple white clapboard farmhouse with black shutters, it was built about 1850 on one of the narrow ribbon farms. At **266 Lakeland Avenue** is Rosecroft, a mansion designed by Albert Kahn in 1912 for the president of Continental Motors.

At 32 Lake Shore Road is the **Grosse Pointe War Memorial**, now a

> For a fuller account of the many fine homes and other sights along East Jefferson and Lake Shore Road, be sure to get "Pointe to Pointe," an informative $3 booklet available at local bookstores.

community center. Originally this was The Moorings, built in 1910 for a founder of the Packard Motor Co. (See p. 127 for visitor information.)

In Grosse Pointe Farms Jefferson becomes a divided boulevard, Lake Shore Road. One of the first houses you see as beautiful Lake St. Clair comes into view on the right is the Paul Deming house, **Cherryhurst.** Built in 1907, it was one of the area's first year-round suburban homes. At 157 Lake Shore is the Gothic Revival **St. Paul-on-the-Lake Catholic Church.** Though it was built in 1899, the parish it serves goes way back to the 18th century. As late as the 1880s, the congregation was still mostly descendants of the French who migrated from Detroit beginning in the 1760s.

Next to the left is the **Grosse Pointe Academy**, a private K-12 school with 400 pupils. It shares the building with a Montessori school. The main building was erected in 1885. This is where the huge log home called "Grant's Castle" stood in the 1770s.

At **Harbor Hill** you can see the development of homes which stands on the site of the palatial home of John Dodge, a giant of Detroit's early auto era. It was never finished due to his death in 1920. Another auto magnate's home can be seen at **8 Carmel Lane**, designed by Albert Kahn for Philip McMillan, a director of the Packard Motor Car Company.

The **Crescent Sail Yacht Club** at 276 Lake Shore is where the house of Packard president Henry Joy stood until 1959. The boat house held Joy's 100-foot yacht.

At **301 Lake Shore** is the shingled home of Carl Schmidt, whose father started the pelt empire housed in what is now Trappers Alley festival marketplace. Built in 1909, it was remodeled in the 1920s.

The grey Queen Anne home (circa 1896) at **365 Lake Shore**, tucked back between two much newer homes, gives an idea of the summer homes that predated the year-round residences on Grosse Pointe.

Perhaps the most spectacular view of all on this drive is that of the private **Grosse Pointe Yacht Club** at the foot of Vernier Road. What began as a ice boating club in 1914 had, by 1929, become what architectural historian Hawkins Ferry called Detroit's climax to 1920s romanticism. "Rising out of the waters of Lake St. Clair on a man-made island, [it] is a vision of Venice replete with a campanile, Gothic tracery, and an arcaded loggia overlooking the lake." The picturesque 187-foot tower has ship bells which strike the hours during sailing season.

This remarkable yacht club, finished just before the Depression, was to be Grosse Pointe's last gasp of gilded grandeur. The Thirties ushered in a sober Georgian neoclassicism, which set the tasteful, albeit dull, tone for most Grosse Pointe construction ever since.

The handsome Grosse Pointe Farms **city hall** (1915) is at 795 Lake Shore. It represents Albert Kahn's most original phase.

Lake St. Clair ★★

Beginning in Grosse Pointe Farms, the lake can be viewed from Lake Shore Rd. The parks are for residents only, but you can park on adjacent side streets and walk along the road.

This heart-shaped body of water, 400 square miles, is sandwiched between Lake Erie and Lake Huron. It separates the Detroit River from the St. Clair River above. The lake is shallow, averaging just 10 feet in depth. A 700-foot-wide shipping channel has been dredged for 18 1/2 miles, giving freighters the needed 27 feet of water to pass through it.

Lake St. Clair was named by La Salle in the summer of 1679 on his first voyage to the region. He was sailing the legendary Griffon, a ship he built near Niagara. Carrying five cannons and a crew of 32, she arrived at the Detroit River August 10. Two days later, on the day of the Festival of St. Claire, the Griffon entered the lake, which was then christened Lake St. Claire in honor of the founder of the Franciscan nuns.

Several lighthouses (not readily visible by the general public) guide the heavy freighter traffic through the lake. One has been at **Windmill Pointe** since 1838. (Once the site of a giant, Dutch-style windmill, Windmill Pointe marks the southwestern terminus of Grosse Pointe Park and of Lake St. Clair.) The present white conical steel tower was erected in 1933, fitted with a small Fresnel lens. An even more modern lighthouse was built in 1941 about midway along the west side of the shipping channel. Its light shines 53 feet above the water. At the northeast end of the lake a pair of lights was installed in 1853 and 1875 to guide boats into the lake channel from the St. Clair River.

Grosse Pointe War Memorial ★★

32 Lake Shore Rd., Grosse Pointe Farms. (313) 881-7511.

Now the hub of recreational and cultural activities in the Pointes, this was originally The Moorings, built in 1910 for Russell Alger, Jr. A founder of the Packard Motor Company, he was the son of the Michigan lumberman who served as McKinley's secretary of war. Albert Kahn, characteristically self-effacing, recommended that the

The Moorings, now the Grosse Pointe War Memorial community center, is an Italian Renaissance villa that shows the Grosse Pointe trend (circa 1910) to country living in the grand manner. Visitors can tour the splendid flower gardens overlooking Lake St. Clair.

Algers engage as its architect Charles Adams Platt of New York. Platt was much admired for his work based on his sophisticated appreciation of Italian country houses and gardens of the Renaissance. He was so immersed in that style that he needed no formal architectural training to design Renaissance villas of perfect proportion, so subtly adapted to the local landscape they seemed to belong there.

Visitors are welcome to see the gardens. A colorful flower garden is behind the house to the left, while a formal garden is to the right. You are welcome to look inside (provided you don't disturb a meeting) and see the stunning views of the lake, framed by elegant, formal interiors (15th-century Florentine, 16th-century Venetian, and Italian Baroque). The main rooms remain very much as Mrs. Alger left them.

War Memorial Events open to the general public include day trips and an eclectic mix of popular and classical music concerts ($6.50). You can bring a picnic to the summer concerts on Lake St. Clair. Call for a schedule.

Edsel & Eleanor Ford House ★★★

1100 Lake Shore Rd. (313) 884-4222. Tours Wed-Sun 1, 2, 3, 4 p.m. Adults $4, seniors $3, under 12 $2.

Built on 87 acres overlooking Lake St. Clair, this splendid mansion takes the prize for formal good taste among the Detroit auto barons' abodes. A large, rambling house designed by Albert Kahn, it mimics on a grander scale those in the Cotswolds 100 miles west of London. Much of the interior paneling and furniture comes from distinguished old English manors. The roof is of imported English stones expertly laid by Cotswold roofmakers. Many of the interior hallways are of limestone, giving one the feeling of entering a centuries-old manor, though the house was actually completed in 1929.

What makes this house especially interesting is that it reflects the Fords' knowledge and love of art and architecture, and that it remains as it was when they lived here. Edsel, Henry Ford's son and the president of Ford Motor, died in 1943. His wife, Eleanor, left the estate virtually untouched. Only some of the priceless paintings — by Renoir, Degas, Titian, Van Gogh — have been replaced by copies. Still, originals by Cezanne, Matisse, Hals, and others remain here. And the original furniture and carpeting is just the way it was.

Large fireplaces abound. But most of the rooms have a stately, formal feel. A striking exception is what the Fords called the "Modern Room." Executed in harmonious Art Deco style in 1938 by Walter Dorwin Teague, this casual gathering place is a most stylishly sophisticated yet comfortable room.

Eleanor left Edsel's personal study unchanged after his early death from stomach cancer. It was in here that he was reportedly seen bent over his desk, weeping in frustration from the abuses heaped on him by his father. Edsel, an intelligent, modest, gentle person with a genuine flair for automobile design, was Henry and Clara Ford's only child. President of Ford Motor since he was 25 years old, Edsel was widely respected by Ford workers and managers. But as the years went by, he was at times sadistically treated by his increasingly curmudgeonly father, who in some instances publicly demolished badly needed auto innovations that his son had spearheaded. Edsel and his co-workers had to watch helplessly as Henry refused to upgrade his Model T while Chevrolet surged into the lead as the nation's best-selling automobile. Ford Motor didn't begin to rebuild until Edsel's son, Henry II, with his mother's backing, wrested control of the company from Henry's thugs after Henry died.

The estate's setting is as remarkable as the manor. Dramatically overlooking the lake, it was planted in native Michigan trees and shrubs by the famous landscape architect Jens Jensen, an influential proponent of looser, more natural landscaping using only native species. The effect is hauntingly serene.

Another treat is daughter Josephine's playhouse, on a path a quarter-mile from the main house. Given to her on her sixth birthday, it is carefully crafted in a similar Cotswold style but executed in 3/4 scale so that the ceiling is only six feet high and the furniture is similarly smaller. Boys weren't permitted in the playhouse, the tour guide informs visitors, but Josephine sometimes spent the night there, alone except for her two bodyguards.

The one-hour tours, led by a professional staff member of the estate, are informative and entertaining.

Kercheval in the Park ★

Kercheval between Wayburn and Beaconsfield in Grosse Pointe Park.

The revival of these three blocks at the border of Grosse Pointe Park and Detroit followed the success of **Sparky Herbert's** restaurant and bar a decade ago. Today this neighborhood shopping strip from about 1920 is an appealing mix of robustly quaint holdovers (**Janet's Lunch, Mulier's grocery, Rustic Cabins bar**), the offbeat (a costume shop, an organic food store, a plant store), and the sleek. Its still slightly funky downhome charm contrasts to Grosse Pointe's other shopping areas farther up Kercheval.

Here are some of the highlights:

Grosse Pointe Reliques
14932 Kercheval. (313) 822-0111. Mon-Sat 11-5.

This crowded consignment shop is full of quality antiques and used furniture at pretty reasonable prices. Several other dealers in furniture, collectibles, and jewelry share space in the back. It's quite an odd contrast to the down-and-out people pawing through old clothes at St. Vincent de Paul next door in Detroit.

Galerie 454
15105 Kercheval. (313) 822-4454. Tues, Wed, Fri 10-6, Thurs 'til 8, Sat 'til 5.

"Corporate art" and "investment are" are bywords at this gallery, which also does framing and restoring. The exhibit space in this stylishly renovated auto showroom is fabulous. In front are shows by area and international artists, with an eclectic mix of contemporary and 19th-century paintings in back. Prints in the bin are under $500, but don't expect to find works by the likes of David Hockney or Jim Dine here; they're in the safe.

James Monnig, Bookseller
15133 Kercheval. (313) 331-7238. Tues-Sat 11-6, Fri 'til 9.

Satisfyingly cluttered used book shop, strong in biography, mysteries, history, art, and children's books. A few hundred vintage videos are for sale ($5-$15). Customers can peruse prospective purchases in the delightful back courtyard.

Rustic Cabins Bar ★
15209 Kercheval, Grosse Pointe Park. (313) 821-6480. Mon-Sat 11 a.m.-2 a.m.

In the early 1930s, when this one-time blind pig went legit, the "cabins" were applied to the facade — two north-woods cabins outlined in round log slabs. Inside, this favorite hangout has barely changed, either. It has original booths and beat-up old tables, lovingly stabilized by the current

The popular Rustic Cabins bar on Kercheval in Grosse Pointe Park still has its original 1932 interior.

owner's dad; a moose head and mounted fish on the knotty-pine walls; and an Art Deco bar. There's pool, foosball, pinball, but no food. Old-timers stop by in the afternoon, a young crowd comes in the evening. Michigan State football coach George Perles was a regular during his coaching days at St. Ambrose.

Mulier's Omer Market ★
15215 Kercheval. (313) 822-7786. Mon-Sat 8-6.

This fourth-generation grocer-butcher has evolved from a neighborhood store geared to nearby Belgians into a gourmet grocer, without losing any of its character. Walk in the door, and you feel you've stepped back in time. They make liver pate, meat loaf, sausage, and Rose Mulier's famous potato salad. Local breads, fresh-squeezed orange juice, and specialty meat cuts are other attractions.

Gypsy's Vintage Bazaar ★
15227 Kercheval. No phone. Mon-Sat, 11-5.

A charming consignment shop, newly expanded and strong in costumes (especially for theatricals), vintage lace, fabrics, and hats. The proprietor just did turn-of-the-century wardrobes for "I Remember Mama" and flapper outfits for a Noel Coward comedy. She says an average Halloween outfit here runs under $10. You could also find everyday clothes and accessories here, along with dishes, tableware, and pictures. A lot of merchandise comes from Grosse Pointe attics cleaned out before moving, which accounts for its unusual age and quality. We saw a stunning 1932 silk wedding gown with Chantilly lace for only $200.

In the same building are **Grosse Pointe Botanical Gardens,** a shop with orchids and unusually large interior plants, and the **Sprout House** health food store.

The Village
Kercheval between Cadieux and Neff in Grosse Pointe. Typical hours are 9:30 or 10 til 5:30 or 6, with some stores open Thursday evening.

The three blocks of Kercheval in the Village form the Pointes' principal shopping district. **Jacobson's** and **Winkelman's** are here; so is a Kroger, disguised to blend in with a streetscape of small shops. In the past five years the Village has lost much of its character, as store owners who own their own buildings realized they could make as much money renting to chains and not be troubled with running a business. **Benetton, Waldenbooks, Laura Ashley, Talbots, Express, Ann Taylor career fashions, Banana Republic, L. J. Hickey** traditional clothiers — all these upscale chains are here.

Of special interest in the Village:

Village Records & Tapes
1711 Kercheval. (313) 886-6039. 10-7 weekdays, Thurs & Fri 'til 9, Sun 12-5.

This service-oriented audiophile shop carries all kinds of CDs and cassettes (no more records) but, as one of its two owner-managers says, "We fancy ourselves a bit of a classical and jazz specialty store." The knowledgeable staff is happy to special-order and, when filling Ticketmaster requests, to find your preferred seat.

Sanders Confectionery ★ ★
17043 Kercheval. (313) 885-8346. Mon-Sat 8 a.m.-10 p.m. Sun 11-6.

Nothing seems to have changed here since the sweet shop's heyday during Prohibition. The 55-year-old Grosse Pointe store is one of the few vintage Sanders still open. You can still enjoy breakfast sweet rolls, sandwiches, ice cream sodas, and pies at the marble soda fountain. Glass cases display candies, sweet rolls, pies, and Sanders' famous hot fudge sauce, hoarded by fans during Sanders' bankruptcy scare.

The Hill

Kercheval between Fisher and Muir in Grosse Pointe Farms. Same hours as the Village.

This tasteful strip of mostly postwar storefronts on a slight rise in Grosse Pointe's flat terrain is Kercheval's third and least intensely retail commercial district. Shops are intermixed with real estate brokers and other offices. Fashion chains are absent. But competition for parking is fierce, due to nearby Cottage Hospital.

Some of the more interesting shops include:

Joy Emery Gallery ★★
1321 Kercheval. (313) 886-1444. Tues-Sat 11-6.

Artists love gallery owner Joy Emery for her down-to-earth enthusiasm and support and her willingness to take a gamble on art she finds interesting, whether it's a proven seller or not — "art," as she puts it, "where there's enough going on that you want to see it more than once." She shows an eclectic range of artists, from realistic to abstract, controlled to messy, including more British artists than other area galleries. Though she avoids shows of exclusively Michigan artists, she shows area artists regularly, including several associated with the Cass Corridor movement: Jim Palkas, Ann Mikolowski, Brian Fekety, and Dick Goode. She coordinated the striking art on view at One23, the restaurant next door.

Hamlin's
89 Kercheval. (313) 885-8400.

Upscale but old-fashioned grocery with gourmet items, takeout salads, and a stunning fruit display.

Pointe Pedlar
88 Kercheval. (313) 885-4028.

This attractive, large kitchen and cookware store is geared to Grosse Pointe's favorite mode of entertaining — at home. There's an unusually large selection of cookbooks, kitchen gadgets, and knives, plus a bakery with French bread and croissants.

Kennedy and Company, interior decorator
76 Kercheval. (313) 885-2701.

Elegant period furniture in lushly dramatic, fully accessorized room settings.

The League Shop
72 Kercheval. (313) 882-6880.

Bridal and gift shop with loads of stand-up silver picture frames (a sine-qua-non of upper-class decor) and enough surprises to be interesting: delicate plates and bowls shaped like vegetables and Herend porcelain from Hungary. Its elegant forms are decorated with butterflies, birds, and patterns, precisely executed in the most vibrant oranges and blues. Don't miss the huge basement display of interesting, traditional table settings and, in another room, nutcrackers.

Brooks Brothers
11 Kercheval. (313) 886-2300.

America's quintessential traditional clothier, in recent years with a women's department, has opened its eastside store here in the remodeled Punch & Judy Theater.

Shopping in Grosse Pointe's "Hill" (pictured here) and "Village" is hardly trendy, but it is quite pleasant, with friendly service and an attractive environment.

Josef's Pastry Shop ★

21150 Mack, Grosse Pointe Woods. (313) 881-5710. Tues-Sat 8-6, Sun 8-1:30

A dozen kinds of Danish, two dozen coffee cakes, a mind-boggling variety of cookies, tortes, petits fours, eclairs, fruit tarts, etc. Of the breads, the brioche, Irish soda bread, and croissants are especially highly recommended. Mack, which is at or near the city line Grosse Pointe shares with Detroit, is lined with many service businesses.

RESTAURANTS

Sparky Herbert's ★★

15117 Kercheval, Grosse Pointe Park. (313) 822-0266. Mon-Sat 11:30-midnight, Sun brunch noon-3. Full bar, extensive wine list. All major credit cards.

This multifaceted place — part pub, part fine dining, part whimsy — looks like a Yuppie watering hole, but all sorts of Grosse Pointe types, young and old, dressed-up and very casual come here. The Key Lime Pie may be its best-known dish, but the hot chili ($1.95 a cup) and burgers on homemade rolls also win raves. Entrees on the dinner menu ($11.95-$18.95, including salad, starch, and vegetable) change frequently. Current favorites, along with steak and grilled swordfish, are curried chicken tenderloins and blackened grouper. But diners at any time can order sandwiches, soups, and appetizers ($4.95-$7.95).

Janet's Lunch ★

15033 Kercheval, Grosse Pointe Park. (313) 331-5776. Mon-Fri 6 a.m.-7 p.m., Sat 'til 2 p.m. No credit cards.

An incredibly diverse and loyal area clientele stops in at the three-sided lunch counter in this classic, ungentrified diner, now run by Janet's daughter. The grill's right out in front, so you can see that the fried potatoes aren't frozen product. Breakfasts are terrific, and the stacked roast beef or pork sandwiches with gravy ($3.20) are lunch favorites.

Cafe le Chat ★★

672 Notre Dame at Kercheval, behind the Merry Mouse gourmet shop. (313) 884-9077. Mon & Tues 11:30-5 (lunch & tea only). Wed-Sat 11:30-11. Cocktails & wine with food only. Visa, MasterCard, AmExpress.

The small, cozy, 35-seat restaurant in the Village is a popular spot for Grosse Pointe "ladies who lunch." Lunch favorites are the chicken strudel (dark meat wrapped in filo dough, topped with Hollandaise sauce) for $6.75 and the classic chicken Caesar salad for $5.95. At dinner the mood is romantic. The menu ($13.95-$18.95, including a starch and vegetable) changes monthly, but usually includes rack of lamb, a veal dish, and a seafood and pasta entree of the day.

One23 ★★

123 Kercheval, Grosse Pointe Farms. (313) 881-5700. Mon-Sat: lunch 11:30-5, dinner 5-11, Fri & Sat 'til midnight. Full bar. Visa, MasterCard, AmExpress.

It's worth coming here just to see how contemporary art can look fabulous in a polished, semi-traditional setting. Gallery owner Joy Emery next door has chosen eclectic pieces by Michigan artists to pick up the subtle blues, purples, browns, and greens in the Pewabic tile borders around the booths. Be sure to go downstairs to peek at the room that cleverly imitates the wine cellar of an old Italian country house and the neon dog whose tail wags when people approach.

The fresh art and innovative food have stirred up tradition-minded Grosse Pointe. Dinner entrees (mostly $18.95, including julienne vegetables and potatoes) range from simple broiled fish (swordfish with curry and Szechuan pepper) to a salmon roasted on a cedar shingle. *Monthly Detroit* praised the more complex appetizers (mostly $5.75), especially grilled chicken and duck livers with spinach and currants and salmon cakes in an herbed corn sauce. Many people order a la carte meals of appetizers, soups (two hot bisques and two cold each day), salads (house salad is $1.95), and desserts — the popular creme brulee ($3.50) or, for $4.95 a person, two-person minimum, a sampling of half a dozen desserts.

Lunch favorites include a grilled chicken sandwich on homemade poppyseed roll ($4.75) and grilled scallop salad ($7.25).

Original Pancake House

20273 Mack , Grosse Pointe Woods. (313) 884-4144. Daily 7 a.m.-9 p.m. No credit cards.

The pancakes, waffles, and crepes here are so good and reasonably priced that you often have to wait in line. All the details add up to a perfect breakfast, any time of day: excellent coffee, fresh-squeezed orange juice, whipped butter, crisp bacon, your choice of homemade syrups (maple-flavored, blueberry, or apple) — all served by a cheerful, uniformed staff in a warm, untrendy colonial setting. Prices start at $2.75 for wonderfully light buttermilk pancakes, with loads of possible variations going up to $3.89: blueberry, whole wheat, buckwheat, 49er flapjacks, potato pancakes with sour cream or applesauce, and more. Omelets run from $4.10 to $5.65; fruit or sour cream crepes from $4.10 to $4.25; and waffles from $3.09 (plain) to $4.65 (for a strawberries with ice cream). The people's favorite is the spectacular Big Apple ($5.69), a crispy, cinnamon-topped oven-baked pancake over a mountain of apples, rushed to your table before it deflates.

See also: *Cadieux Cafe in nearby Detroit, p. 75.*

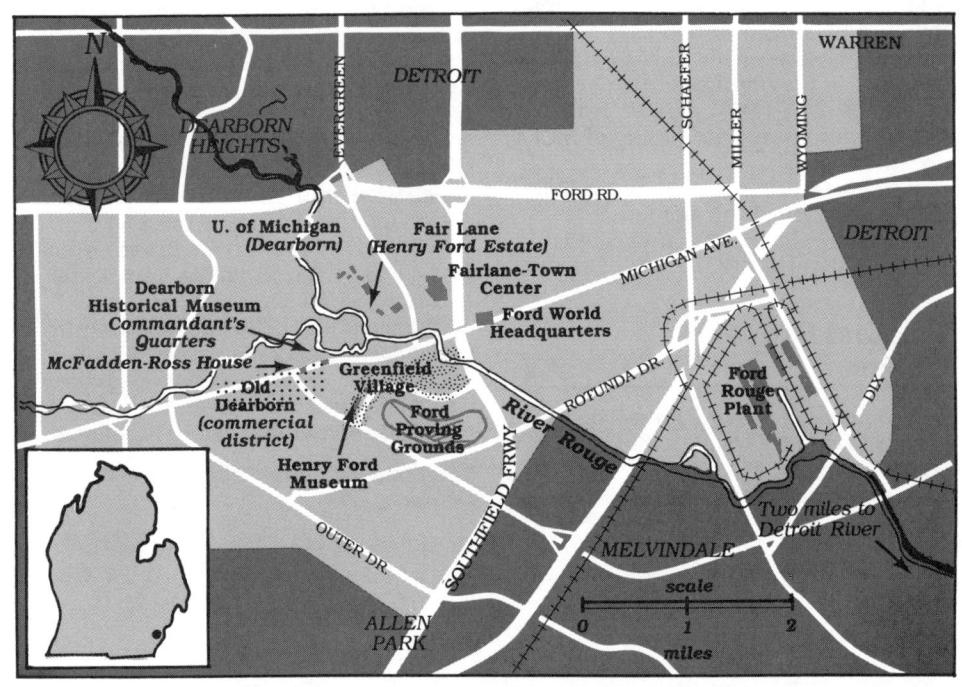

· DEARBORN ·

Dearborn

This city of 90,000 has been shaped by the actions of one man: Henry Ford. He was born and raised on a farm here at the corner of Ford and Greenfield Roads. After moving to Detroit, he came back here in 1916 to build his estate, **Fair Lane**, on a scenic portion of the River Rouge. Then he moved his booming car company here, and built the world's largest factory, the sprawling **Rouge Plant**, which dramatically dominates southeast Dearborn.

Ford also purchased over six square miles of farmland, between the old villages of Dearborn and Springwells. This immense tract of land along and to the east of the River Rouge has, through generous Ford donations, evolved into a huge swath of large-scale institutions and sweeping expanses of green lawn in the middle of Dearborn, dividing the city in two. Just south of Michigan Avenue, Henry Ford established **Greenfield Village** and the **Henry Ford Museum**. They house his immense collections of vehicles, machines, antique furniture and household objects, and buildings themselves. South of them, Henry Ford built an airport and started the country's first commercial airline service, to Cleveland. After accidents with the famous Ford Tri-motor airplane, he gave up aeronautical pursuits and turned the airport into the Ford Proving Grounds.

From Michigan Avenue north to Ford Road, the Ford Motor Company and family has given away large parcels of land along Evergreen Road and otherwise

The Dearborn Trolley is a bus that looks like an old trolley. From May through Oct. 1 it takes passengers on a circular route to Fair Lane estate and Fair Lane Town Center, major hotels, downtown West Dearborn, Greenfield Village and the Dearborn Inn, and Westborn Mall at Outer Drive. Times: Mon-Sat 10-5, Sun noon-5. Fare $1, or 75¢ for seniors and kids 6-12. Call to confirm and get a schedule: (313) 274-6300.

"The Rouge isn't fun any more," the aging Henry Ford said after completing the world's biggest factory. He had become involved in politics, but when his Peace Ship venture to stop World War I failed, he turned to other personal interests that shaped the west side of Dearborn. In the Henry Ford Museum and Greenfield Village he collected relics of America's technological change. He also preserved much of the Upper, Middle, and Lower Rouge Rivers as parkland and harnessed waterpower for small village industries.

helped create the four-year **Dearborn branch** of the **University of Michigan** and the **Henry Ford Community College**. Ford's Fair Lane estate itself is now a conference center for the U-M Dearborn.

Additional Ford gifts are parks — the River Rouge Park along the Upper Rouge River that flows from Southfield, and the idyllic-looking 17 1/2 -mile Middle Rouge Parkway along Hines Drive from Northville. (See p. 182.) Still more land between Evergreen and the Southfield Freeway, just north of Michigan Avenue, has been developed by the Ford Motor Land Development Corporation into **Fairlane Town Center**, the state's largest shopping mall. (See p. 329.) It is connected by a now-defunct monorail with the enormous **Hyatt Regency Hotel**. Looming across the freeway is the Ford World Headquarters, the **"Glass House,"** just north of Michigan Avenue. Immediately north of Fairlane Town Center is another Ford gift, the **Henry Ford Hospital**. Other vast tracts Henry bought are still being developed into office and housing complexes, almost half a century after his death.

Two villages become one town

The city of Dearborn is actually the union of the two 19th-century villages flanking the Ford land. To the east adjoining Detroit was Springwells, at the Detroit city line. Named after Springwells Township, it was briefly renamed Fordson for Henry Ford and his son, Edsel. Three and a half miles west, along Michigan and Garrison between Brady and Military, was the historic core of the village of Dearborn (sometimes called "Old Dearborn" today). The two villages merged in 1929, following an extraordinary decade of growth. In 1920 there were 2,470 residents here. By 1930, the influx of Rouge Plant workers and Ford white-collar employees had rocketed the population to over 50,000. Each year between 1921 and 1927, the school population doubled. Before the 1920s, Dearborn had developed little beyond an assortment of brick manufacturers, despite being on both the important Chicago Road and the Michigan Central Railroad, and despite being right next to Detroit.

Dearborn's claim to fame in the 19th century had been its **military arsenal** moved here from Detroit in 1833. The commandant's quarters on Michigan Avenue and the powder magazine, today both historical museums (see p. 144), are the only remnants of this 11-building complex, which was put out of service in 1875.

By the 1930s, the city's main downtown had developed at Michigan and Schaefer, with big Art Deco stores and an impressive colonial city hall. East Dearborn has an urban feel; indeed, it's only seven miles from downtown Detroit. The solid, ample brick houses

Henry Ford's dark side
As Ford aged, his suspicous side grew, allowing little sympathy for workers. His system pushed them to exhaustion, and the Sociology Department, once a model of enlightenment, spied on them. Dearborn and the Rouge were the scene of terrible labor strife in the 1930s, when the thug-like Harry Bennett virtually ran the company.

The "Dictator of Dearborn"
Mayor Orville Hubbard is widely viewed as having kept blacks, recruited by Ford Motor as foundry and paint shop workers, from living in Dearborn. The 1980 census found virtually no blacks living in Dearborn. Old-timers maintain that Hubbard reflected the wishes of Henry Ford himself. The married Hubbard was a genial and adept politician who managed to openly have a young mistress (the sister of Dearborn's famed broker in surrogate babies, Noel Keane) without alienating his largely Catholic constituency.

north of Michigan Avenue were built for prosperous autoworkers and skilled craftsmen.

West Dearborn has been the more affluent half of the city. Its beautiful big Protestant churches, aura of careful colonial gentility, Jacobson's department store, and two country clubs give it a much more suburban look. West Dearborn was clearly built as the domain of Ford Motor's middle management. Just two blocks from traffic-thick, heavily commercial Michigan Avenue, it's surprising to come upon Morley, Dearborn village's turn-of-the-century show street of fine old houses and big lawns.

Neither retail district is very healthy today. How could they be, with a giant regional shopping center and so much strip commercial development along Michigan Avenue? West Dearborn is livelier, however, and more attractive to pedestrians.

Dearborn's thriving Arab community

The healthiest small-business area in Dearborn today is the booming stretch of West Warren between Miller and Schaefer. Today this is a vibrant center of Muslim Arab culture — a curious development in a city with a racist reputation. But Muslim Arab immigrants, who first settled around the Ford Highland Park plant, had been part of industrial Dearborn's original ethnic mix, all drawn to work at the Rouge.

Fifteen years ago empty storefronts abounded along West Warren here. Then the Arab community in the South End, at Miller and Vernor and Dix, began to grow. In the 1960s and 1970s the wars in Lebanon and the West Bank of Palestine led thousands of people there to join their relatives already in America. After Yemen's feudal isolationist government fell in 1962, Yemeni men came to Detroit to take jobs nobody else wanted, such as working in auto factory paint shops. The Yemenis' fabled honesty led Chrysler to recruit them to clean offices. Dearborn and Detroit already had a big Arab population going back to Arab peddlers in 1908. Most were from Lebanon, and most of them Christian, but with some Muslims as well.

Middle-class Arab-Americans who moved into the substantial brick houses off of West Warren in the mid-1960s soon were joined by wealthier refugees, and by newcomers who had succeeded in business here. West Warren is now lined with businesses catering to the Arab community. New ones are opening up all the time; vacancies are rare. And property values are rising: six- and eight-room 1920s-style houses nearby have risen to from $60,000 to $90,000 and up. Arab families tend to be large, with four to seven children, even more for the Yemeni. Fordson High is now 65 per cent Arab. Arabs make up about 22 per cent of Dearborn's population today.

Dearborn and racism
The two words are automatically associated in many Detroiters' minds, owing largely to the long tenure (1945-1979) of Mayor Orville Hubbard. Urbanologists attribute Dearborn racism to a more general border phenomenon going back to the 1930s, in which suburbs adjoining the city adopt various measures to keep at bay the city's underclass masses. Today nearby Detroiters (3/4ths black) comprise 40% of Fairlane Town Center shoppers. But they are prohibited from using Dearborn parks, along with all other non-residents. The Dearborn police department has a history of stopping and questioning blacks.

Though there are well-publicized cases of severe cultural conflict among immigrant families (largely over girls dating), many young Arabs consider it a great advantage to be able to grow up bilingual and bicultural — in American schools, with non-Arab teachers, and in warm, close Arab families. The family ideal is for the children of gas station- and restaurant-owners to go to college and into the professions, notably law.

Many locals from West Dearborn are offended by the continuing influx of Arabs. Among other things, they're bothered by the sight of Arab matrons in their traditional head covering. "It's not American," they complain. The long head scarf, a custom akin to Italian and Greek married women wearing black, has no political significance other than tradition and cultural pride. But it reminds many outsiders of Iranian fundamentalists on TV, and they don't like it.

Dearborn Mayor Michael Guido, a successor in Orville Hubbard's political machine, has patched things up with the Arabs after circulating a much-publicized and ill-advised campaign pamphlet addressing "the Arab problem" caused by their increasing numbers. He now realizes that these immigrants are ultimately a great economic asset. They are notably hard workers and entrepreneurial self-starters in the best American tradition. Furthermore, family pride and a highly developed sense of shame make street crime practically non-existent among Arab Muslims here.

Dearborn via train
Amtrak's Dearborn station is off Michigan Ave. between East and West Dearborn, not too far from hotels and Greenfield Village. Schedules don't allow for a day trip from points west, but an overnight works well. The morning train from Chicago and Kalamazoo arrives at 2:35 p.m., with time to tour Fair Lane before dinner. A train leaves Dearborn at 5:25 (Fri-Sun only), after a full day at Greenfield Village, and arrives in Chicago at 10. Call 1-800-872-7245 for fares.

POINTS OF INTEREST

Greenfield Village ★★★★

On Village Rd. east off Oakwood Blvd. From Michigan Ave. in West Dearborn, turn south onto Oakwood at the green-roofed Westborn Market. From I-94, take the Southfield Freeway north and follow signs for the Village. (313) 271-1620. For 24-hour taped info, call (313) 271-1976.
Open *daily 9-5. Buildings are closed Jan-mid-March, but the exterior can be viewed for free with a ticket to the Henry Ford Museum.*
Admission: *adults $10.50, seniors $9.50, youths 5-12 $5.25, under 5 free. 2-day unlimited-admission ticket to Museum and Village $9 youths, $18 adults. The Museum/Village* **annual pass** *($22 adults, $11 youths) makes frequent visits affordable.* **Memberships** *($35/adult, $60/companions, $70/family) allow unlimited admissions to museum and village, a 10% discount at the excellent store, and a monthly newsletter and advance notice on special events.*

This outdoor museum, a famous American tourist sight, is a direct outgrowth of Henry Ford's great interest in how technology had changed the lives of ordinary Americans. As Ford entered his sixties, he developed a passionate interest in the tangible manifestations of American history. Part of the great wave of antique-collecting that swept the U.S. in the 1920s, Ford had a very different collecting agenda from most of his wealthy contemporaries who sought out the pinnacles of achievement in the arts and crafts. In the Henry Ford

In the peak summer season, all Greenfield Village's houses are open, the sheep are out grazing at the **Firestone Farm,** you can ride a **steamboat,** and **demonstrations** are under way. The dates of full operation change yearly; call first to plan your visit. In winter (Jan.-mid-March) the buildings are closed, but visitors to the Henry Ford Museum can walk around the village at no extra charge.

Museum and Greenfield Village, Ford wanted mainly to document the ordinary life of the past, that of farmers and shopkeepers and artisans, the middling people. He focused on America's industrial transformation in the late 19th and early 20th centuries. He collected some things barely 20 years old.

Not only did Ford spend millions to obtain the many buildings and artifacts assembled here, but he also personally spent months actively seeking them out. He supervised their placement here, and would spend hours in these historic places — often alone — savoring their connection with the past.

Manufacturing demonstrations have always been important at Greenfield Village. New displays emphasize the experience of the people who once lived and worked in these buildings, rather than merely the physical settings.

Village highlights include:

◆ **Wright Cycle Shop.** Here, in the famous birthplace of aviation, Orville and Wilbur Wright built kites, gliders, and ultimately the world's first successful flying machine. By 1903, the American bicycle craze of the 1890s was on the wane. The Wrights eked out a living selling bicycles and bicycling paraphernalia from the store and repairing bikes in the room behind it. In the very back, they built their flying machines. Displayed among the belt-driven machines used to make the various components is a replica of the center section of that first plane. Moved from Dayton, Ohio, in 1936, the building has been restored to look much as it did in 1903, the year of their first motorized flight. The Wrights' house here also represents that period.

◆ **Susquehanna Plantation.** Redone and reopened in 1988, this Maryland plantation house, interpreted as it would have been in 1860, is now used to examine the economic and social basis of slavery — who the slaves and masters were, their various roles, and the relationships among them.

◆ **Glass, pottery, printing, tinsmithing, and textile demonstrations.** Using 19th-century techniques, craftspeople show how these important products were made.

◆ **Ford's birthplace.** This simple Greek Revival farmhouse was built by Henry's father William in 1861. It's popular because of the public's widespread fascination with Henry Ford. Exhibits tell about his life.

◆ **Bagley Avenue Shed.** This is a replica of the shed for wood and coal behind his house, in which Henry Ford and his associates built their first car, the Quadricycle, in 1896. (A parking lot near Grand Circus Park occupies the site today.) Before he could drive it around the streets of Detroit, Ford had to widen the door with an axe to get the car out. Here you can see the Quadricycle as well as the belt-driven machines with which the men laboriously made engine parts and other components. The cluttered scene enables you to appreciate Ford's ingenuity in building a car from scratch.

◆ **Ford Mack Avenue Factory.** In 1903 the first production-model Fords were manufactured in the original of this scaled-down building. Using an innovative team method of construction (Ford's revolutionary production line was still years away), this factory turned out up to 18 cars a day and quickly made Henry wealthy. The 4 hp vehicles started at $800 apiece.

◆ **Mrs. Cohen's millinery shop.** A Detroit widow ran this shop at the turn of the century to support her family. Visitors enjoy seeing hats made and trying them on.

◆ **Armington & Sims Machine Shop.** Many visitors are unexpectedly fascinated by the awesome turn-of-the-century steam engines demonstrated here.

◆ **Menlo Park Compound.** In this complex of six rather plain New Jersey buildings, one has the opportunity to relive one of the most extraordinary phenomena in American history. Thomas Edison's 1880 laboratories were the world's first commercial research and development center. Edison gathered chemists, machinists, craftsmen, glass blowers, and other specialists (the boarding house they lived in is also here) and gave them a wide assortment of tools and materials. The results were spectacular. Though the laboratory was used only 10 years, 420 of Edison's 1,093 patents came from here, including the electric light bulb, phonograph, and electric sewing machine.

◆ **Plympton House.** This small, rude, one-room house nicely reveals how a typical colonial New England family lived in the 1600s. It was the South Sudbury, Massachusetts, home of Thomas Plympton, his wife, and seven children. What makes the display especially effective is the recorded discussion among family members in the strikingly different dialect of that time.

Antiques Classes and Special Events. For a catalog on the Museum and Village's vast array of special weekend events, plus classes. lectures, and one-day workshops on antiques and related subjects, write Public Programs Department. Henry Ford Museum/Greenfield Village, 20900 Oakwood Blvd., Dearborn, MI 48121-1970. Weekends include American popular dance, black history, rock 'n' roll roots, quilts and textiles, farm days, and much more.

◆ **Noah Webster House.** This house, built in 1823 for $3,400 when Webster and his wife were in their sixties, is spacious for someone of such modest means. Here Noah Webster completed his dictionary. An upstairs room displays the extraordinary number of his accomplishments, from founding Amherst College to serving in the state legislature. The house has been recently reinterpreted to go beyond pretty rooms and highlight the Websters' activities. (She managed the household while he wrote.)

◆ **Cotswold Buildings.** The only non-American structures in Greenfield Village, this delightful 17th-century stone cottage and barn was brought from southwestern England — all 175 tons of it.

◆ **Eagle Tavern.** Transported from Clinton, Michigan, this is a splendid recreation of 19th-century American institution, complete with ladies' parlor, sitting room, and bar. Here you can buy weak versions of authentic drinks from the 1850s such as a "Jersey Lightning" ($1.75). In back, a restaurant serves huge, reasonably-priced meals from recipes of the era such as stewed rabbit ($7.95) and pork loin.

◆ **Elias Brown General Store.** This is one of the very best reconstructions of a classic American 19th-century general store to be found. The store building was moved from Waterford, Michigan, in Oakland County; the contents, dating from about 1860, came from a store in Minaville, New York. Note the paper bags above the counter, an innovation that began in 1864.

Greenfield Village's mammoth size is both a strength and a weakness. A visitor's reactions to this long parade of Americana may well eventually become muted after dutifully plodding to place after place after place. The situation is not helped by often superficial, uninspired signage and recorded accounts. And while some interpretive guides stationed at the more important individual buildings are quite helpful, others add little insight into what you are seeing.

Several eateries, a bakery, and a restaurant are sprinkled throughout the village. The food is far from great, but it is palatable, and sometimes pretty good. The best things we tasted were the bakery's brownies and coffee. The **Great American Emporium** gift shop has many toys and games for children, in addition to reproductions of antiques and jewelry in the collection here, handcrafts made in the village, and an outstanding book store like that in the Henry Ford Museum.

You may want to see only about half of Greenfield Village. Even so, this will take you a good two to three hours. It also may be helpful to break up your walking tour with a **train ride** on the village's splendid steam locomotive that circles the entire complex. $1.50 gives you unlimited rides for the day. Or you can take a horse-driven **carriage ride** ($5 per person) or **bus ride** ($3 per person); both last 30 to 35 minutes. All three rides provide an ongoing description of what you pass.

Henry Ford Museum ★ ★ ★

See Greenfield Village above for directions, phone, and prices.

Henry Ford's squadrons of pickers spread over the Midwest and New England to come up with an astounding array of artifacts for this vast (12 acres of display space) and prestigious indoor museum adjacent to Greenfield Village. The dignified Georgian exterior combines an adaptation of Independence Hall with the look of a well-heeled college campus of the 1920s — quite a contrast with the homey functionalism of some of its strengths, such as the world's greatest collection of 19th-century farm and kitchen implements. The exhibit on the history of lighting, from candles through electric bulbs, is immense enough to be a substantial museum in itself. The same could be said for the large collection of airplanes and cars. Nowhere will you find a more complete historical collection of American tractors. Taking up the most space of all is a vast array of old steam engines, tangible symbols of the harnessed power which transformed life a century ago.

Unfortunately, the hundreds of signs explaining the often arcane items in the museum are in small print, displayed so low visitors sometimes resort to getting on their knees to read them.

Over the years the museum staff has worked to give shape to this huge, at times bewildering, hoard of items. The evolution of the auto industry is brilliantly elucidated by

"The Automobile in American Life" is a lavish series of displays which nostalgically illuminate the car's effect on American streetscapes. This tableau about the drive-in combines a 1956 Chevrolet Bel-Air from the museum's famous car collection with a vintage McDonald's sign. Nearby are a meticulously appointed 1946 diner and parts of a Kalamazoo drive-in theater where visitors see "Car Culture," a 12-minute movie with promotional ads for American cars and a scene from "American Graffiti."

> You don't have to have a museum ticket to shop at the **Museum Store** (open 9-5 daily). Its outstanding book section is especially strong on automobiles and roadside architecture, Henry Ford and Ford Motor, antiques, crafts, Detroit history, and inexpensive Dover paper toys and coloring books. Many of the dolls, crystal, china, and other gift items reproduce objects in the Museum's collections.

using a sequence TV monitors showing short historical film clips with the autos of the period as a backdrop.

Shorter on insight but higher in flash is the grandiose new exhibit called **The Automobile in American Life**, a pioneer in the use of big pieces of roadside architecture. Here is a vintage McDonald's, complete with oversized golden arches, a Holiday Inn guest room, and a diner plucked from Marlboro, Massachusetts, lovingly refurbished to its pristine state in 1946, when an egg salad sandwich cost 15¢. A similar treatment has been given a gleaming green and white 1940 Texaco service station, where you can even peer into the garage and see the tools used at the time. Gradually more of the museum will consist of similar exhibits that use objects to tell stories and relate technological change to people's own lives. "Made in America," on production technology and the growth of the labor force, is due to be ready in 1992.

The most extraordinary theme area of all, however, is **The Streamlining of America**, a dazzling, well-told set of displays on how, beginning in the 1920s, everything from toasters to tractors was redesigned to meet a new ideal of windswept elegance. After the Depression hit, manufacturers relied heavily on styling to stimulate languishing demand for new products.

In counterpoint to these mammoth display areas, the museum also holds an assortment of fascinating isolated items. There's the 1961 Lincoln limousine in which John F. Kennedy was shot, and the rocking chair in which Lincoln was shot. You can see the huge, 600-ton 1941 "Allegheny" steam locomotive, one of the last and largest of a proud era. And in the aviation section is a Lunar Roving Vehicle, one made by NASA to transport astronauts on the moon.

At the supervised **Activity Center** children can talk on a hand-cranked wall phone, pedal a high-wheel bike, work on a moving assembly line, and do other hands-on things. At the end of the walk from the entrance, the **American Cafe** and soda fountain is open 9-4:30, year 'round. No museum ticket is required. Here the hot dogs cost a hefty $1.70 but the $5.25 beef stew lunch is hearty and filling. Visitors can also bring bag lunches to eat at the Corner Cupboard within the museum. The **Plaza Store** within the museum sells handcrafts (many made in Greenfield Village) and a wide range of toys for children and adults.

Henry Ford Estate (Fair Lane)

West off Evergreen between Michigan Ave. and Ford Rd. Park at the Visitors' Center. (313) 593-5590. Tours Mon-Sat 10, 11, 1, 2, 3, Sun between 1 and 4:30 on the half-hour. Closed Jan. 1-April 1 except Sun. $6/adult, $5/seniors and students, 5 and under free.

By the time his estate was completed in 1914, Henry Ford's interests and activities were already expanding beyond manufacturing cars. In fact, his wife, Clara, and son, Edsel, moved into Fair Lane without him in December while he was taking his peace ship to Europe in an attempt to stop World War I.

The 56-room mansion is disappointing architecturally. It's a strange amalgam of Frank Lloyd Wright's naturalistic Prairie School style and the medieval-influenced Scottish baronial style. Ford changed architects in midstream, and it shows.

Unfortunately, the Ford heirs auctioned off most of the furniture after

Henry and Clara died. University of Michigan-Dearborn offices occupy 30 per cent of the mansion. So it's rather difficult to get a good sense of how the Fords really lived here, as you can, for instance, at the Edsel and Eleanor Ford estate in Grosse Pointe Shores.

The home seems a bad fit for Henry Ford's down-to-earth tastes. Not surprisingly, the most used room was the rustic Field Room. Its raw-timbered ambience is unlike the ornate interiors in the rest of the house.

Clearly where Ford put his creative genius was not in the house but in its huge hydroelectric power plant. It occupies a separate structure and is connected by a long underground tunnel with the mansion. He teamed up with his friend Thomas Edison to create an extraordinary 110-kilowatt electric system — quite a feat given the small size of the River Rouge. Almost half of the 1 1/2-hour tour is devoted to this plant. Visitors learn perhaps more than they ever wanted to know about its design. The independence provided by having his own power plant must have fulfilled a deep-seated need in Ford; he went on to build another 20 hydroelectric plants on small rivers in southeastern Michigan. (See p. 181-2.)

The grounds are the high point of a visit to Fair Lane. The mansion overlooks a beautiful, wooded portion of the River Rouge at the point of a delightful small waterfall. It is said that after seeing garbage floating past his mansion, Henry Ford was personally responsible for getting the cities of Plymouth and Northville upstream to stop dumping raw sewage in the river.

The 1,600 acres of surrounding farmland were transformed by the famous landscape architect Jens Jensen into a series of naturalistic meadows and forests. With the aid of a well-designed 25¢ map of the grounds, you can take your own tour of this vast area. The map is available near the information board by the parking lot, or at the gift shop or reception desk inside Fair Lane. Nature

As the River Rouge winds idyllically past Henry Ford's Fair Lane estate, it is quite a contrast to the same river as it passes Ford's Rouge complex, where it has been dredged straight to accommodate freighters and is so polluted it never freezes.

was one of Ford's many passions. An avid bird-watcher, he installed hundreds of birdhouses — eight heated in winter! Almost 600 deer roamed the woods and fields. Clara Ford's taste was for the more formal English gardens. She appropriated one of Jensen's meadows to create a fantastic rose garden that gained national attention in its day. Today you can see its ruins, for it would cost $400,000 a year to maintain.

It's worth having lunch at **The Pool**, a restaurant in the dramatically illuminated space which was initially the mansion's swimming pool. It's open weekdays from 11 to 2. A variety of sandwiches is under $5, and homemade soup and a trip to the salad bar is only $3.95.

Bryant Branch Library

2210 Michigan Ave. at Mason in West Dearborn. (313) 274-6226. Mon-Thurs 9-9, Fri & Sat 9-5. Park in rear off Mason.

The feeling of living in Henry Ford's town is vividly conveyed here in this beautiful small library. Finished in 1924, it was the first in Dearborn, then mushrooming from a village into an affluent city. A bust and portrait of Henry Ford, flanked by portraits of Revolutionary War heroes, still survey one main reading room. In the grand front entry hall one mural, done by the gifted Paul Honore in a lush romantic 1920s' style similar to Howard Pyle and Maxfield Parrish, illustrates "The Application of Knowledge" in a factory and harbor setting much like the Rouge itself. A drab-looking and apparently dull-minded worker leans on his shovel in front of his horse, while a lightbulb-like light of knowledge is held up by a genie-savant in futuristic garb.

The library building was planned by the ladies' garden club of Dearborn, with the active participation of Clara (Mrs. Henry) Ford, who donated the land. Its architect was Edward Tilton of New York, a specialist in libraries and designer of the beautiful McGregor Library in Highland Park. Two fireplaces feature Pewabic tiles — almost an essential for quality Detroit-area buildings of the day. In the west reading alcove, originally for children, delightful fireplace tiles depict scenes from Walter Crane's book illustrations, using Mary Chase Stratton's famous glazes of brilliant blue.

Westborn Market ★

21755 Michigan at Oakwood in West Dearborn. Park off Oakwood. (313) 274-6100. Daily 9 a.m.-9 p.m.

This longtime Italian fruit stand has blossomed into an stylish international food market with cheese, wine, crackers and cookies, and most of the leading brands of fancy foods at good prices. But the fruit and produce, beautifully displayed and surprisingly inexpensive, is still the main draw.

Don't come here for the newest fad vegetables or exotic fresh herbs. Westborn is aimed at middle-income customers like Dearborn's Italian families, who appreciate good food but have a family to feed. Like most fruit markets, it operates on a low-markup, high-turnover principle. Smock-clad cashiers operate six checkout lanes here. The selection of budget and mid-price wines has "all the good names," says a knowledgeable owner of a fine restaurant, and good but little-known budget wines like Prince Pirate. There's also a big selection of breads from area ethnic bakeries. Fresh flowers, fruit baskets, and gifts are sold at **Westborn Flowers** across Michigan Avenue.

Corner-copia

21903 Michigan Ave. at Oakwood Blvd. in West Dearborn, just across Oakwood from the Westborn Market. (313) 565-0875. Mon-Sat 10-5.

A large, well-organized antique and second-hand store, the Corner-copia is especially good for 1920s and 1930s dining sets and other furniture, mostly in near-perfect condition, from Dearborn households now being dispersed. Jewelry and small household items are also on hand. Don't miss the basement.

Commandant's Quarters, Dearborn Historical Museum

21950 Michigan Ave. at Monroe Blvd. in downtown West Dearborn. (313) 565-3000. May-Oct. Mon-Sat 9-5. Nov-April Mon-Sat 1-5. Free.

This impressive stone house was built beginning in 1833 to lodge the commandant of the U.S. Arsenal here. Originally the arsenal, relocated from expanding Detroit, was surrounded by 12-foot walls and included 11 buildings. It was not a military fort, but a place to store arms and materiel that might be needed to defend Michigan and Wisconsin. Its location on the old Chicago military road was strategic. After the military moved out in 1875, the house went through various incarnations. The dismal cells from its years as a police station are still in the basement.

Since 1950 it has been a city museum. Several rooms (parlor, sitting room, lady's and gentleman's bedrooms, office, cellar kitchen) have been appointed to look the way they might have when various commandants lived here between 1833 and 1875. Others are used for displays on local Indians, the Civil War, Lincoln, World War I, and local history.

McFadden-Ross House

915 Brady St., 1/2 block north of Michigan Ave. at the east edge of West Dearborn. Same hours as Commandant's Quarters. Also free.

This, the other part of the Dearborn Historical Museum, once was the Dearborn Arsenal's powder magazine. Hence its four-foot walls and location away from the rest of the arsenal. In 1883 it became a private residence. Today it is mainly used for local school classes, although there are some Victorian rooms, a display of tools and utensils, and Victorian fashions on view to casual visitors. A basement display highlights brickmaking, Dearborn's chief 19th-century industry.

Alcamo's Market ★

4423 Schaefer 2 blocks south of Michigan in downtown East Dearborn. (313) 584-3010. Mon-Sat 9-6, Fri 'til 7. Easy to miss. Look for the red awning. Park in lot on Schaefer and Osborn.

When you walk in the door of this celebrated Italian specialty store, you're overwhelmed by the beguiling fragrances of spicy salamis, garlic, cheeses, coffee beans, and breads. There are two aisles of imported pastas in this spiffily updated old-time grocery, along with Italian specialties like fava beans, imported Italian cookies, crackers, appetizers, and sauces; gorgeous produce; and some Greek food, too.

West Warren Bakery/ Kowalski Sausage

15708 W. Warren at Montrose, 2 blocks west of Greenfield in Detroit. (313) 584-2610. Mon-Sat 5 a.m.-7 p.m.

In this stable westside Detroit Polish neighborhood between East Dearborn and Dearborn Heights, two longtime retail neighbors have recently combined. Kowalski's sells takeout Polish favorites like stuffed cabbage in addition to its well-known kielbasa and such. The bakery's good pumpernickel and rye breads are only 75¢ a loaf. There are Polish specialties like angel wings and jelly donuts, and a fabulous sourdough French bread, great for toast, also baked as submarine rolls that are served next door at the highly regarded Judy's Cafe. They're chewy with a crunchy crust that holds in the juice from tomatoes, and only 20¢ apiece. Order ahead to be sure of availability.

Michigan China Company

15700 W. Warren, corner of Montrose, in Detroit 2 blocks west of Greenfield. (313) 581-4399. Fri & Sat 10-5.

In the same block as Judy's Cafe and the West Warren Bakery is this corner storefront jam-packed with closeouts of thick, sturdy restaurant china — plain white bowls, mugs, fancy Chinese platters — at a third of their normal price.

Ford Rouge Complex ★★★

Surrounded by Schaffer Hwy., Dix Ave., Miller Rd., and Rotunda Dr.

This historic colossus of American industry is sadly no longer open for tours, but you can drive around the complex to take in its awesome magnitude and powerful visual forms.

The Rouge is the place where Henry Ford put it all together. It was the world's first vertically integrated factory, an idea much copied but later discredited as too centralized and massive. Iron ore came in by ship to Rouge Steel, and cars rolled out the connected auto plant.

Dredging the shallow River Rouge for three and one half miles up from its mouth at the Detroit River enabled freighters to deliver the limestone, coal, iron pellets, and other materials to the 1,100-acre site. The huge factories Ford built here turned the raw materials into the steel, plastic, rubber and glass parts which were then assembled into Ford automobiles. By the 1920s this was the world's biggest manufacturing complex; 10,000 cars a day were made here.

Ford's historic Highland Park Plant, where he introduced the assembly line, was only five years old when he started planning for the much bigger Rouge plant in 1914. It was built not far from the farm where he grew up. The 1,100 acres were marshy farmland when Ford sent his agents to buy up the component parcels all in a single day. The Rouge's first products were submarine-chasing Eagle boats made at the tail end of World War I. By the late 1920s, 75,000 workers were making Model As here, turning raw materials into completed vehicles in just 33 hours.

It was an extraordinarily bold move for Henry Ford to invest the hundreds of millions of dollars needed to make this giant car-manufacturing complex, including a state-of-the-art steelmaking plant. Another Rouge plant turned 210,000 bushels of soybeans a year into paints, plastics, and binders. An electrical power plant added in 1920 was one of the world's largest. One plant made the tires for Ford cars, while another made the glass windshields. Yet another made the famous Ford V-8 engine, Henry Ford's last engineering triumph.•

But the Rouge was also the scene of terrible labor strife. The aging Henry Ford lost interest in industrial production. "The Rouge isn't fun any more," he explained as he turned his interests to Greenfield Village, McGuffey's Readers, and an idealized (and ironically pre-industrial) American past. As Henry Ford aged, the dark, suspicious side in him grew, allowing little sympathy for the workers, who were pushed to exhaustion

At the Ford Rouge complex, iron came in on ships and finished cars rolled out. Once 90,000 workers coming from 49 countries were employed here. Since the 1960s, the workers' neighborhood just east of it has become a point of entry for the largest Arab community in the U.S.

and spied upon. At Ford Motor Company, Henry's capable son, Edsel, was cruelly frustrated, while Henry empowered the notorious Harry Bennett and his security department — virtual thugs and spies who infiltrated many potential organizing meetings. Symptoms of oppressive working conditions were many. Innocent protesters were slaughtered during the 1932 Hunger March. In the 1937 Battle of the Overpass, Bennett's goons flagrantly beat up Walter Reuther and other union organizers passing out leaflets even though photographers were present. Their photographs helped turn public opinion in the union's favor. Finally, a strike in 1941 prompted the company to recognize unionized workers.

Labor difficulties, along with the threat of German bombing attacks at the huge complex, led Ford management to decentralize operations after

> **A drive around the Rouge**
>
> A drive around the Rouge, or at least along Miller Road and across the Dix Avenue bridge, is well worthwhile. You could conveniently follow it with a good, inexpensive meal at the Red Sea Middle Eastern restaurant, in the neighborhood where dozens of groups of immigrant Rouge workers first made their home.
>
> Start at the north. Take Miller from Michigan Avenue, or take the Rotunda Drive exit from I-94 (Exit 209). As Miller Road passes high over the rail lines, a vast panorama of this awesome industrial complex opens up, with the powerful forms of the Rouge's eight tall stacks as a backdrop. Unfortunately, it's almost impossible to park near here and take in the view. A little farther on, by Gate 4, the main gate, you can pull over to look at the Dearborn Historical Society's marker — which neglects to mention the historic Battle of the Overpass that took place on a bridge near here (now removed), similar to the current overpass you see leading to the employee parking lot. None of the autoworkers we talked to here knew of the historic incident that occurred here.
>
> Turn west onto Dix Avenue just as it passes over the River Rouge. The drawbridge here raises to let big freighters come in from the Great Lakes. The once-meandering river is now dredged straight and so polluted with chemicals that it never freezes in the winter. In the distance you can see freighters unloading at the huge steel foundry to the north.
>
> Along Dix west of here is an ugly, striking landscape created by piles of raw materials and byproducts of industry. Firms like a refinery and Detroit Tarpaulin are mixed in with factory-gate bars and junkyards advertising for wrecked cars.

World War II. The Rouge's equipment grew outdated until its very existence was threatened during the auto depression of the early 1980s. Workers at the complex dwindled to about 15,000.

But a 1983 labor-management agreement prompted the company to invest $500 million to modernize its steel mill, which now makes galvanized (rust-resistant) steel. It's the new blue-colored plant you see at the south end of Schaefer near Dix. Finally it is making a profit, and Ford has sold it.

Indeed, the entire Rouge complex seems to be experiencing a renaissance. The soybean and tire plants were scrapped long ago, but the electrical plant still generates enough power to serve a city the size of Boston. Mustangs roll off the assembly line at the rate of one a minute. Each year freighters carry 5 million tons of coal, iron-rich taconite pellets, and limestone to the complex. The blast furnaces can produce over 2 million tons of iron and the steelmaking facilities 3.7 million tons of ingots a year. An engine plant makes 612,000 of the 1.9 liter, four-cylinder engines for Ford Escorts each year.

Dearborn's Southend ★★

Stores are on Dix and Vernor just east of Miller Rd. Take Miller south from I-94 or Michigan Ave. Many stores are open from 9 a.m. to 9 p.m., 7 days a week.

The eight stacks of the Rouge's huge steam generating plant form the backdrop for this 70-year-old working-class neighborhood, once a true American melting pot of dozens of nationalities working at Ford. Three decades ago the South End had 44 bars to serve plant workers and neighborhood residents. Now new Arab immigrants have replaced the older-generation autoworkers who have moved to better neighborhoods. One South End Ford worker was Jimmy Darwish, a Muslim Arab and the father of Tiffany, the "bubble-gum rock" pop star, also a Dearborn native.

Now that the South End is Arab, there's just one party store left, and no bars at all. (Islam discourages the use of alcohol.) The bars have been replaced by Arab bakeries, groceries, and meat markets. They serve neighborhood residents plus the larger Islamic community which attends the big Moslem Mosque on Vernor at

Dix. **Basali**, a very big name among Beirut bakeries, has come to the new shopping complex here.

Despite their current violent image from TV news, most Arabs are notably friendly, expressive people who set great store in generosity and hospitality. Outsiders are cheerfully welcomed to these Arab shops. If you're curious enough to ask, you'll be treated to interesting discourses on Arab food and culture, along with free samples.

The **Sunni mosque**, greatly expanded over the years, attracts Muslims from all over metro Detroit — up to 3,000 for some Friday-night prayer services, and far more on holy days. The call to prayer can be heard from the mosque five times a day (geared to sunrise and sunset). Storekeepers uncover small prayer rugs on their counters and take a few moments to pray.

The Muslim autoworkers and South End blue-collar residents who started building the mosque in 1939 have mostly moved on "into business" the second stage of Arabs' preferred career pattern that ends up, one or two generations later, in "the professions," especially law.

Now the South End is the reception area for a continuing stream of immigrants. The Lebanese and West Bank Palestinians, escaping wars at home, come as families. Yemeni men usually come alone, dreaming of saving enough money to return and live comfortably with their families in their beloved but impoverished homeland. This accounts for the large number of single men in skullcaps (a Yemeni tradition) who frequent the South End's coffeehouses, intended for Arab men only. Just in the past few years are the Yemeni beginning to acknowledge that they'll never save enough to realize their dreams, and they are accepting the reality that their and their families' futures are here in American society at large.

The South End storefronts with the graceful Arabic ogee arches are the result of a community development program in the early 1970s. So is the powerful **mural** on Salina at Dix, depicting the immigrants' story. Some of the area's rooming houses and apartments owned by absentee landlords are depressing. The simple owner-occupied homes, however, are neat and trim. Many boast beautiful big gardens full of vegetables and roses, in the best Mediterranean tradition.

You have to go out of your way to get here, but it's an easy detour from I-94 or I-75, and many of the shops are open 12 hours a day, seven days a week. "This is an ethnic neighborhood," explained one hard-working shopkeeper. "If I close, all my customers go someplace else." The **Red Sea** Yemeni restaurant serves huge portions of good food in pleasant surroundings. (See p. 151.)

Arabian Village Bakery ★★
10045 W. Vernor at Dix. (313) 843-0800. 7 days, 9 a.m.-9 p.m.

This highly regarded, home-style bakery sure isn't fancy — there's no display case at all, so you have to ask for a look and a taste of what's just come out of the oven. But it offers a lot, at reasonable prices. For a dollar each, there are meat pies and baked kibbee (cracked wheat) stuffed with lamb. You can warm them up in the oven for healthy fast-food meals, or fry them. (For takeout eating on the run, the clerk will microwave them and squirt on a hummus sauce.) There are *zahtar*, delicious flat breads flavored with oregano, sumac, and sesame. There are *kaak* (3/$1), spice cookies attractively stamped with decorative molds. And the small attached grocery sells hummus, pocket bread, tabooli, and spices, along with everyday groceries and novelties for neighborhood kids.

Arabian Gulf Market
1001 W. Vernor near Dix.

At Middle Eastern groceries like this, you'll find many kinds of rice — in bulk (mostly 47¢ a pound) or in huge bags, imported olives at $1.29 a pound, chunks of pressed tobacco, unusual baked goods and candies, exotic tins of olive oils and fruits, and other staples of Middle Eastern cooking, along with brass coffee boilers for making thick Turkish coffee. "Are you sure that's what your mother wants?" we heard the storekeeper ask a girl buying some rice. "Better call her to make sure!"

Dearborn Sausage
2471 Wyoming 1 block north of Vernor. (313) 842-2375. Retail hours: Thurs & Fri 8-4:30, Sat 8-noon.

Dearborn Sausage, a holdover from the South End's years as a multi-ethnic melting pot, is well known for its high-quality smoked hams, smoked slab bacon, natural-casing all-meat hot dogs, and spiral-sliced glazed hams — over a dollar a pound less than Honey Baked, and better, some say.

ACCESS (Arab-American Community Center for Economic and Social Services) ★★
2651 Saulino Court, which intersects with Dix 7 blocks east of Miller. (313) 842-7010. Mon-Fri 9-5 or by appointment for group tours. Lessons offered in the dabke (Arab circle dance), Arabic language, and mandolin-playing.

A good introduction to the culture of the far-flung Arab world is provided in this outstanding small museum. Currently it is mostly in the hallway of this former Catholic school, now an active community center with medical and social services to help the 60,000 Arabs within 10 miles of here adjust to U.S. life. The well-written displays use interesting artifacts and striking graphics. You'd expect to find this quality only in the best professionally-run museums.

Displays feature textiles and embroidery, calligraphy (a skill respected by Islam because writing transmits the Word of God in the Koran), Islamic architecture (including unusual medieval "skyscrapers" in Yemen), Islamic contributions to science (Arab Muslims were the first to study the human body), and coffee.

The "Christianity and Jews" display points out that the first Christians came from the Arab world (Aramaic, the language of Jesus, was one-third Hebrew and two-thirds Arabic), and that Islam embraces Judaism and Christianity. Abraham, Moses, Noah, and Jesus are Islam's first four prophets, and Arabs honor Miriam (Mary) as the holiest of women. Only Mohammed, the fifth prophet, was an Arab. "We consider Jews Muslims; they cemented the world to God," says ACCESS's Don Unis. "The antagonism between Arabs and Jews is very recent, and very sad."

Look in the library for displays on Arab musical instruments and Dearborn's Arab community.

Arab business district on West Warren ★★
Arab businesses are currently concentrated on eight blocks along Warren between Schaefer and Miller, with residential areas north and south of Warren. This area is expanding rapidly.

The 60-year-old storefronts of West Warren are blossoming with Arab businesses, thanks to the big influx of Arabs in the adjoining neighborhood. Signs are in English and Arabic on most of the restaurants, groceries, bakeries, fruit shops, video stores, and service businesses on Warren between Miller and Schaefer, near the Detroit city limits Don't miss **Aladdin Furniture**, near the Camelot Theater on Warren at Miller. The Arabian Nights meet Marie Antoinette in its rococco molded plastic bedroom suites and lamps with bulbous, fringed shades and gilt figures as bases.

Prices at the fruit stores, groceries, and bakeries are often astonishingly low. "Shopping is a social event," we were told, "and the price is always questioned." Among Arabs, it's never rude to bargain.

Most restaurants on this fiercely competitive street are good, with similar menus. Many are quite popular with non-Arab customers. The restaurant scene here is in constant flux. New ones are opening all the time, ownership changes frequently — it's not a high-status line of work among Arabs — and some restaurants that still have good reputations among outsiders have gone way down hill.

From the car, everything blurs together on this busy street. The area is best seen on foot — window-shopping, buying food, stopping for pastry or coffee. Most stores stay open late for after-dinner shopping.

Here are some east Dearborn shops which are recommended by good cooks:

Cedars Bakery
10451 W. Warren. (313) 582-2306.

This is one of several bakeries recommended by knowledgeable locals.

Bon Juice ★
10621 W. Warren. (313) 581-0287. Open 'til 9 p.m.

This snazzy juice bar with tables offers fresh fruit juices and concoctions like Kashta (sweetened milk curds; $2) and the Energizer (a refreshing combination of bananas, strawberries, milk, and honey; $1.50).

Afrah Pastry ★★
12741 W. Warren. (313) 582-7878. Daily 8 a.m.-11 p.m.

Not as big or as well-known as Shatila, but well thought of by locals, Afrah offers a smaller selection of beautiful honey-filo-nut pastries, and some French pastries, at lower prices. The bird's nest with pistachios (60¢) is excellent. Tables make this a nice place to stop in an interesting area.

Coffee and Nut Gallery
13029 W. Warren next to the Cedarland Restaurant.

The smells of coffee beans and spices in this tiny grocery are wonderful.

Cedars Fruit Market
13110 W. Warren. (313) 582-8057. Daily 9-9.

Fresh fruit is important to Arabs. Here you can get fresh figs, fresh dates (they're crunchy, tart and sweet at the same time) and apricots, in addition to citrus, broccoli, potatoes, onions, and Arab favorites like zucchini, parsley, tomatoes, and green pepper at very good prices. Many Arab fruit markets are bare-bones operations, with simple wood display tables and fruit boxes on the floor, along with stray leaves and paper.

New Yasmeen Bakery ★★
13728 W. Warren. (313) 582-6035. Daily 5 a.m.-6 p.m.

Some feel the Syrian bread here is so good, it's worth the trip to Dearborn. A local says the spinach pies here are "the best in the world."

Garo's Pizza Mitza
14422 W. Warren. (313) 581-8200. Daily 11 a.m.-midnight.

This conventional pizza takeout also makes distinctive little meat "pizzas" ($1) on bread with lots of parsley and pepper. You can eat them here or do what one Ann Arbor professor does: freeze them for an easy meal later with salad.

Shatila Bakery ★★
6712 Schaefer south of Warren opposite L'Opera banquet hall.. (313) 582-1952. Mon-Sat 8 a.m.-11 p.m., Sun 8-7.

Generous hospitality and entertaining at home is a hallmark of Arab culture, and it focuses on coffee and delicious pastries. Shatila is a super-clean, modern bakery, owned by a noted pastry chef from Beirut. It has coffee and a few tables, a great place for people-watching since the line at the counter is a big area gathering spot. All signs are in Arabic. Specialties are an extensive variety of traditional honey-nut-filo pastries and beautiful French pastries with whipped cream — not a surprise when you consider that 19th- and early 20th-century Lebanon was dominated by the French. In fact, it's the French colonial government which shoulders the blame for stirring up rivalries between previously peaceful people by elevating the Maronite Christians above the Muslims.

Joe and Ed's Schaefer Market
5635 Schaefer near Ford Rd. (313) 846-5725. 9:30 a.m.-1 a.m.

Larger than most convenience stores, Joe and Ed's has a big selection of Middle Eastern food, from produce and breads to canned goods and bulk rice and beans.

RESTAURANTS

Dearborn Inn
20301 Oakwood Blvd. 1 mile south of Michigan, 1/2 mile north of Rotunda Dr. (313) 271-2700. Mon-Sat lunch 11-2, dinner 6-10, Sun brunch 10-1:30, Sun dinner 5-9. Full bar. All major credit cards.

Traditional in menu and atmosphere even after its renovation, the Early American Room wins high marks for friendly service, consistency, and a comfortably elegant atmosphere — complete with harpist at dinner. Dinner entrees are priced from $16 to $26, with starch and vegetable. They include prime rib ($22.95) and popular, somewhat newer items like fresh salmon in dill ($21.95) and shrimp diavolo.

Peacock Restaurant ★
4045 Maple 4 blocks south of Michigan. Maple parallels Schaefer 1 block west. (313) 582-2344. Mon-Fri 11-2:30 lunch, 5:30-10:30 dinner. Sat 5-11, Sun 5-9. Full bar. Major credit cards.

This Indian restaurant bowls over many critics and fans with its fragrant spices. To sample a variety of Indian dishes, try the lunch buffet ($7.95), or groups of four or more can order a dinner of several breads, appetizers, and main dishes ($12.50/person). Also, there's a combination dinner ($11.95 vegetarian, $13.95 with lamb or chicken). Or share entrees ($6-8) Chinese-style. Advice and tastes are cheerfully provided. Dishes are individually spiced (no premixed curry powders, of course), to customers' desired level of heat.

Village Cafe
3337 Greenfield at Rotunda in Springwells Village shopping center. (313) 271-8040. Mon-Thurs 11 a.m.-11 p.m., Fri 11 a.m.-2 a.m., Sat & Sun 5 p.m.-2 a.m. Full bar. Visa, MasterCard, AmExpress.

What started out as Uncle Sam's Middle Eastern restaurant on Dix has moved west and upscale. It's all mauve and pink and jade, with brass accents and pretty floral posters. Lebanese food is still featured here, along with an expanded menu that includes charbroiled sirloin with soup and salad ($12.75-$17.95), cheese- and spinach-stuffed chicken ($10.95), and seafood and pasta dishes. Favorite Lebanese dishes appear as salads (mostly $5), skewered meat entrees ($10-$14), and appetizers (mostly $3.50-$4 small, $5.50-$7.50 large).

Middle Eastern atmosphere is missing here — unless you count the **beledi** (belly dancing) and Arab music combo that performs Fridays through Sundays from 9:30 p.m. to 2 a.m. Many Muslims hate belly-dancing because it reinforces the harem stereotype and demeans women.

Red Sea Restaurant
10307 Dix at Salina in Dearborn's South End. (313) 843-8211. 24 hours daily. No alcohol or credit cards.

Locals recommend this modest, pleasant place over other South End restaurants. In addition to good renditions of standard Middle Eastern fare, it offers distinctive Yemeni

Outstanding cooking and a homey, friendly atmosphere draw loyal customers from all over to Judy's Cafe. Judy Gardner (left), Marcus Lucas, and Shannon Linting are the amiable crew.

dishes, seasoned with Indian spices. Especially recommended: *gullabah*, a spicy lamb stew with onions and peppers. Servings here are incredibly generous. You can eat for days on the leftovers. The Red Sea is a good stop when touring the Rouge and the South End Arab neighborhood and cultural museum, and it's convenient, via Vernor and Livernois, to Historic Fort Wayne, Tiger Stadium, and downtown Detroit.

Judy's Cafe ★★

15714 W. Warren in Detroit, between East Dearborn and Dearborn Heights. On north side of street between Forrer and Montrose, 2 1/2 blocks west of Greenfield and less than a mile east of the Southfield Frwy. (313) 581-8185. Tues-Fri 11-8, Sat 8-2. Closed for long holiday weekends, Xmas week, summer vacation, and Tigers Opening day. Carryouts available. No alcohol or credit cards.

Eating here is like dropping in on your neighbor for a cup of coffee — a neighbor who has a plain, homey kitchen — and being surprised with a gourmet meal, not fancy but uniformly excellent. Very likely a lively discussion is going on between the cook behind the counter (owner Judy Gardner), her cheerful staff, and regular customers. If that doesn't entertain you, there's a shelf of magazines and books to read.

The eclectic, international menu, replete with customers' recipes, is all worked out in complicated chart form, not unlike a school lunch menu. If it's the second Tuesday of alternate months beginning with February, there's homemade spaghetti with meat balls ($5.50) or spinach salad with Asiago cheese ($4.50) or a barbeque turkey sandwich ($4.50) — the latter two with Max's Cuban black bean soup. Homemade desserts (mostly $1.50) are good, too.

Don Carlos ★

13701 W. Warren at Neckel, 1 block west of Schaefer. (313) 582-2024. Mon-Thurs 11-9, Fri 11-10, Sat noon-10, closed Sun. No alcohol. Visa, MasterCard, AmExpress.

Critics rave over what the *News's* Sandra Silfven calls the "adventuresome" Mexican menu at this tiny former coffee shop. It's become the original of a Detroit-area chain. "By far the best [Mexican food] we've found in the Detroit area," exclaims the *Detroit Monthly's* Mel Gourmet. Burritos are fixed 15 different ways here ($3.25-$4.95, add $1.75 with rice and beans). Other specialties are chicken mole (a quarter chicken in a spicy chocolate gravy; $7.95 with beans and rice), and fish huachinango (pan-fried red snapper with garlic, pickled onions, tomatoes, and cilantro; market price).

Cedarland Restaurant ★

13027 W. Warren near Appoline. (313) 582-4849. Daily 11 a.m.-midnight. No alcohol or credit cards.

Of all West Warren's Middle Eastern restaurants, this big, unpretentious place may well be the best. It's inexpensive and affordable for big

Arab families, whose intergenerational closeness is wonderful to see.

Each booth is decorated with plastic flowers and little Lebanese and American flags. Whole chickens turn on a rotisserie behind the counter. A big plate of Arabic salad (lettuce and vegetables in a jewel-like dice) is under $4, and most of the expected dishes are $5 or under: parsley tabooli, good lamb shishkebab and shwarma (shaved seared meat like gyros), felafel (ground spiced chickpea patties), and hummus (spread of chickpeas, sesame paste, and garlic). The complimentary appetizer here is bigger than most. Arab-American teens are the wait staff, and they are terrific – super-friendly and helpful.

Lebanon Restaurant

12807 W. Warren near Appoline. (313) 584-1100. Mon-Fri 9 a.m.-midnight, Sat & Sun 9 a.m.-3 a.m. No alcohol or credit cards.

Somewhat fancier, more formal, and more expensive than family places like Cedarland, the Lebanon is more popular with non-Arabs. The food is very fresh and appealing, and the prices reasonable: appetizers like hummus, meat pies, felafil, lamb's tongue, and fatoush from $1.50 to $3, shish kebab with potatoes or rice $6.75, and a wonderful Arabic salad for $4.

Al-Ameer Restaurant

12722 W. Warren near Miller. (313) 582-8185. Mon-Thurs 10 a.m.-midnight, Fri & Sat 9 a.m.-2 a.m., Sun 11 a.m.-midnight. No alcohol. Visa, AmExpress.

Neighborhood residents think highly of this new small restaurant on the most interesting part of West Warren. The decor is simple, with white walls and scenic posters, and the food is fresh, good, and relatively inexpensive. The friendly waiters may not know much English, so it helps to be familiar with Middle Eastern dishes when ordering.

See also: *The Pool at Fair Lane (p. 143), The American Cafe at the Henry Ford Museum (p. 142).*

LODGINGS

Dearborn Inn

*(313) 271-2700.
20301 Oakwood Blvd. From I-94, north on Southfield Frwy. (M-39), exit on Oakwood Blvd. Go west 2 miles, on left side.*

167 rooms on 4 floors of main hotel. Weekdays $130, weekend $69/night including full breakfast. Outdoor pool. 2 exercise rooms. HBO, Disney, pay movies ($6.35). 2 restaurants. On 23 scenic acres close to Ford Motor headquarters and Greenfield Village. Henry Ford built the Georgian-style inn in 1931 to house those who arrived at the nearby Ford Airport. Marriott just renovated it — in keeping with its colonial atmosphere — to the tune of $25 million. Replicas of famous American homes, added behind the hotel in 1936-7, include the Edgar Allen Poe cottage ($250 a night) and the larger Walt Whitman, Patrick Henry, Oliver Wolcott, and Barbara Fritchie homes (divided into suites, $175 single/ $190 double).

Guests may stay at the Dearborn Inn's replica of the Edgar Allen Poe cottage on 192nd St. in New York. There, in genteel poverty, Poe wrote his most famous poems.

Village Inn of Dearborn
(313) 565-8511.
21725 Michigan Ave. east of Oakwood Blvd. From I-94, take either Michigan Ave. or Oakwood Blvd. exit.
30 rooms, 2 floors. $32 single; $38 double (winter); $34 single; $40 double (summer). HBO. Walking distance to Westborn Market, downtown West Dearborn, several restaurants.

Fairlane Inn
(313) 565-0800.
21430 Michigan Ave. east of Oakwood. From I-94, go north on Southfield Frwy., exit on Michigan Ave Go 1 mile west. On right.
100 rooms, 2 floors. $45 single; $55 double. Outdoor pool. HBO & ESPN. Restaurant. Easy walking distance to Westborn Market and downtown West Dearborn.

Hyatt Regency Dearborn
(313) 593-1234.
Fairlane Dr. (in Fairlane Town Center mall complex). From I-94, go north on Southfield Frwy., exit on Michigan Ave, west 1/4 mile to Evergreen, turn north, then east on Fairlane Rd.
15 floors, 766 units.$140 single; $165 double; weekends $99. Indoor swimming pool, sauna, jacuzzi, exercise room. HBO & ESPN, + pay movies ($7). 3 restaurants. Revolving lounge on top floor. Great views of Detroit and Dearborn.

Ritz Carlton Dearborn
(313) 441-2000.
300 Town Center Drive in Fairlane Town Center mall complex. From I-94, go north on Southfield Frwy., exit Ford Rd., left onto Hubbard Dr.
308 units, 11 floors. $130 single; $145 double (and up); weekend packages $79-$150. Indoor pool, sauna, jacuzzi, complete fitness center. HBO & ESPN. 2 restaurants. Good views from upper floors of downtown Detroit, Ambassador Bridge, and Windsor. Luxuriously appointed with Persian rugs, loads of fresh flowers, dazzling chandeliers, lots of marble and wood paneling, this may be Michigan's most elegant hotel. Afternoon tea served from 2 to 5 p.m. daily. Two ambitious, expensive restaurants, the elegant **dining room** and the less formal **grill,** both highly regarded by local restaurant critics.

Royal Oak

Who would have thought that dowdy Royal Oak would become the center of the hippest commercial activity in the Detroit metropolitan area? This bedroom community of 72,000 residents, almost all of them white, was in the 1930s nationally known for the isolationist, anti-Semitic rantings of Father Charles Coughlin, pastor of the Shrine of the Little Flower at the corner of Woodward and 12 Mile Road.

Located just north of Detroit, Royal Oak became a suburb mainly for white automobile workers beginning in the 1920s, a spillover from the increasingly crowded residential sections of Detroit. Royal Oak at the turn of the century had been largely swamp and forest, with just a few hundred residents. The place was supposedly named for a giant oak that Governor Lewis Cass slept under early in the 19th century. John Starr, son of a settler from New York, was the area's first prominent citizen, thanks to the popular cowbells he manufactured. By 1831 Starr built a log cabin here and in 1845 a frame house that is still standing at 3123 North Main. Because his cowbells could be heard for miles around, owners of cows all over the country bought them.

Royal Oak burgeoned in the 1920s from 6,000 to 23,000 residents. The city never attempted to attract industry. Its residents were content to live in a community of modest single-family homes, 90 per cent of which in 1929 were owner-occupied. In the Forties it grew again, to over 46,000. But Royal Oak's biggest

Stylish Washington Square at Washington and Fourth is a local landmark. Finished in 1927 during Royal Oak's boom years, it now houses the Royal Oak Music Theater, the rock nightspot Metropolitan Musicafe, and the striking Swidler Gallery of jewelry and ceramics. On the Sherman Drive side is Keith Fahmie's Les Auteurs bistro, one of metro Detroit's most inventive restaurants.

boom was in the Fifties, when it skyrocketed from 47,000 to over 80,000 residents. After peaking at 86,000, it has declined to about 70,000.

Now it is booming again, this time with a curious blend of businesses featuring funk, punk, antiques, galleries, and trendy restaurants. It's the kind of interesting blend one might expect in downtown Ann Arbor, but high rents and dreadfully tight parking there have tended to discourage innovative bootstrap businesses in recent years.

Another dramatic development has finally unfolded in Royal Oak: the completion of I-696, which will join for the first time the eastern and western suburbs north of Detroit. I-696 puts Royal Oak very much at the center of metropolitan traffic. Ironically, it could also push up downtown rents, strangling the diverse commercial vitality that today makes the area so exciting.

Antiques in Royal Oak
Over a dozen shops are scattered in and around downtown Royal Oak. They cover everything from American general-line to Art Deco, old prints, and books. Stop in at any one for a joint listing and helpful map. Most are open Tues-Sat 11-5, and over half have Sunday hours.

POINTS OF INTEREST

Detroit Zoo

Ten Mile at Woodward. (313) 398-0900. Enter from Woodward. Open Wed-Sun, Nov. through April; 7 days a week, May through Oct. Adults and teens 13 and over $5; 5-12 and seniors $2.50; 4 years and under free.

After years of alleged mismanagement and graft, the Detroit Zoo, one of the country's pioneering zoos, is on the rebound. The central Rackham Fountain is being renovated, the elephant and rhinoceros exhibit has been refurbished, and the farmyard is open again, too.

And the world's finest zoo chimpanzee compound has recently opened. The zoo's most spectacular exhibit, it encompasses four acres, big enough to resemble the natural habitat of its 11 chimps. It cost $8 million. Such a setting should allow the chimps to establish a natural social order, so that visitors can see them acting as they would in their indigenous habitats. This thrust has been a major focus of zoo director Steve Graham, who avoids naming the zoo's animals and treating them like pets. No more cute chimps in jackets doing tricks! Several good viewing points encircle the compound. Visitors can see the chimps in three different settings: forest clearing, meadow, and rock outcropping. The chimps will stay outside a good 300 days a year, but when the weather is too severe, they can be viewed in two large indoor rooms behind one-way glass.

More people actually come to ride on the zoo railroad than to see the animals. The free train carries visitors from the Main Station 1 1/4 miles to the African Station. And

At the Detroit Zoo's new 4-acre chimp compound, the world's finest, chimpanzees have the space and privacy to lead the lives of wild animals, with little human interference.

> **Feeding times:**
> **Penguins:** daily 10:30, 11:30, 1:30.
> **Polar bears:** May to mid-Oct. 1:30.
> **Sea lions:** late May-mid-Oct. 11-2 Wed.-Sun.
> **Lemurs:** early June-mid-Oct. 2:30.

there are also tractor-pulled 45-minute tours of the zoo.

Another popular exhibit is the **Holden Museum of Living Reptiles**, constructed in 1960. The **Penguinarium** houses four species of penguins (blue, king, macaroni, and rockhopper) in three different habitats. The outer, triangular ring of the exhibit is water. The penguins can swim around continuously, giving visitors a wonderfully intimate underwater view of the birds.

The **Wilson Aviary Wing** provides a big free-flight space for birds even as large as the rare Andean condor, with a 10-foot wingspan. In this horseshoe-shaped space are a waterfall, stream, pond, and hundreds of tropical plants. The birds have unrestricted use of this scenic space, which visitors traverse on a walkway.

The zoo opened in 1928 to huge and wildly enthusiastic crowds. Detroit's first zoo in 1883 had been something of an accident, brought about when a small traveling circus had gone bankrupt and its keepers had skipped town. To house the abandoned animals, a zoo was quickly constructed where Tiger Stadium is today. But it closed a year later, after visitors kept taking animals until there was little left to see.

The current zoo was quite innovative by the standards of American zoos, which tend to follow the lead of more forward-looking European ones. Detroit's was the first American zoo to emphasize barless exhibits rather than more confining and jail-like cages typical of the day. This is perhaps most dramatically seen in one of the zoo's first exhibits — the dramatic, enormous polar bear exhibit. Instead of fences, large moats protect visitors from the huge bears. A moat proved ineffective on opening day in 1928. A bear leaped the moat and approached Detroit's mayor, who affably — and foolishly — reached out to shake its paw.

Washington Avenue Commercial District ★★★

Washington Ave. between 11 Mile and Lincoln, plus Second through Sixth Streets east to the railroad tracks.

A decade ago, Royal Oak's twin commercial boulevards, Main Street and Washington Avenue, were in decline like most aging American downtowns upstaged by shopping malls. That trend began to reverse itself in 1980 when energetic Patti Smith started her vintage clothing shop on Washington. Hip and affordable, Patti Smith Collectibles attracted customers from far and wide with both its interesting vintage clothing and its inexpensive original designs. Smith set a successful example, and her Sixties-style community-minded spirit has been infectious. There has been an extraordinary influx of interesting shops, many started by entrepreneurs who can afford the district's low rents.

Here are some of the most notable shops in the area:

Swidler Gallery ★★
308 W. Fourth in the Washington Square building. (313) 542-4880. Tues-Thur 10-6, Fri 10-9, Sat 10-5.

This ceramics and art jewelry gallery has quickly become one of the Midwest's most impressive ceramic galleries, with one-of-a-kind pieces costing over $1,000 as well as much less expensive production pieces. Most of the works are functional and in earth tones. The same designer who did such a great job renovating Gayle's Chocolates designed the interior of the 1927 Washington Square Building.

Patti Smith (second from right) set a spirited example for the hip, offbeat transformation of downtown Royal Oak with her Washington Avenue store. The new and vintage women's clothes at Patti Smith Collectibles, modeled here by the staff just outside the store, are freewheeling but wearable and quite reasonably priced. Smith is not to be confused with Patti Smith the punk rocker and poet, who also lives in Detroit now with her husband and children.

LA Express ★
222 Sherman Dr. at the rear of Washington Square. (313) 544-2372. Mon-Sat 10-9.

The takeout arm of Les Auteurs bistro offers an inviting variety of inventive food, from chicken and beef chili ($3.50) to confit of duck pizza ($13.50 large, $7.50 small). Two of the most popular dishes are the LA Pizza and the black-eyed bean salad ($1.75 small, $2.50 large).

Patti Smith Collectibles ★★
407 S. Washington. (313) 399-0756. Mon Tues 11-6, Wed 11-11, Thurs-Fri, 11-9, Sat 10-6.

This very popular women's apparel and jewelry shop carries one-third vintage and two-thirds small company and local artists' designs. Many come here especially for the Twenties and Thirties vintage clothing.

Dave's Comics and Collectibles
407 S. Washington. (313) 548-1230. Mon-Wed 11-8, Thurs-Fri 11-9, Sat 11-7, Sun 11-4.

The Royal Oak store of this funky regional chain not only sells new and used comics but antique toys, many from the Fifties. A colorful display of vintage children's lunchboxes is at the back.

Gayle's Chocolates ★★
417 S. Washington. (313) 398-0001. Mon-Sat 10-6.

Gayle's is a jewel of a shop, one of the most pleasing Art Deco makeovers to be found. The designer, Ron Rea, also renovated the interesting Washington Square Building up the block. Outstanding hand-dipped chocolates ($1.35 each) are the main attraction. Some say Gayle's are the best available. You can also buy excellent espresso and cappuccino, hot chocolate, or steamed milk and honey. A front area with tables lets you sit back and enjoy the decor.

Vertu ★
511 S. Washington. (313) 545-6050. Tues-Sat noon-6.

Vertu is known for its interesting collection of Art Deco-influenced small appliances (toasters, waffle irons, mixers, etc.) and chrome furniture from the 1930s and 1940s. More generally it deals in objects of modern design (largely furniture and ceramics) from 1900 to 1960. The owner is very knowledgeable about mid-20th-century design.

World of Kites ★
525 S. Washington at Sixth. (313) 398-5900. Tues-Fri 10:30-6, Sat 10-5.

Here you'll find over 250 kites and an amazing variety of kite accessories: kite ferries which go up and down the kite string ($10.95), kite parachutes ($2.50), kite bombs ($1.95), and even kite strobe lights to light up your kite in the sky at night ($29.95).

Neon Images ★★
108 W. Fourth. (313) 543-5063. Mon-Fri 11-5, Sat 12-5.

Owner Darcy Salbert searches far and wide for old neon clocks, then refurbishes them to like-new condition and sells them for $175-$700. You can also find old gum ball machines ($25-$200), slot machines ($1,500), and new small neon advertising signs ($75-$350).

Chosen Books
120 W. Fourth. (313) 543-5758. Noon-10 daily.

The only gay bookstore in metro Detroit has relocated here from Palmer Park. The shop is well-stocked with books, magazines, cards, novelties, gifts, videos, and various paraphernalia.

The Stamping Grounds ★
228 W. Fourth. (313) 543-2190. Mon-Sat 10-5.

Rubber stamps here are taken as serious fun, a means for inspired creative expression, and not just a passing fad or cute gift item. There are plenty of nifty examples and idea books to get you started, and special inks for stamping on fabrics and special purposes. The selection of rubber stamp designs goes way beyond the usual lines to include offbeat new releases and lots of alphabets. Even cheap plastic stamps and 39¢ pencil-toppers aren't scorned.

A new addition are lots of paper cutouts — paper dolls, cut-and-make toys, and architectural models, largely from Dover's excellent and inexpensive series, but from other publishers, too.

The Lotus Import Co. ★ ★
204 W. Fifth. (313) 546-8820. Mon-Wed 10-6, Thur & Fri 10-9, Sat 10-6.

Lotus carries ethnic jewelry, clothing, and decorative accessories from all continents, with quite a few Asian selections — all appealingly displayed in this visually rich shop. The Indonesian clothing — patchwork coats, dresses, shirts, blouses, jumpers ($50-$200) — are made from old sarongs of ikat fabrics. There is also a good selection of African masks ($45-$600).

Dos Manos ★
210 W. Sixth. (313) 542-5856. Tues, Thurs & Fri 11-6, Wed 11-11, Sat 11-4.

Dos Manos sells well-chosen, affordable handcrafts from Latin America exclusively. You can buy Oaxaca rugs ($65-$128), wall hangings from Mexico, Mexican pottery, copper decorative pieces, jewelry, and cotton placemats. Colorful Colombian hammocks are $60, and terra cotta planters in the shapes of frogs and turtles are $30 to $50.

Main Street Commercial District ★★

Main between Third and Lincoln, downtown Royal Oak.

Bright Ideas ★
220 S. Main (2 blocks south of 11 Mile). (313) 541-9940. Tues-Fri 10-9, Sat 10-6, Sun noon-5.

The Midwest doesn't have many contemporary home furnishings stores featuring original new Italian, Swedish, and German designs. Bright Ideas has them, plus smaller accessories like halogen lighting.

Carol James Gallery ★★
301 S. Main. (313) 541-6216. Tues-Wed 10:30-5:30, Thurs 10:30-9, Fri 10:30-5:30, Sat 10-5:30.

An exceptionally pleasing contemporary arts and crafts gallery, Carol James carries glass, decorative and functional ceramics, wood, jewelry, and fiber by 75 craftspeople. Particularly noteworthy are the blown glass paperweights and perfume bottles ($55-$365).

Cinderella's Attic
320 S. Main. (313) 546-7209. Mon-Wed 11-7, Thur-Fri 11-8, Sat 11-6.

A branch of the Dearborn shop, the Attic has punk overtones. It has vintage and rock 'n' roll clothing, vintage and new jewelry, plus toys related to TV shows from the 1950s.

Incognito
323 S. Main (at Fourth). (313) 548-2980. Mon-Sat 11-9, Sun 12-5.

Rock 'n' roll clothing takes up most of the space in this shop, but there is also an extraordinary selection of sunglasses in over 300 styles.

Noir Leather ★
415 S. Main. (313) 541-3979. Mon-Fri 11:30-8, Sat 11-7.

Beyond clothing, downtown Royal Oak can boast of some genuinely eccentric shops. Noir Leather is the most notorious. Here, finally, is a shop to serve all your bondage and sado-masochistic needs. Handcuffs sell for $38. Ominous-looking black leather masks, which cover the entire head except for eyeholes and a zipper across the mouth, are $99. Spiked belts are $22. Crops, which owner Keith Howarth, a gentle soul, says are especially popular, go for $11 to $16. There are also a variety of restraint devices, nipple clamps, black lingerie, and considerable paraphernalia for punk enthusiasts.

Pop Regalia
110 E. Fifth. (313) 399-3851. Mon-Sat 12-7.

Vintage clothes and jewelry from the Twenties through the Sixties.

Royal Oak Farmers' Market and Flea Market

316 E. 11 Mile Rd., 1 1/2 blocks east of Main St. (313) 548-8822. **Jan-April** *Sat 7 a.m.-11 a.m.* **May & Oct** *Tues, Fri, Sat 7 a.m.-11 a.m.* **June-Sept** *Tues, Thurs, Fri, Sat 7 a.m.-11 a.m.* **Nov-Xmas** *Tues, Fri, Sat 7 a.m.-1 p.m.*

Many discriminating Oakland County cooks shop for in-season produce and fruit at this year-round, 110-stall market. Most stalls are indoors, and there's a big parking lot.

Sundays year-round from 10-5 it changes into a highly regarded **flea market** that's really much better than the name connotes. A number of the 75 dealers have permanent booths set up, from which they sell everything from dried flowers and crafts to precious metals and coins. Lots of clothes (both old and new) and antiques and collectibles are always on hand. Patti Smith got her start selling vintage clothing here.

Shrine of the Little Flower

2123 Roseland at Woodward, just north of 12 Mile Rd. (313) 541-4122.

This 2,500-seat church, completed in 1933, and the adjacent 111-foot Crucifixion Tower topped by a 35-foot statue of Christ, are the legacies of Father Charles Coughlin,

Royal Oak's famous radio priest. Moved by his parishoners' plight during the Depression, he became a populist and espoused free coinage of silver and a brand of "paternalistic Christian socialism" that by 1937 had come very close to fascism (the alliance of government, business, and labor). In 1932 Coughlin was already so influential that Roosevelt sought his endorsement. "The New Deal is Christ's Deal," Coughlin announced. But by 1935 he was denouncing Roosevelt as a tool of Jewish bankers, no better than the despised Republicans. His National Union for Social Justice, founded to support the political career of muckraking journalist Upton Sinclair, threatened to become a third party. Today it's hard to imagine that his brand of politics, with its blatant anti-Semitism, could be considered respectable, but it was.

It all began in 1926, when Coughlin took over the little Catholic parish of newly arrived autoworkers in booming Royal Oak, which had been a Protestant farm town. He found his parishoners knew little about their own religion. So he asked to get air time on infant radio station WJR and became the first Catholic priest with a radio show. The genial, theatrical priest, already a proven promoter, soon generated so much interest that cars were lined up for a mile to come to his church on Sundays. He attacked the Federal Council of Churches, which had suggested abstinence as a way to limit family size, as spreading Communist propaganda to emasculate a free people. CBS started broadcasting his program in 1930, and the money started rolling in to build this impressive church. (Coughlin had 106 clerks just to deal with his mail.) The building incorporates blocks of stone from every state. Each is inscribed with the state's name and flower.

From the mid-1940s to the mid-1950s Tom Hayden, liberal California politician and former New Left radical, attended the Shrine's parochial school. Here, early on, he rebelled against the Catholic Church's authority.

RESTAURANTS

Lepanto
316 S. Main. (313) 541-2228. Tues-Sat lunch 11:30-3, dinner 5:30-10. Entrees $5.75-$8 (lunch); $5.95-$13 (dinner). Full bar. MasterCard, Visa.

Before Royal Oak's renaissance, this was a bar called Alden's Alley. Now it's an intimate, attractive, new-style Italian restaurant. Almost instantly it became a great hit with its sleekly sophisticated decor and well-thought-out food, starting with soups, appetizers, and individual pizzas, all good and made with the freshest ingredients. The simple green salad is excellent, but the cannelloni ($6.95 for lunch, $8.95 for dinner) is way too salty. Don't miss *foccacia*, the wonderful flat bread with rosemary ($1.75/lunch, $2.25/dinner).

Detroit News restaurant reviewer Sandra Silfven raves about the bagna cauda ($5.95/ $8.95), a dish of fresh vegetables and foccacia dipped in a warm garlic and anchovy sauce. It serves two. The *Free Press*'s Molly Abraham calls the pasta dishes "glamorous" and the noodles "exquisitely light." Both praise the classic Italian desserts.

Les Auteurs
222 Sherman in Washington Square. 2 blocks south of 11 Mile; 2 blocks west of Main. (313) 544-2887. Lunch Mon-Sat 11-30-2:30; dinner Mon-Thurs 5:30-10:30, Fri & Sat 6-11:30, Sun 5:30-9:30. Arrive before 6:30 on weekends to avoid a 15-60-minute wait. Closed 1st weeks in Jan & July. Entrees: $4-$12 (lunch); $8-$20 (dinner). Full bar. Visa, MasterCard.

This chic, instantly popular Royal Oak restaurant symbolizes the apogee of Royal Oak's commercial renaissance. Superb food is served in a stylish but casual ambience. One favorite on the frequently changed menu is black bean cake with smoked chicken and fresh tomato salsa ($7.50 as a dinner appetizer). Other best bets are the thin-crusted California pizza with sun-dried tomatoes, goat cheese, roasted garlic, and fresh basil ($7 at lunch/$8.50 as a dinner appetizer and $14 as a main course) and mushroom fettuccine with grilled chicken breast, wild mushrooms, gorgonzola cheese, and chive sauce ($9.75/ $17). Herbed bread sticks are always on the table; lunch entrees (meat and seafood) include a house salad. There's a whole range of wonderful desserts ($3.50-$5.50); not all are rich. Many offerings are also available takeout at the adjoining LA Express. From the dining room — or the sidewalk — you can see the pastries being made. There's weekend jazz in the atrium cocktail area.

In what's a spreading sign of laid-back sophistication, you can ask for

Owner-chef Keith Famie has won international attention with Les Auteurs, his "American bistro" in Washington Square. It's simple and direct in presentation, chic and crowded. It's also comfortable and fun, affirms columnist Mike Duffy, a dyed-in-the-wool eastsider ever alert for phoney pretensions when he ventures west into Oakland County.

Crayons and draw on the paper tablecloth. Some of the more amazing customer efforts are framed on the walls. "Les auteurs" — cookbook authors who are owner-chef Keith Famie's personal heroes, from James Beard to Paul Bocuse — are commemorated in framed displays.

Inn Season
500 E. Fourth, east of Main St. (313) 547-7916. Mon-Sat 11-10. Entrees $4.25 -$8.95. Sandwiches $2.50-$4.95. No alcohol, credit cards, or smoking.

This pleasant vegetarian/seafood restaurant has a number of good dishes to recommend it. The Burrito Magnifico ($4.95) is large and delicious, and the tostada ($4.75) is equally good. The popular 4th Street Burger with a grain patty ($3.95) is somewhat bland without the additional cheese ($4.75). Fresh seafood supplements the vegetarian fare, which also includes such unusual items as Japanese twig tea and beets with garlic sauce.

Niki's
703 N. Main north of 11 Mile). (313) 546-5061. Mon-Sat 6 a.m.-9 p.m., Sun 6-4. No alcohol or credit cards.

This small, unpretentious Greek restaurant is a wonderful place for a cheap, quick, healthy lunch. The delicious $2.59 Greek salad comes with equally delicious, warm, fresh pita bread. Gyros and hamburgers head the sandwich menu, and full meals range from Greek favorites like moussaka and spinach pie to fried chicken and pork chops. Most meals are under $5, including potato, vegetable, and soup or salad.

Southfield

Southfield is today one of Detroit's major commercial and residential suburbs, but it didn't even become a city until 1958. Although it borders Detroit, Southfield only had a population of about 10,000 as late as 1950.

When J.L. Hudson began **Northland Shopping Center** here in 1950, it marked a pivotal shift of population and money out of Detroit that continues today. This pioneering shopping mall, designed by Victor Gruen and finished in 1952, would soon be widely copied, not just in the Detroit area, but nation-wide. (See pp. 329, 331.)

Many people who moved here in the 1950s were Jews from nearby northwest Detroit. The rapid Jewish migration northwest out Woodward from central Detroit today continues northwest from Southfield into Farmington Hills and West Bloomfield Township. The remaining Jewish population in the close-in suburbs of Southfield, Oak Park, and Ferndale is aging.

Southfield lacks focus because there was no older town to give it a center. Its predominant image from the freeways that are its main streets is of office buildings. There is more office space here — 22 million square feet — than in the downtowns of many major American cities. These big offices bring in 180,000 commuters a day. Firms such as IBM, Michigan Bell, NCR, EDS, Pitney Bowes, Lear Siegler, and Federal Mogul have major facilities here.

Reflecting the rapid pace of development and change in America's suburbs, this relatively new city is already beginning to look worn. As its wealthier residents keep moving north and west to posher, newer housing, some worry Southfield is vulnerable to decline. Nevertheless, it continues to grow in population — over 82,000 by the late 1980s and still climbing.

In a familiar urban migration pattern in which middle-income African-Americans follow Jews, more black families are moving into Southfield to take advantage of its excellent schools. Today blacks make up a quarter of the overall population and about half the school-age population. In a metropolitan region where suburbs are highly segregated, Southfield today is one of the most integrated communities in the Detroit area. Community groups want to keep it that way by adopting the successful strategy of Oak Park, Illinois, a close-in Chicago suburb, which recruits white families to maintain a stable racial balance.

Detroit's Jewish community numbered an estimated 80,000 in 1981. In 1900, Detroit's 5,000 Jews lived around Hastings Street on downtown's east side, in the neighborhood blacks later ironically named Paradise Valley. Migration from eastern Europe increased the Jewish population to about 35,000 in 1920. By 1940 refugees from Hitler's Germany had raised the number to about 85,000. The insightful Holocaust Museum in West Bloomfield (p. 197) powerfully conveys this part of Jewish history.

POINTS OF INTEREST

Bargains and treats along along Southfield Road ★

Three stores near the corner of Southfield and 14 Mile roads form the secret of one stylish hostess's carefree, budget-conscious entertaining. Other stores along Southfield offer great selection and/or bargains.

Pepperidge Farms Thrift Store
1950 Southfield at the corner of 14 Mile. (313) 642-4242. Mon-Fri 9-7, Sat until 6, Sun 11-4.

Big discounts on rolls, cookies, cakes, breads, and frozen entrees, which can be frozen, then thawed and beautifully presented to good effect.

Honeybaked Ham
31190 Southfield at 14 Mile in The Corners shopping center. (313) 540-0404. Mon-Sat 10-6.

This popular ham is fully baked and spiral sliced around the bone, with a crunchy honey-baked glaze. At $4.09 a pound, it's not cheap, but it's easy to serve and very good.

Sara Lee Kitchens
31255 Southfield just north of 13 Mile. (313) 647-8280. Mon-Fri 9-7, Sat 'til 5, Sun 11-4.

Excess or irregular cakes, muffins, bagels, etc., delivered twice a week, are sold at 25-30% off. (Irregular often means that the weight varies from that stated on package.)

Borders Book Shop ★★
31150 Southfield at 14 Mile in The Corners. (313) 644-1515. Mon-Sat 9-9, Sun 11-5.

At 100,000 titles, the so-called Birmingham Borders (actually in Bloomfield Township) is even bigger than the famed Borders flagship store in Ann Arbor. In the 1970s, as chains came to dominate bookselling by discounting hot titles, Borders based its success by offering knowledgeable service and an outstanding back list of older titles and university press books, plus a 30% discount on selected *New York Times* hardcover best-sellers. Now it's growing into a mid-American chain.

The Tennis Company
26441 Southfield, on the southeast corner of 13 Mile next to Damman Hardware. (313) 258-9366. Mon-Sat 10-6, Thurs till 8.

Widely known as the best racket shop in town, with big discounts (up to 40% off) on an extensive selection of tennis, squash, and racquetball rackets and clothes.

Baking by the Auers
29207 Southfield Rd. between 12 and 13 Mile in Southfield Commons. (313) 424-8660. Tues-Sat. 8-6.

Baker David Auer does a serious job of French baking. Besides French bread, he has gained a wide following for his delicious brioche (65¢ a roll), his equally delicious oat bran muffins (50¢ each), and his round French rolls (25¢ each).

OfficeMax
24725 Southfield Rd. just south of 10 Mile behind Arbor Drug on the west side. (313) 557-3620. Mon-Fri 8-9, Sat 9-9, Sun 11-6.

New to Detroit, with another store in Madison Heights, Office Max is a "category killer" in the heretofore complacent office supply business. Everyday discounts on office supplies, equipment (including copiers), and furniture range from decent to astonishing ($3.76 for 12 legal pads, for instance).

Cloverleaf Market ★
28905 S. Telegraph just south of 12 Mile, next to the Amoco station. (313) 357-0400. Mon-Sat 8 a.m.-11 p.m., Sun 8-8.

Jimmy Lufty has transformed the wine department of his family's unpretentious party store into a mecca for wine connoisseurs, who come there for remarkably low markups on cases of premium wines from all over the world. Lufty keeps overhead low (no romantic trappings here) and buys in quantity, often direct from Europe. Half a dozen top Michigan wineries are represented. The ground floor displays everyday wines (mostly $6 to $12/bottle, mostly from small producers) that are ready to drink. Upstairs, cases of the better wines are stacked up on metal shelves to towering heights — 1,500 cases of classified Bordeaux, for example, and 1,000 cases of premium Burgundies, quantities that exceed what many wholesalers carry.

Modern Bakery & Pastry Shop ★

13735 W. Nine Mile, 1 1/2 blocks west of Coolidge in Oak Park. (313) 546-4477. Open 7 days, 6 a.m.-9 p.m.

The terrific rye and pumpernickel breads from Zingerman's famous Ann Arbor deli come from here. Big, two-pound loaves are $2; for something different, try the rye with chernushka (black caraway seeds). This full-line bakery has cookies, donuts, wedding cakes — "everything," assures owner Martin Weiss, the baker since 1953. Other specialties include kaiser rolls ($3.48/dozen), onion rolls ($3.72/dozen), challah, whole wheat, and French breads, and sissel, a heavy rye bread.

RESTAURANTS

The Stage Deli & Restaurant ★★

13821 W. Nine Mile Rd between Greenfield and Coolidge in Oak Park. 2 blocks west of Coolidge at Westhampton. (313) 548-1111. 7 days 11-8, breakfasts (anytime): $1.20-$4.95; sandwiches $1.50-$4.60.

Tucked in an inconspicuous commercial strip on Nine Mile, this place shares with Maxie's in Detroit the reputation for having the best corned beef sandwiches in the Detroit area. Over 30 years old, the Stage still makes just about everything it serves. There are no microwaves on the premises. "People sometimes get ticked because it takes longer," says its manager, "but I want the food really cooked." The two most popular sandwiches are Dinty Moore (corned beef, lettuce, tomato, and Russian dressing) for $4.55 and the West Side Story (corned beef or pastrami with cole slaw and Russian dressing), also for $4.55. The homemade matzoh ball soup is $1.95 a bowl. The $5.25 Mark Beltaire Salad Bowl (crisp lettuce topped with turkey, ham, Swiss cheese, and Stage house dressing) is also very popular.

The Stage's West Bloomfield counterpart, upscale but authentic, is Stage & Company on 6873 Orchard Lake Road just south of Maple.

Golden Mushroom/ Mushroom Cellar ★★★

18100 W. 10 Mile at Southfield Rd. (313) 559-4230. Mon-Thurs 11:30-11, Fri & Sat 11-midnight. Full bar, outstanding but overpriced wine list. A la carte entrees: $8-$15 (lunch); $19-$30 (dinner).

Luxurious in every detail (down to the bottled water that constantly replenishes diners' glasses), the Golden Mushroom ranks as one of the state's very top restaurants. Chef Milos Cihelka is one of three grand masters in Michigan; graduates of his kitchen have enormously raised the quality of Detroit-area restaurants. He especially enjoys preparing wild game; roast boar, venison, smoked roast chicken, or pheasant may be on the menu, depending on current availability. His Norwegian salmon with dill sauce has won a gold medal. The roast rack of lamb is also extraordinarily good.

Downstairs, the Mushroom Cellar offers a casual setting, lower prices, a big lunch menu, from burgers to upstairs specials for somewhat less money, and pizza, kebabs, and such at dinner.

Sweet Lorraine's Cafe ★★
29101 Greenfield north of 12 Mile. (313) 559-5985. Mon-R=Thurs 11-10:30, Fri & Sat 11-midnight. Full bar, about 20 wines by the glass and 20 imported beers. Visa, AmExpress, MasterCard.

This cheerful Art Deco bistro is one of the entire area's most enjoyable spots. It's known for its inventive menu with many daily specials, its soups (curry raisin is a favorite), pasta and vegetarian dishes. Specialties include pecan chicken ($7.95/ lunch, $9.95 dinner), a pounded chicken breast covered in pecan crumbs in a mustard sauce, Jamai-can spicy steak ($11.95/ $13.95), and shrimp and scallops Monet ($10.95/ $11.95) with julienned vegetables, tossed in ginger-dill sauce. Entrees include starch (often rice pilaf or redskin potatoes), garnish, and, for $1.50 extra, soup or a garden salad. The complimentary breadbasket with changing daily specialties like anise bread is a delight.

LODGINGS

Hampton Inn Southfield
(313) 356-5500. (800) 426-7866. 27500 Northwestern Hwy. at Telegraph. From I-696, Telegraph exit, turn right at first light onto Northwestern Service Dr.
53 rooms; 2 floors. $54-$58 single; $60 double; weekends $48 (with reservations). Indoor pool, whirlpool, exercise room. Free continental breakfast. Showtime & ESPN.

Holiday Inn of Southfield
(313) 353-7700. (800) HOLIDAY. 26555 Telegraph, just north of I-696.
417 rooms, 16 floors in more expensive tower portion. $59-$79 single; $67-$87 double; weekends $69. Holidome with indoor pool, jacuzzi, weight room, game room, ping pong, pool table. Showtime & ESPN. Pay movies ($6.35). Restaurant , lounge.

Michigan Inn
(313) 559-6500. (800) 482-3440. 16400 J.L. Hudson Dr. on the north edge of the Northland shopping center. Just east of Northwestern Hwy. between 8 and 9 Mile Rds.
412 rooms, 14 floors. $89 single; $99 double; weekends $69. Indoor/ outdoor pool, sauna, exercise room. Pay movies ($6.95). 2 restaurants, lounge.

Grosse Ile

Picturesque and historic, this island 12 miles downriver from downtown Detroit has been a haven for the well-to-do as far back as the 1860s, when summer estates were first built here. Today it would be hard to buy an east riverfront home for under $300,000. One local explains that the prices have been driven up by Japanese executives working at the nearby Mazda plant in Flat Rock and by wealthy Indian doctors.

The 1980s building boom here dismays most of the old-time residents. The population today has grown to over 10,000, with fewer and fewer patches of undisturbed woods. Traditionally this has been a tight-knit, self-contained community. It has its own school system, post office, and even a Kroger supermarket. But at the rate of recent development, houses or condos may even some day be built on the island's northern tip, for years the dumping ground of Wyandotte Chemical across the river.

The island remains a striking place to drive around, especially on the magnificent East River Drive along the Detroit River facing Canada. Some splendid old cottages and mansions are here, along with a few incredibly gauche new homes. From the southern end of the drive, you can look east and see Amherstburg, Ontario, across a mile and half of river. Just south of Amherstburg is Boblo Island (Bois Blanc). The observation tower of the popular amusement park is readily visible. The Thorofare, a dredged, navigable stream used by pleasure boats, cuts diagonally through the main island. As in Grosse Pointe on the other side of Detroit, there are unfortunately no public parks on the island where visitors can enjoy the river view.

Historical tour & map
Be sure to pick up a copy of "A Tour of Grosse Ile" for just $1.50 during your visit to the historical society in the Depot. It includes a large map and describes 74 sights on the island.

A 12-island cluster
Grosse Ile (pronounced "gross eel") is the largest of the many islands in the Detroit River. It is 7 1/2 miles long and about 1 1/2 miles wide. Actually, 12 islands cluster together here and are collectively considered Grosse Ile.

The Gothic Revival cottage Littlecote reflects the modest sensibility of the mid-19th century gentleman farmer who made his living in the city but wished to live in harmony with nature in his rural retreat.

European visitors in the 17th century

Grosse Ile attracted the interest of the very earliest settlers to Michigan, in part because of its natural beauty, in part because its high shoreline made it an appealing and relatively safe place to live. There are 17th-century accounts of the island from passing travelers. Before Cadillac founded Detroit by building Fort Pontchartrain in 1701, he considered first building it here. If there had been enough available timber nearby, he might well have done so.

During the Indians' 153-day siege of Detroit in 1763, Chief Pontiac sent braves to Grosse Ile, which served as their base from which to attack rescue ships from Niagara. Two days after the Declaration of Independence was signed in 1776, the Potawatomi tribe deeded the island to Alexander and William Macomb. Eventually it came into the sole possession of William Macomb, the era's wealthiest Detroit merchant. (He also owned Belle Isle.) After flying first the French and then the British flags, Grosse Ile became a part of the U.S. in 1796. The last Indians were forced off in 1799. In 1810 50 people lived on the island, mostly farmers.

Farms, rural retreats, and lavish mansions

Although the last Grosse Ile farm didn't disappear until 1960, the island has been a residence for the affluent for many decades. In the 1850s and 1860s, Detroiters began building country villas like **Littlecote** at 24531 East River Drive. It was a "charmingly rustic dwelling . . . far from the bustle of the city." And it "epitomized the new vogue for country living," according to architectural historian Hawkins Ferry. Detroit's leading 19th-century architect, the Gothic Revivalist Gordon Lloyd, designed it for Detroit judge Samuel Douglass, who stayed weeknights in Detroit until the train reached Grosse Ile. Lloyd and his client followed the lead of the influential landscape architect Andrew Jackson Downing, whose popular books "presented a glowing vision of picturesque villas nestled in a landscape that was a 'refined imitation' of nature." Littecote's Gothic touches include scalloped bargeboard trim, ornamental chimneys, numerous porches, and recessed bookcases with pointed arches. Douglas liked to farm and read about science.

The biggest wave of suburbanization, in the early 20th century, came with the automobile. Ransom Olds, founder of Oldsmobile and later REO, built a splendid mansion in 1916 on adjacent Elba Island. Now apartments, it is just north of where Groh Road meets East River and can be reached by taking Elba Road off of East River. The Vernors of ginger ale fame had a mansion on the river just northeast of Horse Mill Road.

Commercial strip
The island's commercial district is along Macomb Street, which stretches east and west between Meridian and East River. There's even a Kroger to serve the small population on these islands.

Getting there
From I-75, take the West Rd. exit in Woodhaven east 3 miles to Jefferson. Turn right (south) a mile to Van Horn Rd. and the free bridge.
A 1913 toll bridge connects the north tip of the island to Biddle St. and Wyandotte. Fare is 75¢ each way. Both are swing bridges because they span the Trenton Channel, which freighters must sometimes use.

In a wave of fairly lavish suburban development on Grosse Ile around 1920, auto magnate Ransom E. Olds built this Italian Renaissance mansion on Elba Island, just off the southern part of East River Rd. It was outfitted with features befitting the status of a modern American industrial baron: a built-in pipe organ, solarium and outdoor swimming pool, game room, and third-story ballroom.

Parke Lane at the north east end of the island was named for the pharmaceutical magnate who subdivided it. He sold two of the parcels to two of the legendary Fisher brothers, founders of Fisher Body. Only one of the mansions, at 19123 Parke Lane, still stands, the last of the summer residences built here.

Cameron Waterman, whose mansion is at Horse Mill and West River, is perhaps best known today for the fact that his sons invented the outboard motor. The patent was later sold to Evinrude. It was first tested in 1904 right here in the Detroit River.

On 10653 West River between Horse Mill and Church is the striking **Pagoda**, a boat house of oriental design. It was built in 1939 by Harry Bennett, the thug who increasingly ran Ford Motor in the 1930s as old Henry's mind began to go. Complete with underground tunnel to the river with concealed entrances, it was on the market in 1989 for $299,000.

POINTS OF INTEREST

East Side Station (Grosse Ile Historical Museum) ★

Parkway and East River Dr. Thurs 9:30-noon; Sun 1-4. (Closed January-March.) No phone.

This quaint depot museum consists for the most part of artifacts from the homes of people who have lived on Grosse Ile. It has the cluttered, unpretentious atmosphere of a volunteer effort. Labels and explanatory descriptions are in short supply, but its rich array of items makes a brief tour fun. Here you can see the trumpet once used to signal the passing postman in Trenton that there was mail to pick up on the island. There are pieces of wood from the Treaty Tree under which the Macombs gained possession of the island from the Indians in 1776. There are the usual old clothes, old tools, old dolls, old bottles, and some unusual things like a bulky 3-inch pre-1940 TV and a typewriter made by Hammond with a semicircular keyboard. In front is a big anchor from an old Great Lakes steamer. Behind the Customs House (also open for inspection) are big navigational lights once used to guide ships through the Livingstone (downstream) Channel on the Detroit River.

The trim brick Michigan Central depot, built in 1904, was used only for passenger traffic on and off the island, but the old 19th-century customs house behind it was used when the Canadian Southern Railroad shipped cargo (much of it cattle) from Chicago across Ontario to Buffalo beginning in 1873. To get across the Detroit River, they built bridges to Stone Island, just east of Grosse Ile, and ferried the railroad cars the rest of the way across to Gordon, Ontario, north of Amherstburg. A railroad tunnel under the river here was attempted in 1879 but soon abandoned because the limestone formations under the river weren't strong enough. The ferry service stopped in 1883, but passenger rail service continued until 1924, at its height amounting to three trains a day to the island.

Grosse Ile Municipal Airport

South of Groh Road at Meridian.

Until 1969 this decaying facility was a U.S. Naval Air Station. Now it is used by private and corporate aircraft. During World War II both American and British pilots were trained at the airport. In 1928 the first all-metal dirigible was built and flown here. The field was first built by the then fledgling Curtis Wright Company, which started a flying school.

You can grab a bite to eat, and there's a tavern just across Groh.

Grosse Ile Lighthouse

North of Parke Lane and Ridge Rd. overlooking the Detroit River.

This attractive octagonal lighthouse, owned by the local historical society, unfortunately is inaccessible by land because of the private property leading up to it. It was built in 1906 and stands 40 feet high. The Coast Guard stopped using it in 1963. It can be glimpsed from East River Drive as you approach Horse Mill Road to the north.

Westcroft Gardens ★★

21803 W. River Rd. just south of Church Rd. (313) 676-2444. Normal hours: Tues-Fri 8-4:30, Sat 10-6. Sun hours: April-July 2-4, Sept & Oct please call, Nov & Dec 10-5. Jan. & Feb. hours: Mon-Fri 9-2.

"In late May and early June, when the azaleas and rhododendrons [here] go crazy with color, this is truly one of the magical places in Detroit," said the *Detroit Guide*. Parts of the four-acre display garden of this large nursery are in bloom from the end of March through June with ornamental trees and shrubs (including magnolias, dogwood, and pieris japonica), spring wildflowers, ground covers, and perennials. All these are sold here, plus annuals, herbs, water plants grown in a pond, fall mums and pumpkins, even poinsettias, Christmas trees and greens. Spring, fall, and Christmas are all busy.

But Westcroft is known for its azaleas and rhododendrons, guaranteed winter-hardy in southern Michigan up to 100 miles north of here. These spectacular shade- and acid-loving shrubs are native to the mild Carolina highlands. The southern varieties are a different strain from the cold-climate plants the late Ernest Stanton used in developing his hybrids here at Westcroft. Gassed in World War I, he was advised to work outdoors for his health. After studying horticulture, he established the nursery here on his parents' farm, which had produced hay for horses in Detroit.

As yet, plants at Westcroft's 12 acres of greenhouses and nursery are sold only locally. But it wholesales its Greenleaf compound for keeping clayey Michigan soils acid and loose for azaleas and rhododendrons.

Elizabeth Park

At the Free Bridge leading from Van Horn Rd. to Grosse Ile.

This attractive island park in the shipping channel is mainly a marina, but there are picnic tables and nature paths for the general public.

RESTAURANTS

The Hungry Crab

8905 Macomb. (313) 671-1695. Tues-Thurs 11-10, Fri 11-11, Sat 4-11, Sun 4-9. Cocktails. Visa, MasterCard, AmExpress.

Seafood and generous portions mark this large restaurant, unrelated to the Chuck Muer empire despite its name. The popular $4.75 lunch buffet includes one seafood and two meat entrees plus an ample salad bar. Burgers and fries ($3.50 and up), fresh lake perch ($6.95), and under-$5 specials are also available. Dinners run $8-15, including salad, vegetable, potato, and roll. Wednesdays bring the $12.95 all-you-can-eat seafood buffet.

Water's Edge

At the Water's Edge Country Club on West River just south of the bridge. (313) 671-0789. Open April 1-late Oct. 11 a.m. to about 10 p.m. Wine and beer. No credit cards.

For a snack or light meal with some atmosphere, this clubhouse of Grosse Ile's municipally owned country club is your best bet. The lively waterfront concession overlooking the marina has a kitchen (no microwaved fare) where hamburgers ($2.50), patty melts, and croissants stuffed with chicken and tuna salad ($3.25) are prepared. Beginning in 1917 the remodeled farmhouse here had been the home of William S. Knudsen, the Danish-born Ford engineer who later proved instrumental in reviving General Motors in the 1920s.

Tokyo Sushi-Iwa

22601 Allen Rd. at West in Woodhaven, about 3 miles from the Grosse Ile bridge. Take Van Horn due west of the Free Bridge, turn north onto Allen for a mile. The restaurant is near K Mart. (313) 676-4711. Mon-Fri lunch 11:30-2. Daily dinner 5-9:30, 'til 10:30 Fri & Sat. Cocktails. Visa, MasterCard, AmExpress, Diners.

This huge Japanese restaurant chain located its first U.S. restaurant three miles from its Flat Rock plant on Vreeland Road just west of I-75. The 250-seat restaurant, awarded three stars by the *Free Press*'s Molly Abraham, is the real thing, not a tourist version of a Japanese restaurant. In the cocktail lounge, song lyrics for Japanese and pop sing-a-longs appear on a screen. There's a sushi bar, regular seating at tables and booths, and a room with tatami mats where diners sit at low tables with their feet in little pits. The menu ranges from steak (a Japanese favorite, but served with rice, not potatoes) and tempura to less familiar dishes like buckwheat noodles with dried seaweed or steamed or raw fish. Lunch favorites shrimp tempura or steak run $8 (with soup, rice, and vegetables). Dinners, including soup, salad, and rice, range from $10 for grilled chicken to $25 for specially ordered banquets.

Plymouth

What makes this small, attractive suburb worth a visit are its two increasingly interesting commercial districts. They contain a variety of noteworthy shops and a couple of exceptional places to eat.

Most towns of 10,000 don't come close to the vitality of Plymouth's downtown and Old Village. The health of this central city is robust because it also serves the sprawling, 55,000-strong bedroom community of adjacent Canton, and it is close to affluent Northville and Northville Township. Once rich farmlands, Canton Township has recently evolved into a series of modest tract housing developments for white-collar workers and commuters. But the lack of a commercial center in Canton has made Plymouth's downtown the *de facto* downtown for the area.

Outsiders often think that Plymouth must be a major production center for the car of that name. Actually, cars haven't been made here since 1916, when the ill-fated Alter Motor Car Company shut its doors after making just a thousand automobiles. The name "Plymouth" was attached in 1827 to what was then a rude hamlet because of its historical and patriotic connotations. The name has had an effect on the community. You'll find more colonial-style buildings here than in many similar towns. The hotel is called the Mayflower. During World War II, the town sent aid to its namesake in England, and the two have been sister cities ever since, exchanging delegations to major events.

Early stage stop

Early Plymouth was bisected by an old Indian trail that became a road linking Detroit and Ann Arbor. The road is still known as Ann Arbor Trail (Plymouth Road in Washtenaw County). The town was a stage stop with two hotels as early as 1832. The Middle River Rouge curls along Plymouth's northeast boundary. It provided power for the grist and lumber mills that sprang up along its banks. In the 1920s, Henry Ford transformed six of these mills into water-powered auto parts factories supplying his huge Rouge complex. (See p. 181.) The one in Plymouth and the two just north of town are now Wayne County roads and parks facilities.

Two railroads eventually were built through Plymouth, making it a fairly busy train town in the Iron Horse's heyday. One line went from Detroit through Lansing to Lake Michigan, one from Monroe to Holly.

Michigan's sweet corn capital
Still remaining in western Canton Township, just south of Plymouth, are the large farms which make Wayne County the leading sweet corn producer in the state.

Maps and events
For free walking/shopping maps of downtown Plymouth and Old Village, plus a calendar of events, see the Chamber of Commerce (313-453-1540) at 960 W. Ann Arbor Trail (across from Kellogg Park, next to the Little Professor).

The boy pictured in Daisy's 1947 American Boys Bill of Rights responded to post-World War II anti-gun sentiment by proclaiming his right to learn to shoot safely.

BB-gun capital of the world

For years, because it was home of the Daisy Air Rifle Company, Plymouth was known far and wide as the air rifle capital of the world. The first mass-produced air rifle was also made in Plymouth, but not by Daisy. This was a mostly-wood model made by Markham Manufacturing beginning in 1885. You can still see the Markham factory, a brick building on Main Street just east of the railroad tracks, where Plymouth Landing restaurant and offices now are. If you look south down the other side of the tracks at that junction, you can see a much bigger brick building on Union Street, the old Daisy headquarters and factory.

Daisy was initially the Plymouth Windmill Company, but when sales declined, the firm decided to make and give away an all-metal air rifle to any farmer who would buy its windmill. The air rifle sold briskly while windmill sales languished. So the company stopped making windmills and changed its name to the Daisy Manufacturing Company in 1895.

The name "Daisy" came from Plymouth Windmill's general manager. When shown one of the all-metal guns by its designer, he admired its accuracy and power, saying, "Boy, that's a daisy!"

Daisy went on to become Plymouth's largest employer and a force in local projects. By the 1930s it was producing over 90 per cent of the world's air rifles. An especially important Daisy employee was Charles Lefever, who designed the popular pump air rifle and the basic Daisy mechanism in use from 1912 to 1950. Lefever also was responsible for that important American innovation, the plunger-type water pistol.

Daisy departs

Plymouth was stunned when, in 1958, Daisy's board voted to move its entire operations to Rogers, Arkansas. Disgruntlement with the policies of Democratic governor Soapy Williams is one reason given for the move. Others say that when Burroughs and Kelsey-Hayes built large plants nearby, wages were driven up, and Daisy moved to take advantage of cheaper Arkansas labor.

With the departure of Plymouth's major employer, it looked like the town faced a major recession. But the building of a giant Western Electric parts and repair facility and Ford car air conditioner and heater plant on Sheldon Road cushioned the blow.

White-collar suburb

Locked into a small two-square-mile area, Plymouth hasn't had room to grow. Surrounded by a hostile township which has repeatedly thwarted the city's efforts to break out of its confines, little Plymouth is another victim of Michigan's pro-township annexation laws. The town's population has hovered around 10,000 for three decades now, half that of the township. It's a predominantly white-collar suburb, and, like most other Detroit suburbs, it has hardly any blacks — a grand total of 3 in 1980. Plymouth's streets of modestly attractive homes are typically lined with big trees; they have an unusually pleasant aura of small-town America.

Until the early 1980s, Western Electric had a major repair facility here on Sheldon Road, but abandoned it after the AT&T breakup. It is now headquarters of Highland Appliance. The city today has two big employers. The big Ford plant on Sheldon Road makes air conditioners for Fords. Unisys (formerly Burroughs), on Plymouth Road to the east, makes computers. Each employs from 1,500 to 2,000 workers. Winkelman's clothing chain also is headquartered here.

The Plymouth Ice Sculpture Spectacular draws half a million people to downtown Plymouth between the second and third weekends of January. Up to 200 ice sculptures by amateurs and by professionals from as far away as Japan line the streets and the walks of Kellogg Park.

Shop hours downtown are mostly from 10 to 6 daily, until 9 Friday, and closed Sundays. Some Old Village stores are open Sunday.

POINTS OF INTEREST

Kellogg Park

Downtown, Ann Arbor Trail at Main St.

This shady triangular park creates a pleasant center to the city. It was donated by John Kellogg, who arrived in 1832 with a chest full of gold coins, having just sold a hotel and warehouse in Palmyra, New York. Its location on the Erie Canal had made Palmyra prosper. Kellogg promptly bought much of the land which is now Plymouth. A fountain today sits in the center of the park where a 15-ton boulder nicknamed "Plymouth Rock" once sat. Hauled from Northville Road, it is dedicated to those who served in the war with Spain. It now sits across Penniman Street in front of the once splendid **Markham House,** built by Phil Markham in 1903. By the 1980s, the mansion had become sadly dilapidated, but plans call for a thorough restoration in connection with an adjacent $6 million condominium development.

Markham's invention and manufacture of an all-wooden air rifle inspired the Plymouth Windmill Company to get into the air rifle business and eventually manufacture the competing Daisy. Markham designed this house himself, including the fancy millwork, and decorated it with stained glass windows and velvet drapes. Out back he had goldfish ponds and three pet deer. Markham had offended locals by having a mistress, whom he married once his wife died. This friction caused him to move to Hollywood, California, where he bought raw land which soon became the center of that famous town.

Opposite the park on Penniman is the **Farmers Market**, where fresh produce is sold Saturdays from 8 a.m. to 1 p.m., May through October. Next door, at the **Penn Theatre**, not-quite-first-run movies are shown, usually at 7 and 9, for $1.50.

Penniman Street ★★

Between Harvey and Main Streets

This pleasant block just west of Kellogg Park is home to Plymouth's fiercely independent weekly newspaper, the *Community Crier*, and some of Plymouth's choicest establishments. The **Penniman Deli** still has the atmosphere of the old-fashioned meat market it used to be; it is handy for takeout vegetable and pasta salads to eat in Kellogg Park. Other highlights include:

Folkways Trading Company ★★
844 Penniman. (313) 459-0444. 10-5:30, Fri until 9, closed Sun.

At this delightful gift shop you can buy anything from a 75¢ whistle to baskets, garden ornaments, cards, and toys. The owner clearly has an eye for the interesting and distinctive: French damask towels with grape motifs, gleaming copper pots from Turkey, windup toys and nesting dolls, children's books, unusual seasonal novelty items (Halloween masks, Easter baskets, etc.) and cards and gift wraps. It shares space with the highly regarded **Cafe Bon Homme**.

Penniman Showcase of Art & Crafts ★
827 Penniman. (313) 455-5531. Mon-Thurs 10-6, Fri until 9, Sat until 5.

The work of some 150 American craftsmen in porcelain, stoneware, fibers, and jewelry is most attractively displayed. The richly colorful blown glass display is a special treat. Prices range from $20 to $500. Many items in this crowded shop are in pinkish pastel colors, whose effect is curiously beautiful rather than sickeningly sweet.

Maggie & Me ★
880 Ann Arbor Trail, a block south of Penniman. (313) 459-5340. Mon-Sat 10-6.

Two-thirds of the clothes at this highly regarded shop are designed and manufactured in-house by Maggie. It's an updated and contemporary line with a very soft touch, says Maggie, a 12-year veteran designer-retailer who is fascinated with the side effects of the women's movement. Lace mixed with menswear fabrics, sometimes even heavy suiting, is her trademark, and she also uses a lot of hand-dyed silk ribbon and roses. Everything is in natural fibers, one size fits all, with lots of black and jewel tones — amethyst, garnet, topaz, "colors as they come out of the earth," Maggie says. It's not a professional look, but "play clothes," imaginative and fanciful, a relief from the everyday business grind. Her signature item is a cotton sweatshirt in spring, fall, and holiday versions, priced from $69 to $300 and loaded with lace, beads, and roses, to be worn with anything from jeans to a lace skirt.

Old Village ★★

Area between Starkweather, Pearl, Mill, and Spring Streets in north Plymouth, towards Northville and just east of the train tracks. From Main St.

In Plymouth's Old Village, varied antique and specialty shops occupy old commercial buildings and houses.

turn north onto Starkweather or Mill.

This interesting, eclectic commercial district dates from the simultaneous arrival of two railroad lines to Plymouth in 1871. It turned out to be a busy railroad area, with as many as 18 passenger trains arriving a day. But businesses here, centered on Liberty between Starkweather and Mill Streets, never seriously competed with downtown Plymouth. What you find here now, and in houses along Starkweather and Mill, is a rather funky, heterogeneous collection of shops not unlike the colorful array found in Royal Oak. It's not a terribly intense, high-rent area, and occasional shops seem more like hobbies than totally serious businesses. A number of antique shops are worth visiting here, mostly on the old brick commercial block of Liberty.

At the northernmost part of the district is the highly regarded **Sweet Afton Tea Room**. (See Restaurants). Also of special interest are:

Plymouth Antique Mall
900 N. Mill. (313) 455-5595. Daily including Sunday, 11-7.

An interesting collection of dealers, currently 12, in a newer building.

Pringles Pastries
795 N. Mill. (313) 453-4226. Mon-Sat 9:30-6.

Nearly everybody nearby loves this bakery and pastry shop. Cheesecakes and tortes, sold whole or by the slice, are a specialty, but cookies, muffins, and a full line of baked goods are available, along with coffee. Blackbottom cupcakes are catching on.

LaDonna's
638 Starkweather. (313) 459-7474. Mon 1-6, Tues, Wed, Fri 10-5:30, Thurs 1-7.

Previously owned ladies' designer clothing, less than two years old, can be had for a third or a fourth of its original price. The best selection by far is in sizes 8 or 10. Dresses run $30 and up.

Born Again Resale
900 Starkweather. (313) 459-8942. 10-6, Fri until 8, Sat until 4, closed Sun.

This shop is strongest in women's and children's clothing. Sweaters run $5 to $25, two-piece suits $15-$60, and dresses $10 to $50.

Presbyterian Thrift Shop
187 Liberty. Open Thursdays 10-3

Used clothing and all sorts of other things is sold by a convivial group of churchwomen.

Plymouth Yard Hobbies
904 Starkweather at the tracks. (313) 455-4455. Mon-Sat 11-7, Sun 11-3.

The old C & O freight depot here is crammed with model railroad paraphernalia.

Village Paperback Exchange
950 Starkweather. (313) 459-8550. Mon-Sat 10-6, Fri until 8, Sun 12-5.

A well-stocked shop, especially with lowbrow fiction.

Plymouth Historical Museum ★

155 S. Main St. in the old post office. (313) 455-8940. Thurs, Sat, Sun 1-4. Admission $2.

Few cities as small as Plymouth have put as much energy into their local historical museums. There is a modest gift shop here, a reconstruction of a late 19th-century Victorian parlor, dining room, and kitchen, and two rows of shops which use local artifacts to reconstruct 19 trades and professions from early Plymouth. There's a delightful collection of paper dolls in the basement, and some noteworthy Indian artifacts.

Three exhibits are especially eye-catching. In the BB-gun room you can see the locally manufactured Daisy and Markham BB-guns and fascinating advertising for them. One 1910 Daisy Air Rifle ad begins:

> *Every Live American Boy Wants a DAISY AIR RIFLE*

"Boy, you ought to have a gun this summer," the ad orders. "Make up your mind to get one, and learn to shoot straight."

The only known remaining Alter automobile is displayed in the basement. People often think of Plymouth as the place which manufactures the car with that name. In fact, the Alter was the only car ever made in Plymouth. Only a thousand were made. Named after the Wisconsin man who designed it, the Alter was manufactured between 1914 and 1916. Its 27 horsepower 1916 model sold for $685. It's not clear why the company went under (management cited "insufficient capital"), but it was hardly an isolated case of auto company failures in this era. Ford, with its practice of lowering its prices as its volume skyrocketed, was crushing the competition with its cheap, reliable Model T.

Another auto-related display in the basement has recently been constructed by employees at the nearby Sheldon Road Ford plant. In a room labeled "Nankin Mills" is a wonderful model of the countryside along the Middle Rouge River showing the village industries Henry Ford built.

Two bargains in the **gift shop** are a $2 paperback on the history of Daisy Air Rifle and an especially well written hardbound history of Plymouth by Sam Hudson for $8.

RESTAURANTS

Cafe Bon Homme ★

844 Penniman, downtown. (313) 453-6260. Mon-Fri 11:30-10, Sat 12-10:30. Full bar, wide-ranging wine list at all prices. MasterCard, Visa, AmExpress.

This pleasant, popular cafe, although somewhat overpriced, has become an important addition to downtown Plymouth. For lunch you can order dishes like Louisiana Crab Cakes ($10.95), made of king crab, potato, red and green peppers, and served with lobster sauce, or chicken strudel ($8.95), made with mushrooms, gruyere cheese, vegetables and chicken wrapped in filo dough and served with tarragon sauce. Recommended dinner entrees include swordfish steak garnished with sea scallops ($19.95) and Tournedoes au Beurre Rouge ($20.95).

Plymouth Fish & Chips ★

578 Starkweather in the Old Village. (313) 455-2630. Mon-Wed 10-8, Thurs-Sat 10-9, Sun 12-7. No credit cards or alcohol.

The $4.95 order of fish and chips is a fabulous takeout meal to enjoy in Kellogg Park, or you can eat at a table in this fish market. You get three big pieces of fried scrod, very fresh and tasty, plus a generous serving of potatoes fried in peanut oil and a cup of terrific dilled coleslaw, not too sweet. (Marzetti's slaw dressing with onion, fresh dill, parsley and a little white wine is the secret.)

Sweet Afton Tearoom ★★

985 N. Mill St., (off Pearl) in the Old Village. (313) 454-0777. Wed-Sun 11-5. Reservations advised for between noon and 2. No credit cards or alcohol.

This authentically executed British tea room is exceptionally pleasant, with excellent tea, scones, and other dishes to boot. The environment is decidedly feminine. As the menu explains, the tradition of afternoon tea dates from the 1840s "as people of the era ate large breakfasts and did not eat again until 8 or 9. Ladies often found themselves feeling frail by afternoon."

The solution was tea with nibbles, although Sweet Afton also offers a couple of popular beef pies. The small, rather bland Shepard's Pie ($4.95) comes with ground round on the bot-tom, corn, and a topping of daintily textured mashed potatoes. It's greatly enlivened by the accompanying little pot of Branston pickle relish. The Wellington meat pie ($5.25) has beef chunks and vegetables in a flaky crust. The intriguing Ploughman's Lunch ($4.50), explains the menu, is a typical mid-day feast for British farmers: a hefty chunk of white cheddar with a big slice of warm bread, butter, pickled onions, and a hot cup of soup. For $3.50 you can get 6 finger-sized sandwiches with sweet gherkin pickles. Two scones with American Spoon jam and Devon cream are $3.95. The garden salad ($2.95), served with a delicious blueberry muffin, is unadverturous but filling. After 2 p.m., two scones and tea is $5.

The Victorian atmosphere, in which the waitresses' wear long skirts and frilly aprons, is quite pleasant. The place seats only 34, so reservations are recommended.

LODGINGS

Plymouth Radisson

(313) 459-4500.
14707 Northville Rd. From I-275 at 6 Mile Rd., go west 1 1/2 miles to Northville Rd., left 1 1/2 miles, on right.

538 rooms on 5 floors. $70 single; $80 double. Indoor pool, sauna, whirlpool, exercise room, game room, jungle gym for kids. Showtime & ESPN. Restaurant and lobby bar. Comedy club Thurs, Fri, & Sat evenings. Reservations usually required.

Mayflower Hotel

(313) 453-1620.
827 W. Ann Arbor Trail at Main St. (downtown Plymouth).

100 rooms, 3 floors. $63.50 single; $73.50 double; includes breakfast. suites $125 and $150. Cinemax. 2 restaurants & pub. Some rooms have a view of Plymouth's main square, Kellogg Park. Downtown location is close to numerous shops.

Northville

This picturesque suburb, once a farm town, was first settled in 1825. It was best known for a harness racetrack and a giant, troubled state mental hospital. But in recent years, thanks to its excellent freeway access, Northville has become an upscale bedroom community for executives at Ford and other large firms. The town of 22,000 spans northern Wayne County and southern Oakland County. Most of Wayne County is quite flat. Hilly Northville is the county's highest spot, 375 feet above Lake St. Clair.

Northville features an exceptionally pleasant downtown, thanks to one of Michigan's most successful preservation efforts. On bustling Main Street east of Center (which is the in-town section of Sheldon Road) is the nicely restored and heavily used **Marquis Theatre**, a turn-of-the-century opera house. The downtown commercial district has become so popular that it's difficult to find a parking space. But the shopping is a disappointment unless you go for the "country things" theme. Still, there are three outstanding restaurants and a delightful general store called **Grandma Betty's** (124 N. Center, Mon-Sat 10-6, except Fri 'til 8 & Sat 'til 5). In the adult half are coffee beans, fruit juices, bulk spices, low-cholesterol foods, and small gift items. In the kids' half are candies and toys. An attorney with definite ideas about what she wants in her shop, Grandma Betty eschews all competitive and violent games. She takes particular pride in her old-fashioned bins of candies that kids can come in and buy for as little as 2¢ apiece.

Victorian Northville's residential show street was **West Dunlap Street** one block north of Main. Today its several blocks of richly varied 19th-century houses have been stunningly restored and landscaped.

The magic well
Right at the bend of Main St. just past the Ford plant you'll see a well. Hundreds of people come here to fill their jugs with the reportedly exceptional spring water flowing from beneath. They are unaware that some years ago the well's spigot was connected to the city's main water system.

Theater and racing
To find out about upcoming live professional theater productions at the Marquis Theatre, call (313) 349-0868. Harness racing at Northville Downs runs from October through May. Call (313) 349-1000 for post times.

Northville has one of the more attractive downtowns in Michigan. Weak on interesting shops, it is strong on good restaurants and ambience.

POINTS OF INTEREST

Maybury State Park ★

Main entrance: 8 Mile Rd. between Beck and Napier roads, 5 miles west of I-275. (313) 349-8390. Mailing address and horsemen's entrance: 20145 Beck Rd., Northville 48197. Open 8 a.m.-10 p.m. year-round. $3 daily vehicle permit or $15/year state parks sticker.

Though these hilly 945 acres just west of Northville include hiking, riding, and biking trails and picnic sites, the park is best known for its real working farm, unique among Michigan parks and open to the public year-round. A trip to Maybury is well worth while to anyone interested in observing what an authentic American farm in the 1930s was like. At that time, tractors had been introduced but draft horses still did much of the work. Park rangers — experienced, knowledgeable, and good at explaining farm life — grow the grain and hay to feed the animals they raise, and tend a big vegetable garden, with some herbs, too. As at most farms, breeding stock stays on the farm during the winter, while the young are sold off.

This is no display farm, with asphalt paths and suburban landscaping. The farm buildings were here long before the property became part of the Northville tuberculosis hospital opened in the 1920s. When the hospital closed, the property became a park. The state parks department decided to operate the farm, with its century-old barn, to interpret farm life to city people.

Visitors are welcome to watch at feeding time. (Year-round it is 4 p.m.) Seasonal activities depend on the weather. Maple sugaring is sometime in March. Plowing with Sam and Sarge, the team of big Belgians, comes later in spring. Sheep are sheared the middle two weeks of May. Honey is harvested in September. Rangers try to do a lot of farm work for weekend visitors.

Baby animals are abundant during spring and summer. Pigs bear monthly litters from February to November, calves over the year, sheep and goats in spring. Visitors can buy not only honey, fresh eggs, and beeswax candles, but pigs and ducks.

The rest of Maybury's meadows and dense woodlots feature 4 miles of bike trails and 12 miles of hiking trails. Scattered picnic sites reflect contemporary parks thinking. Rather than being clustered close to parking, they are scattered and separated for greater privacy and separation from vehicles, which means considerable walking from your car. Be sure to pick up a map at the entry gate..

◆ **Cross-country skiing** is on 17 miles of one-way trails, most quite hilly and challenging. The concession at the west parking lot (just behind the farm) rents equipment, sells snacks, and offers a warming fire. Open in season noon-6 weekdays, 9-6 weekends. (313) 348-1190.

◆ **Sledding and tobogganing** is on a long hill 1/3 mile from the east parking lot. A shelter has a fireplace.

◆ **Horsemen** use the Beck Road entrance to enter the 8 miles of riding trails. A riding stable

Like most working farms, the one at Maybury State Park sells off the animals born each season, keeping only breeding stock. Piglets, lambs, calves, kids, chicks, ducklings, and goslings are for sale to the public.

rents horses for $10/hour weekdays, $12 weekends and holidays. Open 9 a.m.-dusk year-round, closed Mon.

Mill Race Historical Village

Griswold St. just north of Main, east of Center near downtown. (313) 349-0868. Open June-October, Sun 1-4. Visitors may walk around outside any time. Free admission.

On the banks of the scenic River Rouge where the big, old Northville Mills once stood, the Northville Historical Society has moved six 19th-century structures to create a semblance of a village from that era. Unfortunately an ugly chain-link fence separates the attractive village from the beautiful river.

The houses have been furnished authentically and fully. They include a splendid 1851 Greek Revival home which used to stand at Main and Griswold, a fine 1868 Gothic Revival home from Cady Street, an 1890s cottage from Center Street and an 1830s-era saltbox, also from Cady Street, being furnished as an inn. An 1845 Presbyterian church, an 1873 one-room schoolhouse from Currie Road, a replica of a blacksmith shop, and a new gazebo complete the ensemble.

Ford's Village Industries: Northville Plant

On the Rouge River, Main at Griswold, just east of downtown.

One of the striking ironies of Henry Ford's life is that the same man whose giant factories brought unprecedented masses of workers to the cities actually detested the urban environment. "The great modern

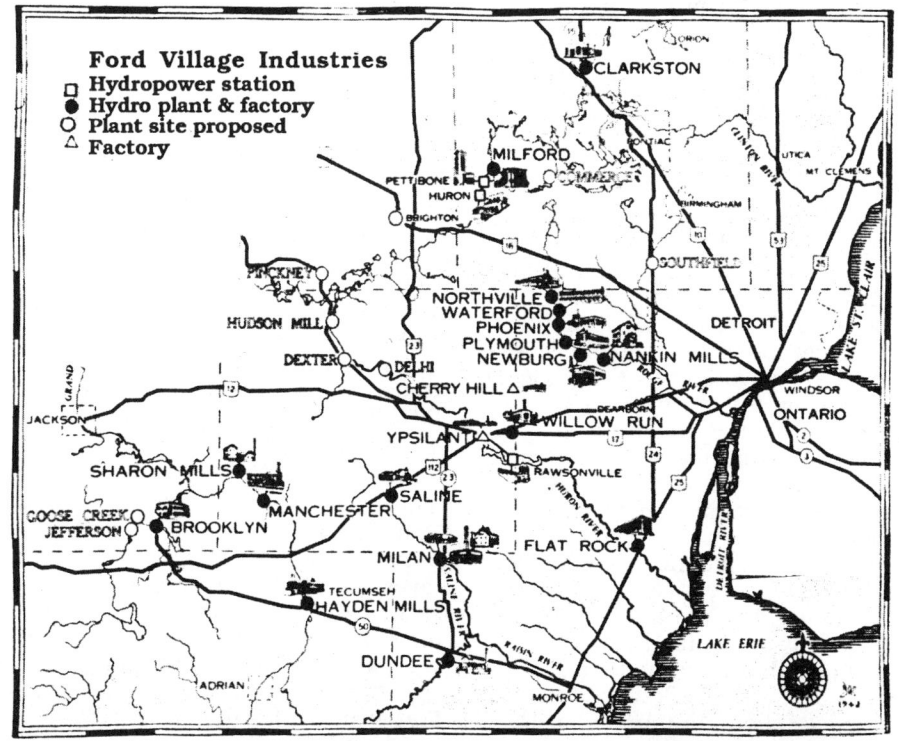

1942 Ford Motor Co. map

city," he once said, "is an abnormal development." Unlike many social thinkers, Ford actually put his money where his mouth was.

Between 1918 and 1944, Ford created 24 "village industries" in small villages or out in the countryside of southeast Michigan. These mini-factories employed nearby residents to make parts for Ford vehicles. Most were simple brick buildings, but occasionally they were installed in 19th-century gristmills. Typical employees were farmers who were given time off to plant and reap.

Ford located his little factories on small rivers so that part or all the electricity needed could be created with a mill wheel connected to a generator. Through his friendship with Thomas Edison, Ford became infatuated with small hydroelectric systems, probably because it suited his interest in self-sufficiency. He built an extraordinarily elaborate hydroelectric system for his own Fair Lane estate. For years it powered all the rest of Dearborn.

Ford's twenty-four small water-powered factories, some of them in historic mills, are dotted along the Middle Rouge, Raisin, Huron, and Saline rivers. Ford was so proud of these hydroelectric systems that he sometimes enclosed the turbines in glass to make them visible. When he walked into the plant manager's office of this Northville plant just after it was completed, he tersely noted that one couldn't see the big mill wheel on the other side of the windowless wall. By the time he revisited the plant the next day, a big picture window was in place. Today the mill wheel remains a Northville landmark.

With few exceptions, these small plants were money-losers for Ford. After Henry's death in 1947, most were quickly dismantled or sold. This plant in Northville on the Middle Rouge River, the very first one built, was an exception. An unusually efficient plant, it was later expanded and kept running until 1989. For years engine valves were built here, and later, gas tanks.

Because of the serene, park-like setting with ducks and geese wandering about year round, the Northville plant was enviously dubbed the "country club" by Ford workers at the big plants. We're told that a spirit of hard-working camaraderie existed here through the years. The ducks and geese actually became such a fixture that the union contract specified that Ford was responsible for keeping them fed, even during strikes.

Middle Rouge Parkway/ Ford Mills

Along Edward Hines Drive. Entered off major east-west roads between Northville and Plymouth and off major north-south roads from Plymouth to Dearborn. West entrance: 7 Mile and Sheldon roads in Northville. East entrance: Ford Rd. west of Evergreen in Dearborn. For a map showing facilities, contact Wayne Co. Parks, 33175 Ann Arbor Trail, Westland, MI 48185. (313) 261-1990.

This remarkable 17 1/2-mile park along the floodplain of the Middle Rouge River includes an 11-mile bike path and 12 miles of hiking trails. It takes about 35 minutes to drive the entire length, but it is more interesting to explore on foot or by bicycle. If you choose to walk or bike along the river starting in Northville, you might first want to pick up a delectable lunch at **Edwards Caterer** (see p.184). If you drive, don't speed: Hines Drive is heavily patrolled.

The parkway has rest rooms along the way, 4 fishing lakes, and picnic shelters. In the winter 2 major sledding hills, 2 tobogganing runs, and 6 skating rinks are in use.

The park is also the setting for four of Henry Ford's village industries. (For background, see p. 181.) Farthest north is the **Phoenix Plant** (14973 Northville Rd.), today a Wayne County maintenance yard. Built in 1922, it had a 35-horsepower generator driven by the river. This mill was unique in that Henry Ford decided that all its 50 to 100 workers should be single or widowed women. Unlike male Ford workers, they got two rest periods a day. They made voltage regulators and later ID badges here.

Downstream at the **Wilcox Mill** (230 Wilcox Rd.) in Plymouth, a 30-horsepower hydroelectric generator was used to produce screw taps. Farther south in Livonia the **Newburgh Mill** (37401 Edward Hines Dr.) was the last to be located on the Middle Rouge. It was opened in 1935 at the site of an old cider mill. When the lake above the dam was low and the water power reduced, a steam engine also provided electricity here. Some 30 local farmers built the plant and then worked here making twist drills for Ford plants around the world. Production ceased in 1947. The garages are now used for stables of the Mounted Division of the sheriff's department.

Of all the Ford water-powered plants along the Middle Rouge, by far the most striking is **Nankin Mills** (Farmington Rd. at Edward Hines Dr.). Built just after the Civil War, this stately old white wood structure was Ford's second village industry, started in 1921. It made script dies, stencils, ID badges, and engravings. You can see the glass-enclosed turbines Henry Ford had built to show off the power source for his factory.

RESTAURANTS

MacKinnon's ★★★

126 E. Main St. (downtown Northville). (313) 348-1991. Mon-Fri 11-10 (Fri until 11), Sat lunch 11:30-4, dinner 5-11. Full bar. Visa, AmExpress, MasterCard.

MacKinnon's attracts diners from throughout the region to this inconspicuous storefront in downtown Northville. The food is excellent and the atmosphere charming. Like many of the best Detroit-area restaurants, it emphasizes wild game. Noteworthy dinner dishes include wild turkey tenderloin broil with spiced berry sauce and poppyseed bread timbale ($15.95), charcoal duck with raspberry sauce ($16.95), and grilled scallops Santa Fe ($15.95). All dinners include bread, salad, and sauteed vegetable. For lunch, try the crab pasta du chef ($6.95) or the baked chicken strudel ($5.95), each with soup or salad.

Little Italy ★★

227 Hutton (one block north of Main St. and one block east of Sheldon in downtown Northville). (313) 348-0575. Tues-Sat 5-10, Fri & Sat until 11. Entrees $10.95-$21.95. Wine. Visa, MasterCard.

This excellent Italian restaurant is in the house occupied not too long ago by the famed, perfectionistic Elizabeth's. Now owned by the family behind West Bloomfield's Ristorante di Maria, it's a more relaxed blend of rusticity and sophistication, antique and contemporary. Veal is a specialty, and the veal de mare ($17.95) takes the prize: veal with lemon butter, white wine, and olives topped with 3 jumbo shrimp. There are also homemade pastas and simple dishes like ravioli, gnocchi, and ziti.

homemade pastas and simple dishes like ravioli, gnocchi, and ziti.

Edwards Caterer

116 E. Dunlap (one block north of Main and one block east of Sheldon). (313) 344-1550. Mon-Sat 8:30-7, Sat 'til 5.

Edwards prepares food for some of the fanciest parties in the affluent northern suburbs of Detroit. But you can also sit down here to eat a sandwich or salad, as well as take out a lunch for a delicious picnic. Popular sandwiches are the chicken tarragon ($3.95) and the smoked turkey with tomato chutney and honeycup mustard ($4). A scrumptious variety of pasta, vegetable, and seafood salads ($3 to $4.25 a serving) change daily. The muffins and scones (89¢ each) are outstanding, as is the fresh-ground coffee (80¢ a cup).

LODGINGS

Atchison House Bed & Breakfast
(313) 349-3340. 501 W. Dunlap.
5 rooms, 3 with private, 2 with shared bath. Weekend rate: $60-70 double. Business rates weekdays. No smoking. 1882 Italianate house on a quiet street of splendid historic homes, with easy walking distance to downtown. Beautifully restored and decorated by innkeeper-owners. Furnished in period antiques. Evening refreshments served in the library.

Novi Hilton
(313) 349-4000.
21111 Haggerty Rd. near I-275 exit at Eight Mile Rd., Novi (3 miles from Northville).
240 rooms with contemporary decor. Weekend rate (Fri-Sun): $65 when available, includes breakfast. "Celebrate" package any day, but not for business: $105, includes champagne & continental breakfast. Free HBO. Exercise room, sauna, hot tub, fair-sized glass-domed pool. Casual and fine dining restaurants, nightclub with band and dancing 6 nights/week. 6 nights/week.

Skylight Inn
(313) 321-6336.
21100 Haggerty Rd. at 8 Mile near I-275 exit.
128 rooms. $43 single, $49 double.

The unusual variety of mid-19th-century houses on West Dunlap Street, Victorian Northville's "show street," have been splendidly fussed over and landscaped in recent years. Visitors can stay here at the Atchison House Bed and Breakfast (above).

Birmingham

During the past decade, a vibrant, chic downtown has become the hallmark of Birmingham, the prestigious residential suburb of 24,000 that is 17 miles out Woodward from downtown Detroit. This recent development is something of a paradox, because Birmingham's reputation had always been based on its attractive homes and good schools, not on fashion and glitz. Yet today many of Michigan's most fashion-forward shops and most of the state's top art galleries are here.

Birmingham, blessed with virtually the only functioning downtown in this booming suburban region of central Oakland County, has become the shopping mecca for one of the ten wealthiest counties in the United States. It's alive with new trends and creative ideas, with activity, with cafes and unusual shops, prestigious offices, even a luxury hotel and legitimate theater. Oddly, the restaurants, though competent and occasionally terrific, don't hold a candle to what Detroit has to offer.

Stylish people come to see and be seen, both in downtown Birmingham and at nearby Somerset Mall in Troy, just past the city's northeast edge at Big Beaver and Coolidge. Business owners, ever abreast of the latest trends, like to say that Birmingham is Michigan's equivalent of Washington's Georgetown or Toronto's Yorkville. There's even enough urban intensity downtown to satisfy some transplanted New Yorkers.

High property values threaten diversity

To many outsiders, Birmingham is a town with a homogeneous population of upper-middle-class white gentiles. Actually, because it is an older suburb with housing of many ages and types, Birmingham has a much wider mix of ages and family types than upscale new suburbs where married professionals and junior executives in their thirties and forties predominate.

Though Birmingham has small $100,000 ranch houses, more typical are the gracious, beautifully landscaped, but seldom showy, colonial and Tudor houses built between the 1920s and 1950s off Maple Road west of beautiful little Quarton Lake and the connecting Rouge River. A fairly typical house here (4 bedrooms, 2 1/2 baths, small den, family room addition) sells for $300,000 to $400,000. Prices go up nearer the lake. A similar 1920s house half a mile away in less prestigious Royal Oak recently sold for just $134,000.

Great garage sales
Garage sales in the Birmingham area are indeed fabulous. Most start on Thursday or Friday, others are one day on Saturday. Check the classifieds in the Eccentric (now part of the Observer-Eccentric chain). It appears Monday and Thursday.

Helpful maps
For detailed Oakland County maps — a help in finding things in this booming area — contact the Oakland Co. Planning Division, 1200 N. Telegraph, Pontiac, MI 48053. (313) 858-0723. A set of 4 maps is $1.50.

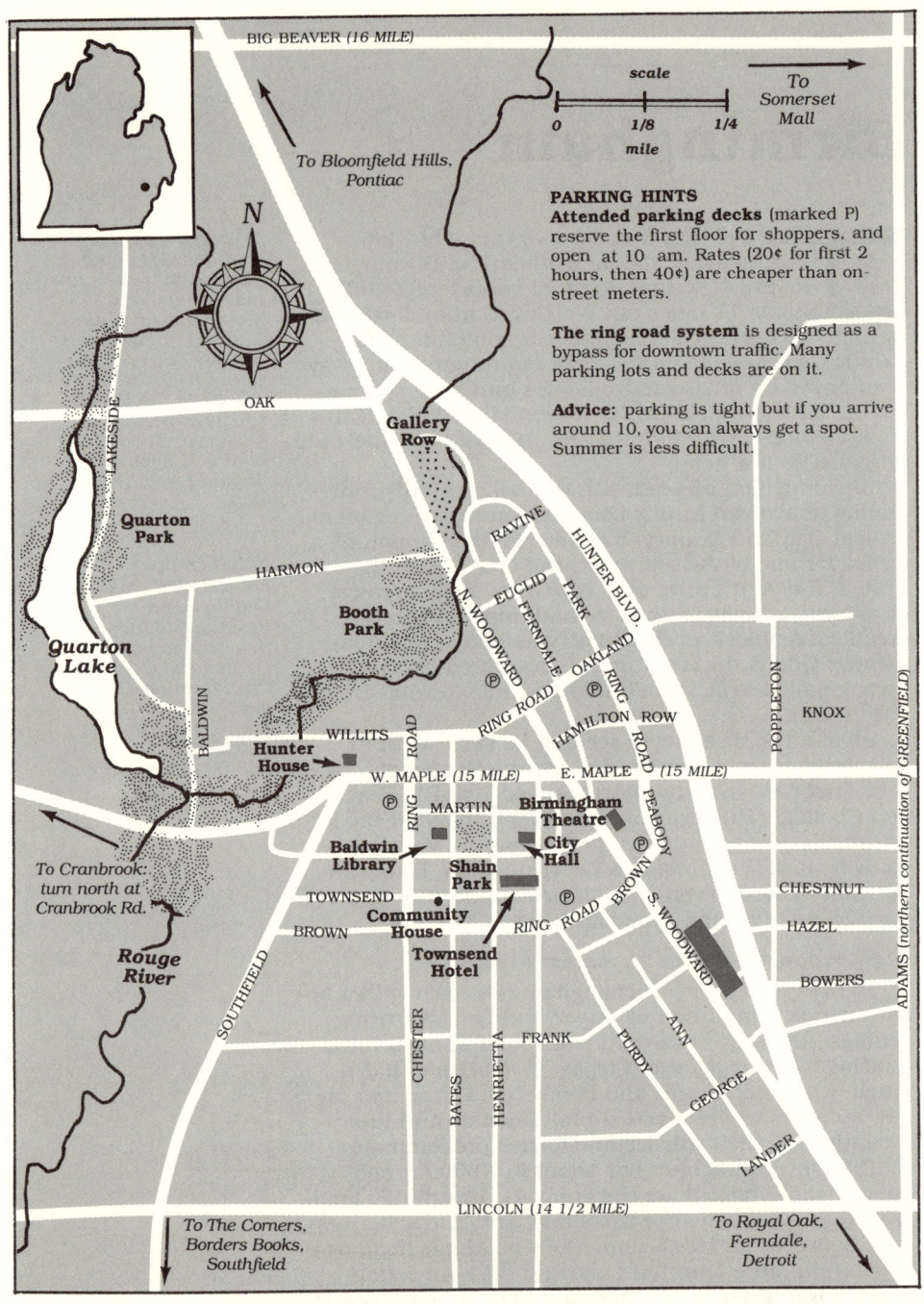

Just west and south of downtown are dense neighborhoods of 1,500-square-foot 1920s bungalows, Cape Cod cottages, and "storybook houses" on 50-foot lots. Detective writer Elmore Leonard lived in this interesting area until he got divorced and hit the literary jackpot; screenwriter Kurt Luedtke (former *Free Press* editor, now known as the writer for the Oscar-winning "Out of Africa") lives here today. Today these smallish houses have been improved, beautifully landscaped, and occasionally transformed into sophisticated statements of personal style with things like bright heliotrope shutters, and terraced courtyards and inventive topiary instead of minuscule front lawns. They run from $150,000 (unimproved) to $350,000 (deluxe rehab). Particularly stunning transformations are on Frank, one block south of Brown, and around the corner on Purdy.

The city of Birmingham, encompassing about four and a half square miles, is only part of what is regarded as Birmingham. In fact, at least three-fourths of the area that has Birmingham schools or a Birmingham mailing address is not in Birmingham at all but in Bingham Farms, Franklin, Beverly Hills, Troy, West Bloomfield Township, Bloomfield Hills, or Bloomfield Township. All the pleasant, quintessentially Birmingham postwar colonials on shady streets between Cranbrook and Lahser are actually in Bloomfield Township. The only indication that they aren't in Birmingham is their quaint, hard-to-read wood street signs. Rock star Bob Seger, incidentally, lives on one of these sedate streets.

First house in Oakland County

Birmingham was transformed from a sleepy agricultural town when the interurban railroad arrived

For movies
the Maple Theater wins raves for its sophisticated art and foreign films, attentive audiences, and terrific treats: popcorn with real butter, Gayle's chocolates, capuccino and espresso, mineral water, muffins, and premium ice cream bars. Audiences here actually stay to watch the credits. The three-screen theater is on Maple just west of Telegraph, behind Bloomfield Plaza, in Bloomfield Township. Call (313) 855-9090 for upcoming program information.

Downtown Birmingham's retail district is attractively landscaped and intense, with retail in every streetfront space and occasionally in upper- and lower-level spaces, as here on Pierce Street. Recently retail fashion chains, able to pay higher rents, have displaced many independently owned local stores, to widespread local concern.

in 1896. That made made the commute to downtown Detroit a mere 40 minutes — only 10 or 15 minutes longer than what it is under optimum traffic conditions by car today. The first settler, John Hunter, had come in 1819 to farm, and a small village soon emerged.

"Piety Hill" was an early nickname for Birmingham, reflecting the hopes of a local Methodist preacher. Indeed, Birmingham's churchy, community-minded character still continues today. The village stayed rural until the 1920s, when Woodward was paved. Then it nearly tripled between 1920 and 1930, growing from 3,694 to 9,539. The next big boom occurred after World War II. From a 1940 population of 11,196, it swelled to a high of 25,525 in 1960.

A concentration of high-quality art and antiques

During the past decade, Birmingham has become a major Midwestern center of important art galleries that focus on everything from museum-quality ancient artifacts to contemporary art by regionally and internationally known artists. Catalyst for its many art galleries was the Donald Morris Gallery on Townsend, which moved from Detroit in 1975.

The combined economics of high rents and a wealthy clientele mean you can see high-quality antiques here that out-state dealers seldom stock. Shops here have a lot of 18th- and early 19th-century English and American furniture, silver, and paintings, but little of grandmother's oak or salt-and-pepper collectibles.

Mourning the loss of that small-town feeling

Many people who have lived here for ten or twenty years regard as invaders the high-fashion pedestrians who frequent downtown Birmingham to see and be seen. Many of these fashion plates are outsiders, from newer suburbs not blessed with attractive, pedestrian-oriented downtowns. They take over local streets and parking spaces, not unlike a college town occupied by waves of students. Downtown Birmingham of yore, before Benetton and Banana Republic, had a genuine, small-town friendliness.

Comfortable, small-town Birmingham still exists — in the neighborhoods, at the Community House community center and **Peabody's Restaurant and Bar** at Hunter and East Maple. It's a beloved, affordable Birmingham institution where a Greek salad for two costs $7.25 and a good fish dinner $6.95. Older people start lining up for dinner at five. Between 5 and 9 there's almost always a wait. (No reservations.) At the **Whistle Stop** diner (501 South Eton, near the railroad tracks) businessmen and electricians, teachers and cops chat at the counter over coffee and homemade pie and carrot cake that's locally famous.

Name reflects industrial aspirations
Roswell Merrill platted the village in 1836. He named it "Birmingham" in hopes that it would become an industrial center like its English namesake. Nothing was to become farther from the truth. Birmingham has profited from the Motor City while distancing itself assiduously from Detroit's workaday industrial character. (Grosse Pointe, the home of many Fords, carries the irony one step farther. Its logo on many signs is a horse and carriage.)

But high rents have driven most of the unpretentious, service-oriented small-town stores out of downtown. The Kresge's is gone, and a Haagen Dazs ice cream parlor and a contemporary furniture store have replaced Huston Hardware. Down-to-earth stores like these were important in preserving residents' cherished illusion that, even though they may move in chic circles, they live in a small town that isn't all that different from the home towns they knew before they started up the ladder of success and social advancement. Idiosyncratic, non-fashion shops with low profit margins are also leaving. The kite shop is now in Royal Oak. And Maximus, the bookstore next to the Birmingham Theatre that was a casual hangout for all ages and sorts of people from all walks of life, including a considerable number of literati and smart high school kids, failed to attract a buyer when its owners divorced. That space now houses a Ralph Lauren Polo Shop, owned by a longtime local retailer who appreciates the drawing power of designer labels.

Majestic, elm-lined streets can still be seen in parts of Birmingham. Drive out Lincoln (14 1/2 Mile) west from downtown Birmingham. As you approach Southfield Road, American elms arch over many side streets to form stately tunnels. It's an amazing sight in the late 1980s, considering the ravages of Dutch elm disease. The city of Birmingham has slowed its spread by spraying and by removing diseased trees promptly.

Victims of success

"We have become a victim of our own success because land values have gone so high," laments former mayor Dante Lanzetta, a GM opinion researcher. The scarcity of developable land means Birmingham is beginning to see West Coast-style tear-downs, in which perfectly adequate homes on desirable lots are torn down for larger houses. High property values hurt homeowners who aren't wealthy, Lanzetta worries, and they hurt start-up businesses which are charged high rents. Chains move in, with a loss of commitment to the community, a loss of personal service to shoppers, and the loss of a distinctive, one-of-a-kind image. Everyday retail services like supermarkets, which work on a low profit margin, are threatened here. To buy a replacement part for a vacuum cleaner, Birmingham residents now have to go to Royal Oak.

Even if Birmingham and its super-low-density neighbor, Bloomfield Hills, are able to control overdevelopment within their own city limits, they are left to deal with the byproduct of the overdevelopment all around them: traffic — 80 per cent of it pass-through traffic not generated by residents, sometimes with the threat of gridlock.

Birmingham businesspeople now worry that high rents are strangling the retail vitality of their downtown. Customer traffic in 1989 was down. Sales per square foot don't come close to a mall. Furthermore, office space is overbuilt, and some new retail space is empty. Independently owned stores are being priced out of the market. It's hard to tell whether downtown Birmingham will now decline in the face of strip malls to the north and west, or of less expensive downtown retailing environments like Royal Oak.

POINTS OF INTEREST

Woodward and Maple ★★

So trendily fashionable has this area become that the very name "Maple Road" has come to connote hyper-awareness of fashion trends. Chains pay top dollar for high visibility here. Vehicular traffic is constant.

K. C. Larson Gallery ★★
209 N. Woodward (upstairs). (313) 647-0135.

A stimulating, eclectic mix of unusual things in room-like settings: folk art (new and old), odd pieces of furniture like heavily carved stools and library chairs that turn into steps, textiles and rugs, very large animal sculptures, Victorian and Edwardian antique jewelry, and books collected for their visual value as art objects. The carefully arranged tableaux of jewelry, books, and small objects are wonderful. A brightly painted, wavy wood snake with fins, at least 15 feet long, hangs over it all.

The Duke Gallery focuses on Arts and Crafts furniture (shown here) and Art Nouveau and Arts and Crafts pottery and Art Nouveau lighting.

Duke Gallery ★
209 N. Woodward (upstairs, to the rear). (313) 258-6848.

Ned Duke and Ann Darden Duke say they have Michigan's largest selection of Arts & Crafts furniture, lighting, pottery, and art glass in the state, and it's an impressive assemblage indeed. Other distinctive 20th-century design movements are also represented: Art Nouveau, Art Deco (Ann helped found the Detroit Area Art Deco Society), and Art Moderne. The work of Frank Lloyd Wright, Gustav Stickley, Charles Eames, and Louis Comfort Tiffany is often found here.

Territorial Sculpture
330 Hamilton. (313) 647-8011. Mon-Sat 10-6.

Indian and Inuit (Eskimo) art.

Deco Doug
124 S. Woodward (upstairs over the Mole Hole). (313) 443-3347. Tues-Sat 12-6 unless at a show.

Jewelry, radios, clocks, accessories, and some furniture, exclusively Art Deco from the 1920s into the 1950s.

In the same building, with about the same hours, are:
Second Story
Vintage watches.
It Was, It Is
Vintage clothing. (313-540-5744)
Art Loft
Contemporary jewelry and painting.

Linda Dresner
99 W. Maple. (313) 642-4999.

This is "the reigning champ of high-end [i.e., $1,200 a dress] women's clothes," proclaimed *Detroit Monthly*. " If you have to have

---

Birmingham **shop hours** are generally from 10 to 5:30 or 6, Monday through Saturday, Thursday evenings until 8, unless otherwise noted. **Gallery hours** are typically Tuesday through Saturday, 11 till 5 or 6.

the look, whether it's Montana, Yamamoto, or Krizia, this is where to go." "Intimidating? Yes! I wouldn't go in unless I weighed 98 pounds and had megabucks," comments a well-heeled and casually fashionable shopper.

It's the Ritz ★
193 W. Maple. (313) 642-5355.

Frank and Debbie Caruso offer European jeans (including the popular Pepe line) and crazy, funky clothes for anyone from 12 to 80 who wants a high-impact, offbeat look.

Caruso Caruso
195 W. Maple. (313) 645-5151.

Here at the Carusos' other shop, the fashionable but subdued Europrep look holds sway.

Merchant of Vino ★
254 W. Maple. (313) 433-3000. Mon-Wed, Sat 10-7, Thurs until 9, Fri 'til 8, Sun 10-4.

Like its progenitor in Southfield, the Birmingham branch is three things. It's Detroit's leading wine store, a premium deli, and a fancy foods store like Hudson's Marketplace. Here is anything you'd need for instant entertaining — or takeout to a nearby park — from prepared dishes like chicken provençal and salads to fresh produce and breads. The fresh fruit and vegetable section is gorgeous. The store is spacious, well-organized, and surprisingly competitively priced.

Twigs
268 W. Maple. (313) 644-8944.

Tightly focused on new trends, like many new-generation Birmingham stores. Here you'll find striking, amusing New Wave jewelry and accessories (belts, purses, and scarves) from New York's Artwear Gallery and other designers from the coasts.

Jacobson's
336 W. Maple, with menswear and furniture stores at 325 N. Woodward. (313) 644-6900.

Jacobson's big Birmingham stores, which occupy two large buildings at the north end of downtown, are the largest in this unusual chain of 23 upper-end department stores in Michigan, Florida, and Ohio. The Jackson, Michigan-based company is geared to customers with annual incomes over $50,000, but to simply label Jacobson's "upscale" ignores distinctive attributes like its longstanding commitment to downtown locations and its emphasis on service. Jacobson's staffs more salespeople per square foot of space than most stores, and it rewards personal attention and sales productivity with incentives and recognition. Employees know upper management by sight and name, and each store's merchandising mix is fine-tuned to the local clientele.

Stewart's Fabrics
275 E. Maple. (313) 646-0665.

A fixture on trendy East Maple, Stewart's has a big selection of wools, silks, and classic fabrics.

Seegerpeople
336 E. Maple. (313) 646-9010.

This 10-store chain features three-dimensional "photographic sculpture," cleverly mounted cutouts of portrait subjects in action (talking, dancing, gesturing) or wearing outfits appropriate to their varied roles. The effect of multiple figures in animated poses is an appealing alternative to stuffy group portraits. Cost: $20 per figure, including portrait sitting.

Merrill, Pierce, and Townsend

On these intimate streets just west of Woodward and south of Maple, the auto-dominated atmosphere changes to favor the pedestrian. Pierce Street, which parallels Woodward, is distinguished by Birmingham's Tudor city hall with its winsome brickwork. Despite the presence of chains such as **Banana Republic** and **Jos. S. Bank Clothiers,** there is a more personal feel, with a higher percentage of local retailers. However, some continue to fall victim to high rents and a recent drop in Birmingham customer traffic.

Michigania
205 Pierce (downstairs).
(313) 647-1444. Mon-Sat 10-6.

Everything here is made in Michigan or related to Michigan — good gift-giving possibilities for out-of-state visitors and relatives. Strong on crafts and jewelry, Michigania also carries a wide assortment of premium Michigan foodstuffs from American Spoon and others, and a big selection of books, plus some posters, prints, games, and audiocassettes.

Birmingham Bookstore
263 Pierce. (313) 647-2665. Mon-Sat 10-5:30, Thurs & Fri until 9, Sun 11-3. In summer, Tues & Wed open until 9.

Good general, independent bookstore, nice for browsing, with personal service and special orders. Attractive children's section with seating.

Merrillwood Building
251 E. Merrill.

Azar's Gallery of Oriental Rugs
(313) 644-7311.

This large, ground-floor store with new and old oriental rugs is the most visible tenant of the Merrillwood Building, a large retail and apartment complex. Upstairs shops include three antique dealers and a good yarn shop:

Leonard Berry
(313) 646-1996. Mon-Sat 11-4.

Lamps and furniture, mostly English mahogany, with some pine. Lamps and shades custom-made in size, shape, material of your choice, also objects as lamp bases.

Chase Antiques
(313) 433-1810. Mon-Sat 11-5.

General line of 18th- and 19th-century English furniture and accessories, including silver, brass, paintings, icons, scientific instruments, and some rugs.

Edna Tillman Antiques
(313) 433-3746. Mon-Sat 11-4.

Moderately priced American country furniture (in pine, cherry, and walnut) and accessories. Benches a strong suit.

The Weaving Room Gallery
(313) 540-3623. Mon-Sat 10-5.

Choice yarns and lots of stylish hand-knit items.

Donald Morris Gallery ★★
105 Townsend. (313) 642-8812.

Morris primarily sells the established 20th-century American and European masters: Picasso, Miro, Leger, Dubuffet, and Calder, to name a few. The gallery also handles classic African art and turn-of-the-century decorative arts, including work by the Wiener Werkstaette, Josef Hoffman, and Charles Rennie Macintosh. Michigan's only member of the Art Dealers Association of America, this is the state's most expensive gallery, with prices often into the hundreds of thousands of dollars.

G. R. N'Namdi Gallery ★
161 Townsend. (313) 642-2700. Tues-Sat 11-5:30.

Paintings, sculpture, and a good number of collages, all characteristically vibrant and colorful, by contemporary artists with national and international reputations, including many of African and African-American descent. Al Loving, Howardene Pindall, and Richard Hunt are represented here. N'Namdi, a Wayne State psychologist-turned-art dealer, recently opened his Birmingham gallery to complement his gallery in the David Whitney Building in downtown Detroit. There's no difference between them in the quality or subject matter of shows.

Hill Gallery ★
163 Townsend. (313) 540-9288. Tues-Sat 11:30-5:30.

Building on its longtime base of museum-quality American folk art (mostly historic, some contemporary) and interesting regional artists, Hill has become a leading Michigan gallery. It now also shows contemporary paintings and, especially, sculptures by nationally well-known artists like Ellsworth Kelly, Richard Serra, and Lee Krasner.

The Townsend Hotel ★★
100 Townsend. (313) 642-7900.

Tea is served in the elegantly homey lobby, on Royal Doulton china with an assortment of mini pastries and finger sandwiches, on Tuesday through Saturday afternoons from 3 to 5. $7.50 a person. The fresh flowers, colorful chintz-covered furniture, and freely painted mural offset the potential stuffiness of the 18th-century-style panelled room with its crystal chandeliers. (See also Lodgings, p. 200.)

You can check out the lobby any time on your way past the desk to **Marley's Boutique** (open 10-9 daily, until 5 Sundays). There a creative melange of handmade clothes: patchwork vests, fanciful skirts and sweaters, denim jackets appliqued with rhinestone maps or lace, and rainbow cocoons of knit coats hang in a magical environment created by artificial grape vines and flowers that festoon nearly all the wall and ceiling space. Folk art furniture and accessories and costume jewelry all reflect a soft-edged, witty sensibility that runs from the romantic to the affably outrageous. Most of this "art-to-wear" is produced by artists working in California and New York. The necklaces of antique charms and hearts, reproduced so cleverly you're sure they're really old, are especially wonderful.

Shain Park

Between Martin and Merrill, Henrietta and Bates.

Birmingham's village green, just behind the city hall on Pierce Street, is a convenient location for relieving shopper's fatigue. In good weather the play equipment is almost always in use by toddlers and parents. Quiet resting spots are provided by benches around Detroiter Marshall Fredericks' striking statue, **"The Freedom of the Human Spirit."** In his many area commissions, Fredericks, a student of the renowned Swedish sculptor Carl Milles at Cranbrook, adhered to Milles's principles, which combined a stylized, Art Deco neoclassicism with Northern mysticism.

Birmingham's major public buildings are on or near the park. For a W.P.A. muralist's interpretation of pioneer Birmingham history, take a peek in the lobby of the **post office** at Martin and Bates. (The postal service itself is moving soon.) The **Baldwin Library** across from it was designed in a 1920s interpretation of Tudor in brick to complement the city hall. A contemporary new section by Birmingham's internationally known Gunnar Birkerts was wrapped around its back to become the new entrance, overwhelming the original building in scale and upsetting many residents.

A block down Bates from the library is the **Community House**, home to Birmingham's many service clubs and community education classes. Enrichment opportunities abound in this area — here, at Cranbrook, and at the Birmingham-Bloomfield Art Association on Cranbrook Road, a powerhouse in art education.

Gallery Row/ "Old Woodward"

N. Woodward between Harmon & Oak, a few blocks north of downtown.

Birmingham's biggest concentration of galleries, along with many interesting shops, occupies this long block. Don't overlook second-story shops on the upper end. Salvatore Scallopini across the street is a fine spot for a quick meal or snack.

D. & J. Bittker Gallery ★
536 N. Woodward. (313) 258-1670.
Antique Chinese furniture and contemporary Chinese art.

Cantor-Lemberg ★
538 N. Woodward. (313) 642-6623.
This gallery of contemporary paintings, drawings, and graphics shows artists who are locally and nationally prominent. A $30,000 Frank Stella work may hang on one wall, and on another a $2,000 mixed media work by Steve Murakishi, Cranbrook's graphic arts department head.

Halsted Gallery ★
560 N. Woodward. (313) 644-8284.
This gallery has a national reputation for its 19th- and 20th-century photography. It also carries out-of-print and rare books on photography.

Xochipilli ★
568 N. Woodward. (313) 645-1905.
It's pronounced "ZO-sha-pee-lee," and it's named after the Aztec god of the arts. Director Mary Wright elicits raves from area artists as one of the most interesting, committed, supportive, and discriminating gallery directors around. She shows paintings and sculpture by contemporary artists from in and around Michigan.

Sign of the Mermaid
570 N. Woodward. (313) 540-4210.
Fine china and crystal (Ceralene, Limoges, Baccarat), silver and marquetry picture frames (the kind that create elegant, intimate clutter), cards, and terrific service: free gift wrap, shopping by phone, and hand deliveries.

Artspace ★
574 N. Woodward. (313) 258-1540.
This consignment resale gallery carries 19th- and 20th-century paintings, drawings, sculpture, prints, and decorative arts — "quality fine art," the owner underscores, and not discarded decorative accessories. Prices start at $200. We saw an Alex Katz unique cutout for $40,000 and a pair of Warhol silkscreen prints for $5,000. Shoppers can find some bargains, especially if the work's owner is desperate for cash. A Peter Max print that would normally go for $1,500 was sold for $500 because the owner, an actor, desperately needed cash to pay his union dues.

Donna Jacobs ★
574 N. Woodward. (313) 540-1600.
This fascinating gallery specializes in ancient art: Greek, Roman, Egyptian, Etruscan, Near Eastern, and Pre-Columbian objects. These include pottery, glass, bronzes, stone, Coptic textiles, and jewelry — beautiful Middle Eastern mosaics and wearable Egyptian necklaces. These museum-quality pieces sell for as little as $35 (for a small, 2,000-year-old terra-cotta oil lamp from the Holy Land). $45 buys 2,300-year-old Egyptian ushabti, little figures set in tombs to serve the dead.

> **Most gallery hours** are Tuesday through Saturday, 11 a.m. to 5 or 6 p.m.

Madeline's Antiques ★
790 N. Woodward. (313) 644-2493.
It's a treat to see the mellow wood of these 18th- and early 19th-century English antiques, beautifully accessorized with antique silver, boxes, and art from oil paintings to silhouettes.

Feigenson-Preston Gallery
796 N. Woodward (rear). (313) 644-3955.
The late Jackie Feigenson (pronounced "FAY-guhn-son") won widespread respect as the first commercial gallery director to focus primarily on Michigan artists, rather than just as additions to a stable of New York or European artists. A major emphasis has been on the exciting Cass Corridor group. Now her longtime associate Mary Preston, who moved the gallery from the Fisher Building to Birmingham in 1988, says, "After all these years in business [since 1976], the majority of

our artists who started in Detroit are living in New York. Staying in the Midwest, artists don't put the right pieces in the career puzzle together. I'd like to help change that." Of her Detroit artists, only Brad Iverson remains in the area; Tom Bills, James Chatelain, and Ruth Leonard are in New York. The gallery now shows works by contemporary American artists regardless of Michigan connections, including Ursula von Rydingsvard, Jane Hammond, and David Kapp.

Mettal Studio
798 N. Woodward. (313) 258-8818.

Highly original sculptural art jewelry by Center for Creative Studies alums Patrick Irla and Cary Stefani.

Brava
800 N. Woodward. (313) 645-0311.

Women's clothes, boldly contemporary yet classic, in bright colors and relaxed, natural fabrics. Moderately priced for Birmingham.

In Situ/ Arkitektura ★
800 N. Woodward (upstairs). (313) 646-0097. Mon-Sat 10-5:30, Thurs until 9.

This striking store sells reproductions of classic 20th-century modern design. It was started in 1984 by the grandson of Eliel Saarinen and two other alums of nearby Cranbrook, where the great Swedish designer lived and worked for many years. In addition to Saarinen designs, In Situ (formerly Arkitektura) sells authorized reproductions of classic furniture by late, great architect/designers like Le Corbusier, Mies van der Rohe, and Charles Rennie Macintosh, and current names like Robert Venturi, Stanley Tigerman, Michael McCoy, and Joe D'Urso. Prices range from $10 to over $10,000, but few of these careful reproductions are cheap. A Saarinen dining chair is $1,700, a table by Le Corbusier $1,500, and a Tizio lamp $300. In Situ also carries the Swid Powell line of architect-designed china, crystal, and silver by the likes of Venturi, Charles Gwathmey and Robert Siegel, Richard Meier, and Michael Graves.

Russell Hardware Co. ★
1036 N. Hunter at Woodward, 1/4 mi. south of Big Beaver. (313) 644-3955. Mon-Fri 8-5, Thurs 'til 8. Closed Sat.

This three-generation hardware store has long specialized in door and cabinet hardware, from basic builders' lines to exclusive and hard-to-find brass fittings and door knockers, reproduction antique doorknobs, unusual door locks, contemporary architect-designed handles, and such. Lately they have gotten into sink and faucet hardware and bathroom accessories like towel bars and soap dishes.

Renovators and designers who are fussy about details come way out of their way to find things like the right doorbell or replacement knob, custom address plaques, classic house numbers in white on blue enamel, sleek and sophisticated lavatory handles or plump, old-fashioned white spoke ones marked "H" and "C." Nylon cabinet pulls come in up-to-the-minute shapes and colors. Russell's has the generic porcelain drawer pull in a huge variety of sizes

But not everything here is just for show; Russell's also carries most possible sizes and varieties of hinges, door closers, thresholds, weather stripping, and the like. Showroom displays are attractive and well-organized, and the staff most helpful.

Plate by Swiss architects Robert and Trix Haussmann.

> No place could be more appealingly urbane for a shopping break or lunch than the **Phoenicia** (see p. 198). The sophistication of prewar Beirut lives on here, in the serene second home of this longtime Detroit Lebanese restaurant, a favorite among Middle Eastern Detroiters who know good food. It's just across Woodward from 555. Fading shoppers can be revived with the sugar and caffeine hit of its strong Turkish coffee and famous bird's nest filo-honey dessert.

South of Brown Street ★★

South of Brown Street is the upscale, 15-story 555 Woodward, a visually overwhelming office-commercial-restaurant-apartment complex so long it straddles two streets. **Hattie's,** Birmingham's doyenne of exclusive women's shops, with everything from sportswear to ball gowns, is here. Past 555, the densely built-up downtown leaves off. But on the east side of South Woodward, across from **New York Carpet World** and a few other mass-market retailers, shopping becomes becomes more broadly appealing, with a string of stylish discount and middle-of-the-market stores. Here you can enjoy strip-center prices while still in the glow of the civilized pedestrian ambience of downtown Birmingham.

Chudik's
294 E. Brown. (313) 647-1300.

This old-line furrier also carries better sportswear, Ultrasuede, coats ($75-$550), suits, and dresses ($64-$500). For friendly service, plus great sales and affordable quality, many stylish, affluent locals think Chudik's has it all over Birmingham's most exclusive shops.

Domicile
808 S. Woodward, (313) 642-4260).

Roughly comparable to the Workbench chain, this locally owned contemporary furniture store, carries Techline modular furniture and storage units, sectionals, and a big variety of kitchen chairs. It also does custom work in laminate and marble.

Wells Freight & Cargo
820 S. Woodward. (313) 642-4642.

The last of a small local chain, it offers big discounts on discontinued or overstocked china, glassware, and tableware.

Expressions ★
950 S. Woodward. (313) 647-8882.

A popular hit since its January, 1989 opening, Expressions carries wildly eclectic furniture (country, Deco, painted folk) and upholstery fabrics. It's the 42nd store in a New Orleans franchise chain offering custom upholstered furniture and design services at unusually low prices. Room settings here are funny, inventive, and fully accessorized with unusual vases, lamps, and folk art accents, many of which are exclusive to Expressions. The mostly cotton fabrics, from mills like Schumacher and Waverly, are vibrant and punchy, whether in chintz, stripes and plaids, or freely drawn foliage and floral motifs. They're all in stock, which means only 45 days for delivery of custom upholstered pieces. The prices (typically $13-$15 a yard) are roughly a third of their cost if special-ordered through an interior designer. (Calico Corners can be even cheaper, though. See p. 213.)

Cecille's
850 S. Woodward. (313) 642-5855.

A discount drug store which offers especially good prices on designer fragrances and big names in cosmetics.

Garys Flowers and Antiques ★
415 E. Frank at Ann, just east of Woodward. (313) 642-2612. Usually open Tues-Sat 10-5; call to confirm.

This is the kind of casual, original, funny place you'd expect to find in Royal Oak. Here, tucked away in what was once a modest print shop, the ebullient Gary Kalm (he's known as "Gary Flowers") has created a de-

Quarton Lake (actually an old mill pond on the Rouge River) is an idyllic place for picnics, taking walks, or relaxing.

lightfully luxurious if somewhat disheveled space where ornate antiques and crystal chandeliers coexist with flowers in a fluidly changing world. Gary's taste in flowers leans to soft, natural, uncontrived bouquets. He does landscape design (the lush treatment of his once-plain building reflects his style), restoration and conservation of silver, gilding (which he studied in London), and rehabilitation of crystal chandeliers. "Every year I try to do something new," he says.

Quarton Lake ★

North of W. Maple 1/4 mile west of downtown Birmingham. North from W. Maple onto Baldwin and bear left onto Lakeside. Park along the lake.

Long, narrow Quarton Lake is created by a small dam on the Rouge River, once used to power a mill. Kids like to fish at the dam. The lake is the focus of a delightful, shady, informal park just a few blocks west of downtown Birmingham. Visitors are welcome to sit on a bench and eat a bag lunch while enjoying the huge trees reflected in the water. But beware parking limits! On summer evenings the banks of the lake are lined with people sitting out and enjoying this one-time mill pond. South of Maple a **wood-chip path** continues along the river. Some of Birmingham's most beautiful 1920s houses face Quarton Lake on the west. It's not uncommon for rising executives to mark promotions by moving closer to the lake.

Holocaust Memorial Center ★★

6602 W. Maple in West Bloomfield Township, 2 1/2 miles west of Orchard Lake Rd. In the Jewish Community Center across from Henry Ford Hospital. (313) 661-0840. Mon-Thurs 10-3:30, Sun noon-3:30. 1 1/2 hour public tour Sun 1 p.m. No admission charge.

The murder of 6,258,484 Jews by Hitler's Nazis during World War II is documented in a chilling, almost low-key manner in this multifaceted, superbly designed museum. The visitor to this $7 million center begins the self-guided tour hearing the sweet, haunting voice of a mother singing a Jewish lullaby. Entering a darkened, ominous-looking tunnel, you pass a video of Hitler bombastically shouting to a throng of Germans his racist message and world view. Displays put into historical context Germany's suffering after World War I and the punishing peace imposed by the French. It becomes clear how humiliation and economic distress led many Germans to turn on their Jewish fellow Germans as scapegoats.

Displays use a sophisticated combination of historical artifacts, photos, dioramas, and film footage, so that no visitor can escape the Holocaust's horror. What comes across is the almost incredible act of the systematic extermination of millions upon millions of men, women, and children by an industrialized, western society quite similar to our own, and also the out-front sadism that the Nazis practiced. These victims not only died but experienced extraordinary suffering before death.

This obviously isn't a pleasant place to visit. Children under 14 aren't advised to come. But the Holocaust museum exposes us to sad truths about the human race and what we are capable of, telling us something we should never forget.

Habatat Gallery ★

32255 Northwestern Hwy. in the Tri-Atria center, midway between Middlebelt and Orchard Lake roads, in Farmington Hills. (313) 851-9090. Tues-Sat 10-6.

In the new field of contemporary glass art, the Habatat Gallery has developed a national reputation. The field got its start at workshops held in a garage behind the Toledo art museum in 1962, when a Libby Glass chemist gave University of Wisconsin art professor Harvey Littleton technical information enabling artists to work in glass using only small kilns, without big factory facilities. New developments have been constant ever since. Art glass is so varied, it's hard to describe. Some artists exploit the sensuous quality inherent in glass, while others negate it. Glass can be cast, blown, sandblasted, or slumped. Some glass is clear, some is brilliantly colored, some is like a painting.

Prices can run from $200 (little things stocked as holiday gifts) up to $25,000 for works by leading glass artists like Dale Chihuly, Joel Philip Myers, Howard Ben Tre, and Klaus Moje.

Orchard Lake Road shopping

The five miles of Orchard Lake Road between Lone Pine Road and I-696.

This road in affluent, booming West Bloomfield Township and Farmington Hills looks like it could be a shopper's paradise. The huge amount of building out here makes for an unusual blend of class and mass merchandising on this 1980s version of Telegraph Road. Here you can find near a K Mart a store that sells kitchen ranges costing as much as a mid-priced car — the **Kitchen Studio** at 2011 Orchard Lake Road. A branch of famed New York City discounter **Loehman's** anchors the 35-store Hunter's Square at Orchard Lake and 14 Mile. **The Boardwalk** between Maple and Northwestern Highway is a consummate strip shopping center with class.

But fast rush-hour traffic out in the booming suburban wilds of West Bloomfield and Farmington Hills lasts from shortly past three to six-thirty and later. "Mean-spirited yuppies in a hurry," one resident says. It's an intense, unmellow, upsetting scene if you're not used to it and become trapped in traffic.

RESTAURANTS

Phoenicia ★★

588 S. Woodward, just south of downtown. (313) 644-3122. Mon-Thurs 11-10:30, Fri-Sat 11-11, closed major holidays. Entrees: $5.95-$7.95 (lunch); $7.25-$21.95 (dinner). Full bar. Major credit cards.

This serene, sophisticated Lebanese restaurant is considered by many the best Middle Eastern restaurant in a metro area blessed with outstanding Middle Eastern cooking. Favorites here include the shish tawook or marinated chicken breast ($6.25 lunch, $12.95 dinner), shawarma (strips of marinated lamb, served with hummus and onions with sumac; $7.95/$13.95), and rack of lamb ($18.95 at dinner). Meals include salad, rice, and bread. As appetizers, Middle Eastern appetizers like stuffed eggplant, baba ganoush, and tabooli run around $4. Its bird's nest filo-honey-nut dessert ($2.25) is great with Turkish coffee.

Monchelle Lamoure Chocolatier & Cafe

149 Pierce (downstairs). (313) 647-4140. Mon-Sat 10-5:30, Thurs until 9. Afternoon tea 2:30-5. No alcohol. Visa, MasterCard, AmExp.

This tiny, pretty chocolate shop/cafe reminds you of France or Austria without being heavy-handedly phoney. Lunch selections include soups with bread ($2-$4); chicken, Waldorf, chef, and spinach salads with fresh French bread ($5-$6); and sandwiches like Honeybaked ham with Swiss on rye ($5.25). Or you can just have coffee or tea (served in flowered bone china cups; $1, $1.50 for capuccino) and a chocolate truffle (95¢) or torte.

Norman's Eton Street Station

245 S. Eton, just south of E. Maple at the tracks. (313) 647-7774. Mon-Thurs 11-11, Fri 11-midnight, Sat noon-midnight, Sun 10:30-9. Major credit cards. Full bar.

As a comfortably elegant, beautifully landscaped restaurant since 1985, Birmingham's gorgeous Tudor-style Grand Trunk depot is a knockout, inside and out, and popular with all kinds of people. In summer the big terrace with umbrella tables is full even on week nights. The airy mahogany bar in the big, open former waiting room is usually busy. Expect a line on weekends, when singles predominate. (Reservations taken for parties of 6 or more.) The menu touches all the bases: burgers ($5), burritos ($7), salads from Caesar to taco to oriental chicken ($6-$8.25), baked and broiled chicken, prime rib, and popular bar appetizers. Favorite entrees (with salad and bread) include seafood fettucine ($11.95 lunch, $14.95 dinner) and chicken and shrimp teriyaki ($11.25/ $12.95.)

Punchinello's

184 Pierce. (313) 644-5277. Mon-Thurs 11-11, Fri & Sat 11-midnight. Major credit cards. Full bar. Entrees: lunch $6-$13, dinner $15-$17.

Punchinello's gets high praise from Molly Abraham's reliable *Restaurants of Detroit* for its sophisticated simplicity. She says it's refreshing in this trendy environment. The menu changes daily. Lunch includes favorites like Greek salad, reuben or tuna salad sandwiches, omelettes, a three-cheese grilled cheese sandwich with onion and tomato on pita bread ($5.25), smoked fish salad ($8.95), and a delicious dish of polenta and Italian sausage with fresh tomato sauce ($7.95). Dinner entrees (osso bucco, grilled and baked fish, sauteed sweetbreads with pilaf, various pasta dishes) average $15, which includes a salad, bread, potato, and vegetable. The huge angled windows of this former sporting-goods shop offer window-side diners a terrific view of sidewalk traffic along two busy streets, as does the summer outdoor cafe.

Salvatore Scallopini

505 N. Woodward at Harmon, across from Gallery Row. (313) 644-8977.

Mon-Thurs 11-9, Fri & Sat 11-10, Sun 1-8. No alcohol. Am. Express.

The lively Birmingham branch of Larry Bongiovanni's popular Detroit-area chain of Italian delis is smaller than the rest, and it really does feel — and smell and taste — like a modern but friendly neighborhood Italian deli, complete with braids of garlic and big cans of olive oil, transplanted to an American suburb. Locals on the run buzz in to pick up popular dishes like the chicken parmesan or meatball sandwich ($5), subs ($5-7), and the homemade pasta special ($4.50 at lunch, $4.95 at dinner for a lot of pasta plus salad and bread, topped with a modest dollop of one of six sauces; most people pay $1.10 extra for more sauce). Simple dishes of breaded or sauteed veal and chicken appear at dinner for $8.50 to $9.25. A few tables and a counter are crowded in here, and outside in good weather. Minestrone ($2.25 a bowl with bread) is excellent.

The Lark

6430 Farmington Rd. one block north of Maple and a mile west of Orchard Lake Rd. in West Bloomfield Township. (313) 661-4466. Tues-Sat 6 p.m.-9 p.m. Fri and Sat have seatings at 6 and 9. Full bar, outstanding wine list. Major credit cards. Reservations required.

The relaxed ambience of a Portuguese country inn prevails, with hand-painted tiles, fireplaces, a herb garden, and lots of fresh flowers. The Lark is one of the Detroit area's best (and most expensive) places to eat. Every detail is perfect. Since opening in 1981, only one dish has remained on the menu throughout: rack of lamb Genghis Khan. Another favorite is the bouillabaisse-like cata plana, a mixture of shrimp, mussels, clams, and chorizo sausage. Entrees cost $42.50 to $50 including selections from the wonderful hors d'oeuvres cart; choice of soup, fresh appetizer, or pasta; salad; and sorbet.

See also: *Peabody's (p. 188), Whistle Stop (p. 188), tea at the Townsend Hotel (p. 193).*

LODGINGS

Barclay Inn
(313) 646-7300 (800) 541-9742
Southeast corner of Maple and Hunter, downtown Birmingham.
125 rooms, 5 floors. $75-$90 single or double; $59-$69 weekends. HBO & ESPN, pay movies ($6.35). Restaurant. Health club 10 minutes away ($10). Upper floors have good views of downtown Birmingham.

Birmingham Village Inn
(313) 642-6200
300 N. Hunter, downtown.
4 floors, 64 rooms. $62-$73 single or double. Weekends: $49 single; $53-$57 double. Free continental breakfast, morning newspaper. Showtime & ESPN. Restaurants within one block. Balconies on some rooms overlook the city.

Townsend Hotel
(313) 642-7900
100 Townsend (downtown Birmingham). North on Woodward to Maple, left (west) 1 block to Pierce, south (left) 3 blocks to Townsend.
87 rooms, 4 floors. $135 single, $145 double; suites $165 single, $175 double. VCR, Showtime. Elegant, European-style hotel on a quiet street in the heart of downtown Birmingham. Restaurant and bar. Some rooms look onto Shain Park.

Bloomfield Hills

When Bloomfield Hills showed up in a study of relative wealth and poverty in the suburbs as the second-wealthiest incorporated place in the U.S., it shouldn't have surprised anyone. Kenilworth, near Chicago, was number one.) This beautifully hilly suburb of 2,000 homes (average price: well over $400,000) consists of a mere 4.5 square miles. The housing stock is far more homogeneous, newer, and thus more expensive than that in larger, older, more urban counterparts such as Grosse Pointe Farms, Bryn Mawr, or Shaker Heights.

Homes of corporate CEOs and celebrities

Bloomfield Hills, long the preferred residence of Detroit's business executives, is the home of the heads of the automotive Big Three, along with CEOs of major Detroit corporations and various celebrities. GM's Roger Smith, Ford's Donald Peterson, Chrysler's Lee Iacocca, and their probable successors all live in Bloomfield Hills, along with the head of K Mart, Pistons' star Isiah Thomas, soul queen Aretha Franklin, and WJR's popular radio deejay J. P. McCarthy.

Detroit's old, inherited money has pretty much stayed along Lake St. Clair in the Grosse Pointes. Bloomfield Hills, by comparison, is less conservative in style, if not in politics; less stuffy, some would say; more fashionable: and more diverse in ethnic composition than you might expect. Glittery charity fundraisers play a big role in many residents' lives. Contrary to the stereotypical moat at Eight Mile Road between Detroit and the suburbs — a stereotype nourished by Detroit Mayor Coleman Young — a good deal of Young's campaign money comes from this area's wealthy Democratic minority.

Home-delivered free-range eggs

Privacy, prestige, and service is what living in Bloomfield Hills is all about. Its residents have little time for even the pretense of the small-town lifestyle in neighboring Birmingham, according to Bloomfield Hills native and longtime city manager Robert Stadler. "By the time they can get to Bloomfield Hills and can afford it, they're too damn busy. Running next door for a cup of coffee doesn't exist." Residents receive fabulous services. The city's "bare pavement" policy of snow removal insures that every street is salted. Three-fourths of all homes are connected with the city's emergency dispatch system. The entire area is served by old-

Different from Grosse Pointe
Bloomfield Center first became a suburb in 1896 when a railway was built linking the village with Detroit. But most of the 2,000 homes here are much more recent. Newer and more secluded than Grosse Pointe mansions, in recent decades they have attracted new money, including the region's executive elite.

fashioned milkmen, now independent entrepreneurs. They walk right into residents' kitchens to fill orders for Borden dairy products, top-rated Guernsey Farms ice cream, and Amish poultry and eggs.

Gateway to the lake region

The famous Cranbrook schools (see p. 204) occupy 315 stunningly landscaped acres in the very heart of Bloomfield Hills, at the intersection of Cranbrook and Lone Pine roads. While most of the terrain in the Detroit area is boring and flat, it begins to get hilly in Bloomfield Hills. This is the beginning edge of the band of glacial lakes arcing across southeast Michigan from Coldwater and Jackson to Pontiac and into Lapeer County. They were formed by stranded ice chunks of the retreating Saginaw lobe of the last glacier 10,000 years ago. Just beyond Bloomfield Hills, other beautiful large homes cluster around Island Lake, Lower Long Lake, Wing Lake, and Orchard Lake.

The fieldstone walls, ornamental ironwork, and statuary around Cranbrook House, newspaper magnate George Booth's home, set the tone for a high level of landscaping in adjacent parts of Bloomfield Hills. Cranbrook's neighbors along Lone Pine and Cranbrook roads have magnificent trees and ivy-covered garden walls pierced by decorative gates — a delight for walkers and bicyclists.

The interesting terrain and lush landscaping make for pleasant drives on Bloomfield Hills' winding streets. Ivy grows up many trees, and woodsy thickets frame many houses. A bike ride would be better yet, to let you stop and admire architectural details.

Not surprisingly, some of the most original domestic architecture in Michigan is here. (There are also some pretty ordinary-looking if expensive homes.) Houses around Cranbrook and Christ Church Cranbrook are especially striking. Occasional iron gates and stone or brick walls make for an English country look that's engaging rather than forbidding. Frank Lloyd Wright designed the house at 5045 Pon Valley Road (off Lone Pine Road in Bloomfield Township), finished in 1951.

A few of the oldest remaining houses, mostly along Woodward, date from 1896, when the interurban railway to Birmingham first allowed wealthy commuters to establish estates in these scenic hills. Before that it had been a farming village founded in 1810 by Amasa Bagley. He followed an Indian trail to an opening where he established a farm.

$250,000 a lot

Today, Bloomfield Hills is zoned almost entirely residential, with few lots smaller than two-thirds of an acre. The few available lots still available today range from three-fourths of an acre (typical current market price: $250,000 west of Woodward, $150,000 east of it) to three acres.

The town's one commercial area is along Woodward, which has a limited amount of shopping (in malls and plazas, rather than a pedestrian-oriented town center), a few office buildings, restaurants, and the Kingsley Inn hotel at Woodward and Long Lake Road. The 1920s Tudor-style Machus Red Fox — now known as Fox & Hounds — is the last place where Teamsters boss Jimmy Hoffa was seen alive.

POINTS OF INTEREST

Christ Church Cranbrook

Lone Pine Rd. at Church St. and Cranbrook Rd. (across from Cranbrook House). (313) 644-5210. Main sanctuary open to visitors 8:30-5 daily. Call church to find out which Sundays bell tower is open. Summer carillon concerts Sundays at 4 p.m.

This imposing, English Gothic-style Episcopal church was donated by Cranbrook founder George Booth. The designer was Oscar Murray in the office of Bertram Goodhue. Goodhue and his longtime partner Ralph Adams Cram were the leaders in the Late Gothic Revival of the first three decades of the 20th century — a movement that greatly influenced the popular notion of what churches and college campuses should look like. Cram's influential theory held that the natural development of Gothic architecture had been cut off by the simultaneous appearance of the Classical Renaissance and the Reformation. He urged the contemporary architect to take up its development at the time of Henry VIII in the 16th century and to adapt its logic to contemporary, 20th-century culture, making the style his own.

The result was churches like Christ Church Cranbrook: smoother in texture and simpler in silhouette, without bands of contrasting ornament. It was consecrated in 1928.

The 118-foot tower holds a large **carillon** whose 62 English-made bells range from 48 to 9,408 pounds. The current carillonneur, Don Cook, holds hour-long **concerts** every Sunday at 4 p.m. beginning the last Sunday in June and ending the first Sunday in September. Visitors can listen from their cars or loll on the pleasant park-like grassy space in front of the church. On selected Sundays there are tours of the tower, from which you can get a spectacular view of Bloomfield Hills and a particularly nice view of Cranbrook next door.

The imposing interior contains examples of the works of artists and artisans from every century since the 12th. Especially noteworthy is the elaborately carved woodwork throughout. Large stained glass windows portray the part women have played in civilization (on the west wall) and scenes from the life of Jesus (east wall).

Cranbrook

Off Lone Pine and Cranbrook roads just west of Woodward. See individual sights for particulars. A map of the grounds and general brochure about the Cranbrook Educational Community is available from the Public Relations office in Cranbrook House, or call (313) 645-3142.

This educational complex on 315 rolling acres has several claims to renown. Internationally Cranbrook is known for its Academy of Art, a graduate school of art, design, and architecture. Locally it is known for its distinguished private elementary, middle, and upper schools, as well as for its popular art and science museums.

Finally, Cranbrook is also known throughout the world for the total aesthetics of its environment, with its careful integration of buildings, gardens, sculpture, and interiors. The noted architectural photographer Balthazar Korab, who lives nearby, expressed this nicely. "Cranbrook is my place of recreation. Walking there, you find yourself in a different atmosphere. It's like a large private estate that has been opened to us pedestrians, where you can inhale a time past, an era of great patrons and great ideas. There is a great unity there — not like on a university campus, where you have just groups of diversified buildings. The gardens, the grounds, and the buildings have a definite, luxurious cohesiveness."

Two remarkable men, a patron and an artist, joined their energies to create this special place. The patron was George Booth, a leading proponent of the Arts and Crafts movement that influenced American popular taste between 1900 and 1917, only to be overwhelmed by machine-made revival styles after World War I. The artist was Eliel Saarinen.

The Arts and Crafts philosophy stressed a greater unification of life and art through handcrafted artistic production by individual craftspeople. In part this was a reaction to the crass pretentiousness of Victorian sensibilities, in part a reaction to Western industrialism which was rapidly dwarfing the significance of individual creative endeavors. In Detroit one of the Arts and Crafts movement's manifestations was the Pewabic Pottery center; another was the Society of Arts and Crafts (now the Center for Creative Studies), a school and studio that grew into one of the nation's largest professional art schools.

Booth was keenly aware of being the grandson of a master coppersmith from Cranbrook, Kent. He him-

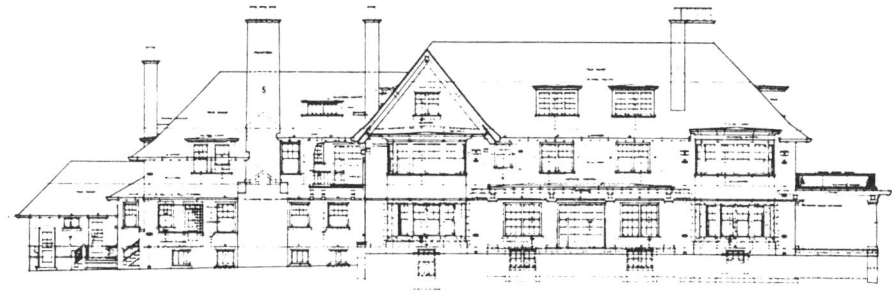

Architect Albert Kahn's elevation of the Tudor-style Cranbrook House (1907). The house suited George Booth's Arts & Crafts sensibility. As an arts patron, he continued the tradition of handcraftsmanship of his grandfather, a master coppersmith from Cranbrook, Kent.

self owned a successful Windsor ornamental ironwork factory when he married Ellen Scripps, the daughter of the owner of Detroit's *Evening News*. Booth went on to head the newspaper in 1906.

By 1904 Booth was secure financially. He bought a rundown Bloomfield Hills farm, commissioning Albert Kahn to build a large mansion there. **Cranbrook House** is now the Cranbrook Community's administrative offices. Influences of the Arts & Crafts sensibility are throughout the house. In 1918 George Booth and his son Henry designed a delightful small house of worship and community activity center called The Meeting Place. It was built up close to Cranbrook Road, with no front yard to speak of. It became the nucleus of Cranbrook's **Brookside** elementary school, a memorable building complex showing the flexibility and rustic charm of the cottage style. It's worth walking by it to see its wonderful iron gate, Scandinavian-style brickwork, and numerous sculptural details.

A trip Booth took to Rome in 1922 was the catalyst for the Cranbrook which would gain worldwide attention. There he saw the American Academy and decided to create a school of architecture and design. Coincidentally, the well-known Finnish architect, Eliel Saarinen, was finding it difficult to practice in his native land due to the civil war and economic depression there. Looking west, he entered a Chicago Tribune competition. His famous design for a tall office building, though it came in second place, stirred a great deal of interest in the U.S. That design, never built, became the paradigm for the tapered American skyscraper which defines the skyline of New York City and many other cities.

In the ensuing enthusiasm for his work, Saarinen, already 50 years old, was invited to Chicago in 1923 to work on plans for the development of the Chicago waterfront. Soon after that he became a visiting professor of architecture at the University of Michigan, where George Booth's son Henry was studying. The senior Booth and Saarinen met. Quickly plans were made to have Saarinen design the educational community Booth envisioned for Cranbrook. Saarinen, along with his wife and children, moved to Bloomfield Hills in 1925 to lay the groundwork for the Cranbrook community.

Saarinen's first designs were for an Academy of Art and Cranbrook School for boys in 1925. In 1928 he designed his own house and a second along Academy Way off Lone Pine Road. Saarinen and Booth had begun to bring distinguished artists to assist in creating the many designs within the complex and to teach at the Academy. It opened in 1931.

Saarinen's work at Cranbrook varies greatly. The early work on Brookside School and the faculty houses consists of his individualistic stone and brick variations on traditional Scandinavian design. But with Kingswood, the girls' school, he moved beyond historical eclecticism in favor of a simplified, organic architecture somewhat akin to Frank Lloyd Wright's work. His plan included Kingswood's interior furnishings, designed by Saarinen's wife, Loja, a weaver, and their talented children, Eero, who started by designing furniture, and Pipsan, an interior designer. By 1943, when the art museum was finished, Saarinen's style had evolved into something severely plain and monumental.

The Cranbrook Academy quickly gained a reputation as one of the world's top artistic communities. The dynamic Maija Grotel headed ceramics, Charles Eames and Saarinen set up the design department,

A hallmark of the Arts & Crafts philosophy was the integration of all arts and crafts in designing the total environment. Textiles — in curtains, pillows, table runners, and tapestries — were elevated to an unaccustomed status. Eliel Saarinen's wife, Loja, established a weaving studio at Cranbrook that did much commission work in addition to producing her own and her husband's designs.

LOJA SAARINEN
CRANBROOK ACADEMY OF ART
BLOOMFIELD HILLS, MICHIGAN

Harry Bertoia headed metal-working, and Carl Milles directed sculpture for twenty years. Saarinen himself directed architecture and urban planning, which was discontinued after his death.

One of Cranbrook's high points was just before World War II, when Saarinen's son Eero and Charles Eames created a new, leaner interior design look in frankly machine-made furniture. By the 1950s Cranbrook graduates Florence Knoll and Harry Bertoia, along with Eames, had popularized the look to such an extent in their furniture manufactured by Knoll International and Herman Miller that it has become the very essence of International-style "modern" design, installed and imitated in offices, schools, and waiting rooms throughout the world. Originals and faithful copies of their work now fetch high prices at shops like In Situ/ Arkitektura in nearby Birmingham. (See p. 195.)

The Academy continues today to be an important advanced art institute, with internationally known artists in residence in nine departments: architecture, ceramics, design, fiber, metalsmithing, painting, photography, printmaking, and sculpture.

Cranbrook remains one of the crowning achievements of Eliel Saarinen's work. He continued to practice architecture in Bloomfield Hills with his son, Eero, until his death in 1950. Eero's office remained here until his death in 1961, just as he was in the process of moving it to New Haven, Connecticut.

Writes Columbia professor David De Long of Saarinen's Cranbrook, ". . . there is a consistent sense of architectural order that is always humanly scaled. Saarinen showed an underlying concern for the exterior spaces themselves, creating a series of courts and gardens defined by building elements and linked by walks and roads."

It all makes for a wonderful place to take walks at every time of year. Covered with fresh snow, it's a magical place. In spring and summer the formal gardens at Cranbrook House are a special delight. The outstanding buildings, many with engaging decorative details, and the numerous Carl Milles sculptures combine with the hilly terrain and mature landscaping to create a memorable environment.

Three Cranbrook buildings are open to the public:

Cranbrook House & Gardens ★★

380 Lone Pine Road. (313) 645-3149. Gardens open: June-Aug. daily 10-5, Sun 1-5. May & Sept. daily 1-5, Sun 1-5. Oct. weekends only, 1-5. $2. House open Thursdays April -Sept. Combined house and garden tour: $5.50. Call 645-3149 by Tues. for Thurs. lunch reservations. Park at Christ Church Cranbrook.

The 1908 mansion designed by Albert Kahn features leaded-glass windows and tapestries and art objects collected by Cranbrook founders George and Ellen Booth. The stunning, impeccably maintained gardens around the house are marked by dramatic vistas, fountains and cascades, sculptures and architectural fragments. Its picturesque stone walls are repeated in the 1920s houses outside Cranbrook's gates as well, lending a cultivated and yet casual unity to this beautiful corner of Bloomfield Hills. The 500-member Cranbrook House and Gardens Auxiliary maintains the gardens, guides visitors, and hold plant sales to keep up the grounds.

The garden's charms are thus described: "*Spring* brings the 'Golden Glade' with thousands of daffodils,

Swedish sculptor Carl Milles's large, many-figured compositions, such as the Orpheus Fountain in front of Cranbrook Academy museum (above), are on a grand, Baroque scale. Here the figure of Orpheus himself, included in the Stockholm version, is missing, but the emotional effect of his music is shown in the surrounding figures' varied responses. Their release through music from their base, material nature illustrates Milles's spiritualist philosophy. Milles directed Cranbrook's sculpture department from 1931 to 1951. His figures, often drawn from mythology, combine a simplified, Art Deco-ish classicism with Northern mysticism. The 60 sculptures he made for Cranbrook are the largest collection of his works except for his studio-home in Sweden. Marshall Fredericks, creator of "The Spirit of Detroit" and many other area sculptures, was a Milles student and protegee.

native Michigan wildflowers, masses of tulips, and blossoming redbud and dogwood trees. *Early summer* displays include peonies, roses, herb and rock gardens, and numerous perennial borders. *Late summer* shows off annuals in the Sunken Garden with patterned designs. *Fall* offers spectacular vistas of rich color."

Academy of Art Museum ★

Enter on Academy Way, 500 Lone Pine Rd. (313) 645-3312. Turn right and park behind the museum. Daily except Monday 1-5. Adults $2.50; $1.50 students and seniors. Call for information on frequent lecture series and special exhibits by noted artists.

On permanent view are works by the Cranbrook Academy's many prominent faculty and students, including Carl Milles, Harry Bertoia, Maija Grotell, Florence Knoll, Marshall Fredericks, Eero Saarinen, Marianne Strengel, Ray and Charles Eames, and Tony Rosenthal, whose huge rotating cube is familiar to two decades of University of Michigan students. Many examples of Eliel Saarinen's decorative work and architectural drawings are here.

Special exhibits focus on contemporary trends in the visual arts.

Institute of Science ★

Enter on Academy Way, 500 Lone Pine Rd., and proceed straight back to Institute Way. Park in the lot by the entrance. (313) 645-3200. Mon-Thurs 10-5; Fri-Sat 10-10, Sun 1-5. (Adults $3, $2 students and seniors.

This exhibit museum is filled with displays illuminating key aspects of the physical sciences, botany, biology, anthropology, and archeology. Here you can find one of the most extensive and well arranged mineral collections in the country. One room is devoted to hands-on exhibits, mostly demonstrating scientific principles.

The **hall on American Indian culture** is especially noteworthy. Full-scale teepees are on display, along with many artifacts and dioramas showing what life was like in Indian villages of various tribes.

The **observatory** is open to the public Saturday evenings after dark. Planetarium and laser shows are held on weekends. Two **gift shops** are here, one especially for children.

LODGINGS

Holiday Inn of Bloomfield Hills

(313) 334-2444.
1801 S. Telegraph, just south of Orchard Lake Rd. From I-75, take exit 75 (Square Lake Rd.), west 4 miles to Telegraph, right 1 mile, on right.
150 rooms, 2 floors. $62 single; $64 double. Weekend (winters only) $49. Outdoor pool. Exercise room opens July, 1990. Showtime, ESPN. Restaurant & lounge. Interior rooms open onto especially pleasant courtyard, usually booked up well in advance in summer.

Kingsley Inn

(800) 544-6835.
1495 N. Woodward (just south of Long Lake Rd.)
220 rooms, 3 floors. Rooms $89 (weekdays), suites $98, $69 weekends includes $20 toward meals.
Showtime, indoor swimming pool, exercise room, restaurant, and lounge.

St. Christopher Motel

(313) 647-1800.
3915 Telegraph at Long Lake, 3 miles north of Maple.
22 units on 1 floor. $35-$40 single or double. Many restaurants nearby. A vanishing breed in suburbia, this is a mom and pop motel.

Troy

The young city of Troy provides perhaps the most dramatic contrast to the city of Detroit. As Detroit's population declines, Troy is booming. In fact, Troy is said to be one of the country's top five job generators. Some 94,000 people work here, outnumbering the 80,000 residents.

The village of Troy didn't even become a city until 1955. Like nearby Rochester and Auburn Hills, it was named for New York State cities by New York immigrants. They first settled the area in 1821. Few 19th-century industries located here because there weren't enough streams which could be harnassed for waterpower. But the rich soil and flat terrain made it superb for farming. After the Detroit United Railroad began service in 1898, farmers shipped milk daily to Detroit creameries. They also grew sugar beets, which went by rail to a Mt. Clemens sugar factory.

The area remained rural until the 1950s and didn't attract much attention until exclusive Somerset Mall came to Big Beaver and Maple in 1967, joined by giant K Mart's headquarters in 1972. Volkswagen of America is also headquartered here, as is GM's highly touted new Saturn division. Today Big Beaver Road (14 Mile) is lined with sleek, occasionally jazzy office towers punctuated by restaurants and watering holes geared to businesses and office workers. It's a good stretch to avoid at rush hour. Troy's population, just 20,000 in 1960, jumped to 67,000 in 1980, and will easily exceed 80,000 by 1990.

Much of the commercial growth comes from small and medium-size firms serving the auto industry. They have flourished due to the downsizing of the Big Three automakers, who contract for many of the services they once provided in-house. Troy could be hit hard during an economic downturn, for the car companies can quickly economize by dropping outside contracts until business picks up. It's clearly a boom time now, with $300,000+ homes being built by the hundreds.

Metro Detroit's most upscale shopping center is toney Somerset Mall on Big Beaver at Coolidge. Anchors are Saks Fifth Avenue and Bonwit Teller (the only one between Philadelphia and Chicago). The mall claims to be Troy's cultural hub, with considerable justification. For a calendar of upcoming exhibits, plays, fashion shows, free concerts and tastings, and the like, call (313) 643-6360. For more on the mall, see p. 329.

The Troy Motor Mall *is thought to be the biggest concentration of auto dealers in the world. It's on Maple Rd. between Coolidge and Crooks, across from the Oakland-Troy Airport in Troy's southwest corner. A service drive connects 12 big auto dealers. Most began to locate here in the late 1960s when they outgrew their space in nearby Birmingham.*

RESTAURANTS

Cafe Jardin ★
Somerset Mall, 2815 W. Big Beaver at Collidge. I-75 to Big Beaver heading west. Open mall hours: Mon, Thurs, & Fri, 10-8:30, Tues & Wed 10-5:30, Sat 10-5:30, Sun noon-4:30. Main dishes $3-$8. Wine. All major credit cards.

Popular place to eat for Somerset Mall's affluent shoppers. The chicken fruit salad ($6.95) is a favorite, as is Michigan Chicken — grilled chicken breast with a warm chutney of MacIntosh apples and Traverse City cherries ($7.50). The *Detroit News's* Sandra Silfven recommends the Caesar Salad ($6.25).

Nicky's
Top of Troy Building, 755 W. Big Beaver. Just off I-75. Tues-Fri 11-2 a.m., Sat 6-2, Mon 11-midnight. Lunch $5-$10, dinner $10.95-$19.95.

Housed on the first floor of Troy's tallest building, Nicky's is one of Troy's more popular restaurants. For lunch the Perch Oriental, a stir-fry with vegetables and almonds, is popular ($9.50). For dinner the broiled salmon ($16.50), veal Oscar ($16.50), and 1-lb. T-bone ($19.95) are favorites.

LODGINGS

Drury Inn
(313) 528-3330. (800) 325-8300. 575 W. Big Beaver at I-75.
154 rooms, 4 floors. $55-$60 single, $61-$66 double. Breakfast included. Outdoor heated pool. Health club around the block ($6). Showtime & ESPN. Pay movie ($6.35). Adjoining restaurant.

Red Roof Inn
(313) 689-4391. 2350 Rochester Court. Take I-75 to Rochester Rd. (exit 67), turn left (it's behind Mountain Jack's restaurant).
109 rooms, 2 floors. $33.95 single; $41.95 double. In-house movies 4 times each evening.

Troy Hilton Inn
(313) 583-9000. (800) 445-8467. 1455 Stephenson Hwy. From I-75, go west at 14 Mile to first light (Stephenson Hwy.), right one mile, on left.
404 rooms, 4 floors. $114/weekdays, $75 weekends. $69 Weekend Getaway package includes champagne, $20 off hotel restaurant meals. Indoor pool. Showtime & ESPN. Pay movie ($7.30). Some rooms with view overlooking courtyard.

Pontiac

This city of 70,000 is best known regionally these days as the home of the Silverdome, the big enclosed stadium where the Detroit Lions play football. This century, Pontiac has followed an up-and-down path like that of Flint 30 miles to the northwest. Like Flint, Pontiac was an active carriage-manufacturing center at the turn of the century, when three-fourths of the men worked in carriage factories. Early on General Motors bought up three Pontiac auto manufacturers. Thus Pontiac, like Flint, became highly dependent on the giant corporation. Like Flint, Pontiac experienced a great housing shortage in the 1920s, when sales of GM cars, trucks, and buses made here soared.

And finally, like Flint, Pontiac has suffered with GM's decline over the past decade. Pontiac is the county seat of affluent Oakland County, one of the five wealthiest counties in the U.S. But this manufacturing city, prosperous two decades ago, has been left a pocket of poverty in the middle of booming suburbia by the auto slump.

Pontiac's racial makeup (37 per cent black and at least 6.5 per cent Hispanic in 1980) contrasts to the suburbs around it, which are 95 per cent white. Today Pontiac makes headlines with its residents' big anti-drug marches. Activist Dick Gregory says they're the most enthusiastic he's seen in his national crusade to free urban neighborhoods of drugs.

Driving into Pontiac from Woodward from Bloomfield Hills, America's second-richest suburb, doesn't present the startling contrast of going from Detroit into Grosse Pointe. Pontiac's south side along Woodward is a parkway of offices and major institutions, with large and attractive ranches and colonial homes behind them.

But as you enter central Pontiac, Woodward changes into Wide Track Drive, which splits to surround the downtown core. Wide Track whooshes you around the **Phoenix Center** (a big, new mixed-use urban renewal project that has a park and amphitheater atop several layers of parking) and past downtown in an instant.

The city government demolished much of downtown and the blighted area around it in the mid-1960s, in a radical attempt to revive Pontiac's central city. The effect on the casual visitor is negative, even eerie. Vast stretches of undeveloped land surround a partially new but not very healthy-looking central commercial district, giving a ghost-town look to the scene. With the backlash against development in the nearby suburbs, some day astute developers may finally come to Pontiac, with its low land prices, excellent location, incentives for development, and considerable open space.

Ottawa hunting grounds to truck-making center

The area around Pontiac was long ago a popular camping ground for the Ottawa Indians. Chief Pontiac is said to have summered here. Fertile land and hundreds of glacially formed lakes made it a good place for hunting and fishing. Today most of the lakes are surrounded by cottages and expensive custom homes. Nine lakes are within the city limits of Pontiac itself.

Detroit speculators first established a village here in 1818. Since 1820 Pontiac has been the seat of Oakland County. After Durant included Pontiac's Oakland Motors and Rapid Motor Truck Company in the General Motors conglomerate, the city's population more than quadrupled from under 15,000 in 1910 to almost 65,000 in 1930.

Rapid Motor Company became the nucleus of the present GM Truck and Bus Group. It grew to mammoth proportions when GM chairman Alfred Sloan bought the Yellow Cab Company and merged its operations with GM's Pontiac facilities, making the city the country's largest truck manufacturer.

The Pontiac automobile was initially the name of a model made by GM's Oakland Motors. First produced in 1926, the Pontiac was priced midway between a Chevrolet and Oldsmobile to compete with the popular Essex. The new car proved an enormous success, selling a record 77,000 units its first year.

GM has stopped making Pontiacs here, although the division's headquarters remains. The last Pontiac to be built here was the ill-fated Fiero, small, sporty, but with an unfortunate tendency for its engine to catch fire. It was discontinued in 1988, a big disappointment for the autoworkers who made it. They had developed an unusual esprit de corps.

Pickup trucks are GM's major product in Pontiac today. Full-size Chevy and GMC pickups are assembled in the big plant in the southeastern corner of town. Smaller Blazers and Jimmys are made in the plant at 600 South Saginaw.

Not all of Pontiac consists of now-declining autoworkers' housing. Around the small lakes and out toward Lake Angelus are larger homes on bigger lots. Off West Huron (the central east-west street crossing through downtown) is **Indian Hills**, a designated historic district of 1920s executive homes in Tudor, Craftsman, and colonial styles of the day. Ottawa, the most impressive street here, joins Huron a mile west of the center of town.

POINTS OF INTEREST

Pontiac Silverdome

1200 Featherstone. North of M-59 and south of Featherstone in east Pontiac, just west of Opdyke Rd. Tickets: (313) 456-1600; Detroit Lions tickets (313) 335-4151. Call (313) 858-7358 for group tours.

The Silverdome, completed in 1975, belongs to the first generation of enclosed stadiums pioneered by Houston's Astrodome. Architects O'Dell Hewlett Luckenbach designed the air-supported roof, a first for stadiums, which made the Silverdome much less expensive than other early enclosed stadiums: $691 a seat, compared with $923 for the Seattle Kingdome and $2,300 for the New Orleans Superdome. In 1985, a heavy, wet snow pressed the roof down against a light fixture; the snag collapsed it. The stadium was empty, and the roof soon repaired.

In the early 1970s, when Pontiac was much more prosperous, voters approved the bond issue to build the Silverdome, with the Lions in place as the key tenant. The subsidy is a large burden for a city as small as Pontiac. It turns out that the Silverdome has helped hotels and motels in surrounding Oakland County more than Pontiac businesses. Events here range from professional football and stadium tours for the likes of the Rolling Stones and The Who to camper shows, thrill shows, and mud bogs.

Pine Grove Historical Museum

405 Oakland Ave. 1/2 mile north of Wide Track Dr. (313) 338-6732. Mon-Fri 10-4. $3 adults, $1.50 kids and seniors. Advance reservations for groups of 10 or more.

This well-preserved Greek Revival house, just off the old Saginaw Trail, was built by Moses Wisner, a pre-Civil War Michigan governor, between 1844 and 1853. Three-fourths of its furnishings actually are Wisner family antiques. Once this stately farmstead sat on a thousand acres; today it remains a pristine anachronism, removed from the neighboring used car lots and auto parts shops on this busy thoroughfare.

A lawyer, Wisner attended the famous founding Republican Party convention in Jackson in 1854. In 1858, he became governor (then a part-time job) and redecorated this house, where he conducted much of the state's business. He formed a Civil War infantry regiment, but died of typhoid fever in 1863.

The unusual side wing features a colonnade of fluted Doric columns. In addition to the handsomely detailed ten-room house, the 1 1/2-hour tour includes the privy, smokehouse, root cellar, summer kitchen, carriage house, and a one-room schoolhouse (circa 1860), moved to the grounds from Drayton Plains. The house has been slowly restored to its 19th-century appearance.

Oakland County Farmers' Market

2350 Pontiac Lake Rd. west of Telegraph, east of County Center Dr. in Waterford Twp. northwest of Pontiac. (313) 858-5495. May-Oct: Tues, Thurs & Sat 6:30 a.m.-1 p.m. Nov & Dec Thurs & Sat 6:30-1. Jan-April: Sat 6:30-1.

Vendors in over 100 selling spots, mostly enclosed, offer a big array of produce, bedding plants in season, herbs, and cider, honey, and baked goods. Highly recommended by good cooks in the area.

Calico Corners ★

1933 S. Telegraph, Bloomfield Twp. Between Square Lake Rd. and Orchard Lake Rd., on the east side of the road, just north of Toyota.

(313) 332-9163. Mon 9:30-8, Tues-Sat 9:30-5:30, Sun 1-5.

Discriminating, budget-conscious home decorators drive for hours to shop at Michigan's two Calico Corners, here and at 21431 Greater Mack in St. Clair Shores. You can find here, if you're lucky, bolt ends and seconds of top-of-the-line Brunswig & Fils and Clarence House upholstery and drapery fabrics for $9 and $10 a yard, which sell for up to $60 a yard. Prices on regularly stocked fabrics like Calico Corners' exclusive Brandywine line of chintzes by Waverly are $13 a yard; other stores sell Waverly fabrics (the moderate-price division of Schumacher) for $27, special-ordered. Other first-quality fabrics, available in 7-10 days from the central warehouse, typically run $11 to $12 a yard, a third of what you'd pay through a decorator. Good rates on upholstery work are available through the knowledgeable, helpful staff.

Antiques and junk in Pontiac and Clarkston

Take Woodward from Bloomfield Hills through Pontiac; it becomes Oakland and then Dixie Hwy.

This stretch, from Woodward along Dixie Highway toward Clarkston, features a spectacular selection of closeouts and junk, along with a wildly contrasting cross-section of American life. On Oakland you pass an automotive alley and Pine Grove, the incongruously trim historic house. Dixie Highway is said to be so named because Civil War troops trained near Saginaw marched south on it to war. Some 75 and 80 years later, Kentuckians streamed north on it to work in Michigan onion fields and tank and aircraft plants. For a change of pace from this hectic commercial strip, you could visit the pretty village of Clarkston, with its many restored Greek Revival cottages.

Dixieland Antique Flea Market ★
On the west side of Dixie Highway at Telegraph. (313) 338-3220. Open Fri 4-9, Sat & Sun 10-6.

Places like this are American versions of Arab bazaars, where hundreds of colorful characters hawk their wares on weekends, indoors and out. Goods here range from actual antiques and collectibles (some fairly pricey), coins, and vintage clothes to new things like socks, quilts, produce, cheap giftware, and some of the biggest lamps and vases imaginable, covered with mirrors and gold finish for an almost blinding effect. At one booth a lawyer dispenses free legal advice 12 to 3 Saturday.

Midwestern Antiques Emporium
West side of Dixie Highway just north of the intersection with Walton and Williams Lake Blvd. (313) 623-7460. Tues-Sun 10-5.

5,500 square feet of space is occupied by 40 to 50 dealers in oak, country, glass and china, lamps, clocks, and more.

The Whoopee Bowl ★★
9580 Dixie Hwy., 1 1/2 miles north of I-75, outside Clarkston. (313) 625-3180. Sun-Thurs 9-6, Fri & Sat 9-8.

This celebrated surplus store is full of seconds and odd lots, hardware and parts, mostly new but some used. "We buy — sell — swap," it advertises. "If we ain't got it, it's gonna be hard to find." No Odd Lots store could match the grungy atmosphere of this cavernous series of rooms. The search is one half of the fun, the bargains the other: sheets of heavy-duty sandpaper for $1.50/lb., library discards for 25¢ a book, irregulars of large deep-blue mixing bowls for 75¢, big flower pots for a dollar, a room of vinyl auto upholstery at $3.50 a yard, 54" wide. This is the underside of our consumer society: fads that have come and gone (Ms. Pac Man, sticker albums, plastic paint-it-yourself suncatchers), outdated calendars and desk pads, barrels of garish orange and blue translucent beads, floor mats for past models of GM cars, streaked plastic tractor seats, boxes of wood spindles, rolls of seat belt webbing, pieces of leather and mirror glass.

Artists and do-it-yourselfers love the bins of hardware, knobs, and fittings. There's also plenty of stuff like jewelry and jewelry parts, miniatures and dollhouse accessories, functional and decorative ceramics, toys, and craft kits and supplies.

RESTAURANTS

Pike Street Restaurant★★★
18 W. Pike St., south of Huron and north of Orchard Lake Rd. in downtown Pontiac. (313) 344-7878. Lunch Mon-Fri 11-3; dinner Tues-Thurs 5-10; Fri-Sa 5-11. Full bar, outstanding wine list. All major credit cards. Entrees $5.50-$9.50 (lunch); $16.50-$23.50 (dinner).

This attractive restaurant features delicious food emphasizing Michigan ingredients. Roast loin of whitetail venison ($23.50) is served with apple-sage stuffing and wild leeks, fiddlehead ferns, and stuffed morels. Sauteed pickerel comes with a Posen potato crust. (Potatoes from the vicinity of Posen, Michigan, are unusually yellow and starchy.) Lunch entrees are accompanied by a simple but outstanding spinach/pear/mushroom salad. Wild mushroom soup is among the excellent soups ($3) that change daily. Jamaican red bean soup is always offered.

Co-owner Jim Fitzpatrick, who worked in Pontiac for years as a GM executive, has handsomely renovated this old brick Michigan Bell facility in downtown Pontiac. Co-owner and chef Brian Polcyn combines his own inventive flair, boyhood love of Polish home cooking, and training in classic French cooking, to transform it into one of Michigan's best restaurants — "remarkably affordable," says the *Free Press's* Molly Abraham, compared with many peers.

La Familia Martinez
Relocating; call (313) 332-6851.

Trini & Carmen's
Northwest of downtown Pontiac at 1715 N. Telegraph (west side) almost at Dixie Hwy., just north of the RR viaduct next to Wendy's. (313) 332-6851. Mon-Thurs 11-11, Fri & Sat 11-midnight, Sun noon-midnight. Full bar. All major credit cards.

The Martinez family and its 12 children have provided Pontiac and north Oakland County great family eating spots, fun and inexpensive, for over two decades. The portions are so huge, $10 can feed a family. The original place, La Familia Martinez on South Woodward, had to move and hasn't found a new place yet. Trini & Carmen's had the same menu, anyway. Widely known specialties include margaritas by the liter; a huge Burrito el Grande with steak ($6.25); Nachos Supreme ("the first in the area") that resemble a Mexican pizza with piles of chicken, beef, beans, green peppers, tomatoes, and cheese on top; and for dessert, munuelos — deep-fried tortillas filled with cheese and honey. The avocado in the gazpacho is real here, of course. Mexican beers and coffee drinks are also available.

West End Restaurant
975 Orchard Lake Rd. at Old Telegraph. Old Telegraph parallels Telegraph to the east just south of the Orchard Lake Rd. overpass. If you're coming from the south on Telegraph, it's just north of the Honda dealer. (313) 334-5980. Mon-Sat 11-10, Sun noon-8. Call to confirm if arriving after 9 p.m. No, bar; bring your own. AmExpress, Diners.

This unpretentious Asian restaurant is more like a family or club of regulars than a normal business. The owner-chef, Nguyen Huy Han, a former South Vietnamese official, shares with customers his philosophy (based on world harmony) and, at year's end, his profits. The changing menu offers an eclectic range of good and simple, mostly Asian, dishes between $4 and $7. Han used to run another restaurant at 129 North Perry downtown, more as a social service venture with inexpensive, filling lunches. It's closed while he looks for capital to bring it up to code, remodel it, and reopen as a nonprofit institution.

Clarkston Cafe

18 S. Main between Depot and Washington in downtown Clarkston. (313) 625-5660. Mon-Thurs 11 a.m.-11 p.m. Fri & Sat 11-midnight. Closed holdiays. Full bar. AmExpress, MasterCard, Visa.

In this friendly, old-fashioned country setting in the attractive small town of Clarkston, a two-part menu at lunch and dinner features both casual soup-and-sandwich fare and sophisticated dishes with game, wild mushrooms, and the like. Six to eight specials daily augment the regular menu.

Most food is prepared on the premises — all the pasta, salmon smoked here that appears as an appetizer or a salad with dill dressing ($5.95 at lunch, $6.95 dinner). The $4.75 soup and salad lunch features a variety of great bean and pea soups; lunch menu fixtures include sauteed pork loin with morel sauce and a side of fettucine Alfredo with sun-dried tomatoes ($7.95) and fettucine carbonara with homemade sausage ($6.50). Lunch entrees include soup or salad. Dinner choices often include roast rack of lamb with rosemary, or veal and home-cured ham with three-peppercorn sauce for $16.95 including fettucine, soup, salad, and excellent French bread, which is served with most meals.

LODGINGS

McGuire's Motor Inn
*(313) 682-5100.
120 S. Telegraph. On US-10/US-24, 2 blocks south of M-59. $34 single, $36-$38 double. 41 rooms. Heated outdoor pool. HBO & Showtime. Refrigerator.*

Rochester/ Auburn Hills

Rochester, Rochester Hills, and Auburn Hills — these three suburbs just east of Pontiac are part of metro Detroit's fastest-growing area, and one of the more affluent. Their combined population of about 75,000 is increasing rapidly as new homes and corporations locate in the region. It's a challenge even for local fire and police to keep up with the new streets and subdivisions being added. Rochester differs from most Oakland County boom towns in having a historic center dating back to its earlier identity as a prosperous farming village. Auburn Hills, on the other hand, has completely suppressed its earlier identity as Pontiac Township, avoiding association with the troubled city of Pontiac and borrowing instead the name of the neighboring town of Auburn Heights.

A major landmark in this fast-changing area is **Oakland University**, founded in 1959 thanks to a gift of land and money from the Wilson family who lived in adjacent Meadow Brook Hall. Its five schools have a combined enrollment of 12,000. First operated under the auspices of Michigan State, Oakland is now an independent state university with a reputation for a strong undergraduate curriculum. The well-known **Meadowbrook Theater** on campus offers eight professional performances a year between October and May. Call (313) 377-3300 for information.

Much more recent is **The Palace of Auburn Hills**, the super-luxurious home of the Detroit Pistons basketball team. The Palace has quickly become one of the most popular big venues for major pop and rock concerts coming to metro Detroit. A hot local topic is the traffic tie-ups The Palace will continue to create until the road infrastructure catches up with residential and commercial development.

Meadow Brook and Michigan State

It came as no surprise that Matilda Dodge Wilson donated Meadow Brook and $2 million to Michigan State University to start a new college on her country estate. Her connection to the school went way back to when she got advice on developing Meadow Brook's poultry flock — from a young extension agent named John Hannah. Hannah was just as compelling and exciting as a chicken expert to Michigan farmers as he later was as Michigan State's visionary, empire-building president. He sold her on the land-grant colleges' philosophy of outreach and service.

POINTS OF INTEREST

Meadow Brook Hall ★★★
On the Oakland University campus off Walton Rd. or Adams Rd. 3 miles northeast of downtown Pontiac. From I-75, take Exit 79 (Pontiac Rd.) east one mile to University Dr. (313) 370-3140. Self-guided tours year-round Sun 1-4. Guided tours July-Aug Mon-Sat 10:15-3:45. Closed holidays. $4, $3 for seniors, $2 for children under 13. Also open daily in early Dec; call.

Of the major auto magnate mansions in the Detroit area, this is the

Built in the late 1920s for $4 million, Meadow Brook Hall is surprisinginly homey for a 100-room mansion. Dodge heir Matilda Wilson closely supervised its construction, proud that her Tudor home was built with mostly American materials.

warmest and most pleasing. It's a remarkable feat to make a 100-room Tudor mansion feel comfortable and inviting. The credit goes to Matilda Dodge Wilson, the daughter of a German immigrant who ran the Dry Dock Saloon on Detroit's riverfront. Secretary, second wife, and widow of the great automaker John Dodge, she was left over $150 million after he died of the flu in 1921. John and Matilda had used the Meadow Brook farm property as a country retreat. At age 41 she married again, this time to a wealthy lumber broker, Alfred Wilson. In 1926 she began building the long planned Tudor home at Meadow Brook. Industrious and strong-willed, Matilda was closely involved in Meadow Brook's design (by Smith Hinchman & Grylls), construction and decor. Matilda preferred the more modern, active life of a do-er and church woman to the glamorous life of her sister-in-law Anna Thompson Dodge in Grosse Pointe's and Palm Beach's high society. Entertaining, chatty, informative biographies of John Dodge and Matilda are for sale at Meadow Brook.

Happily, the interior of this magnificent home is still quite close to what it was when Matilda lived here. Although she ultimately spent $4 million on the home, she resisted overpowering effects. In a very natural way, priceless works of art occupy the same rooms as works of purely personal interest. Most of the rooms, big and small, pleasingly combine fine works of art (including paintings by Van Dyke, Reynolds, and Rosa Bonheur), ornate carved wood and plaster architectural detailing, carpeting, and furniture. Matilda's vast Louis XV bedroom makes anything on the set of "Dallas" look like small potatoes.

Milford

The old industrial and farm town of Milford, in west Oakland County, was first settled in 1827 to take advantage of the water power of the Huron River and its Pettibone Creek tributary. Today it is a most attractive place to visit. Milford's setting and that of Highland, its smaller neighbor a few miles north, is idyllic, in the midst of the hilly, park-studded belt of glacial lakes northwest of Detroit.

Abundant recreational land

Milford is now suburbanized, and the area is developing and gentrifying fast. The village's population remains about 5,000, but the entire township is 12,000, 20 per cent more than in 1980, and still growing. Milford feels like it's still partly a country town, thanks to the streams, wetlands, and vast tracts of recreational land that surround nearly half its periphery. In areas of marginal farmland like this, a good deal of land reverted to the state during the Depression from nonpayment of taxes, forming the nucleus for natural areas and parks. The Proud Lake and Highland state recreation areas were acquired for a song in the 1940s. And in 1948 the new Huron-Clinton Metropark Authority opened Kensington Metropark on 4,300 acres of mostly farm land as one of the jewels of its ambitious parks system.

West of Milford, further expanses of woods and fields are part of the General Motors Proving Grounds. It was founded here in 1924 because the varied glacial terrain (from steep hills to flatlands) were convenient to big GM facilities in Flint, Lansing, and Detroit. Nearby Camp Dearborn, owned and operated by the city of Dearborn, was started by Henry Ford as a summer vacation spot for Dearborn residents.

All this undeveloped land keeps suburban sprawl at bay, even though Milford is only four miles north of I-96 and eight miles east of U.S. 23. The fast-food strip, south of town along Milford Road, doesn't encroach on the historic downtown. But subdivisions of $400,000 mini-mansions are advancing up Milford Road from I-96, and village leaders are being pushed, pulled, and sued in a series of development controversies. Police in this recently placid place are hard-pressed to deal with increasing drug-related thefts and break-ins. They're frustrated with what they call residents' "Mayberry-type attitudes" in denying the need to deal with the realities of their increasingly urbanized situation.

Maps and information
For a plump, free advertising directory/guide of the Milford/Highland area with local maps, contact the Huron Valley Area Chamber of Commerce, 371 North Main, Milford, MI 48042. Open 9-12 weekdays. (313) 685-7129. For a big, overall map showing the state recreation areas (not in detail) and Kensington Metropark (in detail), contact Huron-Clinton Metropolitan Authority, Box 2001, Brighton, MI 48116-8001, or call 1-800-24-PARKS.

Getting there
From I-96, take the Milford Rd. exit north 4 miles to Milford, or the Kent Lake Rd. exit through Kensington Metropark into town. From the north, take US-23 to M-59, go east 7 miles to Milford Rd., then 4 miles south through Highland to Milford.

A 19th-century farm and mill town

At the edges of the village of Milford, Greek Revival stone and brick farmhouses, modest in size and cheerfully restored, are now mixed in among new homes along the Huron River and Pettibone Creek, which meet just south and west of the pleasant business district. The most interesting-looking old neighborhood is just east of Main Street, between Liberty and Commerce. At Commerce and Union, the **Milford Historical Museum** (313-685-7308) is open from 1 to 4 p.m. Wednesdays and Saturdays.

A waterfall and lots of water power

A big local employment base keeps Milford from becoming just a bedroom community. The GM Proving Grounds employs 3,500 in its Safety Research and Development Lab, Vehicle Emission Lab, and top-secret testing facilities for prototype and production cars. A Kelsey-Hayes plant employs 900 making brake valves. Henry Ford started the plant by the upper mill pond on Pettibone Creek to make carburetor.
A stepped waterfall, quite dramatic by Michigan standards, marks the main **dam and historic mill site**. Once it powered factories making woolens, agricultural implements, lumber, and furniture. Today you can see it at Mill Valley, 100 West Commerce (just west of Main Street), which houses a number of small businesses. During regular weekday hours, the gate is open, and you can go just below the dam and enjoy the beautiful view.

Milford's mortician-poet

The genial director of Lynch & Sons funeral home, Tom Lynch, past president of the local chamber of commerce, is also a nationally acclaimed poet. His very first book of poetry, "Skating with Heather Grace," was published by the prestigious Knopf Poetry Series. (Heather Grace is his daughter.) He is one of four mustachioed mortician brothers who followed in their father's footsteps. In his accessible, often humorous poetry Lynch incorporates material about death, his funeral work, Irish mythology, and life in small-town Milford. His funeral home is east of downtown at Liberty and First, in a rambling, grey frame house.

POINTS OF INTEREST

Downtown Milford

Main Street (Milford Rd.) between the Huron River and Commerce Rd. Most stores open Thurs & Fri evenings, closed Sun.

Downtown Milford today still has a nice balance of old, small-town businesses and new gift shops and boutiques geared to an increasingly affluent clientele in the surrounding area. A sign of the times is an old Quonset hut whose facade has been embellished with vaguely colonial storefronts, behind which are a doll shop, a bright, informal women's clothing shop, and a custom jewelry shop. Planters, benches, and even a fountain are gentrified amenities downtown, but Milford is still relaxed and small-town enough that the owner of Martin Furniture feels free to post a "Gone fishing" sign on his door for a week. Next door, the **Shutter Shop** features an odd mix of musical instruments, hobby supplies, and unusual new and old toys.

If you're the kind of person who likes shopping in low-key, small-town settings rather than hitting the malls or walking long distances in oversized discount stores, you could fill most ordinary needs here and get good personal service, too. Milford has a

Dancer's, a D & C variety store, a good shoe store, **Arms Brothers** menswear (established in 1837, the year after the great Michigan land rush, it's the state's oldest men's clothing store), an attractive children's shop, plus a bakery, a new wine and cheese shop, antique and gift shops, a goldsmith, and a stylish store with mineral specimens and fossils. The **Red Doggie Saloon** on Main Street (you can't miss it; a large black and white dog is on the roof) is an un-gentrified bar, reputed to be a favorite of cruising motorcyclists, with good hamburgers.

Just south of the central business district, on Main Street and the north bank of the Huron River, is attractive **Central Park**, with wooden play structures, grills, and tennis courts.

Eco Sports Canoe Livery/ Henry Ford Hydroelectric Plant ★

275 W. Liberty, Box 281, Milford, MI 48042. Follow signs from downtown Milford or Commerce Rd. (313) 685-3410 or (313) 887-2521 (home). $12/day, $6/first hour. Weekdays $1 less.

This rather amazing spot is worth a short visit whether or not you intend to go canoeing. Henry Ford built a brick hydroelectric plant here, tucked away in a leafy and highly picturesque spot just below Milford's lower dam. It's just above where Pettibone Creek joins the Huron. At least 30 feet of fall within a half a mile afforded 19th-century Milford splendid water power. The canoe livery that now occupies the plant has provided a path and footbridge to a glade overlooking the stream. It's a wonderfully sensuous

> A **Huron River canoe map** comes free for the asking from Huron-Clinton Metroparks. Call 1-800-24-PARKS or (313) 685-1561. Campgrounds for canoeists are at Kensington and Proud Lake. See p. 235 for more on Huron River canoeing.

The streams and wetlands surrounding Milford are home to egrets (left), great blue herons (right), and bitterns (below). They can often be seen by canoeists on quiet days.

oasis in mid-summer.

Slow current here allows canoeists to paddle upstream and back on the Huron 10 miles through Proud Lake Recreation Area, almost up to Commerce Lake. Or they can go downstream through Kensington Metropark and Island Lake Recreation Area.

Dropoffs and pickups are available for an additional fee, ranging from $4 at Kensington to $15 at Dexter, two days downstream. Possible trips range in length from 1 1/2 hours to five days (all the way to Lake Erie). There are **canoe camps** downstream at Kensington Metropark, Island Lake State Park (5 miles away), and Hudson Mills near Dexter.

Wildlife is abundant along the Huron here. On weekdays, you're more likely to see American bitterns, their necks waving like reeds, great blue heron, and speedy, long-legged leatherback turtles. Unusual water lilies are plen-tiful. The Huron is stocked with trout at Proud Lake; canoeists have brought back some big ones.

Dee Segula Studio

569 W. Liberty (west off Main St. north of Central Park). Call ahead: (313) 685-3533.

Segula is widely known for her shimmering, playful versions of jumping jack pull puppets — fanciful animals and party ladies that look like they're made of marbled and hand-tinted or handmade papers, with pewter fasteners. Actually the paper is applied to formica. They range from simple to elaborately mounted, from $50 to $3,000. Lately she's been using the same techniques, images, and iridescent tones in jewelry ($18-$150).

Detroit Polo Club

2270 N. Milford Rd., 3 mi. north of Milford. Game info: (313) 682-4356. Membership info: (313) 682-4356. Lessons available. Games: 2 p.m. most Sundays, June-Oct. Call to confirm. $3 admission, 12 and under free.

Visitors are most welcome by this friendly, enthusiastic crew, and a $3 program explains in entertaining style polo basics to know-nothings. There's food service on a pleasant terrace. Since the club first acquired its 33-acre Milford site in 1972, U.S. polo has developed greatly, here and elsewhere.

Though the costly sport is known as the sport of kings, this crew enjoys a spirit of rough-and-tumble camraderie that's reflected in the club history of its improvised early years. Until 1973, we're told, club members, "like the Asian horsemen who conceived the sport over 2,000 years ago, wandered and played on whatever field was available. Half-trained mounts in rusty two-horse trailers would visit Grand Rapids or Cleveland, and the green locals would get whipped pretty good in the games but hold their own in the post-game parties. If a player had two horses who had seen a polo ball 10 or 12 times, he was well mounted."

Today the club has 20 members, professional players, over 140 horses, and two major U.S. polo cups to its credit. It has built a huge barn and training center. Right next door, a member is developing an equestrian center with huge covered arena and Grand Prix jumping course that will be the best such facility in the Midwest, he claims.

Highland Recreation Area ★

Entrance and contact station (where you can get a map) off M-59 between Ormond and Ford roads, about 4 miles east of the village of Highland and 1 1/2 miles east of Duck Lake Rd. (313) 887-5135. 8 a.m.-10 p.m. $3/day vehicle fee, or $15 annual state park sticker.

Incredibly, these 5,500 acres of gorgeous wetlands, lakes, wooded hills, and meadows are under-used even though they're not far from booming suburbia. The main entrance off M-59 leads to **Haven Hill Lake** (with a picnic site and a 24-site rustic campground for horseback riders and others) and to **Teeple Lake** (picnicing and a small swimming beach). Between the two small lakes are three marked **cross-country ski trails** (12 miles altogether) with a warming room and ski rental concession (open weekends 10 a.m.-dusk; call first).

For fabulous **fall color and views**, take the steep, paved, dead-end road leading to the hilltop nature center (closed due to state budget cuts). It overlooks Haven Hill Lake. Just north of the lake, the 700-acre **Haven Hill Natural Area** includes every forest type found in southern Michigan. Over 100 species of birds have been sighted here, including colonies of the uncommon Brewster's warbler. Most of Highland's east side is closed to hunting.

In the center of the recreation area, hiking trails lead to three other **panoramic vistas**. They aren't indicated with signs, but if you pick up a map at the entrance, you can see where to reach them off Beaumont Road.

A **chain of four lakes** off Pettibone Lake Road at the area's west edge offer attractive picnic sites. (The secluded rustic campground has been closed for lack of use.) Fishing for pike and bass at all Highland's 10 lakes is considered good.

Alpine Valley Ski Area

5775 E. Highland Rd. (M-59) at Bogie Lake Rd., 3-4 miles east of the village of Highland. (313) 887-2180. 24-hour snowline: 887-4183.

This scenic downhill ski area, southern Michigan's largest, has augmented the natural glacial hills to create two new 1,100-foot-long slopes with a 300-foot vertical drop. In all, 25 slopes and trails use 10 chairlifts and 13 rope tows to provide a variety of terrains from easy to challenging (by southern Michigan standards). The snowmaking system, which can produce 500 tons of snow an hour, is said to be the biggest in southeast Michigan. The lodge has many stone fireplaces, two cafeterias, and a lounge with cocktails, dancing, and entertainment. New in '89-'90: a half-pipe for snowboarders.

Hours and chairlift tickets : Weekends and holidays: 9 a.m.-11 p.m, $18. Weekdays: 10 a.m.-11 p.m., $13-$14. Saturday midnight skiing begins in January: 9 p.m.-2 a.m., $16. Beginner tickets (no chairlifts) $10-$11, free weekdays daytime. Equipment rental: $12-$14. NOTE: Tickets purchased before 3 p.m. are good only until 5:30. Slopes close between 5:30 and 6. Call 887-7111 for group reservations. Ski lessons: 887-6010.

Proud Lake Recreation Area ★

Main entrance off Wixom Rd. 1 1/2 miles south of Commerce Rd., about 3 miles east of Milford. (313) 685-2433. 8 a.m.-10 p.m. $3/day vehicle fee, or $15 annual state parks sticker.

In these 3,614 acres of state land just east of Milford, the Huron River has been dammed to create a little chain of lakes that forms the park's focus. Proud Lake is wonderful for canoeing, fishing (trout are released in spring for fly fishermen), hiking, birdwatching, and easy cross-country skiing on flat terrain. Hardwood forests, pine plantations, marshes, meadows, and a quaking bog are accessible via **trails** which loop around the nature study and picnic area near the park entrance and extend out — 21 miles in all, with 5 miles of **cross-country ski trails**. A 130-unit **modern campground** (mostly unshaded and often full on summer weekends) overlooks Proud Lake. The **canoe livery** (313-685-2379) is off Garden Road, the dirt road that intersects with Wixom Road at the enrance. Canoes put in at the Wixom Road bridge here. Just north of the entrance is the small **Power Beach** swimming area and picnic grounds.

Kensington Metropark ★

Headquarters: 2240 W. Buno Rd. (at north end of Kent Lake), Milford, MI 48042. From I-96 (4 mi. east of U.S. 23), take Kensington Rd. or Kent Lake Rd. exits and follow signs a short distance to park. (313) 685-1561 or 800-24-PARKS. Park hours: 6 a.m.-10 p.m. Trail hours: 6 p.m.- dusk. Closed Thanksgiving & Xmas. $2/day or $10/year per vehicle for all Metroparks.

This hilly, wooded, 4,300-acre park surrounds twisting, island-filled Kent Lake, created by damming the Huron River. Though the lake and park are heavily used, they offer so many different micro-environments and activities that you needn't feel part of a big mob scene.

Four island picnic spots (one accessible only by boat) and fishing areas on inlets offer a get-away-from-it-all feeling with super-convenient access from metro Detroit, Ann Arbor, and Flint. Picnic areas, 14 in all, are cleverly sited. Spring Hill, near the nature center, has a spectacular view. Others are in woods or overlook water and wetlands.

The combination of water, hills, trees, lawns, and wetlands makes for a beautiful landscape which offers plenty of shade on hot days. Most of this was farmland or pasture when the park was formed in the 1940s, so the trees, though good-sized, don't have that primeval look except in old woodlots (mostly west of Kent Lake) and the nature study area.

East side of lake

◆ **East Boat Launch.** Grassy hillside and picnic spots overlook colorful sailboats. Sailors like Kent Lake because its 10 m.p.h. speed limit eliminates power boats with big wakes.

◆ **Martindale Beach.** Never full except on the three big holiday weekends. Pleasant, grassy setting, with a good view of sailboats.

◆ **Hiking-Biking Trail.** A loop of 8 miles of asphalt path around Kent Lake connects most major sights. Challenging hills.

◆ **Shorefishing area.** Shady, secluded area not bothered by boats. Bluegill, crappie, walleye, pike, bass.

◆ **Farm Center.** Open year-round; summer hours 9-6 weekdays, 9-7 weekends. Call for reduced off-season hours. The new buildings, asphalt paths, suburban landscaping, and snack bar are most un-farmy, but the smells from the pigs, ducks, geese,

Special events at Metroparks range from slopping the pigs at the farm center to hearing the fabulous Detroit Symphony Orchestra free of charge. Find out about them in the free Metroparks newsletter (1-800-24-PARKS).

chickens, goats, rabbits, cows, and horses are the real thing, and you can see the animals up close. The baby animal barn is a special attraction. Though there's a small vegetable and herb garden, the animals take center stage; you don't ever get the broader picture of farm operations. There are excellent interpretive displays about things like cows' four-part stomachs, "an egg start to finish," and how domestic ducks are descended from mallards.

Hayrides and sleighrides at the Farm Center for families and individuals: weekends (weather permitting) from 12:30-4:30 p.m. $1.50/adult, $1/child or senior for a 20-minute ride. No reservations necessary.

West side of Kent Lake

◆ **Maple Beach.** This area, on a peninsula jutting out into the lake, is much more intensely developed than Martindale Beach, with a broader sandy beach and a snack bar.

◆ **Boat rental.** Just west of Maple Beach. Rowboats (12 to 16-foot): $2.50-$4/hour, $10-16 daily max. Sailboats: $6/hour, $30 weekday max. 4-person paddleboats: $6/hour.

◆ **Island Queen Excursion Boat.** 50-minute rides leave from the boat rental every hour between noon and 6 p.m. $1.75/adult, $1.25/children and seniors. Morning and evening charters $25-$100/hour.

◆ **Nature Center.** The interpretive building on a lagoon backs up to woods and a tamarack bog. Six miles of trails in 7 loops start here; open

daylight to dusk.
- **Golf/cross-country skiing.** The hilly terrain challenges skiers and wins raves from golfers. 18 holes: $11 weekdays, $13 weekends. 9 holes: $7 weekdays, $8 weekends. Senior and junior discounts.
- **Winter sports.** Ski on golf course with marked trails, rental equipment, food bar. Skate at Maple Beach boat rental building, lighted weekend evenings. Toboggan and sled run with warming shelter at Orchard Picnic Area. (No equipment rentals.)

General Motors Proving Grounds

Entrance on Hickory Ridge Rd. about 2 miles west of Milford via General Motors Rd. Proving Grounds stretch from Commerce Rd. south to Stobart Rd. between Hickory Ridge and Pleasant Valley Rd. Off-limits to the general public.

Behind the high security fences around these 6 square miles west of Milford, 3,500 people work. They are not only test drivers of top-secret new prototype cars on the 128 miles of roads, but engineers and analysts in laboratories devoted to safety research, noise and vibration control, fuel economy and emissions testing, and tire and wheel design. Durability test schedules are conducted at all times of day and year, on roads that are hot and dry, wet, and snowy. (Subsidiary labs in Arizona, Colorado, and Canada test for desert, super-cold, and high-altitude conditions.) Tests include an 8,000-mile run over rough Belgian blocks, a 28,000-mile test over varied roads, and runs through salt spray and corrosives and through a shed that's 100 degrees at 100% humidity. Every eight hours, test cars are examined by inspectors. In labs, parts being developed are analyzed

At the 6-square-mile GM Proving Grounds in Milford, GM prototype and preprototype cars are driven on rigorous schedules over 128 miles of road ranging from banked, high-speed ovals to steep, 27% grades and rutted dirt tracks. The proving grounds and associated laboratories employ 3,500.

under precise scientific conditions.

The Proving Grounds were established in 1924 by Alfred Sloan as a microcosm of real-world conditions that was convenient to GM facilities in Detroit, Flint, and Lansing. The glacial knob-and-kettle terrain provides both steep, 27% grades and flatlands for high-speed, banked test tracks.

Island Lake Recreation Area

Entrance off Kensington Lake Rd. just south of I-96 exit 151. (313) 229-7067. 8 a.m.-10 p.m. $3/day vehicle fee, or $15 annual state park permit.

Immediately south of Kent Lake in the very popular Kensington Metropark, this recreation area offers a less developed, less heavily used alternative along a beautiful 7 1/2-mile stretch of the Huron River. The dead-end interior road winds alongside and across the river and connects the park's scattered picnic sites and main activity areas at **Lower Kent Lake**, **Spring Mill Pond**, and **Island Lake**. Each has swimming beaches. The trees aren't really big here, but the marshes make for some spectacular fall color, visible from the **14-mile loop trail** that goes through marshes, fields, and woods and up hills overlooking the valley. Midway along the interior drive is a **balloon launch site**, Meadow Port, where hot-air balloons can often be seen up close early mornings and evenings.

Canoes can put in at Kent Lake or along the river midway through the park. **Canoe rentals and snacks** are available at Lower Kent Lake (313-685-2379). Call for information on the **rustic canoe campground**, accessible only by canoe. There are also **18 shady semi-modern campsites** (flush toilets but no electricity) overlooking Island Lake, close to swimming, and 25 closely spaced rustic campsites nearby. Reservations advisable.

RESTAURANTS

Appeteaser

335 N. Main. (313) 685-0989 Mon-Thurs 11-10, Fri-Sat 11-11, Sun 11-9. Entrees: lunch $4.25-$8.50; dinner $5.50-$18.95. Full bar. Visa, Mastercard, AmExpress, Diners.

A pretty, airy, three-level place with bare brick walls softened by rather elegantly set tables, complete with cloth napkin fans. The menu runs the gamut from burgers and steaks to freshly prepared specialties like Chicken Hawaiian (breast of chicken with coconut breading served over rice pilaf; $6.95), sauteed liver with strawberries ($7.95), and shrimp and scallops with peapods ($13.95, dinner only).

Hector & Jimmy's

780 N. Milford Rd. (313) 685-8779. Mon-Thurs 11-10, Fri 11-11:30, Sat noon-11:30, Sun noon-9. Full bar. MasterCard, Visa. Entrees $3.95-$13.95, mostly $4.95-$7.95.

This popular place is an American family tavern, where you'll see everything from babies in high chairs to businessmen in suits. The fried chicken salad ($5.25) is especially popular, as are the bar-b-que platters ($9.95-$13.95). Many entrees come with salad or slaw and choice of potato.

LODGINGS

Huron Valley Motel
(313) 685-1020.
640 N. Milford Rd. just north of downtown Milford.
13 rooms, $35-$50/night. TV, air-conditioning, some refrigerators.

Monroe

Located just up the beautiful River Raisin from the marshes along Lake Erie, Monroe is a settled old industrial city, originally French. Today the historic city center, punctuated by frequent church spires, seems curiously remote from the outlying shopping malls and busy highways (I-75, Telegraph, and Dixie Highway) that go past it from Toledo to Detroit.

Hunters and bird-watchers are attracted by the huge flocks of migrating waterfowl which come to the marshes along Lake Erie, home of some of the state's best bird-watching. For centuries Indians harvested wild rice in these marshes. Beautiful lotuses blossom here every August, giving a spectacular view to visitors who head east out Dunbar Road just south of town.

Monroe was the site of the famous River Raisin Massacre of 1813, when Indians murdered 60 wounded American soldiers after a battle during the War of 1812. Some still visit it today because it was once the home of that dashing Civil War hero and Indian fighter General Custer. Monroe's excellent museum of local history and the county library have extensive collections of interesting Custer material. Monroe is also known as the "Floral City" because of the nurseries once located here. Most are now gone. Some know the city as the birthplace of the La-Z-Boy Chair Company, still headquartered but not manufacturing here. Many more are aware that Monroe is the home of the 1988 Miss America, Kae Lani Rae Rafko, the hula-dancing cancer nurse, and the 1988 Miss Michigan, Molly McIntyre, who says, "Monroe is a great pageant town." Indeed, competing dance and baton studios place huge ads in the Monroe yellow pages advertising long lists of contest winners they have taught.

Monroe is an old city, one of Michigan's most historic. Only Detroit was incorporated earlier. But unlike the Motor City, Monroe has remained peculiarly stagnant over the decades, leaving a good many old churches and Greek Revival houses in the central area looking very much as they did over a century ago. Right past downtown flows the wide, majestic River Raisin, entering Lake Erie four miles downstream. **St. Mary's Park,** just north of the river from downtown, offers a pleasant riverside spot to picnic. You can pick up a coney island at downtown's most popular and quaintest eatery, Coney Island Lunch (4 W. Front) and

Lake Erie's rebirth
Sport fishing has become big in the past decade, after anti-pollution measures led to Lake Erie's remarkable renaissance. Monroe now calls itself the "walleye capital of the world" (perch is good, too). It has a dozen charter-boat services. Call the Chamber at (313) 242-3366 for charter information.

Muskrat dinners a local tradition
The Indians taught Monroe's French the custom of eating muskrat (pronounced "mushrat" in these parts), and it is still considered a delicacy here. Trapped before the spring thaw, muskrat is still often featured at winter dinners of fraternal orders and charitable organizations.

saunter across the pedestrian bridge (constructed by Michigan Bell for a trunk line) to the park.

A French town

Monroe was founded by Detroit French who grew disenchanted with life there under the British after France lost control of the city in 1760. They migrated to this spot because Indian villages were located on the River Raisin just upstream from Lake Erie. Unlike the British, the French-Canadians had a knack for living harmoniously with the Indians. There are still quite a few French families in Monroe descended from these 18th-century settlers to this far reach of French Canada. A quick phone-book survey reveals many French names. Some natives can still even speak in the area's distinctive French accent, and double cousins are not uncommon among members of these old families. Many French ribbon farms remain — narrow parcels running perpendicular to the river.

Originally the French called the settlement River Raisin. It was called Frenchtown by the subsequent American settlers, then renamed Monroe by Governor Lewis Cass in honor of President James Monroe's 1817 visit to Detroit. (The President didn't, as hoped, take the time to see his namesake.) Some important battles of the War of 1812 with the British had occurred in Monroe, including the infamous River Raisin Massacre. (See p. 233.) Both sides of the river are dotted with historical markers commemorating these events.

Key port for settlers

By far the most colorful and exciting era in the city's history occurred between 1825 and 1837. Monroe was then a key port. Through it poured thousands of Easterners who settled Michigan, Indiana, and Illinois. The harbor they used back then was not at the mouth

Monroe and the Toledo War
At one point in the 1835 border dispute between Michigan and Ohio over control of Toledo and the mouth of the Maumee River, a thousand Michigan militiamen camped at Monroe, poised to push south. In the end Congress deferred to more powerful Ohio. In return for giving up Toledo, Michigan received the Upper Peninsula, with its then-undiscovered mineral wealth. But the passions of Ohioans and Michiganders ran high before this compromise was worked out.

Monroe is a settled old town that hasn't been gentrified. Many of its 19th-century houses are in close to original condition — a delight for old-house lovers. Fine homes are on the north bank of the river and just south and east of downtown.

of the Raisin, which was too shallow, but on Lake Erie a little south of the river, at the foot of La Plaisance Road. Known as Bolles Harbor today, then it was called LaPlaisance Harbor.

The Erie Canal, opened in 1825, brought settlers to Buffalo. There they boarded sailing ships or steamers to make the sometimes dangerous and usually uncomfortable 10-day voyage to Monroe. From Monroe they typically took the Chicago Turnpike (now M-50) to Dundee, Tecumseh, and points west. Most settled on farmland, which sold for as little as $1.25 an acre.

Monroe's early promise unfulfilled

It isn't clear why Monroe has grown so little over the decades. Early on, it rivaled Detroit as Michigan's leading city. Its advantages were several:

♦ As Lake Erie's westernmost port and Michigan's only port on this important link with the East, Monroe quickly generated a great deal of cargo and passenger traffic.

♦ The city is located next to some of the richest farmland in the world.

♦ Monroe was linked by rail with Chicago as early as Detroit (1848).

Nonetheless, the town never grew into a major metropolis. It numbered only 5,000 residents by the turn of the century.

One local historian points out that newspaper editorials of the 1830s and 1840s called for improving the port to promote the city's growth. Newspaper editorials still make the same argument today.

Port history

Hopes remain alive that Monroe will once again become a significant shipping port. The mouth of the River Raisin replaced LaPlaisance Bay as the area's chief port in 1835, when a ship canal was dug across the mud bar shielding the mouth of the river. But by then Toledo had developed its port, and it quickly came to dominate western Lake Erie.

In the 1930s the river channel at the mouth of the River Raisin was deepened and a 22-acre **turning basin** was dug a little up river just behind today's new **Port Authority building** at 2929 East Front Street, east of I-75. The improvements spurred some activity, most notably when Renault started shipping 10,000 of its cars a year through the port. Today several big facilities are close to the port: the big Ford stamping plant right across the river, Cargill's North Star steel plant just to the south, and the Detroit Edison's huge generating plant. The **Detroit Edison plant**, whose twin 800-foot smokestacks are a regional landmark, is the second- or third-largest fossil fuel plant in the world. It gobbles up a trainload of coal a day and receives almost a million tons of coal a year by boat. Still, on most

Slow growth
Early on a major Michigan port, Monroe failed to become a leading Michigan city, as these population figures show:

1840	1,703
1860	3,892
1880	4,930
1900	5,043
1920	11,573
1940	18,478
1960	22,968
1980	23,531

Prime bird-watching
The Lake Erie marshes near Monroe offer some of Michigan's most outstanding bird-watching — often from the comfort of your car. Beginning with the Nature Conservancy's extensive Erie Marsh Preserve just north of the Ohio line, three protected areas of marsh and lagoons provide nesting and stopover habitats for migrating wetland birds and residents.

Pick up "Bird Watching at Its Best," an excellent free brochure, at Michigan information centers on interstate entries to Michigan. Complete directions to these spots are included.

An old Monroe billboard advertising La-Z-Boy chairs, invented by two local cousins in 1928. Though the big firm is still headquartered here, it has moved its manufacturing facilities to other states.

days you won't see a freighter around the port. The 21-foot river channel is still too shallow for the biggest vessels (a deepwater port is 27 feet), and freighters longer than 770 feet can't turn around in the basin.

Some say the reason Monroe didn't grow more is that historically it has been a closed, conservative city whose leading citizens have not welcomed development. This is not the case any more, but growth from new plants such as Cargill's North Star Steel Company have been offset by the closing of plants such as the giant Consolidated paper mill on Elm Street and the now-empty Steel Castings plant at Monroe and Seventh.

By far the largest Monroe-area employer is **Ford**, whose plant on Elm near Lake Erie employs 1,710 workers. Parts of this plant were built back as early as 1929, when it processed steel. The car company has expanded the plant to 1.4 million square feet to make wheels, catalytic converters, stabilizer bars, coiled springs, and body stampings for the entire Ford line. Although the plant looks like it is in the middle of nowhere, it is just 35 miles south of Ford's Wayne Assembly, Dearborn Assembly, and Michigan Truck plants. It uses steel made by North Star across the river to manufacture its coil springs and stabilizer bars.

Paper and flowers

Paper mills were the city's major industry around the turn of the century. Only two remain, both on Elm Street: Jefferson Smurfitt and Monroe Paper, which makes the paperboard used for such things as the classic cylindrical canisters of Morton Salt. Once nurseries were so large here that Monroe was called the "Floral City." The remnants of some of these old nurseries has been bought out by **Snow's Nursery** at 5485 West Dunbar.

More on Monroe
Free historic tour brochures at the Monroe County Historical Museum cover architectural highlights, churches, and traces of Custer. For a packet of maps and visitor brochures, contact the Chamber of Commerce, 22 W. Second, Monroe, Mich. 48161. (313) 242-3366.

Politically the town votes conservative Democrat, a tendency said to date back to the days of President Grover Cleveland and before. Like Flint, it's a blue-collar town. But unlike Flint, which has invested millions in promoting tourism, Monroe has so far done little to take advantage of its considerable natural resources: the scenic River Raisin, many historic buildings, a state park with a long beach on Lake Erie, and extensive marshes that beckon bird hunters and bird-watchers.

POINTS OF INTEREST

Monroe County Historical Museum ★★

126 S. Monroe St. (313) 243-7137. May 1-Sept 30: Tues-Sun 10-5. Oct 1-April 30: Wed-Sun 10-5. Free.

Housed in the old post office, this interesting general museum of local history has many memorabilia about General George Armstrong Custer, the most famous person associated with Monroe. One section is devoted to the dashing soldier who spent much of his youth in Monroe and visited it often afterwards. Custer is best known as the merciless Indian fighter whose foolhardy pursuit of a Sioux band ended in the entire annihilation of his 225-man unit at Little Big Horn in 1876. But before that he had been a genuinely heroic Civil War officer, promoted to general at the unheard-of age of 23 because of his aggressive, courageous leadership at a time when the timidity of many Union generals was driving President Lincoln to distraction.

Here you can see Custer's swords and beloved rifles, a map he made of a Confederate camp while he was held aloft by balloon, various portraits (which suggest the arrogance that might have been the root of his undoing), and his big buffalo robe worn during the Washita Campaign of 1868 when he defeated a bigger band of Sioux. Dresses and furniture belong-

Monroe's museum and county library have a wealth of interesting material about the town's controversial hero, General Custer.

ing to his spunky wife, Libbie Bacon Custer, suggest the lifestyle of this Monroe belle who accompanied her husband out west and became a successful New York journalist after his death. Custer, whose ambition it was since childhood to fight Indians, had the job of routing the tribes who were understandably outraged after repeated betrayals by the U.S. government. The man with the flowing yellow hair still fascinates history buffs. People come from around the world to visit the museum and the Custer collection of the Monroe County Library. (See p. 234.)

The museum, outstanding for a

town of Monroe's size, has much more than Custer memorabilia of interest. One display shows how, 6,000 to 12,000 years ago, more than 100 species of large mammals in this area mysteriously disappeared, including the mammoth, the mastodon, the great sloth, and the American camel and horse, leaving only the great bison. This forced the local Indians, whose spear and arrowheads are shown, to hunt much smaller animals.

A sequence of dioramas shows what it looked like at Frenchtown (Monroe's former name) in 1813 when American troops were surprised by the British and disastrously surrendered, leading to the famous massacre of some 60 wounded soldiers by Indians.

In one corner is the interesting office of the Monroe dentist who patented the device which would become the country's leading dispenser of laughing gas. A folk art altar, hand-carved by a grieving father after his daughter's death, is remarkable. A nifty collection of old Monroe shop signs includes the arresting Louis Shoe Repair sign of vivid red and green glass dots. On another wall is a huge shotgun called a punt gun. The gun was not shouldered, but attached to a small boat that glided quietly across the marshes near Monroe until a flock of sitting ducks was sighted.

A display about the pride of Monroe, Kaye Lani Rae Rafko, Miss America, 1988, features the revealing green sequined Hawaiian costume she made for her hula dance in the pageant's talent competition. Today she has returned to Monroe and to nursing, married her boyfriend (whom she met picking strawberries), and hopes to start a hospice in the area.

The museum's charming gift shop sells a colorful poster of General Custer staring at the viewer. Under his portrait are the words:
**I WANT YOU
FOR THE U.S. CALVARY
Join me and the illustrious 7th.
Help put down the militant Sioux.
[signed] George A. Custer**

Loranger Square

Intersection of First and Washington Streets downtown.

At this downtown intersection you can see the early, New England-style courthouse square carved out of the corners of the four adjoining blocks. This square, unique in Michigan, is one sign of how much older Monroe is than other cities in the state. The unusual, impressively ornate 1880 **County Courthouse** is on the square's southeast corner. In front is a cannon that dates to the reign of George II of England. Across First Street is the site of the **First Presbyterian Church,** built in 1846. Next to the church on First is the **Dorsch Memorial Library**, located in the former home of Dr. Eduard Dorsch, a Bavarian physician who fled after the failed 1848 German revolution. He is said to have introduced the American lotus to Monroe's marshes.

On the square's northwest corner, a plaque commemorates the spot where a **whipping post** once stood. Another sign of the antiquity of Monroe, whipping posts were a rarity in the Midwest. The New England custom of whipping minor criminals was abolished here in 1835.

Downtown

Centered at the intersection of Front St. with Monroe and Washington, extending south from the River Raisin.

Monroe's downtown of interesting old buildings and vintage storefronts has seen better days. Locals say that the downtown has already lost most of the retail shops it is going to lose; the only direction left to go is up. With a beautiful river running right alongside it and many handsome old buildings, this may well again become a splendid district some day. The new Riverwalk flanks the south side of the Raisin between Macomb and the

> **The walking tour brochure** available at the museum takes you on an interesting walk through Old Monroe's historic commercial and residential district. The heart of old Monroe is from Elm and Front streets along the river south to Fourth, along Cass, Monroe, Washington, Macomb, and Scott. Take-out coffee and sweetrolls from Paul's Bakery, 6 E. Front, can be enjoyed on benches in front of the library, looking out on the pleasant historic Loranger Square at First and Washington.

pedestrian bridge to St. Mary's Park.

Along Washington Street (one street over from Monroe) are some attractively restored commercial buildngs north of the courthouse. Others remain hidden behind the ugly grillwork facades popular in the 1950s and 1960s to bring old storefronts "up-to-date." In this case, **Kline's** department store (known for its frequent good sales) has outdone itself. It faces both Washington and Front, and it has obliterated not just one but two blocks of historic stone-trimmed storefronts.

The **Monroe Bank & Trust** is a fine example of early 20th-century Beaux Arts architecture. It's worth a peek inside to see the imposing interior. A map on the kiosk outside orients visitors to major Monroe sights.

Moving west on Front Street, you pass Monroe's most elegant restaurant, **Kennon's**. It is Front Street's only business to make use of the River Raisin right behind it. A small terrace here is opened during warmer days for patrons.

At 15 East Front is **Frenchie's** coin and stamp shop, with the added attraction of a Rolls Royce in its front window and a newly made, flashingly bright pressed copper ceiling. At **Paul's Bakery** across the street, you can buy tasty fresh pastries and coffee to go.

North of the river across the Monroe Street bridge is the impressive **Custer Monument** at Elm and Monroe. Edward Potter's bronze equestrian statue of the hero at the Battle of Gettysburg was unveiled in 1910 by his widow, by then a well-known New York writer, with President Taft at her side.

South on Monroe Street are several noteworthy establishments. The tidy, well-organized **Thrift Shop** at 119 S. Monroe is run by a charitable organization that sells its merchandise (used clothes, furniture, dishes, etc.) at amazingly cheap prices. It's open Monday through Saturday from 9:30 to 3:30, except for closing at 11:30 on Tuesday and opening at 11:30 Saturday. At 317 S. Monroe, **Monroe Hobbies** (open Mondays and Wednesdays 11:30-6; Fridays 11:30-9, and Saturdays 10-6) has an impressive array of items for the hobbyist. Next door at **Spainhower's Auction House** can be found a rather wild variety of antique items for sale. (Open 9-5 Monday-Saturday. Call 313-242-5411 about upcoming auctions held every three weeks or so.)

Finally, if you walk west on Front Street past Monroe Street, you'll soon see the home of the *Monroe Evening News* at 201 W. First. Giant glass windows let the passing public see its big web presses in action. Around 2:30 on weekday afternoons, you can see that day's edition roaring off the presses.

River Raisin Battlefields and Massacre Site

Along the River Raisin on E. Elm St. just west of the I-75 exit. The new battlefield interpretive museum and park, at E. Elm just west of Detroit St. (between M-50 and I-75), is due to open in May, 1990. Call (313) 243-7137 for hours.

The War of 1812 again pitted the British and Indians against the Americans. At stake was the extent of American holdings on the continent. Many who urged their fellow Americans to take up arms felt Canada could be easily added to U.S. possessions. One of the major battles in that often ineptly led war occurred at the River Raisin between Dixie Highway and Detroit Street.

The British had retaken Detroit. Therefore, control of the Detroit-Toledo road through Monroe was of key importance. In January, 1813, an American army led by the elderly General James Winchester moved up from Kentucky to break the British hold. It was badly mauled here in an early-morning surprise attack by British and Canadian soldiers. Nearly 280 Americans were killed, and a brigade of 600 militiamen was ordered to surrender by the captured General Winchester. Wounded Americans, left in the homes of Monroe settlers, were set upon by Indians a day later. Over 60 were murdered. This was the famous "River Raisin Massacre" which ignited the American troops. A series of metal markers along the river explains its the major incidents.

Monroe, then called Frenchtown, was almost totally devastated by the battle and subsequent massacre. It was another five years before most settlers returned.

> A "Battlefield Trail" of historical markers is described in a brochure at the Monroe County Historical Museum.

Navarre-Anderson Trading Post ★★

N. Custer Rd. at Raisinville Rd., 4 miles west of downtown Monroe. From M-50 (S. Custer Rd.) turn north onto Raisinville Rd. and cross the river. (313) 243-7137. Open Memorial Day-Labor Day, weekends 1-5; other times, by appointment for groups. Free.

The centerpiece of this three-building complex of relocated historic buildings is the plain, steep-roofed, story-and-a-half house built in Monroe in 1789 by fur trader François Navarre. It's believed to be the oldest surviving house in Michigan, and it has been restored and furnished with simple French-Canadian furniture to look as it might have when the Navarres lived there between 1789 and 1802. The interior trim is barn red (the French liked color), with white walls and ceiling to reflect candlelight. The house had no kitchen, so the 1810 house moved beside it has been interpreted as a summer kitchen. A French-Canadian barn is under construction nearby. The brick schoolhouse built on this site in 1860 has been interpreted as a **country store** from between 1910 and 1920. Faithfulness to period is more accurate than in most country store recreations.

Custer Collection, Monroe County Library

3700 S. Custer Rd. (M-50) at Raisinville Rd. (313) 241-5277. Mon-Fri 9-4.

Much of this 35,000-item collection of photos, paintings, films, tapes, and all manner of printed matter on the events shaping the life of Custer was assembled by Lawrence Frost, Monroe podiatrist, mayor, and Custer expert. The library welcomes Custer scholars and the general public; call for group appointments.

St. Mary's Academy

W. Elm Ave. between Monroe and Telegraph.

This impressively large Catholic complex sits back on a grand sweep of lawn and trees. The western part is the Mother House of the order of nuns which governs Marygrove College in Detroit. The eastern part was St. Mary's Academy, a girls' boarding school. Much of the original 1932 Art Deco decor remains intact, and visitors are welcome to look at the chapel and entrance foyers. The academy is becoming a Japanese finishing school for the daughters of Japanese executives between here and Detroit.

Sterling State Park

2800 State Park Rd., off Dixie Hwy. 1 mile northeast of I-75 exit 15. (313) 289-2715. 8 a.m.-10 p.m. $3/day, or $15 annual state park sticker.

Sterling State Park, just north of Monroe, is western Lake Erie's only park with camping and swimming. From the beach, swimmers and sunbathers get a stark view of the giant cooling towers of the Fermi Nuclear Plant four miles north. (Such towers, almost a symbol of nuclear power, are actually identical to those of coal-fired power plants. They release steam — vaporized water, not particulate smoke — into the air.)

Half of this 1,000-acre park consists of water — lagoons that are excellent habitats for migrating and nesting shore birds. A causeway leads to the large **beach**, beachhouse, parking area and, behind it, the partly shaded **picnic area** and **playground** on a rise offering a panorama of Lake Erie. The park has **288 modern campsites** without privacy or shade, overlooking the boat basin.

In early spring the **lakeside walkway** is crowded with walleye shore-fishermen. **Fishing docks** also extend out into two lagoons. A big, protected **boat launch** offers excellent access off the Sandy Creek Outlet.

At Sterling State Park most bird activity can be observed from the comfort of your heated car — a big plus on wet, raw spring days. (Birds are actually less disturbed by the familiar outlines of cars than by pedestrians.) Tom Powers' *Natural Michigan* points out, "Several roads closely border the park's four lagoons, which attract egrets, Great Blue Heron, smaller shorebirds, Coots, Mergansers, Blue-winged Teal and many other species." A 2.6-mile loop along the Marsh View Nature Trail surrounds the park's largest lagoon. (It's open for cross-country skiing in winter.) A mile walk leads to its observation tower.

Fermi 2 Power Plant & Visitors Center

On Enrico Fermi Drive off Dixie Hwy., 7 miles north of downtown Monroe. (313) 586-5228. 3-5 weeks advance reservations required for free group tours conducted Mon-Sat between 9 and 5. Individuals may join scheduled group tours.

These tours of Detroit Edison's only nuclear power plant get high marks from University of Michigan radiation experts for straightforward information about nuclear power and about the much-publicized delays and cost overruns in starting up Fermi 2. The visitor facilities here aren't as glitzy as those at the Cook Nuclear Information Center south of St. Joseph. In fact, they go back to the 1958, when Fermi 1 was under construction here. That pioneering atomic reactor, a developmental fast neutron breeder reactor, was one of the first full-scale atomic power plants in the U.S., part of Eisenhower's Atoms for Peace nuclear energy program. It is considered a historical landmark by the American Nuclear Society.

Fermi 1 was decommissioned in 1975, after a severe core meltdown accident that was controlled without environmental contamination by the containment vessel. The incident was the basis for much anti-nuclear literature, including the book *The Day We Almost Lost Detroit*.

Fermi 2's notoriety and frequent shutdowns stem from the 15-year time lag between its initial design and its completion in 1987. High interest rates and labor and delivery problems had postponed the project until 3 Mile Island had created a mugh tighter regulatory environment. As a result, much of Fermi 2 had to be redesigned, requiring a longer approval and shakedown period. At first, Detroit Edison's corporate culture proceeded as if Fermi 2 could be run like any other power plant. In fact, these new nuclear power plants are, in the words of one nuclear expert, "extremely complex, high-tech systems, perhaps to the point where the human mind has difficulty in handling them." Detroit Edison's nonchalant attitude caused the Nuclear Regulatory Commission to scrutinize Fermi 2's design and operations even more closely, putting it on the "troubled plant" list and sometimes shutting it down. Under current management, Fermi 2 has had a large number of trouble-free days and been removed from the list. Today it supplies 10 per cent of Detroit Edison's electricity.

The visitor center tours combine a film on how nuclear energy is produced, a tour of the facility (some adults-only tours include the protected area where the turbine generator produces electricity), and lots of chances for questions-and-answers with coordinator Susan Webster, a former Navy reactor operator and Fermi 2 technician. Not surprisingly, the tour emphasizes safety and environmental issues. There's a scale model of Fermi 2's drywell or primary containment system.

Manufacturers Market Place

14500 La Plaisance at I-75 (exit 11), 2 1/2 miles southeast of downtown Monroe. Mon-Sat 10-9, Sun 11-7. For information: (616) 728-5170.

The parking lot of this nautical-themed 38-store outlet mall is usually full, with lots of buses and out-of-state license plates. But there aren't nearly as many bargains here as you might think. Its discounts of 30 to 70 per cent seem almost standard these days. Well organized and slick, most of the stores here seem sterile and exude little of the bargain-basement promise of grubbier, more male-oriented outlets like the Whoopee Bowl in Clarkston or Ginsberg's Surplus City in Jackson, where you can occasionally find incredible bargains and truly wierd stuff.

This Manufacturers Market Place, somewhat smaller than its sister in Birch Run near Frankenmuth, is more comparable to the new one in Holland. The manager-developers of them all are the Horizons Group of Muskegon, and all feature a food court and candy and snack shops. Tenant stores here include **Harve Benard**, **Van Heusen**, **Maidenform**, **Leggs/Hanes/Bali**, **Bass** and **Mushrooms** shoes, **Sneakers 'n Cleats**, **American Tourister**, **Toy Liquidators**, **Corning/Revere**, **Sportsland USA**, and **Salem China Factory Outlet**. Locals we talked to noted as places with especially good deals **Carter's Childrenswear**, **Wearever's Kitchen Collection** (great on kitchen gadgets), **Socks Galore**, **The Paper Factory** (giftwrap and school supplies), and the large **Westpoint Pepperell** store (which opens at 9 a.m. and is the only one in Michigan).

RESTAURANTS

Monroe Inn ★★

14493 S. Telegraph south of Dunbar, west side of road. (313) 241-6580. Fri & Sat evenings 5-8, sometimes other evenings, too. Call first. Full bar. Checks.

If you're fascinated by remnants of the past, this delightful restaurant is well worth a trip while it's still open. A roadhouse, it was built just before the Great Crash of 1929, and is run by the founders' delightful daughters. They are keeping it open "on a limited basis," mostly serving friends, until they are able to consummate a satisfactory sale. From the outside the place has a slightly spooky feel, as if caught in a time warp. The neon sign is off (birds created problems with it), and maintenance has been deferred. It is indeed in a time warp — somewhere in the 1950s, but not the 1950s popular teen culture, rather the sophisticated but unpretentious 1950s of Irma Rombauer and *The Joy of Cooking*.

The decor is simple and serene, the presentations striking, the service gracious, the food uniformly excellent. The menu is short: breaded pickerel ($8.95) and sirloin steak ($9.50). Both include a fresh fruit cup, roll, and salad. Dessert (extra) is a mint ice cream parfait. Don't think of hurrying. The menu warns:

> "If you are in a HURRY, don't waste your time in a good restaurant. A Beanery will do as well. An ORCHARD CANNOT BE GROWN OVERNIGHT, neither a culinary masterpiece be produced in five minutes."

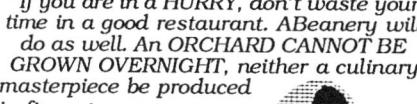

Detroit Beach Restaurant ★

2630 N. Dixie Hwy. (north of I-75 exit 15, past Sterling State Park, at the entrance to Detroit Beach subdivision). (313) 289-9865. Tues-Sun 11 a.m.-1 a.m., Fri & Sat til 3 a.m., Mon closed. Beer & wine. No credit cards.

Free Press reviewer Molly Abraham calls this 25-year-old family-run Italian restaurant "a genuine find." The setting isn't fancy. (Joe's French-Italian Inn just up the road is Monroe's popular place for Italian food with atmosphere, booze, and credit cards.) But everything here is made on the premises, and, according to Joe Conte, one of the four siblings who now own and run the restaurant, you get "a ton of food for the price." Low prices reflect low overhead; the Contes have never advertised. Pizza is a mainstay, with the homemade tomato sauce that appears in nearly every dish and a huge variety of toppings. Pizzas begin at $2.70 for a 12" plain cheese pizza and $5.10 for 16". But the place is also known for a popular mostaccioli casserole ($4.65) and for homestyle Italian specialties like gnocchi (potato dumplings in tomato sauce) and veal ($7.45 for veal parmesan, $9.75 for pan-fried scallopini in a mushroom-wine sauce). All entrees include salad, crusty homemade bread, and bread sticks.

Kennon's Restaurant

33 E. Front St. (313) 242-9590. Mon-Sat 11-9, Fri & Sat until 10. Full bar. Visa, MasterCard, AmExpress.

Kennon's, a newish restaurant in a 19th-century downtown storefront, offers the best views and most sophisticated menu items in a town that embraces new ideas slowly. The rear dining room looks out onto the broad River Raisin and the two attractive downtown bridges; the lower-level patio is at the new downtown Riverwalk. Lunch selections run from $3.25 for a chicken salad sandwich with a cup of soup (bread and soups are all homemade here) and $4 for a marinated grilled chicken with fries, slaw, or soup, to $6 for chicken pasta with artichokes and mushrooms and $7 for lake perch with salad and rice pilaf. Dinner menu favorites (all with salad and potato or rice) cover all the bases, with seafood and veal selections, BBQ ribs ($8.50 a half slab), a 14-ounce New York strip steak for $9.95, and shrimp and chicken linguine for $9.95.

Dessert here would make a nice stop for a walking tour of historic Monroe. Kentucky pie, hot fudge cream puffs, and carrot cake ($2.25-$2.50) are popular selections.

Reasonably priced Kennon's stands out in food and atmosphere when compared with other Monroe restaurants of its kind.

Coney Island Lunch

4 W. Front St. (313) 241-4904. Mon-Sat 8-3. No alcohol or credit cards.

Standard diner fare (burgers, eggs, soup, and a good $1.25 coney island) are served in a vintage grill that's a downtown landmark. The old wood booths have classic Seeburg Wall-O-Matic jukebox selectors.

LODGINGS

Cross-Country Inn
(313) 289-2330.
1900 Welcome Way. I-75 to N. Dixie Hwy. (exit 15), east 1/4 mile, left onto Welcome Way (on left).
120 rooms, 2 floors. $34.27 single, $43.63 double. Outside heated pool. Game room. Movie Channel. & ESPN. Adjacent Bob Evans restaurant.

Day's Inn
(313) 289-4000.
1440 N. Dixie Hwy. I-75 to Dixie Hwy. (exit 15), southeast of intersection.
115 rooms, 2 floors. $35.95 single; $54 double. Indoor pool, sauna, whirlpool, game room. HBO & ESPN. Restaurant & lounge.

Holiday Inn
(313) 242-6000. (800) HOLIDAY.
1225 Dixie Hwy. Take I-75 to Dixie Hwy. (exit 15), northeast of intersection.
127 rooms, 4 floors. $50 single; $60 double. Weekends $39 (available only with reservations through 800 number). Large indoor pool, sauna, game room. Restaurant and lounge. Dinner theater. Showtime & ESPN.

Ypsilanti

Ypsilanti is the third-oldest town in Michigan, after Detroit and Monroe. The city of 24,000 has many fine old mansions and a beautiful riverside park. The scenic Huron River bisects Ypsilanti north and south. There are lots of ingredients here for a delightful city, but Ypsilanti is still recovering from the traumatic disruption which occurred half a century ago when the huge Ford Willow Run bomber plant was built on its eastern edge. The sudden arrival of tens of thousands of mostly poor, rural Southerners to work in the bomber plant created housing and social problems still visible today.

Before World War II this was a quiet, uncommonly beautiful small city of 12,000. The first teachers' college west of the Alleghenies located here in 1852. Now called **Eastern Michigan University**, the old Michigan Normal College has become a thriving state university.

Ypsilanti was a trading post when first settled back in 1809. The town was platted in 1825 by Detroit's flamboyant, rum-guzzling Judge Augustus Woodward and his associates. Woodward was prone to the arcane and complex. It was he who designed Detroit's cobweb street layout of 1806 and christened the new University of Michigan the *Catholepistemiad*. The eccentric judge shrugged off the more ordinary names of Waterville or Palmyra suggested by others for the new town and

For information about events, including the Gus Macker 3-on-3 Basketball Tournament in May, the Frog Island Zydeco, Blues, and Jazz Festival in June, Drum Corps North in July, and the big Ypsilanti Heritage Festival in August, contact the Ypsilanti Conference and Visitors' Bureau, 125 N. Huron, Ypsilanti, MI 48197.

(313) 482-4920.

This 1880s engraving of the Forest Ave. Sanitarium at 42 Forest evokes the settled 19th-century charm Ypsilanti once had, back when prosperous small-town industrialists built their stately homes and students at the "Normal" were serious young women aspiring to be teachers. That placidity vanished when the town was successively invaded by bomber plant workers and floods of post-war college students with cars.

named it after the contemporary Greek general who was then a hero in the battle for Greek independence against the Turks. Outsiders often incorrectly pronounce the city's name "YIP-si-lan-tee." "IP-si-lan-tee" is correct, and "Ypsi" is its common nickname.

Strategically sited

From the start, the little town had two major strategic advantages. First, it was located on the old Sauk Indian trail which became the Chicago Road connecting Detroit and Chicago. (Today that road is U.S. 12.) Secondly, Ypsilanti benefitted from being on the Huron River. Pole boats could travel up it all the way from Lake Erie to the new town. More importantly, the Huron provided consistent water power, which was immediately harnessed, first for lumber mills, then for flour and woolen mills. Quickly the town became an outfitting site for settlers pouring into the region.

In 1849 the city outbid Niles, Jackson, and Marshall for the new state teachers' college, which remains a major part of the community's economy. By 1890 four paper mills lined the Huron in Ypsilanti. **Peninsular Paper** at 1000 North Huron still operates. Founded in 1867, this paper mill prospered by supplying newsprint to the *Chicago Tribune*. When that contract gave out, the mill converted to making paper for books and pamphlets. It survives to this day by occupying the highly specialized niche of manufacturing a variety of colored papers used for such things as the end leaves of fine books. The mill was bought in 1974 by the Curtis Paper Division of James River Corporation.

"The real McCoy"

Like many Michigan towns in the 19th century, Ypsilanti capitalized on the vogue in therapeutic mineral baths and boasted several spas. Nationwide, the town was probably best known for the long john underwear produced in the woolen mill and sold in great quantities all over the country. Its most famous resident was a black man named Elijah McCoy. The son of a freed slave who was a cigar maker, McCoy learned engineering in Scotland in the 1860s and eventually patented over 60 inventions. His lubricating cup for steam engines was so venerated, the story goes, that buyers would ask, "Is this the real McCoy?,' thus perhaps introducing that well-known phrase into the vernacular.

A more visually conspicuous mark was left by the inventor of trading stamps, S & H Green Stamp magnate Shelley Byron Hutchinson. In 1902 he built a mansion of weirdly diverse architectural styles at **600 North River** south of Cross. It still gets stares from passers-by. Located in a neighborhood of modest homes, the 33-room house perches on a hilltop with

Surprise discovery
In 1905, Greek Prince Hohenhole, husband of Princess Ypsilanti, happened to be traveling across Michigan on the Michigan Central Railroad. It was then a local custom for children to pick flowers from the famed Ypsilanti depot gardens and give them to the ladies on trains stopping at the station. "The prince," wrote Ypsilanti historian Harvey Colburn, "attracted by this, inquired the name of the station. 'Ypsilanti!' Great excitement among the prince's party. The prince begged that the train be held five minutes, left the car, purchased picture postcards, addressed them to the princess and sent a note to the postmaster requesting that they be postmarked plainly."

The old 1889 water tower at the intersection of Washtenaw and Cross has long been an Ypsilanti landmark. Made of limestone and shingles, it stands 171 feet tall on the highest point in the region, providing a steady 50 pounds of water pressure. At its top is a quarter-million gallon metal container, still in use. It was once topped by a Victorian cupola, which blew off during a 1920s windstorm. Once a year, during Ypsi's Heritage Festival, the observation deck near the top is open to visitors. The view is spectacular.

three acres of grounds. It was built with an indoor swimming pool, elevator, two-story ballroom with orchestra loft, and a dining room patterned after the one in Kaiser Wilhelm's castle. The mansion is now occupied by **High Scope**, a nonprofit educational research and advocacy firm. Its research, documenting the considerable benefits of Head Start-type preschool enrichment programs for the disadvantaged, saved Head Start from the Reagan Administration's budget-cutting axe in the early 1980s.

Other prosperous Ypsilanti businessmen had earlier built their showy mansions along Huron Street closer to downtown. The district is quite a contrast to Ann Arbor's much more subdued 19th-century mansions built by frugal German businessmen and cultivated professors who lacked the exuberant ostentation of Ypsilanti's industrialists. Many Ypsilanti residents remain sensitive about living in the shadow of neighboring Ann Arbor, with its nationally known university and more affluent citizenry. Not without reason, Ann Arborites are viewed here as smug and condescending.

EMU's impressive growth

Ypsilanti has been greatly boosted in recent years by the surprising growth of **Eastern Michigan University** under the impressive leadership of its immediate past president, John Porter. The commuter-oriented campus extends from Washtenaw and Cross north to the river, on Ypsilanti's near west side. Enrollment is over 20,000. A big new business school downtown is expected to help revitalize the central city. Downtown is beginning to recapture some of its more pleasing historic look as 1950s-style metal grilles come down to reveal original 19th-century facades. One building which apparently will keep its gaudy metal attached front is the City Hall, surely one of the Midwest's ugliest city halls. Unfortunately the previous occupant, a bank, removed the fine gables and other architectural details, leaving little more to behold under the metal mask than a blank wall.

Auto town

Despite the big university and the 4,000-employee St. Joseph Mercy Hospital just northwest of town, Ypsilanti's economy is largely dominated by the automobile industry. In addition to a variety of sizable auto parts manufacturers in the vicinity, there are three huge auto plants. The biggest is GM's Hydra-Matic Plant at the old Willow Run facility, the region's biggest employer with 9,700 workers. Adjacent to it is a plant that makes Chevrolet Caprices and employs some 4,000. Inside Ypsi proper and separated from Ford Lake by I-94 is a Ford plant employing about 5,400 workers who make electric components.

These auto plants are a legacy of the giant Willow Run bomber plant built in 1941. Until then Ypsilanti had been a quiet city of just over 10,000. Because of the severe labor shortage caused by the war, Southerners were vigorously recruited from Kentucky, Tennessee, and northern Alabama to supply the over 40,000 workers needed for the plant. They came up through Cincinnati on what has long been known as the "Dixie Highway." Their trials and tribulations were movingly told in Harriet Arnow's highly acclaimed novel, *The Dollmaker*. "Ypsi-tucky" is the name still sometimes applied to the east part of Ypsilanti Township, populated by people with roots in eastern Kentucky. It has the highest concentration of white Southerners in the state. The heart of Ypsi-tucky stretches from Emerick Road to the west to Van Buren to the east just south of I-94.

Ypsilanti's population of 24,000 hasn't changed much from the 1950s, so it has come to be dwarfed by surrounding Ypsilanti Township, with almost twice the population of the city and over seven times the area.

The curse of one-way thoroughfares

Like many smaller Michigan cities, Ypsilanti bears the scars of the auto-oriented 1950s and 1960s, when major arteries in the central area were converted into hectic one-way thoroughfares. These changes have introjected a highway-like pace in the central city. Cross Street across from EMU, for example, feels like a

Father of the innovative Tucker automobile and hero of Francis Ford Coppola's recent movie, Preston Tucker lived in the big white house at 110 North Park, just north of Michigan Ave., three blocks east of the Huron River. As owner of the Ypsilanti Machine Tool Co. on Grove St. behind his house, he built a remote gun turret for the Army here, in addition to racing Indy cars and customizing automobiles.

four-lane freeway, providing no parking and creating a psychological barrier between the campus and the retail district which serves it. Equally inhospitable is the potentially inviting drive along Huron Street in front of the city's fine old homes along the Huron River. Today it is also a one-way, fast-paced thoroughfare.

POINTS OF INTEREST

Huron Street Historic Buildings

North Huron between Michigan Ave. and Cross.

Ypsilanti is blessed with lots of fine 19th-century houses. Many on North Huron back up on the scenic Huron River. Here are a selected few:

◆ **Quirk Mansion** (1860) *300 N. Huron.* Built by a prominent banker and paper magnate, this house with its four-story tower and patterned slate mansard roof is one of the city's most ostentatious. Nancy Quirk Williams, Gov. Soapy Williams' wife, grew up here. Today it houses offices.

◆ **Ladies' Library Building** (pre-1860) *130 N. Huron.* This Greek Revival house was donated in 1890 to the Ladies' Library group for its growing book collection. It is now used for offices.

◆ **Ballard-Breakey House** *125 N. Huron.* The front portion of this austere Greek Revival house may have been built as early as 1830, making it one of the oldest houses in the state.

◆ **Saint Luke's Episcopal Church** (1858) *120 N. Huron.* This Gothic Revival church no longer has its big tower, once a landmark. The tower's bell is now in a courtyard north of the sanctuary.

◆ **Watling Dental Office** *119 N. Huron.* This distinctive, small sandstone building was built before the turn of the century by the first dean of the University of Michigan Dental School, who lived in the 1865 Italian villa next door.

◆ **Cornwell-Beyer Mansion** (1880s) *203 N. Huron.* Built by a paper mill magnate, this was said to have once been the biggest house between Chicago and Detroit.

◆ **Miles House** (1845) *219 N. Huron.* This is the city's earliest cobblestone house, a type of construction imported from western New York by early local settlers. The Queen Anne roof, dormers, and decorative woodwork were later additions. Local legend says the Underground Railroad used a tunnel here that went to the river.

◆ **Towner House** (1830s) *303 N. Huron.* Another impressive Greek Revival building. The Gothic porch decorations were added later. It is now a children's museum, open during the Heritage Festival.

> Other streets for beautiful old houses are just west of Huron and south of Cross; South Huron just south of downtown; and North River and East Cross east of the river.

Ypsilanti Historical Museum

220 N. Huron St. near Cross. (313) 482-4990. Thurs, Sat, Sun 2-4. Free.

Housed in one of the impressive mansions perched above the banks of the Huron, this museum has unfor-

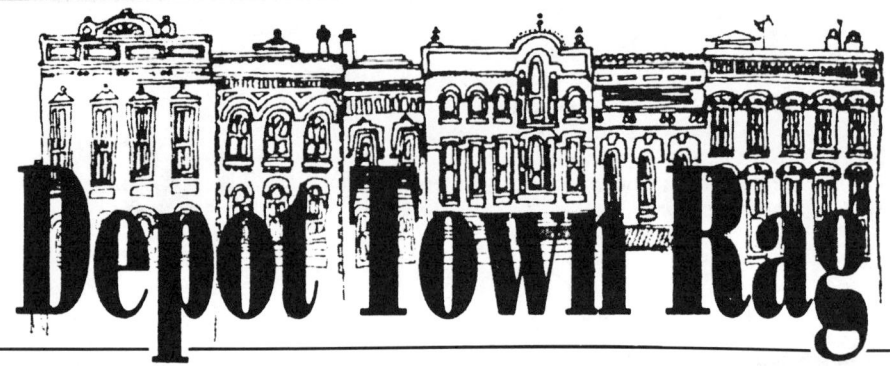

tunately used much of its space to recreate the familiar Victorian upper-middle-class household. It's hard to get excited about another mock-Victorian home.

Fortunately, the museum also has an "Ypsilanti Room," where an amusing assortment of local artifacts is on display. You can see the famous long underwear that gave the city a national reputation in the 19th century, accompanied by a poster touting the woolen garments as "the perfect underwear for progressive people" and revealing the jingle:

*Never rip and never tear,
Ypsilanti underwear*

Other display cases are devoted to Civil War paraphernalia, including swords, medals, rifles, photos, and World War I memorabilia.

Ypsilanti is where two Indian trails, the Sauk and the Potawatami, intersect to cross the Huron River. So it's no surprise that many arrowheads were found near here. One avid collector of long ago, Jacob Thumm, who started when young, has left the museum a splendidly rich assortment of the flint projectiles.

The museum has happily found room to include some of the more offbeat items that can make local museums diverting. Upstairs there are the gloves worn by a local lady, Nora Babbitt, when she shook hands with Mrs. Tom Thumb. And there are remnants of a pedal-driven dentist's drill which makes one wince just to look at it. A majestic old Tiffany window from the library building down the block leans against the wall of a

"The Depot Town Rag," an unusually meaty neighborhood newsletter, is a good introduction to area businesses and the active historic preservation scene. Pick it up monthly at Depot Town stores.

front room upstairs. And a back room is full of old dolls. Kids are said to be most intrigued by the large doll house a man made from crates for his daughter during the Depression.

Depot Town

East Cross St. between the Huron River and River St. Many stores open Sundays 11-5; some antique shops are closed Mondays and Tuesdays.

This architecturally interesting 19th-century commercial district features some popular bars, several antique and resale shops, a food co-op, and other attractions. Depot Town actually became for a while the city's main downtown after the railroad arrived in 1838 from Detroit. It prospered as a regional shipping center. The passenger and freight depots are still here. The **Michigan Central passenger station** on North River Street, now one story high, is a pale shadow of the ornate three-story building and tower built here in 1863. It was then said to be the finest station between Detroit and Chicago. A fire and train collision have reduced it to its present humble state.

Across the tracks, the **freight depot** is a long Italianate structure from 1875. It is now headquarters for **Ypsilanti's Farmers' Market**, open Wednesdays and Saturdays from 8 a.m. to 3 p.m.

Grassroot efforts have dramatically renovated the 1850s and 1860s brick storefronts along Cross Street. Many of the upper stories are now apartments, and the area, with its own sprightly neighborhood publication, has a sense of camaraderie. The 1859 **Follett House** at 17-25 E. Cross was known as one of the finest hotels on the Michigan Central line. The third-floor ballroom hosted Buffalo Bill, Tom Thumb, and other 19th-century celebrities.

The **Side Track** at 56 East Cross is a very popular watering place, with excellent hamburgers and a massive back bar. **Aubree's Saloon** across the street features live Detroit blues on weekends. The **Old Town Restaurant** at 38 East Cross is also popular. Around the corner of North River Street is the **Ypsilanti Food Co-op** (Mon-Fri 10-7; Wed 'til 9; Sat 9-7; Sun 12-5) where bulk natural foods can be found. Yet to be renovated on the very east end of Depot Town is the **Thompson Block**. Built about 1860, it was a barracks during the Civil War.

Riverside & Frog Island Parks

Southwest and north of Cross St. Bridge.

The fine homes above Huron Street once had gardens extending down to the river. The city has acquired 16 acres of these old backyards to create Riverside Park. It has a pavilion, a dock extending into the water, play equipment for kids, and picnic tables. Connected by footbridge is Frog Island Park, which was a real island in the 1800s when a millrace separated it from East Ypsilanti. This was the point of the river's greatest fall in the area, and thus an important millsite. Today the flat, grassy park has a track, soccer field, and amphitheater. The popular Frog Island Zydeco, Jazz, and Blues festival is held here every June.

Miller Motors ★★

100 N. Cross Street at River (313) 482-5200. Mon-Sat 9-5:30 (except for lunchtime). Call first to make sure it's open.

In front of this old Hudson auto dealership is the vintage HUDSON sign, and in the show window is a spiffy-looking 1947 Hudson coupe. This isn't a mirage — or a museum. It's the business of Jack Miller, whose father started selling Hudsons here in 1933. Miller still trades in Hudsons, though production ceased in 1957, and his place is one of the best in the world to get unused Hudson parts, still in their original cartons, some half a century old. They have been bought up from old warehouses around the country.

In the service area behind the sales room are an array of Hudson cars, part of Miller's private collection. These include a 1953 Hudson Hornet, the 1946 Hudson pickup Miller drives to work in the summer, a 1946 Hudson convertible, and 1956 pink and grey Hudson which Miller says "could be bought." In an adjoining area Miller repairs old Hudsons. He also sells Hudson memorabilia as well as die cast scale models of vintage cars and tractors ($5.75 and up).

Miller Motors in 1946, with two new Hudson coupes in front. Miller Motors remains in business, much as it looked in this photo, despite the fact that Hudsons haven't been made for over 30 years.

Hudson aficionados often stop by to chat. Miller affably shares his wealth of knowledge about Hudsons with visitors. He explains that they were first manufactured in 1909 and named after financial backer J. L. Hudson, the Detroit department store magnate. The Hudson name was sullied in the mid-1950s when Nash took over the firm and turned out what some consider gaudy imitations of the real thing. But the Hudsons of the 1940s were extraordinary automobiles, Miller points out, fast but stable highway cars engineered and built extremely well.

Looking around the showroom is a treat in itself. The walls are covered with old Hudson promotional posters, as well as photos and other antique artifacts. Visitors are welcome to browse. And you can also kick the tires of what a *Car and Driver* article called the "vaguely eccentric" array of used cars other than Hudsons.

Nationally-known Materials Unlimited and Schmidt's top the list of 12 Ypsilanti-area antiques dealers — in Depot Town (mostly open Wed.-Sun.), on Michigan Ave. downtown, and out by Schmidt's west of town. On the low, low end, a wild assortment of stuff can be found weekends at the Giant Flea Market (214 E. Michigan at Park).

Materials Unlimited ★★
2 W. Michigan Ave. (313) 483-6980. 7 days a week 10-5.

This is one of the finest places in the Midwest to find exceptionally attractive architectural artifacts, both new and old: beautiful old stained glass windows, ornate brass door hinges, carved oak column capitals, 19th-century building ornaments, etc. Proprietor Reynold Lowe also sells some antique furniture here, as well as eccentric items such as wooden masks and cigar store Indians. For those with an interest in architecture and historic restorations these three spacious floor are great fun to browse through.

Schmidt's Antique Shop/Gallery ★★
5138 Michigan, 4 miles west of Ypsilanti. From US 23, take Mich. Ave. exit east. From I-94, take Mich Ave. exit west. Schmidt's is south of I-94, just west of Morgan Rd. (313) 434-2660. Mon-Sat 9-5, Sun 11-5. Auction: first Saturday of month, 11 a.m.

This rather dowdy-looking establishment with the cement block showroom is actually one of the largest dealers in English antiques in the country. It has 16,000 square feet of antiques, in many places stacked on top of each other to the ceiling. Some 75 per cent of the items are English, and most of the rest are American. Much of the furniture is middle-quality, in Chippendale, Hepplewhite, Sheraton, Empire styles of tables, chairs, sideboards, etc. Today wardrobes are especially popular, to hide TVs. Decorative items are also in abundance: candlesticks, crystal, pottery, Wedgwood teapots, figurines, chandeliers, and vases.

A serious buyer would do well to negotiate rather than pay the full price on floor items. The monthly auctions are consignment items (often estate sales) and sometimes stick to a given theme such as pewter or maps. Call ahead to find out what's coming up. It's a spectacle to attend one of the auctions just to take in the crowd, the auctioneers' humor, and some of the weird items that go up for bids.

Yankee Air Force Museum/ Willow Run Airport ★★

Willow Run Airport, off Beck Rd. Take exit 190 from I-94. (313) 483-4030. Tues-Sat 10-4, Sun 12-4. $3/adult, $2.50 seniors & students, $1 children 3-12.

Part of the fun of visiting this military air museum is roaming around Willow Run Airport, a remarkable place built in the early 1940s to test the long-range B-24 bombers built in the huge adjacent factory. Today the airport has a rather seedy, almost disreputable look to it. The carcasses of old planes are strewn around the fringes of the giant field, some partially devoured for spare parts. Big old four-engine propeller-powered cargo planes still lumber into the air from the long runways. Many rush critically needed parts to keep auto plants around the country running.

Just west of the field is the gigantic **GM Hydra-Matic Plant**, so big that specially-made superhighways funnel workers in and out of the complex. This was initially the famous **Willow Run Bomber Plant**. Built by Ford Motor Company in 1941, it was the largest building ever built, covering 70 acres and sprawling for 3/4 of a mile. The big plant proved to be a big boost to American morale after Pearl Harbor. Architect Albert Kahn built it in an L-shape to keep it from spilling into Wayne County, which Ford considered unfriendly Democratic territory with higher taxes.

When the giant facility was being planned, it wasn't clear whether or not the Allies would lose Great Britain to the Nazis, so the plant had to make quickly thousands of bombers big enough to fly missions across the Atlantic to reach Germany. The factory was supposed to turn out one of these B-24 "Liberators" an hour, but production difficulties seriously delayed output. This goal wasn't achieved until 1943. Between 1942 and 1945, some 42,000 women and men worked in the plant, including midgets especially hired to fit parts in the nose section and other hard-to-reach areas. By the time the bomber plant closed in June of 1945, 8,685 Liberators had been produced.

After the war, the plant was bought by the new Kaiser-Frazer auto company. After that company failed, GM purchased the plant in 1953 to make automatic transmissions. The big Hydra-Matic plant has actually been expanded over the years to 4.8 million square feet, making it one of the very largest plants under one roof in the world. It now employs about 9,300 workers. Next door is a Chevrolet assembly plant which makes Caprices. Meanwhile, the adjoining airport itself became one of Detroit's major commercial air facilities and remained so until Metropolitan Airport was expanded in the 1960s.

On the airport's other side, off Beck Road, is the **Yankee Air Force Museum**, housed in a cavernous 1941 hangar. It has the interestingly scruffy atmosphere of a bootstrap creation of dedicated fans. Although the museum was only organized in 1981, the huge hangar is already crowded with aging military aircraft. Some are in the process of being renovated. A common sight on a weekend is an elderly volunteer mechanic, no doubt an Air Corps veteran, working on an engine.

Some of the 28 planes here already fly. One is a 1945 C-47, the cargo version of the classic DC-3. Another is a 1943 B-25 gunship that saw action in Europe, providing close ground support and flying 90 bombing missions. This is the same model used in the Doolittle raid of Japan. Museum members are hard at work on a classic B-17 "Flying Fortress," the Allies' largest heavy bomber during most of World War II. Also on display in the hangar is another classic military aircraft: the F-86 Sabre jet, a major fighter during the Korean War.

On the second floor of the hangar complex are rooms with memorabilia on display: Air Force patches and medals, old newspaper clippings, paintings and photos of planes in action, engines, shells, radios, flights suits, goggles, and so on. One room features women in aviation; another is devoted to material on the giant Ford bomber plant itself, with photos of the assembly line.

Just outside the hangar are even more planes, highlighted by the hulking, rather ominous presence of a camouflaged B-52 bomber. Some museum planes are flown here three times a year: at its big Memorial Day weekend air show, at a June air show, and on Founders' Day in mid-September.

The **gift shop** is well stocked with books on aviation, toy and model airplanes, postcards, T-shirts, and other souvenirs.

RESTAURANTS

Haab's
18 W. Michigan between Huron and the river downtown. From I-94, take exit 183. (313) 483-8200. Sun-Thurs 11-9, Fri & Sat 11-10. Full bar. Major credit cards. Lunch $3-$8; dinner $6-$16.75.

For decades Haab's has drawn customers from Ann Arbor and elsewhere. It's known for prime rib ($8.45 at lunch; $14.95 at dinner), and New York strip steaks are also popular (12 oz. for $13.45). Dinners include super salad, starch, bread loaf. Lunches and sandwiches include one side. Haab's is also a longtime franchisee of "chicken-in-the-rough," a specially prepared fried chicken that comes with french fries, biscuit, cole slaw ($7.45). Fresh catch and 18 seafood dishers are also available.

Old China
505 W. Cross, just south of Eastern Michigan campus. (313) 482-8333. Tues-Thurs 11:30-9:30, Fri 11:30-11, Sat 4:30-11, Sun 4:30-9:30. No alcohol; bring your own. Visa, MasterCard, AmExpress. Entrees $3.25-$5 (lunch); $7-$16 (dinner).

A plain Chinese restaurant, the Old China has long been a favorite of many in the Ann Arbor-Ypsilanti area. The sizzling rice soup ($6.75) is great. It has shrimp, chicken, abalone, and fresh vegetables, but it's the distinctive almost-burnt rice crust that really makes it delicious.

Sidetrack
56 E. Cross at River in Depot Town. (313) 483-1035. 11 a.m.-1 a.m. Mon-Sat. Full bar.

One of those old saloons that still has a massive Victorian back bar and an unpretentious, neighborly atmosphere, the Sidetrack does more business with its tasty, low-priced food than with drinks. It's known for excellent hamburgers ($2.50) but the soups, made from scratch daily, are also good.

LODGINGS

Radisson Resort
(313) 487-2000. 1275 Whittaker Rd. south of downtown and I-94, on Ford Lake. Whittaker is the southerly extension of Huron St. I-94 to Huron (exit 183), straight past light to Whittaker, left 1/2 mile, on left. 236 rooms, 8 floors. $115-135 weekdays, $89 weekend depending on availability. Indoor pool. Golf course (fee), running and biking trail. Showtime and pay movies ($6.35).

Ann Arbor

A city of 110,000, Ann Arbor has long had a bigger national presence than its numbers would suggest. As home to one of the Midwest's few top-echelon universities, the University of Michigan draws students and faculty from all over the country and world. At the same time Michigan has for decades fielded top-ranked football (and more recently basketball) teams, giving Ann Arbor name recognition to sports fans across the country.

U-M students account for a third of the population here. Their arrogant jaywalking habits pose a severe test in self-control for even the most mild-mannered motorists. The U-M, together with its enormous hospital complex, is far and away Ann Arbor's biggest employer. But this overgrown college town is increasingly taking on a glittery veneer of high-tech hustle as well.

Main Street and downtown Ann Arbor, long dominated by conservative German merchants, is now full of fashionable new restaurants, bars, and shops. Traffic these days is intense throughout the day, and streetside parking is scarce.

A town of hills and trees

Ann Arbor was founded in 1824 as a part of that great early 19th-century settlement surge by land-hungry Easterners from New York and New England. The first crude cabins actually huddled around Allen's Creek, a tributary of the pretty Huron River. The little creek is now covered over, in effect a storm sewer, following the dip that separates downtown from the city's west side.

Part of the city's attractiveness is due to its hilly landscape, unusual for Michigan. It results from two glacial moraines intersecting in the vicinity. Even more important is the number of trees. They grow so densely here that most parts of Ann Arbor look like a forest from the air. The city has long had a full-time forester whose department both plants and tends to ailing trees. A substantial fund left by a thoughtful citizen, Elizabeth Dean, has paid for the planting of thousands of trees over the years.

In the 19th century, a German town

Earlier than in most Midwestern cities, Germans settled in Ann Arbor. They migrated beginning in the early 1830s, from the southwestern part of Germany called Swabia. It was a backward region, like most of Germany then. Germans came to dominate Ann Arbor retailing, banking, and building trades until recent

Parkers beware!
With the most vigilant and well-staffed crew of parking enforcers in the state, don't be surprised if you find a ticket on your car even if your meter has only expired for a couple of minutes. Bring plenty of quarters!

The Ann Arbor Antiques Market attracts buyers from all over the Midwest. Organizer Margaret Brusher selects quality dealers (350 each month) to appeal to all budgets. April through November, usually the 3rd Sunday of the month, from 5 a.m.-4 p.m. (April is the 4th Sunday, November the 2nd.) At the Saline Fairgrounds, 5055 Ann Arbor-Saline Rd. at Pleasant Lake Rd. $3/person.

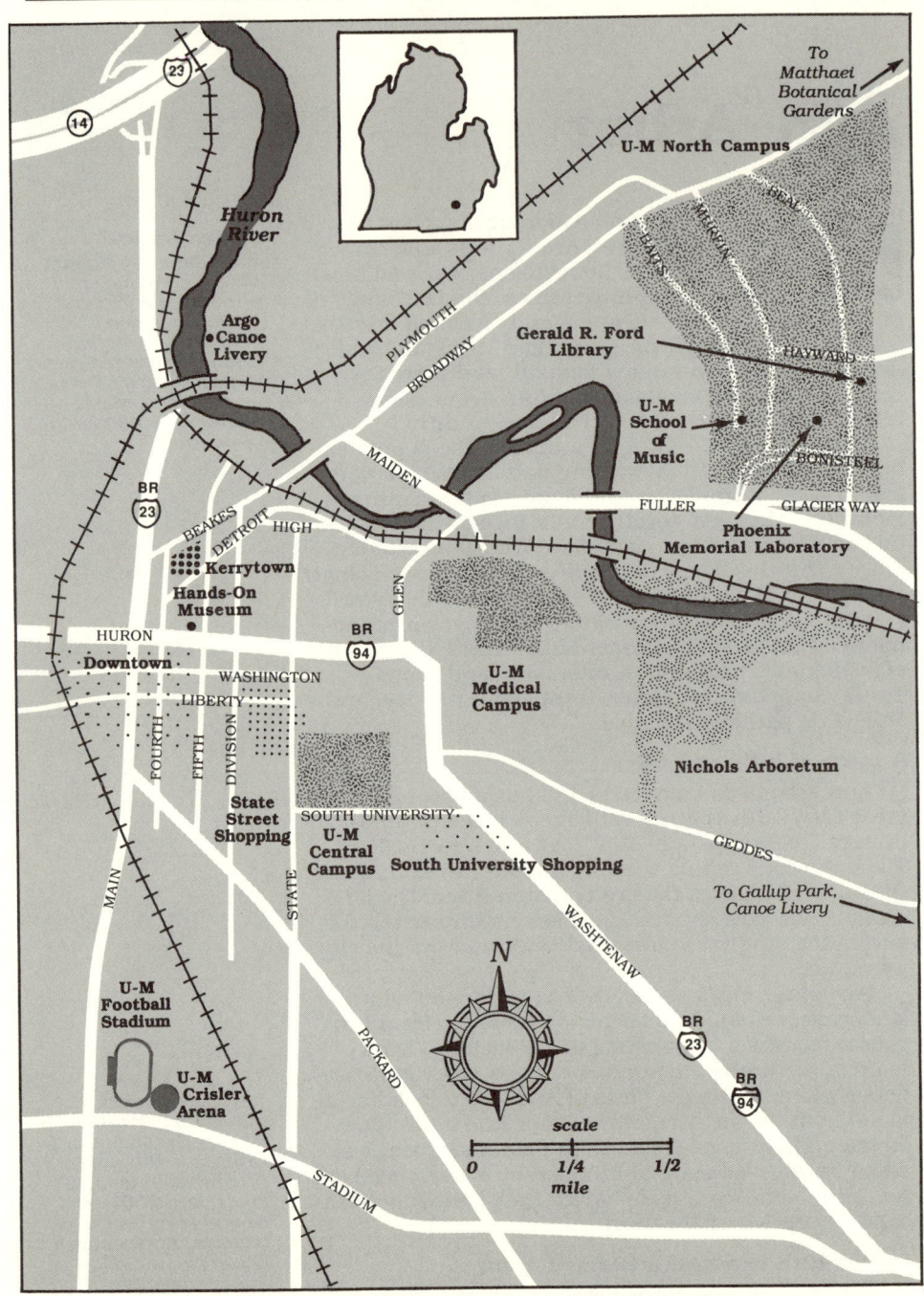

· CENTRAL ANN ARBOR ·

years. Work-oriented, these German families routinely used to take their sons out of school and put them to work after their confirmations at age 14. This attitude toward higher education, shaped by German respect for trades and crafts, continued up into the 1920s. It accentuated the town-gown split college towns like Ann Arbor are already prone to develop. Drawn together by their love of music, Germans and academics did join over a hundred years ago to form the University Musical Society. It today provides a cultural smorgasbord of concerts by nationally and internationally known performers.

Skilled German workmen settled predominantly in what is now called the **Old West Side**, a modest neighborhood of two-story homes just west of downtown and south of Huron Street. Over the past decade it has a become popular, even trendy place for young Ann Arbor professionals to live, with plain two-story frame houses commanding prices of $100,000 to $150,000 and more. Simple houses that once sported tight-clipped evergreen shrubs and neat-as-a-pin lawns now have been expanded, landscaped, fenced, and repainted to attain a subtlety and visual richness their practical original owners never dreamed of. The Old West Side does live on at the **Washtenaw Dairy** at Ashley and Madison, a great neighborhood gathering place with excellent donuts and ice cream cones.

A surprising number of old German businesses are run by their founders' descendants. **Schlenker Hardware**, on West Liberty between Ashley and First, still serves up nuts and bolts from century-old cabinets, along with detailed how-to advice. **Vogel's Locks** at 113 West Washington, begun as a machine shop, also retains a 19th-century pace, as does the downtown's remaining work clothes shop, **Ehnis & Son** at 116 West Liberty, and **Ann Arbor Implement** in an old flour mill on South First. Two popular German restaurants, owned by different branches of the Metzger family, continue to thrive: the **Old German** at 120 West Washington and **Metzger's**, on East Washington near Fourth Avenue. They're good places to observe the

Ann Arbor's Old West Side offers visitors a chance to see just how much can be done renovating, expanding, and enhancing simple housing stock. The neighborhood west of downtown was built by and for German tradesmen and factory workers around the turn of the century.

*A free map of Ann Arbor and the U-M, in*cluding one-way streets and all university buildings, is available, along with a bimonthly events calendar and Visitor's Guide, from the Ann Arbor Convention and Visitors' Bureau, 211 E. Huron, Ann Arbor, MI 48104. (313) 995-2781.

hometown establishment. And the two biggest German churches, **Zion Lutheran** and **Bethlehem United** Church of Christ, are still among the largest in town.

Liberal, but . . .

Ann Arbor has had a reputation as a bastion of liberalism ever since the big student protests at the U-M in the 1960s. In 1961 Ann Arbor activists, including former *Michigan Daily* editor Tom Hayden, founded Students for a Democratic Society (S.D.S.). It soon became a key component in the New Left. Later in the 1960s, John Sinclair's White Panther Party moved into two big houses on Hill Street and launched a multifaceted assault on establishment culture that centered on drugs and rock music.

In national elections with high turnout among young voters, Ann Arbor has voted consistently for the more liberal of the presidential candidates in every election since 1960 and has elected liberal state officials like Perry Bullard and Lana Pollack. It has adopted a famously lenient $5 fine for marijuana offenders and passed one of the country's most lavish public transportation millages to support a superb bus system. Citizens are willing to spend lots of money on bike paths and parks, and Ann Arbor has been far more aggressive in building subsidized housing than other affluent cities.

In fact, however, the town is a lot less liberal than its image. Local elections have produced few Democratic mayors, even during the most activist phases of local politics in the 1960s and 1970s. Here, as in many places, the people who shape the community's image don't represent the populace at large. What actually has distinguished Ann Arbor politics in recent years is the vigor and vehemence with which savvy neighborhood groups rise up to fight nearby developments.

Today Ann Arbor has some of the most expensive housing in the state. Because of the limited number of university dorms, over half of all Ann Arborites live in apartments, and rental prices also have skyrocketed. Many residents who loved their town's laid-back, irreverent, casual flavor in the Seventies now bemoan the "Birminghamization" of Ann Arbor. They refer to what is disparagingly seen as the sterilely homogeneous and affluent atmosphere of that Detroit suburb. In the past few years, locally owned shops around campus have increasingly been replaced by chains as the cost for retail space escalates. Glitzy big office/condo developments and parking structures intrude on what was a comfortingly small-town cityscape. Another casualty of high rents has been nightspots with live contemporary music, which flourished in the 1970s.

Music and theater program information
The Ark. *To get on mailing list for bi-monthly calendar, send a postcard to The Ark, 637 1/2 S. Main, Ann Arbor, MI 48104.*
Michigan Theater, *home of the Ann Arbor Symphony, also sponsors series of drama, concerts, "serious fun," children's entertainment, and films (first-run, revivals, and reruns) on a new 70mm projection system. (313) 668-8480.*
Performance Network. *Call (313) 663-0681 weekdays for program information or to get on mailing list.*
University Musical Society. *(313) 764-2538.*
University of Michigan School of Music *(also includes dance and theater). Hotline: (313) 763-4726. For free bi-monthly subscription to Music at Michigan, write Luise Kienzle, Circulation office, 2309 Moore Bldg. University of Michigan, Ann Arbor, MI 48109 or call (313) 763-0965.*

The 1886 train station, now Chuck Muer's Gandy Dancer restaurant, is one of Ann Arbor's many handsome native fieldstone buildings, mostly 19th-century churches.

Robust downtown

Still, the downtown here is a picture of economic health compared to most other Michigan cities. A quarter of a century ago, Ann Arbor was virtually devoid of interesting new restaurants. Today Ann Arbor may well have more good restaurants per capita than any other Midwestern city. With its restaurants and bars, it has become such a magnet for people out on the town that downtown streets and the summertime sidewalk cafes on Main Street are lively until late at night.

Another attraction is entertainment. Through university-sponsored series, the world's very finest performers in classical music come to town regularly. Events at the top-caliber **School of Music**, mostly free, are an underexploited cultural treasure; tomorrow's stars may be performing here as students today. Free faculty concerts include nationally known performers. Jazz pianist Jim Dapogny and the multifaceted pianist/composer Bill Bolcom, winner of a Pulitzer Prize, teach there. Bolcom occasionally performs American popular songs with his wife, soprano Joan Morris, at local events. Student performances in drama, dance, and opera (all part of the School of Music) are of increasingly high quality.

Several university and private organizations sponsor film series, though the quality has fallen off in recent years and can't be compared to the Detroit Institute of Arts film series. **The Ark** is a nationally known center for folk performers, with acts almost every night. **Performance Network** stages frequent plays of social criticism, theatrically avant-garde, none conventional. And **Kerrytown Concert House** presents high-caliber classical music, jazz, and chamber theater in an intimate setting.

High tech's increasing presence

In recent years Ann Arbor has become an economic hotspot in the Midwest with a number of new high-tech facilities. An expensive, big new state-supported robotics center, the **Industrial Technology**

A train ride to Ann Arbor can really make sense. Parking is difficult here, and visitor destinations are concentrated in the pedestrian-oriented central city. Call Amtrak (1-800-872-7245) for rates and schedules, which suit day and overnight trips from Detroit and Dearborn and overnight trips from the west.

The Ann Arbor Art Fair is Ann Arbor's big event. It is Wednesday through Saturday in the third week of July (9 a.m.-9 p.m., 'til 5 on Saturday). Actually it's three fairs that take over the entire central city. One, the Ann Arbor Street Art Fair on South University is one of the top art fairs in the U.S. and constantly improving. For complete information, pick up guides at the fair itself. Call (313) 995-7281 for general visitor and parking information.

Instiltute, has been built on the university's North Campus. Funding to the university's once slumbering engineering school has been sharply increased. The most tangible manifestation of this trend is **Irwin Magnetics**, a highly successful manufacturer of hard disk drives for PCs. Other important high-tech centers in Ann Arbor include **Environmental Research Institute of Michigan**, a nationally eminent remote sensing firm once connected with the U-M, and the big research and development headquarters of **Warner-Lambert** pharmaceuticals.

Another important part of the Ann Arbor scene is the huge university medical complex, which includes a big hospital, medical school, and research facilities. In the late 1970s, as the once prominent but then aging U-M medical complex declined in national importance, a strategic decision was made to invest the hundreds of millions of dollars it would take to put it back in the forefront of medical research and practice. This very difficult goal has by and large been accomplished. The medical faculty has been upgraded, the facilities modernized, and, the new **University of Michigan Hospital** are packed with patients.

Events and exhibits in Ann Arbor
The critically annotated and most complete listing of everything from major concerts to free U-M lectures, nature walks, and organized bike rides is in the Ann Arbor Observer monthly city magazine, available at newsstands and paper boxes for $1.50 an issue, $14/year. (313) 769-3175.

POINTS OF INTEREST

Downtown ★★★
Between Huron and William from Ashley east to Division. Main and Liberty are the main shopping streets.

Ann Arbor has the most interestingly diverse downtown in the state. Within just a few square blocks there are lots of noteworthy shops, very good restaurants, and lively nightspots. Many traditional old German businesses such as the Ehnis & Son work clothes shop and Vogel's Locks are still here, giving historical continuity to the area. But gradually the old is giving way to the new, most poignantly, perhaps, in the case of the transformation of the beloved old Quality Bakery into the Quality Bar, with an upper-level deck costing $250,000.

Art Deco Design ★★
116 W. Washington. (313) 663-3326. Tues-Sat 11-6.

Nine-tenths of the artfully displayed Art Deco furniture, accessories, and jewelry here was made between 1925 and 1939, but select 1950s pieces add extra zing. Prices are reasonable, and reproductions are few and far between.

Del-Rio Bar ★★
122 W. Washington at Ashley. (313) 761-2530. Opens Mon-Fri at 11:30 a.m., Sat at noon, Sun at 5:30 p.m. Closing 1:45 a.m. daily.

A venerable outpost of Ann Arbor counterculture, this employee-run bar attracts all types with its hamburgers, vegetarian burritos and soups, and salads — all excellent. It's a popular place for listening to jazz Sundays from 5:30 to 9 p.m.

16 Hands ★
119 W. Washington. (313) 761-1110. Mon-Fri 11-6, Sat 10-6, also Fri evening 8:30-10.

Originally a consortium of 8 local craftspeople, this fine crafts shop now shows handmade jewelry, furniture and wood accessories, leather goods, weaving, blown glass, and other media by talented artists., mostly from southeast Michigan.

Bird of Paradise ★★
207 S. Ashley. (313) 662-8310. Sun-Thurs 6 p.m.-2 a.m. Fri & Sat from 5 p.m. Music starts at 9:15 or so except for a piano soloist at 5:30 Fri & Sat.

Bassist Ron Brooks's attractive jazz club features good Ann Arbor and Detroit-area jazz musicians seven nights a week, with very occasional national acts. There's a bar, and deli food available.

Hertler's
210 S. Ashley. (313) 662-1713. Mon-Sat 8-5:30.

This former feed barn and farm supply store was one of the first downtown stores to gentrify. You can still get bales of hay and seed in bulk here, but joining them now are Jotul stoves, birdhouses, upscale garden implements, and a large array of country-oriented gift items.

The Blind Pig ★
208 S. First St. (313) 996-8555. Upstairs space open with live music Mon-Sat 9 p.m.-2 a.m. Sun is women's night with a deejay and dance music. 8 Ball Saloon (in basement) open 1 p.m.-2 a.m. daily except for 3 p.m. Sun opening.

Good rock 'n' roll bands, along with some reggae and blues, play here six nights a week. But the current owner has banished the Pig's old, laid-back cafe atmosphere, along with the good soup and sandwiches, in favor of full-scale music club with a more hard-driving, party-time pursuit of fun.

Additional art galleries
Ann Arbor has a big variety of other galleries and art exhibit spaces, including the **Clay Gallery** in Nickels Arcade, the School of Art's **Slusser Gallery**, the internationally known stable of artists at the **Alice Simsar Gallery, Le Minotaure** gallery of current French art, and the home gallery of interesting regional artists at **Clare Spitler Works of Art**. Pick up a brochure on all major galleries at Selo/Shevel, 16 Hands, the Artful Exchange, or the Art Association. For a complete monthly exhibit guide, see the Ann Arbor Observer Galleries and Exhibits listing.

Downtown parking hints
Natives swear up and down about tight central-city parking but don't use the two big structures, which are safe and almost always not filled. The new structure entered from Ann and Ashley is attractive as well, with a glass-faced elevator offering an interesting view. The huge structure at Fourth and William is conveniently located at downtown's south edge. Hourly parking at both is metered (30¢/hour).

Ann Arbor Art Association ★
117 W. Liberty at Ashley. (313) 994-8004. Mon noon-5:30, Tues-Fri 10-5:30, Sat 10-5.

Ann Arbor's legacy from the crafts boom of the 60s is a large number of committed craftspeople who have polished and refined their work over the years. The gallery shop in this one-time carriage factory presents an interesting mix of accomplished local artists — largely painters, weavers, jewelers, printmakers. As the crafts scene has become slicker and more professional, much of the art here retains a less commercial sincerity that is refreshing.

In the attractive exhibition space opposite the shop are high-quality, interesting shows featuring mostly well-known area and regional artists.

Rider's Hobby Shop
115 W. Liberty. (313) 668-8950. Mon-Fri 10-8, Sat 10-6.

Next door to the wonderful West Side Book Shop (see "Books in Ann Arbor"), this, the original Rider's, remains remarkably well stocked with a full line of model trains and scenery; remote-control planes, cars, and boats; plastic kits; and one of the largest selections of strategic adventure and role-playing games around. It's worth a visit if only to gaze at the large model airplanes hanging from the ceiling.

The Conservatory ★★
111 W. Liberty. (313) 994-4443. Mon-Sat 10-6, Fri 'til 9 or later.

Products of good design, not gift fads, are the focus of this shop run by an architect and his jeweler wife. The ambience is delightfully serene. The eclectic assemblage of items ranges from the crisply contemporary to the old-fashioned and ethnic. It's known for unusual basketry, paper products and note cards (such as $21.50 bark-covered blank books), jewelry, and decorative accessories like ornate wax seals ($6-$23).

Ehnis & Son
116 W. Liberty. (313) 663-4337. Mon-Sat 8-6.

This is a real working man's clothes store, descended from a harnessmaker who developed shoes as a sideline. Shelves of Red Wing boots and shoes are part of the old-time interior.

The Round Table
114 W. Liberty. (313) 761-3977. Mon-Fri 6:30-2, Sat 6:30-11.

Still holding its own amid a recent plethora of new ornate restaurants is this old Ann Arbor institution, where you still get two slices of storebought bread and two pats of "genuine margarine" with every meal. The decor is minimalist formica, but the $3.50 hot lunches are popular with all sorts of folks. At the back is a big round table, where the county's judges and other local patriarchs often dine.

Selo/Shevel Gallery ★★
329 S. Main. (313) 761-6263. Mon-Sat 10-6, except Thurs 'til 9 and Fri 'til 10.

The attractive space of this extraordinary crafts gallery is filled with a choice selection of handcrafted jewelry, blown glass, wood boxes and the like by many of America's leading craftspeople. African masks, sculpture, and textiles are highlights of the folk art here. Tucked into a front corner is **It Pays the Rent**, filled with beautiful wrapping papers, small gift items, and greeting cards ranging from the handmade or sentimental to the ribaldly comic.

See also "Bookstores in Ann Arbor," p. 265.

The Peaceable Kingdom ★
210 S. Main. (313) 668-7886. Mon-Sat 10-6, Fri 'til 9.

This warm, clever, personal shop has become an Ann Arbor institution with its delightful potpourri of imaginatively displayed things, from small inexpensive toys, collectibles, and gadgets to imported and contemporary American folk art. Prices range from funny novelties for a quarter up to $200 (for masks from Africa and Mexico) and $600 for well-known Ann Arbor artist Charla Khanna's compelling one-of-a-kind dolls.

Harry's Army Surplus
201 E. Washington at 4th Ave. (313) 994-3572. Mon-Fri 9-8, Sat 9-6, Sun 11-5.

A wild assortment of customers frequents this little brother of the giant original Harry's in Dearborn. Punks and visiting rock musicians seek out the large assortment of military insignias, leather jackets, and military boots. Campers like to check out the tents and camping accessories. Kids like to fondle the heavy Army practice grenades and ogle the shiny, dangerous throwing stars and huge selection of knives. Visitors from the Soviet Union favor the Army surplus clothing. There are even flags from over 100 countries.

The Artful Exchange ★
215 E. Washington. (313) 761-2287. Tues-Thurs 11-5, Fri 'til 6:30, Sat 10-5.

An eclectic variety of fine art — paintings, sculpture, drawings, ethnic art, prints but no reproductions, is sold on consignment at this well-regarded shop. Prices start as low as $5 and go up into the thousands, for "investment art" by the likes of Chagall, Dali, and Calder. Many works by well-known University of Michigan art school faculty members are here, especially of the older generation that included Frank Cassara, Chet LaMore, Emil Weddige, and Richard Wilt.

Now there's jewelry here, too — some old jewelry sold on consignment, some of artist Vicki Schwager's new jewelry, and some purchased new by owner Judy Crofton.

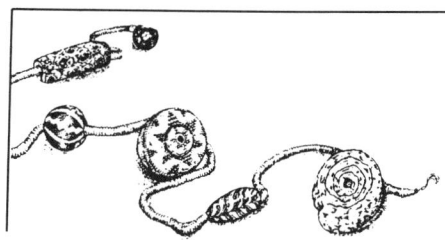

The Bead Gallery ★★
309 E. Liberty between Fifth and Division (lower level). (313) 663-6800. Mon-Fri 10-6, Sat 10-4.

The fabulous array of beads here, and the money to be saved by custom-making necklaces and earrings to suit your taste and wardrobe, is enough to turn a woman from a consumer into a creator, even without special skills. Ceramic beads from Thailand, old glass beads, antique jade buttons, gemstones, Ethiopian silver beads, millefiore Venetian beads, glass and wood beads of all colors and kinds — the range is enormous. There are books and instructional sheets and sample necklaces in the store to inspire and teach, and findings like pin backs and clasps are for sale, too. Existing necklaces can be redesigned and restrung, with neat closings to permit a choice of adjust-able lengths. For a beautifully finished ethnic look, hand-braiding or hand-wrapping can be done.

Another unusual specialist is located just upstairs: **Creative Tattoo**. A degree-holding artist and former art teacher, Suzanne Fauser has won national awards with her beautiful tattoos. She has also relieved a lot of embarrassment by modifying ill-advised tattoos.

Collected Works
325 E. Liberty between Fifth and Division. (313) 995-4222. Mon-Sat 10-6, Thurs & Fri 'til 8, Sun 12-5.

This popular natural-fibers clothing shop, mostly for women but with some sweaters, shirts, and pants for men, creates a relaxed, sophisticated look by playing off ethnic prints and textures against basic solid colors in unstructured clothing, often knit. Prices range from inexpensive to moderate. It's known for ethnic classics like Peruvian sweaters, Indonesian print skirts, and colorful knit caps.

Hands-on Museum ★
219 E. Huron at Fifth Ave. (313) 995-KIDS. Tues-Fri 1:30-5:30; Sat 10-5; Sun 1-5. Adults $2.50; children $1.50.

Housed in the landmark 1879 fire station across from City Hall, this four-story museum is a popular destination for field trips, with over 150 exhibits. Some are rather tedious. Others are a delight. Some favorites are the wonderfully multi-faceted stroboscope; the neat video system that prints out your picture for 25¢; the hot-air balloon powered by two toasters; the amazing reflection hologram microscope; and the pendulum-driven mechanical motion machine. In the computer room are 14 computers, each programmed with an educational game. Adults might want to wear earplugs on busy days here.

The 1879 fire house is home to the popular Hands-On Museum, with a good gift shop of mostly science-related toys and projects.

Kerrytown/
Farmers' Market area ★★

The market itself runs between Detroit and N. Fourth Ave. just north of Catherine, and the Kerrytown shopping complex is just to the north of it, fronting also on N. Fifth Ave. Shops are extend down E. Ann and N. Fourth (both north of Huron) and along Detroit St.

Thirty years ago, Ann Arbor liberals wanted to tear down much of this area of plain old houses on the near north side for urban renewal, but area residents (then mostly black) joined up to preserve the neighborhood with the Republican mayor, who owned the moving and storage firm where Workbench now is. Now the older residents live next to newcomers who can afford the pricey new condos and rehabs, tucked away on North Fourth and Fifth. The small workers' houses on **Braun Court** now house ethnic restaurants, generally quite good.

Retailing around here also reflects the area's affluent present (in the Kerrytown shops and Zingerman's deli) and its low-income past, gloriously represented by the incomparable **Treasure Mart** consignment store and the **People's Food Co-op**. It anchors an increasingly interesting row of alternative-culture stores along Fourth Avenue between Catherine and Ann: **Wildflour Bakery**, **Birkenstock** shoes, **Crazy Wisdom** New Age paraphernalia.

Kerrytown parking hints
One-way streets make the market area confusing to the out-of-town motorist. The easiest way to get to Kerrytown itself from downtown is on North Fourth Avenue. (From Main, turn east to Catherine and north on Fourth.) Even so, it can be hard to find parking in small, scattered lots, and next to impossible on Saturday mornings. One fail-safe alternative: park in the roomy, light-filled Ashley-Ann structure (entered off Ann just west of Main), and walk 3 1/2 short, interesting blocks. While you're parking, enjoy the views of downtown and the northwest side from the upper decks.

A great **playground** for kids to run off steam is at Wheeler Park, at the foot of North Fourth and North Fifth avenues. The evening pick-up basketball games here draw good players.

Kerrytown Shops ★
Faces N. Fifth and N. Fourth Ave. just south of Kingsley. Call (313) 662-4221 for special events and basic information. General shop hours: Mon-Fri 9:30 or 10 a.m.-7 p.m., Sat 9 a.m.-6 p.m., Sun 11-5. Food market shops open at 8 a.m. weekdays, 7 a.m. Sat, 10 or 11 Sun.

Situated in an old lumberyard and warehouse next to Ann Arbor's popular Farmers Market, Kerrytown is a lively complex of over 30 shops, food stalls, and eateries, including the noteworthy **Kerrytown Bistro** and **Diamond Head Cafe.**

Kerrytown has been around since 1968, long before the festival marketplaces concept swept American central cities. It is anchored on the Fourth Avenue side by **Workbench**, the contemporary furniture franchise chain, and in the north building by what may be the state's best cookware shop, **Kitchen Port**, also strong in the tabletop area. The smaller shops sell candles, Asian and Indian imports, interesting greeting cards and paper goods, hand-thrown pottery, futons, yarn, and plants, among other things.

On the first-floor food market, the city's best fish market, **Monahan's**, made a reputation by tracking down sources of very fresh fish to suit the particular tastes of Ann Arbor's fish-loving epicures and foreigners, especially the Japanese. It's across from **Ascione Produce**, plentifully supplied with beautiful fruits and vegetables. Nearby there's a good wine shop, **Partners in Wine**, and the **Moveable Feast's Kerrytown shop**, where the well-known restaurant's locally celebrated sourdough French bread sells for $2 a loaf. Here you can also sit down and enjoy the Feast's takeout salads, pates, perfect flakey sandwich croissants ($2.50-$3), and its famously rich desserts, such as chocolate-rum-walnut Gateau Nancy.

Upstairs in the food market building, **Key Largo** carries tropical clothing, swimsuits, and resortwear year-round, along with sun lotions, jewelry, children's toys, and plenty of flamingos on accessories. Thanks to intelligent buying, it does a much better job of it than many shops of a similar ilk. Down the hall at **Prager,** the two owners travel to Indonesia to search out mostly older, one-of-a-kind Indonesian folk art that you seldom see elsewhere. Prices range from $5 (for made-to-export wood earrings) to $5,000 for an architectural sea horse from a prince's water palace. Here you'll find carvings, baskets, textiles, and, also from India and Africa, ethnic jewelry.

Ann Arbor Farmers' Market ★
Open-air sheds run from Detroit and N. Fifth Ave. to N. Fourth. Wed & Sat 7 a.m.-3 p.m.

This extremely popular market is more the place to find unusual herbs and perennials and choice vegetables than to pick up bargains like 50-pound bags of onions or absorb an Old World atmosphere of mingling ethnic groups. Launching the weekend with a Saturday morning trip to the market is a tradition among academics of all ages. Nearby shops open early for a rich if hectic shopping experience.

DeLong's Barbecue
314 Detroit at N. Fifth Ave. (313) 665-2266. 11 a.m.-1 a.m., 'til 3 a.m. Fri & Sat, closed Tues.

There's no space to eat here, but the takeout pork and beef barbecue and spicy fried trout sandwiches are delicious.

People's Food Co-op
212 N. Fourth Ave. (313) 994-9174. Mon-Fri 9-9, Sat 8 a.m.- 7 p.m., Sun 10 a.m.-8 p.m.

The co-op has become much more user-friendly during the 1980s, with a vastly improved self-serve system for packaging your purchases in ecologically correct recycled brown paper bags. The produce (available in organic and non-organic) now looks terrific, and includes foods never seen in super-markets, such as coffee beans from Nicaragua.

What with the wide selection of pasta, beans, granola, rice, unusual cheeses (including no-salt and rennetless), herbs, coffees, teas, and even select bottled condiments, crackers, and prepared foods, the co-op has expanded its clientele. Ironically, food at this nonprofit cooperative is often expensive, but the quality is quite good. Even the bulk granola costs 20 per cent more than at a comparable, privately owned store.

Extended hours make this a convenient evening stop, when parking is easier. The bulletin board and handouts give a quick overview of area alternative-culture happenings.

Zingerman's Delicatessen ★★★
422 Detroit at Kingsley. (313) 663-3354. Mon-Sat 7 a.m.-8:30 p.m., Sun 9 a.m.-8:30 p.m.

Depending on who you talk to, this is the best deli in Michigan or in the entire Midwest. Sandwiches (over 40 in all) are huge and delicious; the $6.25 corned beef Reuben is the bestseller. The extensive takeout counter offers tempting salads and favorites, from deli classics like coleslaw ($1.90/side), chicken soup, and noodle kugel ($1.75/slice) to inventive potato salads, the popular Thai noodle salad, and salmon-dill pasta salad ($4.50/side) made with Irish smoked salmon. With Uhsinger's sausages from Milwaukee and unusual cheeses from around the world, the deli counter is absolutely top-of-the-line. The selection of olive oils, vinegars, and mustards is outstanding. The owners do a great job of searching out unusual jams, relishes, and gourmet goodies of all kinds.

The fun, information-packed free handouts are a short course in food. Call (313) 663-0974 to get on the mailing list. This feels like a real deli and not a gourmet shop, especially

People who care about good breads go out of their way to Zingerman's for its hearty German- and Jewish-style breads: New York rye from the Modern Bakery in Oak Park, challah bread, Dimpflmeier's traditional German breads from Toronto, bialys, onion rolls, kaiser rolls, and bagels.

if you stop by in the leisurely morning hours, when it's favored by various tradesmen, downtown workers, and academic types. The main way it differs from New York delis is the astounding politeness and patience of the knowledgeable staff, which prides itself on providing advice and samples to sometimes obnoxiously fussy customers. For serious shopping and sampling, best time your visit to a lull — mornings, mid-afternoons, or early in the week.

For awhile, Zingerman's was so crowded it was a pain to enter the place, but they have expanded and streamlined their service, quickening it appreciably. The adjacent eating area is now positively spacious. It's nice to see an enormously successful establishment like Zingerman's that continues to put its energy into improving what it offers rather than starting up clones elsewhere.

The Treasure Mart ★★
529 Detroit St. between Kingsley and Division. (313) 662-1363. Mon-Sat 9 a.m-5:30 p.m., Mon & Fri 'til 8:30.

Ann Arbor's legendary resale shop has a sprawling array of home furnishings at all price levels, often at prices far lower than an antique shop would charge. The quality of its used furniture, collectibles, lighting, china, linens, framed pictures, and the like reflects the broad range of Ann Arbor lifestyles, from the quite ordinary or tastefully impoverished to the sophisticatedly affluent. Some terrific bargains are here, due to sometimes erratic pricing and a monthly markdown system. With a large and fast-moving stock, this place is truly addictive. Some customers stop by daily; more than a few local dealers have launched successful businesses by buying and selling here.

State-Liberty shopping district ★★★
State Street between William and Washington, as well as adjacent North University, Washington, William, and Liberty (the pedestrian shopping street linking downtown and the campus area).

Just a few blocks east of downtown lies a lively, cosmopolitan commercial district spawned by its proximity to the U-M central campus. On its often-crowded sidewalks are a colorful mixture of college students, street people, tweedy professors, expensively dressed shoppers, and punks. In the past five years State Street as a concentration of upscale specialty stores has been strengthened by the addition of new national stores (**Benetton** in a spiffy minimall at State and Liberty, **Laura Ashley** and **Talbot's** on Washington). But State Street is much better known as a fabulous center of book and record stores. (See separate entries, **Bookstores in Ann Arbor** and **Record stores in Ann Arbor**.)

The area is anchored by a **Jacobson's** department store along with

---
State Street parking hint
The best place to find a space is the staffed city structure entered off Maynard (by Jacobson's) or Thompson near Liberty. The metered Tally Hall garage off Washington between Division and State is another good choice, but you can't tell it's full until you get to the top. Both are 30¢ an hour.

Borders Book Shop (see Bookstores in Ann Arbor). Prominent historic landmarks include **Nickels Arcade**, an unusual 1915 arcade of elegant little shopfronts that runs through from State opposite North University to Maynard, and two movie theaters, the 1928 **Michigan Theater** (see below) and the jazzy 1940 **State Theater** on State at Liberty. The State, after being ignominiously carved into a cinema fourplex, was recently converted into **Urban Outfitters**, part of a youth-oriented clothes and lifestyle accessory chain. The new tenants have accorded the old theater more respect than it's had in years. The landmark neon sign, visible for blocks down both State and Liberty, is now fully operational, and the inside remodeling shows off the structural bones of the balcony in an interesting way.

On Maynard Street is one of America's subtlest **McDonald's**, set back from the street by a landscaped courtyard. Its distinctive, almost church-like look was the giant hamburger chain's effort to propitiate citizens infuriated over the demolition of the beautiful old home it replaced.

Look up from here, and you see Ann Arbor's tallest building, 26-story **Tower Plaza**. Its construction in the late 1960s so alarmed Ann Arbor residents, who are fond of thinking they live in a small town, that new zoning laws were quickly passed to prevent any further buildings of this scale. Originally apartments, Tower Plaza is now exclusively condos.

Van Boven's
326 S. State at North University, at the entrance to Nickels Arcade. (313) 665-7228. Mon-Sat 9-5:30, Fri 'til 7.

This fine men's shop, a longtime Ann Arbor fixture, specializes in traditional, classic looks: blue blazers, tweed sport coats, and such. Its shoe store (for men and women) is just inside the arcade.

Caravan Shop
At the Maynard St. entrance to Nickels Arcade. (313) 668-6047. Mon-Sat 9-5:30.

The colorful sidewalk scene on State and Liberty by the University of Michigan campus is the most cosmopolitan and liveliest in the state. Well known as an outstanding center of book and record stores, the State Street area has more recently become a rather exciting area for specialty shopping.

Hundreds of thousands of people around the world must remember the "All is vanity" poster in the arcade window here. Thousands of students pass it going to the Nickels Arcade post office. Seen one way, it's a woman at her vanity mirror; look again, and it's a skull. It's still here, along with the display of tiny china animals and gifts from around the world, such as Chinese bowls, Russian lacquer boxes, baskets, Swiss music boxes, and Italian porcelains.

Renaissance
336 Maynard. (313) 769-8511. Mon-Sat 10-6, Fri 'til 7.

The costly European men's and women's clothing here, largely Italian, has a stylishly classic, contemporary look. A suit here will cost from $800 to $1,200; the men's leather goods are the only local store to advertise regularly — not small ads, either—in the *New York Times* Midwest Edition. It's part of a changing cluster of expensive shops at Maynard and William that also includes, next door, custom jeweler **Matthew Hoffmann,** a self-taught phenomenon who has parlayed winning personal charm and enthusiasm into a base of loyal customer-friends and classy shops in Chicago and New York.

Jacobson's
612 E. Liberty and Maynard. (313) 769-7600. Mon-Sat 9:30-6, Thurs & Fri 'til 9.

This highly regarded, upscale department store chain, based in Jackson, is notable for remaining in Michigan's central cities when most other department stores fled to the malls.

Michigan Theater ★
Liberty at Maynard. Call (313) 668-8480 for program information.

Ann Arbor's 1928 picture palace was threatened with conversion to a shopping arcade. Now it is Ann Arbor's successful community-owned theater, much used for concerts, occasional plays, and films. The interior gilding and other decoration has been restored. Weekends before the main event the original Barton Theater Organ is often played by members of the Motor City Theater Organ Society, the group that heroically patched the old theater up during its hard times. It's a chance to see movies the way they were once meant to be seen.

Espresso Royale ★
324-6 S. State at North University. (313) 662-2770. Mon-Fri 7 a.m.-midnight, Sat & Sun 9 a.m.-midnight.

At this popular new coffee house in Follett's bookstore's old space, a dollar buys a delicious cup of cappucino and 80¢ a cup of espresso. Muffins, bagels, croissants, and unusual European treats like poppyseed bread are also available. This college-town chain has recreated slick, high-tech Italian cafes without being offensively cute or self-conscious about it.

Drake Sandwich Shop ★★
709 North University near State. (313) 668-8853. Mon-Sat 10 a.m.-10:45 p.m., Sun 3 p.m.-10 p.m.

This legendary campus sweet shoppe looks much as it did when owner Truman Tibbals remodeled it in the 1930s. The pressed metal ceiling, pale green booths, and cluttered, darkened atmosphere are just as generations of Michigan students remember them.

Here you can get a wonderful glass of fresh-squeezed limeade in the summer or hot chocolate in the winter, and sandwiches, cakes, and pies. Impulse items include packaged teas and teapots and novelty candies like moon rocks (actually they resemble Michigan's beautifully colored glacial stones). Another specialty is good chocolates, searched out by chocolate-lover Truman Tibbals and sold by the ounce. The double almond bark (2 oz. for $1.10) is outstanding.

Steve's Ice Cream
State and William. (313) 994-4220. 7 days noon-midnight.

This popular ice cream store has the best super-premium ice cream in town, with a great many toppings. New Englanders take their ice cream very seriously; this is Michigan's only store in the Boston-based chain.

South University area ★
South University between East University and Forest.

This three-block-long commercial district is the most heavily used by U-M students. If you are unfortunate enough to arrive by car at the top of the hour when classes are getting out, you may find you have a bit of a wait, as there is no doubt in these students' minds that pedestrians come first around the campus. In terms of general retailing interest, South Universi-

---
South U. parking hint
The metered 30¢/hour city structure on Forest just south of South University is your best bet here.

ty has declined in recent years as fast food spots have proliferated here.

Middle Earth ★★★
1209 South University. (313) 769-1488. Mon-Sat 10-7, Thurs & Fri 'til 9, Sun noon-5.

This is one of the most entertaining shops in the entire state. Nostalgia candy like Pez and Double Bubble competes for space with a striking display of beautiful jewelry, some quite expensive, including thousands of earrings. You'll find an outrageous variety of constantly changing paraphernalia which owner Cynthia Shevel calls "cheap thrills." These have included a Nixon shower head (the water came out of the mouth), a Jim and Tammy Bakker T-shirt with PTL spelled out "Pass the Loot." But political novelties have fallen on hard times lately, Shevel says. "Bush is so boring, and Dan Quayle they've kept so quiet, nobody knows he's around."

T-shirts are a big deal here, with imprints like "Chernobyl at Night" (with a glow-in-the-dark patch) and art T-shirts from the Mona Lisa and Monet to M. C. Escher. The first shop in town to sell bawdy greeting cards, Middle Earth still has the most ribald selection, though there are plenty of lovely, artistic cards any mother would love to receive. Another speciality is over 20,000 post cards featuring almost every eccentric topic imaginable.

Village Corner ★
South University and Forest. (313) 995-1818. 7 days 8 a.m.-1 a.m.

Unlike most Ann Arbor retail, which has become steadily more gentrified over the years, the VC obstinately keeps its scruffy, vaguely counter-culture ambience. Clerks, often outlandishly clad, wait on you in amusingly surly fashion. As a variety store mainly for students, the VC has a good selection of convenience and takeout food (fresh fruit, sandwiches, good bread and cheese) and groceries.

In a totally different guise, the Village Corner is a nationally known wine shop with one of Michigan's most sophisticated and wide-ranging selections of wine, from inexpensive to very fine — 4,000 kinds, along with 600 kinds of spirits. In the wine section, salespeople are knowledgeable and willing to take the time to advise customers on their selections, even if it's a $5 bottle to accompany spaghetti and meatballs. Prices are reasonable, and deals on cases of wine are especially good.

Clear and informative shelf descriptions of wines are likely written by Village Corner owner Dick Scheer, a well-known wine authority and judge. Ask for the free annotated catalog and newsletter.

Steve's Lunch
1313 South University east of Forest. (313) 769-2288. Mon-Fri 8 a.m.-8 p.m., Sat & Sun 9-8.

Steve's, a small, crowded diner long known for its good omelets, also serves a good bi bim bob (Korean stir-fry with fried egg).

Coffee Break
1327 South University near Washtenaw. (313) 761-1327. Mon-Fri 7 a.m.-8 p.m., Sat 8 a.m.-7 p.m., Sun 8-8.

A Korean couple runs this cafeteria-style restaurant, which serves donuts, sweet rolls, and lunch specials, including a huge portion of superb bi bim bob for $4.50.

Rick's American Cafe
611 Church just south of South University. (313) 996-2747. Mon-Fri 4 p.m.-2 a.m. (happy hour 4-8), Sat 8 p.m.-2 a.m., Sun closed.

Rick's, part of a Champaign-based chain, is one of the region's most popular nightclubs, thanks in part to the live music booked by Lee Berry of Prism Productions. The noisy atmosphere and collegiate crowd makes this something like a giant fraternity party. In addition to popular rock bands, Rick's features good Chicago blues musicians well worth hearing.

Red Hot Lovers
629 East University just south of South University. (313) 996-3663. Mon-Sat 11 a.m.-9 p.m., Sun noon-9.

This popular eastern outpost of the Chicago-style hot dog serves Old Vienna franks ($3.19) with all the expected trimmings: sauerkraut, hot peppers, cheese, onions, tomatoes, mustard, ketchup plus fries and cole slaw. And it throws in some 1970s Ann Arbor surprises: a marinated tofu dog ($3.59 with fries and slaw) that's surprisingly good when loaded up with extras, and Gary Grimshaw's classic vintage blues and rock posters on the walls. Crowded and noisy.

Bookstores in Ann Arbor ★★★

Centered on State near Liberty.

Few places in the country have as lively, high-quality concentration of bookstores, both new and used, as does central Ann Arbor, anchored by the fabulously successful Borders. Ann Arborites buy more books per person than any other city in the United States, according to surveys. The bookstores are open occasional evenings, and most are open Sunday afternoons, too.

Connoisseurs of used and rare books would do well to pick up a listing of some area book dealers, including several distinguished home book shops, from West Side Books or the State Street Book Shop. Jan Longone's **Wine and Food Library** ★★ deals exclusively in out-of-print and rare publications on wine, food, and gastronomy, and is internationally known. It's by appointment only; call (313) 663-4894.

Borders Book Shop ★★★
303 S. State at Liberty. (313) 668-7652. MonSat 9-9, Sun 11-6.

Ann Arbor was almost a trade book wasteland in 1971 when the two Borders brothers, former grad students, started their store in an obscure second-story retail space on William. Thanks to its knowledgeable, helpful clerks, relentlessly attentive manager Joe Gable, pleasing ambience, and outstanding back list, the Ann Arbor Borders, with over 80,000 titles, has gradually grown to become perhaps the finest bookstore in U.S. and the flagship of a high-quality chain. There's also an impressive selection of maps and better posters.

Shaman Drum Bookshop ★
313 1/2 S. State. (313) 662-7407. Mon-Fri 10-5:30, Sat 'til 4:30.

This intimate, second-story shop, just down the street toward campus from Borders, specializes in scholarly books in the humanities, chosen by its highly knowledgeable staff. Here you can find a good many important books in religious studies, classical studies, poetry, Native American culture, anthropology, and literature and literary studies.

State Street Book Shop ★
316 S. State. (313) 994-4041. Mon-Sat 10-5:45.

The fanciest of Ann Arbor's used bookstores, State Street specializes in angling books, first editions, maps, and prints, in addition to its general-line stock. The basement features 50¢ paperbacks and $2 hardcovers.

David's Books ★
622 E. Liberty at State. (313) 665-8017. Mon-Sat 9:30 or so-9, Sun 12-9.

Upstairs at Liberty and State is this legendary, somewhat scruffy store, crowded with some 50,000 used books at quite reasonable prices, plus a good collection of new chess books.

Wooden Spoon
200 N. Fourth Ave. at Ann. (313) 769-4775. Mon, Tues & Thurs 9:30-4, Wed & Fri 9:30-6, Sat 7:30-5, Sun 1-5.

The Wooden Spoon is located near the Farmers' Market in the very spot where the legendary Joe's saloon once was. Its many rooms have a distinctly dusty, well worn aura. Specialities include cookbooks, books on gardening, literary criticism, history, and arts and crafts.

West Side Book Shop ★★
113 W. Liberty just west of Main. (313) 995-1891. Mon-Fri 11-6, Sat 10-5.

This delightful shop fits the traditional image of a bookstore: antique in a comfortable way, cluttered, accented with old prints, and personal — conducive to browsing and chatting. Its specialties are nautical topics, exploration, and photography. The 1891 building was designed with rich detail befitting its arty earlier image as a photographer's studio.

After Words ★
219 S. Main near Liberty. (313) 996-2808. Mon-Sat 10-10, Sun 12-8.

Attractively laid out and good for browsing, this good-sized store carries only new remaindered books at big discounts.

Community Newscenters ★
330 E. Liberty west of Division. (313) 663-6168. 7 days 7:30 a.m.-11 p.m.
1301 South University at Forest. (313) 662-6150. 7 days 8:30 a.m.-11 p.m.

Both Ann Arbor stores of this Lansing-based chain have an outstanding selection of magazines as well as a selection of paperback and hardcover books that's surprising for newsstands. The extraordinarily long hours of these lower-level stores are an impulse browser's delight.

Michigan Book & Supply
317 S. State at North University. (313) 665-4990. Mon-Fri 9-6, Sat 9:30-5, Sun 12-5.

The longtime Kresge space is now occupied by one of three Ann Arbor bookstores catering to the textbook needs of U-M students.

Barnes & Noble Bookstore
In the basement of the Michigan Union, on State at South University. (313) 995-8877. Mon-Thurs 9-7, Fri 9-5, Sat 10-4, Sun 12-4.

This spiffy big textbook store also has, among its general reading books, a special section with English and American paperback editions of the classics.

Ulrich's Book Store
East University at South University. (313) 662-3201. Mon-Fri 8:30-5:30, Sat 9:30-5.

Now the oldest textbook store in town, Ulrich's also has a good art supplies department and a big selection of U-M insignia items and inexpensive posters.

Record stores

Concentrated in the State and Liberty area.

Music-lovers from across the U.S. consider this area the best place to shop for recordings because of the outstanding comparison-shopping permitted by the concentration of high-quality stores. Most record stores are open evenings and Sunday afternoons.

Liberty Music ★★
417 E. Liberty at Thompson. (313) 662-0675. Mon-Sat 10-5:30.

The granddaddy of Ann Arbor's great record stores, Liberty has been one of North America's best-known classical music shops for decades. Other specialties are show tunes, band music, spoken word, children's, and international. The personal service (including mail order) is incredible, and you can get a musical education from the staff. Ann Arbor native Evans Mirageas, now with the Boston Symphony, says he learned much more under the tutelage of Liberty's staff than from four years at the U-M School of Music.

SKR Classical ★★
539 E. Liberty at Maynard. (313) 995-5051. Mon-Thurs 10-8, Fri & Sat 10-9, Sun 12-6.

SKR's relatively recent classical music store is a Schoolkids' subsidiary, managed by the *Ann Arbor News*'s passionately opinionated music critic Jim Leonard. It has the state's biggest collection of classical compact disks and a great many tapes. It also has scores and many pirate tapes of live performances.

Schoolkids Records & Tapes ★★★
523 E. Liberty at Maynard. (313) 994-8031. Mon-Sat 9:30-9:30, Sun noon-8.

Early on, Schoolkids learned that having a great back list in the right town can build a market dramatically. Its strength is its breadth and depth in everything from rock and jazz to country and new age, including esoteric labels and foreign pressings. Though CDs are now the main focus, its record collection is still pretty amazing. The folk and jazz, victims of the CD revolution, aren't quite what they used to be. Prices are below that of most big U.S. chains.

Discount Records
State and Liberty. (313) 665-3679. Mon-Thurs 9-9, Fri & Sat 9-10, Sun 12-8.

A college-town chain, Discount covers all the pop and classical bases and keeps local prices competitive. Its big stock of singles is unusual.

State Discount
309 S. State. (313) 994-1262. Mon-Fri 9-9, Sat 10-6, Sun 12-6.

A campus general store, State is known by music buffs not as a source of toothpaste and snack food but as the cheapest place in town to buy just-released, mass-volume CDs.

Wazoo Records ★
336 1/2 S. State at North University. (313) 761-8686. Mon-Fri 10-8, Sat 10-6, Sun 12-6.

This upstairs store has a well-organized stock of used vinyl and CD records and tapes (mostly rock and jazz) in remarkably good condition, at reasonable prices ($3.50 for most vinyl records). The only scratchy records you'll find here are rare ones, reports a regular customer, who also appreciates the good prices paid for used records.

PJ's Used Records and CDs ★
619 Packard between Hill and State. (313) 663-3441. Mon-Thurs 10-9, Fri & Sat 10-10, Sun noon-8.

PJ's is an interesting used record store run by knowledgeable jazz, R&B, and blues enthusiasts. "Opinions rendered on all subjects," they advertise.

Earth Wisdom Music
Inside Seva Restaurant at 314 E. Liberty. (313) 769-0969. Mon & Tues 11-7, Wed-Sat 11-8:30, Sun 11-2:30 or later.

A purveyor of New Age music for meditation, relaxation, guided imagery, and dance, Earth Wisdom has been around since before the genre became a form of Muzak for the 80s.

Nichols Arboretum ★★
Geddes Ave. entrance is between Oxford and Oswego, just east of the main campus. Open 6 a.m.-10 p.m. School-year parking is very tight; plan on driving by a few blocks to find a space, or, failing that, use the Forest St. parking structure and walk.

These hilly 126 acres of meadow and woodland are laced with paths and planted with over 2,000 kinds of woody plants from all over the world. Its calming, unregimented aura is enhanced by the absence of vehicles, picnic tables, benches, signs, and, in winter, sleds. It's a favorite place for walks the year round; spring is especially spectacular, with wildflowers blooming in the woods, 30 varieties of flowering crabapples, 120 kinds of lilacs, and special plantings of rhododendrons and peonies. The steep contours create some 26 different growing conditions, allowing for a great variety of plants. In spring, many kinds of migrating warblers stay in the bushes out toward the railroad bridge over the Huron River, reached by following the car-free riverside road east.

The Arb owes its existence to a U-M undergraduate in the 1880s, Walter Nichols. While still a student, he purchased 27 acres of raw land on what then was the edge of town for the purpose of raising vegetables to sell at market. He held onto the land

Cobblestone Farm

Parks in Ann Arbor are a point of great local pride. They include a terrific variety of environments and activities: a **skateboard halfpipe**, a **play castle** at the Mixer Playground, the 19th-century **Cobblestone Farm** with a historic house, gardens, and animals, **summer band concerts** at West Park's band shell, (illicit) gambling at **Island Park**, **U-M crew practice** at Argo Canoe Livery, two challenging **golf courses**, three **swimming pools**, winter natural-ice **hockey rinks** plus two artificial rinks, an occasionally operating **19th-century gristmill**, and over a hundred parks. If you come here often, it's well worth checking out. For further information, call (313) 994-2780 weekdays, or stop by the parks office at City Hall, N. Fifth Ave. between Huron and Ann. For recorded facility program information, call (313) 769-9140 24 hours.

after graduating and leaving Ann Arbor. In 1907 he gave the nucleus of the arboretum to the university.

You can also walk through the oak-shaded **Forest Hills Cemetery**, one of Michigan's most picturesque cemeteries in the romantic mode of the mid-19th century. It is entered through the Gothic-arched stone gates at Geddes and Observatory. Most of Ann Arbor's prominent past citizens are buried here.

Just east of the Arb are a number of informal, English-style lanes with highly picturesque (and pricey) homes, mostly from the 1920s. **Ridgeway** and **Highland Road** are especially charming. Bob McNamara lived in the big Tudor house on Highland at Highland Lane when he was president of Ford. **Inglis House**, a sort of a French provincial chateau built by a Detroit industrialist and used as a guest residence by the University of Michigan, is on Highland at Regent Drive. To see a remarkable, angular **Frank Lloyd Wright house** built around a hilltop, continue east on winding Highland Road, and bear left onto Orchard Hills Drive.

Gallup Park ★

Entrances on Fuller Rd. just west of Huron Parkway (north of river) and on Geddes Ave. where it descends to the Huron (south of river). General park information: (313) 994-2780. Canoe livery phone: (313) 662-9319; call for hours. Park open 6 a.m.-10 p.m. Free.

Sweeping expanses of water and sky make this 83-acre, barrier-free park the closest thing Ann Arbor has to an in-town lake. It lies on both sides of a big pond created by the dammed Huron River. Where steep, wooded glacial hills meet the river, the natural scenery is varied and fairly spectacular, in a low-key Michigan way.

Walkways and bridges connecting manmade islands in the river make for a serene walk or bike ride. Fishing spots abound here. Swimming isn't allowed, but **windsurfers** are out in force every weekend of good weather, and the **canoe livery** rents canoes, paddleboats, and bicycles. It also has a snack bar. A quiet, remote **nature trail** along the south bank leads west from the bridge almost a mile to Dow Field, the easternmost portion of the U-M Arboretum.

On Fuller Road just west of the north entrance is a Greek Revival **cobblestone house,** an outstanding example of the upstate New York cobblestone architecture brought here by settlers from that state.

Some of Ann Arbor's choicest residential areas lie just south of the park, on either side of Geddes going toward the campus. Joggers love Devonshire (just east of the southern park entrance) for its light traffic and leafy beauty. Immediately south of Gallup Park along Huron Parkway is the scenic **Huron Hills Golf Course/Ski Center** (313) 971-9841.

In winter, the moist tropical air and scents in the conservatory at the Matthaei Botanical Gardens are a special treat, and children love the goldfish pond. The gift shop is geared to indoor and outdoor gardeners.

Matthaei Botanical Gardens ★

1800 N. Dixboro Rd.(between Plymouth and Geddes) (313) 763-7060. Grounds open sunrise to sunset. Conservatory open daily 10-4:30; adults $1.

This University of Michigan facility has an unusual variety of plants in several appealing environments. In the dome-covered conservatory are tropical and desert plants. Surrounding the conservatory are cultivated **gardens**, each with a different theme, such as ornamental plants, medicinal plants, and herbs. The maze-like herb garden is particularly striking.

Along four **nature trails** centered along a stream are some 730 kinds of wildflowers, trees, and grasses. In one section of this 300-acre site is an authentic **prairie**, showing what much of southwestern Michigan looked like before man cultivated the area.

Domino's Farms

Off Plymouth Rd. just east of US-23. (313) 995-4258. From Plymouth, look for the Domino's Farms sign at the relocated Earhart Rd.

The most impressive and pleasing view of Domino's Pizza's huge headquarters is from either of the two divided highways that intersect nearby, US-23 or M-14. From either, Frank Lloyd Wright's idea of a Prairie House harmonious with the landscape is clear. But once you get up close to it, the 6/10 of a mile long, low, 1.2 million-square-foot building seems overpowering and ominously out of scale in a Brave New World sort of way. The building, designed by the internationally known architect Gunnar Birkerts of Bloomfield Hills, houses everything from Domino's distribution facilities to corporate offices and an Exhibition Hall of various museums and archives.

The building comes off best at the entrance, just behind the row of flags representing the countries in which Domino's operates. Here you can see the complex detailing of the intersecting planes of the upper-story terrace outside Domino founder Tom Monaghan's luxurious 2-story office. It has leather walls and floors and gold bathroom fixtures. (Monaghan prefers to work in an adjacent austere cubicle, an arrangement reflecting both his exuberant glorification of the trappings of success and his ascetic, humanitarian streak. He once considered becoming a priest.)

Weekend group tours ($1/person) include the office, board room, fitness center, and pizza store. Call (313) 995-4258 at least two weeks in advance.

The copper-roofed Domino's Farms complex, intended to pay homage to Monaghan's hero Frank

---

Domino's Farms Map — For a handy Domino Farms map and brochure on its visitor attractions, and for special information, call (313) 995-4258.

Lloyd Wright, is one of his many pet projects, reminiscent in their imaginative sweep of the aging Henry Ford.

Raised in an orphanage and sporting an aw-shucks grin much of the time, the pizza magnate is widely admired as a classic Horatio Alger story. Starting with an Ypsilanti pizza place across from the Eastern Michigan campus, he plugged away doggedly for years. He introduced the insulating corrugated cardboard pizza box. His quick preparation system allowed the crucial 30-minute delivery promise. He promoted spirited contests between stores in his Pepperoni Press. By the early 1980s his pizza chain had evolved into a multi-billion-dollar Goliath, privately owned, with a distinctive, gung-ho, family-like corporate culture.

Monaghan doesn't just sell $2 billion worth of pizza a year. Among many other things, he also:

♦ owns the Detroit Tigers.

♦ collects Frank Lloyd Wright memorabilia, paying record prices for some items and causing other Wright collectors to accuse him of inflating the market.

♦ buys expensive old cars, which he displays at Domino's Farms.

♦ has started a small demonstration farm near here which is supposed to show that the small-scale farmer can do quite well if he or she just grows the right things.

♦ owns a local radio station, which he promptly re-named WPZA.

Along the way, this genuinely nice guy, loyal to his old associates and staff, a family man who believes in putting his principles into action, has managed to alienate a huge spectrum of people. Tiger fans are angry that he traded Kirk Gibson and wants to replace beloved Tiger Stadium. Neighbors of Domino's Farms are furious over the congestion caused by the "Blessed Christmas" light show, which he stubbornly pushes as a statement of his beliefs.

A wide variety of Ann Arborites view Monaghan as an oafish, right-wing clown in a city where others with wealth and power keep a low-key presence. Outdoor-lovers are upset at his developing a good deal of rustic Drummond Island near the Straits of Mackinac into a Domino's resort. The lavish VIP party he held there years ago, at which celebrity guests were given big gifts, still is the object of criticism in newspapers. Museums and collectors of Frank Lloyd Wright artifacts are upset because Monaghan's expensive purchases have inflated prices beyond their budgets. Monaghan's donations to Right-to-Life causes have infuriated Pro-Choice forces. And now, the sacred 30-minute Domino's delivery guarantee itself is under attack as a cause of traffic accidents.

No wonder Monaghan has said he wants to sell his pizza empire, since a Boycott Domino's movement seems to be gaining steam. As a result, the future prospects of Domino's Farms and its myriad visitor attractions, so much the product of his enthusiasms, is uncertain.

Petting Farm ★

In the big red barn by the white farmhouse opposite Exhibition Hall, at the end of the Domino's complex. (313) 996-0599. Wed-Fri 11 a.m.-1 p.m., Sat & Sun 1-4. Group tours by appointment. Free.

The big barn Ann Arbor farmer Walter Zeeb built in 1925 has been moved a ways down the road in this wierdly transformed landscape, but the magic is that it smells and looks just like a barn should. It feels much better than many touristic farm operations, and it has all the expected farm animals. The big Shire horses take visitors on free weekend hayrides every 20 minutes. Fun and informative animal shows at 1, 2, and 3 Saturdays and Sundays get visitors acquainted with farm animals.

The Domino's Center for Architecture & Design ★

In Exhibition Hall at the far end of the Domino's complex. For information or to schedule a guided tour, call (313) 995-4504. Tues-Fri 10-5:30, Sat & Sun noon-5. $2 adults, children free. Reduced fees while a portion of the Wright collection is loaned to the Smithsonian through Sept, 1991. BookStore closes at 5 p.m.

This exhibit of artifacts, architectural plans, and photos of the works of Frank Lloyd Wright was developed here because Domino founder Tom Monaghan has admired Wright's work since he was a youth.

It is not a place we would suggest travelers go out of their way to visit unless they already have a great interest in Wright's work. The famous architect was a fascinating individual — pretentious, exasperating, usually over his head in debt, promising more than he could deliver, and yet incredibly fertile creatively over a great span of time. But the center focuses only on fragments of his work. His approach to design was more totally integrated than perhaps any other architect's. Wright designed leaded glass, furniture, and lighting, and supervised the design of textiles, murals, and even gardens to go with his houses. The museum here takes his furniture and other artifacts out of the context of the dramatic architectural spaces for which they were designed. The emotional impact of his design is therefore drained.

The large black-and-white photos of original interiors try to make up for the lack of context. Here you can see big photos of Wright's amazing Imperial Hotel in Tokyo (now demolished), along with a few leaded glass windows, chairs, tables, benches, and sconces from it.

There's a chair he designed from the late, famous Larkin Administration Building in Buffalo (1904), supposedly the first time anyone thought to put casters on an office chair. Monaghan paid the most ever for a decorative item when he paid $198,000 for a highback chair from the 1902 Ward Willits Residence. You can see abstract covers Wright designed in 1927 for *Liberty Magazine*, but which were never published.

One of the few remaining intact Wright dining sets is here at the Center, the 1899 set from the Joseph Husser Residence. There's a table from one of Wright's most famous houses, Fallingwater, and a film on its design and construction which visitors can view. Architects admired Wright's delicate style of drawing, and a number of presentation drawings are on display.

Downstairs from the Center, the most impressive **BookStore** carries a delightful selection of jewelry, stained glass, post cards, posters, and even some striking T-shirts connected with Wright's work. Its collection of books and magazines on all facets of architecture and design, from preservation to vernacular and contemporary architecture, is outstanding. The management plans on having one of the Midwest's best selection of books on architecture and design. Adjacent to it is a much smaller shop of Detroit Tigers souvenirs and related items, including Tom Monaghan's autobiography, *Pizza Tiger*.

Domino's Classic Cars ★★

Domino's Farms Exhibition Hall, in last building of complex. (313) 668-7319. Mon-Sat 10-5:30, Sun noon-5:30. Admission $5 adults, $3 seniors, $2 children 6-12.

Tom Monaghan only started collecting cars in 1984, but he used his millions to quickly build a very fine collection. Best known is his 1931 Bugatti Royale, carmaker Ettore Bugatti's personal car, for which Monaghan paid $8.1 million in 1986. A rare Duesenberg on display cost the pizza baron a million dollars.

The museum's changing collection also includes wonderful classic American cars — for example

a 1922 Model T truck. The cars are on display in the 20,000-square-foot museum.

The collection was assembled by Monaghan and his ex-partner, George Crocker. They met when bidding against each other at car auctions. The two car lovers agreed to jointly assemble an all-time great car collection. But after Monaghan decided to sell Domino's Pizza, he broke off this partnership, sold many of his cars, and reduced floor space almost by half.

The remaining cars are well presented against a neutral dark-grey background with hundreds of small spotlights to highlight their special features. No ropes separate the visitor from the irreplaceable collection. Amid all the cars are antique jukeboxes, a collection of classic bicycles, operable kiddie cars, specialty vehicles like dune buggies, and toy autos and trucks.

The adjoining gift shop is exceptionally fine. There's a large collection of car-related books as well as car-inspired art, toys, and novelties, all presented in striking displays.

Eskimo Art, Inc.
Exhibition Hall, Domino's Farms. (313) 665-9663. Tues, Wed, Fri 10-2

This interesting shop sells the soapstone, ivory, and bone carvings

The 1931 Bugatti Royale at Domino's Classic Car Museum is one of only six ever built. This luxury touring limousine, built for royalty and the super-rich, sold for $45,000 when new. Over 7,000 pounds, it is one of the largest cars ever made, with a 14-foot wheelbase and an engine that gets 7 miles to the gallon. Behind it are the flags of countries in which Domino's operates, leading to the entrance of corporate headquarters.

made by the seminomadic Eskimos of the Canadian Eastern Arctic region. Geographically remote, these 9,000 Eskimos occupy over half a million square mile. Their lives revolve around hunting and fishing. Their art, often made of the animals they hunt, has been little affected by outside civilization. Its smooth, round, simple forms show life through the keenly observant eyes of hunters. In recent decades, a few artists and collectors have encouraged the Inuit or Eskimo people to continue their traditional art and helped them find new markets for it. Ann Arbor microfilm pioneer Eugene Powers started the nonprofit Eskimo Art in 1953.

Prices range from $35 for very small carvings to $4,000, with most between $100 and $200. The popular $14 Eskimo Art calendar features reproductions of stone block prints, stencils, and lithographs.

The University of Michigan

The architecture of the Michigan campus is a heterogeneous mix reflecting the university's long history. The imposing portico of Angell Hall (1924) presents a collegiate and stately face to State Street.

The University of Michigan is the first of the giant state universities. Classes began here in 1841 on 40 acres of donated land, but today the campus sprawls over much of eastern Ann Arbor. The U-M differs from most other big state universities in one important way: for over a century now, it has maintained one of the most distinguished faculties in the country. In fields as diverse as anthropology, geology, philosophy, history, law, psychology, hospital administration, Chinese studies, medical illustration, and industrial engineering, the faculty consistently rank among the very top in the country.

The effect on Ann Arbor of having such a distinguished university has been enormous. Its reputation attracts many of the country's top students, a fair number of whom end up settling in Ann Arbor. The faculty also is one of the country's most successful in winning researching grants, which now pump a quarter of a billion dollars a year into the city and state. Furthermore, sizable corporate and governmental research, testing, and development complexes have sprung up on the fringes of town because of the university. Due almost entirely to the U-M's presence, Ann Arbor has been a boom town for years and has been insulated throughout this century from most of the economic downswings other Michigan cities have experienced.

Michigan's legislature, with sharply fewer U-M grads these days, shows little regard for this important state asset. State funding has slipped greatly. To maintain quality the U-M has had to hike tuition. Over $10,000 a year for out-of-state undergraduates, it is the highest of any state university in the U.S. Fund-raising has also been intensified, and it now brings in $70 million a year. By trimming peripheral programs and carefully focusing resources, the university has done a remarkable job of remaining among the country's elite.

First U.S. research university

Two mid-19th-century developments laid the foundation for the U-M to become world-famous. Its first president, Henry Tappan, took the reins of the struggling, dissension-wracked state school in 1852 and imposed on it his progressive vision for a new kind of American university. Instead of the classical curriculum followed by the elite universities of the East, Harvard, Yale, and Princeton, Tappan instituted the German research model for Michigan, emphasizing advancing knowledge rather than rote memorization of established knowledge. Tappan also scouted the East and Europe for the best faculty he could find. The proud, impolitic Tappan was ultimately hounded out of office in 1863, but by that time the University of Michigan was already gaining national attention.

Early generous funding

The other key ingredient to the university's meteoric rise was the generous funding by the 19th-century state legislature. Because so many early Michigan settlers were relatively well educated New Yorkers and New Englanders, Michigan supported public education much more than most other states. In 1835 a portion of the tremendous revenues coming into state coffers from land sales was earmarked for education, giving the university an ample source of revenue for years. The U-M was not only able to pay competitive salaries for top faculty, it grew quickly until by the1880s it was the largest university in the land.

Today the U-M has about 35,000 students, half of them in the university's many graduate programs.

Parking
It's difficult, and enforcement at U-M lots is just as rigorous as the city's. Many university lots have metered visitors' sections, but you may do best to head to a large structure and be prepared to walk. It's 30¢/hour. Bring lots of quarters. Some suggestions:
♦ *the visitors' section of the Power Center structure on Fletcher between N. University and Huron.*
♦ *the city-operated structures on Maynard St. structure near Jacobson's or on Washington west of State (Tally Hall).*
♦ *The city structure on Forest just south of South University.*
♦ *On North Campus, visitor sections behind the Art & Architecture Schools and North Campus Commons.*
♦ *All-day visitor permits for $4 enable you to park in staff lots and structures. (But they often fill up, too.) Available weekdays at the Parking Office in the structure at 508 Thompson between Jefferson and Madison. (313) 764-8291.*

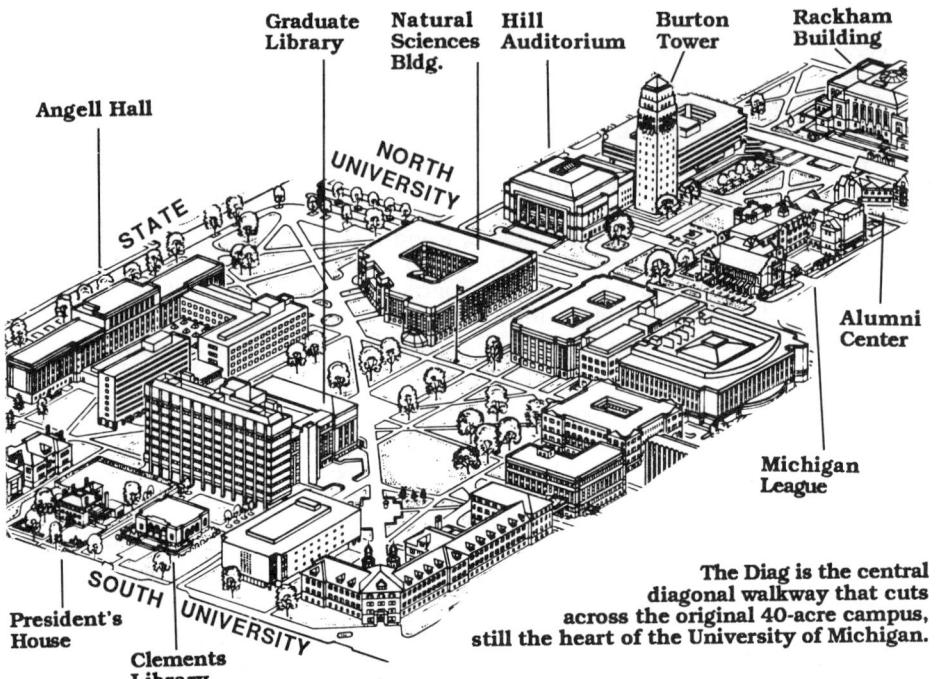

The Diag is the central diagonal walkway that cuts across the original 40-acre campus, still the heart of the University of Michigan.

POINTS OF INTEREST

Central Campus ★★
Original 40 acres bounded by State, North University, East University, and South University. Campus Information Center: (313) 763-4636. University operator: 764-1817.

Ann Arbor won the state university in 1837 because owners of a local land holding company offered the state 40 acres of farmland on the edge of town. This flat, unremarkable field remains the focal point of the campus. Here you will find, fronting State Street, **Angell Hall** with its eight great Doric columns. One of many buildings on campus designed by Albert Kahn, it was built in 1924. The imposing neoclassical style was a reaction to criticism of Kahn's simpler, more original **Natural Sciences Building** (1917) just northeast of it on North University. Ironically, today the Natural Sciences Building is considered far more distinguished architecturally. Connected with two much newer buildings behind it, Angell Hall is the heart of the university's liberal arts college.

Traversing the original 40-acre campus is a diagonal walk from northwest to southeast, connecting the shopping district on State and Liberty with that along South University. Midway is the famous **Diag**, a plaza in front of the Graduate Library that has been the site of countless student demonstrations and rallies. If it's a pleasant day outdoors, this is a good place between noon and 1 p.m. to see Michigan students and the myriad causes currently being espoused.

Other nearby points of interest are:

Harlan Hatcher Graduate Library
*The 1919 North Building is entered (via many steps) from the Diag. The attached, 8-story **South Building** (1970; handicapped-accessible) is entered from the rear. (313) 764-9356. In-session hours: Mon-Thurs 8 a.m.-midnight, Fri 8 a.m.-10*

p.m., Sat 10 a.m.-6 p.m., Sun 1 p.m.-midnight.

Just south of the Diag are the entrance steps to the big brick **Graduate Library** building. With over 6 million volumes, the U-M has the 5th-largest academic library system in the country. The 1919 front building was designed by Kahn in a strong, simple style that combines classical details with Louis Sullivan-style tapestry brick ornament. Changing exhibits about subjects from African-American authors to the French Revolution are in its foyer. The second-floor **Reference Room** has an impressive high vaulted ceiling. At either end of it are large allegorical murals, *The Arts of Peace* and *The Arts of War*, painted for the 1893 Chicago World's Fair by the noted Detroit artist Gari Melchers.

Rare Books and Special Collections
Seventh floor, South Building. (313) 764-9377. Mon-Fri 10-12 & 1-5, Sat 10-12.

Here visitors can see a plate from the beautiful *Birds of America* by Audubon, one of the library's first acquisitions. The book's $970 price caused an outcry among state legislators in 1839. Today the book is worth over a million dollars. Changing exhibits usually feature books from the collection. Visitors are welcome to request to examine items from the collections in the reading room.

One part of this rare book section is the nationally famous **Labadie Collection of Radical Literature**, begun in 1870 by Detroit anarchist Jo Labadie. He donated it to the university in 1911. It has grown to become a major resource for scholars from around the world who study extremist groups from the far left to the far right.

On the 8th floor, the collection of **ancient papyri** is the largest in the U.S.

Map Room
8th floor, South Building. (313) 764-0407. Mon-Fri 10-12, 1-5, Sun 1-4.

The public is free to look at any of the quarter of a million maps here, including quite a few old Michigan maps and city plans. With glass walls to the south, west, and north, the Map Room is also a fine place to get a **panoramic view** of the surrounding campus and city.

The 1919 Graduate Library has been the backdrop for countless rallies. At the first of the school year, the Diag is alive with banners and balloons of student organizations recruiting new members.

President's House
South University at Tappan.

Looking almost straight down from the south windows of the Graduate Library, you can get a sense of why the university's president and his family feel like they are living in a goldfish bowl. The back yard of the President's House, which faces South University Avenue has a high fence, but this has been an ineffective screen since the 8-story addition to the library was added.

The President's House is actually the oldest building on campus and one of the first to have been built. In 1840 four identical two-story professor's houses were constructed in the Greek Revival style. This one alone remains. The roof was later raised to add a third floor, and elaborate Italianate brackets were attached. Ann Arbor's first flush toilet was installed here in 1871.

Clements Library ★★
909 S. University at Tappan. (313) 764-2347. Mon-Fri 10:30-12, 1-5.

Next door to the President's House is the jewel-like Clements Library, the repository of many rare books, manuscripts, maps, and other primary source material. Its collection focuses on all aspects of early American history from the Age of Discovery to the end of the 19th century. Its designer, Albert Kahn, considered it the finest creation in his acclaimed 45-year career. Finished in 1923, the library is patterned on an Italian Renaissance villa at Caprarola. The style was chosen to reflect the age of great explorers and cartographers who opened up the Americas.

It's worth looking beyond the ornate bronze grilles on the entrance doors and visit the grand main reading room, where special exhibits are usually on display. The high curved ceiling, hung with giant chandeliers, is elaborately detailed. The room is lined with fine wooden bookshelves, the volumes arranged in chronological order from the 15th to the 19th century. Antiques are on display throughout. A grandfather clock comes from George Washington's 1782-83 headquarters at New Windsor, New York. It was a gift from Carl Van Doren, who used the library to write his *Secret History of the Revolution*. A collection of Amberina glassware, fashionable in the 1880s, was made by the New England firm which eventually moved to Toledo, Ohio, and became Libbey Glass.

At the west end of the room is one of the most popular paintings of 18th-century England, Benjamin West's *The Death of General Wolfe*. West, an American, became a famous painter of historical scenes in the court of George III and went on to organize the Royal Academy. The painting shows British General Wolfe, fatally wounded, surrounded by his staff. The year was 1759, just after Wolfe had completed a decisive victory over the French at Quebec, sealing British control over North America.

Martha Cook Building ★
South University and Tappan

Right across South University from Clements Library is one of the most lavishly furnished dormitories anywhere, the Martha Cook Building for women students, built in 1915. It was a gift of alumnus William Cook. Born in Hillsdale in 1858, Cook got his undergraduate and law degrees at Michigan and went on to author at age 27 *Cook on Corporations*, still a classic in its field. Over the entrance is a statue of Portia, the heroine of Shakespeare's The Merchant of Venice. In Cook's view, she was "Shakespeare's greatest lawyer." The interior is quite a sight — with its Tudor and Elizabethan panelled oak walls, vaulted ceilings, and handsome period furniture.

The customs at Martha Cook are far more formal and ritualized than in any other dormitory on the Michigan campus. Traditions continue such as afternoon teas, limited male visiting privileges, a dress code, and evening meals begun and ended in unison.

Law Quadrangle ★
Facing South University and State, to Tappan and Monroe. (313) 764-1358.

Right across the street from Martha Cook is an even grander gift from Cook: the Law Quadrangle, home of the U-M's top-ranked law school. This picturesque court of Gothic buildings was built between 1923 and 1933.

The Law Quad's quality of workmanship was rare even in the 1920s. The striking reading room of the **old Law Library** at the south side of the quadrangle (open 8 a.m.-midnight) has richly ornamented blue and gold plaster medallions decorating the ceiling. Heavy beams across the ceiling rest on elaborately carved blocks of wood. On each of the tall, narrow windows above the paneling is a colorful stained-glass seal of a college or university.

When the law library needed to be expanded, it presented the problem of how to deal architecturally with the imposing Gothic unity of the existing Law Quad. Architect Gunnar Birkerts' widely praised solution was an underground building that permits much natural light, along with dramatic views up at the Law Quad. Visitors are welcome to enter the foyer of the **new Law Library** at Tappan and Monroe.

Michigan Union ★
S. State at the head of South University. Mon 7 a.m.-1 a.m., Tues-Sat 7 a.m.-2 a.m., Sun 9 a.m.-1 a.m. Anyone can call with university-related questions to the Campus Information Center on the 1st floor (same hours): (313) 763-4636.

Across the street at State and South University is the venerable Michigan Union, built in 1920 as a meeting place for male U-M students. It was the first such student union in the county. For many years women were only allowed entrance through a side door, and then only for special

The Law Quad viewed from the west: collegiate Gothic at its most impressive, made possible by an alumnus' profits from Cuban sugar and street railways.

events. The **billiard room** was the last male bastion to fall, in the late 1960s. The big room remains one of the Union's most interesting areas. With oak paneling and quality tables, it retains the atmosphere of gentlemen's gaming rooms in decades past. Some of the country's best players still drop in to play here.

In the slickly remodeled Union basement is a a big **Barnes and Noble student book store** and large **food court** (open weekdays 7 a.m.-midnight, weekends from 9 a.m.)

Renovations have turned the upstairs into much more of a student lounge and meeting place than it had been for years. The **Campus Information Center**, up from the main entrance to the left, is staffed throughout the Union's long hours (from 7 a.m. to 1 a.m. most days) to field all questions about the U-M; it has a good deal of printed information about university doings (763-4636). Behind it, the informal, all-hours, food-permitted **Art Lounge** responds to student requests for exhibits of everything from student art to photos of Guatemala.

Michigan League ★
911 North University on Ingalls Mall. (313) 764-3177. Building and newsstand open daily 7 a.m.-11 p.m.

The Union's female counterpart as a student center was the 1929 Michigan League on North University.

Smaller than the Union, it remains a popular place because of its well-stocked newsstand at the front desk, large and excellent cafeteria, and basement grill. The League also houses the 700-seat **Lydia Mendelssohn Theater**, Ann Arbor's most congenial space for theatrical performances. The League's meeting and reception rooms are popular for everything from brown-bag lunches to weddings.

The tastefully decorated League has always been impeccably maintained under watchful feminine management, while the male-run Union, in contrast, has in past years been a mess. In the manner of a fine old-fashioned hotel, there are comfortable lounge areas for visitors here. On the fourth floor are 21 overnight **guest rooms** which many knowledgeable campus visitors make reservations well in advance to secure. Also, in warm weather don't miss the nice courtyard garden tucked in back.

Alumni Center
Fletcher at Washington. (Entrance faces the League). (313) 764-0384. Mon-Fri 8-12, 1-5. Sat 9-12.

Free one-hour **campus walking tours** for any interested visitor are given here by student volunteers weekdays at 10, 11, 12, 1, and 2 and Saturdays at 11 from September through April, with reduced summer hours. No appointment necessary. Visitors can also pick up free copies of the alumni magazine and a wide variety of U-M publications here. The center, finished in 1982, was designed by Washington architect Hugh Newell Jacobson, noted for contemporary buildings that adjust gracefully to sensitive historic environments.

Burton Tower ★
Behind Hill Auditorium on Ingalls Mall. University Musical Society: (313) 764-2538.

Across from the League is the Burton Tower, a campus landmark designed by Albert Kahn and finished in 1936 for the School of Music facilities and the University Musical Society, whose ticket office is here. At its top is the **Baird Carillon** with its 53 bronze bells weighing from 12 pounds to 12 tons. It was part of a carillon-building boom that swept U.S. college campuses beginning about 1915. **Half-hour concerts** begin weekdays at noon when school is in session. During that time you can go up to the top and see the single player pound hand and foot levers in quick succession to ring the bells. The tower offers a fine view of the campus.

On the eighth floor, instruments in the **Japanese music room**, with its tatami mats, can be heard when School of Music students practice there Tuesdays between noon and 9 p.m., September through April. Likewise, the **gamelan** or Indonesian orchestra can be heard in practice on the fourth floor Thursday afternoons and evenings.

Thomas M. Cooley Fountain ★
Ingalls Mall, between Burton Tower and the League

The centerpiece of Ingalls Mall is this delightful Art Deco fountain by Swedish sculptor Carl Milles. It shows Triton, the Greek god of the sea, frolicking with his children. Benches and flowers in season make this a pleasant place for a takeout lunch while listening to the carillon.

Hill Auditorium
North University between Thayer and Ingalls Mall. Box office: (313) 764-8350.

Hill has hosted just about every significant classical musical ensemble in the world. Although it is huge, with 4,300 seats, its acoustics are extraordinary, among the best in the country. Finished in 1912, it is a product of Albert Kahn's most original phase, showing the influence of Louis Sullivan in his use of strong geometric forms accented by tapestry brick ornament.

Rackham Building ★

E. Washington at Ingalls Mall west of Fletcher. Mon-Sat 8 a.m.-11p.m. Information desk: (313) 764-4415.

The administrative home of the university's graduate school, designed by Smith, Hinchman and Grylls and finished in 1935, is a visual feast inside. Its vivid colors are based on Roman and Greek designs. Pompeiian red walls contrast with the high blue-green ceiling stenciled with polychrome and gold decorations. The first-floor **auditorium** with its dramatic blue ceiling with gold stars is also a treat. On the third floor, extensive **galleries** exhibit mostly work of U-M students and faculty.

Horace Rackham, a Detroit lawyer who drew up the papers for the Ford Motor Company in 1903, made $12.5 million on his $5,000 investment in the fledgling firm and donated $10 million to the university for this splendid building.

Power Center for the Performing Arts

Fletcher and Huron.

This concrete and glass building reflects Felch Park's trees and its historic neighbors on Huron by day, and by night turns into a glowing glass box. The fat round columns echo the towering steam smokestack of the U-M power plant behind it. It's a striking building, one of the most distinguished architecturally on campus, designed by the noted Connecticut firm Kevin Roche-John Dinkeloo Associates. (Dinkeloo is a U-M architecture alum.) Donor Eugene Power, founder of University Microfilm, pioneered the mass microfilming of documents.

U-M Exhibit Museum ★★★

1109 Geddes Ave. where it intersects with N. University. (313) 764-0478. Tues-Sat 9-5, Sun 1-5. Free.

Not many other natural science museums in the country match the rarity and breadth of items on display here. The very number of displays can be overwhelming, however, and some of the explanatory signs are beyond most visitors' interest and knowledge levels.

Still, much here will likely interest most visitors. Over the decades the staff has meticulously constructed dozens of dioramas, miniature three-dimensional scenes which vividly re-evoke what life on Earth was like in the distant past. You can view a lush scene from a Pennsylvania coal forest 300 million years ago when giant insects abounded: dragonflies with 30-inch wingspans, and huge roaches crawling among gigantic palm trees. Another diorama shows what New England looked like 10 million years ago when it was populated with camels, primitive elephants, short-legged rhinoceroses, and rodents the size of woodchucks. You can see a part of Los Angeles 15 millions ago when sabertooths the size of African lions roamed the region.

A series of seven dioramas reveals the evolution of life, beginning way back in the Cambrian age 575 million years ago when crab-like creatures were the most sophisticated beasts around. You also get an intriguing glimpse into the villages of the various tribes of Indians who inhabited Michigan before Europeans arrived.

Displays reveal that the first paleo-Indians only arrived around here 10,000 years ago. Then the area was mainly covered with spruce-balsam forests supporting few large game animals except caribou, which these Indians hunted with lance-like spears. Any notion that Indian tribes here lived in tranquility before the white man's arrival is jarred with maps showing how the Potawatomi in the 17th century were driven out of this region by the Ottawa and other tribes, and how a variety of tribes came and went over the centuries.

An area of special interest to children is the dinosaur section, seven skeletons strong, highlighted by the looming remains of a big allosaurus that roamed Utah 140 million years ago. The flesh-eating giant had forbiddingly long claws and sharp, menacing teeth. More subtle but also evocative are the various fossil footprints dinosaurs made millions of years ago.

The museum also has a nifty **gift shop** on the ground floor, full of all sorts of small items to delight kids, along with some interesting jewelry, nature publications, and folk art.

The 4th-floor **planetarium** has changing shows ($1/person, no children under 5) on Saturday mornings at 10:30 and 11:30 and weekend afternoons at 2, 3, and 4. Weekday showings are by advance reservation only.

Group tours, which attract busloads of schoolchildren, are $1/person, with a $20 minimum. Make reservations at (313) 764-0478.

Kelsey Museum of Archaeology ★★★

434 S. State, across from Angell Hall. Mon-Fri 9-4, Sat & Sun 1-4. Call (313) 764-9304 for general information and special exhibits.

This small but important museum has two special attractions. The first is the 1891 building itself, made of local fieldstone in the Richardsonian Romanesque style. Originally called Newberry Hall, it was built to house the private Student Christian Association. Clearly great pains were taken in choosing beautiful stones for the structure. The green copper roof, decorative glass and woodwork, and imposing front turret combine to make this an architectural gem.

Inside is stored one of the most important collections of ancient Greek, Egyptian, Roman, and Near Eastern artifacts in the U.S. Only a fraction of the 90,000-piece collection is on permanent display, and what you see is very choice indeed. Colorful Egyptian mummy masks, exquisite Attic black-and-red-figured vase paintings, rare and amazingly intact Roman glass are all presented in a comfortable, intimate setting which encourages close study. Most surprising of all, perhaps, are the early Egyptian sculptures. Dating from 1000 to 200 B.C., they reveal remarkable artistic skill.

Much of the credit for this remarkable collection goes to a professor of Latin at the University of Michigan, Francis Kelsey. He started buying Mediterranean antiquities for the university in 1893. In addition, he was able to mobilize the excavation of the Roman town of Karanis in Eqypt, long covered by desert sands. Its rich debris was in danger of being mined as fertilizer in the 1920s. The Kelsey-led archaeological expedition discovered enormous quantities of normally perishable materials which the arid climate and sand covering had preserved. Glass, textiles, wood, and papyri were all found in abundance. The Karanis excavation has given the museum one of the world's most extensive collections of Roman glass and one of the few remaining wooden doors from the Roman era. In

At the Kelsey Museum visitors get a close look at stunning exhibits from one of the world's most important collections of of ancient Greek, Egyptian, Roman, and Near Eastern artifacts.

one Karanis house alone, some 20,000 Roman coins were found stashed away.

Changing exhibits are on widely varied topics such as Egyptian mummies and "Art and Holy Powers in Early Christian Homes." To schedule **docent-guided tours** (50¢ a person) for small or large groups, call (313) 763-3559.

U-M Museum of Art ★★

525 S. State at South University. (313) 764-0395. Sept-May: Tues-Fri 10-4, Sat-Sun 1-5. June-Aug: Tues-Fri 11-4, Sat-Sun 1-5. Free.

This is considered among the top ten university art museums in the country. Its strength is in the breadth of its holdings. There are well over 20,000 works in the permanent collection, including pieces by Durer, Delacroix, Rodin, Picasso, Rembrandt, Corot, Millet, Monet, Cezanne, Miro, Klee, and David Smith. Well-known paintings on permanent display include Expressionist Max Beckman's *Begin the Beguine*, the Italian Baroque painter Guercino's *Esther before Ahasuerus*, and Carl Wimar's dramatic portrayal of the American West, *Attack on an Emigrant Train*.

Collections of Whistler prints and German Expressionist paintings are outstanding, and there is a large collection of fine work from China and Japan. One especially remarkable work is "Autumn Colors At Ju-shan." Drawn about the year 1700, it shows in great detail a walled town and fishing villages in front of mountains along a river bank.

Other strengths are the 20th-century British and American sculpture and 19th-century landscapes. Another strong collection, prints, drawings, and photographs, is finally highlighted in the new Works on Paper Gallery in the basement.

The small **gift shop** has a choice assortment of cards, art publications, posters, handmade and ethnic jewelry, folk art and craft collectibles.

The ground floor of the U-M Museum of Art, one of the top university museums in the country with over 20,000 pieces. There are important works here from many eras, both Oriental and Western.

The enthusiastic, high-caliber staff of volunteer docents conducts free **group tours**; call (313) 747-2067 to schedule. Each Sunday at 2 pm., a different adult-oriented **gallery tour** focuses on one part of the collection. Lunchtime **art breaks** (Tues & Thurs at 12:10 and 12:30) explain one object or part of a show.

Michigan Stadium and Crisler Arena

Stadium Blvd. at Main St. Ticket information: (313) 764-3177. Athletic Department: (313) 747-BLUE. Michigan Stadium is open daily except home football games 10 a.m.-3 p.m.

The U-M is the only top-ranked academic university which has also over the decades consistently fielded a top-ranked NCAA football team. The team's heritage is long and distinguished. Only 11 times in the past 89 years has the team lost more games than it won; it has completed 15 seasons without a loss.

The stadium the Wolverines play in is also remarkable. It is the biggest collegiate stadium in the country. Even more remarkably, the 101,701 seats are consistently sold out. The field lies directly over Allen's Creek. If you put your ear down on the 50-yard line when the stands are empty, you can still hear the creek running.

Men's NCAA basketball has been more erratic at the U-M over the years. Only in the past quarter century has it become a fairly consistent power. Before its remarkable 1989 national championship, the team's zenith was in 1964, when Cazzie Russell and Bill Buntin led the Wolverines to the NCAA finals. There, although ranked number one in the country, they were defeated by UCLA. Demand for tickets after that season so far outstripped available seats in Yost Field House that much bigger Crisler Arena was completed in 1967. Dubbed "the house that Cazzie built," it seats 13,601. Concerts also are held here, as are NCAA wrestling and gymnastic matches.

Yost Field House, a very handsome and under-appreciated building designed by Smith Hinchman and Grylls in a Renaissance-derived style with rich brick detail, is now used as the ice hockey arena. The U-M **hockey team practice** throughout the year is between 3:45 and 5:45; visitors are welcome.

The **M Go Blue Shop** (open weekdays 11-8, weekends 10-4) inside Yost sells a wide range of Michigan clothing, not just the usual sweatshirts and mufflers, but $37 hockey jerseys, team guides, videotapes, books, and paraphernalia to benefit U-M athletic scholarships.

Tickets for individual games are close to impossible to get for football, and basketball games ($10) are often sold out well in advance. But hockey ($6/$4) and baseball ($2) don't require advance arrangements. Call 764-3177 for schedule and ticket information. For information on minor sports, men's and women's, call (313) 747-BLUE.

North Campus

Between Fuller and Plymouth roads north of the river. Accessible from Huron via Glen or Division.

This outlying 800-acre campus across the river from the Central Campus to the northeast was planned in the 1940s, when residential neighborhoods blocked future growth of the university in central Ann Arbor. Famed architect Eero Saarinen planned the new campus, which includes the College of Engineering, School of Music, and, in a single building, the School of Art and College of Architecture and Urban Planning.

The **Art School snack bar**, open from 8 a.m. to 10 p.m. weekdays, Saturdays 8 to 5, may well be the most interesting place to eat out here, with a good selection of deli sandwiches, fresh bagels and donuts, trail mix, and the like. The halls are lined with projects of art and architecture students.

Phoenix Memorial Laboratory

Bonisteel Blvd. near Beal. (313) 764-6220.

The two-megawatt experimental nuclear reactor built here in 1954 was one of the first university reactors in the postwar surge of research interest in peaceful applications of

Gerald R. Ford Presidential Library ★
1000 Beal south of Bonisteel Blvd. (313) 668-2218. Mon-Fri 9-4:30.

This is one of only seven presidential libraries in the country, located here because Ford was a 1935 graduate of the U-M. Scholars from around the world come here to delve into myriad issues affected by the Ford presidency.

The library's estimated 15 million pages of documents brought from Washington include all of Ford's White House papers as well as the papers of certain key advisors such as economist Arthur Burns and energy chief Frank Zarb. Some papers remain classified and are kept in locked vaults, but most are available for public scrutiny. A semi-permanent display explains the library's function to visitors; occasional special exhibits are organized here.

Bentley Historical Library
1150 Beal at Bonisteel. (313) 764-3482. Mon-Fri 8:30-5, Sat 9-12:30. Limited free parking by the library.

The library houses the **Michigan Historical Collection**, one of three main archives for primary source materials on Michigan history. Reference librarians are accustomed to helping genealogists and other amateur historians who are researching their houses and communities.

Gerald Ford's papers during his 25 years as a Congressman from Grand Rapids are also here. Changing displays in the foyer **exhibit case** highlight subjects from the collections.

The library's longtime former director, Bob Warner, now head of the U-M library school, made history as the head of the National Archives by refusing to surrender the Watergate tapes to Richard Nixon.

Earlier in the page: atomic energy. Half-hour tours are available by appointment Monday through Friday.

Stearns Collection of Musical Instruments ★★
In the new Margaret Dow Towsley south wing of the Moore Building, the main part of the School of Music, at the end of Baits Dr. (Baits is off Broadway at the top of the hill, about 1/4 mile west of Plymouth Rd. Or, from Murfin on North Campus, take Duffield to Baits.) (313) 763-4389. Thurs & Fri 10-5, Sat & Sun 1-8 except for May and June. Free.

The core of this unusual collection is 1,400 instruments collected by wealthy Detroit drug manufacturer Frederick Stearns and donated to the university in 1899. They include some extremely rare Asian and African instruments along with European instruments like a Baroque cello in almost-original condition and a recorder from Leipzig at the time of Bach.

The collection, now over 2,000 and growing, is intended to be encyclopaedic, representing instruments of all sorts from throughout the world. New additions, including the first Moog synthesizer to be sold, reflect an effort to collect 20th-century materials. Interesting lecture-demonstrations are held at 2 o'clock on the second Sundays of September, October, January, and February.

Eva Jessye Afro-American Music Collection
Lobby of the Moore Building, School of Music. See directions for Stearns Collection. Mon-Fri 9-5, Sat & Sun 1-8 except for May and June.

Changing exhibits feature material on African-American musicians from this collection of African-American original manuscripts, opera scores, recordings, books, and photographs. There is a special emphasis on jazz and Duke Ellington. Jessye conducted the chorus for the 1935 premiere of Gershwin's "Porgy and Bess."

RESTAURANTS

DOWNTOWN

The Earle

121 W. Washington at First St. (313) 994-0211. Mon-Thurs 5:30-10, Fri 5:30-midnight, Sat 6-midnight, Sun 5-9 but closed in summer. Full bar, outstanding wine list. Major credit cards. A la carte entrees (including a starch) $10-16.

A decade ago, The Earle was the Ann Arbor vanguard of earthy French and Italian provincial cooking, served up for a sophisticated, well-traveled clientele who would appreciate amenities like dinner music on the piano and an award-winning wine list. The Earle remains both popular and excellent. It is comfortably housed in the lower level of the old Earle hotel. Specialties include a fresh salmon fillet in puffed pastry lined with a spinach-dill mousse ($15.95), changing veal, duck, and lamb dishes, and pastas like *vermicelli alla puttanesca alla napoletana* (with garlic, capers, anchovies, and black olives). Budget-conscious diners order the $10-11 pastas or the cheaper appetizers to allow for the noteworthy desserts. At the wine bar, you can sample an unusual variety of wines by the glass.

Gratzi

326 S. Main between Liberty and William. (313) 663-5555. Mon-Thurs 11:30-11, Fri & Sat 11:30-midnight, Sun 4-10. Entrees $5-$9 (lunch); $9-$16 (dinner). Full bar. Visa, AmExpress, MasterCard.

Dramatically housed in the old Orpheum Theater, this loud, convivial Northern Italian restaurant quickly became a hot spot in the region. The light food is quite good, and the decor is striking, with its two tiers of seating and theatrical flair. Come early, or be prepared to wait. Chef's specialties currently include *linguine del golfo* (shrimp, mussels, and sea scallops in a pesto sauce) and *pello al mar salla con funghi*, a sauteed chicken breast dish. The thin-crust pizza is also popular here.

Moveable Feast

326 W. Liberty just west of downtown. (313) 663-3278. Lunch 11:30-2 Tues-Fri; dinner 6-9:30 Tues-Sat. Entrees $5-$8 (lunch); $12-$23 (dinner). Wine. Major credit cards.

Housed in an elegant, mansard-roofed brick house in the Old West Side, the Moveable Feast has consistently been one of Ann Arbor's best fine restaurants. The French-accented menu, changed frequently, is international in scope. A celebrated sourdough French bread, perfect flakey croissants (including filled lunch croissants), and famously rich butter cakes, all baked in the Feast's own bakery, may be purchased to take out. Simple lunches, very moderately priced, may feature cappellini pasta with roasted eggplant and fresh tomato sauce ($5.50) or sauteed medallions of pork tenderloin with leek compote and mustard sauce ($5.75).

Dinner may be ordered a la carte or as four-course prix fixe meal for $35.50, which includes an appetizer, soup or salad, entrees such as sauteed Provini veal chops with gingered mushrooms, or sauteed medallions of lamb with goat cheese and fresh basil, and choice of dessert. An especially good value is the Tuesday through Thursday bistro supper ($35 for two): soup, salad, or appetizer, an entree, and dessert.

Old German Restaurant ★

120 W. Washington at Ashley. (313) 662-0737. Mon-Wed, Sat 11-8:30, closed Thurs, Fri 11-9, Sun 11-8. All major credit cards. Full bar.

More than anyplace else, the Old German is a living link to the traditional lifestyle of Ann Arbor Germans. A fire gutted the place, and rebuilding gave it a new look, all brick and beams, again accented by a superb collection of mostly antique beer steins and plates. Owner Bud Metzger made it a point to rebuild the lunch counter, used by workers from the factories that used to dot the west side. The big round corner table is a real *Stammtisch,* a communal table for hometown regulars from many walks of life.

There are no portion-controlled servings of meat here — the Old German buys entire quarters and, by careful planning, uses every bit, just like good housewives used to, down to small pieces for goulash and meat patties and bones for broth. The meat-oriented menu is long and a little overwhelming. The Swiss steak and bratwurst with pan-fried onions are good, and some of the best dishes are the daily specials: pork loin with sauerkraut ($4.75 at lunch, $7.75 for dinner on Tuesday), veal-stuffed noodle with German potato salad ($4.50/$6.50), and smoked pork shank ($7.75 at dinner) that perfumes the entire restaurant.

KERRYTOWN AREA

Fuji Restaurant ★★

327 Braun Court, off N. Fourth Ave. between Catherine and Kingsley opposite the Farmers' Market. (313) 663-3111. Tues-Sat 11-2, 5-10. Visa, AmExpress, MasterCard. Full bar.

The ethnic restaurants in the row of workers' houses on Braun Court are good, and many people consider this Japanese restaurant the best. The look and taste of things here are so well thought out and serene, you tend to leave feeling calm and happy. Seating is at Western-height tables, but everything expected of a Japanese restaurant is here: sake, Japanese beer, a sushi bar, excellent tempura made with salmon, chicken, fish, pork, lobster, or vegetables. Dinners run from $7.50 for some noodle dishes to $18.50 (for a lobster combination), with most between $9.50 and $11.50.

Lunches average $5. All meals come with soup, lettuce salad, and rice.

Zingerman's Delicatessen ★★★

422 Detroit at Kingsley, east of Kerrytown. (313) 663-3354. Mon-Sat 7 a.m.-8:30 p.m., Sun 9-8:30. No credit cards; Checks accepted. No alcohol.

This high-energy place is a fabulous deli, covering all the basics including chicken soup and bagels and lox, and featuring a cross-cultural array of creative home cooking. The (at last count) 59 huge and delicious sandwiches are the main attraction. Most popular is the Reuben (#2): hot corned beef, imported Swiss cheese, sauerkraut, Russian dressing, on toasted rye ($6.10). In second place is the grilled Georgia Reuben (#18) made with turkey breast and cole slaw ($6.10). See p. 259 for a fuller listing. Seating for 56 in a neighboring house, and terrace seating in good weather, makes for much shorter waits.

Gandy Dancer ★

401 Depot between N. Division and N. State. (313) 769-0592. Lunch Mon-Sat 11:30-4, dinner 5-11, 'til midnight Fri & Sat. Sun brunch 10:30-2, dinner 3-10. Entrees $4-$9 (lunch); $11-$18 (dinner). Full bar. Major credit cards.

Ann Arbor's most popular destination restaurant is in the striking old fieldstone Michigan Central railroad station. Detroit's successful Chuck Muer seafood chain has treated the building handsomely, with dignity and general good taste. Passing trains are announced by ringing a bell.

The menu changes daily but always features fresh fish, accompanied by a starch and vegetable, for $6.75-$11 (lunch) and $6.75-$15 (dinner). Soup and salad are extra ($2-$$3.75). A big favorite is the $18 bucket filled with lobster, crab, mussels, corn on the cob, and redskin potatoes. Other choices include rack of lamb, filet mignon, and pasta dishes. A jazz trio plays for Sunday brunch.

CAMPUS AREA

Cottage Inn

512 E. William between Thompson and Maynard. (313) 663-3379. Mon-Sat 11 a.m.-1 a.m., Fri & Sat 'til 1:30, Sun noon-1:30. Full bar. Visa, MasterCard, AmExpress.

A 40-year-old campus pizza spot, the Cottage Inn has been expanded and updated for broader appeal, with comfortable booths and a warm, lively atmosphere. Today it's one of the few places in town where parents on a budget can relax over dinner and a beer with their kids. The pizza comes with lots of cheese. A big bowl of Greek salad makes a meal with a pizza for two (for $12.75) or four ($15.25). Greek, antipasto, and spinach salads ($4.45-$4.75) are enough for two or three. Dinner dishes like lasagna, chicken stir-fry Alfredo, chicken Florentine (a breast marinated in wine, baked with marinara sauce and cheese on a spinach bed), and various pasta combinations are mostly under $7, including bread and soup or salad.

Angelo's Restaurant

1100 Catherine at Glen by University Hospital. (313) 761-8996. Mon-Fri 6-4, Sat 6-2, Sun 7-2. No liquor or credit cards.

Breakfast at Angelo's is an Ann Arbor tradition, featuring thick slices of homemade bread or raisin toast. French toast is good (regular $3.50, deep fried with strawberries, blueberries, and whipped cream $4.15), but so are the eggs and omelets. For lunch the pork sandwich ($3.50) is the classic, but the salads are good, too. The main problem with this widely popular diner, in the shadow of the giant U-M medical complex, is the crowds and parking. When its own little lot across Glen is full, space is very hard to find except on weekends.

Krazy Jim's Blimpy Burgers

551 S. Division at Packard) (313) 663-4590. Mon-Sat 11-8. No liquor or credit cards.

Another Ann Arbor institution, Krazy Jim's has been serving up its famous, greasy Blimpy Burgers since 1954. Jim Shafer still owns and runs the place. Not far from the U-M athletic campus, it gets a fair number of jocks and coaches, and there's generally a 30-minute wait between noon and 2. The burgers range from the double ($1.10) to the quint ($3.20). The concept here is "build your own burger," with 245,760 possible combinations starting with a choice of buns (plain, onion, Kaiser, pumpernickel). French-fried zucchini, caulilower, and mushrooms are also featured.

Le Dog ★

410 E. Liberty between Division and Thompson. (313) 665-2114, Mon-Fri 11-3, Saturday hours (May-Oct only) noon-4. Closed Jan-March.

This glorified hot dog stand (takeout only) is probably Ann Arbor's most unique eatery. The most popular items are hot dogs ($1.20) and Polish sausage ($1.45, cheese, chili, and/or sauerkraut 20¢ each extra). But chef Julius Dobos, blessed with an inspired Hungarian flair for food, makes a very tasty lobster bisque Thursdays and Fridays for only $2.40 a bowl and treats his customers with a sometimes dazzling array of pre-ordered choices like veal tarragon. This man understands what "small is beautiful" is all about, and enjoys a three-month winter vacation as a result. The whole place fits into the old 8 by 20-foot Ice Cream Caramel Corn Castle. It's conveniently located between downtown and the State Street area, not far from the pleasant urban park at Liberty and Division.

Cajun Rice, a mixture of sausages, vegetables, and spicy sauce with fresh dill pickles, is available throughout the week, also for $2.40. Seasonal $1 specialties include fresh fruit shakes (peach, strawberry, blueberry, etc.) and hot mulled cider.

Michigan League Cafeteria

911 N. University, 2 blocks east of South State on the U-M campus. (313) 764-3177. Mon-Sat lunch 11:30-1:45; dinner 4:30-7:30. Sun dinner 11:30-2:15. Entrees $2.70-$4.50. No alcohol or credit cards.

Long popular with senior citizens, this pleasant University of Michigan cafeteria is a good choice for children, too. The food is good and reasonably priced. There's prime rib every night. Chicken pot pie is another favorite. Unusual vegetable dishes such as corn pudding or carrots with cranberries are a specialty. Thursday evenings from October through July feature international or early American dishes.

ELSEWHERE

Siam Kitchen ★

In Westgate Shopping Center on West Stadium at Jackson. (313) 665-2571. Mon-Sat lunch 11:30-2, dinner 5-9, 'til 10 Fri & Sat. Entrees: $4.95-$6.75 (lunch), $5.95-$13 (dinner). No alcohol.

This popular restaurant offers tasty stir-fried dishes with the unique blend of spicy, hot Thai flavors. Especially good dishes include shrimp with broccoli and chicken strips marinated in coconut milk.

Cousins Heritage Inn ★★★

7954 Ann Arbor St. in Dexter, just east of downtown. From Ann Arbor, take Dexter Rd. west; it turns into Ann Arbor St. (313) 426-3020. Lunch 11-2 Mon-Fri; dinner 6-9 Tues-Sat. Wine. Visa, MasterCard, Diners, checks.

A perfectionistic pair of ex-teachers and a chef trained at the Golden Mushroom, run this outstand-ing little restaurant, considered one of the best in Michigan. It's in a pleasant mid-19th-century house in thevillage of Dexter. Wild game is the specialty here. The dinner menu, which changes frequently, recently featured roast pheasant; a yellowfin tuna saute with scallops, shrimp, and lobster sauce ($20), and mule deer and Russian black boar with wild rice pancakes, braised cabbage, and cranberry relish ($22). All meals, lunch and dinner, include a house salad, starch (some are pretty exotic: brown rice pilaf with pine nuts, and quinoa, a high-protein Central American grain), and varying vegetables — super-sweet fresh corn (a signature vegetable, flown in from Florida), carrots, and pea pods served with basmati rice, for instance.

Lunches are very reasonable — $8 for beef tenderloin tips with wild mushrooms, $7.75 for seafood pasta with shrimp and smoked whitefish. Soups are wonderful, and desserts, from fruit cobblers to Jacques Pepin's iced souffle, appeal to an unusually wide range of tastes. The intelligently chosen 70-item wine list is wide-ranging for its size.

For a delightful outing from Ann Arbor, take the sinuous, scenic Huron River Drive to Dexter. And stop at **Pat Garrett and Friends**, an inspired gift shop in downtown Dexter.

See also: *Del Rio (p. 254), Round Table (p. 256), DeLong's Barbeque (p. 259), Drake Sandwich Shop (p. 262), Steve's Lunch (p. 263), Coffee Break (p. 263).*

LODGINGS

Campus Inn
(313) 769-2200.
615 E. Huron at State near campus and downtown.
205 units on 15 floors. $80 single; $90 double. $80 weekend special for 2 includes $25 gift certificate towards meals. Outdoor pool. Sauna. HBO. 3 ballrooms. Excellent but expensive restaurant, Victors, and a casual cafe. Upper floors have terrific views of the central city and U-M campus.

Bell Tower Hotel
(313) 769-3010.
300 S. Thayer across from Hill Auditorium.
56 rooms on 4 floors; 10 suites. $79 single; $89 double; suites $95-$190. No swimming pool, but $4 university swimming facility nearby. Within the hotel is the highly regarded (and expensive) Escoffier restaurant; many other restaurants nearby. One of the Midwest's few luxury European-style hotels with an exceptionally pleasant and refined ambience.

Michigan League
(313) 764-0446.
911 N. University on U-M campus.
21 rooms, 1 suite on 4th floor of U-M facility with cafeteria, coffee shop. Single: $55; double: $65. Many rooms have fine views of the central campus.

Weber's Inn
(313) 769-2500. (800) 521-1413. 3050 Jackson Rd. 1/2 mile west of I-94.
160 units on 4 floors. $68 single; $72 double. Medium-sized indoor swimming pool, exercise room, sauna, whirlpool, and game room. Free Showtime movies.

Ann Arbor Marriott Inn
(313) 769-9800 (800) 228-9290.
3600 Plymouth Rd. near Green just west of US-23.
227 units on 5 floors. $89 single; $104 double; $69 weekend rate for 2 includes breakfast. Medium-sized indoor pool; large outdoor pool. Sauna, whirlpool, game room. HBO, ESPN, and $6.95 pay movies. Reasonably good in-house restaurant and lounge. Some rooms overlook pool. Views from 5th-floor rooms.

Best Western Wolverine Inn
(313) 665-3500. (800) 528-1234.
3505 S. State at I-94 Exit 177; on northeastern corner of intersection.
119 units on 2 floors. $39 single; $45 double whirlpool and sauna. Free HBO and ESPN. Next to Bill Knapp Restaurant, and near Briarwood mall.

Holiday Inn Holidome
(313) 665-4444. (800) HOLIDAY.
2900 Jackson Rd. just west of I-94. From I-94 exit 172 (Jackson Rd.), turn west. 1 1/2 blocks on right.
223 rooms and 3 suites on 5 floors. $64 single; $74 double. $69 weekend special for 2 includes breakfast, gift package. Indoor & outdoor swimming pools, sauna, whirlpool, game room. Lounge with live entertainment Tues-Sun. TV movies: Showtime & pay movies ($6.35). Two in-house restaurants.

Red Roof Inn
(313) 996-5800. (800) 848-7878.
3621 Plymouth Rd. just west of US-23.
109 units on 2 floors. $35.95 single; $41.95-$43.95 double. Room TVs have free in-house movies, ESPN. Free local calling. Non-smoking rooms available. Free morning coffee and newspaper. Big Boy Restaurant is next door. Red Roof Inns are noted for their thick, soundproof walls which reduce the chance of being kept up by a noisy TV or party.

The Homestead Bed and Breakfast
(313) 429-9625.
9279 Macon Rd., Saline. 8 miles south-west of Ann Arbor.
5 rooms share 2 baths. $45-$55 Includes full breakfast. 1851 brick farmhouse, comfortably furnished with antiques and lots of books. Innkeeper is a knowledgeable native.

Fenton

This small city of about 8,000, nestled among several lakes, was once home of a large wooden implement factory and later a cement factory. But today it is primarily a bedroom community of Flint, 14 miles due north.

Here is the **Miceless Mansion**, a white, 12-room house at the corner of Shiawassee and Adelaide streets. A.J. Phillips built it in 1890 for his wife, who so abhorred the little rodents that he constructed especially solid walls to prevent their entry. The adjoining Victorian mansions belonged to Phillips's three sons. Phillips owned the local factory which made an extraordinary variety of wooden implements: snow shovels, ironing boards, ladders, hammock and swing sets, among many others. The screens his factory made were the first to be used in the White House. Phillips was an energetic, if eccentric, man who kept two offices in town. One is where the post office is today. The other, which he donated to the city for a library, is now Fenton's historical museum. (See "Points of Interest" below.) Philllips used it as a sort of hideaway, a place where he could indulge his interests in wine and women. (He died of cirrhosis of the liver in 1904.)

The downtown that disappeared

Fenton wins the prize for the state's most unsuccessful urban renewal project. In 1976, after several defeats, citizens here voted to raze almost the entire brick downtown and build a new "square" in its place. Some blame the approval of this misguided project on the fact that a five-inch snowfall on the day of the election reduced the number of old-timers who voted. It is also charged that the project was spearheaded by citizens who directly profited by removing the old brick buildings. In any case, the structures were razed, and only a small part of the grandiose new commercial center which was supposed to replace it has been built. What's worse, the new complex interrupts Fenton's main avenue, Leroy Street. "It cut the city in half," complains one resident. To the casual visitor the central area is confusing. Now called "Fenton Square," the downtown includes a bank, a Dancer's department store, a pharmacy, and a few other stores and service businesses. It lacks the critical mass to seem like a real downtown. "Everyone hates downtown," one person summed it up. In contrast, the central residential district around downtown still looks like an attractive turn-of-the-century small town.

Maps and information
For free maps of Fenton and nearby Seven Lakes State Park, plus brochures about events and visitor destinations, contact the Chamber of Commerce, 207 Silver Lake Rd., Fenton, MI 48430. (313) 629-5447. A helpful map on the entire Holly, Fenton, and Linden area including golf courses, recreation areas, local beaches, and ski areas is $2.

Continental brand screen door made in A.J. Phillips' Fenton factory. The eccentric Fenton businessman made the fist screens used in the White House.

As commercial development strings out along a long, ugly commercial strip to the north, the city's original downtown is left stranded to the south of Fenton Square. Today it is an attractive shopping complex, called **"Dibbleville"** after the town's original name. The oldest of its buildings, at the corner of South Leroy and Shiawassee Avenue, went up in 1868. The entire district of old homes and commercial buildings is on the National Register of Historic Places.

Gazebo concerts
There are nightly concerts at Fenton's exceptionally pleasant gazebo near downtown from the last week in June through the first week in August. They begin at 7 p.m.

A fateful card game

Dibbleville was named after its founder, Clark Dibble. He chose the spot in 1834 because two Indian trails intersected here near the Shiawassee River. A few years later two men named Fenton and Leroy bought the village from Dibble. A card game was played to determine which man the city would be renamed after, with the loser having the honor of naming the main street.

In the 1850s a railroad was built from Detroit, making Fenton briefly a railhead. Wagons came from as far away as Flint (15 miles to the north) and Saginaw to ship their goods by rail. That gave Fenton a boost. So did Lake Fenton just to the north. By 1900 it had become a popular vacation spot, with two hotels and a lake steamer.

In this century a big cement factory, using marl from the bottoms of the region's many lakes, was the major employer. In the 1950s, when US-23 was completed, Fenton became more and more of a bedroom community for people commuting to Flint and the far reaches of the Detroit metropolitan area. Today the city's largest employers are Creative Foam (which employs 200 fabricating foam for auto car seats and furniture) and a 190-employee Lear Siegler car seat factory.

The **Fenton Hotel** at North Leroy and Grange Hall Road, built in 1856, is one of Michigan's oldest hotels still in operation. Now exclusively a restaurant and bar, it serves lunch and dinner daily. Across Leroy Street, the acclaimed Michigan Bean Company restaurant used to occupy the imposing old wooden Fenton Grain Elevator, erected in 1868. It was once owned by the Michigan Bean Company. Farmers brought their grain and beans here to be processed and bagged. Locals speculate that the fine restaurant recently installed here was a bit too much of a drive for Detroit-area patrons happy to pay its fancy prices, yet too expensive for the local citizenry.

The Fenton Museum, former office of A.J. Phillips, whose factory made every thing from ironing boards to swings.

POINTS OF INTEREST

Fenton Museum ★
301 S. Leroy St. (313) 629-0549. Open Mon-Fri 12-4, Sun 1-4.

This local museum has the quaint, informal ambience of a true small-town historical museum which is the repository of a wide assortment of local artifacts. Here you can see the wooden cradle used by the infant of the town's first settler, along with a detailed model of Fenton High School made by the shop class of 1952, and an amazingly well preserved dress of the wife of town founder Clark Dibble.

This was once A. J. Phillips's office, and you can see his factory's many wood products and the old catalogs that promoted them. His oak desk is in the front room, which he air-conditioned by opening doors to the basement and cutting a big hole through the floor.

Dibbleville
South Leroy at Shiawassee. Typical store hours: Mon-Sat 10-5:30.

Today this shopping complex of post-Civil War brick buildings features an interesting antique and gift shop called **The Iron Grate**, a chocolate shop, a nice bakery/ice cream/sandwich shop, a top-notch carryout, and a country gift shop. A district of historic homes adjoins it.

Gazebo and Millrace ★
Leroy at Mill streets (between Dibbleville and downtown.

Next to the noisily rushing waters of the Shiawassee River, this big, old-fashioned gazebo is dramatically situated just below the serene mill pond. Built in 1980, it's a civic project in which residents justifiably take great pride. The gazebo has quickly become a Fenton focal point (City Hall is next door and the post office across the street) and a favorite spot for weddings. It is a great place for a picnic. Just south on LeRoy you can pick up a tasty takeout lunch or snack at **Brick's Oven Bakery** or at the **Fenton House Carryout**.

Fenton Depot/ Chamber of Commerce
Silver Lake Rd. at Pine St. (313) 629-5447. Mon-Fri 9-4:30.

The Chamber of Commerce occupies this attractive little depot. It was built in 1882 after the original 1856 depot burned down. It still looks very much the same, except for the newer hipped roof. The original light fixtures, paneling, ticket counters, and some furniture remain. The railroad line between Fenton and Detroit made Fenton especially important because this was the end of the line. (A turntable to turn the locomotives around was just to the east.) The line, now owned by the the Canadian Grand Trunk, extends north to link up with the Grand Trunk line between Port Huron and Chicago.

Seven Lakes Vineyard, Orchard & Cider Mill
1111 Tinsman Rd near Eddy Lake Rd., northeast of Fenton and near Seven Lakes State Park. (313) 629-5686. Mon-Sat 10-5, Sun noon to 5. In winter by appointment.

Harry Guest and his son, Chris, have planted 20,000 French hybrid grape vines on their 100 hilly acres, which include 35 acres of woods and 15 acres of apple trees. Since 1983 they have been producing estate-bottled wines commercially: vignoles, aurore, chancellor, and seyval. Vignoles and their Cady Lake blended white wine have done especially well. Visitors are invited to taste the wine.

Home winemakers (like the Guests had been before they launched Harry's retirement project) may buy bottles and fresh grape juice by the jug or barrel in September and October. Eight varieties of apples are also for sale. You can pick your own. From late September to Thanksgiving a very good apple cider is available on weekends, along with doughnuts.

You are welcome to **picnic** at the tables here. Maps of the **walking trails** are available.

Balloon Corporation of America

2084 Thompson Rd. (313) 629-0040.

Located just north of Fenton, BCA offers a 45- to 60-minute balloon flight over this scenic countryside for $175 per person. Other special flights are available. Call for reservations.

RESTAURANTS

Fenton Hotel

302 N. Leroy at Grange Hall Rd. (313) 629-2632. Mon-Sat; lunch 11-4, dinner 5-11, 'til midnight Fri & Sat. Entrees: $2.95-$7.95 (lunch); $7.95-$29.95 (dinner). Full bar. Visa, AmExpress, Diners, MasterCard.

The interior of this old 1856 railroad hotel is not nearly as charming as the nearby Holly Hotel, but it is a locally popular "fine dining" restaurant. It is best known for the frog legs, available all week but all-you-can-eat on Mondays and Tuesdays for $8.95. The 16 oz. prime rib for $15.95 is another favorite.

Fenton House Carryout ★

413 S. Leroy in the Dibbleville Minimall. (313) 629-0661. Mon-Thurs 11:30-10, Fri & Sat until 11, Sun noon-9. No credit cards or alcohol.

Despite the name, this unpretentious spot, run by a Greek-Italian family, has a few tables for diners The food elicits raves from locals who bemoan the chains that dominate Fenton restaurants. Portions are huge; the $3.95 croissant sandwich (club, turkey, Italian, or tuna) is more than one person could usually eat. Dinners for two (enough for three!) come with homemade bread sticks and a Greek salad: a wonderful whole herbed lemon chicken is $11.50, lasagna $9.50, a slab of moist, well-seasoned pork ribs for $16.95. A la carte also available.

LODGINGS

Best Western of Fenton
(313) 750-1711, (800) 528-1234. 3255 Owen Rd. Take U.S.-23 to Owen Rd. exit 78, southeast corner of intersection.
62 rooms, 2 floors. $48 single; $56 double. Suites $75-$85. Freeway location. Indoor pool. VCR rental ($3.50 + $2/tape). Small refrigerators in rooms. Restaurants within walking distance.

Holly

This attractive town of about 5,000 nestles in the low hills and lakes at Oakland County's very northwestern corner. It's a pastoral contrast to the densely populated suburbs to the southeast. The well-preserved downtown has become quite a tourist attraction, highlighted by the infamous **Battle Alley** between Saginaw and Broad, a block southeast of the center of town. There, decades ago, brawls among taverngoers were common. If anything, the trend today is too far toward the sedate. While taverns have dwindled to a precious few, there are more than enough cute gift shoppes filled with small, mock-Victorian knick-knacks. Antique shops also abound, spilling across the railroad tracks into the adjoining residential neighborhood.

A well deserved Battle Alley attraction is the **Holly Hotel**, now a restaurant. Built in the mid-19th century, it combines very good food with an exceptional Victorian decor that feels authentic without becoming a silly parody of that era. There is also a comfortable old-fashioned bar.

Like most towns in southern Michigan, Holly was settled in the 1830s by emigrants from upstate New York. However, a New Jersey settler named it for Mt. Holly, New Jersey. The Shiawassee River flows along the town's southern boundary. It was dammed in 1843 for a sawmill and later a gristmill, which burned down in 1900. This region is studded with lakes. Three are within the city limits alone. Back in 1887, 25¢ steamboat excursions took people from Simonson Lake in the center of town through a canal to Bush Lake to the north and back.

Festival town
The well-regarded **Michigan Renaissance Festival**, held weekends in August and September, presents costumed parades; mounted jousts; period plays, music, and dance; children's activities; and food (Renaissance and otherwise). It's held on a large parcel of land off Dixie Highway north of Holly; all-day admission is under $10 for adults, about $5 for children. It is one of four similar festivals professionally produced by a Minneapolis firm. (313) 645-9640.

The **Carry Nation Festival**, held on and around Battle Alley the weekend after Labor Day, commemorates the temperance militant's visit to Holly with street performances, a parade, and crafts and food booths. Free.

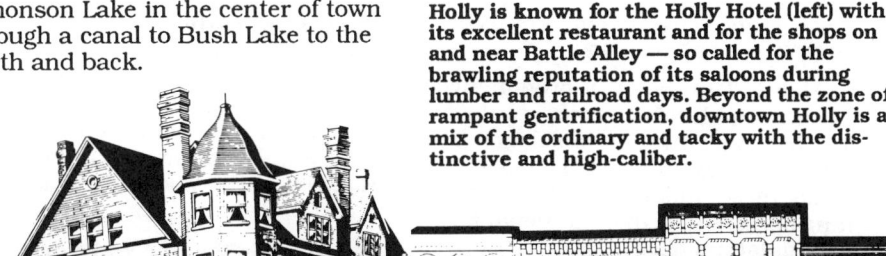

Holly is known for the Holly Hotel (left) with its excellent restaurant and for the shops on and near Battle Alley — so called for the brawling reputation of its saloons during lumber and railroad days. Beyond the zone of rampant gentrification, downtown Holly is a mix of the ordinary and tacky with the distinctive and high-caliber.

Holly is the site of the state's first railroad junction, and both lines are still in operation. The Grand Trunk heads northwest out of Detroit; the C&O heads up from Toledo through Saginaw to Ludington, where a ferry takes the cars across Lake Michigan. Flint lumber baron Henry Crapo, later Michigan governor, helped bring that railroad to completion. **Crapo Park** is located on the spot where he had a big lumberyard next to downtown along the C&O tracks.

Today Holly's biggest employer is Delta Tube, with about 180 employees. A division of Richfield Iron Works of Flint, it makes the rugged metal bins that automakers store parts in. Second-biggest is the Georg Fischer Foundry. Owned by a Swiss firm, it makes products that improve sand mold casting done by foundries. Their product line, which ranges in price all the way from $15 to $20 million, is sold mainly to the Big three automakers, as well as Navistar, John Deere, and Caterpillar.

Stimulated by a number of festivals each year, Holly has developed a considerable touristic infrastructure. One festival celebrates the time ax-wielding temperance crusader Carry Nation staged her felonious assault on Battle Alley taverns, smashing whiskey bottles right and left.

*Weekends between Thanksgiving and Christmas, the **Dickens Olde Fashioned Christmas Walk** on and around Battle Alley brings Dickens' "Christmas Carol" to life with costumed carollers on the street and in shops; jugglers and other street performers; skits with Scrooge and Tiny Tim; and outdoor food booths selling chestnuts, sausages, baked potatoes, and the like.*

POINTS OF INTEREST

Battle Alley

Between Broad (Milford Rd.) and Saginaw, on the southeast side of downtown Holly. Typical hours (unless otherwise noted): Mon-Fri 10-5, Sat until 6, Sun 12-5.

Holly's 19th-century prominence as a rail and lumber center resulted in a big concentration of saloons between here and the nearby depot. Today these buildings house shops ranging from kitschy to unusual and even outstanding. They carry women's fashions, old coins, decorative and kitchen accessories, Hawaiian clothing and accessories, and Hong Kong imports.

Battle Alley Arcade
108 Battle Alley.

A handful of shops sell candies, dolls, handmade items, antiques, and Christmas decorations. You can stop in here for a free tasting of wines from the up-and-coming **Seven Lakes Vineyard** nearby. Found architectural materials have been used to create the wierdly interesting storefronts.

Pampered Lady
103 Battle Alley.

An unusual array of little luxuries from perfumes, oils for mixing your own fragrances, bath products, jewelry, vintage and new clothing, "wearable art," and vintage hats.

Balcony Row Antiques ★★

216 S. Broad. (313) 634-1400. Thurs-Sun 1-5.

Globetrotting proprietors Evelyn Raskin and Jim Hilty, who had a hand in restoring the Holly Hotel and developing Battle Alley, don't buy anything they don't like. As a result, with some choice furniture, china, and art objects from Europe and the U.S. (going back to the 18th century and even much earlier) and ancient Egypt. Nothing's very recent, except perhaps some autographs in Hilty's extensive collection.

In some ways this place is more like a museum than a store. You can read a letter from Voltaire apologizing for missing a lunch date, or go through a tunnel with dioramas illustrating the history of tools and agriculture, in which cavemen-style paintings adorn the cavern-like walls. There's also a book shop strong on military history, rare books, and documents. The name commemorates the old opera house, replaced by a plain block post office now completely covered over with an assemblage of found architectural artifacts.

Water Tower Antique Mall

310 Broad St., around the corner from Battle Alley. (313) 634-3500. Mon-Sat 10-5, Sun 12-5.

Sixty dealers or thereabouts in three interconnected buildings offer a great variety of merchandise, from primitives to Art Deco.

Detroit Model Railroad Club

104 N. Saginaw, just north of Maple St. (Holly Rd.) in downtown Holly. Call (313) 634-9167 for dates of 4 weekend open houses (3 in fall, 1 after Easter).

Since it bought the old Holly Theater here in the early 1970s, the Detroit Model Railroad Club has been working on a huge layout in "O" gauge, twice the size of the usual HO model trains, and correspondingly more realistic in detailing. Every Tuesday evening, club members come to work on the scenery, which is a cross-section of the U.S., with valleys, countryside and cities, and lots of switchyards for plenty of switching action. Visitors are welcome to drop by and see what they're up to. Radio controls guide eight trains on 2,000 feet of track. Weekend open houses (1 in spring and 3 in fall, including 3 days after Thanksgiving) run from 10-6 and cost $1.50 for adults, 75¢ for children.

Holly Recreation Area ★

Headquarters and maps: 8100 Grange Hall Rd. just east of Dixie Hwy. From I-75 north of Pontiac, take Grange Hall Rd. exit 101 and go east about 2.5 miles. (313) 634-8811. State park sticker required: $3/day or $15/year.

This spread-out recreation area east of Holly includes nearly all the wonderfully diverse terrains and habitats that go with Michigan's belts of glacial landscapes: lakes (over 20, good for fishing, with no motors allowed), high hills with mature woods and big trees, wetlands, and open fields. It makes for very good nature observation and bird-

Holly and Fenton sit in the belt of glacial lakes formed by huge ice chunks broken off the melting Saginaw Lobe of our most recent glacier as it retreated northward. This hilly, gravelly land is poor for farming but wonderful for recreation — skiing at Mt. Holly and elsewhere, hiking, fishing and swimming at numerous lakes. The 7,000-acre Holly Recreation Area (below) has three scenic trails (great for fall color) and an unusually private campground.

watching, especially on quiet weekdays along the shores of McGinness and Valley lakes, according to Tom Powers' *Natural Michigan*. Altogether, 190 bird species have been seen here.

There's a good mix of trees for fine fall colors. Off the drive from the Grange Hall Road park entrance to Wildwood Beach is a **scenic overlook**. Three **hiking trails** total 25 miles; a short one circles two heavily used lakes, while the others extend into more remote areas. Ask for a map at the headquarters. In winter there are 10 miles of **cross-country ski trails** around the beach and campground areas (parts are easy and parts are challenging) and 15 miles of **snowmobile trails** in a separate area west of I-75.

Heron Beach is on Heron Lake, close to the day-use park entrance on Grange Hall Road. It is big, often very crowded, and treeless. Boats and canoes can be rented here. At the end of a road that winds alongside Heron and Wildwood lakes is the much nicer **Wildwood Beach**, small, quiet, and shady. Picnic areas along this road either offer hilltop views or wooded shoreline settings.

Near a third interconnected lake is the **McGinniss Lake Campground**, with 160 large lots made unusually private by many trees and shrubs. Tom Powers calls it an "undiscovered gem." It seldom fills up, even on summer weekends, and it has all the amenities of a modern campground — showers, flush toilets, a dump station, and 80 year-round sites with electrical hookups — without cramped conditions.

Mt. Holly

13536 S. Dixie Hwy. north of Grange Hall Rd. From I-75 and U.S. 23, take Fenton exits and go east on Grange Hall Rd. (due east from downtown Fenton) to Dixie Hwy. (313) 634-8260. Snowline: 1 (800) 582-7256.

Fifteen trails are served by four rope tows and seven chairlifts, including a slow, easy-to-ride beginner's lift. Lessons include Kinder-Sparks Ski Instruction for 4-10-year-olds. Mt. Holly claims to have the area's largest, most efficient rental system. Three lounges include one with live entertainment and drinks.

Hours: weekdays 10 a.m.-11 p.m. Weekends & holidays 9 a.m.-11 p.m. Rates: weekdays $14 chairlift, $10 rope tows. (Holly-Daze specials start Jan. 3, $11 tow, $11 rentals, $4 lessons.) Weekends & holidays: $17, $12. NOTE: tickets purchased before 3 p.m. are good only until 5:30. Slopes close for re-grooming between 5:30 and 6. Equipment rental: $14.

RESTAURANTS

Historic Holly Hotel ★★

110 Battle Alley at Broad in downtown Holly. (313) 634-5208. Mon-Sat lunch 11-3, dinner 5-10, until 11 Fri & Sat; Sun noon-8. Full bar, good wine list. Visa, MasterCard, AmEx, Diners.

The wonderful Victorian decor of this splendid hotel's dining room was painstakingly reconstructed from old photos, even to the point of having identical chairs custom-made. The hotel burned twice, both on the same day (January 19, in 1918 and 1978), and the restaurant has an annual half-off fire sale to commemorate the coincidence. The food here is very good. Dinner favorites include Beef Wellington ($18.50), roast lingonberry duck ($16.95), and poached salmon with champagne sauce ($18). Dinners include bread, soup, salad, and vegetable. At lunch, chicken strudel ($5.50) and Victorian onion soup with cheese and puff pastry ($3.50) stand out on a menu that also includes croissant sandwiches and soup ($6.50), omelettes ($4.75), large salads ($4), and fresh fish specials (about $8).

Flint

People associate American automobiles with Detroit, but Flint, the birthplace of General Motors, actually has the highest concentration of autoworkers in the country. Buick, GM's early linchpin, helped make the city a boom town for years. Then came Chevrolet and AC Sparkplug. But in recent years Flint has been a profoundly troubled city, with high unemployment and high crime. Before the 1980s it was already losing population, and its central city was in decline. Then came GM's great shrinkage. Once 82,000 people in the region worked for GM. Now only about half that many are employed at the giant Flint GM plants that once made all the Buicks and Chevrolets in America.

As GM's domestic market share has dropped from roughly one half to one third, Flint's population has plummeted from almost 200,000 in the 1960s to about 140,000 today. Until World War II, the city was 90 per cent white, a heterogeneous mix of ethnic groups typical of auto towns that boomed in the early 20th century. Then many black Southerners came to Flint to relieve the labor shortage at the car plants. Today blacks comprise almost half of the city's population.

You can still see magnificent, well maintained mansions on the wooded estates of Hawthorne Drive and Parkside on the southwest side of town. But in a city that once made national news for its acute shortage of housing, there are now large empty areas where dilapidated homes have been torn down.

Propping up a depressed downtown

GM's downturn has not caused but has certainly accelerated the central city's dismaying decline. Despite the infusion of tens of millions of dollars into Flint's downtown to build massive projects — a splendid riverfront park, the giant AutoWorld theme park (now defunct), the University of Michigan at Flint, and a

The name "Flint" came from part of a Chippewa phrase meaning "flint stones in the river."

Flint's metro area of roughly 430,000 includes a number of attractive small towns turned into bedroom communities. The most prestigious is **Grand Blanc**, with two private golf clubs, including Warwick Hills, home of the Buick Open. But the best concentrations of historic buildings and neighborhoods are in **Davison, Fenton, Flushing, Gaines, Linden,** and **Otisville.**

Heavily subsidized new downtown developments like the Water Street Pavilion (center foreground) and Hyatt Regency hotel (right center) complement Flint's big 1920s office buildings to give downtown an impressive silhouette, especially at night. Downtown retailing, however, is minimal, having been usurped by two large regional malls.

festival marketplace, among others — this looks like a pretty dead place, vivid testimony that big bucks alone can't turn a downtown around.

Attractions in central Flint

Still, downtown Flint has **Buckham Alley,** home of a theater and an alternative art gallery/performing space. And it has some some unusually friendly taverns such as Churchill's, Billy's, and the Torch, with good food and a great cross-section of society: businesspeople, cops, lawyers, city workers, artists, and street people.

Despite the depressing scarcity of retail business along downtown Saginaw Street, the city's main boulevard, the central area has some interesting sights. In a renovated former hotel known as **Northland Center** there is one very good restaurant (Top of the Park) with a splendid view. The **Cultural Center** along Kearsley east of the Flint River and I-475 has a first-class historical museum, a very fine art museum, and the splendid Whiting Auditorium with an impressive schedule of local and national entertainment. There are pleasant downtown walkways and nooks along the Flint River. And even Flint's detractors admit that there's no local shortage of activities. Amateur and semi-professional dramatics organizations are big in Flint, and Mott Community College and the University of Michigan's Flint campus sponsor a host of lectures, classes, and concerts, including the Flint Symphony.

Out by the AC Spark Plug plant on the east side, Angelo's is the premiere spot for Flint's dry-style coney island, deemed the state's best by *Detroit Free Press* columnist Bob Talbert. There are two fascinating **tours of GM assembly plants. Crossroads Village,** an ambitious county-operated "living village" north of town, is the center of several recreation attractions.

But civic leaders' costly attempts to make this industrial city a tourist attraction have flopped sadly, and it's hard to see how future efforts will fare much better. "Flint is a blue-collar town and nothing but," says one native. "When it tries to be something else, it doesn't work."

Fur-trapping post and lumber town

Flint is located at a shallow place on the Flint River. This fording point was first used by Indians, who created a trail roughly from Detroit all the way up to the Upper Peninsula. A Canadian fur trader named Jacob Smith, faced with increasing competition in Detroit, followed that trail 70 miles north from Detroit to the Flint River and opened a trading post here in 1819. He was given 11 square miles of land in the heart of the future city by Governor Lewis Cass in return for help in getting the region's Indians to sign over vast tracts of land to the American government. Fur trapping here

A surprising array of cultural events can round out a trip to Flint. Five active theater groups range from the Buckham Alley alternative theater to semi-professional dinner theater. Big-name entertainment is booked at the Whiting Auditorium. For a 6-month calendar, call weekdays 1-800-482-6708 (in Michigan) or (313) 232-8900. For a week's recorded events and exhibit schedule, call (313) 232-2211 anytime.

For Flint autoworkers accustomed to bringing in well over $30,000 a year, the loss of jobs and benefits has been ironically more devastating than in parts of the state like rural Hillsdale and Cass counties, where generations of people have learned to live on little.

The big carriage industry insured Flint's prosperity when pine for its big lumber mills ran out. Carriage making led to its role as the town that made General Motors.

reached its peak in the 1830s and declined rapidly after the 1840s.

Forests of white pine around here made Flint a lumbering center from the 1850s until the 1870s, when the supply was exhausted. Easterner W. H. Crapo (pronounced CRAY-po) made Flint stand out among lumber towns. He arrived in 1856, already wealthy from the whaling business, built one of the state's larger sawmills, and became a Republican governor in the 1860s.

"Vehicle City"

Lumbermen of the era were only interested in the light, floatable pine. They left considerable stands of oak. As the the pine era ebbed in the final quarter of the 19th century, the sturdy oak helped Flint become a leading carriage and cart manufacturer. Many other lumbering boom towns suffered lengthy declines after the timber ran out, but Flint made a smooth transition to manufacturing. In 1900 Flint, by then dubbed "The Vehicle City," was pouring out 150,000 carriages and carts a year, rivaled only by South Bend, Indiana, for Midwestern dominance in this important field.

One Flint company made only carriage wheels, selling them to carriage manufacturers all over the country. Another company made whip sockets and so completely dominated the market for this little item that Flint also came to be known as the "whip socket center of the world." Yet another firm was a major producer of farm wagons.

The amazing Billy Durant

The person who most helped put Flint on the map as an important cart and carriage manufacturing center was Billy Durant, surely one of the most remarkable people in American history. A Flint native and grandson of Governor Crapo, he had promotional and empire-building abilities that were truly extraordinary. He first used them to build a Flint-based cart and carriage manufacturing empire with J. Dallas Dort.

Durant was a hypnotic salesman. When he started the Durant-Dort Carriage Company in 1886, the dapper entrepreneur had only the prototype of a new, smoother-riding two-wheel cart, yet he sold several hundred before production ever began. South Bend touted itself as the place that sent carriages "all over the world." Not to be outdone, the Durant-Dort company claimed that its vehicles went "to all parts of the universe." In this small city of 13,000 at the turn of the century, the payroll of Durant's firm alone was larger than all the earlier Flint lumber mills combined.

By the early 20th century Durant left Flint a rich man to play the stock market in New York. In the meantime, a Scotsman named David Buick had built a very successful plumbing business in Detroit, inventing a number of useful hardware parts and processes for the growing indoor plumbing industry sweeping America. An inventor at heart, Buick gave up his lucrative business to tinker with gasoline engines. Soon he turned his attention to making cars and started the Buick Company in 1903. But it quickly ran out of money. Eventually the company was bought by the Flint Wagon Works, which built a big new plant in Flint to house the struggling auto manufacturer.

The Buick's main claim to fame was its durability, an important feature in an era of crude, bumpy roads. In a dramatic demonstration that captured national attention, a Buick was driven from Flint to Detroit and back at just under 30 miles an hour without mishap. But the company kept losing large sums of money, and an initially reluctant Billy Durant was lured back to Flint from New York to head the struggling firm.

Three well-known anti-establishment activists hail from Flint. Most prominent today is Michael Moore, an autoworker's son ("born to install rocker panels on Buicks," he is wont to say) and founder of the defunct *Flint Voice*, now making headlines with his documentary hit "Roger and Me." The *Wall Street Journal* called it "deliciously funny and utterly unfair."

John Sinclair, rock manager, arts critic, and founder of the White Panther Party in the 1960s, also grew up in Flint, as did Stewart Rawlings Mott, maverick younger son of Flint's reactionary benefactor C. S. Mott. Stewart Mott, who used to send friends newsletters telling off his family, has devoted himself to liberal causes from ecology to population control.

This portrait shows the calm confidence and kindness that made General Motors founder Billy Durant (1861-1947) so well liked and effective at sales. After years of neglect, Durant's role in General Motors and Flint is being officially recognized. A bronze statue of Durant was recently installed in front of the Durant-Dort Carriage Co. office at 316 W. Water.

Durant creates General Motors

Durant is often portrayed as merely a superb salesman or promoter, but clearly it took more than a great salesman to build Buick into one of the major auto firms and then use it as a springboard to create General Motors. He chose unusual talent to run his increasingly complex empire — future auto giants such as Walter Chrysler and C. W. Nash. He convinced Albert Champion to relocate to Flint his spark plug factory from Massachusetts and and C. S. Mott to move his axle company from New York. And later, after gaining control of Chevrolet, Durant moved that company, too, from Buffalo to Flint.

Durant created GM in 1908. Just a year later it encompassed 20 companies, including Buick, Olds, Cadillac, and Oakland Motors (later renamed Pontiac). After the bankers financing Durant's dizzying empire pushed him out in 1910, he teamed up with Louis Chevrolet to make a low-priced car that would eventually outsell Fords. Then, in a move of breathtaking audacity, he used the Chevrolet company to buy back GM. Eventually his aggressive deal-making again caused his ouster from GM in 1921. His final car venture, the Flint Motor Company, began making "Durants" in 1923, but folded after two years. Its big plant was sold to GM. As the Fisher Body Plant No. 1, it was the site of the famous 1937 sitdown strike which would lead to the unionization of autoworkers. The plant has recently been partially razed and rebuilt as the Great Lakes Technology center, employing 1,300 GM engineers and draftsmen relocated from Troy.

The same extraordinary, restless energy that led Durant to build empires also proved his downfall when the Depression devalued the vast stockmarket holdings which he had acquired trying to keep the sagging stock market propped up. After losing his fortune, he managed a Flint bowling alley with the same genial good spirits and optimism he brought to all his endeavors. Into his eighties he dreamed of creating a bowling alley empire across the country.

From housing shortage to demolition

If you drive past Buick City on Industrial Drive, east of North Saginaw on Flint's north side, you will see a stand of tall oak trees. This is now **Oak Grove Park**, but during Flint's most acute housing shortage, between 1912 and 1920, it was the site of a tent city, where autoworkers lived year-round until they could find housing. With the twin success of Buick and Chevrolet, Flint's population surged from under 40,000 in 1910 to over 150,000 in 1930. Families were living not just in tents but in tar paper shacks and piano crates.

GM itself helped alleviate the housing shortage when, in 1919, it began building **Civic City** around

The Flint sitdown strike of 1937, brilliantly executed by well-disciplined strikers, led to the eventual unionization of the entire domestic auto industry. It was initiated by workers at GM's Fisher Body, the least well-to-do of Flint's enormous population of auto workers, and aided by a pro-labor governor and President Roosevelt.

Bassett Park on the west side. This still-pleasant neighborhood allowed GM workers to buy homes with generous company financing. The lucky occupants were mostly Buick workers. Having arrived before World War I, they were the first wave of autoworkers to come to Flint. Many came off the soil-poor farms north of Saginaw and Bay City.

The second wave of auto workers came after World War I, when Chevrolet was becoming a nationally prominent manufacturer. They came from the coal mines of Pennsylvania and from southern Ohio and lived in tiny one-story bungalows on the west end. Over the years, most of these houses were added onto so much that the original homes are hardly recognizable.

The third wave began coming in the mid-1920s, when Durant recruited workers from Arkansas, Tennessee, and southern Missouri for his ill-starred Flint Motor Company. These people, who would later work in Fisher Body No. 1, were the hardest hit of all Flint workers by the Depression. Not surprisingly, it was the Fisher and Chevrolet workers, not the better established and more conservative Buick workers, who fought to organize the UAW in 1937.

In dramatic contrast to the chronic housing shortages that faced Flint this century, you can now see vast, empty areas where housing has recently been razed. On Industrial Drive across from Buick City were big rooming houses. Now all you see are big fields. Mary Street east of Saginaw was once crowded with houses, all of which are now torn down.

Still a major auto city

Most of Flint's present GM facilities are a direct legacy of Billy Durant. Although feeling is widespread among many residents here that GM has abandoned Flint, there is still a massive amount of General Motors activity and a substantial amount of new investment in the city where the country's largest concentration of auto workers lives. GM plans to spend $475 million in capital investment in Flint through 1993. Its 1988 Flint payroll was $2.47 billion.

By far the biggest GM facility is **Buick City**, stretching over a mile and a half on the north side just west of the Flint River. It includes both Buick's headquarters and the plant where the LeSabre is made. (See p. 311 for tour information.) Across the river to the southeast is the headquarters of GM's **AC Spark Plug Division** (see p. 310). Here AC makes the spark plugs, fuel pumps, filters, and instruments which go into GM cars. AC has also taken over the old Chevrolet plant just southwest of downtown. On this 80-acre site all the engines and pressed metal parts for Chevrolets were built until the 1950s. Now AC uses sections of the old plant to build exhaust systems, fuel tanks, and other components.

In the southwest corner of Flint, visible to motorists on I-75 and I-69, is the huge GM **Truck and Bus Group** where Chevrolet Blazers and GMC Jimmy and Suburban vehicles are built. (See p. 310 for tour information.) At the south end of town, the big Fisher Body plants are being replaced by a much smaller **Great Lakes Technology Center**, where 1,300 GM engineers will design future models. Some locals see the demolition of Fisher Body No. 1 as GM's revenge for the masterful 1937 sitdown strike, which proved the key to unionizing GM. The sad truth is that the plant's removal is much more symbolic of GM's decline over the past decade, when it dropped from 46 to 35 percent of domestic market share. Even though the plant was profitable, the company no longer enjoys a big enough market share to need it.

Flint is also the home of **General Motors Institute**, an engineering college just west of downtown near the old Chevrolet plant. G.M.I. was founded in 1919 by GM but is now independent. Its 2,600 students go to school for 12 weeks, then spend the next 12 working for a corporation, earning from $35,000 to $75,000 over the five years it takes to get a degree. GM's AC Spark Plug Division is the biggest participant in this unusual higher education program, in which some 400 firms enroll students from 48 states and 12 foreign countries.

The Mott legacy

Flint's biggest benefactor was Charles Stewart Mott, who died at 97 in 1973. His legacy can be seen in many of the imposing civic buildings around central Flint. Mott took his father's Utica, N.Y., wheel factory to Flint as Durant was building up GM, then sold it to GM for stock before World War I. The money from this stock, plus interests in U.S. Sugar, several banks, and various municipal water-supply systems, made him a billionaire by the time he died. Mayor of Flint three times between 1912 and 1919, Mott made an unsuccessful bid for governor in 1920. A conservative Republican who supported far-right political causes, he was quite civic-minded and devoted to Flint. Early on he helped build a local hospital, buy land for city parks, and establish a YMCA camp. In 1935 he began a program to use the public schools year round, night and day, in a novel and hugely successful adult education program that was widely copied nationally. The Mott Foundation spent an incredible $100 million over 35 years to support this community education program.

The Mott Foundation, now endowed with about half a billion dollars, has focused much of it on central Flint. It helped relocate the University of Michigan's Flint campus downtown, paid for about a fifth of the AutoWorld project, subsidized low-income housing projects, and supported the building of Riverside Park downtown. The big foundation has also given critical parcels of land to the city so that, for example, a state office building could be built downtown. The foundation is now greatly cutting back on these types of massive attempts to revitalize Flint.

For free visitor maps to Flint and more information, call weekdays 1-800-482-6708 (in Michigan) or (313) 232-8900.

POINTS OF INTEREST

Sloan Museum ★★★

1221 E. Kearsley in Flint's Cultural Center. From I-75 and the south, take I-475 north to Exit 8A (Longway Blvd.), turn right at 1st light, turn right at next street (Forest). Park on your right. (313) 762-1169. Tues-Fri 10-5, Sat & Sun 12-5. Open Mon in July & August. $2 adults, $1 students, children, seniors, groups.

The highlights of this excellent city museum relate to Flint's extraordinary history. Vivid displays show how lumbering turned the small city into a 19th-century boom town, generating for the state more money than all that was made in the Gold Rush out West. Other displays show how Flint later became, along with Detroit, a center of the American auto industry. Finally, there is one of the choicest selections of majestic old American automobiles to be found anywhere.

The fascinating centerpiece of the section on Flint's important lumbering era is a vast miniature model of a Michigan lumber company, from the lumberjacks' camp to the big mill which cut the logs into boards.

Display captions here are unusually well written. "Michigan's lumbering era lasted slightly over four decades," concludes one. "Thousands of square miles of fine-grained white pine were cut. It had been the largest virgin white pine forest in the world when the lumbermen moved in. When they left, there remained only miles and miles of stumps."

There are two memorable full-scale displays of Flint's early auto years. One is the preserved ornate dining room of Flint banker A.G. Bishop, showing a manikin of Bishop with that amazing entrepreneur, Billy Durant. The time was 1905, and the

The Sloan Museum's outstanding collection of historic autos includes the Chevy 490. Its success was a major factor in Chevrolet's early success.

event was the agreement insuring that Buicks would keep being being made in Flint rather than Jackson. Durant had already helped make Flint the country's leading carriage manufacturer. Just three years after he took over Buick, it had become the country's leading auto manufacturer, making more cars than Ford and Cadillac combined.

Another memorable display is starkly realistic. It is a tar paper shack, a symbol of the desperate housing shortage in Flint as its auto industry burgeoned. In 1910, Flint's population had jumped in just six years from 15,000 to 39,000, making it America's most congested city. One thousand homeless workers camped on the banks of the Flint River, unable to buy or rent a place to stay. Tar paper shacks, tents, and empty piano crates were common housing, even in winter. Inside the museum's shack are revealing panoramic photos of these squalid scenes.

The display of historic autos here is a delight even for nonenthusiasts. It plays off the gleaming cars against an appealing background of advertising signs and blown-up photos of old gas stations and the like. You can see the sporty, bright red 1910 Buick "Bug," Buick's 106 mph racing car. One of its racing team members was none other than Louis Chevrolet. Durant later teamed up with him to create Chevrolet Motors after Durant was shoved aside by the banker-dominated GM board of directors.

The oldest production-model Chevrolet in existence, the unsuccessful 1912 Classic Six, looks like it just came out of the factory. More

historically significant is the famous Chevy "490," which became the world's top-selling line by 1918. Most eye-catching of all, perhaps, is the futuristic 1959 Cadillac Cyclone, a non-production concept car which still looks modern today. In its nose-cone, radar devices signal the driver as objects approach the vehicle.

The Sloan Museum also features dozens of realistic dolls representing a variety of historical figures, dioramas portraying the early European exploration of North America, and large-scale illuminated anatomical models of the human body.

> Call (313) 762-1169 for information on special one-day **workshops** for adults and children; **events** like the huge 1,000-vehicle antique auto show the 4th week in June; seasonal holiday activities; and 5 annual **special shows** such as animated prehistoric sea monsters, the science of sport, a living history of Vietnam, and the art of the eye.

Flint Institute of Arts ★★

1120 E. Kearsley, in Flint's Cultural Center. From I-475 from the south, get off at the Court St. exit, turn right, go to 2nd light, turn left onto Crapo. At the next light, turn right onto Kearsley. Museum is past library. Park in front. (313) 234-1695. Tues-Sat 10-5, Sun 1-5. Free.

Generous donations from wealthy Flint citizens have built this into the state's second most prominent city art museum, behind only the Detroit Institute of Arts.

There is an exceptional collection of **19th-century French paintings**, mostly landscapes, by Corot, Courbet, Sisley, Renoir, Toulouse-Lautrec, and others. The gallery spaces are themselves uninspiring, except for the room with the **Bray Renaissance Gallery**. This Renaissance-style hall, with an ornate coffered ceiling and marble floor, houses an impressive collection of 15th- to 17th-century European works of art, including furniture, paintings, and tapestries. The museum's collection of Oriental vases and sculptures is also noteworthy.

Another highlight is the stunning **paperweights collection** donated by a wealthy local patron. Popular in the 19th century, some are true works of art. The Bray Collection includes some of the finest French mid-19th century pieces beautifully displayed in special illuminated cases.

Temporary exhibits draw on the 5,000-object permanent collection and traveling shows. They appeal to a very wide variety of tastes. One six-month stretch featured carousel animals, American Indian artifacts and historic photographs, 20th-century prints, early American art, seagrass baskets from South Carolina, and miniature textile art.

The **gift shop** includes decorator items, handmade contemporary jewelry, scarves, art books, toys, cards, and souvenirs.

Longway Planetarium ★

1310 E. Kearsley in the Cultural Center. From I-475 from the south, take Longway Blvd. exit, go 2 blocks east to Walnut and turn right. The planetarium parking lot is opposite the end of Walnut. (313) 762-1181. Regular astronomy shows ($3/adults, $2 for kids and seniors) and laser light shows ($5/$4) are scheduled Thurs-Sun, with weekend matinees. Call for details.

Michigan's largest planetarium has a 60-foot domed screen for an especially realistic depiction of the skies. It's the same size as the big planetaria in Chicago and New York. Entertaining multi-media shows change every three to five months and explore the skies, ancient mythology and the constellations, science fiction, and space travel, in addition to a regular show about the current season's sky. Non-educational laser light shows feature laser animations set to music such as Sgt. Pepper's Lonely Heart Band.

Corridor displays include a glowing black light mural, 55 feet long, of planets, comets, and constellations, and exhibit cases on star evolution, the solar system and other astronomical subjects. An excellent gift counter has astronomy- and space-related T-shirts, stickers, books, posters, and hard-to-find educational items. **Gift** and **exhibit areas** are open 9-5 weekdays. Individuals are welcome to tag along with any school group coming to see shows during the week.

Riverbank Park ★★

Downtown Flint at Saginaw and the Flint River, along Water, First, and Second Avenues.

This $22 million project is one of the most elaborate modern urban parks in the country. It was designed by Lawrence Halprin Associates, a well-known West Coast design firm. The park is the outgrowth of needed flood control measures because the Flint River is prone to severe flooding. (There was a particularly bad flood in 1947.) Originally the Corps of Engineers was going to construct concrete banks to control the water. Instead, the park was created as a buffer; it becomes flooded during times of high water.

The 4 1/2-block park has flower gardens, picnic sites, a playground, a large amphitheater, and a fish ladder for the big salmon migrating upriver in the fall. There is even a water-powered Archimedes screw which lifts water to create multiple waterfalls.

Walkways on both sides of the park provide good views of the river and of the surrounding urban area. To the northeast is the Northbank Center, a recently renovated, stately building which houses both the **Children's Museum** and **Top of the Park Restaurant**. Behind Northbank Center is the defunct **Autoworld**. On the opposite bank is the new location for the **University of Michigan-Flint**. Downriver on one side towers the Hyatt Regency Hotel. Across the river is **Carriage Town.**

In the fall it's exciting to see the **fish ladder** and watch for giant coho and chinook salmon swimming upriver from Lake Huron to spawn. The greatest migration is usually from late September through October. Sightings are common, but don't expect to see a salmon every few minutes.

Fishermen enjoy the park, especially during the salmon migration, but **fishing** is good here throughout the year. The river is much cleaner than it used to be, thanks to improved waste control by Buick and other plants. There are plenty of big pike, walleye, smallmouth bass, white bass, and catfish.

John Sellenraad's nifty pictorial **monument** commemorates the 50th anniversary of the UAW Flint Sitdown Strike. It's across the river from the University of Michigan Flint, at the park's east end. The handsome display features big, rather primitive mural paintings on Pewabic tiles. One shows the great Flint Sitdown strike of 1936-37 at Fisher Body Plants 1 & 2. The other shows workers in an automobile plant. Below the paintings are a chronology of gains won by the UAW for its workers, such as overtime pay in 1939. An amusing touch is the benches in front of the displays: tan concrete car seats.

For a picnic in the park, Windmill Place is handy for an international selection of takeout fast food.

Windmill Place

877 E. Fifth at N. Saginaw. (313) 234-2640. Mon-Thurs 10-8, Fri & Sat 10-9, Sun 12-7.

Just north of downtown Flint and west of the closed Autoworld, Windmill Place is a pleasant, popular food court of 13 eateries including Chinese, Greek, Italian, Hungarian, Middle Eastern, and Southern bar-b-que. The choices for the hungry browser are wide and interesting, everything from coney islands (a Flint staple) and outstanding Middle Eastern sandwiches and salads (spicy enough to satisfy purists) to corned beef and pastrami at **Jack's Deli** (also known for its banana and coconut cream pies), a good cabbage roll at the **Hungarian Gourmet,** stuffed potatoes, salads and muffins, fish and chips, cookies, candy, and Stroh's ice cream. There is also a video game room for kids, and shops with gifts T-shirts, and cosmetics upstairs.

Flint Farmers' Market

Fifth Ave. at Boulevard Drive, across from the post office and just east of the Flint River. Tues, Thurs & Sat year-round, 7 a.m.-5:30 p.m.

Flint's farmers' market is interesting and lively even in winter, what with two meat vendors, a fish shop, two poultry dealers, several flower stalls, several egg producers, and dealers who import bulk produce such as 50-pound bags of potatoes ($3.50) and 10-pound bags of white onions ($3).

Don't miss **Ed Janego's sausage stand**. He's been making and selling sausages for over 25 years. Janego promises his hot pork sausage ($3.09/lb.) will "curl your tongue."

The Children's Museum

432 N. Saginaw at Second Ave. (north of the Flint River), in the basement of Northbank Center. (313) 238-6900. Mon-Fri 10-5, Sat & Sun 1-5. $2 for adults and children.

At this career-oriented hands-on museum, kids from 3 to 12 can play doctor in a simulated doctor's office, be a TV anchorman in a realistic set with real TV cameras and operating monitors, play judge wielding a gavel behind an impressive bench, or be a pilot in a real airplane. There are 15 occupational settings in all.

The museum also has a gallery of 18 striking-looking holograms (three-dimensional laser-produced pictures) with explanatory diagrams on how they are made.

Durant-Dort Carriage Factory/Flint Chamber of Commerce

316 W. Water, across from Riverbank Park north of the river. (313) 232-7101. Mon-Fri 9-5, closed 12:30-1:30.

The 1895 offices of the Durant-Dort Carriage Company have been handsomely restored by the Chamber of Commerce. Visitors are welcome to stop in and pick up information on events and destinations in Flint, and to look at the collection of historic office furniture, including desks of former General Motors presidents. The adjacent area has some of Flint's oldest and most interesting buildings.

Durant's carriage company, which became one of the largest in the country, was in a sense the forerunner of GM. Although Durant was dedicated to carriages and despised the noisy arrival of the automobile, he built Buick quickly into a major U.S. car company, the keystone of GM.

The Durant-Dort Carriage Co., which made simple road carts and carriages like this, became the springboard for General Motors.

Water Street Pavilion

Water St. at the Flint River in downtown Flint.

The future of four-year-old Water Street Pavilion is uncertain. The colorful festival marketplace had not yet proven viable for shops and small eateries, so serious thought is being given to turning it into offices, leaving in place the popular Italian restaurant Figlio's.

This interestingly complex festival marketplace was the creation of the Rouse Company, masters of this genre. Rouse has done similar projects in Baltimore, Boston, Toledo, and elsewhere. It has a **food court** (though the slightly older Windmill Place had already attracted some of the best mom-and-pop food operations), a stage area with a huge video tower, a most attractive outdoor **ice skating rink,** and an assortment of specialty shops that mostly have failed. The biggest retail success here was not the trendy Benetton fashion franchise (it closed), but the **Great Divide,** which sells paraphernalia from the state's rival universities, Michigan State and the University of Michigan.

As part of a major effort to try and help put downtown Flint back on its feet, the project was heavily subsidized by the city. "AutoWorld, the Hyatt, the Water Street Pavillion — they all keyed off of one another," said the Pavilion's manager. It was part of an unprecedented (and in retrospect unlikely) plan to transform a single-industry town into a vacation destination. Without AutoWorld, Water Street Pavilion didn't succeed. A bustling lunchtime wasn't enough to make up for traffic that remained almost dead in the evenings and lackadaisical on weekends, despite heavy promotion.

Paul's Pipe Shop ★

736 S. Saginaw in downtown Flint. (313) 235-0581. Mon-Sat 9-7.

One of the last of a dying breed, this is a first-class, independent pipe shop. Paul's is, no doubt, the biggest in the Midwest, with over a million pipes ranging from a $4 corncob to a $5,000 Dunhill.

The driving force behind this remarkable operation is 76-year-old Paul Spaniola, who has been in the business for over 60 years. Paul's family came from Italy in 1897. He started his own business in 1928 in nearby Swartz Creek and came to Flint in 1947. An expansive entrepreneur, Paul is known around the world among pipe-smoking connoisseurs for several reasons: his remarkable stock of pipes, his record as five-time holder of the world pipe-smoking title (the winner is the person who can smoke his pipe the longest), and his own personally finished "Cayuga" pipes, which he boils in a special South American nut oil and claims flatly is "the best pipe you ever smoked."

Pipes cram the shop; even more are stored on the second story. In the basement, Paul blends his own popular pipe tobaccos in a specially climate-controlled and gloriously aromatic back room. The favorite is his "58th Anniversary" blend — $2.15 for 2 ounces. Cigars fill another climate-controlled room.

Paul's Pipe Shop should keep going after Paul retires. Some of his 12 children help out.

Indian Earth Art & Crafts

124 W. First, west of Saginaw in downtown Flint. (313) 239-6621. Mon-Fri 9-4:30.

Beadwork, basketry, and paintings, along with nostalgic items like toy birchbark canoes and teepees, are for sale in the shop of the Genesee Valley Indian Association, a social services and cultural organization for area Native Americans. There's also a small museum with informational displays. Work is underway for a living village to be finished, possibly by 1991, at the Happy Hollow Nature Center on Hammerberg Road west of Flint.

Buckham Fine Arts Project

134 1/2 W. Second St. just west of S. Saginaw in downtown Flint. (313) 239-239-6334. Wed-Sat 11:30-5.

A handsomely worn, 40 x 60 foot loft in downtown Flint is the home of an artists' cooperative that draws discriminating artists from Ann Arbor and Detroit for what its founders call "cutting edge" shows — work that museums or commercial galleries aren't likely to show. The gallery, with over 200 running feet of wall space and a vaulted ceiling, permits the building of unusually big constructions — "transformations," in the words of coordinator Eva Wattenmaker, because they transform the gallery into a totally different environment. Three times a year the exhibition schedule is interrupted for performance art, dance, and jazz.

Buckham Alley is quite unlike local artists' organizations that are dominated by refined wives of the well-to-do. The close, committed group of participating artists includes students, art teachers, factory workers, and a wide cross-section of the area populace. Two blue-collar artists

1950 ad for Paul's Pipe Shop.

incorporate elements of the industrial environment in their work; other factory workers explore totally different directions. A visit here, and to the Buckham Alley Theater and Torch Bar and Grill (see Restaurants) around the corner in tucked-away Buckham Alley itself, will surely expand most outsiders' conception of what Flint has to offer. Ask for printed information about other nearby galleries in central Flint.

Vernor's Mural/ Haloburger ★

800 S. Saginaw at Fourth in downtown Flint.

The elaborate terra cotta front section of Bill Thomas's popular downtown Haloburger restaurant was built as a Vernor's Gingerale outlet in the 1920s. Customers could sit down and enjoy cream ales and other fountain treats, then take home a case of Vernor's.

Plump, bearded gnomes in peaked green caps push barrels of gingerale up to their castle warehouse painted on the wall next to the side parking lot. The Thomas family has restored and protected this nostalgic landmark. See Restaurants, p. 317.

GM Truck & Bus Flint Assembly Plant tour ★★★

Van Slyke at Atherton, southeast of town. From I-75, take the Bristol Rd. exit, go east to Van Slyke, turn north to plant. (313) 236-4978. Free one-hour tours 9:30 & 11:30, Tues and Thurs. Reservations required.

GM's popular Blazer and Suburban pickup trucks are made here. They are so much in demand that each one being built (at the rate of 38 an hour) has already been sold. At up to $28,000, they're not cheap, with standard V-8 engines and plush interiors. In Texas they're called "Texas Cadillacs." Indeed, Texas is the biggest customer for these fancy trucks, followed by Saudi Arabia.

The tour of the huge 3 million-square-foot assembly plant is conducted by two affable plant veterans who know their way around. It's a pleasantly informal tour, which encourages questions. The pace suits the inclinations of the group, ranging all the way from 2 to 80 people Here you get to see the classic assembly line in action, starting with a bare frame that crawls steadily along at about 1/2 mile an hour as workers put more and more parts on it. Unlike the heavily roboticized Buick City, this is a relatively old-fashioned plant where workers do most of the procedures. It is one of the last plants in the country to use the old "body drop" way of construction. The completed body is lowered onto the chassis from a second level about 30 feet above. A tour highlight is seeing the body swing down swiftly onto the chassis, where a team of workers quickly secures the two sections.

There are 5,000 workers here on two shifts. Chances of a recent high school graduate getting a job here (starting pay $14.20 an hour) are slim to none; most workers have a decade or more longevity.

It takes about 14 hours to make one truck. Another line makes crew cabs and chassis cab trucks. At the end of the line, trucks are given stationary 30 mph test "drives" to check them out.

AC Spark Plug

1300 N. Dort Hwy. just north of Longway Blvd.

There aren't many plants bigger than this 4.3 million-square-foot behemoth located on a strip of land on Flint's east side, two miles long and half a mile wide. AC Spark Plug was founded by Albert Champion of Boston, Massachusetts, another of the important people Billy Durant brought to Flint before 1910 to supply his General Motors auto companies. Now half of AC's 24,000 workers are in Flint. A lot more than spark plugs is made here: fuel pumps, cruise controls, radiator and gas caps, among others. Tours of the big facility were terminated in 1989, when state-of-the-art spark plug equipment was installed, creating fear of industrial spies.

Another big Flint AC facility is located in the "hole" just west of downtown where Chevrolets were originally manufactured. Gas tanks, engine valves, and radiator supports are made there. AC has recently merged with GM's Rochester Division, famous for its four-barrel carburetors. Headquarters of the combined divisions remains in Flint.

Buick City Tour

3 miles north of downtown Flint between Industrial Ave. and I-475. (313) 236-4494. Free tours, 1 to 1 1/2 hours, are Tues & Thurs at 9:30 a.m. and noon. Make reservations well in advance. No children under 6, no cameras.

Buick City is one of the most interesting industrial tours in America. You can see the Buick LeSabre built almost from scratch in the country's most totally integrated auto assembly plant, a mimicking of Japan's Toyota City. The very size of the operation is impressive. Buick City is a 123-acre complex, — and at that, it's only part of the 450-acre, two-mile-long Buick complex. The main plant has 1.8 million square feet and 15 miles of conveyor lines turning out 480 cars per daily shift. A second shift has been added, and over 2,000 laid-off workers have been recalled.

This most modern of auto factories is located on the very site of Flint's first Buick operations back in 1904 when Billy Durant quickly turned it into a national giant.

Buick sales suffered greatly in the 1980s, the result of quality and image problems. Few young workers are in evidence, as there has been virtually no hiring since 1979, the year that kicked off a dramatic decline in the American auto industry.

But Buick sales have recently been increasing, and word is out that the Buicks now produced are of much better quality than those of just a few years ago. A 1988 workers' newsletter at the entrance boasted of a record low 2.9 defects per car, down from 7 or 8 half a decade ago. Part of the reason may be the huge GM investment in robots. The tour visitor sees them at virtually every stage of the assembly line. You even see unattended robots winding their way down aisles carrying things like engines from one part of the plant to another. In this plant, most of the difficult operations seem to be performed by robots, which our enthusiastic tour guide said are the most sophisticated in the industry. There is a striking contrast between the robots' intense activity and the workers' leisurely pace. Some have time to read a newspaper between their repetitious duties. It's strange to see a factory where the humans do the simple tasks like placing windshields on a conveyor belt one after another, while a vision-guided robot does the sensitive job of attaching the windshield to the frame.

The labyrinthine conveyor belt is another wonder to behold. It's a far cry from Henry Ford's straightforward original assembly line. Buick City's computer-guided line operates on several layers, so that a part manufactured in one section of the plant will be automatically elevated to an overhead line and transported in timely fashion to another location. Another impressive innovation borrowed from the Japanese is "just in time" parts delivery. Some 200 to 300 trucks arrive per shift at the many portals circling the factory, so that a part arrives within 300 feet of where it will be used. This way the plant keeps only a two-hour supply of the parts needed in making the LeSabre.

Crossroads Village & Huckleberry Railroad ★★

Bray Rd. north of Coldwater Rd. east of I-475. From I-475, take Carpenter Rd. (exit 11) and follow signs. (313) 763-7100. Summer season: mid-May through Labor Day. Mon-Fri 10-5:30, weekends & holidays 11-6:30. Also open first 2 weekends in Oct. (Fri-Sun) and from the day after Thanksgiving up to Christmas. Summer rates: adults $6.95, children 4-12 $4,95, seniors over 60 $5.95.

Crossroads Village is a collection of some two dozen historic buildings arranged to resemble a Genesee County village from between 1860 and 1880. During its main summer season this "living village" is focus of many events and unusual demonstrations of antique technologies. Weekends in early October and between Thanksgiving and Christmas extend the season. A special attraction is a 45-minute ride on the **Huckleberry Railroad,** a narrow-gauge steam engine and train with open-air cars. At a sawmill, blacksmith shop,

The jolts and gritty smoke of a ride on the Huckleberry Railroad at Crossroads Village dispel many notions about the romance of train travel in the good old days. The "huckleberry" name goes back to when this stretch of track went past huckleberry marshes. The train was so slow, the joke went, that passengers in the first car could get out, pick huckleberries, and have plenty of time to hop back on as the last car passed.

grist mill, and cider mill on the village's periphery, generally competent costumed workers make simple tools, cornmeal, and cider, which visitors can purchase.

This ambitious undertaking has some wonderful aspects. The train ride's grit and jolts do much to deromanticize 19th-century train travel, and watching the old mechanical technologies in action sheds a perspective on how hard people had to work under noisy, dangerous conditions to make basic products.

Bees swarm around the apple pulp at the cider mill. Belts whirr overhead in the grist mill. The smell of coal smoke and sawdust at the

sawmill irritate your eyes. Most historic recreations are only for looking, and never confront all your senses with these realities.

Other things at Crossroads Village, however, can be so annoying that they can threaten to spoil the whole visit. The staged train robbery melodrama is too corny, even for some children. Twentieth-century touches like half-barrels planted with marigolds and a supposed general store full of Christmas ornaments imported from the Far East spoil the illusion of going back in time and can lead some visitors to question just how authentic anything in the village is. The village's business center is a fancy, three-story block befitting a town of thousands. Yet the houses are spread out on big lots, as if in a rural hamlet without a train and train-related commerce.

Highlights include:

◆ **Atlas Mill.** A pre-Civil War grist mill sits on a splendidly lazy "mill pond" that's actually part of Mott Lake. The whole building shakes when the watergate is opened up to move the grindstones and make cornmeal.

◆ **Carousel.** Music from an antique organ that imitates a whole band accompanies the chariots and 36 horses of this 1912 carousel manufactured by Charles Parker, "America's Amusement King." Rides are 50¢. Tucked away beyond the chapel and sawmill, it's easy to miss.

◆ **Sawmill** with demonstration.

◆ **Cider mill** with demonstration.

◆ **Restored, 19th-century buildings** authentically furnished with antiques, including a lawyer's office and

Historic Genesee County buildings threatened by demolition continue to be moved to Crossroads Village and restored. The three-story brick buildings (far right) were moved when Fenton replaced much of its downtown with a shopping center. At the Attica Hotel (far left) visitors may see restoration in progress. The 1854 Buzzell House from Flint (center) is one of several buildings with authentic period furnishings.

home, a church, a school, and a recreated doctor's office. (These are quite well done, unlike the historic buildings with commercial uses.)

◆ **Durant barn** with toymaking demonstrations.

◆ **Print shop** in the Manwaring Building downtown. The Crossroads Chronicle is a good read in the lively, folksy style of small-town journalism.

For a **daily schedule** of hourly demonstrations and special performances such as band concerts and magic shows, consult the map given to you on arrival. **Weekends** have more activities, plus a big, very moderately priced outdoor chicken broil. Every summer weekend features a **special show** of some sort at no extra charge: barbershop singing; banjo music; Revolutionary and Civil War encampments; the Michigan Storytellers Festival; a flea market; shows featuring quilts, carriages, mules, antique machinery; a special for rail fans; a harvest festival; and a hot-air balloon event.

If you plan to spend a half day or more, Crossroads Village is an excellent entertainment value. In the immediate vicinity are Pennywhistle Place (a nifty children's play area; $2.50 admission); free swimming at Mott Lake; and Stepping Stone Falls, a lighted waterfall and picnic area (also free).

Pennywhistle Place ★★★

Bray Rd. near Coldwater Rd. just south of Crossroads Village. (313) 785-8066. Open Memorial Day-Labor Day. Mon-Sat 10-8, Sun noon-8. $2/person, adults and children.

Kids may well want to stay for hours at this bright, exciting creative play environment. There's a range of challenge levels, from easy activities for younger kids like the Ball Crawl, Cloud Bounce, and two-story Slab Slide to slightly scary ones like climbing high on a net and swinging from platform to platform on a gliding cable. One favorite is the Music Machine, a giant step-on calliope-type affair. There are shaded benches, and drinks, hot dogs, and snacks available.

Bluebell Beach

Entrance on Bray Rd. just south of Coldwater Rd. and Crossroads Village in the Genesee Recreation Area. Open Memorial Day-Labor Day. Free.

There's little shade to be found, but this popular beach on Mott Lake is convenient to Crossroads Village and Pennywhistle Place, and it's free.

Stepping Stone Falls

Branch Rd. 1/2 mile north of Carpenter Rd., roughly across Mott Lake from Crossroads Village. Open Memorial Day-Labor Day, Mon-Thurs noon-11, Fri-Sun noon-midnight. Free.

This man-made waterfall is where the Flint River has been dammed to form Mott Lake. A wooded picnic area overlooks the falls, which flow over a series of rectilinear platforms and steps. By night, the path to the falls is lined with lights, and the falls themselves are illuminated by changing colored lights behind and in front of the water.

Timberwolf Campground

1007 N. Irish Rd. in the Genesee Recreation Area. (313) 640-1600 (in season); 736-7100 otherwise.

196 campsites (some with electricity, more without, all with showers) are in a wooded area along the Flint River. Hiking trails, boat launch, playground, picnic area. Only campers can use a nearby beach on a spring-fed lake in a woods. Ten minutes to downtown Flint. Operated by the Genesee County Parks and Recreation Commission along with an equally large campground in the **Holloway Reservoir Regional Park** about 7 miles east of here.

Wolcott Orchards & Cider Mill

3284 W. Coldwater between Clio and Jennings roads on the north edge of Flint but south of I-475. From I-475, take the Clio Rd. exit, go south to Coldwater and turn west. (313) 789-9561. Daily, year-round, 9-6.

Wolcott's features a wide variety of apples, including less common varieties such as Talman Sweet, Maiden Blush, Winter Banana, Greening, and Steel Red. The orchard has been in business for almost 100 years; part of its cider mill is that old, too. Because it is open all year, it stocks a variety of other items: donuts, nuts, flours, juices, and more.

RESTAURANTS

Top of the Park ★★★

432 N. Saginaw (Northbank Center), 12th floor. (313) 232-8888. Mon-Fri 11-10:30, Sat 5:30-10:30. Entrees $5.95-$12.95 (lunch); $15.95-$29.95 (dinner). Full bar, 80-bottle wine list (longest in the area). MasterCard, Visa, Diners' Club.

Top of the Park offers excellent food in pleasing surroundings, with a fine view of the Flint River and central Flint. Ask to be seated along the south wall. At lunch, new age music blends well with the contemporary decor. The bread, baked on the premises, is especially tasty.

The menu changes regularly. Recent lunch favorites included poulet en fillo (chicken and broccoli wrapped in filo pastry with hollandaise sauce; $6.95) and grilled breast of duckling sauced with sliced strawberries, coconut milk, and Grand Marnier ($9.50). For dinner, there was Filet of Waronoff (aged prime tender-loin marinated in bourbon, brandy, peppercorns, and mustard, with a Bordelaise sauce; $24.95) and paupiettes of swordfish with carrots and fennel ($18.95). Dinners include house salad, sorbet intermezzo, potato, and vegetable.

Figlio's

1 Water St. at S. Saginaw in the Water Street Pavilion. (313) 767-0000. Full bar, 20-bottle list of mostly California wines. Mon-Thurs 11:30-10, Fri 11:30-midnight, Sat noon-midnight, Sun 12-8.

Figlio's bistro (pronounced FEE-li-o's) is part of a small Minnesota-based chain. It is one of the better restaurants in central Flint. Though the future of the Water Street Pavilion is in doubt, Figlio's place seems assured, with a long-term lease and a good business. You can watch the pasta being made daily. Soup and salad is a good lunch value at $3.95. Also popular: tortellini pasta salad with olive oil, Italian salami, red and yellow peppers, and parmesan cheese ($5.95): calzone (turnovers) filled with Italian sausage, ricotta cheese, and red onion, and smoked chicken salad with curried mayonnaise, chutney, and grapes in a fresh pineapple half. For dinner fettucine alfredo ($6.25) and blackened redfish ($11.95) are specialties.

Battiste's Temple Dining Room

755 S. Saginaw in the Masonic Temple basement in downtown Saginaw. (313) 235-7760. Mon-Fri 11 a.m.-2 p.m., closed in July. No credit cards.

Battiste's is open only for lunch on weekdays. If you eat at this plain, obscure spot, you are truly eating with the natives. No one else knows about it. This vast dining room, seating over 200, is in the basement of the hulking Masonic Temple. The big room is alive with convivial conversations of the regulars, many of them retirees, who come for the decent food at rock-bottom prices. For under $4 you can get pot roast of beef with buttered noodles, tossed salad, rolls, and butter, or breaded shrimp, french fries, and cole slaw. Bar-B-Q beef on a bun, with french fries and salad (under $3) is a big favorite, as are the homemade pies ($1.25 a slice).

Take a moment, if you have time, to browse in the upstairs lobby of the Masonic Temple, where you'll see framed old newspapers front pages heralding the Temple's 1911 opening.

Floogles

1174 Robert T. Longway Blvd. just west of I-475 (in the Hampton Inn). (313) 235-6661. Mon-Sat 8 a.m.-10 p.m., Sun 10-8. Entrees $4.50-$4.75, sandwiches $4. Full bar. Major credit cards.

This popular Flint eating place has a striking new Art Deco interior with lots of skylights, window walls, and plants. The Bar-B-Q ribs ($11.95 and prime beef($9.95 and $12.95) are the most popular entrees.

Angelo's Coney Island and Grill

1816 Davison at Franklin, east of downtown between Kearsley Park and AC Spark Plug. (313) 238-3761. Daily 5 a.m.-3 a.m.

This extremely popular greasy spoon has been around since 1949. Angelo himself died in 1972. It's famed for its dry coney island hot dogs ($1.15), made with ground meat and spices without the usual bean sauce. They taste rather salty, but people love them. "Flint-style" coneys are even catching on elsewhere in Michigan. Also good are the $1.15 hamburgers. Chili ($1.35/bowl) is another favorite. Angelo's makes a homemade soup daily (vegetable beef, chicken noodle, beef barley, etc.). What's left over is served on Saturdays.

Bill Thomas' Haloburger

14 locations. See below. Typically open Mon-Sat 7 a.m.-10 p.m., until 11 on Fri & Sat; Sun 7:30 a.m.-8 p.m. 24-hour location at 800 S. Saginaw downtown.

The Haloburger is a very good hamburger — and a very good value. It's served at the 14 locations of this family-owned alternative to franchised fast food. The late Bill Thomas started as an employee and later owner of the Flint Kewpee Sandwich franchise, then went independent in 1967 and dreamed up, with the help of his son, the memorable angelic cow logo.

The newly expanded downtown Haloburger at **800 South Saginaw** at Court Street is pretty memorable, too, with its Vernor's gnomes and castle mural preserved on an outdoor wall. (See p. 311) The restaurant is a favorite gathering place of cops, lawyers, firemen, and government employees nearby. Sometimes you'll even see the jury, judge, defendant, and attorneys all here at lunch. It's open 24 hours a day, except for Sunday morning, when it closes at 5 a.m. and reopens at 4 p.m.

For I-75 travelers, the attractive **Pierson Road** Haloburger northwest of downtown Flint has a beautiful wooded site.

Haloburgers are made with fresh beef, your choice of fixings, in regular (82¢), 1/4 pound ($1.62), and 1/2 pound ($2.55). Other options are soup, grilled and fried chicken, and a chef salad (large is $2.58) are other options. Breakfasts include eggs, pancakes, French toast, and even oatmeal.

The Torch Bar and Grill

522 Buckham, around the corner from Second St. and one block west of Saginaw in downtown Flint. (313) 232-0626. Mon-Sat 11 a.m.-2 a.m. Cocktails, beer.

This old bar has a homey, friendly, living-room atmosphere that has evolved over the decades. It's light-filled, with a nice view of Buckham Alley, but without hanging plants — they couldn't survive the smoke. The big food draw is the half-pound Torchburger ($2.35), deemed Flint's second-best burger after the Haloburger, but chili and soup, steak and onions, coneys, and fries are also served. The diverse clientele includes downtown businesspeople, lawyers, cops, people with their kids, and artists associated with the Buckham Fine Arts Project around the corner, where artist/tavern owner Gary Gebhart shows his work. This is a place, says a manager, "where everybody knows everybody, and if you don't, you soon will."

See also: *Windmill Place p. 307, Flint Farmers' Market p. 307.*

LODGINGS

Hyatt Regency Flint
(313) 239-1234. (800) 228-9000.
S. Saginaw at Riverbank Park, south of the Flint River in downtown Flint. Take I-475 to Court St. exit, left onto Court, then right onto Saginaw (north) 8 blocks.
16 floors, 369 rooms. $87 single; $97 double; $65 weekend special for 2. Indoor pool, jacuzzi. HBO, pay movies ($6.35). Restaurant (Stetson's), many others nearby.

Best Western Mr. Gibby's Inn
(313) 733-7570. (800) 529-1234.
3129 Miller Rd. at I-75, west of downtown Flint. Take I-75 to Exit 117B (Miller Rd.). On southeast corner of intersection.
110 units; 2 floors. Summer rate: $50 single; $55 double. (Winter rates less.) Outdoor pool. Hot tubs. HBO & ESPN. Mr. Gibby's restaurant (prime rib and seafood specialties). Polynesian pool bar in summer.

Red Roof Inn
(313) 733-1660. (800) 843-7663.
3219 Miller Rd. at I-75, west of downtown Flint. From I-75, take exit 117B (Miller Rd.). Southwest of intersection.
2 floors, 107 units. $38-42 double. Free movies in evening. Fast-food restaurants nearby.

Sheraton Flint
(313) 732-0400. (800) 325-3535.
I-75 at Pierson Rd. exit, northwest of downtown Flint. Take I-75 to exit 122 (Pierson Rd.). Northwest of intersection.
5 floors, 196 units. $59 single; $65 double. Indoor pool. Whirlpool, sauna. Exercise room, game room. Tennis courts. Views of garden area. Fenced play yard for children. HBO, Showtime, ESPN. 2 restaurants.

Walli's Motor Lodge West
(313) 789-0400.
I-75 at Pierson Rd. exit, northwest of downtown Flint. Take I-75 to exit 122 (Pierson Rd.). On southeast corner of intersection.
67 units; 2 floors. $32 single, $39 double. HBO & ESPN. Walli's restaurant.

Best Western Flint
(313) 733-7570. (800) 529-1234.
I-75 at Pierson Rd. exit, northwest of downtown Flint. Take I-75 to Exit 122 (Pierson Rd.). Just west of overpass.
73 units; 2 floors. $39 single; $44 double. Exercise room. Sauna, whirlpool. HBO. Fast-food restaurants nearby.

Walli's Motor Lodge East
(313) 743-8850.
1341 S. Center Rd. near Lapeer Rd. in suburban Burton. From I-69 exit Center Rd., 1 1/2 blocks south, on east side.
69 units; 2 floors. $36 single; $38 double. HBO & ESPN. Walli's restaurant (home of the Walliburger) open 24 hours., small cocktail bar.

Howard Johnson's East
(313) 744-0200. (800) 654-2000.
932 S. Center Rd. in suburban Burton, east of Flint. Take I-69 to Center Rd. exit. Across from Courtland Mall at Center and Court.
176 units; 2 floors. $43 single; $46 double. Indoor pool. Whirlpool. Tennis courts. HBO & Showtime. Full-service restaurant.

The Country Inn of Grand Blanc
(313) 694-6749.
6136 S. Belsay Rd. between Perry and Hill, on the north outskirts of Grand Blanc.
3 rooms with private or shared bath. $45-65. Turn-of-the-century house in country setting, furnished with antiques.

Port Huron

This city of 34,000, Thomas Edison's home town, is strategically sited where Lake Huron pours into the St. Clair River. It offers some of Michigan's more scenic and historic sights.

The French built Fort St. Joseph in 1686 to seal off the upper Great Lakes from the English. That makes Port Huron one of the earliest outposts in the American interior. The fort only existed two years before it burned to the ground. The next settlers, about a century later, were also French, part of the French exodus from Detroit following British occupation of the city.

The Americans built Fort Gratiot here in 1814 on the same site as Fort St. Joseph, also to keep the British out of Lake Huron and beyond. Friction with British-controlled Canada had changed to cooperation by 1891, when the long underground St. Clair Railroad Tunnel was built beneath the St. Clair River to join Sarnia with Port Huron. The two-mile-long tunnel was a major feat, receiving national attention. It brought shipments much faster from points west to markets in the East.

Located just south of John Street, the tunnel is still quite active. For the high railroad cars which can't fit through the tunnel, ferry service is in operation 24 hours a day to get them across the St. Clair River. The line's owner, Grand Trunk, has its car repair shops in Port Huron at 25th and Minnie streets. With a 435-person work force here, it has long been a major local employer.

The Black River winds southeast through town to the St. Clair River, joining it right near the middle of

The 1.4-mile-long Blue Water Bridge conects Port Huron with Sarnia, Ontario. Pedestrians on this majestic bridge are rewarded with fabulous bird's-eye views of Lake Huron, north Port Huron neighborhoods, the St. Clair River, and Sarnia.

downtown. This necessitates three manned drawbridges. The Black River is only big enough to accommodate pleasure craft, but their masts can back up traffic just as effectively as a mighty steamer.

A pleasant backwater

Despite its strategic position, Port Huron has been something of a backwater over the decades. Military concerns disappeared after the Civil War, and no industrial giants sprang up here as they did in Midland or Battle Creek or Kalamazoo. Its population grew gradually to a height of about 37,000 around 1975 and has slipped back slowly to 34,000 today. The one big event, which attracts thousands, is the **Mackinac Race Day** in late July, when a flotilla of sailing boats races to Mackinac Island.

The downtown is pleasantly quaint, if a bit tired-looking. Not too many American downtowns still have both their J.C. Penney and Sears stores like Port Huron does, nor their home-owned department store. At **Sperry's** at Huron and Grand River, the polite elevator attendant wears gloves. Next door is **Diana's**, a true 1926 gem of a sweet shop (see p. 322). Port Huron draws shoppers from the east side of Michigan's Thumb to the north as well as from Canada.

Papers mills and a brass factory

Two sizable paper mills still operate in Port Huron. Dunn Paper, with about 225 employees, is on Lake Huron just north of the Blue Water Bridge. Now owned by James River, it makes gift wrap for companies like Hallmark and American Greeting. Port Huron Paper, with 325 employees, is on the Black River off Washington Street. Founded in 1888, it was recently purchased by Eddy Paper and makes microwave popcorn bags as well as wrappers for fast-food restaurant hamburgers.

None of the big auto companies established a plant here as they have in most larger cities in southeast Michigan. The dominant firm since World War I has been **Mueller Brass** at 20th Street and Lapeer Avenue. This million-square-foot industrial complex got its start in Port Huron during World War I when the U.S. Government invited a Sarnia company called Mueller Metals to start manufacturing munitions for the U.S. The founder was the son of a German master machinist who emigrated from Germany in 1852. Mueller Brass was the first commercial producer of brass forgings in the U.S. It is best known, however, for developing solder fittings which made it possible for copper pipes to replace threaded galvanized steel in American plumbing.

Today Mueller makes all sorts of brass, copper, and aluminum products, many for very specialized tasks. In 1979 Mueller was acquired by Sharon Steel, which

For a free map and events calendar, contact the Port Huron/Marysville Chamber of Commerce, 920 Pine Grove, Port Huron, MI 48060. (313) 985-7101.

Russo-Germans in Port Huron
Not many years ago a group of Russo-Germans lived in central Port Huron. Their ancestors had emigrated to Russia from Germany in the 1700s, when Catherine the Great promised them free land and freedom of religion. Between 1910 and 1915, many immigrated to the U.S., and some ended up here, living just south of the Black River. Once a distinctive ethnic enclave, by now these Germans are dispersed throughout the area.

Freighters from all over the world travel through the upper Great Lakes. Port Huron's riverfront parks let you see these enormous vessels up close, thanks to the narrow St. Clair River here. About 30 big boats a day pass by from the end of March until the end of December.

in turn is owned by Victor Posner's NVF Corp. Employment has sagged to about 950 in recent years as newer Mueller plants have been built in the South.

A $1.2 million donation built **McMorran Place**, a sizable convention center on Huron (M-25) at the south edge of downtown. The money came from the two daughters of a local businessman who had served in Congress from 1903 to 1913. McMorran was such a stickler for promptness that he always wore two watches. In 1960 the 1,200-seat auditorium was built, followed by an arena and then a pavilion. In 1965 the 150-foot tower was erected. You can climb its steps on summer afternoons to get a good view of the city.

POINTS OF INTEREST

1858 Grand Trunk Depot ★

Just south of the Blue Water Bridge. From Pine Grove Ave. take Thomas Edison Parkway just north of the tracks. Parking spaces and boardwalk by the river.

Port Huron's strategic location where Lake Huron flows into the St. Clair River provides an exceptional visual setting in this new park by the historic train station. To your left as you face Canada looms the enormous **Blue Water Bridge** overhead, and beyond that the great expanse of **Lake Huron**. Directly ahead, the river is surprisingly narrow, less than a quarter mile wide. It therefore runs quite swiftly, 7 or 8 miles an hour.

The river's narrow width brings the big freighters up close as they pass. Sarnia's northern suburb, Point Edward, is also easily viewed. Freighters are typically tied up at its harbors.

Standing starkly near the railroad tracks is the recently restored 1858 **Grand Trunk Depot**. It was from here in 1859 that Thomas Edison, a Port Huron boy of 12, embarked to sell fruits, nuts, magazines, and newspapers on the train to Detroit and back. He used much of his earnings to buy chemicals for the small laboratory he set up in the train's baggage car. After the Battle of Shiloh, he made a killing selling nickel copies of the *Detroit Free*

Press for a dollar each to the clamoring crowds here eager to read the list of who had died in the battle.

The Grand Trunk Railroad later built a much more impressive Port Huron depot farther down the tracks. The 1858 depot, re-clad in stucco, became the office for the adjacent New Egyptian Cement Company. Now the cement plant is gone, the stucco removed, and under the care of the **Thomas Edison Inn**, the depot can once again be seen as it was over a century ago.

Just south of the old depot is the new Thomas Edison Inn, a pricey 150-suite dining/hotel complex built by the owners of the popular St. Clair Inn downriver. Just south of the inn's parking lot is where **Fort Gratiot** (1814-1879) stood.

Blue Water Bridge ★★

U.S. entrance is the northern terminus of I-94. Toll: 75¢ per car.

Rising 152 feet over the St. Clair River to allow freighters to pass underneath, the Blue Water Bridge is 1.4 miles long, with a main span of 871 feet. Completed in 1938, it connects Port Huron with Sarnia, Ontario. Its height gives you a splendid view of Lake Huron to the north and the St. Clair River to the south. Also interesting are the bird's-eye views of Port Huron neighborhoods. Just to the north you see the Dunn Paper facilities. You can also walk across the bridge.

Sarnia, Canada

I-94 to the Blue Water Bridge. No passport necessary for American citizens.

Port Huron's neighbor across the St. Clair River is a pleasant, if rather unexciting place to visit. No longer are there great buys on Commonwealth products to lure Americans across the border. If anything, the flow is reversed, and Canadians flock to Port Huron's K Mart for good deals.

American beer drinkers may find it worthwhile to pick up a case of the more potent and robust Canadian brew, but the price is steep (about $1 a bottle) and a small duty must be paid when re-entering the U.S. An elaborate government-run information center is just to the south of the Canadian side of the bridge.

The economy of Sarnia (population 80,000) is based on the petrochemical industry, whose fascinating-looking plants sprawl for some 20 miles below the city along the St. Clair River. At night, the spaghetti-like complex of lights and tubing are quite a sight from the American side. The most important catalyst for this area becoming the center of Canada's chemical industry was the building of a World War II plant to make synthetic rubber.

Sarnia was a lumber town in the early 19th century. Later oil was discovered south of Sarnia. Its economy was also stimulated by the arrival of the Grand Trunk and Great Western tracks in the late 1850s.

Sarnia became a deepwater port in the 1920s. The most prominent sight on its waterfront is the huge grain elevators from which freighters receive their cargo.

Lighthouse Park ★★

Off Omar St. between Robinson and Riverview 5 blocks north of the Blue Water Bridge. From Pine Grove north of I-94, take Garfield east to the park.

Here, next to the oldest surviving lighthouse in Michigan, is another good vantage point from which to enjoy the splendid view of Lake Huron as it enters the St. Clair River. Lights illuminate an asphalt path leading to the sandy beach. If it is a foggy day, it's an eerie sight to see giant northerly freighters quietly churning past and becoming quickly engulfed in the mist on the Lake.

On the short path to the beach, you pass a small Coast Guard complex, complete with a pair of classic old two-story structures: the 1874 lightkeeper's dwelling of red brick and the white clapboard Coast Guard station. Also in the complex is the 86-foot-tall **Fort Gratiot Light**. It still flashes a warning to freighters coming south into the river, a tricky maneuver because of the river's narrow width and swift current. The white brick lighthouse was first built in 1825. It was destroyed by a storm in 1828 and rebuilt a year later. Now part of a Coast Guard complex, the lighthouse is just north of where Fort Gratiot used to stand.

Pinegrove Park   ★★

East off Pine Grove between Prospect and Lincoln, a few blocks north of downtown.

This city park also fronts the St. Clair River and provides a wonderful view of the big bridge, the Canadian shoreline, and boat traffic. On the concrete walk right at the riverbank you can see fishermen with big landing nets fishing for walleye and steelhead. Four decades ago, there used to be a little post office here, from which a small boat embarked to deliver mail to the freighters as they passed by. (This service is now provided near the Ambassador Bridge in Detroit.)

At the park's northeastern edge, perched strangely on the riverbank, is the **Lightship Huron,** a retired floating lighthouse whose light could be seen for 14 miles. The 97-foot-long ship served six miles north of Port Huron from 1935 until 1970. North of the lightship you can see a red **pilot house,** quarters for the American freighter pilots who take the wheels of foreign vessels heading into U.S. waters. The vacant lot behind the pilot house was where Thomas Edison's family home stood. Student archaeologists from Michigan State University have found old bottles on the site which they think were used by the young inventor in his lab.

Looking south across the river, you can see the beginning of Canada's 20-mile-long **"chemical valley,"** Canada's greatest concentration of chemical factories. They are responsible for creating most of the pollution in the lower St. Clair River.

Diana Sweet Shop   ★★

307 Huron between Grand River and McMorran downtown. (313) 985-6933. Mon-Thurs 7:30 a.m.-6 p.m., Fri 7:30-9, Sat 7:30-6. MasterCard, Visa, AmExpress. No alcohol.

Fine woodwork abounds in this beautifully preserved 1926 sweet shop. The ornate wallpaper, the lighting, the pressed metal ceiling, the pictures — all combine to create an extraordinary atmosphere.

Named "Diana" after the goddess of the hunt, it is still owned and operated by the sons of the founder. Sweet shops also served sandwiches. They flourished in the 1920s as the tempo of American urban life sped up and people stopped going home for lunch. Elegant interiors were a mark of success. Diana's preserves not only the decor but the menu: sandwiches, ice cream, pastries, and fudge.

Don't miss the original 1926 "Violano Virtuoso" up front as you enter. For 25¢ it will play five tunes, plucking at a violin and hammering on strings.

The Diana Sweet Shoppe still has the same extraordinarily ornate, inviting interior as when it opened in 1926. The menu, emphasizing simple sandwiches, ice cream, and fudge, hasn't changed much, either.

Museum of Arts & History ★

1115 Sixth St. between Wall and Court, south of the Black River and downtown. Sixth is one block west of M-25, the main artery. (313) 982-0891. Wed-Sun 1-4:30. Free admission, donations welcome.

This sizable museum is housed in the impressive 1904 Carnegie library, which in 1917 became Michigan's first county library. The museum, dating from 1968, has a little bit of everything, from 7,000 B.C. Indian artifacts to recent paintings for sale by local artists.

As in many local history museums, interpretation of what you see is weak. There is a remarkable array of Indian stone points and tools from the region, ranging in stages from the 7000-5000 B.C. Aqua-Plano era to the Late Woodlawn era of 800-1600 A.D. Also on display are some fine examples of the curiously beautiful Indian "birdstones." There are small-scale models of old Fort St. Joseph and Fort Gratiot and the fruits of a careful archaeological excavation of Fort Gratiot: insignias, gun flints, an old soda pop bottle, buttons, clay pipes, and a cannon ball, among others. Another display centers on Thomas Edison's life in Port Huron.

The natural sciences section has arrays of stuffed animals, rocks, and lots of butterflies. Upstairs is an ornate Victorian room with some striking quilts and a rather large gallery of Great Lakes items.

Most haunting are the objects brought up by divers from wrecks. The *Daniel J. Morrell* broke in two north of Harbor Beach in 1966, drowning 28 of the 29-man crew. Along with pictures of the boat hangs a life jacket and a piece of life raft that drifted to shore. The *S.S. Regina* was one of nine boats that went down in the horrendous November storm of 1913. A diver in 1986 found a brass lantern, the shipbuilder's plate, and part of the cargo of spoons from the wreck. The steamer *Pewabic* has been lying in 176 feet of water since 1865 after colliding with its sister ship. On display are examples of its cargo of interesting-looking copper ingots, plus an ornate spittoon, a ship's bell, and a walking stick.

The cluttered pilot house of a Great Lakes steamer has been reconstructed, using salvaged items from various old boats. You can stand up to the big pilot wheel and ring the boat's bell.

RESTAURANTS

Fogcutter Restaurant

511 Fort St. at Michigan. (313) 987-3300. Mon-Fri 11 a.m.-10 p.m. Sat 12-11, Sun 12-7. Entrees (including salad and veg.) $5.95-$8.95 (lunch), $9.95-$19.95 (dinner). Full bar. MasterCard, Visa, AmExpress, Discovery.

Local business executives like to eat here, atop the People's Bank in downtown Port Huron. The food is rather mediocre, but the view from all three sides is terrific. To the west you see the river and Sarnia, to the north you see northern Port Huron, the Blue Water Bridge, and Lake Huron, and to the south, downtown Port Huron. The favorites here are steak and seafood.

Victorian Inn ★★

1229 7th at Union, 2 blocks west of M-25. Union is one-way away from M-25, so turn west on Court and take 7th south to Union. (313) 984-1437. Tues-Sat lunch 11:30-1:30, dinner 5:30-8:30. Entrees $5.50-$6.50 (lunch); $15-$20 (dinner). Full bar. Pub in basement. Visa, MasterCard, Discovery, Diners.

This elaborate Queen Anne house, beautifully and authentically restored, is also a four-room bed and breakfast. Table settings and starchy white service uniforms carry out the historic theme. The 50-seat restaurant has become not only the leading local fine dining choice but a popular destination attraction. Its limited menu of American fare with a continental touch changes frequently. Typical dinner items include filet mignon with shiitake mushrooms ($20.50) and sausage-stuffed quail, with lighter crepes, omelets, and strudels for lunch. Dinner entrees include salad, vegetable, rolls, and starch. Soups are very good here, and the homemade desserts are noteworthy. Reservations recommended.

Jambalayas' ★★

2525 24th St. at Dove, 2 miles southwest of downtown. Take Dove St. exit from I-94. From M-25, take 24th St. north just north of Lincoln Park at the south edge of town. (313) 985-5553. Mon-Sat 6 a.m.-9 p.m. Sandwiches $2.85-$4.25. Hot entrees $1.75 (cup of gumbo)-$6.50 (shrimp platter). No alcohol or credit cards.

This jazzed-up diner near an industrial park is a surprising new arrival, what with authentic Creole cooking. It came about when one owner discovered that Sarnia's International Bakery could make the right kind of bread he wanted for po'boys, French toast, and muffuletta. A muffuletta ($6.50, $3.50 for 1/2) is a giant sandwich on a round, flat loaf layered with Genoa salami, ham, provolone and Swiss, and homemade olive salad. Shrimp creole ($5.95) is a popular dish. The *Detroit Free Press's* Molly Abraham recommends the chicken-and-sausage jambalaya. ($5.25) include lots of rice, bread, and salad.

See also: *Diana Sweet Shoppe downtown, p. 322.*

LODGINGS

Colonial Motor Inn
(313) 984-1522.
2908 Pine Grove Ave. Take I-94 almost to the Blue Water Bridge, go north onto M-25. It's just north of Garfield, about 1 1/2 miles from downtown.
107 rooms, 2 floors. $43.95 single; $47.95-$51.95 double. Outdoor pool. Game room. In-house movies. Short drive to Lighthouse Park, bridge.

Econo Lodge of Port Huron
(313) 984-2661.
1720 Hancock at the M-25 turnoff at the terminus of I-94. 1 1/2 miles north of downtown.
100 rooms, 2 floors. $43.95 single; $47.95 double. Suites $103.95-$153.95. Indoor pool, sauna, jacuzzi. Playground for kids. Bowling alley next door. In-house movies. Short drive to Lighthouse Park, bridge.

Thomas Edison Inn
(313) 984-8000.
500 Thomas Edison Parkway. From I-94's turnoff onto M-25 just before the Blue Water Bridge, go right onto Hancock, right onto Pine Grove, left in 1/2 mile to Thomas Edison Parkway.
49 rooms, 3 floors. $80 parking lot side; $100 downriver views; $105 Blue Water Bridge view. Indoor pool. whirlpool, sauna, exercise room, tanning booths. Dining room and lounge. Dancing Thurs, Fri, & Sat evenings.

Victorian Inn
(313) 984-1437.
1229 7th St. Directions: see p. 324.
Bed and breakfast with 4 guest rooms in a large Queen Anne house. $45-50 for rooms with shared bath, $55-60 with private bath includes continental breakfast. Good restaurant on first floor, casual pub in cellar.

Detroit-Area Nightspots

Here are some of the most noteworthy clubs in metro Detroit. See also Ann Arbor for the Bird of Paradise (jazz), The Ark (folk), and The Blind Pig (rock), and Rick's (rock and blues).

ROCK 'N' ROLL

Alvin's Finer Delicatessen
5756 Cass just north of Palmer, across Cass from Wayne State. (313) 832-2355. Bar and deli open Mon-Sat 11 a.m.-2:30 a.m. Live music Mon, Fri & Sat starts at 10.

This is Detroit's most famous rock joint, where the region's best bands play. Alvin's also occasionally books blues, jazz, and reggae groups. It seats 200, and there is a bar and deli food. Closed on Sundays.

ClubLand
2115 Woodward at Grand Circus, downtown. 961-5450. Thurs-Sun 9 p.m.-2 a.m. Cover $5 Thurs-Sat.

Housed in the gloriously ornate 1925 State Theater, ClubLand has quickly become one of Detroit's hottest dance clubs. It has a 3,000-square-foot dance floor, room for a crowd of 3,500, and the largest video display system in the country with 64 27-inch monitors and 3 10x14-foot front projection monitors. In-house dance troupe. Creative video skits. Small cafe. Guest musicians.

Lilli's 21
2930 Jacob, 3 blocks south of Holbrook and just east of Jos Campau in Hamtramck. (313) 875-6555. Bar and restaurant open Mon-Fri 11 a.m.-midnight, Sat & Sun 7p.m.-2 a.m. Live music Fri & Sat begins around 11:30. Cover $4-$6.

Lilli, the bar's owner, a onetime Dodge Main worker and concentration camp inmate, started booking punk and rock acts here years ago. Now her children run the place. On weekends its solid rock acts draw a good number of suburbanites who don't want to go all the way downtown. Two bands play every weekend. It's original music, from New Music to hard rock. The clientele is mixed, too, from punks to suits. Burgers and short-order specials served.

Clutch Cargo's at St. Andrew's Hall
431 E. Congress between Beaubien and Brush in Bricktown, 2 blocks north of the RenCen. (313) 961-MELT. Hall number 961-8137. Fri 11 p.m.-5 a.m., Sat 9 p.m.-5 a.m.

This turn-of-the-century Scottish men's clubhouse, staid by day, rocks at night. With its big 1,200-seat ballroom, St. Andrew's is able to book up-and-coming national and international rock acts. Some of the most interesting new rock music can be heard here.

BLUES, SOUL, FOLK, and R&B

Soup Kitchen Saloon
1585 Franklin at Orleans in Rivertown, 4 blocks east of the RenCen. From Jefferson, turn south onto Orleans. From I-375, exit Jefferson Ave. East. (313) 259-2643. Live music Wed & Sun 8 p.m., Fri & Sat 9:30 p.m. Cover $2-$15, averaging $7.

The emphasis at this locally legendary saloon is Chicago-style electric blues, with a fair number of folk and Southern blues performers as well. The top blues artists come here: Albert Collins, James Cotton, Willie Dixon, John Scofield, Hiram Bullock, to mention a few. Right on the riverfront, the 150-year-old Soup Kitchen is Detroit's oldest saloon. The first-floor entertainment area seats 125. Good barbecue and Creole food.

Sully's

4758 Greenfield between Michigan and Ford Rd. in Dearborn, 1 mile east of Southfield Frwy., 1 mile north of I-94. For schedule, call (313) 846-5377. Bar phone (313) 846-1920. Live music typically Thurs 9 p.m., Fri & Sat 10 p.m. Cover $5-$15.

Important rhythm and blues place, often featuring interesting new acts. Some folk music, too. Seating 175 to 200, it is big enough to book major artists like Dr. John and Albert King.

Club Pentha

Fisher Building, West Grand Blvd at Second Ave in the New Center. (313) 972-3760. Wed-Sat 9 p.m. $5 cover on weekends.

First-rate soul music, with an emphasis on vocals, for a sophisticated Buppy crowd in an atmosphere of quiet elegance.

JAZZ

Alexander's Lounge

4265 Woodward at Canfield, between Orchestra Hall and the DIA. (313) 831-2662. Live acts Fri & Sat 9-2. Cover $6.

Next to the opulent Whitney restaurant, this is the best fusion jazz club in the state. It seats 150. A full kitchen serves steaks and Italian food.

Bo-Mac's Lounge

281 Gratiot. Between Broadway and Randolph, downtown near Harmonie Park. (313) 961-5152. Live jazz Thurs 8-12, Fri & Sat 9:30-2. No cover.

At this small, friendly black bar, a very hot Hammond organ quartet plays in a vintage 1950s atmosphere. Organist Ben Baber is joined by various friends. In addition to drinks, down-home food such as greens, macaroni and cheese, and pork chop sandwiches is served.

New World Stage

1435-37 Randolph in Harmonie Park between Gratiot and E. Grand River. (313) 964-0527. Sat 10 p.m.-3 a.m. Cover $7-$12.50.

Detroit's only jazz loft attracts jazz fans all the way from Toronto. The space is a rehearsal studio during the week, but an exceptionally comfortable place to hear jazz Saturday night. They play straight-ahead jazz here, booking acts like Sun-Ra, Donald Walden, and Barry Harris. The good music is the focus, but there is limited bar service and Creole food.

Pro Sports Tickets

Detroit Lions

Season: September-December.
Pontiac Silverdome. On Opdyke Rd. and Featherstone on Pontiac's east side, 1 mile west of I-75. From I-75, take M-59 west, Opdyke exit. Tickets $18 (bleachers $7.50). Credit card orders: (313) 335-4151 or Ticketmaster (313) 645-6666. Prepaid parking $5.

The Lions play in the largest-capacity enclosed stadium in the country, the 80,000-seat Silverdome. (See page 213.) Due no doubt in part to their losing ways in recent years, Lions tickets are the cheapest in the NFL. Stadiums in many NFL towns are sold out, but a casual visitor to Detroit may well be able to pick up a ticket at the last minute, though the seat will likely be a lower-level corner or end zone. Be sure to order prepaid parking ($5) if available. The Lions sell about 40,000 season tickets at $180/season.
Dining options: *see Pontiac (p. 215).*

Detroit Pistons

Season: November-April.
The Palace of Auburn Hills, 5 miles northeast of downtown Pontiac at the intersection of I-75 and M-24. Take exit 81 (Lapeer Rd. M-24). Tickets $10.50-$100. Parking $5. Credit card orders: (313) 377-8600 or Ticketmaster (313) 645-6666.

Because the Pistons have become such a strong team, last-minute tickets are hard to get for more one or two people together. The Palace, seating 21,454, is a pleasant arena for watching basketball. (See p. 217.) In the arena is the Palace Grille restaurant.
Dining options: *see Pontiac (p. 215).*

Detroit Tigers

Season: April-September.
Tiger Stadium, Michigan at Trumbull, 1 mile west of downtown Detroit. From I-94, take Tiger Stadium exit. Tickets: $10.50 boxes, $8.50 reserved, $6 grand stand, $2 bleachers — available only at the stadium two hours before game time. Season tickets (box seats): $760. Ticket orders ($2 handling charge): (313) 963-7300. Business office (313) 962-4000.

Tiger Stadium is one of the better places in the country to watch major league baseball. It's one of the last of the ancient stadiums with atmosphere and a certain intimacy, compared with the more gradually sloped seating of the newer stadiums. (See p. 84 for Tiger Stadium's history and uncertain status.) The 11,000 bleacher seats, an extraordinary value, offer about as good a view as the grand stand. The stadium provides no parking, and there's a fairly wide range of prices correlating roughly with the distance from the stadium.
Dining options: *see southwest Detroit (p. 86), downtown Detroit (p. 37), Cultural Center (p. 101), Rivertown (p. 50).*

Detroit Red Wings

Season: October-March.
Joe Louis Arena in downtown Detroit. Location on the PeopleMover allows you to park and dine anywhere on the route. Take the Lodge Freeway (U.S. 10) south to Joe Louis Parking exit. Tickets $9 (upper bowl) and $16 (lower bowl). Ticket orders: (313) 567-7372 or Ticketmaster (313) 645-6666.

If at all possible, get the $16 lower bowl tickets, or you'll have a long look down in this 19,000-seat stadium.
Dining options: *see downtown Detroit, p. 37.*

Detroit-Area Shopping Malls

Shopping malls came early to Detroit and caught on big. In the flush of the 1950s postwar auto boom, suburban Detroit was a shopping center developer's dream, thanks to the huge metro population, rapid suburbanization, and high average family earnings. Hudson's **Northland** (1952), just across the Detroit line at Eight Mile Road and Greenfield in Southfield, was designed by the noted urban planner Victor Gruen. It became the nation's pioneering model for shopping malls.

Mall retailing in Michigan is overwhelmingly dominated by five of Al Taubman's 19 super-regional malls: Fairlane Town Center (Dearborn), Lakeside (Sterling Heights), Briarwood (Ann Arbor), Twelve Oaks (Novi), and one in Grand Rapids. The Taubman Company is the nation's most profitable mall manager and developer. The rigor of its tenant selection and maintenance is legendary.

Of metropolitan Detroit's 15 regional malls, **Somerset Mall** in Troy is the toniest, **Northland** in Southfield the largest (in square feet) and most historic, and **Twelve Oaks** in Novi has the best all-around mall for selection and atmosphere. **Fairlane Town Center** in Dearborn is almost as big as Northland, with more stores (225), including a Saks in addition to the usual Taubman anchors (Hudson's, Penney's, Sears, and Lord & Taylor).

The early 1990s promise to bring a lot of new activity to the Detroit retail market. Its last new player, Lord & Taylor, came in 1978, just before the auto downturn. But now the powerhouses in the industry, including Bloomingdale's, Macy's, Nordstrom, and Neiman-Marcus, are quite interested in metro Detroit.

Behind the Taubman fortune
Shopping mall magnate Al Taubman of Bloomfield Hills also owns the prestigious Sotheby Parke-Bernet auction gallery and the A&W root beer chain. He made his first millions building gas stations for prominent Detroit businessman/philanthropist Max Fisher. Taubman's mall empire was built in the 1970s with the fortune he made in southern California real estate. He, Fisher, and Henry Ford bought the huge, county-size Irvine Ranch, partly developed it, and resold it.

POINTS OF INTEREST

Somerset Mall

Big Beaver at Coolidge, Troy, MI 48084. 1 1/2 miles northeast of downtown Birmingham. Big Beaver is the same as 16 Mile Road. (313) 643-6360. Write or phone for mall directory. Sun 12-5; Tues, Wed, Sat 10-6; Mon, Thurs, Fri 10-9.

On some days the customers are the fashion show here at Detroit's most exclusive mall. Its 50 stores number **Saks Fifth Avenue** and **Bonwit Teller** as anchors; specialty chains based on status brands like **Gucci, Godiva,** and **Mark Cross** further set the tone. When Bonwit's opened branch stores like this, incidentally, it lost its cachet in Manhattan to the revived Bergdorf Goodman.

Other noteworthy shops in Somerset Mall are the well-known

Brooks Brothers, Brookstone, Laura Ashley, Jaeger, and Cache. shops. You can also find a Williams-Sonoma cooking store, Eddie Bauer outdoor gear, and Sharper Image here.

Not all stores here are clones, however. Locally owned and regional leaders in their fields include Furs by Robert and Anna Bassett's Claire Pearone women's fashions, which has the area exclusive on Christian Lacroix's deluxe ready-to-wear. Roz and Sherm's serves up a good deal of astute fashion advice along with its men's and women's fashions and the area's best collection of high-fashion shoes.

"Somerset has also become known as the 'cultural hub' of the City of Troy," its press agent states. "Informal modeling is a daily occurrence in our restaurants. Every Sunday there is a free jazz or classical music concert from 2 to 4 p.m." Mall management is happy to send a newsletter with upcoming events and art exhibits.

The mall has three restaurants: the "contemporary California French" Cafe Jardin, Houlihan's Bar, and Sebastian's seafood restaurant. Also here are the adjacent 250-room Somerset Inn (313-643-7800) and Somerset Dinner Theatre (313-649-6629).

Somerset Mall is kitty-corner from K Mart's world headquarters, also at Big Beaver and Coolidge — one of those class-versus-mass contrasts so common around the Detroit area.

Somerset is a small mall (385,000 square feet) not by design but because its developer, Sam Frankel, was locked in a 15-year dispute with the city of Troy over expanding the 20-year-old mall. A 1989 compromise permits him to double the mall, adding a second floor and possibly Nieman Marcus as a third anchor. He is also allowed to build Somerset North (850,000 square feet) across the street, with three more upscale anchors (including possibly Bloomingdale's), provided he pays for new road construction. In return, he's giving up plans for twin nine-story office towers, an 18-story hotel, 236 condos, and a performing arts center.

Twelve Oaks Mall

27500 Novi Rd. Novi, MI 48050. Just north of I-96 at Novi Rd. and 12 Mile Rd., 2 miles west of I-275. (313) 348-9400. Phone or write for directory/map. Mon-Sat 10-9, Sun 12-5.

The Taubman Company's Twelve Oaks is a 170-store, 1.2 million-square-foot super-regional mall on two floors. What makes it the best all-around mall, shoppers say, is its civilized, pleasant atmosphere and its range of stores, from upper-end names like Talbots, Laura Ashley, Sharper Image, and Ann Taylor to more common, popular-priced chains. The anchors Hudson's, Sears, Penney's, and Lord & Taylor are common to other Taubman malls. But Twelve Oaks' location, convenient to both the fast-growing western and northern suburbs, puts it in an enviable position in attracting a huge, affluent customer base.

The interior landscaping here is unusually lush. Mall-cruising teens here are considered less objectionable than at some other big malls closer to Detroit.

Liz Claiborne chose Twelve Oaks for her very first specialty shop. Her intelligently chic clothes sell well in the Midwest, and especially here. At 13,000 square feet, Liz Claiborne is the mall's largest single individual store. Loyal Claiborne fans flock here to check out the complete line.

Other new concept stores have chosen Twelve Oaks to represent them in the big Detroit market: the Disney store and Macy's Fantasy lingerie shop and Aeropostale active sportswear, which is styled with World War II aviators' flair. At the same time, two independent, upscale local stores have recently forsaken stylish downtowns (Active Lady in Ann Arbor and Fini in

Birmingham) in favor of Twelve Oaks, because of its heavy, high-quality customer traffic.

Northland Center

21500 Northwestern Hwy. between 8 Mile and Greenfield, Southfield, MI 48075. (313) 569-6272. Call or write for directory/map. Mon-Sat 10 a.m.-9:30 p.m., Sun 11 a.m.-7 p.m.

Northland opened in 1954 as the first of a series of pioneering Detroit-area shopping centers developed by the J. L. Hudson Company. It was the first large shopping center designed by the noted architect and planner Victor Gruen. He planned it as a pleasant series of landscaped courtyards and colonnades, lined with shops and accented by sculptures, clustered around Hudson's department store. Northland achieved great fame and influence as a popular illustration of Gruen's notion that shopping centers ideally could become cultural centers and meeting places of the modern age.

The separation of pedestrian and vehicular traffic was a new idea for an American shopping center. Northland "was such a magnet that many Detroiters had the habit of visiting it, even on Sunday when only the restaurants were open," wrote John Burchard and Albert Bush-Brown in *The Architecture of America: A Social and Cultural History.* Gruen designed three more centers for Hudson's. At the same time, in designing Southdale Center in Minneapolis (1957), he sought to lessen the effects of Minnesota's extreme climate and came upon the idea that revolutionized shopping centers from that time on: he enclosed it under a roof. Northland itself was enclosed in 1976, and its lush outdoor landscaping of rhododendron, azaleas, magnolias, and other flowering shrubs and trees fell victim to the change.

Today Northland, with 180 stores anchored by Hudson's and Penney's, is Michigan's largest mall, but without its early charm. Over 60 per cent of its shoppers come from Detroit, now that Hudson's early and aggressive suburban expansion killed off its own downtown store and left Detroit the only older major U.S. city without a downtown department store. Despite recent perceptions of increased crime based on two isolated incidents in Southfield, crime at Northland is way down, to less than half of its 1986 level.

Other shopping

For interesting, convenient shopping in downtown business districts oriented to pedestrians, see listings for **Ann Arbor, Birmingham, Detroit** (Downtown and Eastern Market chapters), **Grosse Pointe, Hamtramck, Milford, Northville, Plymouth, Royal Oak,** and **Ypsilanti** (Depot Town).

For smaller specialty malls, see also:

◆ In Ann Arbor, **Kerrytown**: 30 specialty shops and food stores near downtown.

◆ In Detroit, **Trappers Alley**: festival marketplace with 70 gift and clothing shops adjacent to Greektown. The **Renaissance Center's World of Shops**: 13 clothing stores and dozens of other shops and restaurants geared to downtown employees and visitors. **New Center**: anchored by Crowley's department store with several additional clothing stores and some unusual specialty shops in the sumptuous Fisher Building and the GM Building.

◆ In Monroe, **Manufacturers' Marketplace,** a 45-store off-price mall just off I-75 between Toledo and Detroit.

Recommended Reading

Abraham, Molly. **Restaurants of Detroit.** Detroit Free Press. 1989.

The Free Press's Abraham rates 200 good Michigan restaurants, mostly in the Detroit area. Along with discerning reviews of the food, she provides basic background information about the chefs, the atmosphere, and excellent cross-referecing at the end.

Anderson, James and Iva Smith, editors. **Ethnic Groups in Michigan.** Detroit: The Michigan Ethnic Heritage Studies Center, 1983.

This collection of dozens of articles on Michigan ethnic groups covers large and small groups (Chaldeans, Belgians, and Maltese in Detroit) and tiny obscure ones (Byelorussians, Manx), with insight on who came, why, and what they did when they got here. Available for $10 from the publisher, 80 Farnsworth, Detroit, MI 48202.

Arnow, Harriette. **The Dollmaker.** New York: Macmillan. 1954.

A now-classic American novel of the travails of a poor Kentucky family moving to Detroit to work in a big WWII defense factory. It contrasts rural self-sufficiency with the allure of store-bought goods and glitter.

Babson, Steve. **Working Detroit.** Wayne State University Press. 1984.

A sympathetic and compelling account, full of photos, of how one of the most anti-union cities in the country became, through bloody struggles, a bastion of unionism.

Conot, Robert. **American Odyssey: A Unique History of America Told Through the Life of a Great City.** New York: William Morrow. 1974.

Fascinating, ponderous, and largely negative sweeping view of life in Detroit, with special sympathy for the common man.

Farmer, Silas. **The History of Detroit and Michigan.** Detroit Free Press. 1884.

Long out of print, this highly respected history of Detroit from a 19th-century historian's perspective is full of interesting information and striking etchings. Available in most major libraries.

Ferry, Hawkins W. **The Buildings of Detroit: A History.** Wayne State University Press. 1980.

A highly informed, critical view of Detroit's architecture by a scion of the Ferry Seeds family.

Fine, Sidney. **Violence in the Model City.** University of Michigan Press. 1989.

The definitive study of the 1967 Detroit riots, the nation's largest and most puzzling, by a renowned University of Michigan historian considered a master of primary research from documents and interviews. Compelling reading for the many people affected and intrigued by the riots.

Gustin, Lawrence R. **Billy Durant: Creator of General Motors..** Flushing, MI: Craneshaw. 1984.

A well-researched, interesting biography of one of America's most extraordinary entrepreneurs.

Holli, Melvin G., ed. **Detroit.** New York: New Viewpoints. 1976.

Intelligently compiled anthology of original documents and articles on Detroit. Insightful introductions provide much background.

Hudson, Sam. **The Story of Plymouth, Michigan: A Midwest Microcosm.** Plymouth, Michigan. 1976.

An unusually interesting local history of the town Daisy air rifles made famous.

Hyde, Charles K. **An Industrial History Guide.** Detroit: Detroit Historical Society.

A small but splendid guide to the Detroit area's many important old industrial sites, most of them today abandoned. Available in the gift shop of Detroit's History Museum.

Hyde, Charles K. *The Northern Lights..* Lansing: TwoPeninsula Press. 1986.

Beautiful color photographs accompany short descriptions of the 155 lighthouses along the coasts of Michigan.

Lacey, Robert. *Ford: The Men and the Machine.* New York: Little Brown. 1986.

Superb history of the Ford clan, beginning with Henry. Lacey tells a fascinating story extremely well.

Love, Edmund G. *Hanging On.* Detroit: Wayne State University. 1988.

Intimate, revealing look at life in Flint during the Depression, with an especially insightful view of the famous sit-down strikes from the point of view of the citizenry.

Love, Edmund, G. *The Situation in Flushing.* New York: Harper & Row, 1965.

A delightful reminiscence by the author of *Subways Are for Sleeping* of growing up in a village just outside of Flint in the first quarter of the century.

Marwil, Jonathan L. *A History of Ann Arbor.* Ann Arbor Observer, 1987.

An insightful, short history of the home of the University of Michigan.

Meyer, Katharine Mattingly, and McElroy, Martin C. P., eds. *Detroit Architecture.* Wayne State University Press. 1986.

Highly informative guide to the important architecture, both recent and old, around the Detroit area.

Nawrocki, Dennis with Thomas Holleman. **Art in Detroit Public Places.** Wayne State University. 1980.

With photos illustrating each work, this splendid little book illuminates the Detroit area's many fine outdoor statues and sculptures around Detroit.

Nowlin, William. *The Bark Covered House.* Dearborn Historical Commission. 1973.

Fascinating first-person account of early Michigan pioneering life by a man whose family cleared land in 1834 in what is today Dearborn.

Powers, Tom. *Michigan State & Natural Parks: A Complete Guide.* Davison, MI: Friede Publications. 1989.

Critical evaluations of campgrounds (such as which ones are treeless, which have good privacy) and beaches (which have shade, which are uncrowded) make this guide invaluable. Park maps included.

Powers, Tom. *Natural Michigan.* Davison, MI: Friede Publications, 1987.

Competently prepared guide to 150 natural areas in Michigan, including state parks, nature centers, swamps, trails, and preserves.

Serafino, Frank. *West of Warsaw.* Hamtramck: Avenue Publishing, 1983.

Interesting, readable history of Hamtramck's Poles, and a look at the city's past and future economy, written from an affectionate but unusually objective hometown perspective.

Silfven, Sandra. *Pocket Guide to Detroit & Michigan Restaurants.* Rochester Hills, MI: Momentum Books. 1989.

Detroit News restaurant reviewer Sandra Silfven writes much briefer evaluations than Molly Abraham (typically four to six lines per restaurant) but her comments are incisive and useful, and she includes lots of restaurants (about 500).

Tutag, Nola Huse. *Discovering Stained Glass in Detroit..* Detroit: Wayne State University Press. 1987.

A handsome book with both beautiful color photos of many extraordinary windows and authoritative background on their symbols and makers.

Wylie, Jeanie. *Poletown: Community Betrayed.* Urbana: University of Illinois Press. 1989.

The first major look at the destruction of the recently vibrant Poletown neighborhood south of Hamtramck for the new GM plant, by a historian actively involved in the fight against it.

INDEX

AC Spark Plug 310-311
ACCESS 149
Afrah Pastry 150
After Words 265
African-Americans 3, 46, 60, 68, 84, 99, 100, 101, 139, 163, 211, 240, 283
    Art 31, 68
    Restaurants 74, 92, 101
    Theater 30, 95
Al-Ameer 153
Al's Fish & Seafood 63
Al's Lounge 87
Alcamo's Market 145
Alexander's Lounge 326
Alpine Valley Ski Area 223
Alvin's Finer Delicatessen 326
Ambassador Bridge 81-82
American Coney Island 37
AMUSEMENT PARKS 81
Angelo's Coney Island 316
Angelo's Restaurant 286
Ann Arbor 249-288
    Downtown 254-257
    Restaurants 254, 256, 258, 262, 263, 264, 284-287
Ann Arbor Antiques Market 249
Ann Arbor Art Association 255
Ann Arbor Farmers Market 259
Ann Arbor Marriott Inn 288
ANTIQUE SHOPS 25, 129, 144, 156, 159, 176, 190, 192, 194, 196, 214, 233, 246, 249, 260, 291, 294
Appeteaser 226
Aquarium 56
Arabian Gulf Market 148
Arabian Village Bakery 148
Arabs 31, 60, 61, 63, 65
    Restaurants 101, 151, 152, 153, 198-199, 307
Ark 252-253
ART DECO ARCHITECTURE & DESIGN 17-19, 69, 123, 129-130, 142, 159, 190, 234, 254
Art Deco Design 254
Artful Exchange 256
ART GALLERIES 25, 30, 31, 32, 129, 131, 157, 188, 190, 192-194, 255, 256, 279, 309-310
Art Loft 190
ART, PUBLIC 17, 21, 29, 31-32, 35-36, 53-55, 68, 69, 94, 97, 118, 143-144, 193, 198, 207, 233, 236, 278, 295, 307, 310, 328-331
ART MUSEUMS 90-92, 208, 280, 281, 305-306
ARTS & CRAFTS ARCHITECTURE AND DESIGN 70-72, 89, 190, 204-208, 212
Artspace 194

ASTRONOMY 208, 280, 306
Atchison House Bed & Breakfast 184
Athens Bookstore 27
Athens Grocery and Bakery 27
Attic Theater 106
AUTO PLANT TOURS
    Buick 311
    Cadillac 119-120
    GM Truck 310
AUTO FACTORES (HISTORIC)
    Cadillac 78
    Dodge Truck 103
    Ford 77-78, 103-105, 145-147
    Lincoln 78
    Packard 76, 78
    Plymouth 78
AUTOMOBILES, CLASSIC 141, 246, 304-305
AUTOMOBILE MUSEUMS & SHOWS 82-84
Azar's Gallery of Oriental Rugs 192

B & S Produce 63
Bagley Memorial Fountain 28-29
BAKERIES 26-27, 117, 132, 148, 150, 164, 165, 176, 233, 258, 291
Baking by the Auers 164
Balcony Row Antiques 294
Balloon Corporation of America 292
BALLOONING 226, 292
Barclay Inn 200
Barnes & Noble Bookstore 265
Battiste's Temple 315
Battle Alley 294
Bead Gallery 257
Beaubien House 24
Belgians 60, 122, 130
    Restaurants 75
Bell Tower Hotel 288
Belle Isle 44, 45, 52-57
    Aquarium 56-57
    Dossin Great Lakes Museum 55
    Livingstone MeM. Lighthouse 58
    Nature Center 58
    Scott Fountain 55
    Whitcomb Conservatory 57
    Zoo 57-58
Bentley Historical Library 283
Best Western Fenton 292
Best Western Flint 317
Best Western Mr. Gibby's Inn 317
Best Western Wolverine Inn 288
BICYCLE RIDES 124, 182, 224
Bill Thomas Haloburger 310, 316
Bird of Paradise 256
BIRDWATCHING 221, 223, 226, 227, 229, 235, 266-267
Birmingham 185-200
    Restaurants 188, 198-200
Birmingham Bookstore 192
Birmingham Village Inn 200
Blanche House Bed & Breakfast 113

Blind Pig 255
Bloomfield Hills 201-208
Blossoms 24
Blue Nile 39
BLUES CLUBS see 325
Blue Water Bridge 321
Bluebell Beach 314
BOAT TRIPS 42, 80, 139, 224
Bo-Mac's Lounge 326
Boblo Island 80-81
Bon Juice 150
Bonstelle Theater 89, 95
Book Building & Book Tower 35
BOOKSTORES 27, 31, 36, 129, 142, 159, 192, 264-265, 270
Borders Book Shop 164, 264
Born Again Resale 176
Brava 195
Bricktown 25
Bright Ideas 160
Britt's Cafe 37
Brooks Brothers 131
Bryant Branch Library 143
Buckham Fine Arts Project 309-310
Buddy's Pizza 120
Buhl Building 19
Buick City 311
Burton Historical Collection 94
Burton Tower 278

Cadieux Cafe 75
Cadillac Detroit-Hamtramck Plant 119
Cadillac Division, GM 78, 119-120
Cadillac Square 28-29
Cafe Bon Homme 177
Cafe Jardin 210
Cafe le Chat 132
Calder Stabile 36
Calico Corners 213
CAMPING 223, 226, 235, 296, 314
Campus Inn 288
Campus Treasure Shop 97
CANOEING 221, 223, 267, 296
Cantor-Lemberg 194
Capital Poultry 66
Caravan Shop 261
Carl's Chop House 42
Carol James Gallery 160
Caruso Caruso 191
Cass Corridor Food Co-op 98
Cecille's 196
Cedarland Restaurant 152-53
Cedars Bakery 150
Cedars Fruit Market 150
Center for Creative Studies 93
Central United Methodist Church (Detroit) 32
Charles Freer House 98
Charles Warren House 99
Chase Antiques 192
Chene Park 43-44, 46-47

CHILDREN'S MUSEUMS 92, 257, 307-308
Chosen Books 159
Christ Church Cranbrook 203-204
Christ Episcopal Church (Detroit) 49
Chrysler-Jefferson Assembly Plant 70
Chudik's 196
Ciaramitaro Brothers 61, 62, 65
CIDER MILLS 291-292, 314
Ciemniak Meat Market 118
Cinderella's Attic 160
Clarkston Cafe 216
CLOTHING SHOPS
    Men 109, 110, 130, 131, 160, 191, 209, 260, 261, 262, 328-331
    Women 25, 31, 110, 130, 131, 158, 159, 160, 175, 176, 191, 193, 195, 196, 198, 209, 221, 236, 257, 259, 260, 262
Cloverleaf Market 165
Club Pentha 107, 326
ClubLand 33, 325
Coast Guard Lighthouse Depot (Detroit) 48
Cobo Hall 22
Coffee and Nut Gallery 150
Coffee Break 263
Collected Works 257
Colonial Motor Inn 324
Community Newscenters 265
CONCERTS, OUTDOOR 21, 46, 107, 127, 204, 224, 267, 278, 290, 313
Coney Island Lunch 238
Conservatory 255-256
Corktown 85
Corner-copia 144
Cost Plus Wine Warehouse 63
Cottage Inn 286
Country Inn of Grand Blanc 317
Cousins Heritage Inn 287
CRAFTS 30, 72, 110, 117, 141, 142, 159, 160, 175, 192, 193, 198, 206, 208, 221, 253, 254, 255, 256, 271
Cranbrook 204-208
    Academy of Art Museum 208
    Cranbrook House & Gardens 205, 207-208
    Institute of Science 208
Cross-Country Inn 238
CROSS-COUNTRY SKIING 180, 222, 223, 225, 267, 296
Crossroads Village 312-313
Cuisine de Pays 75
Custer Collection 234

D. & J. Bittker Gallery 194
Dave's Comics and Collectibles 158
David Mackenzie House 99
David Whitney, Jr. House. 100
David's Books 264
David Whitney Building 30

INDEX 335

Day's Inn Detroit 113
Day's Inn Monroe 238
Dearborn 134-154
    Restaurants 140, 142, 143, 151-153, 154
Dearborn Historical Museum 144-145
Dearborn Inn 153
Dearborn Inn (restaurant) 151
Dearborn Sausage 149
Dearborn's Southend 147
Deco Doug 190
Dee Segula Studio 221
Del-Rio Bar 254
DeLong's Barbecue 259
Depot Town 244
Detroit 5-113
    Civic Center 22
    Cultural Center 88-102
    Belle Isle 52-58
    Downtown 15-42
    East Side 59-75
    Financial District 17
    Historic Auto Factories 76-78
    New Center 106-112
    Lodgings 113
    Restaurants 37-42, 50-51, 65, 73-75, 86-87, 92, 97, 101-102, 110, 112
    Rivertown 43-51
    Southwest 79-87
    Theater District 33-35
Detroit Artists Market 30
Detroit Beach Restaurant 237
Detroit Council of the Arts 32
Detroit Focus Gallery 25
Detroit Gallery of Contemporary Crafts 110
Detroit Film Theater 91
Detroit Garden Center 49
Detroit Historical Museum 93
Detroit Historical Society 94
Detroit Institute of Art 90-92
Detroit Lions 327
Detroit Model Railroad Club (Holly) 295
Detroit People Mover 17
Detroit Pistons 327
Detroit Polo Club 222
Detroit Public Library 94
Detroit Recorder's Court 28
Detroit Red Wings 327
Detroit River 20-21, 44-47, 81-82, 87, 171
Detroit Science Center 92
Detroit Symphony Orchestra 100
Detroit Tigers 84, 269-70, 328
Detroit-Windsor Tunnel 24
Detroit Youtheater 91
Detroit Zoo 156-157
Diana Sweet Shop 322
Dibbleville 291
Discount Records 266
Diva Boutique 31

Dixieland Antique Flea Market 214
Domicile 196
Domino's Farms 268-271
    Classic Cars 270-271
    Center for Architecture & Design 270
    Petting Farm 270
Don Carlos 152
Donald Morris Gallery 192
Donna Jacobs 194
Dos Manos 159
Dossin Great Lakes Museum 55-56
Drake Sandwich Shop 262
Drury Inns 210
Duke Gallery 190
DuMouchelle Auction Gallery 25
Dunbar Hospital 99
Durant-Dort Carriage Factory 308

Earle 284
Earth Wisdom Music 266
Eastern Market (Detroit) 60-66
East Side Station 169
Eastern Michigan University 239, 241-242
Eco Sports Canoe Livery 221
Econo Lodge of Port Huron 324
Edison, Thomas 140, 321, 323
Edna Tillman Antiques 192
Edsel & Eleanor Ford Home 128
Edwards Caterer 184
Ehnis & Son 256
Elizabeth Park 171
Elizabeth Street Cafe 41
Elmwood Cemetery 67-68
Elwood Bar & Grill 41
Epicurean Cafe 38
Eskimo Art 271
Espresso Royale 262
Ethnic festivals (Detroit) 21
Expressions 196

FABRIC SHOPS 191, 196, 213
Fair Lane 142-143
Fairlane Inn 154
FARMERS' MARKETS 60-66, 160, 175, 213, 244-45, 259, 307
FARM FOR VISITORS 139, 180, 224, 269
Favor Ruhl 98
Feigenson-Preston Gallery 194
Fenton 289-292
    Restaurants 292
Fenton Depot 292
Fenton Hotel 292
Fenton House Carryout 292
Fenton Museum 291
Fermi 2 Power Plant 235
Figlio's 315
FILM 91, 187, 252, 262
Fisher Building 106, 109
Fisher Mansion 72-73
Fisher Theater 107, 109

FISHING 47, 48, 53, 222, 223, 224, 226, 227, 235, 307
Flint 297-317
    Restaurants 315-316
Flint Children's Museum 307
Flint Farmers' Market 307
Flint Institute of Arts 305-306
Flood's Bar & Grill 26
Floogles 315
Fogcutter Restaurant 323
FOLK MUSIC see 325- 326
Folkways Trading Company 175
Ford Auditorium 22
Ford, Henry 135, 236, 138-139, 142-143, 146, 181-182
Ford Highland Park Plant 77
Ford Motor Co. 135, 136, 139, 247
Ford Northville Plant 181
Ford Rouge Complex 135, 145-147
Ford's Village Industries 143, 181-183, 220-221
Fort Wayne 82
Fox Theatre 33-35
French 7-8, 124, 227-228, 234
Frog Island Park 245
Fuji Restaurant 285

G. R. N'Namdi Gallery 31, 192
Galerie 454 129
Gallery Row 193
Gallup Park 268
Gandy Dancer 285-286
GARDENS 49, 50, 52, 57, 127, 170, 202, 207-208, 266-267, 268
Garo's Pizza Mitza 150
Garys Flowers and Antiques 196
Gayle's Chocolates 158
General Motors Proving Grounds 225-226
General Motors Building 106, 108
Gerald R. Ford Presidential Librar 283
Germack Pistachio Company 66
Germans 60, 66, 249-252, 319
    Restaurants 40
Giant Flea Market 246
Giovanni's 87
GM Truck & Bus Flint Assembly Plant Tour 310
Gnome 101
Golden Mushroom 165
Govinda's 75
Grand Circus Park 31
Grandma Betty's 179
Grand Trunk Depot (1858) 320-321
Gratiot Central Market 65
Gratzi 285
Grayhaven Marina Village 60
Great Lakes Indian Museum 84
GREAT LAKES SHIPPING & FREIGHTERS 44-45, 55-56, 81-82, 318, 323
Grecian Gardens 40

Greeks 26-27, 40
Greektown 26-28
Greenfield Village 138-141
Grosse Ile 167-171
    Restaurants 170, 171
Grosse Ile Historical Museum 169-170
Grosse Ile Lighthouse 170
Grosse Ile Municipal Airport 170
Grosse Pointe 121-133
    Restaurants 130, 132-133
Grosse Pointe Yacht Club 126
Grosse Pointe Reliques 129
Guardian Building 18
Gypsy Dome Rainbow Tearoom 30
Gypsy's Vintage Bazaar 130

Haab's 248
Habatat Gallery 198
Haloburger 311, 317
Halsted Gallery 194
Hamlin's 131
Hampton Inn Southfield 166
Hamtramck 114-120
    Restaurants 120
    Taverns 117
Hands-On Museum (Ann Arbor) 257
Harbortown 50
Harbortown Market 50
Harmonie Park 30
Harmonie Park Playhouse 30
Harry's Army Surplus 256
Hart Plaza 20-21
Hattie's 196
Hector & Jimmy's 226
Heidelberg Street Project 68
Henry Ford Estate 142
Henry Ford Museum 141-142
Hertler's 255
Highland Recreation Area 222
Hilal Books 31
Hilberry Theater 95, 96
Hill Auditorium 278
Hill Gallery 192
Hispanics 79, 80, 86, 211
    Restaurants 86-87, 152
Historic Fort Wayne 82-84
Historic Holly Hotel 297
HISTORIC HOMES 48-50, 70, 72, 85, 98-100, 125-26, 127, 128, 139-40, 142-43, 145, 167-168, 169, 174, 179, 181, 203, 205, 207-208, 212, 213, 217-218, 228, 233, 234, 240, 243, 251, 267
HISTORICAL MUSEUMS 82-84, 93, 138-141, 141-142, 144-145, 169, 177, 213, 220, 231-232, 243-244, 291, 304-305, 313, 323
Holiday Inn Holidome Ann Arbor 288
Holiday Inn (Monroe) 238
Holiday Inn of Bloomfield Hills 208
Holiday Inn of Southfield 166
Holiday Inn Windsor 44

Holly 293-296
    Restaurants 292
Holly Recreation Area 295
Holocaust Memorial Center 197-198
Holy Trinity Church 85
Homemaker's Pantry 101
Homestead 288
Honeybaked Ham 164
HORSEBACK RIDING 180
Hotel Pontchartrain 113
Hotel St. Regis 106, 113
Howard Johnson's East (Flint) 317
Huckleberry Railroad 312-313
Hudson Motor Co. 245-246
Hudson's, J.L. 29, 163, 328
Hungarians 79
    Restaurants 87, 307
Hungry Crab 171
Huron Valley Motel 226
Hyatt Regency Dearborn 154
Hyatt Regency Flint 317

ICE SKATING 47, 225
Incognito 160
India Brass 32
Indian Earth Art & Crafts 309
Indians, American 84, 208, 244, 279, 309
Indian Village 13, 70, 88
Inn Season 162
In Situ 195
**INTERIOR FURNISHINGS &
    ACCESSORIES** 19-20, 131, 159,
    160, 190, 192, 195, 196, 198, 236,
    246, 258, 259
International Institute (Detroit) 92
Irish 27, 80, 85
Island Lake 226
Italians 60, 145
    Restaurants 73-74, 87, 112, 161, 183,
    237
It's the Ritz 191
It Was, It Is 190

Jacobson's 130, 191, 262
Jacoby's Since 1904 40
Jambalayas' 324
James Monnig, Bookseller 129
Janet's Lunch 132
JAZZ see 326
Jefferson Avenue (Detroit) 48, 68, 125
    Historic buildings 48-49
JEWELRY SHOPS 25, 159, 190, 191,
    193, 195, 255-256, 257, 262, 263
Jews 89, 163
    Restaurants 165
Joe and Ed's Schaefer Market 151
Joe Louis Arena 22
Joe Muer's Seafood 74
Joe's Wine and Liquor 65
Joe Wigley Meats 65
John King Books 36

Josef's Pastry Shop 132
Joy Emery Gallery 131
Judy's Cafe 152

Kahn, Albert 103-105, 108-109, 125,
    128, 274-276, 278
K. C. Larson Gallery 190
Kellogg Park 174
Kennedy and Company, 131
Kennon's Restaurant 237
Kensington Metropark 223
Kerrytown 258-259
Kingsley Inn 208
Kowalski Sausage 118, 145
Krazy Jim's Blimpy Burgers 286

Lake St. Clair 126-127
LA Express 158
LaDonna's 176
La Familia Martinez 215
Lafayette Coney Island 38
Lafayette Park 66-67
Laikon 40
Lake Shore Road 125
Lansdowne 38
Lark 200
Le Dog 286
League Shop 131
Lebanon Restaurant 153
Lelli's 112
Leonard Berry 192
Lepanto 161
Les Auteurs 161-162
Liberty Music 265
Lighthouse Park 321-322
LIGHTHOUSES 58, 127, 170, 322
Lilli's 21 325
Lincoln Motors 78
Linda Dresner 190
Lindell A.C. 38
Lindos Taverna 40
Lines: New Writing 91
Little Italy 183
Little Things 25
Livingstone Memorial Lighthouse 58
Lofts at Rivertown 50
London Chop House 38
Longway Planetarium 306
Loranger Square 232
Lotus Import Co. 159
Louisiana Creole Jambalaya 65
Lynn Portnoy 25

MacKinnon's 183
Madeline's Antiques 194
Maggie & Me 175
Maltese 79
Manoogian Mansion 69
Manufacturers Market Place 236
Map Room 276

338 INDEX

MAPS
    Belle Isle 54
    Dearborn 134
    Detroit metro area 4
    Southeast Michigan 3
Mariners' Church 21
Marley's Boutique 193
Marquis Theatre 179
Martha Cook Building 276
Materials Unlimited 246
Matthaei Botanical Gardens 268
Maxie's Leftfield Deli 86
Maybury State Park 180
Mayflower Hotel 178
McFadden-Ross House 145
McGuire's Motor Inn 216
Meadow Brook Hall 217
Meadowbrook Theater 217
Merchant of Vino 191
Merrill-Palmer Institute 98
Merrillwood Building 192
Mettal Studio 195
Mexican Town 86
Michigan Book & Supply 265
Michigan Central Station (Detroit) 80
Michigan China Company 145
Michigan Gallery 86
Michigan Inn 166
Michigan League Cafeteria 287
Michigan Soldiers & Sailors Monument 29
Michigan Society of Architects/
    Beaubien House 24
Michigan Stadium 282
Michigan Theater 262
Michigania 192
Middle Earth 263
Middle Rouge Parkway 182
Midwestern Antiques Emporium 214
Milford 219-226
    Restaurants 226
Milford Historical Museum 220
MILITARY MUSEUMS & SITES 82-84,
    144-145, 231-232, 233-234, 247
Miller Motor 245-246
Mill Race Historical Museum 181
Millender Center 24
Modern Bakery 165
Monchelle Lamoure Chocolatier &
    Cafe 199
Money Museum 20
Money Tree 39
Monroe 227-238
    Restaurants 237-238
Monroe County Historical Museum 231
Monroe Grocery and Bakery 27
Monroe Inn 237
Monument 118
Moross House 49-50
Motown Museum 90, 110-112
Moveable Feast 258, 284
Mr. Fofo's Deli 112

Mt. Elliott Park 43-44, 47
Mt. Holly 296
Muccioli Studio Gallery 25
Mulier's Omer Market 130
Museum of African-American History 92
Museum of Arts & History 323
Mushroom Cellar 165

National Auto History Collection 94
National Conference of Artists 31
National Museum of the Tuskegee
    Airmen 84
National Toy Gallery 94
NATURE CENTERS 58, 180, 224
NATURE WALKS 58, 142, 197, 222,
    223, 224, 235, 266-267, 268, 292, 296
Navarre-Anderson Trading Post 234
Neon Images 159
New Center (Detroit) 106-112
New Center Commons 107
New Center One 110
New Detroiter 74
New Hellas 40
New Palace Bakery 117
New World Stage 326
New Yasmeen Bakery 150
Nichols Arboretum 266
Nicky's (Troy) 210
Niki's (Royal Oak) 162
Niki's Taverna 40
1940 Chop House 50
Noir Leather 160
Norman's Eton St. Station 199
Northland Center 163, 330
Northville 179-184
    Restaurants 183-184
Novi Hilton 184

Oakland County Farmers Market 213
Oakland University 217
OfficeMax 164
Old China 248
Old German Restaurant 284-285
Old Shillelagh 27
Old Village, Plymouth 175
Old Woodward 193
Omni Hotel 24 113
One23 132
Opus One 25, 41
Orchard Lake Road shopping 198
Orchestra Hall 100
Original Pancake House 133

Packard Motors 78
Palace of Auburn Hills 217
Pampered Lady 294
PARKS 20-21, 30, 31, 45, 46, 47, 52-58,
    69, 81-82, 171, 174, 180, 182-183,
    193, 197, 221, 223-225, 227, 235,
    245, 258, 267, 306, 321-322

Patti Smith Collectibles 157, 158
Paul's Pipe Shop 309
Peabody's Restaurant 188
Peaceable Kingdom 256
Peacock 151
Pegasus at the Fisher 112
Pegasus Taverna 40
Penniman Showcase of Arts & Crafts 175
Penniman Street (Plymouth) 175
Pennywhistle Place 314
Penobscot Building 19
People's Food Co-op 259
People Mover (Detroit) 17
Pepperidge Farms Thrift Store 164
Petting Farm, Domino's 270
Pewabic Pottery 70-72
PEWABIC TILE 17, 18, 73, 75, 144, 204
Phoenicia 196, 198-199
Phoenix Memorial Laboratory 282
PICNICKING 21, 45, 46, 47, 52, 171, 174, 180, 182, 197, 222, 227, 235, 292
Pike Street Restaurant 215
Pine Grove Historical Museum 213
Pinegrove Park 322
PJ's Used Records 266
Plymouth 172-178
    Restaurants 177-78
Plymouth Antique Mall 176
Plymouth Fish & Chips 177
Plymouth Historical Museum 177
Plymouth Motors 78
Plymouth Radisson 178
Plymouth Yard Hobbies 176
Pointe Pedlar 131
Poles 114-117, 145
    Restaurants 120
Polish Art Center 117
Polonia 120
Pontchartrain Wine 39
Pontiac 211-216
    Restaurants 215-216
Pontiac Silverdome 213
Pop Regalia 160
Pope John Paul II, Monument to 118
Port Huron 318-325
    Restaurants 322, 324-325
Power Center of Performing Arts 279
Prager Indonesia 259
Presbyterian Thrift Shop 176
Preservation Wayne 92, 99
Pringles Pastries 176
Proud Lake Recreation Area 223
Punchinello's 199

Quarton Lake 197
Quattro Punti 39

R. Hirt Jr. Company 63-65
Radisson Resort 248
Rafal Spice Company 65
Rattlesnake Club 51

RECORD SHOPS 130, 265-266
Red Hot Lovers 264
Red Roof Inn Ann Arbor 288
Red Roof Inn Flint 317
Red Roof Inn Troy 210
Red Sea Restaurant 151
Renaissance 261
Renaissance Center 22-24
RESALE SHOPS 32, 97, 129, 130, 144, 176, 214, 233, 260
Rhinoceros 43
Rick's American Cafe 263
Rider's Hobby Shop 255
Ritz Carlton Dearborn 154
River Place Inn 113
River Raisin Battlefields and Massacre Site 233
Riverbank Park (Flint) 306
River Bistro 24
Riverfront Cafe (Detroit) 38
Riverfront industries (Detroit) 46
River Place Inn 113
Riverside Park (Detroit) 81-82
Riverside Park (Ypsilanti) 245
Rochester 217-218
ROCK 'N' ROLL CLUBS *see* 325
Roma Cafe 73-74
Ronnie's Meats 65
Roostertail 69-70
Rouge Plant (Ford) 145-147
Round Table 256
Royal Oak 155-162
    Main Street Commercial District 160
    Restaurants 161-162
Royal Oak Farmers' Market 160
Russell Hardware 195
Russell St. Deli 65
Rustic Cabins Bar 129

Salvatore Scallopini 199
Sanders Confectionery 130
Sara Lee Kitchens 164
Sarkis Gallery 93
Sarnia, Canada 321
SCENIC DRIVES 44-45, 124, 182-83, 287
    Industrial scenery 87, 147
Schmidt's Antique Shop/Gallery 246
Schoolkids Records & Tapes 266
Scots 25, 83
Scott Fountain 55
Second Story 190
Seegerpeople 191
Selo/Shevel Gallery 256
Seven Lakes Vineyard 292
Shain Park 193
Shaman Drum Bookshop 264
Shatila Bakery 150
Sheraton Flint 317
SHOPPING MALLS 163, 209, 328-331
Shorecrest Motor Inn 113
Shrine of the Little Flower 160-161

Siam Kitchen 287
Sidetrack 248
Sign of the Mermaid 194
Silver's/People's State Bank 19
Sindbad's 74
16 Hands 254
SKR Classical 265
SLEDDING 180, 225
SKIING, DOWNHILL 223, 296
Skylight Inn 184
Sloan Museum 304-305
Small World Shop 32
Smiley Bros. Music Co. 98
Solidarity House 69
Somerset Mall 328
Soup Kitchen Saloon 43, 325
Southfield Road 164
Southwest Detroit 79-87
Sparky Herbert's 132
Sports, Professional 327
St. Andrew's Hall 25, 325
St. Aubin Park 43-44, 45-46
St. Christopher Motel 208
St. Florian Church 119
St. Mary's Academy 234
Spirit of Detroit 21
Stage Deli 165
Stamping Grounds 159
Star of Detroit 42
State Discount 266
State Street Book Shop 264
Stearns Building 50
Stearns Collection of Musical
    Instruments 283
Stemma Bakery 26-27
Stepping Stone Falls 314
Sterling State Park 235
Steve's Ice Cream 262
Steve's Lunch 263
Stewart's Fabrics 191
Stroh River Place 47
Student Center Building 97
Sully's 327
Summit Steak House 23, 24
Susan Hoffmann Pastries 27
Sweet Afton Tearoom 178
Sweet Lorraine's Cafe 166
Swidler Gallery 157
SWIMMING 52, 54, 222, 223, 224, 226,
    235, 296, 314
Swords into Plowshares 32

Taboo 43
TAVERNS 27, 38, 40, 51, 74-75, 87,
    117, 129, 221, 245, 248, 254, 316,
    325, 326
Tennis Company 164
Territorial Sculpture 190
THEATER 30, 93, 106, 107, 179, 217,
    252, 298
Thomas Edison Inn 324

Thomas M. Cooley Fountain 278
Tiger Stadium 84
Tokyo Sushi-Iwa 171
Top of the Park 315
Torch Bar and Grill 316
Townsend Hotel 193, 200
Traffic Jam & Snug 101-102
TRAIN TRIPS 138, 253
Trappers Alley 27-28
Treasure Mart 260
Trini & Carmen's 215
Trolley (Downtown Detroit) 36
Troy 209-210
    Restaurants 210
Troy Hilton Inn 210
Troy Motor Mall 209
Twelve Oaks Mall 329
Twigs 191

Ulrich's Book Store 265
Under the Eagle 120
Unisys 107
University of Michigan 272-281
    Athletics Events & tickets 282
    Central Campus 274-281
    Clements Library 276
    Crisler Arena 282
    Eva Jesse Afro-American Music
      Collection 283
    Exhibit Museum 279-280
    Harlan Hatcher Graduate Library 274
    Kelsey Museum 280-281
    Law Quadrangle 277
    Michigan League 277-278, 288
    Michigan Union 277
    Museum of Art 281
    North Campus 282-283
    Phoenix Memorial Lab 282
    President's House 276
    Rackham Bldg. 279
    Yost Field House 282
    Walking Tour 278

Value Shop 32
Van Boven's 261
Van Dyke Place 74-75
Vernor's Mural 310
Vertu 159
Victorian Inn 323-324
Village Cafe 151
Village Corner 263
Village Inn of Dearborn 154
Village Paperback Exchange 176
Village Records & Tapes 130
VINTAGE CLOTHING 32, 130, 158, 160,
    176, 190, 233, 295

Walli's Motor Lodge East 317
Walli's Motor Lodge West 317
Walter Reuther Library 97

Washington Avenue Commerical
  District, Royal Oak 157
Washington Boulevard (Detroit) 35-36
Water Street Pavilion 308
Water Tower Antique Mall 295
Water's Edge 171
Waterworks Park 69
Wayne County Building 29
Wayne State University 95-97
  Community Arts Gallery 97
  Gullen Mall 96
  Walter Reuther Library 97
Wazoo Records 266
Weaving Room Gallery 192
Weber's Inn 288
West End Restaurant 215
Wells Freight & Cargo 196
West Side Book Shop 265
West Warren Bakery 145
Westborn Market 144
Westcroft Gardens 170
Westin Hotel 23, 113
Whistlestop 188
Whitcomb Conservatory 57
Whitney 100, 102
Whoopee Bowl 214
William Jackson House 99
Willis Gallery 98

Willow Run Airport 247
Willow Run Bomber Plant 247
Windmill Place 308
Windmill Pointe 127
Wine and Food Library 264
WINE SHOPS 63, 65, 144, 164-165,
  191, 258, 263, 291, 295
WJR 109
Wolcott Orchards 314
Woodbridge Tavern 51
Wooden Spoon 264
Woodward and Maple, Birmingham
  190-191
World of Kites 159
Wright, Frank Lloyd 203, 267, 270

Xochimilco 86-87
Xochipilli 194

Yankee Air Museum 247
Your Heritage House 99
Ypsilanti 239-248
  Restaurants 248
Ypsilanti Farmers Market 244-245
Ypsilanti Historical Museum 243-244

Zef's Coney Island 65
Zingerman's Delicatessen 259-260, 285

Dear Reader,

Your suggested additions and corrections are much appreciated. We update this guidebook every year.

Please tell us of interesting things to add, your comments, and your criticisms. If we use your suggestions, we'll send you the newest edition as soon as it's off the press.

Send your letter to:

>Midwestern Guides
>8330 Waterloo Road
>Grass Lake, Michigan 49240

We want to keep improving and enlarging the guide to make it better reflect the richness of this region.

Thanks for your help.

>Mary & Don Hunt